CIS 110/111

Composition and Communication I & II

for the **University of Kentucky**

Editors at the University of Kentucky

Troy Cooper | Sarah Kercsmar | Jessalyn Vallade

Real Communication, Third Edition
by Dan O'Hair, Mary Wiemann,
Dorothy Imrich Mullin, and Jason Teven

Everything's an Argument, Seventh Edition
by Andrea A. Lunsford and John J. Ruszkiewicz

A Speaker's Guidebook, Sixth Edition
by Dan O'Hair, Rob Stewart, and Hannah Rubenstein

macmillan learning
curriculum solutions

Manufactured in the United States of America

1 0 9 8 7 6
f e d c b a

Macmillan Learning Curriculum Solutions
14903 Pilot Drive
Plymouth, MI 48170
www.macmillanlearning.com

ISBN: 978-1-319-10065-0

Acknowledgments

Text acknowledgments and copyrights appear at the back of the book on page 639, which constitutes an extension of the copyright page. Art acknowledgments and copyrights appear on the same page as the art selections they cover. It is a violation of the law to reproduce these selections by any means whatsoever without the written permission of the copyright holder.

macmillan learning
curriculum solutions

bedford/st. martin's • hayden-mcneil
w.h. freeman • worth publishers

Table of Contents

CIS 110 Inform Yourself and Others

CIS 111 Persuade

CIS 110
Inform Yourself and Others

Chapter 1

Verbal Communication

The Nature of Language

The Functions of Language

Language and Meaning

Problematic Uses of Language

Language in Context

chapter outcomes

After you have finished reading this chapter, you will be able to

- Describe the power of language—the system of symbols we use to think about and communicate our experiences and feelings

- Identify the ways language works to help people communicate—the five functional communication competencies

- Describe the ways that communicators create meaning with language

- Label problematic uses of language and their remedies

- Describe how language reflects, builds on, and determines context

This chapter is taken from Dan O'Hair, Mary Wiemann, Dorothy Imric Mullin, and Jason Teven, *Real Communication,* Third Edition, pp. 64–90 (Chapter 3).

Anne Kerry was walking to the bank in her San Francisco neighborhood when she suddenly ran into Scott, an old college friend, accompanied by another young man. "Anne," he said warmly, "I want you to meet my partner, Bryan." Anne was surprised—she hadn't realized that Scott was gay. She asked, "How long have you two been together?" Both men looked at her quizzically before they realized what she was thinking. "No," said Scott, "I became a police officer. Bryan and I work patrol together." "I was embarrassed," said Anne. "I didn't mean to misunderstand their relationship. I just figured that 'partner' meant love interest."

Like many words in the English language, *partner* has a variety of definitions: it can mean anything from "an associate" to "a dancing companion" to "a group of two or more symbiotically associated organisms." But like Anne, many of us immediately jump to another definition: "half of a couple who live together or who are habitual companions." Indeed, the term is widely used by gays and lesbians seeking a label for their loved one. Some heterosexual couples have also embraced the term to reveal their committed state, particularly when they feel that they've outgrown the term *boyfriend* or *girlfriend* or are unwilling to use the terms *husband* and *wife*.

The fact is the labels we choose for our relationships have a huge impact on our communication. The term *partner* can give rise to ambiguity—is the person you introduce with this term a business colleague, someone you play tennis with, or your "significant other"? That ambiguity makes it difficult for others to grasp your intended meaning. Perhaps that's why some Massachusetts gays and lesbians who wed after the state was the first to ratify same-sex marriages avoid the term *partner*. Bob Buckley felt the power of such labels when his partner, Marty Scott, needed medical treatment. When hospital administrators asked his relationship to the patient, Buckley was able to say, simply, "husband" and was immediately allowed to stay with Scott, since spouses are afforded this privilege but partners are not (Jones, 2005).

As our opening vignette shows, the names used to describe our connections with others have power. This is true for all kinds of relationships. For example, calling your father "Dad" reveals less formality in your relationship than calling him "Father." In a stepfamily situation, calling your father's wife "Mom" indicates more closeness than using her first name. Choosing words can get complicated. That's why we dedicate this chapter to studying verbal communication, the way we communicate with language. **Language** is the system of symbols (words) that we use to think about and communicate experiences and feelings. Language is also governed by grammatical rules and is influenced by contexts.

Of course, nonverbal behaviors—pauses, tone of voice, and body movements—accompany the words we speak. Thus they are an integral part of our communication and we examine them in **CHAPTER 2**. But we now focus on the nature of language, its functions, how it creates meaning, problems with language, and contexts that influence our use of language.

■ The Nature of Language

In 1970, a "wild child" was discovered in California. Thirteen-year-old "Genie" had been chained in a small room with no toys and little food for nearly her entire life. Her abusive father gave her no hugs, no loving words, and no conversation. As a result, Genie never developed language. Medical doctors, linguists, and psychologists worked intensely with Genie for over seven years, hoping to give the girl a chance at life in a community with others. But despite their efforts, Genie never learned more than a few hundred words and was never able to form sentences of more than two or three words (Pines, 1997; "Secret," 1997). Genie's sad story highlights the complex nature of language: someone with Genie's background will never fully grasp that language is symbolic, has multiple meanings, is informed by our thoughts, and is shaped by grammar and context. We explore these four points in this chapter.

Language Is Symbolic

What comes to mind when you see the word *cat*? A furry childhood best friend? Fits of sneezing from allergies? Either way, the word evokes a response because it is a *symbol,* a sign representing a person, idea, or thing. Words evoke particular responses because speakers of that language agree that they do. Thus you can use words to communicate ideas and thoughts about particular subjects when you have a common language. Moreover, using words as symbols is a uniquely human ability (Wade, 2010).

Thought Informs Language

Jamal Henderson is preparing to apply to colleges. He keeps his father, Michael, involved in the process because he values his opinion. They both agree that Jamal should attend a "good college." But Michael feels hurt when Jamal starts talking seriously about urban universities in another state. He thinks his son has ruled out his own alma mater, the local campus of the state university system. Jamal and Michael have different thoughts about what a "good college" is. Their language and thoughts are related in their own minds, and each thinks he is using the term appropriately.

Your **cognitive language** is the system of symbols you use to describe people, things, and situations in your mind. It influences your language (Giles & Wiemann, 1987) and is related to your thoughts, attitudes, and the society in which you live (Bradac & Giles, 2005). Michael may think a "good college" is close to home, is involved in the local community, and offers small class sizes. Meanwhile, Jamal may think a "good college" presents the opportunity to live in a new city and to study with people from other countries.

Our thinking affects the language we use. But language also influences our thoughts. If you tell yourself that a coworker is an "idiot," the word may influence your future impressions of him. To illustrate, if he's quiet during a meeting, you might conclude that he knows nothing about the subject under discussion. On a much larger scale, we can have visceral reactions to the words or names assigned to people and places. For example, children assigned linguistically low-status names (like Alekzandra instead of Alexandra) tend to be treated differently by teachers, are more likely to be referred for special education, and are less likely to be perceived as gifted (Rochman, 2011). Indeed, the city of Stalingrad in Russia was renamed Volgograd because of the strong, negative reaction to a name associated with the violent dictator, Joseph Stalin (Roth, 2013).

Language Is Ruled by Grammar

If you are a fantasy or science-fiction fan, you know that the language in today's video games and television must be more than the alien gibberish of old. It must have complete structures that consistently make sense. So Hollywood hires "conlangers"—people who construct new languages with complete grammatical structures like those you see in the HBO series *Game of Thrones'* Dothraki or *Avatar*'s Na'vi (Chozick, 2011).

As your third-grade teacher likely told you, **grammar**—the system of rules for creating words, phrases, and sentences in a particular language—is important. Although good grammar doesn't always equal good communication, using correct grammar helps you communicate clearly. And pronunciation matters, too. For example, if you pronounce the word *tomato* "tommy-toe," others probably won't understand that you are referring to the red fruit that tastes really good on a hamburger. That's because grammar has *phonological rules* governing how words should be pronounced.

Similarly, grammar has *syntactic rules* guiding the placement of words in a sentence. If you shuffle the words in the sentence "I ran to the store to buy some milk" to "Store I to milk to ran the buy some," your meaning becomes unclear. Grammatical rules differ among languages. Native speakers of English, for example, must remember that the grammar of Romance languages (such as French and Spanish) requires a different syntax. For example, in English, adjectives typically precede a noun ("I have an intelligent dog"), whereas in Spanish, adjectives follow the noun (*"Tengo un perro intelegente,"* literally translated as "I have a dog intelligent"). To communicate clearly in Spanish, an English speaker must adjust.

Excellent grammar on its own will not automatically make you an outstanding communicator. Telling your professor in perfect English that her style of dress is a sorry flashback to the 1980s is still offensive and inappropriate. That's because competent communicators also consider the situational, relational, and cultural contexts whenever they use language.

AND YOU?

Have you ever found yourself in a situation where you are entirely sure that you are using a term precisely ("a good restaurant," "a fun party," "an affordable car") only to have someone wholeheartedly disagree? How did you handle this language challenge?

Language Is Bound by Context

Imagine a scenario in which your cousin prattles on and on about her wild spring break in Miami. Now imagine that she's talking to your eighty-year-old grandmother … at your niece's fifth birthday party…in front of a group of devoutly religious family members. These contrasting scenarios illustrate how language is bound by contexts such as our relationship with the people present, the situation we're in, and the cultural factors at play. Does Grandma really want to hear about your cousin's behavior? Is it really OK to talk about this at a little kid's party? What about respecting the beliefs and sensibilities of your family members?

Communication accommodation theory (CAT) explains how language and identity shape communication in various contexts. CAT argues that competent communicators adjust their language and nonverbal behaviors (see **CHAPTER 2**) to the person, group, and context (Giles, Coupland, & Coupland, 1991; Shepherd, Giles, & LePoire, 2001; Soliz & Giles, 2010). We examine the relational, situational, and cultural contexts later in this chapter. But for now, keep in mind that communicating competently involves accommodating to context.

Rubberball/Jupiter images

FIGURE 1.1 It's probably a good idea to avoid regaling your grandmother with tales of your crazy spring-break shenanigans.

■ The Functions of Language

One of the first phrases that eighteen-month-old Josie learned to use was "thank you." Had this toddler already mastered the rules of etiquette? Was she just picking up a habit from her parents? Or was she learning that certain phrases would help her get things she wants: a compliment, a smile, a cookie?

We all learn isolated words and grammar as we acquire language. Josie, for example, probably picked up the expression "thank you" from her parents, her older brother, or her babysitter. But to become a competent communicator, she must learn to use this and other symbols appropriately. If Josie uses "thank you" as a name for her stuffed bear, she's not using it appropriately, so she's not communicating effectively. **Communication acquisition** is the process of learning individual words in a language as well as how to use that language *appropriately* and *effectively* in various contexts. Just as Josie gets a smile from her parents for saying "thank you," using language competently helps us to achieve our goals.

Researchers have identified five competencies (Wood, 1982) for how language behaviors function: controlling, informing, feeling, imagining, and ritualizing. We all develop these competencies when we're young by interacting with family and peers and observing television and other media. These competencies remain important throughout our lives. For that reason, we now look at them more closely.

Using Language as a Means of Control

Language is used as an instrument of *control*, to exert influence over others and our environment. Josie's use of the phrase "thank you" impresses her mother, who reassures her that using the term makes her a "good girl." Such appropriate use of language can make children seem cute, smart, or polite, giving them the ability to present themselves in a positive light. *Control* is actually a neutral term; it is a crucial social skill whether used in a positive or negative way. As an adult, Josie will be able to use language to control her environment by negotiating a pay raise or bargaining with a car dealer. However, she will also need to avoid negative control strategies, such as whining, ridiculing, insulting, threatening, or belittling, as these do not contribute to productive, successful communication.

For anyone who has been the victim of hurtful language and actions, speaking out—harnessing the power of language—can actually restore a sense of control. Tens of thousands of women have been brutally raped in the Congo, and their shame has kept them silent. Cultural taboos about gender and sexual behavior have also prevented them from sharing their stories. However, local and international aid groups have organized open forums to help victims talk about the atrocities, connect with others, and regain control of their lives. Words about such experiences are certainly hard to speak, but once these narratives are spoken, they can empower the speaker (Bartels et al., 2013; Gettleman, 2008).

Using Language to Share Information

Have you ever asked a sick child to tell you "where it hurts," only to receive a vague and unhelpful answer? This is because young children are still developing the next functional competency, **informing**—using language to give and receive information. As an adult, if you've ever been asked for directions, you know that providing people with information that they can understand and understanding the information they're conveying to you are equally important skills.

There are four important aspects of informing: questioning, describing, reinforcing, and withholding.

- *Questioning* is something we learn at a young age and use throughout our lives. Young children hungry for information about their world quickly learn the power of the simple, one-word question "Why?"

- *Describing* helps us communicate our world to others. Parents and teachers may ask children to repeat directions to their school or their home or to detail the specifics of a story they've heard.

- *Reinforcing* information can help us become competent listeners. We might take notes or simply repeat the information to confirm our comprehension.

- *Withholding* information or opinions may be appropriate in some situations. For example, you may withhold your opposition to your manager's plan because you want to keep your job. Or you may elect not to reveal a piece of information that might embarrass a friend.

Together, these four skills form the basis of the informational competency that we use to communicate throughout our lives.

© Zero Creatives/Image Source/Corbis

FIGURE 1.2 We've all been there: a tourist asks you for directions and you mutter, "Um, yeah, you go a little bit up this way and turn around that way...."

Using Language to Express Feelings

Poets, writers, and lyricists are celebrated for using language to capture and express emotions. But most expressions of feelings are less elaborately composed than a Shakespearean sonnet or an angry protest song. In everyday conversation and correspondence, we use language to send messages to others expressing how we feel about ourselves, them, or the situation. Young children can say, "I'm sad," and cry or laugh to communicate feelings. As you mature, you learn how to express a more complex set of emotions—liking, love, respect, empathy, hostility, and pride—and you may even intensify emotion by using words like *obsessed* rather than *love/like* (Goodman, 2013). The functional competency of expressing **feeling** is primarily relational: you let people know how much you value (or don't value) them by the emotions you express.

We all use language to express our feelings, but to be competent, we must do so appropriately and effectively. Many people don't communicate their emotions well. For example, Elliot expresses frustration with his staff by yelling at them; his staff responds by mocking Elliot at a local pub after work. Instead, Elliot could have said, "I'm *worried* that we're not going to make the deadline on this project"; someone on his staff could have said, "I'm feeling *tense* about making the deadline, too, but I'm also *confused* about why you yelled at me." Sometimes, appropriate and effective communication means avoiding expressing feelings that we consider inappropriate or risky in a given situation (Burleson, Holmstrom, & Gilstrap, 2005). For example, when Abby's boyfriend suggests sharing an apartment next semester, Abby changes the subject to avoid admitting that she's uncomfortable taking that step.

Using Language to Express Creativity

What do Katniss Everdeen, George Michael Bluth, Wonder Woman, and Sherlock Holmes have in common? Each is the product of the imagination of a writer or storyteller. And regardless of whether they were conceptualized as part of a novel, comic book, screenplay, or television series, each character and his or her story are primarily expressed through language.

Imagining is probably the most complex functional competency. It is the ability to think, play, and be creative in communication. Children imagine by pretending to be a superhero. Adults imagine, too. The way a song is worded, the way a play is scripted, and the way special effects coordinate with the message delivered in a film—these all stem from imagination. On the job, imagining is the ability to use language to convey a vision for a project to your coworkers (such as architects explaining blueprints and models). In a debate, imagining enables you to think ahead of your opponent, to put words to each side of an argument, and to use language in logical and convincing ways.

Suzanne Hanover/© Universal Pictures/Courtesy Everett Collection

FIGURE 1.3 While a toast might be the perfect way to wish a couple happiness at their wedding shower, in the film *Bridesmaids* Annie and Helen inappropriately use it as an opportunity to compete for the role of best friend to the bride.

Using Language as Ritual

When little Josie says "thank you" for her cookie, it's a sign that she is learning the fifth functional competency: ritualizing. **Ritualizing** involves the rules for managing conversations and relationships. We begin learning these rules as children: peekaboo games require us to learn turn-taking in conversations. When we learn to say "hi" or "bye-bye" or "please," we internalize politeness rituals.

In adulthood, ritualizing effectively means saying and doing the "right" thing at weddings, funerals, dinners, athletic events, and other social gatherings. Simple exchanges, like telling a bride and groom "congratulations" or offering condolences to a grieving friend, are some ways we ritualize language. However, our ritualizing is not always that formal, nor is it limited to big events. In our everyday lives we use ritual comments to support one another in relationships, such as "Have a great day, Honey!" "You're going to nail that speech" or even just "I'll text you later...."

■ Language and Meaning

Imagine three-year-old Damon sitting in a house of worship with his parents. He's having a great time banging his stuffed toys around until his mother grabs them away during a silent part of the service. Clearly upset, Damon calls her a nasty name. Mom's face turns bright red, and she escorts Damon out to the car. Damon associated his language with the concept of being unhappy; he was upset about Mom taking his toys, so he uttered the same word he had probably heard a family member use when unhappy with someone.

(left) MaxyM/Shutterstock; (right) Comstock/Jupiter Images

FIGURE 1.4 The word *school* has multiple denotative meanings: it is not only the place where students learn but also a group of fish.

Semantics involves the relationships among symbols, objects, people, and concepts; it refers to the *meaning* that words have for people, either because of their definitions or because of their placement in a sentence. Damon had probably observed reactions to the use of the nasty name, so he thought it meant "Give me my toys back." What Damon had not learned was **pragmatics,** the ability to use his culture's symbol systems appropriately. He may have gotten a few laughs by using the language in front of his family at home, but he didn't realize that it's inappropriate to use the word in other contexts. When you acquire language, you learn semantics, but when you learn *how* to use the verbal symbols of a culture appropriately, you learn pragmatics.

Key to understanding semantic and pragmatic meaning are three ideas that we now examine: the multiple meanings of words, their varying levels of abstraction, and their usage in particular groups.

Words Have Multiple Meanings

As you saw in the opening "partner" vignette, a single word can have many meanings. A dictionary can help you find the **denotative meaning** of a word—its basic, consistently accepted definition. But to be a competent communicator, you'll also need to consider a word's **connotative meaning**, people's emotional or attitudinal response to it. Consider the word *school*. It has several denotative meanings, including a building where education takes place and a large group of fish. But the word can also carry strong connotative meanings, based on your attitudes toward and experiences with school: it might bring back happy memories of class birthday parties in second grade, or it might make you feel anxious about final exams.

> ### AND YOU?
> What connotative meanings does each of the following words have for you: *religion, divorce, money, exercise, travel, dancing, parenthood*? Why do you have the reaction you do to each word?

Obviously, choosing words carefully is important. Not only must you make sure the denotative meaning is clear (using the word *ostentatious* with a bunch of six-year-olds isn't going to help you explain anything), but you also have to be aware of the possible connotative meanings of the words you use (Hample, 1987). Consider the words people might choose at a party to introduce the person to whom they are married. They could say, "I'd like you to meet my *wife*," or "...my *spouse*" (or *bride, old lady, ball-and-chain, better half*). These terms denotatively mean the same thing— their marital partner. But connotatively, they might generate very different reactions (including possibly offending people). *Spouse* may have a positive connotation in some situations, such as in legal paperwork or a gender-neutral invitation ("spouses welcome"). But in a personal introduction, it may come across negatively, as too formal and lacking affection. Connotative reactions also depend on the people you're speaking to and your relationship to them—the same word may make your friends laugh but anger your family members.

Subtle differences in word meaning can even change your entire interpretation of an event. For example, your grandfather offers to give you $10,000 at your college graduation if you graduate with honors. Is his offer a bribe, a reward, or an incentive? How you and others perceive and process his offer depends on the meaning associated with the language used. You may resent your grandfather if you consider the money a *bribe*, feel proud if you earn your *reward*, or feel motivated by the *incentive*.

Abstraction

Language operates at many levels of abstraction, ranging from very vague to very specific. You might talk in such broad, vague terms that no one knows what you are staying ("Stuff is cool!"), or you can speak so specifically that people may think you are keeping notes for a court case against them: "I saw you at 10:32 P.M. on Friday, January 29, at the right-hand corner table of Harry's Bar with a six-foot-tall, brown-haired man wearing black jeans, boots, and a powder blue T-shirt."

The **abstraction ladder** (Hayakawa, 1964) illustrates the specific versus general levels of abstraction (see **FIGURE 1.5**). The top rungs of the ladder are high-level abstractions: these are the most general and vague. Lower-level abstractions are more specific and can help you understand more precisely what people mean. "Let's watch something interesting on Netflix" is a high abstraction that allows a wide range of choices (and the possibility of some really bad movies). Saying "I'd like to watch a historical drama tonight" (lower abstraction) is more likely to get you something you'll enjoy, whereas naming the exact movie ("Let's watch *Lincoln*") ensures satisfaction.

Higher

ABSTRACTIONS

"You're useless."

"You never help out around the house."

"You keep forgetting to do your chores."

"The trash wasn't emptied last night, and it's your job to do that."

"I noticed you didn't take out the trash in the kitchen, the bathroom, or the bedroom. You agreed that taking out the trash every Monday and Thursday evening would be your job."

Lower

FIGURE 1.5 The abstraction ladder.s

But even though lower abstractions ensure clarity, high abstractions can accomplish certain communication goals. Here are a few examples:

- *Evasion.* Avoiding specific details is evasion. A teenager might tell her parents that she is "going *out* with *some friends*" rather than "going to a party at Nell's house with Fernanda, Justin, and Derek."

- *Equivocation.* **Equivocation** involves using words that have imprecise meanings that can be interpreted multiple ways. Equivocation can help us get out of an uncomfortable situation, as when a friend asks what you think of her new sweater—which you think is hideous—and you reply, "It's …*colorful.*"

- *Euphemisms.* **Euphemisms** are words or phrases with neutral or positive connotations that we use to substitute for terms that might be perceived as upsetting. For example, you might say that your uncle "passed on" rather than "died" or that your mother had a "procedure" rather than an "operation."

Michael Sharkey/Getty Images

FIGURE 1.6 Skateboarders have their own jargon for their fancy flips and tricks. If you're not a skateboarder, an "ollie" might be a foreign concept.

Group Identification and Meaning

Language also informs others about your affiliations and memberships. For example, **slang** is language that is informal, nonstandard, and usually particular to a specific age or social group; it operates as a high-level abstraction because meanings of slang are known only by its users during a specific time in history. A rock concert might be described as "groovy," "totally awesome," or "off the hook"—each expression places the speaker in a particular time or place in the world. Teenagers might alert each other online that they've "GTG" (got to go) because of "POS" (parent over shoulder), and their parents are none the wiser. Slang is often intensified by adjectives that increase emphasis, such as *absolutely, completely, extremely, totally, wickedly,* or *massively* (Palacios Martínez & Núñez Pertejo, 2012).

Related to slang is **jargon**, technical language that is specific to members of a given profession or activity or hobby group. Jargon may seem abstract and vague to those outside the group but conveys clear and precise meanings to those within the group. For example, when a fan of the model game Warhammer 40K speaks of "kit bashing," other fans understand that the speaker is taking parts from two different models and mixing them together. The rest of us, however, would probably just stare blankly.

AND YOU?

What kinds of slang or jargon do you regularly use? How did you become familiar with these terms? And how would you go about explaining these terms to someone who is unfamiliar with them?

WIRED FOR COMMUNICATION

Speaking in Code

There's a large contingent of educators and parents who think the key to securing a good-paying job after college lies with learning a foreign language. Envisioning a future in which China leads the world's economy, they push school boards to teach Mandarin or enroll their children in extracurricular immersion courses (McDonald, 2012). But what if there were another language just as likely to lead to fruitful employment, one that applied to just about every existing and emerging industry that not only could be taught in schools but also learned at home for little cost? And what if that language, already in use around the world, were based primarily on English?

That language—well, technically, *those languages*, since there are many—is computer code. Code essentially refers to the directions given to a computer to make it do what you want it to do. The apps you use to play games on your phone, the programs that spit out your credit card bill each month, the tools that small businesses use to manage supply chains and payroll, even the sensor that dings in your car when you forget to buckle up, all run on code. In every industry, from information tech to communications, manufacturing to agriculture, and food service to shipping, computers and code play a role. The most popular computer languages (like Ruby, Python, and C++) are "spoken" in just about every technologically advanced country, even though these languages are, by and large, based on English language keywords. But most Americans—even the digital natives who were raised on technology—simply don't know how to code, and so employers find themselves duking it out to hire the ones who do. "Our policy is literally to hire as many talented engineers as we can find," notes Facebook founder Mark Zuckerberg. "There just aren't enough people who are trained and have these skills today" (Zuckerberg, 2013). Others are careful to point out that coding is not just for engineers or engineering majors. It's a skill that will benefit anyone in just about any job. Huffington Post CTO John Pavley points out that even for nontech types, coding can open doors to satisfying work. "[N]on-technical people can learn to code, which will open doors to better jobs and a richer understanding of the rapidly changing world around us, where computer chips and software are finding their way into every aspect of our lives" (Pavley, 2013).

Pavley likens the divide between those who can and cannot code to the low levels of literacy during the Dark Ages, when the written word, along with the power it conferred, was the provenance of only a small elite. But there is a movement to bring the power of code to the masses. Organizations like CodeAcademy and Code.org advocate making more computer science courses available to students from kindergarten through high school and offer free coding lessons online for anyone interested in learning a programming language at home (Wingfield, 2013). Some even suggest making learning code an educational requirement along the lines of, or even in place of, a foreign language (Koerner, 2013). Other nations have already taken that step. Multilingual education may take on a whole new meaning.

Think About This

1. In communication terms, what kind of code is *code?* Is it a language like English or Mandarin? Is it verbal communication or something else entirely?

2. Should schools require students to learn code the same way most schools require them to learn a foreign language? If computer languages can be learned fairly easily with a book via a Web-based class, why might it be important to offer them in schools?

3. Is the dominance of English in the programming world significant? What meaning might it carry in non-English-speaking contexts?

4. Consider your envisioned field of study and the career you hope to pursue after college. Do you think having some knowledge of computer code would be helpful for you?

■ Problematic Uses of Language

"I think we're still in a muddle with our language, because once you get words and a spoken language it gets harder to communicate" (Ewalt, 2005, para. 1). The famous primatologist Jane Goodall made this point when explaining why chimpanzees get over their disputes much faster than humans. They strike out at each other and then offer each other reassuring pats or embraces, and voilà, argument over. Not so with people: words can be really hard to forget.

As you've probably experienced, words can lead to confusion, hurt feelings, misunderstandings, and anger when we blurt things out before considering them (and their effects) carefully (Miller & Roloff, 2007). We sometimes engage in hurtful or hateful language, use labels in ways that others don't appreciate, reveal bias through our words, and use offensive or coarse language. And when we put thoughtless or hastily chosen words in e-mails or post them on Twitter or Facebook, they become "permanent," and we may have great difficulty taking them back (Riordan & Kreuz, 2010).

Hateful and Hurtful Language

After twenty-five minutes of hearing ethnic slurs from the crowd whenever he tried to score a goal, soccer star Kevin Prince Boateng kicked the ball into the crowd and walked off the field, accompanied by his teammates (Herman, 2013). Sadly, Boateng's story is not an isolated event: anti-Semitic chants plagued another soccer club, and fans have thrown food and screamed insults at black players in others. Such language that offends, threatens, or insults a person or group based on race, religion, gender, or other identifiable characteristics is **hatespeech** (Waltman & Haas, 2011). Hatespeech employs offensive words to deride the person or group; thus hatespeech often creates vividly negative images of groups in the minds of listeners while downplaying the unique qualities of individuals in those groups (Haas, 2012, p. 132).

Other language choices may not be intended to offend individuals based on cultural factors but are nonetheless hurtful. For example, do sports fans have the right to jeer at the opposing team? Should they be allowed to bellow at referees throughout the game? What about the instance of an opposing team fan reading loudly from the grand jury report of the Jerry Sandusky sexual abuse case at a Penn State game (Pennington, 2012)? Although none of these behaviors are technically against the law, they have communication effects and are often considered **hurtful language**—inappropriate, damaging, mean, sarcastic, or offensive statements that affect others in negative ways.

Labeling

Feminist. The literal definition of the term is "a person who advocates equal social, political, and all other rights for women and men." But who are these people who label themselves feminists? In our years of teaching undergraduates, we've heard plenty of students note that feminists are women who hate men and care only about professional success. But "there is no way to tell what a feminist 'looks' like. Feminists are young, old, women, men, feminine or masculine, and of varying ethnicities" (McClanahan, 2006, para. 5).

CIS 110

AND YOU?

Are you a feminist? What does the term *feminist* mean to you? If you hear someone called a feminist, what ideas or images does this bring to mind?

(left) © Beathan/Corbis; (right) RIZWAN TABASSUM/AFP/Getty Images)

FIGURE 1.7 What does a feminist look like? Stereotypes may cause you to believe that the professional woman on the left is a feminist. But the woman on the right, Mukhtar Mai, is a feminist too. A devout Muslim, she also supports and champions Pakistani rape victims.

Feminists also hail from different religious backgrounds, causing some interesting discussions about the labels believers choose regarding their feminist viewpoints. When a group of Spanish Muslims approached city officials in Barcelona, Spain, about sponsoring a conference on Islamic feminism, one official responded with shock, noting that "Islamic feminism" must surely be a contradiction or an oxymoron (Nomani, 2005). Others have eschewed the feminist label entirely because of its connection to liberal politics. More recently, prominent conservative female politicians have donned the label "mama grizzly" to express the fierceness of pro-life, limited-government women (Torregrosa, 2010).

What these examples reveal is that the labels we choose for our beliefs affect how we communicate them to others (and how others respond). As these examples show, when we place gender, ethnic, class, occupation, or role labels on others, we ignore their individual differences (Sarich & Miele, 2004) and thus limit or constrict our communication. So if you think all feminists are liberal, secular, career-oriented women, you may miss out on the opportunity to understand the feminist views of your aunt who is a stay-at-home mom or your male neighbor who is a conservative Jew.

Biased Language

Some language is infused with subtle meanings that imply that a person or subject should be perceived in a particular way. This is known as **biased language**. For example, addressing an older person as "sweetie" or "dear" can be belittling (even if kindly intended) (Leland, 2008). In particular, older individuals struggling with dementia are sensitive to language that implies that they are childlike ("Did you eat your dinner like a good boy?") because they are struggling to maintain their dignity (Williams, Herman, Gajewski, & Wilson, 2009). In addition, there are many derogatory terms for women who engage in casual sex, though men who engage in similar behaviors in similar situations are afforded less derogatory labels (she is "easy"; he is a "player"). Such biased language perpetuates perceptions of women as less intelligent, less mentally healthy, and less competent than men in similar relationships or situations (Conley, 2011; Jacobs, 2012).

Connect

The federal government and organizations take derogatory labels that hurt and demean others quite seriously. Professional organizations typically provide employees with information regarding their *harassment* and *sexual harassment* policies, which are intended to protect employees from feeling threatened or attacked because of their race, religion, abilities, or other personal traits.

EVALUATING COMMUNICATION ETHICS

Résumé Language

You've just graduated with a B.A. in communication and are on the hunt for an entry-level position in marketing. You know that your résumé is strong in terms of your degree, relevant coursework, and good grades, but you're a bit worried that you may not have enough real-world experience. Since you had to work full time to pay college expenses, you couldn't afford to take the kinds of unpaid internships that look so impressive on a résumé; you waited tables all through college instead and graduated in five years instead of four.

You discuss these concerns with a friend who suggests making some changes in the language of your résumé. First, she suggests changing your entry date for college to make it look like you finished the degree in four years. Second, she suggests you cast your restaurant experience as a type of marketing internship in which you developed "people skills" and "sales skills" that helped you "analyze and synthesize" consumers and products. Finally, she tells you to use your cover letter to describe yourself as "a team player" who is "attentive to detail" and has "proven creativity."

You're worried that some aspects of your résumé might not be impressive enough, but you're not entirely sure that padding your résumé with vague language and empty jargon is the way to go. What will you do?

Think About This

1. Is it crucial that an employer know how long it took you to earn your B.A.? Is it unethical to simply note the date you finished it?

2. Will you follow your friend's suggestion to use vague expressions like "team player"? In what ways might you use more precise terms to describe yourself?

3. Rather than dressing it up as "marketing experience," might there be an honest way to use your restaurant experience to your advantage here?

AND YOU?
Has anyone ever labeled you in a way that truly irritated or offended you? What terms did they use? Are you aware of any biased language that frequently seeps into conversations among your friends, family, or coworkers? How might you consider addressing such biases?

Biased language can also affect others' perceptions of you. For example, if you employ the vague "those guys" to describe coworkers in another department or a group of teens hanging out at the mall, others will likely see you as more biased than people who use concrete terms (for example, "the attorneys in the legal department" or "the high school students at FroYo") (Assilaméhou & Testé, 2013).

When language openly excludes certain groups or implies something negative about them, we often attempt to replace the biased language with more neutral terms, employing what is known as **politically correct language**. For example, the terms *firefighter*, *police officer*, and *chairperson* replace the sexist terms *fireman*, *policeman*, and *chairman*, reflecting and perhaps influencing the fact that these once male-dominated positions are now open to women as well. Critics of political correctness argue that such attempts at sensitivity and neutrality can undermine communication as they substitute euphemisms for clarity when dealing with difficult subjects and place certain words off-limits (O'Neill, 2011). But others note that there is value in always trying to be sensitive—and accurate—when we make choices regarding language.

Profanity and Civility

Comedians curse and audiences laugh; perhaps you have a relative who adds colorful words to his or her stories, which amuses your family members ("That's Uncle Mike for you!"). This was not the case for A.J. Clemente who cursed on air on his first day as a broadcaster for the North Dakota NBC affiliate KFYR. Clemente later explained that he was practicing his lines and nervously uttered the offensive words without realizing that his microphone was on; he also offered an apology for his behavior on Twitter. But in the end, he could not undo the impression he left with his new employer and was ultimately fired (ABC News, 2013; Grossman, 2013). Recent years have seen an increase in swearing over mediated channels (Butler & Fitzgerald, 2011), and some critics believe that public outrage over sex, violence, and profanity seems to have waned in recent decades (Steinberg, 2010). In fact, in the wake of Clemente's outburst, more than fifteen hundred fans wrote supportive notes on the station's Facebook page asking managers to reconsider their decision to let Clemente go. Twitter supporters also showed their support with #FreeAJ and #KeepAJ.

Profanity includes cursing and other expressions considered rude, vulgar, or disrespectful. Such words get their social and emotional impact from the culture and can be perceived positively, neutrally, or negatively (Johnson, 2012) based on factors like the social setting (for example, friends at home watching televised sports) or the relationship. If A.J. Clemente had uttered the exact same words at a bar surrounded by friends, it would not have made national news. Rather, he cursed in a formal, professional environment.

Regardless of whether language is viewed as rude or appropriate based on the relational, cultural, or situational context, it should meet some standards of **civility**, the social norm for appropriate behavior. Crude, offensive, vulgar, and profane language can create uncomfortable and unproductive relationships and work environments (Johnson & Lewis, 2010). Following are five guidelines for the production of more civil language in the workplace (Troester & Mester, 2007), but most of them are applicable outside of the business context as well:

- Use no words rather than offensive ones.

- Use words appropriate to your specific listener.

- Choose temperate and accurate words over inflammatory ones when commenting on ideas, issues, or persons.

- Use objective, respectful, nondiscriminatory language.

- Use clean language at all times when at work.

■ Language in Context

Context is particularly important to our study of language in three ways: language reflects, builds on, and determines context.

- *Language reflects context.* The language we use reflects who we're around, where we are, and what sort of cultural factors are at play—that is, the context we're in. In different contexts, we use different **speech repertoires**—sets of complex language styles, behaviors, and skills that we have learned. Recall from the beginning of this chapter that we need to "accommodate" our communication (that is, adjust our way of speaking with other people). Having several speech repertoires at our disposal allows us to choose the most effective and appropriate way of speaking for a given relationship, situation, or cultural environment.

- *Language builds on context.* At the beginning of this chapter, we wondered about the difference between calling your stepmother "Mom" versus calling her by her first name. It's an example of language building on context. If your stepmother raised you and is your primary maternal figure, you might well call her "Mom." But if your relationship with her is strained, you are close to your own biological or adopted mother, or your stepmother entered your life once you were an adult, you may prefer to call her by her name. As you develop relationships, you learn how people prefer to be addressed (and how you are comfortable addressing them), and you adjust your language accordingly.

- *Language determines context.* We can also *create* context by the language we use. If your professor says, "Call me Veronica," one context is created (informal, first-name basis, more equal). If she says, "I'm Dr. Esquivel," you will likely have expectations for a more formal context (less personal, less equal). This context will then influence your choice of speech repertoires—you're more likely to tell "Veronica" about your weekend plans than "Dr. Esquivel."

With these points in mind, let's consider how language works in different situations, in our relationships, and in our cultures, as well as in mediated settings.

AND YOU?

Consider the various situations you find yourself in over the course of a given day—at home, in the classroom, at a student activity, on the job, and so on. Do you have different speech repertoires for each situation? Does your language change further depending on who is present—your mother, your best friend, your professor?

Situational Context

Different situations (being at a job interview, in a court of law, or at your Uncle Fred's sixtieth birthday party) call for different speech repertoires. **Code switching** is a type of accommodation in which communicators change from one repertoire or "code" to another as the situation warrants. The language you speak is one type of code. If you speak both English and Spanish, for example, you might speak English in the classroom or on the job but switch to Spanish with your family at home because it creates a special bond between family members (Gudykunst, 2004).

Another type of code that you may switch is the linguistic style—the use of slang, jargon, and grammar—that allows you to fit in with a particular group. These language accommodations may be ways to survive, to manage defensiveness, to manage identity, or to signal power or status in different situations (Dragojevic, Giles, & Watson, 2013). For instance, police officers use this type of accommodation when they adopt the street slang or foreign phrases used by citizens in the neighborhoods they patrol and when they use more formal, bureaucratic language when interacting with superiors, filling out reports, or testifying in court.

Similarly, you might decide to use **high language**—a more formal, polite, or "mainstream" language—in business contexts, in the classroom, and in formal social gatherings (as when trying to impress the parents of your new romantic interest). However, you would probably switch to more informal, easygoing **low language** (often involving slang) when you're in more casual or comfortable environments, such as watching a football game at a sports bar with your friends.

Our sex and gender can interact with the situation to affect our language use. For example, women and men adapt their language use to same-sex versus mixed-sex situations. When women speak with other women, they tend to discuss relationships and use words that are more affection-oriented (concerned with feelings, values, and attitudes). Men chatting with other men use more instrumentally oriented language (concerned with doing things and accomplishing tasks) (Reis, 1998). Gender also comes into play in workplace situations. Occupations that have been traditionally defined as "masculine" or "feminine" often develop a job culture and language that follow suit. Male nursery school teachers (a traditionally "feminine job") and fathers doing primary childcare may use feminine language at work; female police officers (a traditionally "masculine" job) may adopt more masculine language on patrol (Winter & Pauwels, 2006).

COMMUNICATION ACROSS CULTURES

Teaching Twain

It is considered a classic of American literature, a truly groundbreaking novel that thumbed its nose at convention when it was published in 1885 and continues to challenge ideas about race, relationships, and language more than a century later.

At a time when respectable books were written in upper-middle-class English—and when slavery was still fresh in American memory—Mark Twain's *Adventures of Huckleberry Finn* told the story of the unlikely relationship between a free-spirited white boy and a fugitive slave, Jim, in everyday language. Twain carefully constructed Jim and Huck's conversations with words, inflections, and phonetic spellings that can shock modern readers. Most notably, Twain uses the "N-word" over two hundred times.

The book itself remains controversial as scholars and critics continue to argue about Twain's characters. It is consistently at or near the top of the American Library Association's annual list of books banned or challenged by parents or school boards. John Wallace, a former public school administrator, calls it "racist trash" and says that its use of the N-word is offensive, no matter what the context or how teachers try to explain it (D. L. Howard, 2004). Yet others come to the book's defense, noting that it was written as satire and that Twain's intention was "to subvert, not reinforce, racism" (Kennedy, 2003, p. 108). Temple University professor David Bradley notes that the word must be taken in the context of the times and situation: "What was Twain supposed to do, call them African-Americans?" (Rabinowitz, 1995, para. 16).

Teachers of American literature often find themselves struggling with self-censorship as they grapple with whether or not to speak the word aloud in class, since it may cause students to feel hurt and offended. This was certainly the case for Professor Alan Gribben of Auburn University at Montgomery, who created a revised edition of the work that replaces the N-word with the word *slave*. Professor Gribben explains: "I'm by no means sanitizing Mark Twain. The sharp social critiques are in there. The humor is intact. I just had the idea to get us away from obsessing about this one word, and just let the stories stand alone" (quoted in Bosman, 2011, para. 2). But critics passionately disagree, accusing Professor Gribben's publisher of censorship and sanitizing history. Author Jill Nelson notes that changing Twain's carefully chosen words to suit contemporary mores and eliminate hurt feelings "is an abdication of a teacher's responsibility to illuminate and guide students through an unfamiliar and perhaps difficult text" (Nelson, 2011, para. 3).

Think About This

1. What meaning does the N-word carry for you? Does it seem appropriate to use it in a scholarly discussion? How do you feel about it being printed (or not printed) in this textbook? Does avoiding printing or saying the word give it more or less power?

2. If an instructor chose to use the word in class, how might he or she do so in a way that would be sensitive to students? Can students investigate the word's meaning and history without using it?

3. What is your opinion on Gribben's new edition? Are his editorial changes sensitive and helpful, or is he sanitizing history?

Ronnie Kaufman/Larry Hirshowitz/Blend Images/Getty Images

FIGURE 1.8 The formal, high language that this young woman employs while at work with her colleagues differs from the more casual, low language that she probably uses when relaxing at home or socializing with friends.

But as we've learned, competent communicators use the most effective and appropriate ways of interacting in a given situation. That may mean putting aside gendered speech "appropriate" for our sex. For instance, a successful male manager uses language that reflects liking and respect when building relationships in the workplace, and a successful female manager uses direct language to clarify instructions for completing an important task (Bates, 1988).

Relational Context

Kathryn Stockett's bestseller *The Help* (2009), along with the 2011 film adaptation, is a fascinating representation of the relationships between black domestic servants and their white employers in Mississippi in the early 1960s. The dialogues (told in different voices) ring true because they reflect the relationships between and among women of different races, social classes, and experiences. We all choose different language to communicate in different relationships: you don't speak to your grandmother the way you speak to your best friend, and we (college professors) don't speak to our students the way we speak to our colleagues. That's because language both reflects and creates the relational context. Let's consider some examples.

Michelle and Chris have been dating for a few weeks. After a movie one night, they run into one of Chris's colleagues. When Chris introduces Michelle as his *girlfriend*, Michelle is surprised. She hadn't thought of their relationship as being that serious yet. The English language allows us to communicate the status of many of our relationships quite clearly: mother, brother, aunt, grandfather, daughter, and so on. But as with the word *partner*, the language we use when communicating about other types of relationships can be confusing. Chris and Michelle are in the somewhat undefined state of "dating." When Chris uses the term *girlfriend* as a label for Michelle, this implies a more defined level of intimacy that Michelle isn't yet sure she feels. Chris certainly had other options, but each has its own issues. For example, if Chris had said that Michelle is a *friend*, it might have implied a lack of romantic interest (and might have hurt Michelle's feelings). The fact is the English language has very few terms to describe different levels of intimacy we have with friends and romantic partners (Bradac, 1983; Stollen & White, 2004).

Dale Robinette/© Walt Disney Studios Motion Pictures/Courtesy Everett Collection

FIGURE 1.9 In *The Help*, Aibleen, played by Octavia Spencer, uses language to show the relationship between herself and her employer in 1960s Mississippi.

Labels can also confer status and create understandings between and among individuals. If you say, "I'd like you to meet my boss, Edward Sanchez," you are describing both Mr. Sanchez's status and the professional relationship that you have with him; it tells others what language is appropriate in front of him. To indicate a more casual relationship, you might introduce him as, "Ed—we work together at Kohl's."

> **AND YOU?**
> How do you label your romantic partner? Do you use different terms around different people in different situations? How do the terms you choose for each other affect your understanding of the status of the relationship?

CONNECT

The different language we use in different relationships is often affected by unique *communication climates* or atmospheres that encompass relationships. This is certainly true when experiencing interpersonal conflict. For example, if you and your brother experience a *supportive climate*, your conflicts will likely be characterized by careful, considerate words and an openness to hearing each other's thoughts.

Cultural Context

Throughout this book, we remind you about the relationship between culture and communication (particularly in Chapter 4). Next we examine particular aspects of how the cultural context shapes our language, including the relationship among culture, words, and thoughts; the relationship between gender and language; and the impact of our region (where we grew up or where we live now) on our verbal choices.

Culture, Words, and Thought

As we have seen, our language use can affect our thoughts. Consider a study of the Pirahã tribe of Brazil (Gordon, 2004). The study shows that the Pirahã language does not have words for numbers above two—anything above two is simply called "many." When researchers laid a random number of familiar objects (like sticks and nuts) in a row, and asked the Pirahã to lay out the same number of objects in their own pile, tribe members were able to match the pile if there were three or fewer objects. But for numbers above three, they would only approximately match the pile, becoming less and less accurate as the number of objects increased. In addition, when researchers asked them to copy taps on the floor, the Pirahã did not copy the behavior beyond three taps. Researchers concluded that the limitation of words for numbers above two prevented the Pirahã from perceiving larger numbers (Biever, 2004).

The study's findings support the **Sapir-Whorf hypothesis** (also known as linguistic relativity theory), which holds that the words a culture uses (or doesn't use) influence the thinking of people from that culture (Sapir & Whorf, 1956). In other words, if a culture lacks a word for something (as the Pirahã lack words for higher numbers), members of that culture will have few thoughts about that thing or concept. Thus language influences or determines how we see the world around us, and speakers of different languages develop different views of the world relative to their language. For example, some languages (like Spanish, French, and German) assign a gender to objects. This is a bit of a foreign concept to many native speakers of English because English is gender-neutral—English speakers simply say *the shoe* whereas a Spanish speaker marks the word as masculine (*el zapato, el* being the masculine article); a French speaker marks the word as feminine (*la chaussure, la* being the feminine article). Marking an object as masculine or feminine changes a speaker's mental picture of the object. For example, German speakers describe a key (a masculine word in German) in traditionally masculine terms (*hard, heavy, jagged, metal, serrated,* and *useful*) whereas Spanish speakers describe a key (a feminine word in Spanish) in traditionally feminine terms (*golden, intricate, little, lovely, shiny,* and *tiny*) (Wasserman & Weseley, 2009).

REAL COMMUNICATOR

NAME: Matt Burgess

OCCUPATION: Author and Creative Writing Instructor

The use of language has always been fascinating to me. When my first novel (*Dogfight: A Love Story*) was published, reviewers said I had an incredible ear for dialogue and the "poetry" of the street. I was flattered to have succeeded at putting the vivid language of my New York City neighborhood onto the printed page.

When I began writing stories in college, I used the more sophisticated terminology of my professors and student peers. But back home in Queens, I felt uncomfortable—almost guilty—using the high language of that urbane, professional context. Then I realized there was no reason to be anxious; the language of different economic, social, and cultural groups is rich with meaning. I really believe that this conscious decision helped my fiction become more realistic and reflective of the worlds around me. For example, when I try to capture the conversations in bodegas, bowling alleys, and barbershops, I use the casual, low language so familiar to me; it's filled with the slang, neighborhood references, and good-humored insults that I grew up around. Nonverbal communication is important to capture, too. Some people deliver an insult with a wink, smile, or vocal tone that expresses love and changes the literal meaning of the words spoken.

Precise language is important to my writing as well. For example, I avoid clichés and highly abstract language. If you say something happened "out of the blue," you don't really mean something came out of a color; this is a lazy language choice. Rather, I use precise words for clarity and interest: "She showed signs of satisfaction as she took possession of her reward" transforms into "Gilda grinned as she snatched the coin." (On a personal note, precise language is important in my marriage, too. When my wife says, "I particularly enjoyed the curry dish you spent an hour making tonight," I appreciate it even more than when she just says, "Thanks for fixing dinner.")

In addition to working on my second novel, I teach creative writing courses to both traditional students and older adults. One of my goals is to help them find their own unique voice as writers to say what they mean accurately and precisely while utilizing the unique words and speaking styles comfortable and familiar to them. This journey with language has been deeply rewarding to me and enriches my life. My hope as an author and teacher is that my readers and students will be able to say the same.

Gender and Language

Cultural factors deeply affect our thinking and perception of gender roles, which are often inscribed with "different languages" for the masculine and the feminine (Gudykunst & Ting-Toomey, 1988). The idea that men and women speak entirely different languages is popular fodder for comedy, talk shows, and pop psychologists, so let's identify what actual differences have contributed to that view.

Women primarily see conversations as negotiations for closeness and connection with others, whereas men experience talk more as a struggle for control, independence, and hierarchy (Tannen, 1992). But either may use powerful, controlling language to define limits, authority, and relationships and less controlling language to express affection. Let's look at a few examples.

- *Interruptions.* Male speakers are thought to interrupt others in conversation more than female speakers, but the situation and the status of the speakers are better predictors than biological sex (Pearson, Turner, & Todd-Mancillas, 1991). For example, female professors can be expected to interrupt male students more often than those male students interrupt female professors, owing to the difference in power and status. But when status and situation are neutral, men tend to interrupt women considerably more often than women interrupt men (Ivy & Backlund, 2004).

- *Intensifiers.* Women's speech patterns, compared with men's, contain more words that heighten or intensify topics: ("so excited," "*very* happy") (Yaguchi, Iyeiri, & Baba, 2010). Consider the intensity level of "I'm upset" versus "I'm *really* upset."

- *Qualifiers, hedges, and disclaimers.* Language that sounds hesitant is perceived as being less powerful (often associated with women's speech). *Qualifiers* include terms like *kind of, sort of, maybe,* and *possibly. Hedges* are expressions such as "I think," "I feel," or "I guess." *Disclaimers* discount what you are about to say and can head off confrontation or avoid embarrassment: "I'm likely imagining things, but I thought I saw . . ." (Palomares, 2009).

- *Tag questions.* Another sign of hesitancy or uncertainty associated with feminine speech is the *tag question,* as in "That waitress was obnoxious, wasn't she?" Tag questions attempt to get your conversational partner to agree with you, establishing a connection based on similar opinions. They can also come across as threats (Ivy & Backlund, 2004); for example, "You're not going to smoke another cigarette, *are you?*"

- *Resistance messages.* Differences in the way men and women express resistance can have serious consequences. Specifically, date rape awareness programs advise women to use the word *no* when a male partner or friend makes an unwanted sexual advance. But a woman might instead say, "I don't have protection," choosing vague or evasive language over the direct *no* to avoid a scene. Men, however, sometimes perceive an indirect denial as a yes. Women's use of clear messages, coupled with men's increased understanding of women's preference for more indirect resistance messages, can lead to more competent communication in this crucial area (Lim & Roloff, 1999; Motley & Reeder, 1995).

CONNECT

Gendered language often affects mixed-sex small group settings. Women are typically encouraged to build rapport, using affectionate language to keep the peace and share power. Men are rewarded for taking charge of a group and using direct, action-oriented language. Competent communicators must be aware of these differences in style and must promote group communication that encourages all members to share and challenge ideas in order to achieve group goals.

AND YOU?

What are your personal thoughts on sex, gender, and language? Do you think men and women speak different languages, or do you feel that we all speak more similarly than differently? How do your thoughts and opinions match up with the research we've cited in this chapter?

In summary, research has corroborated some differences in communication style due to sex (Kiesling, 1998), but many of those differences pale when we consider *gender* (the cultural meaning of sex), context, role, and task (Ewald, 2010; Mulac, Wiemann, Widenmann, & Gibson, 1988; Newman, Groom, Handelman, & Pennebaker, 2008). Relatedly, studying language from a sex-difference approach can be misleading, because it treats women (and men) as a homogenous "global category," paying little attention to differences in ethnicity, religion, sexuality, and economic status (Crawford, 1995). In fact, recent studies focus on how we present our different "faces" in interaction (Tannen, 2009, 2010) and how language choices are more about negotiating influence (power, hierarchy), solidarity (connection, intimacy), value formation, and identity rather than about sex (Tannen, Kendall, & Gorgon, 2007). Decades of research find that we are less bound by our sex than we are by the language choices we make. Thus, regardless of whether we are male or female, we can choose to use language that gives us more influence or creates more connection—or both.

Geography

Our editor from New Jersey assures us that even in such a small state, it makes a big difference if you are from North Jersey or South Jersey. (The status of people from the middle part of the state remains unclear, at least to us.) People in North Jersey eat subs (sandwiches that you buy at 7-Eleven or QuickChek) and Italian ice (a frozen dessert). The night before Halloween, when shaving cream and toilet paper abound, is Goosey Night or Cabbage Night. And "the city" is, of course, New York City. People from South Jersey eat hoagies (typically from a convenience store called Wawa) and water ice. The night before Halloween is Mischief Night. And going to "the city" means taking a trip to Philadelphia.

As this example illustrates, even for speakers of the same language who grow up just fifty miles apart, culture affects their language and their understanding of the world. Other examples are more extreme. Consider our friend Ada, who kindly shared an embarrassing moment with us (and is allowing us to tell you). When she came to the United States from Hong Kong, she knew she had to give up some of her Britishisms to communicate more effectively with her American-born classmates at Wesleyan University. This was never more apparent than when she asked a classmate for a rubber (to correct some mistakes in her notebook). She wanted an eraser; he thought she was asking for a condom. Needless to say, she was a bit perplexed by his response: "Maybe after class?"

AND YOU?
Think back to where you grew up—whether in the United States or abroad. Are there any terms that you use that would cause confusion to others who speak your native tongue? Have you ever been in a situation where you've used a regional term that caused an embarrassing miscommunication?

© Foodcollection.com/Alamy

FIGURE 1.10 Is this a sub or a hoagie? Perhaps a hero or just a plain old sandwich?

Mediated Contexts

Have you ever sent an e-mail or a text message that was misunderstood by the recipient? It has happened to all of us—and that's often because our e-mails, text messages, tweets, and wall postings lack the nonverbal cues and hints we provide in face-to-face conversation. So if you text your spouse to say that you both have to spend Friday night with your slightly quirky Aunt Ethel, and he texts you back "Great," is he really excited? Is he being sarcastic? "Great" could mean either thing, but you can't see his nonverbal reaction to know if he's smiling or grimacing and rolling his eyes. That's why communication in mediated contexts must be extra clear to be effective (DeAndrea & Walther, 2011).

Other characteristics of our online language can also influence communication. For example, people in computer-mediated groups who use powerful language, such as direct statements of their personal goals, are seen as more credible, attractive, and persuasive than those who use tentative language (hedges, disclaimers, and tag questions) (Adkins & Brashers, 1995). However, group-oriented language can be more persuasive and effective than language pushing personal goals. For example, one study of an international adolescent online forum found that students who were elected as "leaders" (Cassell, Huffaker, Tversky, & Ferriman, 2006) made references to group goals and synthesized other students' posts.

Interestingly, sex and gender can influence the language you use with technology. In online games, for example, people who were assigned avatars of their own gender were more likely to use gender-typical language (more emotional expressions and tentative language if assigned a feminine avatar) than those assigned mismatched avatars (Palomares & Lee, 2010). Another study found that people infer a person's sex from language cues online (for example, amount of self-disclosure, expression of emotion) and conform more to computer-mediated partners when they believe them to be male (Lee, 2007).

But technology affects language use in broader ways as well, including the proliferation of English as the language of the Internet. Individuals in Salt Lake City, São Paulo, and Stockholm can all communicate digitally, often in English. Critics often claim that because English dominates the mass media industries, English speakers' values and thinking are being imposed on the non-English-speaking world. Nevertheless, many non-Western countries have benefited from this proliferation, with countless jobs being relocated to places like India and Hong Kong (Friedman, 2007). Every day brings increasing language diversity to the Internet, and Internet-based translators make it much easier to translate material into innumerable languages (Danet & Herring, 2007).

Blend Images/Veer

FIGURE 1.11 Texting your friend "Coffee?" is a perfect way to schedule a quick get-together, but if you're asking your professor to meet over a cup for career advice, it'd be smart to send a more formal email.

Despite the controversies surrounding English, the Internet, and mass media, technology has, in some sense, created a language of its own. The language of text messaging and chat rooms frequently relies on acronyms (for example, IMO for "in my opinion"), some of which people use in other contexts and some of which has even made it into the *Oxford English Dictionary* (Editorial, 2011). Acronyms are useful in texting because they enable rapid keystroking, resulting in speed that makes this "fingered speech" more like spoken language (McWhorter, 2013). However, it's important to keep text language in its appropriate context. If your professor writes you an e-mail asking about your recent absences from class, it's probably not a good idea to respond with "NOYB, IMHO" ("none of your business, in my humble opinion"). That would show not only a lack of respect for your instructor (obviously) but also a lack of understanding regarding context. E-mail etiquette calls for more complete sentences.

■ What About You?

Beliefs About "Talk"

As you've seen in this chapter, individuals value language as a way to gain control in conversations, to share information, express feelings, be creative, and so on. Others, however, are more comfortable with fewer words, even silence.

Complete the following questionnaire about your own beliefs about talking and language use, and rate the frequency that you engage in each behavior. Use the following scale: 5 = almost always; 4 = frequently; 3 = sometimes; 2 = not very often; and 1 = rarely. Then add your scores and consider where you fall on the following continuum.

	1. I enjoy meeting and talking with people.
	2. In general, I consider myself quite a talker.
	3. I don't mind initiating conversations with strangers.
	4. I like to voice my opinion.
	5. In general, I enjoy talking.
	6. I enjoy small talk.
	7. I like people who talk a lot.
	8. When talking, I find myself trying to influence others' opinions and feelings.
	9. I believe talk is one way to increase intimacy.
	10. Small talk is an enjoyable use of time.
	11. I don't mind taking responsibility for breaking the ice when meeting someone for the first time.
	12. I talk more when I feel I'm in control of a situation.
	13. I feel uncomfortable with silences in a conversation.
	14. In general, I like to be the first one to speak in a discussion.
	15. I feel comfortable asking a stranger for information.
	16. When in a discussion, I talk even if I'm unfamiliar with the topic.
	17. I enjoy going out to meet and talk with people.
	18. I find myself turning on the radio or TV just to hear the sound of someone's voice.

67–90: You enjoy and value talk and are not apprehensive about talking; you see talking as a social experience and, as a rule, you are uncomfortable with silence.

43–66: You have a more measured approach to talk, using it to accomplish goals and meet the norms of the situation. You are comfortable with silence and more likely to adjust your rate of talking to that of your partner(s).

18–42: You do not enjoy a lot of talk and prefer to use it with a purpose in mind. Silence is comfortable for you and you do not rush to fill it with words.

Note: Different cultures value talk in different ways, so it might be important for you to adapt your use of language or silence according to the situation. In addition, competent communicators remember that being appropriate and effective means talking up at times, being sociable with talk, but also knowing when to be quiet and let others talk.

Source: Adapted from Honeycutt & Wiemann (1999) and Wiemann, Chen, & Giles (1986).

Back To Our Partners

Our discussion of the word *partner* and its various meanings showed that the labels we choose are powerful—and can complicate our communication.

- The word *partner* has several denotative meanings, as we discussed earlier. But it can also have powerful connotative meanings. Let's look at romantic couples who choose the term *partner*. When some people hear an individual refer to his or her "partner," they may assume the individual is gay or lesbian. And they may have positive, negative, or neutral reactions based on their cultural background. Others may wonder if the individual is trying to hide his or her marital or legal status. Still others may see *partner* as a term that marks equality in romantic relationships.

- Abstraction plays an important role in the use of the term *partner*. Saying "This is my boyfriend" or "This is my business partner" is a low-level abstraction, offering others a clear definition of your status. But the term *partner* is a high-level abstraction, keeping your status and relationship considerably more vague.

- Considering the relational, situational, and cultural context is one way to make the term *partner* less abstract and vague. If you let your chemistry professor know that your "partner" needs some help with an experiment, the instructor understands that you mean your lab partner rather than your romantic partner or the person you play tennis with. Similarly, when introducing the love of your life to your elderly great-aunt, you might want to use a less ambiguous term. Your great-aunt may be of a generation that did not use the term *partner* to apply to a love interest.

■ Things To Try

Activities

1. Take a look at a piece of writing you've produced (an essay, your résumé, or a private Facebook message to a friend). Do you use high or low levels of abstraction? Is your choice of language appropriate for the communication contexts involved? (For example, is your essay written in a way that is mindful of your relationship with your professor and the academic setting?)

2. Describe the similarities and differences you find in the language you use and the language a close friend or family member of the opposite sex uses over the course of a single conversation. What did you notice? Were there any misunderstandings or power struggles in this conversation? How do your findings match up with what the research we presented tells us?

3. Examine the language you use in mediated communication. Are there subtle ways in which you and your communication partners negotiate influence and create connectedness? Are any language choices related to sex or gender? What differences do you find in the language you use in mediated contexts from the language you use in face-to-face contexts?

4. Make a study of your Facebook (or other social networking) pages. Compile a list of the types of language used, including acronyms. Do you ever misunderstand the language in posts from your friends? Have you ever used language that was misinterpreted? Are you ever offended by the posts or "shares" of your friends? Describe how you could post in the future to avoid problems due to language.

Chapter 2

Nonverbal Communication

- The Nature of Nonverbal Communication
- Functions of Nonverbal Communication
- Nonverbal Communication Codes
- Influences on Nonverbal Communication

chapter outcomes

After you have finished reading this chapter, you will be able to

- Describe the power of nonverbal communication
- Outline the functions of nonverbal communication
- Describe the set of communication symbols that are nonverbal codes
- Illustrate the influences culture, technology, and situation have on our nonverbal behavior

This chapter is taken from Dan O'Hair, Mary Wiemann, Dorothy Imric Mullin, and Jason Teven, *Real Communication*, Third Edition, pp. 92–118 (Chapter 4).

MCD©Walt Disney Co./courtesy Everett Collection

No dialogue is needed to convey Carl and Ellie's love for each other.

Can you tell a compelling, believable, and heartwarming love story in just four minutes—without using any words? The Academy Award–nominated *Up* does just that (Docter & Peterson, 2009). After opening with a simple meet-cute between young, quiet Carl and adventurous, talkative Ellie, the sequence that follows offers a montage of life moments, explained simply and graphically: they express affection by holding hands and devotion by the cross-my-heart gesture of their childhood. Their dreams of children are symbolized in visions of baby-shaped clouds, and as those dreams are crushed, their grief is conveyed by Ellie's silent sobs and Carl's quiet gestures of comfort. As the years go by, their plans to travel are shown with paintings and brochures; the financial struggles that thwart them are explained in tiny vignettes that detail home repairs, car troubles, and medical bills. Relying entirely on nonverbal behaviors—beautifully crafted and rendered by the artists at Pixar Studios—and set to a mesmerizing musical score, the sequence manages to clearly convey the events and emotions that shaped these two characters' decades-long romance, as well as Carl's loneliness and isolation after Ellie's death, without a word of dialogue.

The filmmakers at Pixar were no strangers to near "silent" films— their previous offering, the equally stunning and compelling *WALL-E*, included virtually no dialogue for the first forty minutes, in what the British newspaper *The Independent* called "a masterclass in non-verbal communication" (Quinn, 2008, para. 7). During those scenes, the film not only managed to create compelling characters out of a pair of robots and a lone, unspeaking cockroach, but also to explain a fairly complicated story line of environmental devastation in a simple, accessible way.

Telling a story on screen is complicated because filmmaking encompasses nonverbal performances (be it from actors or from animators). These performances include the visual choices made by the artists and directors, from colors used in a scene's background to the characters' clothing. For animators like the team at Pixar, the challenge is even more daunting. They must make inhuman objects—whether computer-generated "people" like Carl and Ellie, monsters like Mike Wazowski from *Monster's University*, or robots (or fish, toys, or insects)—into believable, humanlike characters who can effectively communicate complex information and emotions.

Likewise, in real life, we communicate with many tools other than language. In this chapter, we examine **nonverbal communication**—the process of intentionally or unintentionally signaling meaning through behavior other than words (Knapp & Hall, 2010). This definition encompasses a variety of actions, such as gestures, tone of voice, and eye behavior, as well as all aspects of physical appearance. We begin by examining the nature and functions of nonverbal communication. Then we move to the nonverbal codes that convey messages without words and conclude with an examination of important influences on nonverbal communication.

■ The Nature of Nonverbal Communication

A deaf woman signs a message to a companion. A colleague writes a note to you on a pad of paper during a boring meeting. A man taps his watch to signal to a friend that it's almost time for lunch. In all three instances, communication occurs without a word being spoken. But not all of all these examples are actually nonverbal communication. Studying the essential nature of nonverbal communication reveals why.

Nonverbal Behavior Is Communicative

You communicate nonverbally when you convey a message without using any words. But you also communicate nonverbally when you use nonverbal behaviors *in addition* to words: when you smile, frown, or gesture as you speak or when you use a particular tone or volume while talking (Giles & LePoire, 2006). For example, as a kid, maybe you knew when your parents were angry with you because they called you by your full name while using "that tone."

Consider the examples we gave above. American Sign Language (ASL), a visual language with its own grammatical structure used by hearing-impaired individuals in the United States and English-speaking Canada, is still verbal communication. It may be *nonvocal*, because the communicators don't use their voices. However, it is still a language, because it uses hand signals (rather than spoken words) as symbols and it has grammatical rules. The note that your colleague writes to you uses words, so it too is a form of verbal communication (written rather than spoken). Only the third example is nonverbal communication—tapping a watch signals meaning without use of linguistic symbols. Yet this example reminds us that nonverbal behavior and verbal communication are connected. Had the friends not made a verbal agreement to meet for lunch, the act of tapping the watch might be confusing.

(top) Simon Baker/Getty Images; (bottom) AP Photo/Al Behrman

FIGURE 2.1 Giving someone a big hug is an example of nonverbal communication, but communicating with someone using American Sign Language is not.

Nonverbal Communication Is Often Spontaneous and Unintentional

The best poker players think a great deal about nonverbal communication. They know how to bluff, or convince their opponents that they are holding a better (or worse) hand than is actually the case. A player who figures out an opponent's "tell"—a nonverbal signal indicating a good or bad hand—can profit from this knowledge if he, quite literally, plays his cards right. Mike Caro, a poker professional and author of *The Body Language of Poker*, warns players not to look at the cards as they are laid out on the table. Players who look away from "the flop" have a strong hand, he explains. Those who stare at it—or at their cards—have a weak one. He also advises players to memorize their hand so opponents won't see them looking at their cards and glean cues from this action (Zimbushka, 2008).

Like poker players, we often send nonverbal messages unintentionally—we roll our eyes, laugh, slouch, or blush without meaning to. And our nonverbal behaviors can send powerful, unintended messages without us having much time to think through them (Capella & Greene, 1982). Great poker players know that they can't completely eliminate such behaviors. That's why many of them wear sunglasses while playing: they want to mask their eyes so their opponents can't pick up subtle and unintentional cues from their eye movements.

CONNECT

You make sense of your world and decode nonverbal behavior through *schemas*, your accumulated experience of people, roles, and situations. So if you catch your friend in a lie, you might suspect, on the basis of your relational history, that whenever he avoids eye contact with you, he's lying. But competent communicators must think beyond schemas when determining the meaning of nonverbal communication.

Nonverbal Communication Is Ambiguous

Professional players like Caro might have a system for reading nonverbal behaviors, but even they know that it's more of an art than a science. That's because nonverbal communication is inherently ambiguous. Blinking, stammering, or hesitations in speech can indicate deception. But they can also indicate anxiety or uncertainty. In many cases, you can pick up clues about the meaning of behavior from the situational context. If your friend is sighing deeply and blinking rapidly as she heads off to her biochemistry final exam, she's probably anxious. But you can't know for sure. Perhaps her boyfriend broke up with her twenty minutes ago and she just doesn't feel like talking about it. For this reason, it's best to regard nonverbal behavior (and poker "tells") as cues to be checked out rather than as facts.

Nonverbal Communication Is More Believable Than Verbal Communication

Imagine you're grabbing lunch with your brother, talking a mile a minute about your exciting plans for after graduation. He's staring off into space. You wonder if you're boring him. But when you look closer, you notice that his face is ashen, he isn't making eye contact with you, and he hasn't shaved in a few days. You pause and ask, "Hey, is everything OK with you? You seem...not yourself." Your brother looks up somewhat startled, tries to smile, and says, "What? Oh! Yes, everything's great."

You've just experienced **channel discrepancy**, a situation in which one set of behaviors says one thing and another set says something different. In this case, your brother's verbal communication says he is fine, but his nonverbal communication says he is not fine at all. So which message do you believe? In most cases, you'll believe the nonverbal message. Like most of us, you assume your brother has less control over his nonverbal behaviors, so they are more "reliable" indicators of how he is feeling. Research supports your assumption. Studies show that we tend to give more weight to nonverbal behavior than to verbal behavior when we

- express spontaneous feelings (such as crying) (Burgoon & Hoobler, 2002)

- assess others' motives (as in deception) (Burgoon, Blair, & Strom, 2008)

- express rapport with others (for example, show liking) (Hullman, Goodnight, & Mougeotte, 2012)

- figure out others' meanings when there are few other behaviors to observe (Grahe & Bernieri, 1999; Knapp & Hall, 2010)

However, just because we tend to place more stock in nonverbal communication doesn't mean that we always interpret that communication accurately. Your brother might be fine, just as he says he is. Perhaps he is growing a "playoff beard" along with the rest of his hockey team and is thinking about the next day's game rather than listening to you talk about your plans. Even when we know others very well, we often fail to detect deception or read their nonverbal behaviors accurately (Knapp & Hall, 2010; Van Swol, Malhotr, & Braun, 2012; Vrij, 2006).

Pablo Blazquez Dominguez/Getty Images

FIGURE 2.2 Does this card player have a good or bad hand? Who knows? His poker face reveals nothing.

AND YOU?

Have you ever ignored what someone said because the person's nonverbal behavior seemed to contradict the verbal message? Were you able to determine if the nonverbal communication was accurate?

■ Functions of Nonverbal Communication

Now that we've established the essential nature of nonverbal communication, we can discuss how it helps us interact effectively in relationships. It's impossible to discuss every purpose that nonverbal behaviors serve, but next we highlight the most important ways that nonverbal behaviors work on their own—and in combination with verbal behaviors—to affect communication (Burgoon, Floyd, & Guerrero, 2010).

© Sandy Felsenthal/Corbis

FIGURE 2.3 When a traffic cop holds out one hand, you know to stop; she doesn't have to scream "STOP!" to get the intended effect.

Reinforcing Verbal Messages

Nonverbal behavior clarifies meaning by reinforcing verbal messages in three ways: repeating, complementing, and accenting. **Repeating** mirrors the verbal message through a clear nonverbal cue that represents the exact same idea. For example, you hold up three fingers while saying "three" or shake your head at a toddler while saying "no." You can also reinforce verbal messages with **complementing**, nonverbal behavior that is consistent with the verbal message and often enhances it. For example, when you pat a friend on the back while saying, "You did a great job," you reinforce the message that your friend has done well.

Nonverbal behaviors are also used for **accenting**, or clarifying and emphasizing specific information in a verbal message. For example, suppose you want your friend to meet you at a local pub at 6 P.M. You can make eye contact as you talk (indicating that you are monitoring your friend's attention level) and touch the friend lightly on the forearm as you mention the pub on State Street ("Do you know the one I mean?").

Substituting Verbal Messages

Nonverbal cues can substitute for words. For example, a traffic officer's outstretched palm substitutes for the word *stop*. **Substituting** is common in situations where words are unavailable (communicating with someone who speaks a different language) or when speaking aloud would be inappropriate (at the symphony or during a religious service). Substitution cues signal information you'd rather not say aloud (raising your eyebrows at your partner to signal you want to leave a party) or help you communicate when you don't know the words to use (pointing to the location of pain to your doctor) (Rowbotham, Holler, Lloyd, & Wearden, 2012).

Sometimes you may nonverbally substitute silence for words. If your roommate is driving you nuts with her constant talking (while you're trying to write a paper), you may become silent and look away from her when she asks for your input on last night's episode of *Dancing with the Stars* (Giles, Coupland, & Wiemann, 1992). Silence may also be a sign of deference (as when you don't express your opinion because the other has higher status); it may also signal defiance (as when you refuse to answer someone who angers you) (Ng & Ng, 2012).

> ### AND YOU?
> Have you ever experienced (or been responsible for) a failed attempt at sarcasm or teasing via a text message or social network posting? What, in your opinion, caused this communication breakdown? How might it have been avoided?

Contradicting Verbal Messages

Nonverbal communication functions to **contradict** the verbal when the behavioral cues convey the opposite of the verbal message. Sometimes this is unintentional, as when you clearly look upset but say that nothing's wrong, and you don't realize your nonverbal behavior is giving you away. Other times, contradicting behavior is intentional. For instance, Caroline sighs deeply to get Andy to ask, "What's wrong?" She can keep the attention coming by refusing to answer or by tersely stating, "Nothing." Although such tactics can get another person's attention, they're deceptive because they take advantage of the person's concern in order to serve selfish purposes.

Contradicting behavior is also part of what makes joking around, teasing, and the use of sarcasm (cutting remarks) so powerful. When you roll your eyes and say, "Wow, that was a captivating lecture," you let your classmate know that, despite your words, you found listening to your professor about as interesting as vacuuming. Contradicting behavior can work positively as well. For instance, your friend calls to your beloved dog, "Come here, you smelly, ugly little monster!" Your friend's smile, high pitch, and open arms reveal that your friend really thinks your dog is adorable.

FIGURE 2.4 A smelly, ugly little monster? Certainly not.

AND YOU?

Imagine that you are listening to a friend tell a long story in a face-to-face setting. How might you regulate the interaction to show that you're listening or that you'd like to interject a comment? Would these actions change if the conversation were taking place via instant messaging or in a chat room? How so?

Managing Impressions and Regulating Interactions

Nonverbal cues are used to manage the impressions and regulate interactions of communicators in a variety of relationships and situations (Cappella & Schreiber, 2006). This **interaction management** function occurs from the first time you meet someone and continues throughout the life span of your relationship. For example, you dress professionally for a job interview; your smile, firm handshake, and friendly tone convey your sincerity as you say, "This sounds like a wonderful organization to work for." The hiring manager's smiles and nods—or frowns and silence—in turn influence your behaviors back to her (Keating, 2006). Should you get the job, your nonverbal behaviors help you manage a tense situation with your boss by keeping a respectful distance and lowering your tone of voice. Additionally, nonverbal behavior (like smiles, eye contact, and so on) helps you manage your ongoing, everyday interactions with coworkers.

Nonverbal cues are also used in coordinating verbal interaction at the level of conversation—they help us **regulate** the back-and-forth flow of communication. For example, if you pause after saying "Hello" when answering your phone, you are offering the person on the other end a chance to self-identify and explain the purpose of the call. Face to face, you may hold your hand up while speaking to signal that you don't want to be interrupted or gesture broadly to indicate continued excitement about your topic (Cutica & Bucciarelli, 2011). Additionally, raising your hand in a face-to-face classroom setting lets your professor know that you have a question or information to share.

If conversational regulation doesn't go smoothly, there can be negative consequences. For example, if you successfully interrupt others when they are speaking, you may gain influence, but they may like you less. On the other hand, if you allow interruptions, others may perceive you as less influential (Farley, 2008). Naturally, the situational context plays a role. It's more serious to interrupt (or be interrupted) during a debate or a business meeting, whereas some interruption is acceptable during casual conversations with friends. Matching your regulation behaviors to those of your partner makes interactions go smoothly (Schmidt, Morr, Fitzpatrick, & Richardson, 2012).

Creating Immediacy

Nonverbal communication can also create **immediacy**, a feeling of closeness, involvement, and warmth between people (Andersen, Guerrero, & Jones, 2006; Prager, 2000). Such behaviors include sitting or standing close to another person, turning and leaning toward the individual, smiling, making eye contact, and touching appropriately (Andersen, 1998; Andersen, Guerrero, Buller, & Jorgensen, 1998). Even adding "smiley face" emoticons to your e-mail messages has been found to increase perceptions of immediacy and liking (Yoo, 2007).

Immediacy behaviors help you form and manage impressions, particularly if you want to have more social influence. The implications for interpersonal relationships are clear: physical contact, eye contact, smiling, and other gestures tell your romantic partner, your family members, and close friends that you love and care for them and that you want to be near them. In the professional world, multiple studies find that physicians, nurses, and staff who engage in immediacy behaviors have patients who are less fearful of them and more satisfied with their medical care (Richmond, Smith, Heisel, & McCroskey, 2001; Wanzer, Booth-Butterfield, & Gruber, 2004). And if you are a supervisor at work, combine positive messages with immediacy behaviors to enhance your likeability and credibility (Teven, 2007).

Deceiving Others

In the historical drama *Argo,* Central Intelligence Agency officer Tony Mendez rescues six American agents stranded in Tehran, Iran, during the 1979 Iranian hostage crisis. Mendez executes his rescue without a single weapon. Rather, he deceives Iranian officials by having the agents pose as a Canadian movie crew scouting locations in Iran (Dargis, 2012). Mendez and the hostages (both in the film and in real life) pulled off their deception by carefully learning their "roles" in the fabricated story and by consciously monitoring their nonverbal communication to reveal confidence and poise.

Although most of us will never engage in such a dramatic example of **deception**—the attempt to convince others of something that is false (O'Hair & Cody, 1994)—we will admit to occasionally engaging in it (if we're being honest). Sometimes we deceive to protect others, as when you tell your friend that no one noticed her torn slacks. Other times, we deceive out of fear, as when victims of abuse blame their injuries on falls or accidents. However, deception can have malicious and self-serving motives, as in the solicitor who tries to get your social security number and other personal data in order to commit identity theft.

FIGURE 2.5 Mendez and the other agents had to develop detailed backstories in order to pull off their plan: to convincingly pose as a Canadian film crew in Iran.

■ What About You?

Nonverbal Immediacy Scale

The following statements describe the level of involvement, warmth, and closeness (immediacy) that some people attempt to achieve when communicating with others.

Please indicate in the space at the left of each item the degree to which you believe the statement applies to you in a given conversation with a stranger. Please use the following five-point scale: 1 = never; 2 = rarely; 3 = occasionally; 4 = often; and 5 = very often.

	1. I use my hands and arms to gesture while talking to people.
	2. I touch others on the shoulder or arm while talking to them.
	3. I use an excited voice while talking to people.
	4. I look at or toward others while talking to them.
	5. I don't move away from others when they touch me while we are talking.
	6. I have a relaxed body position when I talk to people.
	7. I smile while talking to people.
	8. I make eye contact while talking to people.
	9. My facial expressions show others I care about the conversation.
	10. I sit close to people while talking with them.
	11. My voice is warm when I talk to people.
	12. I use a variety of vocal expressions when I talk to people.
	13. I lean slightly toward people when I talk with them.
	14. I am animated when I talk to people.
	15. I express myself through facial expressions when I talk with people.
	16. I move closer to people when I talk to them.
	17. I turn my body toward others during conversations.
	18. I nod in response to others' assertions.
	Add your scores for 1–18 here

67–90: You communicate a high level of immediacy in your nonverbal behavior. Be careful not to exceed others', particularly strangers', comfort levels, however (that is, watch out for people who shrink back, look away, or have negative facial expressions, as you may be getting too close or touching too much).

43–66: You communicate immediacy in many situations. Your nonverbal expressions of interest and warmth are likely to make new people in your life more comfortable, too.

18–42: You don't communicate immediacy behaviors very often. Consider increasing your nonverbal immediacy behaviors to help you manage impressions and initiate more satisfying relationships.

Source: Adapted from V. P. Richmond, J. C. McCroskey, and A. D. Johnson, A. D. (2003).

You may be drawn in by a solicitor who sounds warm and friendly, but it is more likely that you will look for the opposite type of behavior to sniff out a liar (Canary, Cody, & Manusov, 2008). People who appear anxious, who avoid making eye contact, who blink frequently, or who have frequent and awkward body movements seem deceptive (Leal & Vrij, 2008). However, research shows that although these cues make us more suspicious, they do not actually make us more accurate at detecting deception (Van Swol, Braun, & Kolb, 2013). This is partly because people's "honest" or "dishonest" demeanor is often inconsistent with whether they are actually telling the truth or lying (Levine et al., 2011). Liars often appear anxious only if concerned about the lie or about getting caught (Canary, Cody, & Manusov, 2008). On one hand, if the lie is unimportant, liars may instead be relaxed and controlled. On the other hand, someone accused of lying may show nonverbal or physiological signs of anxiety even if not guilty. This is one reason why so-called lie detectors (and the newer brain scans) are not reliable measures of deception (Kirchner, 2013).

AND YOU?

When you attempt to deceive others (as when telling a friend you like her new boyfriend when you don't), are you aware of your nonverbal messages? Do you tend to alter your tone of voice or change your eye contact? What types of nonverbal indications do you look for in others in order to figure out if they're telling the truth?

■ Nonverbal Communication Codes

Ask any fans of *The Big Bang Theory* about the brilliant Dr. Sheldon Cooper's greatest struggle and they'll quickly respond with "understanding other people." More specifically, Sheldon confesses to having an immensely difficult time interpreting others' emotions (like sadness or disappointment) and responding empathically. And—played out to great comic effect on the show—he seems completely unable to decode others' sarcasm. (At one point, his friend and roommate, Leonard, has to hold up a sign that says "SARCASM" to help Sheldon navigate a particularly intense conversation with their neighbor, Penny!)

Truth be told, Sheldon struggles to interpret and understand **nonverbal codes,** the symbols we use to send messages without, or in addition to, words. Although we divide these codes into categories for simplicity and clarity, nonverbal behaviors seldom communicate meaning in isolation; as you saw in the last section, clusters of nonverbal behaviors (hugs, smiles, eye contact) function together to regulate behavior or convey immediacy. The codes we examine here are gestures and body movements, facial expressions, eye behavior, voice, physical appearance, space and environment, touch, and time.

Gestures and Body Movements

Did you succumb to the dance craze and Internet meme the "Harlem Shake"? If so, you've joined millions in the silly, shimmying body movements that communicate sexuality one moment and hilarity the next—all without words (Cvitanic, 2013). You have probably heard others call such body movements "body language," but the way you move your body is not a language at all—"Harlem Shaking" has no specific, consistently understood definition. Such behavior is called kinesics—gestures and body movements that send nonverbal messages. When Eva motions her arm to include Jane in a conversation, or Rodney walks into an interview standing tall to project confidence, you are witnessing kinesic behaviors. And although there is not a specific message conveyed, research shows that we're fairly good at deciphering others' emotions from their gestures and movements (Montepare, Koff, Zaitchik, & Alberet, 1999).

There are five main categories of gestures and movements that convey meaning nonverbally (Ekman & Friesen, 1969):

- **Emblems** are often used to substitute for words, because they have a more definition-like meaning for the people who use them. The "thumbs up" and "okay" signs are both emblems that most Americans would recognize and understand. During his inauguration parade, Barack Obama greeted the marching band from his old high school with an emblem fellow Hawaiians would understand: a shaka sign—a pinkie and thumb salute that is widely regarded as a representation of the "aloha spirit."

- **Illustrators** reinforce verbal messages and help visually explain what is being said. Holding your hands two feet apart while saying, "The fish was this big!" is an illustrator. Illustrators can also be used to increase influence in relationships, as when we emphasize our words with pointing or sketching a thought in the air (Dunbar & Burgoon, 2005).

- **Regulators** help us manage our interactions. Raising your hand and lifting your head, for example, indicate that you want to speak. Raising your eyebrows usually indicates you want information from others (Flecha-García, 2010). Both regulators and illustrators often pair with vocal signals to enhance communication, as when you say, "I, I, I..." while holding up your index finger to break into conversation (regulators) or emphasize the word *this* in the preceding fish example (illustrator).

- **Adaptors** satisfy some physical or psychological need, such as rubbing your eyes when you're tired or twisting your hair when you're nervous or bored. Usually not conscious behaviors, adaptors are used to reduce bodily tension. Because they may be more frequent when someone is stressed, impatient, or bored, they are often interpreted as indicators of negative feelings (Goss & O'Hair, 1988).

- **Affect displays** are nonverbal gestures that convey feelings, moods, and reactions. Slumping in a chair may indicate fatigue or boredom; a fist thrust high in the air indicates joy when your team scores a touchdown. Setting your jaw and hitting your fist on the table may indicate your anger or frustration. Affect is also displayed through facial expressions, as discussed next.

REAL COMMUNICATOR

NAME: OCTAVIA SPENCER

OCCUPATION: ACADEMY AWARD WINNING ACTRESS

I've always wanted to work in the film industry, though I never dreamed it would be in front of the camera. But in 1995, I got a small part opposite Sandra Bullock in the hit film *A Time to Kill*, and I was on my way. Since that time, I've had a number of roles on stage, screen, and television.

What I do want everyone reading this interview to realize is that my success is tied to a number of the topics you're studying right now—particularly nonverbal communication. For example, pretty much anyone can read a script out loud, but *how* you read it is what counts in this industry. The tone of voice, the timing, the pause that is just long enough to get people to look up and pay attention—these are the keys to getting (and staying) employed!

Vocal cues alone are incredibly important in acting. When I was the voice of "Minny" on the audio version of the book *The Help* (Kathryn Stockett's New York Times bestseller), I had to study the appropriate accents, timing, and inflections to make my performance truly authentic. Later, when I played the same role for the film, I realized just how much more meaning and feeling I was able to communicate when I could use facial expressions and body movements to express my character.

Most of my roles are comedic and, let me tell you, acting in comedies isn't a barrel of laughs. It's incredibly challenging work. Facial expressions in particular have to be appropriate and come at just the right moment (otherwise, they aren't at all funny). Often there are ten different facial expressions I have to produce in less than one minute to show surprise, hurt, outrage, confusion, acceptance, determination, confidence, liking, disgust, and pleasure. Oh, and it has to appear natural, too.

In addition, the way I tilt my head or hold my body changes the information I'm trying to convey. For example, I played Dr. Evilini, a witch with dual personalities, on *Wizards of Waverly Place*. As one personality, my head was bent, and my voice low pitched with a diabolical, screeching laugh. The other personality had a normal voice, and I kept my body erect, though my eyes were always wide with expression. Because the show's target audience was primarily comprised of children, every movement was exaggerated to ensure its comedic value.

At the end of the day, I am truly grateful to be doing something that I absolutely enjoy—and none of it would be possible without a close study of nonverbal communication.

Facial Expressions

Consider the character Spock, the half-Vulcan, half-human science officer from *Star Trek* who suppresses his emotions at all costs in the pursuit of pure logic. Both of the actors who have played Spock (Leonard Nimoy in the original television series and

Zachary Quinto in the 2013 film) had their human eyebrows replaced with artificial "Vulcan" ones: because Spock's eyebrows—and eye expressions in general—appear less human, his emotions seem less human too.

© Paramount. Courtesy Everett Collection

FIGURE 2.6 With those Vulcan eyebrows, Spock portrays little emotion.

As humans, we are wired to use our faces to indicate emotions (Fridlund & Russell, 2006). Although the reasons behind our facial expressions might be difficult to ascertain, several specific expressions are common across all cultures (Ekman & Friesen, 1971). A smile, for example, usually indicates happiness; a frown, sadness; raised eyebrows tend to indicate surprise, and wrinkled eyebrows, concern (see **FIGURE 2.7**).

Blind children, who cannot learn to mimic facial movements through sight, exhibit sadness, anger, disgust, fear, interest, surprise, and happiness in the same way that sighted people exhibit these feelings (Eibl-Eibesfeldt, 1973). These seven primary facial expressions are thus considered inborn, whereas most other expressions are learned from our culture (Gagnon, Gosselin, Hudon-ven der Buhs, Larocque, & Milliard, 2010). There is some evidence that pride also may be a universally recognized emotion (Tracy & Robins, 2008).

Although we're fairly adept at deciphering these common expressions of emotion, we're not necessarily experts at decoding all facial expressions (Bavelas & Chovil, 2006). That's because the human face can produce more than a thousand different expressions (and as many as twenty thousand if you take into account all of the combinations of the different facial areas) (Ekman, Friesen, & Ellsworth, 1972; Harrigan & Taing, 1997). Moreover, our emotions can be concealed by facial management techniques, conscious manipulation of our faces to convey a particular expression.

One common facial management technique is **masking**, replacing an expression that shows true feeling with an expression that shows appropriate feeling for a given interaction. Actors use masking all the time. But you also use it when you smile at customers at the restaurant where you work even though you're in a horrible mood and wish they'd leave (Richmond, McCroskey, & Payne, 1991).

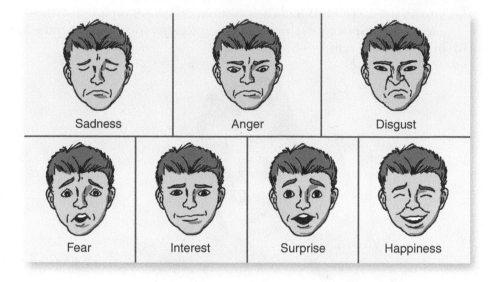

FIGURE 2.7 Cross-cultural primary facial expressions research shows that these seven expressions of emotion exist in all cultures and are inborn.

Eye Behavior

When Rooney Mara portrayed Lisbeth Salander in the film adaptation of *The Girl with the Dragon Tattoo* (2011), she learned to move and gesture in ways to convey the hurt and fury her avenging character experiences. But Mara said that her character's eye behavior was particularly hard to master. Contrary to the norms of interaction, Salander never looks into the face of others, keeping her gaze downcast or sideways (Ryzik, 2012). **Oculesics** is the study of the use of the eyes to communicate—which includes Salander's gaze aversion.

Newborn infants (two to five days old) stare significantly longer at faces offering a direct gaze rather than an averted one. The babies orient themselves more often toward the face that makes eye contact with them. Babies as young as three months old smile less when adults avert their gaze and begin smiling more when adults resume eye contact (Farroni, Csibra, Simion, & Johnson, 2002).

There are some cultural variations in gazing with children. For example, European American parents gaze more at their children, especially between mothers and sons. Mexican American parents, on the other hand, spend less time making eye contact with children. Accordingly, children gaze more directly at fathers in European American homes than in Mexican American homes (Schofield, Parke, Castañeda, & Coltrane, 2008). Perhaps children in Mexican American homes gaze less directly at fathers as a sign of respect for the cultural hierarchy in the family.

The human gaze remains important beyond childhood. You use direct eye contact with a hiring manager in a job interview in the United States to make a stronger impression. In more personal relationships, you look at a friend differently than you look at your significant other and very differently from someone you dislike intensely. Each glance can send a message of liking, loving, attraction, or contempt (see **TABLE 2.1**).

CONNECT

Despite differing cultural norms regarding direct eye contact, it remains an important part of giving speeches and succeeding in job interviews in the United States. In both situations, eye contact signals respect for your audience and confidence in your abilities and preparedness.

AND YOU?

How do you feel about making eye contact with others (fellow classmates or your professor) when speaking in the classroom? With strangers when you lock eyes in the grocery store or on an elevator? When interacting with people who have higher status (such as a hiring manager or boss)?

Voice

When the University of Arizona opened the National Institute for Civil Discourse, they wanted to promote compromise and understanding among groups famously at odds with one another (Dooling, 2011). They quickly found out that it was not only the words used that stood in the way of civility, but it was also the vocal tone. Imagine yourself saying, "I respect your right to believe that" with a calm, balanced tone; now imagine saying the same words with a sarcastic tone while emphasizing the word *right*. You could communicate genuine respect in the first instance or disgust and intolerance in the second.

The vocalized sounds that accompany our words are nonverbal behaviors called **paralanguage**. **Pitch** in language involves variations in the voice (higher or lower) that give prominence to certain words or syllables. Vocal **tone** is a modulation of the voice, usually expressing a particular feeling or mood; you may notice your friend sounds "down" or hear the excitement in your teammate's revelry about your win. Vocal **volume** is how loud or soft the voice is—think of the softness of a whisper or the thunder of an angry shout.

In addition to pitch, tone, and volume, paralanguage also involves behaviors like pauses, hesitations, vocal quality, accents, and the rate and rhythm of speech. It exhibits qualities like hoarseness, nasality, smoothness, or deepness, and it may sound precise, clipped, slurred, or shrill. Teenage girls are sometimes mocked for using uptalk (making statements into questions? "Right?") or for guttural flutter of the vocal cords called "vocal fry," as in comedienne Maya Rudolph's mimicry of poet Maya Angelou on *Saturday Night Live* (Quenqua, 2012).

We all have preferences about which voices are most attractive—angry, demanding voices are usually perceived as annoying—and whiny voices *really* annoying (Sokol, Webster, Thompson, & Stevens, 2005). Look no further than your favorite radio DJs or newscasters to examine the vocal qualities people enjoy the most. These individuals tend to have smooth voices and find a middle ground between precise and fluid speech. Pronunciation matters too—and can identify individuals as coming from another country or region. Thus, our Missouri readers may know that residents disagree on whether to pronounce their home state as "Missouruh" (which tags a speaker as being from a rural part of the state) or "Misoureeee," indicating a more urban environment. Interestingly, politicians often pronounce it both ways to cover their bases (Wheaton, 2012).

Meanwhile, **vocalizations** are paralinguistic utterances that give information about our emotional or physical state, such as laughing, crying, sighing, yawning, or moaning. Other vocalizations simply replace words or create nonword fillers in conversations. You might clear your throat to get someone's attention or use "Shhhh" to quiet a crowd, and most of us tend to insert "umm's" and "ah's" into conversation when we're taking a moment to think. Sometimes such **back-channel cues** signal when we want to talk versus when we're encouraging others to continue talking ("oh," "uh-huh").

Max Hirshfeld/Redux

FIGURE 2.8 NPR music host Bob Boilen uses a precise, accentless voice on the air.

Table 2.1 The power of eye contact

CONVEYING FEELINGS	INFLUENCING BEHAVIOR	REGULATING INTERACTIONS

Vladimir Godnik/Getty Images

© ACE STOCK LIMITED/Alamy

© Image Source/Alamy

A baby's wide eyes might express fear or surprise.

A mother may look at her son as she reprimands him to make sure that he is listening.

In conversations, as one person speaks, the other may use eye contact to show that she is paying attention.

INDICATING INTEREST	CREATING AN IMPRESSION	DEMONSTRATING LEVELS OF POWER

John Henley/Getty Images

Frank Herholdt /Getty Images

ColorBlind Images/Getty Images

A salesperson might maintain eye contact with a customer in an attempt to establish rapport.

A good speaker will use eye contact to gain an audience's trust.

In the workplace, an employee is more likely to make prolonged eye contact with a subordinate than with a higher-ranking colleague.

CONNECT

Using vocalizations like "uh-huh" can help others perceive you as an effective listener. When a loved one discusses a difficult situation, you want to allow the person to speak and not constantly interrupt with your own words. Vocalizations tell your partner that you're listening and that you're actively engaged in the conversation.

Physical Appearance

If you've ever seen a reality television makeover show (from *The Biggest Loser* to *What Not to Wear*), you know that many people wish to alter their appearance to elicit positive changes in their personal and professional lives. Although what you wear—or the way you fix your hair or makeup—may not speak directly to your abilities or define you as a person, it communicates messages about you nonetheless. In fact, the initial impression your appearance makes may affect your future interactions with others (DeKay, 2009).

Most people in Western society are well aware of the significance of appearance. Research shows that society affords attractive people certain advantages. For instance, attractive students receive more interaction from their teachers (Richmond et al., 1991), and "good-looking" job candidates have a greater chance of being hired (Molloy, 1983; Shannon & Stark, 2003). Jurors find attractive defendants innocent more often (Efran, 1974), although discussion and deliberation can mitigate this bias (Patry, 2008). Appearance affects not only perceptions of attractiveness but also judgments about a person's background, character, personality, status, and future behavior (Guerrero & Floyd, 2006).

Perceptions about appearance and attractiveness are inferred not only from physical characteristics like body shape and size, facial features, skin color, height, and hair color but also from the clothing you wear, which can reveal quite a bit about your status, economic level, social background, goals, and satisfaction (Crane, 2000). In fact, your clothing choice can also speak to your communication intentions. When Queen Elizabeth II became the first British monarch to visit the Irish Republic after decades of discord, she wore a suit in emerald green, the proud color of the Emerald Isle. Clearly her choice signaled a hoped-for reconciliation (Dowd, 2012).

We also infer a great deal of meaning from **artifacts**—accessories carried or used on the body for decoration or identification. For example, the expensive Rolex watch that your uncle wears sends a very different message about wealth and status than a ten-dollar watch would. Other artifacts, such as briefcases, tattoos, earrings, nose rings, nail polish, and engagement and wedding rings, also convey messages about your relational status, your gender, and even how willing you are to defy conventions. Tattoos, for example, send a variety of messages. Some descendants of Holocaust survivors inscribe the concentration camp identification numbers of their ancestors onto their forearms to communicate their desire to remember their relatives and never forget the atrocities perpetuated by the Nazi regime (Rudoren, 2012). On a lighter note, research finds that men view a butterfly tattoo on the back of a sunbathing woman as a sign that she may be receptive to his romantic overtures (Guéguen, 2012).

Remember that perceptions of artifacts (and physical appearance in general) can change over time. To illustrate, when the late British politician Margaret Thatcher carried a handbag, it was at first perceived as a sign of weakness, but with her rise to prime minister, the handbag came to be a symbol of tremendous power (Givhan, 2013).

NBC/Photofest

FIGURE 2.9 Reality shows like *The Biggest Loser* aim to help people change their appearance (and health) through weight loss.

Space and Environment

Believe it or not, you also send nonverbal messages by the spaces that surround you and your communication partners. We examine three factors here: proxemics, territoriality, and environment.

Proxemics

Ben's first job involved a coworker Lucas, who was a close talker—a person who stands very near when speaking to others. "During shifts when I'd be on with this guy, I'd always have to try to find some excuse to be away from the counter," Ben said. "If we were both behind the counter together, he'd talk so close that I'd end up completely backed into a corner, with the counter digging into my back, just hoping for someone to rob the place so there'd be an excuse to get out of the situation" (Edwards, 2013). Ben's intense discomfort with Lucas was due to **proxemics,** the way we use and communicate with space.

Professor Edward Hall (1959) identified four specific spatial zones that carry communication messages (see **FIGURE 2.10**).

- *Intimate* (0 to 18 inches). We often send intimate messages in this zone, which is usually reserved for spouses or romantic partners, very close friends, and close family members.

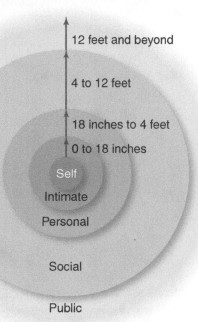

FIGURE 2.10 Zones of Personal Space. The four zones of personal space described by Edward Hall indicate ranges that generally apply across cultures.

- *Personal* (18 inches to 4 feet). In the personal zone, we communicate with friends, relatives, and occasionally colleagues.

- *Social* (4 to 12 feet). The social zone is most comfortable for communicating in professional settings, such as business meetings or teacher–student conferences.

- *Public* (12 feet and beyond). The public zone allows for distance between interactants at, for example, public speaking events or performances.

COMMUNICATION ACROSS CULTURES

What Nurses Wear

It might be strange to think that just a few decades ago professional women with college degrees were expected to show up for work wearing nipped-waist dresses, frilly aprons, and white linen caps. For more than 100 years, variations on this theme signified a woman trained in the medical profession. "The nurse's cap," writes nursing historian Christina Bates (2012), "is one of the most evocative garments ever associated with an occupational group" (p. 22). Well into the twentieth century, nurses' uniforms separated the nurses from the doctors—and coincidentally the ladies from the men—in the health care field. But they also served as important signifiers. Prior to the opening of the first nurses' colleges in the 1830s, nursing was left largely to religious orders and untrained mothers, wives, and sisters. The adoption of a uniform—however odd it may seem today—served to provide some status to the young women who emerged from these nursing schools, separating them from the women who went before them (Bates, 2012).

Today such ensembles are limited, for the most part, to sexy Halloween costumes, but most nurses still wear a uniform of sorts: usually a simple pair of hospital scrubs in any of a number of colors or prints. In contrast to the nurse uniforms of yore, these simple and practical ensembles are for the most part gender-neutral. But even these seemingly nondescript items convey meaning. Research shows that the choice of color or print of scrubs can have an impact on patients' perceptions about a nurse's competence. Among adult patients who were asked to comment on a variety of nursing uniforms, white scrubs were perceived as indicative of higher levels of professionalism, attentiveness, reliability, empathy, and six other traits than were colored or print scrubs. But among children and adolescents, there was little if any discernable difference in the way they perceived different uniforms for nursing professionals (Albert, Wocial, Meyer, Na, & Trochelman, 2008).

Of course, uniforms are not limited to the nursing profession. Police officers, sports teams, military and paramilitary organizations, and of course many schools have dress requirements that are much more strict than those that govern what today's nurses wear to work. By dressing in uniform, members of these groups convey messages about who they are, what their role is, and to which group they belong.

THINK ABOUT THIS

1. Do you think that nurses' uniforms became less gendered as more men entered this traditionally female profession, or do you think men began to think more seriously about the field as the old frilly uniforms gave way to more androgynous scrubs?

2. Why do you think the color of nurses' uniforms had such an impact on adults' perceptions? Why might it have had less of an impact on younger patients? Do you think that those younger patients' perceptions will change as they age?

3. Consider the traditional nurse's uniform in a few different contexts. How is it that a uniform that indicated professional prestige 100 or even 50 years ago now seems so blatantly sexist?

4. The traditional nurse's uniform sent a very concrete message about the woman wearing it in terms of her job and her qualifications. What message, if any, do modern scrubs send? Is the meaning of scrubs concrete or abstract?

Your personal space needs may vary from the forgoing space categories. These vary according to culture too; Hall "normed" these zones for different cultures around the world. How close or distant you want to be from someone depends on whom you're dealing with, the situation, and your comfort level. You might enjoy being physically close to your boyfriend or girlfriend while taking a walk together, but you probably don't hold hands or embrace during class. Gender also plays a role. Research says that groups of men walking together will walk faster and typically leave more space between themselves and others than women will (Costa, 2010). But regardless of your personal preferences, violations of space are almost always uncomfortable and awkward and can cause relational problems (Burgoon, 1978).

Proxemic messages are not limited to the real world. In the online virtual world *Second Life*, you create your own space in which you and your avatar move. Avatars use proxemic cues to send relational messages and structure interaction, much as people do in real life (Antonijevic, 2008; Gillath, McCall, Shaver, & Blascovich, 2008).

EVALUATING COMMUNICATION ETHICS

The Job Killer Tat

You're a few years out of college, working at a public policy think tank that specializes in childhood education research. It's a great position with lots of room for advancement and the ability to be active in an area that really interests you. What's more, the organization is growing rapidly and looking to fill new positions. When your manager mentions that they're seeking someone who can work with policymakers in the state capitol, and asks if you know anyone, you immediately think of your friend Dave. This position is essentially Dave's dream job, and he's more than qualified, having dual majors in early childhood education and communication and having worked freelance as a grant writer for nonprofit organizations. You pass Dave's résumé on to your manager and wish your buddy good luck.

When Dave shows up at your office for an interview, you are astonished. He has forgone a traditional suit and tie and is wearing a short-sleeved collared shirt that reveals the full arm sleeve of tattoos that he has been cultivating since he was about sixteen years old. You had mentioned to Dave that the office environment is very professional and that the position would require him to interact with lobbyists, lawyers, and lawmakers on a regular basis. You know that your boss will not think well of his decision not to cover up his tattoos—or even attempt to find a suit. You're worried that your boss will think you've wasted his time with a candidate who is less than serious and you're angry at Dave for possibly insulting your organization's sensibilities (and for possibly making you look like a fool for recommending him). What do you do?

THINK ABOUT THIS

1. Why might Dave have failed to consider the professional context of the interview? Could his own professional experience as a freelancer have changed his definition of "professional attire"?

2. If you could rewind the situation and start over, would you offer Dave more clear directions on how to dress or would you not recommend him at all?

3. Knowing what you know about Dave's skills and education—and knowing that he would adapt his behavior as directed—would you hire Dave? Or is his failure to figure out what was appropriate ahead of time a deal breaker?

Territoriality

Closely related to proxemics is **territoriality**—the claiming of an area, with or without legal basis, through continuous occupation of that area. Your home, your car, and your office are personal territories. But territories also encompass implied ownership of space, such as a seat in a classroom, a parking space, or a table in a restaurant. Few people like anyone encroaching on their territory. If you're a fan of *How I Met Your Mother*, then you know that nothing good can come from taking the booth that Ted and his crew have unofficially claimed.

Territoriality operates in mediated contexts as well. Just as we do with physical spaces in the real world, we claim our social networking pages by naming them and decorating them with our "stuff," we allow certain people ("friends") access, and we "clean up" our space by deleting or hiding comments. Research shows that young people are more adept at managing their space on Facebook than are their parents (Madden & Smith, 2010). Some clean up their wall regularly, deleting status updates and wall posts as often as they make them. Others take social media "vacations" or "breaks" or simply deactivate their accounts when they are not online so "friends" cannot see their wall, post anything on it, or tag them in photos while they're metaphorically not around (Boyd, 2010).

CONNECT

Territoriality can have an impact on group communication, as we generally feel more in control of situations on our own turf. Think about this the next time a professor breaks you up into random groups. Do you enjoy moving across the room from your usual seat, or do you prefer your group members to come to you? Chances are good that a new "territory" will affect your communication.

Environment

Any home designer or architect knows that humans use space to express themselves. The layout and decoration of your home, your office, and any other space you occupy tells others something about you. For example, the way you arrange your furniture can encourage interaction or discourage it; the décor, lighting, and cleanliness of the space all send messages about how you want interactions to proceed. Even the scent of a space impacts communication: customers stay in stores longer and rate the store higher if the aroma is pleasant (as in the scent of chocolate in a bookstore) (Doucé, 2013). Professors who have neat, clean, attractive offices are rated by their students as more friendly, trustworthy, and authoritative (Teven & Comadena, 1996).

Color also matters. Hollywood location scouts negotiated with Juzcar in southeastern Spain to paint all the bone-white Andaluz stone buildings baby blue to film the feature-length version of *The Smurfs* there. The blue color was so unique—and clearly signaled the popular movie—that tourists flocked there. Although the producers agreed to repaint the buildings white after the filming, the townspeople left them blue because the tourist trade had relieved their unemployment woes (Herman, 2013).

The environment's power to affect communication may explain, in part, the success of shows like *Extreme Makeover: Home Edition* and *Renovation Raiders*. In transforming dreary or cluttered spaces into warm and vibrant rooms, the best makeovers reflect not only a family's practical needs but also its unique personalities and interests. That's because the designers understand that environment communicates to others about who we are.

CLIFF LIPSON/CBS /Landov

FIGURE 2.11 Many people favor "their" spots, which can include a favorite table at the bar, a preferred spot in the lecture hall, or a usual seat in the car.

Touch

Touch is the first communication we experience in life. A newborn baby is soothed in the arms of her parents; she begins learning about herself and others while reaching out to explore her environment. **Haptics** is the use of touch to send messages. We hug our loved ones in happy and sad times, we reassure others with a pat on the back, and we experience intimacy with the caress of a romantic partner.

There are as many different types of touches as there are thoughts about and reactions for being touched. The intimacy continuum (Heslin, 1974) provides insights into how our use of touch reflects our relationship with a communication partner:

- *Functional-professional touch* is used to perform a job. How would your dentist perform your root canal if he or she didn't touch you?

- *Social-polite touch* is often a polite acknowledgment of the other person, such as a handshake.

- *Friendship-warmth touch* conveys liking and affection between people who know each other well, as when you hug your friends or offer your brother a pat on the back.

- *Love-intimacy touch* is used by romantic partners, parents and children, and even close friends and family members. Examples include kissing (whether on the mouth or cheek), embracing, and caressing.

- *Sexual-arousal touch* is an intense form of touch that plays an important part in sexual relationships.

Another classification system for touch distinguishes among a dozen different kinds of body contact (Morris, 1977). TABLE 2.2 illustrates these types of contact in connection with the intimacy continuum.

Clearly, touch powerfully affects our relationships. It is one factor related to sustained liking in healthy marriages (Hinkle, 1999). Our reassuring touch also lets our friends know that we care and serves to regulate social interactions, as when beginning or ending an interaction with a handshake. However, not all touch is positive. Bullying behaviors like kicking, punching, hitting, and poking are inappropriate forms of touch, unless inside a boxing ring.

Gauging the appropriate amount of touch for a given situation or relationship is also critical for communication. For example, dating partners usually expect touch, but someone who wants "too much" (such as constant hand-holding) can be perceived as needy or clingy. Withholding touch communicates a message of disinterest or dislike, which can damage a relationship, whether with a friend, a romantic partner, or a colleague. Obviously, it's important to adjust touch to individual expectations and needs (and culture, as we explain later in the chapter).

Table 2.2 How People Touch

TYPE OF CONTACT	PURPOSE	INTIMACY TYPE
Handshake	Forming relational ties	Social-polite
Body-guide	A substitute for pointing	Social-polite
Pat	A congratulatory gesture but sometimes meant as a condescending or sexual one	Social-polite or sexual-arousal
Arm-link	Used for support or to indicate a close relationship	Friendship-warmth
Shoulder embrace	Signifies friendship; can also signify romantic connectiveness	Friendship-warmth
Full embrace	Shows emotional response or relational closeness	Friendship-warmth
Hand-in-hand	Equality in an adult relationship	Friendship-warmth
Mock attack	An aggressive behavior performed in a nonaggressive manner, such as a pinch meant to convey playfulness	Friendship-warmth
Waist embrace	Indicates intimacy	Love-intimacy
Kiss	Signals a degree of closeness or the desire for closeness	Love-intimacy or sexual-arousal
Caress	Normally used by romantic partners; signals intimacy	Love-intimacy or sexual-arousal
Body support	Touching used as physical support	Love-intimacy

Are you repelled by touches from strangers? What about touches from people who are not your age (children or the elderly)? What about being touched by a colleague or a professor—someone you have a professional relationship with? Does it depend on the situation? Explain your answer.

Time Orientation

Imagine you're late for a job interview. If you are the interviewee, you've probably lost the job before you have a chance to say a word—your lateness sends a message to the employer that you don't value punctuality and his or her time. If you are the interviewer, however, it can be completely acceptable for you to keep the interviewee waiting. In fact, by making the person wait, you assert your status by clearly conveying that you have control.

Chronemics is the use of time in nonverbal communication—the ways that you perceive and value time, structure your time, and react to time. Your *time orientation*— your personal associations with the use of time—determines the importance you give to conversation content, the length or urgency of the interaction, and punctuality (Burgoon et al., 1989). For example, when you are invited to someone's home in the United States for dinner, it's acceptable to arrive about ten minutes after the time suggested. It shows consideration for your host not to arrive too early or too late (and possibly ruin the dinner). Similarly, spending time with others communicates concern and interest. For example, good friends will make plans to spend time together even when it's inconvenient.

In our personal lives, deciding the timing of a message can be tricky. How long do you wait after you've met someone to send that person a Facebook friend request or an invitation to connect professionally on LinkedIn? How long do you wait to text or call someone you met at a party to see if he or she might want to go out on a date? Right after you've left the party may seem too eager, but a week later may suggest you're not really interested. Research shows that we do use people's response rate (how quickly they return e-mails, texts, etc.) as an indication of interest and immediacy, but the situation and context also make a difference (Döring & Pöschl, 2009; Kalman & Rafaeli, 2011; Kalman, Ravid, Raban, & Rafaeli, 2006; Ledbetter, 2008).

CONNECT

Are you punctual or habitually tardy? Do you evaluate others on their use of time? Does it vary when you are in friendship situations versus professional situations? In Appendix A we illustrate the ways to prepare for an interview so that your use of time is viewed positively.

What kind of message does it send if you are habitually late to class? What about showing up late to work? On the other hand, what kind of message is sent by showing up early for a party or to pick up a date?

■ Influences on Nonverbal Communication

Pick any individual nonverbal behavior—let's say a kiss. A kiss can mean lots of different things in different places, between different people in different situations. A kiss is a friendly manner of greeting between the sexes and with friends of the same sex throughout much of southern Europe and Latin America. This is not necessarily the case in the United States and Canada, where kissing tends to be reserved for immediate family, romantic partners, or very close friends. In India, public kissing of any sort has only recently become acceptable (Harris, 2013). You might kiss your romantic partner differently in front of your family members than you would when you're alone. Indeed the very definition of *how* you kiss your partner might range from rubbing noses to exchanging saliva (Berliet, 2013). And if you're sending an e-mail to your eight-year-old niece, you might end it with a big wet kiss, signaled by the emoticon ☺. Clearly, culture, technology, and the situation all serve as powerful influences on our nonverbal behavior.

Culture and Nonverbal Communication

When Mike and his friends visited a beach in Qingdao, China, they were surprised to see a woman emerge from the sea wearing gloves, a wetsuit, and a neon-orange ski mask. Another mask-wearing bather told them, "A woman should always have fair skin; otherwise people will think she is a peasant" (Levin, 2012). The tanning booths and self-tanning creams popular in the United States are clearly not important to beach lovers in China because different cultures view physical appearance differently. Relatedly, if you've ever traveled abroad, you may have been advised that certain nonverbal gestures that are entirely acceptable and quite positive in the United States (for example, "A-OK" or "thumbs up") are deeply insulting and crude in other parts of the world (Matsumoto & Hwang, 2013).

As these examples illustrate, nonverbal communication is highly influenced by culture. Culture affects everything from touch to facial expressions including time orientation and notions of physical attractiveness (see **CHAPTER 4**). For example, in the United States, people tend to make direct eye contact when speaking to someone, whether a colleague, a supervisor, or a professor. Similarly, in the Middle East, engaging in long and direct eye contact with your speaking partner shows interest and helps you assess the sincerity and truth of the other person's words (Samovar, Porter, & Stefani, 1998). However, in Latin America, Japan, and the Caribbean, such sustained eye behavior is a sign of disrespect.

Similarly, culture affects the use of touch. Some cultures are **contact cultures** (for example, Italy) (Williams & Hughes, 2005) and depend on touch as an important form of communication. Other cultures are **noncontact cultures** and are touch-sensitive or even tend to avoid touch. Latin American, Mediterranean, and Eastern European cultures, for example, rely on touch much more than Scandinavian cultures do. Public touch, linked to the type of interpersonal relationship that exists and the culture in which it occurs, affects both the amount of touch and the area of the body that is appropriate to touch (Avtgis & Rancer, 2003; DiBiase & Gunnoe, 2004; McDaniel & Andersen, 1998). Social-polite touch, for example, involves a handshake between

American men but a kiss between Arabic men. And some religions prohibit opposite-sex touch between unmarried or unrelated individuals.

Sex and gender also influence nonverbal communication. Women usually pay more attention to both verbal and nonverbal cues when evaluating their partners and deciding how much of themselves they should reveal to those partners, whereas men attend more to verbal information (Gore, 2009). Women also engage in more eye contact, initiate touch more often, and smile more than men (Hall, 1998; Stewart, Cooper, & Steward, 2003).

Such differences are not necessarily biologically based. For example, mothers may use more varied facial expressions with their daughters because they believe that women are supposed to be more expressive than men or because their childhood environment presented them with more opportunities to develop nonverbal skills (Hall, Carter, & Hogan, 2000). Adult gender roles may also play a part. Since women are expected to look out for the welfare of others, smiling—as well as other affirming nonverbal behaviors—may help women meet situational, gendered expectations (Hall et al., 2000). This may also help explain why women exhibit greater sensitivity to nonverbal messages. They tend to exhibit more signs of interest (such as head tilts and paralinguistic encouragers like "uh-huh" and "ah") and also decode others' nonverbal behaviors more accurately, particularly those involving the face (Burgoon & Bacue, 2003).

Maridav/Shutterstock

FIGURE 2.12 While the "thumbs up" is a friendly sign in America, it's considered rude and offensive in certain parts of the Middle East.

Mediated Nonverbal Communication

At a conference, a colleague told an interesting story about nonverbal communication in mediated contexts. She asked her students to submit their assignments via e-mail by midnight on the date they were due. At 1:00 A.M., she received a frantic note from her student, Aaron, explaining that a computer malfunction had prevented him from sending his speech outline until then. As Aaron typically provided quality work and never missed deadlines, our colleague was not concerned and did not intend to penalize him. So she simply wrote back "Got it" to quickly reassure him that she had received his outline. When she later saw Aaron in class, he said her short response made him worried that she was annoyed about his lateness. "If you had used a smiley face, I would have known what you meant," Aaron said.

When you speak with someone face to face, you've got a number of nonverbal codes at your disposal. Even on the phone, where you have no visual cues, you can use *paralinguistic cues* (vocal tone, rate, pitch, volume, sighs) to offer information. But when you send an e-mail, IM, or text message, many of the nonverbal channels you rely on (eye contact, paralanguage, and so on) are unavailable. However, people have developed a series of creative substitutions for nonverbal cues: capital letters to indicate shouting; creative use of font sizes, colors, and typefaces to provide emphasis; random punctuation (#@*&!) to substitute for obscenities; and animations, figures, diagrams, and pictures to add visuals to messages (Gayomali, 2013). Punctuation (or the lack of it) can help readers "hear" the intonation of what is being said (many people say that they "hear" their friend's texts or posts in that friend's "voice").

As Aaron noted in our example, some individuals expect others to use emoticons in mediated texts to help clarify meaning—whether to express emotion or to signal that something we say is a joke (Walther, 2006). Emoticons can also strengthen the intensity of a message, add ambiguity (was that *really* a joke?), or indicate sarcasm (Derks, Bos, & von Grumbkow, 2008).

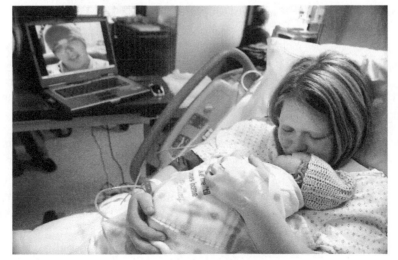

AP Photo/The Advocate Messenger, Clay Jackson

FIGURE 2.13 Technology has become so advanced that a father stationed in Iraq is now able to witness his child's birth in the United States—via webcam!

WIRED FOR COMMUNICATION

War Games Without Weapons, Sometimes Without Words

It's probably no surprise that soldiers benefit from virtual reality training offered in computerized war games. But soldiers abroad need to learn to dodge more than bullets: in different cultures, they need to learn to navigate different norms and rules of nonverbal communication.

American soldiers stationed in Iraq, for example, have discovered the hard way that gestures that are innocent in the United States can be quite offensive in Iraqi culture (and vice versa). For example, showing the soles of your feet is considered rude in Iraq; proximity while speaking, head bowing, and handshakes can also lead to misunderstanding. In one instance, an Iraqi man gestured at a female soldier by rubbing his fingers together. He was indicating friendship; she thought he was making a lewd sexual gesture.

This is where Tactical Iraqi, a virtual reality game created for the U.S. military, comes in handy. *Wired* magazine reports that "players navigate a set of real-life scenarios by learning a set of Arabic phrases, culturally relevant gestures and taboos.... A speech-recognition system records and evaluates the responses. Accurate responses allow the soldier to build a rapport with other characters and advance to the next level" (Cuda, 2006). The point is to help soldiers understand the Iraqi gestures, as well as to know how Iraqis are likely to perceive gestures that are considered innocent in the United States.

Interestingly, the game, though intended for soldiers, has no weapons or combat of any kind. It focuses instead on mutual understanding, with soldiers attempting to gain the trust of their companions in order to rebuild war-torn communities. The game's technical director, Hannes Vilhjalmsson, notes the power of nonverbal communication in this process: "I got a kick out of removing the weapons and replacing them with gestures" (Cuda, 2006). The success of such games has led the U.S. military to invest even more in simulation games—dubbed "first-person cultural trainers"—that help prepare troops for intercultural communication (Drummond, 2010).

THINK ABOUT THIS

1. Do you think soldiers can learn communication skills from a video game? Do you think this method of training would be more or less effective than classroom instruction?

2. Why is establishing competent communication so important for soldiers in Iraq? Do you think such training would have been more or less important for soldiers in Europe during World War II?

3. The company that created Tactical Iraqi is considering a civilian version of the game. Would it be useful to engage different cultures in the United States in virtual reality play? How might its technological format affect its usefulness for various co-cultures (age, education, socioeconomic status, and so on)?

One study in Japan found that college students use positive emoticons as a "flame deterrent"—to try to prevent emotional misunderstandings that might upset others (Kato, Kato, & Scott, 2009). Since we can't hear voice inflection or see facial expressions in many mediated situations, effective use of the keyboard and computer graphics can help to create a sense of nonverbal immediacy. This can be particularly useful in relationship formation and maintenance; for example, a dating Web site that used avatars to restore nonverbal cues improved perceptions of the effectiveness of online interaction so that participants exchanged more information and had a stronger desire to pursue a relationship (Kotlyar & Ariely, 2013).

AND YOU?
Have you ever taken an online or distance-learning course? Were you happy with the instruction and the amount of interaction? It is challenging to both present and respond nonverbally in courses offered online. What are the most effective ways to do this, based on your experience?

The Situational Context

Dancing at a funeral. Raising your Starbucks cup to toast your professor. Making long, steady, somewhat flirtatious eye contact with your doctor. Wearing a business suit to a rock concert. Do these situations sound strange or potentially uncomfortable? The situational context has a powerful impact on nonverbal communication. The situational context includes spheres like the place you are in, your comfort level, the event, current events, and the social environment.

Now imagine dancing at a wedding, toasting your friend's accomplishment, flirting with an attractive friend, or wearing a business suit to a job interview. In each instance, the situational context has changed. Situational context determines the rules of behavior and the roles people must play under different conditions. Competent communicators will always consider the appropriateness and effectiveness of nonverbal communication in a given context.

Two of the primary factors involved in situational context are the public–private dimension and the informal–formal dimension. The **public–private dimension** is the physical space that affects our nonverbal communication. For example, you might touch or caress your partner's hand while chatting over dinner at your kitchen table, but you would be much less likely to do that at your brother's kitchen table or during a meeting at city hall. The **informal–formal dimension** is more psychological, dealing with our perceptions of personal versus impersonal situations. The formality of a situation is signaled by various nonverbal cues, such as the environment (your local pub versus a five-star restaurant), the event (a child's first birthday party or a funeral), the level of touch (a business handshake as contrasted with a warm embrace from your aunt), or even the punctuality expected (a wedding beginning promptly at 2:00 P.M. or a barbecue at your friend Nari's house going from 6:00 P.M. to whenever) (Burgoon & Bacue, 2003). Competently assessing the formality or informality of the situation affects your use of nonverbal communication—you might wear flip-flops and shorts to hang out at Nari's, but you probably wouldn't wear them to a wedding and certainly wouldn't wear them on a job interview.

If your nonverbal communication does not appropriately fit the public–private and formal–informal dimensions, you'll likely be met with some nonverbal indications that you are not being appropriate or effective (tight smiles, restless body movements, gaze aversion, and vocal tension).

Back To Pixar Animation Studios

At the beginning of this chapter, we considered how animators at Pixar use elements of nonverbal communication to tell elaborate stories in films like *Up* and *WALL-E*. Let's reconsider some of the ways nonverbal codes operate in these and other films.

- The directors of *Up* used simple visual cues to highlight the characters so their appearance provides insights into their personalities. Carl is very squarish in appearance, so he's perceived as boxed in, in both his house and his life. Eight-year-old Explorer Scout Russell is round and bouncy—like Carl's balloons, reflecting his optimistic, energetic personality. These nonverbal elements carry subtle yet influential messages.

- Animators study human kinesics to make decisions about how their animated characters should move. To animate the aged Carl, they studied their own parents and grandparents and watched footage of the Senior Olympics.

- If Carl moved like eight-year-old Russell, the credibility of the film would be compromised.

- It takes talented voice actors to bring a script to life. The veteran actor Ed Asner breathed life into Carl, delivering not only his lines, but also believable vocal cues—grunts, sighs, speaking through clenched teeth—that made those lines more human and real. But for the roles of young Ellie and Russell, the directors chose nonactors who would give genuine, unpolished performances full of childish energy—the goal was for them to sound more like real children than actors reading from a script.

■ Things To Try

Activities

1. Record a new episode of your favorite scripted television show. Try watching it with the sound turned all the way down (and closed captions turned off). Can you guess what's going on in terms of plot? How about in terms of what the characters are feeling? Now watch it again with the sound on. How accurate were your interpretations of the nonverbal behaviors shown? How successful do you think you would have been if it were an unfamiliar show, one with characters you don't know as well?

2. Shake up your clothing and artifacts today. Wear something completely out of character for you, and consider how people react. If you normally dress very casually, try wearing a suit, or if you're normally quite put together, try going out wearing sweatpants, sneakers, or a T-shirt; if you're normally a clean-shaven man, try growing a beard for a week, or if you're a woman who never wears makeup, try wearing lipstick and eyeliner. Do you get treated differently by friends? How about strangers (such as clerks in stores) or any professionals (such as doctors or mechanics) with whom you interact?

3. Observe the nonverbal behaviors of people leaving or greeting one another at an airport or a train station. Do you think you can tell the relationship they have from their nonverbal behaviors? Describe the variety of behaviors you observe, and categorize them according to the codes and functions detailed in this chapter.

4. Try smiling (genuinely) more than you usually do—and with people you might not usually smile at. See what happens. Do you feel differently about yourself and others? Do others respond with more smiles of their own? (A group of thirty of our students tried this one day and reported back that they thought they had made the whole campus a happier place—though there were a few people they encountered who remained their solemn selves.)

5. Play with text-to-speech features on your computer. Compare the way the machine reads a passage of text to the way you would read it. Do you have a choice of voices from which to choose, and is there one you prefer? Would you rather listen to an audiobook performance by a noted actor or a computer-generated voice reading the same material?

Chapter 3

Managing Speech Anxiety

What Makes Us Anxious about Public Speaking?

Pinpoint the Onset of Public Speaking Anxiety

Use Proven Strategies to Build Your Confidence

This chapter is taken from Dan O'Hair, Rob Stewart, and Hannah Rubenstein, *A Speaker's Guidebook*, Sixth Edition, pp. 42–50 (Chapter 3).

In my experience, men go to far greater lengths to avoid what they fear than to obtain what they desire.

—Sir Leigh Teabing in *The Da Vinci Code*

Contrary to what most of us think, feeling nervous about giving a speech is not only normal but desirable. Channeled properly, nervousness can boost performance. Grammy-award–winning pop singer Adele has fought stage fright since age sixteen, using such anxiety-reducing methods as belly breathing to channel her nervous energy into powerful performances.[1] She's learned to breathe with her diaphragm instead of her chest, a technique many people faced with delivering a speech find enormously helpful.

The difference between seasoned public speakers and the rest of us is that they know how to make nervousness work *for* rather than *against* them. This chapter introduces specific techniques that speakers use to minimize their tension.

I focus on the information. I try not to think about being graded. I also practice my speech a ton to really make sure I do not speak too quickly. I time myself so that I can develop an average time. This makes me more confident [in dealing] with time requirements. And, because I know that I am well prepared, I really try to just relax.

—*Kristen Obracay, student*

■ What Makes Us Anxious about Public Speaking?

Anxiety is simply a state of increased fear or arousal. Some of us tend to be more anxious about public speaking because of our particular psychological traits, life experiences, or even genetic factors.[2] Researchers have identified several factors that underlie the fear of public speaking: a lack of public speaking experience, or having had a negative experience; feeling different from members of the audience; and uneasiness about being the center of attention. Each factor can precipitate **public speaking anxiety (PSA)**—"a situation-specific social anxiety that arises from the real or anticipated enactment of an oral presentation."[3] Fortunately, we can learn techniques to tame this anxiety and make it work for us.

Lack of Positive Experience

If you have had no exposure to public speaking or have had unpleasant experiences, anxiety about what to expect is only natural. And without positive experiences to fall back on, it's hard to put this anxiety into perspective. It's a bit of a vicious circle. Some people react by deciding to avoid making speeches altogether, yet gaining more experience is key to overcoming speech anxiety.

Feeling Different

The prospect of getting up in front of an audience makes many of us extra-sensitive to our personal idiosyncrasies, such as a less-than-perfect haircut, a slight lisp, or an accent. We even believe that no one could possibly be interested in anything we have to say.

As inexperienced speakers, we become anxious because we assume that being different somehow means being inferior. Actually, everyone is different from everyone else in many ways. However, nearly everyone experiences some nervousness about giving a speech.

> I control my anxiety by mentally viewing myself as being 100 percent equal to my classmates.
>
> —*Lee Morris, student*

Being the Center of Attention

Certain audience behaviors—such as lack of eye contact with the speaker, pointing, or chatting while the speaker is talking—can cause us as speakers to think that we must be doing something wrong; we wonder what it is and whether the entire audience has noticed it.

Left unchecked, this kind of self-consciousness can distract us from the speech itself, with all our attention now focused on "me." We then become more sensitive to things that might be wrong—and that makes us feel even more conspicuous, which in turn increases our anxiety! Actually, an audience rarely notices anything about us that we don't want to reveal.

> It's always scary to speak in front of others, but you just have to remember that everyone is human.... Nobody wants you to fail; they're not waiting on you to mess up.
>
> —*Mary Parrish, student*

■ Pinpoint the Onset of Public Speaking Anxiety

Different people become anxious at different times during the speechmaking process. Some people start to feel anxious as soon as they learn that they will have to give a speech. Others don't really get nervous until they approach the podium. Even the kind of speech assigned (e.g., being called on to deliver off-the-cuff remarks versus reading from a prepared speech) may be a factor in when and how much a speaker feels anxious.[4] By pinpointing the onset of speech anxiety, you can manage it promptly with specific anxiety-reducing techniques (see FIGURE 3.1).

CHECKLIST	
Recognizing and Overcoming Your Underlying Fears about Public Speaking	
Problem	**Solution**
Are you intimidated by a lack of experience?	Prepare well and practice your speech several times in front of at least one other person. This actual experience delivering your speech will help build your confidence.
Are you worried about appearing different from others?	Remember that everyone is different from everyone else. Dress appropriately for the occasion and be well groomed to make a good impression.
Are you uncomfortable about being the center of attention?	Focus on the speech and not on yourself, and remember that the audience won't notice anything about you that you don't want to reveal.

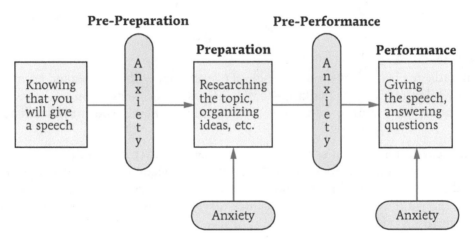

FIGURE 3.1 Where anxiety can occur in the speechmaking process.

Pre-Preparation Anxiety

Some people feel anxious the minute they know they will be giving a speech. **Pre-preparation anxiety** can be a problem when the speaker delays planning for the speech, or when it so preoccupies the speaker that he or she misses vital information needed to fulfill the speech assignment. If you are particularly affected by anxiety at this stage, start immediately to use the stress-reducing techniques described later in this chapter.

Preparation Anxiety

For a few people, anxiety arises only when they actually begin to prepare for the speech. They might feel overwhelmed at the amount of time and planning required or hit a roadblock that puts them behind schedule. Preparation pressures produce a cycle of stress, procrastination, and outright avoidance, all of which contribute to **preparation anxiety.** Research has shown, however, that for most speakers, anxiety is lowest during the preparation phase,[5] suggesting that the best way to gain a sense of control and confidence is to immerse yourself in the speech's preparation.

Pre-Performance Anxiety

Some people experience anxiety as they rehearse their speech. This is when the reality of the situation sets in: They anticipate an audience that will be watching and listening only to them; or they feel that their ideas aren't as focused or as interesting as they should be, and they sense that time is short. If this **pre-performance anxiety** is strong enough, they may even decide to stop rehearsing. If you experience heightened anxiety at this point, consider using **anxiety stop-time**: Allow your anxiety to present itself for up to a few minutes until you declare time for confidence to step in so you can proceed to complete your practice.[6]

> I experience anxiety before, during, and after the speech. My "before speech" anxiety begins the night before my speech, but then I begin to look over my notecards, and I start to realize that I am ready for this speech. I practice one more time and I tell myself I am going to be fine.
>
> —*Paige Mease, student*

Performance Anxiety

For most people, anxiety is highest just as a speech begins.[7] **Performance anxiety** is probably most pronounced during the introduction portion of the speech when we are most aware of the audience's attention. Not surprisingly, audiences we perceive to be hostile or negative usually cause us to feel more anxious than those we sense are positive or neutral.[8] However, experienced speakers agree that by controlling their nervousness during the introduction, the rest of the speech goes quite smoothly.

Each of us will experience more or less speech anxiety at these four different points in the process depending mainly on our level of **trait anxiety**. People with high trait anxiety are naturally anxious much of the time, whereas people with low trait anxiety experience nervousness usually only in unusual situations. Public speaking situations tend to make people nervous regardless of their level of trait anxiety, for the reasons outlined earlier (lack of experience, feeling different, being the center of attention). But it can be more challenging for high trait-anxious individuals than low trait-anxious persons. For instance, researchers have shown that low trait-anxious people get nervous when starting a speech but gain confidence throughout the speech. Regardless of your level of trait anxiety, and when anxiety about a speech strikes, the important thing to remember is that you can manage the anxiety and control the time and effort you put into planning, rehearsing, and delivering a successful speech.

■ Use Proven Strategies to Build Your Confidence

A number of proven strategies can help you rein in your fears about public speaking, from *meditation* and *visualization* to other forms of relaxation techniques. The first step in taming speech anxiety is to have a thorough plan for each presentation. As professional speaker Lenny Laskowski sums it up in the 9 Ps: "Prior Proper Preparation Prevents Poor Performance of the Person Putting on the Presentation."[9]

Prepare and Practice

Preparation should begin as soon as possible after a speech is assigned. If you are confident that you know your material and have adequately rehearsed your delivery, you're far more likely to feel confident at the podium. Once you have prepared the speech, you should rehearse it several times. Recent research shows that students who practiced their speeches in front of small audiences of three to eight people received significantly higher evaluations of their classroom speeches than students who didn't practice or practiced in different ways.[10] And although practicing didn't directly produce lower speech anxiety, the overall better performance outcomes for those who did practice suggest that even the more anxious students were better able to control their anxiety. Speech coach John Robert Colombo emphasizes that the best way to work out your fear of speaking is to *overwork* it[11]—practice as often as you can, and, in the future, accept as many speaking engagements as appropriate.

> Knowing your material is crucial! The worst anxiety comes when you feel unprepared. You just can't help but be nervous, at least a little. If you are confident about what you're speaking, the anxiety fades and you'll feel more comfortable.
>
> —*Shea Michelle Allen, student*

Modify Thoughts and Attitudes

Negative thoughts about speechmaking increase speech anxiety.[12] A positive attitude, on the other hand, produces lowered heart rate and reduced anxiety during delivery of the speech.[13] As you prepare for and deliver your speech, envision it as a valuable, worthwhile, and challenging activity. Remind yourself of all the reasons that public speaking is helpful personally, socially, and professionally. Think of speechmaking not as a formal performance where you will be judged and critiqued, but as a kind of ordinary conversation. In this way, you will feel less threatened and more relaxed about the process.[14] And with each successive speech experience, your thoughts and attitudes about public speaking will be increasingly favorable.

> Just before a speech those feelings of anxiety undoubtedly try to sneak in. The way I keep them from taking over is to not let my mind become negative! As long as I keep positive thoughts of confidence in my head, anxiety doesn't stand a chance!
>
> —*Morgan Verdery, student*

ESL SPEAKER'S NOTES

Confidence and Culture: When English Isn't Your First Language

NASA Goddard Space Flight center

For native English speakers, the fear of being at center stage is normal. If you are a non-native speaker, public speaking anxiety can create an added challenge, but also an opportunity.[1] It is important to know that you are not alone.

Try to think about public speaking as an opportunity to learn more about the English language and how to use it. Following are some tips that all novice speakers, regardless of whether English is their first language, will find helpful:

1. Take your time and speak slowly as you introduce the purpose and the main points of your speech. This will give your listeners time to get used to your voice and to focus on your message.

2. Practice saying any English words that may be troublesome for you five times. Then say the words again, five times. Progress slowly until each word becomes clearer and easier to pronounce. This type of practice will give you time to work on any accent features you might want to improve.[2]

3. Avoid using jargon. Learn to use a thesaurus to find *synonyms*, or words that mean the same thing, that are simpler and easier to pronounce.

4. Offer words from your native language as a way of drawing attention to a point you're making. This helps the audience appreciate your native language and your accent. For example, the Spanish word *corazón* has a more lyrical quality than its English counterpart, *heart*. Capitalize on the beauty of your native tongue.

1. T. Docan-Morgan and T. Schmidt, "Reducing Public Speaking Anxiety for Native and Non-Native English Speakers: The Value of Systematic Desensitization, Cognitive Restructuring, and Skills Training," *Cross-Cultural Communication* 8 (2012): 16–19.
2. J. E. Flege, J. M. Munro, and I. R. A. MacKay, "Factors Affecting Strength of Perceived Foreign Accent in a Second Language," *Journal of the Acoustical Society of America* 97 (1995): 3125ff.

Visualize Success

Visualization is a highly effective method of reducing speech anxiety.[15] It does this by summoning feelings and actions consistent with effective performance.[16] Speech communication researchers have developed scripts for visualizing success and increasing positive expectations associated with a public speaking occasion; one such script is below. The exercise requires you, the speaker, to close your eyes and visualize a series of positive feelings and actions that will occur on the day of your speech.

> Close your eyes and allow your body to get comfortable in the chair in which you are sitting. Take a deep, comfortable breath and hold it...now slowly release it through your nose. Now take another deep breath and make certain that you are breathing from the diaphragm...hold it...now slowly release it and note how you feel while doing this. Now one more deep breath...hold it...and release it slowly...and begin your normal breathing pattern. Shift around if you need to get comfortable again.

> Now begin to visualize the beginning of a day in which you are going to give an informative speech. See yourself getting up in the morning, full of energy, full of confidence, looking forward to the day's challenges. As you dress, you think about how dressing well makes you look and feel good about yourself. As you are driving, riding, or walking to the speech setting, note how clear and confident you feel. You feel thoroughly prepared to discuss the topic that you will be presenting today.

> Now you see yourself standing or sitting in the room where you will present your speech, talking very comfortably and confidently with others in the room. The people to whom you will be presenting your speech appear to be quite friendly and are very cordial in their greetings and conversations prior to the presentation. You feel absolutely sure of your material and of your ability to present the information in a forceful, convincing, positive manner.

> Now you see yourself approaching the area from which you will present. You are feeling very good about this presentation and see yourself move eagerly forward. All of your audiovisual materials are well organized, well planned, and clearly aid your presentation.[17]

Practicing the mental exercise of seeing yourself give a successful speech will help you prepare with confidence and strengthen your positive attitudes and expectations for speechmaking.

Activate the Relaxation Response

Before, during, and sometimes after a speech you may experience rapid heart rate and breathing, dry mouth, faintness, freezing-up, or other uncomfortable sensations. These automatic physiological reactions result from the "**fight or flight response**"— the body's automatic response to threatening or fear-inducing events. These sensations indicate the body is preparing to confront a threat head-on ("fight") or to make a hasty escape from the threat ("flight").[18] Research shows that you can reduce these sensations by using techniques such as meditation and controlled breathing.[19] Just as you would warm up before taking a lengthy jog, use the following relaxation techniques before, and even during, your speech to help slow your heart rate and breathing rate, lower your blood pressure, increase blood flow to major muscles, and reduce muscle tension. These more relaxed physiological sensations help you feel better[20] and result in better concentration and sharper performance.

Briefly Meditate

You can calm yourself considerably before delivering a presentation with this brief meditation exercise:

1. Sit comfortably in a quiet place.

2. Relax your muscles, moving from neck to shoulders to arms to back to legs.

3. Choose a word, phrase, or prayer associated with your belief system (e.g., "Namaste," "Om," "Hail Mary, full of grace"). Breathe slowly and say it until you become calm (about ten to twenty minutes).

Use Stress-Control Breathing

When you feel stressed about speaking, the center of your breathing tends to move from the abdomen to the upper chest, and the chest and shoulders rise—leaving you with a reduced supply of air and feeling out of breath. *Stress-control breathing* gives you more movement in the stomach than in the chest. Try it in two stages.

Stage One: Inhale air and let your abdomen go out. Exhale air and let your abdomen go in. Do this for a while until you get into the rhythm of it.

Stage Two: As you inhale, use a soothing word such as *calm* or *relax*, or a personal mantra, like this: "Inhale *calm*, abdomen out, exhale *calm*, abdomen in." Go slowly, taking about three to five seconds with each inhalation and exhalation.

Begin practicing stress-control breathing several days before a speech event. Then, once the occasion arrives, begin stress-control breathing while awaiting your turn at the podium. And you can continue the breathing pattern as you approach the podium, and once more while you're arranging your notes and getting ready to begin.

> I get very anxious before I'm about to speak, so I have two ways to cope with my nervousness. I take a couple deep breaths through my stomach; I breathe in through my nose and out of my mouth. This allows more oxygen to the brain so you can think clearly. I also calm myself down by saying, "Everything will be okay, and the world is not going to crumble before me if I mess up."
>
> —*Jenna Sanford, student*

Use Movement to Minimize Anxiety

While delivering your speech, channel some of your nervousness through controlled gestures and body movements (see **CHAPTER 14**).

Practice Natural Gestures

Practice natural gestures such as holding up your index finger when stating your first main point. Think about what you want to say as you do this, instead of thinking about how you look or feel. (See **CHAPTER 14** for tips on practicing natural gestures.)

Move as You Speak

You don't have to stand perfectly still behind the podium when you deliver a speech. Walk around as you make some of your points. Movement relieves tension and helps hold the audience's attention. Some actual exercise a few hours prior to your speech can sharpen your mental focus, leaving you more limber and better able to move naturally.[21]

Enjoy the Occasion

Most people ultimately find that giving speeches can indeed be fun. It's satisfying and empowering to influence people, and a good speech is a sure way to do this. All of the time and effort that go into preparing and delivering a speech, from the moment the assignment is made to the moment you step away from the podium, make public speaking both challenging and exciting. Think of it in this way, and chances are you will find much pleasure in it.

Learn from Feedback

Speech evaluations help to identify ways to improve what you do. You can learn a lot through self-evaluation, but self-evaluation can be distorted,[22] so objective evaluations by others often are more helpful. In your speech class, your speech assignments will be evaluated by your instructor, of course, and probably by your classmates as well. Both sources will provide practical feedback to help you improve your next speeches. Ultimately, all speakers rely on audience feedback to evaluate the effectiveness of their speeches.

CHECKLIST
Preparing to Speak with Confidence
Your confidence will grow with each successful completion of a speech assignment, but both confidence and success result mainly from diligent preparation. Follow these general steps as part of your plan for each speech.
•   *Prepare and practice.* Start early, even when selecting your topic, to decide when and where you will practice your speech.
•   *Modify thoughts and attitudes.* Keep positive thoughts, concentrating on what makes sense as you develop your topic, and on the positive outcomes expected from your speech.
•   *Visualize success.* Practice an optimistic frame of mind, seeing yourself with well-developed speech points that you deliver enthusiastically and effectively.
•   *Utilize relaxation techniques.* Use stress-control breathing and natural hand and body movement while speaking.
•   *Learn from the task and enjoy it.* Consider each speech assignment a learning opportunity to enrich future academic and career objectives.

Chapter 4
Selecting a Topic and Purpose

Exploring Topics for Your Speech

Try Brainstorming to Generate Ideas

Identify the General Purpose of Your Speech

Refine the Topic and Purpose

From Topic and Purpose to Thesis Statement

This chapter is taken from Dan O'Hair, Rob Stewart, and Hannah Rubenstein, *A Speaker's Guidebook*, Sixth Edition, pp. 102–108 (Chapter 7).

The late, great baseball player Yogi Berra, famously prone to mangling popular sayings,[1] once said "You've got to be very careful if you don't know where you're going, because you might not get there." Presumably, Berra meant the actual saying: "You must know where you are going in order to get there."

No words were ever truer for the public speaker. Unless you know what you want to say and why you want to say it—your topic and purpose—you won't get *there*—giving a speech that works. Thus one of the first tasks in preparing any speech is to select a topic and purpose that are *appropriate to the audience, occasion,* and *overall speech situation* (*rhetorical situation*). You should be able to answer three key questions with total confidence before delivering any speech: "What precisely is my speech about?" "What is my goal in speaking to the audience?" and "What specifically do I want my listeners to know or do?"

■ Exploring Topics for Your Speech

A good speech topic must pique both the audience's curiosity and your own, too. As you explore topics, consider each one's potential appeal to the audience and its appropriateness for the occasion. Will the topic meet listeners' expectations for the speech?

Assigned versus Self-Selected Topics

In the workplace and in the classroom, including the public speaking course, employers and instructors will assign various kinds of speeches, some of which might have a set topic. Even when the topic is yours to choose, you are usually given some direction as to how your talk should be presented. For example:

- You may be given a *purpose.* You are asked to speak to a youth group about avoiding behaviors harmful to health. The specific behaviors are yours to choose.

- You are given *time constraints.* You are a spokesperson for a neighborhood association and will be addressing the city council on members' opposition to locating a garbage dump nearby. The council has given you five minutes to make your case.

- You are given a *challenge.* The project director asks you to convince an important client group to modify a design and extend the timeline for completion. "Get buy-in and approval," she tells you.

Even in the preliminary stages of choosing a topic, think about the constraints of the speech circumstances. Doing so may help you avoid picking inappropriate or unrealistic topics.

Identify Personal Interests

Selecting a topic you are familiar with and enthusiastic about has several advantages. You'll enjoy researching and learning more about it. You'll bring a genuine enthusiasm to your presentation, which will help convey your competence and encourage the audience to see you as a highly credible speaker.

As seen in TABLE 4.1, personal interests run the gamut from favorite activities and hobbies to deeply held goals and values. Personal experiences provide powerful topics, especially if your telling them in some way benefits the audience. "What it's like" stories also yield captivating topics. For example, what is it like to go hang gliding in the Rocky Mountains or to be part of a medical mission team working in Uganda?

TABLE 4.1 Identifying Topics

FAVORITE HOBBIES	PERSONAL EXPERIENCES	VALUES	GOALS
• Sports • Building computers • Cars • Fashion • Reading • Video games • Music • Travel • Cooking	• Exotic travel destinations • Service in the armed forces • Volunteer work in a foreign country* • Immigration • Life-threatening disease • Surviving disaster	• Building a greater sense of community* • Spirituality • Philanthropy* • Political activism*	• Being a high-tech entrepreneur • Attending graduate or professional school • Starting a family • Staying fit* • Learning more about my religion
SPECIFIC SUBJECT INTERESTS	**SOCIAL PROBLEMS**	**HEALTH AND NUTRITION**	**CURRENT EVENTS**
• Local history* • Medieval history • Politics* • Art* • Religion • Science	• Road rage* • Violence in the schools • Unemployment • Racism* • Lack of affordable childcare	• Diets • Circle contact lenses • Exercise regimens • HMOs • Assisted living • Asperger's syndrome	• Pending legislation* • Political races • Climate and biodiversity • National security
GRASSROOTS ISSUES	**NEW OR UNUSUAL ANGLES**	**ISSUES OF CONTROVERSY**	
• Costs of higher education* • Safer schools* • Caring for the homeless	• Unsolved crimes • Unexplained disappearances • Scandals	• Corporate bailouts • Medical marijuana • Concealed handguns in schools	

*Note: Topics marked with an asterisk are good possibilities for speeches on civic responsibility.

Consider Current Events and Controversial Issues

Few of us have the time to delve into the barrage of events that get reported, yet most of us appreciate learning about them when we can. As an interested and responsible citizen of your community and the world, select events and issues that are most important to you and your audience, and see if you can make a difference. A word of warning, however: people rarely respond to alternative perspectives directed at their core values, so speeches on such topics must be planned very carefully to hold the audience's positive attention and leave them thinking about the ideas presented.

Librarians often refer students to two related publications—*CQ Researcher* (published weekly) and *CQ Global Researcher* (published monthly)—for trustworthy background information on pressing social, political, environmental, and regional issues. Available online as part of your library's electronic holdings, for each topic they include an overview and assessment of the current situation, pro/con statements from representatives of opposing positions, and bibliographies of key sources.

Survey Grassroots Issues: Engage the Community

Audience members respond with interest to local issues that may affect them directly. Town residents want to know why their utility rates have increased dramatically; parents need information on proposed changes to the public school schedules. People are also interested in what other people in their communities are doing. Review your community's newspapers and news blogs for the local headlines. Consider giving a speech about a charitable event you participate in or a campus club you belong to.

Steer Clear of Overused and Trivial Topics

To avoid boring your classmates and instructor, stay away from tired issues, such as drunk driving and the health risks of smoking cigarettes, as well as trite topics such as "how to change a tire." These and other overused topics appear far too frequently in student classroom speeches across the country. Instead, seek out subject matter that yields new or refreshing insight. As one source of ideas, consider searching your favorite print or online publications. Indeed, consider how you can apply relevant secondary research to personal experience to form a topic. Fresh ideas based on first-hand knowledge are more intriguing and provide an opportunity for others to get to know you better.

■ Try Brainstorming to Generate Ideas

Brainstorming is a method of spontaneously generating ideas through word association, topic mapping, or Internet browsing using search engines and directories. Brainstorming works—it is a structured and effective way to identify topic ideas in a relatively brief period of time.

Word Association

To brainstorm by **word association,** write down *one* topic that might interest you and your listeners. Then jot down the first thing that comes to mind related to it. Repeat the process until you have a list of fifteen to twenty items. Narrow the list to two or three, and then select a final topic.

- health ⇒ alternative medicine ⇒ naturopathy ⇒ fraud
- children ⇒ parenting ⇒ working ⇒ day care ⇒ living expenses
- diving ⇒ snorkeling ⇒ Bahamas ⇒ conch shells ⇒ deep-sea fishing
- Internet ⇒ websites ⇒ social media ⇒ Twitter
- exercise ⇒ Zumba ⇒ weight lifting ⇒ swimming

Topic Mapping

Topic mapping is a brainstorming technique in which you lay out words in diagram form to show categorical relationships among them (see **FIGURE 4.1**). Put a potential topic in the middle of a piece of paper and draw a circle around it. As related ideas come to you, write them down as shown in **FIGURE 4.1**. Keep going until you hit upon an idea that appeals most to you.

Internet Tools

Popular Internet search engines such as Google (www.google.com), Yahoo! (www.yahoo.com), and Bing (www.bing.com) offer a wealth of resources both to discover topics and to narrow them. For example, each search engine offers options for specialized searches within particular categories of information sources, such as books, news, blogs, finance, and images. You can further narrow topics by limiting searches to within a range of dates (e.g., 1900–1950), to a geographic region (e.g., Europe), or in a particular language.

Another online tool you can use to find (and narrow) a topic is a library's portal, or its home page (see "From Source to Speech: Narrowing Your Topic Using a Library Portal," on p. 91). If you've already chosen a topic, consult the library's online databases, such as Academic OneFile, to locate credible sources.

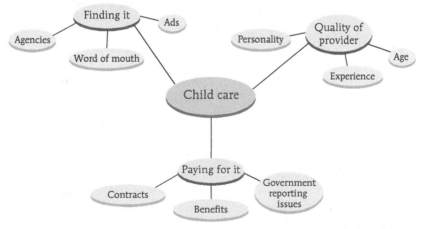

FIGURE 4.1 A Topic Map

FROM SOURCE TO SPEECH

Narrowing Your Topic Using a Library Portal

One of several ways to research your topic is to use a library's online portal. Using reputable tools to generate narrower ideas also guarantees that the new ideas are supported by credible sources. For example, to narrow down the topic of smoking in movies, you could use your school library's home page to locate relevant books and access online periodical databases that offer full-text articles evaluated for reliability by librarians and other content experts.

Navigating the Library Portal through Basic Searches

To search the portal of the Brooklyn Public Library, you could find sources through links on the home page: "Library Catalog" to find books, and "Articles and Databases" to find full-text articles.

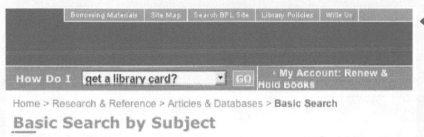

————A basic search within "Articles and Databases" results in multiple hits, all with numerous articles from various databases.

Borrowing Materials | Site Map | Search BPL Site | Library Policies | Write Us

How Do I **get a library card?** ▾ GO ▸ **My Account: Renew & Hold Books**

Home > Research & Reference > Articles & Databases > **Basic Search**

Basic Search by Subject

Search all electronic resources

smoking in the movies | Search

View | View PDF

7. ☐ **CAN CIGARETTE WARNINGS COUNTERBALANCE EFFECTS OF SMOKING SCENES IN MOVIES?**
Author: Golmier, Isabelle; Chebat, Jean-Charles; G◆linas-Chebat, Claire
Journal: Psychological Reports
Pub.: 2007-02
Volume: 100
Issue: 1
Pages: 3(16)
ISSN: 00332941
Subject: SMOKING in motion pictures; MOTION pictures & teenagers; WARNING labels; CIGARETTE industry; CIGARETTE package labels; CIGARETTE smokers; TOBACCO; ORAL habits; TOBACCO use
Description: Publication Type : Academic Journal Language : English AN : 24652953 DOI : 10.2466/PR0.100.1.3-18 Scenes in movies where smoking occurs have been empirically shown to influence teenagers to smoke cigarettes. The capacity of a Canadian warning label on cigarette packages to decrease the effects of smoking scenes in popular movies has been investigated. A 2 ◆ 3 factorial design was used to test the effects of the same movie scene with or without electronic manipulation of all elements related to smoking, and cigarette pack warnings, i.e., no warning, text-only warning, and text+picture warning. Smoking-related stereotypes and intent to smoke of teenagers were measured. It was found that, in the absence of warning, and in the presence of smoking scenes, teenagers showed positive smoking-related stereotypes. However, these effects were not observed if the teenagers were first exposed to a picture and text warning. Also, smoking-related stereotypes mediated the relationship of the combined presentation of a text and picture warning and a smoking scene on teenagers' intent to smoke. Effectiveness of Canadian warning labels to prevent or to decrease cigarette smoking among teenagers is discussed, and areas of research are proposed.

View

8. ☐ **Smoking imagery increasingly prevalent in movies, report finds.**

————This psychology journal article reveals a level of results that general search engines do not find an article that has undergone peer review and can be viewed in full-text, PDF form.

The Brooklyn Public Library

Using Advanced Library Portal Searches

An advanced search allows you to hone in on credible sources that are even more likely to help you. This function will allow you to better distill the specific purpose of your speech and to develop your thesis statement.

The Brooklyn Public Library

1. Linking search terms *cigarettes* and *movies* by the Boolean operator "AND" results in hits containing both these terms.

2. Limiting the search from 2008 to 2014 ensures that only articles in this period appear.

3. Limiting the resource categories yields results that cover only the areas on which you want to focus your thesis.

CHECKLIST
Criteria for Selecting a Topic
1. Is the topic appropriate to the occasion?
2. Will the topic appeal to my listeners' interests and needs?
3. Is the topic something I can speak about with enthusiasm and insight?
4. Can I research and report on the topic in the time allotted?
5. Will I be able to offer a fresh perspective on the topic?

■ Identify the General Purpose of Your Speech

Once you have an idea for a topic, you'll need to refine and adapt it to your general speech purpose. **The general speech purpose** (also called *rhetorical purpose*) for any speech answers the question "What is my objective in speaking on this topic to this audience on this occasion?" Public speeches typically accomplish one of three general purposes: to inform, to persuade, or to mark a special occasion.

The rhetorical situation—the circumstances that call for the speech—often determines or at least suggests what might be an appropriate purpose. For example, a town leader invited to address a civic group about opening up nearby land to wind farm installations may choose a persuasive purpose to encourage the group to get behind the effort. However, if invited to describe the initiative to the town finance committee, the speaker may choose an informative purpose, in which the main goal is to help the finance members understand project costs. Addressing the same topic in different circumstances, the speaker selects a different general speech purpose to suit the audience and occasion.

When the General Speech Purpose Is to Inform

The general purpose of an **informative speech** is *to increase the audience's understanding and awareness of a topic* by defining, describing, explaining, or demonstrating your knowledge of the subject. When selecting a topic for an informative speech, try to gauge how much the audience already knows about it. There's no surer way to lose audience members' attention than to speak over—or under—their heads. Just about any topic is appropriate for an informative speech (see **TABLES 4.2** and **4.3**), as long as you present it with the goal of giving the audience something new to expand their understanding and awareness.

When the General Speech Purpose Is to Persuade

The general purpose of a **persuasive speech** goes beyond informing to *effect some degree of change in the audience's attitudes, beliefs, or even specific behaviors* (e.g., "Only eat wild salmon"). Topics or issues on which there are competing perspectives are particularly suitable for persuasive speeches. Issues such as U.S. policy on the Middle East, the popularity of problem celebrities, and hazing on college campuses naturally lend themselves to a persuasive purpose because people hold strongly contrasting opinions about them. Most any topic is suitable for a persuasive speech as long as the speaker can fashion it into a message that is intended to effect some degree of change in the audience (SEE TABLE 4.4).

Consider the topic of hazing. A persuasive purpose (e.g., "To persuade my audience to report incidents of hazing") would be appropriate if:

- The audience feels considerably different about the topic than you do (e.g., members of the audience are part of a community that tends to ignore hazing).

- The audience holds similar attitudes and beliefs about the topic as you do but needs direction in taking action (e.g., the audience consists of people who want to curb the incidence of hazing and are seeking strategies to do so).

- The audience agrees with your position but is likely to encounter opposing information or circumstances in the near future (e.g., fraternities and sororities tend to fall back on old habits as the new pledge class arrives at school).

Table 4.2 Some General Categories of Informative Topics

OBJECTS	PEOPLE	EVENTS	CONCEPTS	PROCESSES	ISSUES
Their origin, construction, function, symbolic or concrete meaning. For example, history of the personal computer; the many facets of a diamond.	Their biographies, noteworthy achievements, anecdotes about them. For example, Barack Obama's childhood; the professional life of Sheryl Sandburg.	Noteworthy or unusual occurrences, both past and present. For example, major storms of the 21st century, so far; highlights of the 2012 Summer Olympics.	Abstract and difficult ideas or theories. For example, the nature of love; the definition of peace; the theory of intelligent design.	A series of steps leading to an end result. For example, how "fracking" works; how to prepare bananas Foster.	Problems or matters of dispute. For example, U.S. border security; whether reality television is really real.

TABLE 4.3

SAMPLE INFORMATIVE SPEECH TOPICS
• The Role of Sleep in Academic Success
• Taking Distance Courses as a Resident Student
• The Popular Consumption of Pomegranate Juice
• Using Your Smartphone as a Learning Aid
• Booming Careers That Have No Major
• What's Behind the Immigration Issue

Table 4.4

SAMPLE PERSUASIVE SPEECH TOPICS
• Manage Your Sleep Habits to Improve Academic Performance
• Enroll in Distance Courses to Put Slack in Your Campus Schedule
• Drink Pomegranate Juice for Better Health
• Learn by Using Your Smartphone in Class
• Use Your Major to Develop a New Career Area
• Take a Stand on Immigration Reform

When the General Speech Purpose Is to Mark a Special Occasion

Speeches are often a key, if not featured, part of a special occasion. **Special occasion speeches** serve the general purpose to *entertain, celebrate, commemorate, inspire, or set a social agenda* and include speeches of introduction, acceptance, and presentation; roasts and toasts; eulogies; and after-dinner speeches, among others. Special occasion speeches sometimes have secondary specific purposes to inform or to persuade. For example, a speech to mark the occasion of Veterans Day might include a message to contribute to or volunteer with organizations like Wounded Warriors Project.

■ Refine the Topic and Purpose

Once you have an idea for a topic and have established a general speech purpose, you'll need to narrow your focus to align with the nature of the occasion, audience expectations, and time constraints.

CHECKLIST
Identifying Your General Speech Purpose
• If your speech goal is primarily to increase the audience's knowledge of a topic or to share your point of view, your general purpose is to inform.
• If it is primarily to effect some degree of change in the way your listeners view or do something, your general purpose is to persuade.
• If it is primarily to mark a special occasion, your general purpose will be variously to entertain, celebrate, commemorate, inspire, or set a social agenda.

Narrow the Topic

As you narrow your topic, carefully evaluate it according to audience interests and knowledge, the purpose of your speech and its occasion, how long the speech should be, and how much time you have to do research. Imagine, for example, how your approach to the topic "Hit British T.V. Shows in the U.S." may change as you consider the following factors:

- The speech is for an informative speaking assignment.

- The time limit is five to seven minutes.

- You remember seeing an online article about the topic but can't remember where and how you found it.

Just as brainstorming can be used to discover a general topic, it can also be helpful in narrowing one. One way of doing this is to brainstorm by category. What sorts of categories can you break your general topic into? For the general topic of British T.V., some related categories are sitcoms, actors and actresses, and crime dramas. As you brainstorm by category, ask yourself, "What questions do I have about the topic? Am I more interested in what the particular programs are, who stars in them, or why they are so appealing to American audiences? What aspect is my audience most likely to want to hear about?" You can also use topic mapping or trend searching (see p. 90) to narrow your topic.

CHECKLIST
Identifying Your General Speech Purpose
•   What is my audience most likely to know about the subject?
•   What are my listeners most likely to want to learn?
•   What aspects of the topic are most relevant to the occasion?
•   Can I develop the topic using just two or three main points?
•   How much can I competently research and report on in the time I am given to speak?

FROM SOURCE TO SPEECH

Narrowing Your Topic to Fit Your Audience

Why Narrow Your Topic?

Choosing a topic that interests you is only the beginning. A vital step in moving from topic to speech is narrowing your topic and tailoring it to fit your audience and the speech occasion.

A Case Study

Jenny is a member of the campus animal rights club and a student in a public speaking class. She is giving several persuasive speeches this semester: one to her public speaking class, one to the student council, and one in an online video for the website of the animal rights club. For all three presentations, Jenny plans to speak on the broad topic of animal rights and welfare. But she must narrow this topic considerably to fit each audience and the speech occasion, and this means different narrowed topics.

First, Jenny draws a topic map to generate ideas.

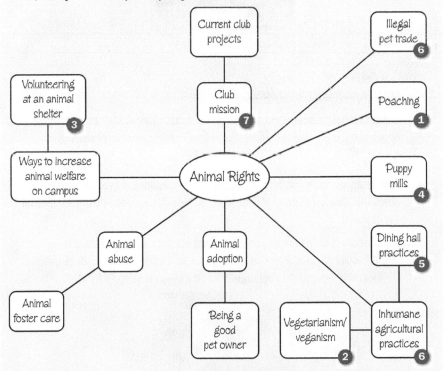

For each presentation, Jenny narrows her topic after considering her audience and the speech occasion.

Public speaking class (25–30 people):

- Mixed ages, races, and ethnicities, and an even mix of males and females

- Busy with classes, jobs, sports, and clubs

- Half live in campus housing, where pets are not allowed

1. Jenny eliminates poaching because it's not an everyday concern for students.

2. She eliminates vegetarianism because she will be unlikely to change listeners' minds in a six-minute speech.

3. Volunteering at an animal shelter may appeal to animal lovers who are not allowed to have pets on campus. Jenny argues that students should donate an hour a week to a nearby shelter, so that busy students can still participate.

Andersen Ross/Digital Vision/Getty Images;

Student council (8–10 people):

- Mixed demographic characteristics

- Similar interests: government, maintaining a rich campus life, an investment in ethics and the honor code, and an interest in keeping student affairs within budget

4. Jenny can eliminate the topic of puppy mills—though the student council may agree that they are harmful, it's not likely that they'll be able to do anything about the problem.

5. Jenny zeros in on dining hall practices because they are directly tied to campus life. A resolution to use free-range eggs in the campus dining hall benefits all students and requires the support of the council—an ideal topic for this audience.

Animal rights club website (open to all searchers of the Internet):

- Most diverse audience—unknown mix of demographic characteristics

- Likely interest in animal rights

6. Jenny can easily eliminate many topics, such as inhumane agricultural practices, because they are too complicated for a brief video clip.

7. She opts for the club's mission as a topic. A very brief welcome message that invites Web visitors to attend a longer information session will appeal to both the curious passerby and the dedicated animal rights activist.

(top) Manfred Rutz/The Images Bank/Getty Images; (bot) Anne Ackermann/Digital Vision/Getty Images

Form a Specific Speech Purpose

After you've narrowed the topic, you need to refine the speech goal. You know you want to give an informative speech, or a persuasive one, but you now need to decide more specifically what you want to accomplish with the speech. The **specific speech purpose** lays out precisely what you want the audience to get from the speech. To determine the specific purpose, ask yourself, "What is it about my topic that I want the audience to learn/do/reconsider/agree with?" Be specific about your aim, and then state it in action form, as in the following, written for an informative speech:

General Topic:	Consolidating student loans
Narrowed Topic:	Understanding when and why consolidating student loans makes sense
General Purpose:	To inform
Specific Purpose:	To inform my audience about the factors to consider when deciding whether or not to consolidate student loans

Although the specific purpose statement is seldom articulated in the actual speech, it is important to formulate it for yourself in order to keep in mind exactly what you want your speech to accomplish.

◼ From Topic and Purpose to Thesis Statement

After narrowing your topic and forming a specific purpose, your next step is to formulate a thesis statement. The **thesis statement** (also called the *central idea*) is the theme of the speech stated as a single declarative sentence that concisely expresses what the speech will attempt to support from the speaker's point of view. Much like a backbone, it serves to connect all the parts of the speech. The main points, the supporting material, and the conclusion all emanate from and relate to the thesis.

The thesis statement and the specific purpose are closely linked. Both state the speech topic, but do so in different forms. *The specific purpose describes in action form what outcome you want to achieve with the speech. The thesis statement concisely declares, in a single idea, what the speech is about.* By clearly stating your speech thesis (what it's about), you set in your mind exactly what outcome you want to accomplish (the specific purpose).

Postpone Development of Main Points

The thesis statement conveys the central idea or core assumption about the topic (see FIGURE 4.2). It offers your perspective on the topic. For instance, the thesis statement "Three major events caused the United States to go to war in 1941" expresses your view that three factors played a part in the U.S. entry into World War II. The speech is then developed from this thesis, presenting facts and evidence to support it. Thus, you should postpone the development of main points and supporting material until you have correctly formulated the specific purpose and thesis statement (see CHAPTER 6).

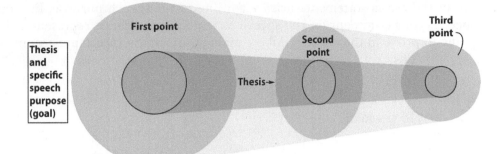

FIGURE 4.2 Main points should relate to and bolster your thesis and speech goals.

ETHICALLY SPEAKING

Ethical Considerations in Selecting a Topic and Purpose

Respect for your audience members and adaptation to their needs and interests should always guide your topic choices. What makes a speech ethical or unethical depends on how it empowers the audience to think or act. In other words, ethical considerations begin with your speech purpose. Speakers who select persuasive purposes should be particularly careful; under pressure to sway an audience, some speakers may be tempted to tamper with the truth. As you review your speech goal, consider the following:

* Have you deliberately distorted information to achieve a desired result?

* Is it your intent to deceive?

* Do you try to coerce the audience into thinking or acting in a certain way?

* Have you knowingly tried to appeal to harmful biases?

Although few hard-and-fast rules exist when it comes to ethical guidelines for selecting topics, some areas are clearly off-limits—at least in U.S. culture:

* The topic shows an audience how to perform actions prohibited by law.

* The topic provides audience members with information that may result in their physical or psychological harm.

* The topic humiliates or degrades the fundamental values of an audience's culture, religion, or political system.

Radu Bercan/Shutterstock

The nature of the thesis statement varies according to the speech purpose. In a persuasive speech, your comment on the speech as stated in the thesis represents what you are going to prove in the address. All the main points in the speech are arguments that develop this position.

Example 1

General Purpose:	To persuade
Specific Purpose:	To persuade the audience to raise money on behalf of green charities
Thesis:	A donation to a member organization of green charities is an investment in a sustainable environment.

Example 2

Specific Purpose:	To persuade the audience that abstinence is the way to avoid the harm alcohol can cause
Thesis:	Abstinence is the best way to avoid the harm alcohol can cause.

Example 3

Speech Topic:	Service learning courses
General Speech Purpose:	To persuade
Specific Speech Purpose:	To persuade my audience that service learning courses are beneficial
Thesis Statement:	To prepare for a difficult job market and enhance your résumé while making a significant difference for other people, you should take one or more service learning courses.

Notice that in each case, after you read the thesis you find yourself asking "Why?" or thinking "Prove it!" This will be accomplished by the evidence you give in the main points (see CHAPTER 6).

The thesis statement in an informative speech conveys the scope of the topic, the steps associated with the topic, or the underlying elements of the topic. It describes what the audience will learn.

Example 1

Speech Topic:	Blogs
General Speech Purpose:	To inform
Specific Speech Purpose:	To inform my audience of three benefits of keeping a blog
Thesis Statement:	Maintaining a blog provides the opportunity to practice writing, a means of networking with others who share similar interests, and the chance to develop basic website management skills.

Example 2

General Purpose:	To inform
Specific Purpose:	To enable audience members to invest their money properly
Thesis:	You can invest wisely in the stock market in just three steps.

Use the Thesis Statement to Guide Your Speech Preparation

The point of creating a thesis statement is to help you identify precisely what your speech is about. As you develop the speech, use the thesis to keep yourself on track. Depicted as the inner core of a cylinder, as in FIGURE 4.2, the thesis is a straight and narrow path to follow from when you first state it to when you reach your last point and fulfill the speech purpose. As you research materials, review them in the light of whether they contribute to the thesis or stray from it. When you actually draft your speech, work your thesis statement into it and restate it where appropriate. Doing so will encourage your audience to understand and accept your message.

Make the Thesis Statement Relevant and Motivating

As you revise drafts of your speech, try to express the thesis statement so that it will motivate the audience to listen. In many cases, creating a relevant thesis can be accomplished quite easily by adding a few key words or phrases. You can preface an informative thesis statement with a phrase such as "Few of us know" or "Contrary to popular belief" or "Have you ever." A persuasive thesis statement can also be adapted to establish relevance for the audience. Phrases such as "As most of you know" or "As informed members of the community" or "As concerned adults" can attract listeners' attention and interest and help them see the topic's relevance.

The exact phrasing or rewording of your thesis statement depends on the audience to whom you are speaking. Once you gain some information about your audience members, you won't have trouble making the topic relevant for them.

CHECKLIST
Formulating the Thesis Statement
• Does my thesis statement sum up in a single sentence what my speech is about?
• Is it restricted to a single idea?
• Is it in the form of a complete declarative sentence?
• Is it stated in a way that is relevant to the audience?

Chapter 5

Analyzing the Audience

This chapter is taken from Dan O'Hair, Rob Stewart, and Hannah Rubenstein, *A Speaker's Guidebook*, Sixth Edition, pp. 83–101 (Chapter 6).

Advertisers are shrewd analysts of people's needs and wants. They extensively research our buying habits and lifestyle choices to identify what motivates us; only then, when their investigation is complete, do they craft the actual advertisement. In at least one sense, to make a successful speech or presentation, you too, must function like an advertiser. To spark interest and sustain the audience's involvement in your message, you also must investigate and appeal to your audience.

Audience analysis is the process of gathering and analyzing information about audience members' attributes and motivations *with the explicit aim of preparing your speech in ways that will be meaningful to them.* This is the single most critical aspect of preparing for any speech. What are your listeners' attitudes with respect to your topic? What might they need or want to know? How will their values influence their response to your presentation? How much do audience members have in common with one another?

Assuming an **audience-centered perspective** throughout the entire speech preparation process—from selection and treatment of the speech topic to making decisions about how you will organize, word, and deliver it—will help you prepare a presentation that your audience will want to hear.

■ Adapt to Audience Psychology: Who Are Your Listeners?

One of the most important psychological principles you can learn as a speaker is that audience members, and people in general, tend to evaluate information in terms of their own—rather than the speaker's—point of view, at least until they are convinced to take a second look.[1] Establishing a connection with your listeners thus starts with seeking to understand *their* outlook and motivations and letting this information guide you in constructing your speech. You may want to convince your classmates to support a four-day school week, but unless you know how they feel and what they know about the proposal, you won't know how to adapt your presentation accordingly.

Being audience-centered does not mean that you must abandon your own convictions or cater to the audience's whims. This practice, called **pandering**, will only undermine your credibility in the eyes of the audience. Think of audience analysis as an opportunity to get to know and establish common ground with audience members, just as you might do with a new acquaintance. The more you find out about someone, the more you can discover what you share in common and how you differ.

Appeal to Audience Members' Attitudes, Beliefs, and Values

The audience members' attitudes, beliefs, and values provide crucial clues to how receptive they will be toward your topic and your position on it. While intertwined, attitudes, beliefs, and values reflect distinct mental states that reveal a great deal about us.

Attitudes are our general evaluations of people, ideas, objects, or events.[2] To evaluate something is to judge it as relatively good or bad, useful or useless, desirable or undesirable, and so on. People generally act in accordance with their attitudes (although the degree to which they do so depends on many factors).[3] If your listeners have a positive attitude toward gun ownership, for example, they're likely to own a gun and want to listen to your speech opposing stricter gun laws.

Attitudes are based on **beliefs**—the ways in which people perceive reality.[4] They are our feelings about what is true or real. Whereas attitudes deal with how we feel about some activity or entity ("Yoga is good" or "Regular church/mosque/synagogue attendance is good"), beliefs refer to our level of confidence about the very existence or validity of something ("I believe God exists" or "I'm not so sure that God exists"). The less faith listeners have that something exists—UFOs, for instance—the less open they are to hearing about it.

Both attitudes and beliefs are shaped by **values**—our most enduring judgments about what's good in life, as shaped by our culture and our unique experiences within it. We have fewer values than either attitudes or beliefs, but they are more deeply felt and resistant to change. We feel our values strongly and use them as a compass to direct our behavior. In addition, we have positive attitudes toward our values and strive to realize them. *Personal values* mirror our feelings about religious, political, social, and civic matters. *Cultural values* (also called "core values") reflect values deemed important by many members of a culture, imbuing it with a distinct identity.

In the United States, researchers have identified a set of cultural values prevalent in the dominant culture, including achievement and success, equal opportunity, material comfort, hard work, practicality and efficiency, change and progress, science, democracy, and freedom.[5] For some of us, the sanctity of marriage between a man and a woman is a cultural value. For others, the value of social justice supersedes that of material comfort. Whatever the nature of our values, they are central to our sense of who we are.

"If the Value Fits, Use It"

Evoking some combination of the audience's values, attitudes, and beliefs in the speeches you deliver will make them more personally relevant and motivating. For example, a recent large-scale survey of values related to the environment reveals that Americans overwhelmingly feel responsible to preserve the environment for future generations, to protect nature as God's creation, and to ensure that their families enjoy a healthy environment. Using this information, the Biodiversity Project, a communications group that helps speakers raise public awareness about the environment, counsels its clients to appeal directly to these values in their presentations, offering the following as an example of how to do this:

> You care about your family's health (value #1), and you feel a responsibility to protect your loved ones' quality of life (value #2). The local wetland provides a sanctuary to many plants and animals. It helps to clean our air and water and provides a space of beauty and serenity (value #3). All of this is about to be destroyed by irresponsible development.[6]

Gauge Listeners' Feelings toward the Topic, Speaker, and Occasion

With any speech, it's important to assess the audience's feelings and expectations toward (1) the topic of your speech, (2) you as the speaker, and (3) the speech occasion. This perspective-taking will help you anticipate listeners' reactions and develop the speech accordingly.

Gauge Listeners' Feelings toward the Topic

Consideration of the audience's attitudes about and familiarity with a topic is key to offering a speech that will resonate with them (see **CHAPTER 4**). Is your topic one with which the audience is familiar, or is it new to them? Do your listeners hold positive, negative, or neutral attitudes toward the topic? That is, do they care a lot, a little, or not at all about your topic? As a general rule, people pay more attention to and feel more positively (e.g., hold more positive attitudes) about topics that are in line with their values and beliefs. The less we know about something, the more indifferent we tend to be. Once you gauge the audience's knowledge level and attitudes toward the topic (using tools such as interviews and polls; see **pp. 119–122**), consider these guidelines to present your topic at the appropriate level:

If the Topic Is New to Listeners

- Start by showing why the topic is relevant to them.

- Relate the topic to familiar issues and ideas about which they already hold positive attitudes.

If Listeners Know Relatively Little about the Topic

- Stick to the basics and include background information.

- Steer clear of jargon and define unclear terms.

- Repeat important points, summarizing information often.

If Listeners Are Negatively Disposed toward the Topic

- Focus on establishing rapport and credibility.

- Don't directly challenge listeners' attitudes; instead begin with areas of agreement.

- Discover if they have a negative bias in order to tactfully introduce the other side of the argument.

- Offer solid evidence from sources they are likely to accept.

- Give good reasons for developing a positive attitude toward the topic.[7]

If Listeners Hold Positive Attitudes toward the Topic

- Stimulate the audience to feel even more strongly by emphasizing the side of the argument with which they already agree.

- Tell stories with vivid language that reinforces listeners' attitudes.[8]

If Listeners Are a Captive Audience

- Motivate listeners to pay attention by focusing as much as possible on what is most relevant to them.

- Pay close attention to the length of your speech.

Gauge Listeners' Feelings toward the Speaker

How audience members feel about you will also have considerable bearing on their attentiveness and responsiveness to your message. A speaker who is well liked can gain at least an initial hearing by an audience even if listeners are unsure of what to expect from the message itself. Conversely, an audience that feels negatively toward the speaker will disregard even the most important or interesting message. We tend to put up barriers against people whom we hold in low regard.

Listeners have a natural need to identify with the speaker and to feel that he or she shares their perceptions,[9] so look for ways to establish a common bond, or feeling of **identification**, between you and the audience. Sharing a personal story, emphasizing a shared role, and otherwise stressing mutual bonds all help to create identification. So, too, does the strategic use of inclusive language such as *we, you, I,* and *me.*

Many times, especially when the topic is controversial, a speaker will create identification by emphasizing those aspects of the topic about which the audience members are likely to agree. When speaking to an audience of abortion rights activists, for example, then-Senator Hillary Clinton called on opposing sides in the debate to find "common ground" by focusing on education and abstinence:

> We should all be able to agree that we want every child born in this country and around the world to be wanted, cherished, and loved. The best way to get there is to do more to educate the public about reproductive health, about how to prevent unsafe and unwanted pregnancies.[10]

Clinton clearly was attempting to reach out beyond her core constituency and achieve some measure of identification with those who oppose abortion. Notice, too, how Clinton uses the personal pronoun *we* to encourage identification with the speech goal and to build a sense of community within the audience. Even your physical presentation can foster identification. We're more apt to identify with the speaker who dresses like us (or in a manner we aspire to) than with someone whose style and grooming seem strange or displeasing.

CHECKLIST
Appeal to Audience Attitudes, Beliefs, and Values
Have you…
• Investigated audience members' attitudes, beliefs, and values toward your topic?
• Assessed the audience's level of knowledge about the topic?
• Considered strategies to address positive, negative, and neutral responses to your speech topic?
• Considered appealing directly to audience members' attitudes and values in your speech?

Gauge Listeners' Feelings toward the Occasion

Depending on the circumstances calling for the speech, people will bring different sets of expectations and emotions to it. For example, members of a **captive audience**, who are required to hear the speaker, may be less positively disposed to the occasion than members of a **voluntary audience** who attend of their own free will. Imagine being a businessperson attending a conference—it's your third night away from home, you're tired from daylong meetings, and now you're expected to listen to company executives explain routine production charges for the coming fiscal year. In contrast, imagine attending a speech of your own free will to listen to a speaker you've long admired. Whether planning a wedding toast or a business presentation, failure to anticipate and adjust for the audience's expectations risks alienating them.

■ Adapt Your Message to Audience Demographics

Collecting psychological data about audience members takes you partway through an audience analysis. Equally important is to learn demographic information about them. **Demographics** are the statistical characteristics of a given population. At least seven characteristics are typically considered when analyzing speech audiences: *age, ethnic and cultural background, socioeconomic status* (including *income, occupation,* and *education*), *religious and political affiliations, gender, group affiliations,* and *disability.* Various other traits—for example, sexual orientation and place of residence—may also be important to investigate.

Appeal to Your Target Audience

Knowing where audience members fall in relation to audience demographics will help you identify your **target audience**—those individuals within the broader audience whom you are most likely to influence in the direction you seek. Mass communicators rely upon **audience segmentation**—dividing a general audience into smaller groups to identify target audiences with similar characteristics, wants, and needs. But whether used by advertisers selling Apple iPads, advocacy groups selling cleaner air, or you as a public speaker, segmentation is a crucial tool for those attempting to reach an audience.

Consider a speech delivered to your classmates about lowering fees for campus parking violations. Your target audience will be those persons in the class who drive, rather than bicycle or walk, to campus. Whenever you appeal to a target audience, however, aim to make the topic relevant to other audience members. For example, you might mention that lower fees will benefit nondrivers in the future, should they bring cars to campus. You may not be able to please everyone, but you should be able to establish a connection with your target audience as well as some others.

Age

Age can be a very important factor in determining how listeners will react to a topic. Each age group brings with it its own concerns and psychological drives and motivations. The quest for identity in adolescence (around the ages of 12–20), for example, differs markedly from the need to establish stable careers and relationships in early adulthood (ages 20–40). Similarly, adults in their middle years (40–65), sometimes called the "sandwich generation," tend to grapple with a full plate of issues related to career, children, aging parents, and an increased awareness of mortality. And as we age (65 and older), physical changes and changes in lifestyle (from work to retirement) assume greater prominence.

Age-specific concerns affect attitudes toward many social issues, from the role that government should play (more younger than older voters want a bigger government) to Social Security and Medicare benefits (more older than younger voters want to preserve existing arrangements).[11]

People of the same generation often share a familiarity with significant individuals, local and world events, noteworthy popular culture, and so forth. Thus being aware of the **generational identity** of your audience, such as the Baby Boomers (those born between 1946 and 1964), millennials (those born between 1980 and 1999), or Generation Z (those born since 2000), allows you to develop points that are relevant to the experiences and interests of the widest possible cross section of your listeners. TABLE 5.1 lists some of the prominent characteristics and values of today's generations.

Ethnic or Cultural Background

An understanding of and sensitivity to the ethnic and cultural composition of your audience are key factors in delivering a successful (and ethical) speech. As a speaker in a multicultural and multiethnic society, you should expect that your audience will include members of different national origins. Some audience members may have a great deal in common with you. Others may be fluent in a language other than yours and may struggle to understand you. Some members of the audience may belong to a distinct **co-culture**, a social community whose values and style of communicating may or may not mesh with your own. (For guidelines on adapting to diverse audiences, see p. 115 "Adapt to Diverse Audiences.")

Table 5.1

GENERATIONAL IDENTITY AND TODAY'S GENERATIONS		
GENERATION	BORN	CHARACTERISTICS
Traditional	1925–1945	Respect for authority and duty, disciplined, strong sense of right and wrong
Baby Boomer	1946–1964	Idealistic, devoted to career, self-actualizing, value health and wellness
Generation X	1965–1979	Seeks work-life balance, entrepreneurial, technically savvy, flexible, questions authority figures, skeptical
Generation Y/ Millennials	1980–1999	Technically savvy, optimistic, self-confident, educated, appreciative of diversity, entrepreneurial, respectful of elders, short attention spans
Generation Z	2000–	Comfortable with the highest level of technical connectivity, naturally inclined to collaborate online, boundless faith in power of technology to make things possible

See, for example, "Millennials, Gen X and Baby Boomers: Who's Working at Your Company and What Do They Think About Ethics?" Ethics Resource Center, 2009 National Business Ethics Survey Supplemental Research Brief, http://ethics.org/files/u5/Gen-Diff.pdf; Dennis McCafferty, "Workforce Preview: What to Expect From Gen Z," *Baseline Magazine*, April 4, 2013, www.baselinemag.com/it-management/slideshows/workforce-preview-what-to-expect-from-gen-z; "Generations in the Workplace in the United States and Canada," Catalyst, May 1, 2012, www.catalyst.org/knowledge/generations-workplace-united-states-canada.

Socioeconomic Status

Socioeconomic status (SES) includes income, occupation, and education. Knowing roughly where an audience falls in terms of these key variables can be critical in effectively targeting your message.

Income

Income determines people's experiences on many levels. It directly affects how they are housed, clothed, and fed, and determines what they can afford. Beyond this, income has a ripple effect, influencing many other aspects of life. For example, depending on income, home ownership is either a taken-for-granted budget item or an out-of-reach dream. The same is true for any activity dependent on income. Given how pervasively income affects people's life experiences, insight into this aspect of an audience's makeup can be quite important.

Occupation

In most speech situations, the occupation of audience members is an important and easily identifiable demographic characteristic that you as a speaker should try to determine in advance. The nature of people's work has a lot to do with what interests them. Occupational interests are tied to several other areas of social concern, such as politics, the economy, education, and social reform. Personal attitudes, beliefs, and goals are also closely tied to occupational standing.

Education

Level of education strongly influences people's ideas, perspectives, and range of abilities. A higher level of education appears to be associated with greater fluctuation in personal values, beliefs, and goals. Higher levels of education lead to increased lifetime earnings, decreased levels of crime, better health outcomes, and greater civic engagement;[12] such factors may be important to consider when preparing a speech. Depending upon audience members' level of education, your speech may treat topics at a higher or lower level of sophistication, with fewer or more clarifying examples and illustrations.

Religion

Beliefs, practices, and social and political views vary by religious traditions, making *religion* another key demographic variable. At least a dozen major religious traditions coexist in the United States.[13] A major change in the United States over the past several decades is the decline in religious observance among adults under age thirty, with fully a third of persons in this group identifying as unaffiliated in 2012.[14] While members of the same spiritual tradition will most likely agree on the major spiritual tenets of their faith, they will not agree on all religiously based issues. People who identify themselves as Catholic disagree on birth control and divorce, Jews disagree on whether to recognize same-sex unions, and so forth. Awareness of an audience's general religious orientation can be especially helpful when your speech touches on a topic as potentially controversial as religion itself. Capital punishment, same-sex marriage, and teaching about the origins of humankind—all are rife with religious overtones and implications.

CHECKLIST
Respond to the Audience as You Speak
Audience analysis continues as you deliver your speech. During your speech, monitor the audience for signs of how they are receiving your message. Look for bodily clues as signs of interest or disengagement:
• Large smiles and eye contact suggest a liking for and agreement with the speaker.
• Arms closed across the chest may signal disagreement.
• Averted glances, slumped posture, looking at a cell phone or other mobile device, and squirming usually indicate disengagement.
• Engage with the audience when it appears they aren't with you.
• Invite one or two listeners to briefly relate their own experiences on the topic.[1]
• Invite one or two listeners to briefly relate their own experiences on the topic.[1]
• Share a story linked to the topic to increase identification.

1. Nick Morgan, Working the Room: *How to Move People to Action through Audience-Centered Speaking* (Cambridge, MA: Harvard Business School Press, 2003), 181–97.

Political Affiliation

As with religion, beware of making unwarranted assumptions about an audience's political values and beliefs. Some people like nothing better than a lively debate about public-policy issues. Others avoid anything that smacks of politics. And many people are very touchy about their views on political issues. Those on the right hold certain views that those on the left dispute, and the chasm between far right and far left is great indeed. Thus if your topic involves politics, you'll need to obtain background on your audience's political views.

Gender

Gender is another important factor in audience analysis, if only as a reminder to avoid the minefield of gender stereotyping. Distinct from the fixed physical characteristics of biological sex, **gender** is our social and psychological sense of ourselves as males or females.[15] Making assumptions about the preferences, abilities, and behaviors of your audience members based on their presumed gender can seriously undermine their receptivity to your message. Using **sexist language**, language that casts males or females into roles on the basis of sex alone, will also swiftly alienate many listeners. Equally damaging to credibility is the inclusion of overt **gender stereotypes**—oversimplified and often severely distorted ideas about the innate nature of what it means to be male or female.

Group Affiliations

The various groups to which audience members belong—whether social, civic, work-related, or religiously or politically affiliated—reflect their interests and values and so provide insight into what they care about:

- *Social clubs* include any grouping of people who gather to share a common interest and activities, from book clubs to college fraternities and sororities.

- *Civic organizations* promote some aspect of social welfare. Examples include Lions' and Rotary clubs, Habitat for Humanity, the Sierra Club, and the National Association for the Advancement of Colored People (NAACP).

- *Professional associations* seek to further the interests of a particular profession, from firefighters and police to lawyers and clergy.

- *Social networking groups* maintain pre-established interpersonal relationships and build new ones online through social networking sites such as Facebook, LinkedIn, and Twitter. Nearly three-quarters of adults online use social networking sites.[16]

- *Online communities* enable people in different geographic locations around the world without pre-established relationships to "congregate" in virtual space to share interests, work toward goals, and provide fellowship.

CHECKLIST
Reviewing Your Speech in Light of Audience Demographics
• Does your speech acknowledge potential differences in values and beliefs and address them sensitively?
• Have you reviewed your topic in light of the age range and generational identity of your listeners? Do you use examples they will recognize and find relevant?
• Have you tried to create a sense of identification between yourself and audience members?
• Are your explanations and examples at a level appropriate to the audience's sophistication and education?
• Do you make any unwarranted assumptions about the audience's political or religious values and beliefs?
• Does your topic carry religious or political overtones that are likely to stir your listeners' emotions in a negative way?
• Is your speech free of generalizations based on gender?
• Does your language reflect sensitivity toward people with disabilities?
• Do you address the concerns of both male and female listeners?

Disability

According to the U.S. Census Bureau, more than 19 percent of the population, or about fifty million people five years and older (excluding persons who are institutionalized), have some sort of physical, mental, or employment disability; some two-thirds of these have a severe disability. Over 14 percent of those enrolled in college and graduate school are counted as disabled.[17] Problems range from sight and hearing impairments to constraints on physical mobility and employment. Thus disability is another demographic variable to consider when analyzing an audience. Keep **persons with disabilities (PWD)** in mind when you speak, and use language and examples that afford them respect and dignity.

■ Adapt to Diverse Audiences

In the United States, over one-third of the population, or nearly 105 million persons, belongs to a racial or ethnic minority group, or one designated by the U.S. Census Bureau as other than "non-Hispanic White." Additionally, 38 million people, or 12.8 percent of the U.S. population, are foreign-born (see **FIGURE 5.1**). California leads the nation, with 27 percent of its residents foreign-born; New York, New Jersey, and Hawaii follow close behind. Nationwide, nearly 20 percent of the population speaks a language other than English in the home; two-thirds of these speak Spanish.[18] Worldwide, there are 195 recognized independent states, and many more distinct cultures within these countries.[19] What these figures suggest is that audience members will hold different cultural perspectives and employ different styles of communicating that may or may not mesh with your own.

How might you prepare to speak in front of an ethnically and culturally diverse audience, including that of your classroom? In any speaking situation, your foremost concern should be to treat your listeners with dignity and to act with integrity. You do this by infusing your speech with the pillars of character: trustworthiness, respect, responsibility, and fairness. Since values are central to who we are, identifying those of your listeners with respect to your topic can help you to avoid ethnocentrism and deliver your message in a culturally sensitive manner.

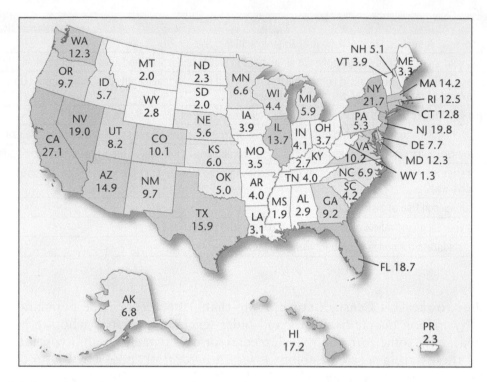

Source: U.S. Census Bureau, American Community Survey (2010), www.census.gov/prod/2012pubs/acs-19.pdf

FIGURE 5.1 Foreign-Born Population as a Percentage of State Population.

■ Adapt to Cross-Cultural Values

Values vary by culture. While dominant cultural values in U.S. society include *achievement and success*, *equal opportunity*, *material comfort*, and *democracy* surveys of several Asian societies[20] reveal such values as a *spirit of harmony*, *humility toward one's superiors*, *awe of nature*, and a *desire for prosperity*. In Mexico, *group loyalty*, *cyclical time*, and *fatalism*, among others, are cultural values. Becoming familiar with differences, as well as points of sameness, in values will help you to anticipate and appeal to those of your audience members.

Cross-cultural scholars offer numerous models that compare and contrast differing values and associated behavioral patterns among various cultures. One that has been particularly helpful to public speakers is Geert Hofstede's *value dimensions model.*

Hofstede's Value-Dimensions Model: Cultural Values and National Differences

Researchers have shown that as with individuals, nations differ in the values held by the majority of their members. Cross-cultural scholar Geert Hofstede has identified five major "value dimensions," or "broad preferences for one state of affairs over another, usually held unconsciously," as being significant across all cultures, but in widely varying degrees; he then ranks fifty countries in terms of how they compare on these dimensions.[21]

Individualism versus Collectivism

The *individualism versus collectivism* dimension refers to how people define themselves in relation to others. **Individualistic cultures** tend to emphasize the needs of the individual rather than those of the group, upholding such values as individual achievement and decision making. In **collectivist cultures,** by contrast, personal identity, needs, and desires are viewed as secondary to those of the larger group. Audience members who share collectivist values may believe that the wishes of parents and the family group must come before their own. The United States, Australia, Great Britain, and Canada rank highest on individualism. Ecuador, Venezuela, Peru, Taiwan, and Pakistan rank highest in collectivist characteristics.

Uncertainty Avoidance

Uncertainty avoidance refers to the extent to which people in a given culture feel threatened by ambiguity. **High-uncertainty avoidance cultures** tend to structure life more rigidly and formally for their members, while **low-uncertainty avoidance cultures** are more accepting of uncertainty in life and therefore allow more variation in individual behavior. Among the nations Hofstede investigated, Greece, Portugal, Guatemala, Peru, Belgium, and Japan rank among the highest in uncertainty avoidance; Singapore, Jamaica, Hong Kong, and the Scandinavian nations of Denmark, Norway, Sweden, and Finland rank among the lowest. Out of a score of 100, the United States scored 46, placing it near the middle of the uncertainty-avoidance value dimension.

Power Distance

Power distance is the extent to which people in a given culture see inequality and authority as normal. Cultures with *high levels of power distance* tend to be more rigidly organized along hierarchical lines, with greater emphasis placed on honoring authority. Those with *low levels of power distance* place a higher value on social equality. Some very high power distance countries include Malaysia, the Philippines, Indonesia, India, and the Arab nations of Egypt, Iraq, Kuwait, Lebanon, Libya, and Saudi Arabia; the Scandinavian nations, New Zealand, and Israel rank lowest, favoring the most equality among persons of different social levels. The United States ranks somewhat above the midpoint range on the power distance dimension, indicating that social rank is a fairly important value in the culture.

Masculinity versus Femininity

The *masculinity and femininity* dimension refers to the degree to which a culture values traits that are associated with traditional or stereotypical views of masculinity or femininity. Traditional masculine traits include ambition, assertiveness, and competitiveness. Feminine traits stress nurturance and cooperation. Ireland, the Philippines, Greece, and South Africa ranks among the highest in masculinity, while the Scandinavian nations rank highest in femininity. With a score of 62 out of 100, the United States weights toward masculinity.

Long- versus Short-Term Time Orientation

The *time orientation* dimension refers to the degree to which a culture values behavior that is directed to future rewards, such as perseverance and thrift, versus behavior that is directed toward the present, such as expecting quick results. China, Hong Kong, Taiwan, and South Korea ranked highest in long-term orientation, while Canada, Great Britain, the United States, Germany, and Australia rank highest in short-term orientation.

Bear in mind that the cultural patterns identified by Hofstede reflect those of the *dominant culture;* they do not necessarily reflect the behaviors of all the groups living within a society. Although individualism characterizes the dominant culture of the United States, for example, various co-cultures—such as Hispanic Americans, Native Americans, and (to varying degrees) African Americans—have been described as collectivist in nature. To find out individual country rankings and compare your home culture with another culture, see www.geert-hofstede.com/hofstede_dimensions.php.

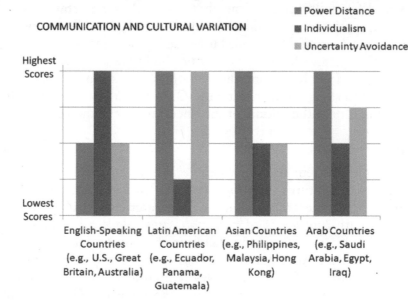

FIGURE 5.2 Values Dimensions by Country

A CULTURAL PERSPECTIVE

Consult Global Opinion Polls

Cross-cultural surveys can be extremely useful for learning about how values vary across cultures. The *Pew Global Attitudes Project* (http://pewglobal.org/) is a series of worldwide opinion surveys conducted in 60 countries. Gallup World View (worldview.gallup.com) surveys 150 countries on attitudes related to issues ranging from well-being to the environment. The *World Values Survey* (www.worldvaluessurvey.org) offers a fascinating look at the values and beliefs of people in 97 countries. Through these resources you can discover how people of other nations feel about work, family, religion, and even who should do the housework.

Charles Taylor/Shutterstock

Focus on Universal Values

As much as possible, it is important to try to determine the attitudes, beliefs, and values of audience members. At the same time, you can focus on certain values that, if not universally shared, are probably universally aspired to in the human heart. These include love, truthfulness, fairness, unity, tolerance, responsibility, and respect for life.[22]

■ Techniques for Learning about Your Audience

Now that you know the kind of information to look for when analyzing an audience, how do you actually uncover it? Unlike a professional pollster, you cannot survey thousands of people and apply sophisticated statistical techniques to analyze your results. On a smaller scale, however, you can use the same techniques. These include interviewing, surveying, and consulting published sources. Often, it takes just a few questions to get some idea of where audience members stand on each of the demographic factors. In the classroom, you can poll classmates and conduct brief interviews with them.

Interview Audience Members

An **interview** is a face-to-face communication for the purpose of gathering information. Interviews, even brief ones, can reveal a lot about the audience's interests and needs. You can conduct interviews one on one or in a group, in person, or by telephone, e-mail, or videoconference. Consider interviewing a sampling of the audience, or even just one knowledgeable representative of the group that you will address. As in questionnaires (see "Survey the Audience," which follows), interviews usually consist of a mix of open- and closed-ended questions.

Survey the Audience

Surveys can be as informal as a poll of several audience members or as formal as the pre-speech distribution of a written survey, or **questionnaire**—a series of open- and closed-ended questions. **Closed-ended questions** (also called *structured questions*) supplied by the interviewer are designed to elicit a small range of specific answers:

> "Do you smoke cigarettes?"
>
> Yes ___ No ___ I quit, but I smoked for ___ years
>
> Answers will be "Yes," "No," or "I smoked for x number of years."

Closed-ended questions may be either fixed-alternative or scale questions. **Fixed-alternative questions** contain a limited choice of answers, such as "Yes," "No," or "For x years" (as in the preceding example). **Scale questions**—also called *attitude scales*—measure the respondent's level of agreement or disagreement with specific issues:

> "Flag burning should be outlawed."
>
> Strongly agree ___ Agree ___ Undecided ___ Disagree ___ Strongly disagree ___

Scale questions can be used to measure how important listeners judge something to be and how frequently they engage in a particular behavior:

> "How important is religion in your life?"
>
> Very important ___ Important ___ Moderately important ___
>
> Of minor importance ___ Unimportant ___
>
> "How frequently do you attend religious services?"
>
> Very frequently ___ Frequently ___ Occasionally ___ Never ___

Open-ended questions (also called *unstructured questions*) are designed to allow a respondent to elaborate on his or her opinion as much as they wish:

> "How do you feel about using the results of DNA testing to prove innocence or guilt in criminal proceedings?"

Open-ended questions, which begin with a "how," "what," "when," "where," or "why," are particularly useful for probing beliefs and opinions. They elicit more individual or personal information about audience members' thoughts and feelings. They are also more time-intensive than closed-ended questions, so use them sparingly if at all in written questionnaires.

Often, it takes just a few fixed-alternative and scale questions to draw a fairly clear picture of audience members' backgrounds and attitudes and where they fall in demographic categories. You may wish to use Web-based survey software, such as Survey-Monkey or QuestionPro, to generate surveys electronically using premade templates and distribute them via e-mail.

Sample Audience Analysis Questionnaire

Part I: Demographic Analysis

1. What is your age? _____ years

2. What is your sex? _____ Male _____ Female

3. Please indicate your primary heritage:

    _____ Native American   _____ African American

    _____ Asian American   _____ European

    _____ Latino   _____ Middle Eastern   _____ Other

4. Please indicate your level of formal education:

    _____ High school   _____ Some college

    _____ College degree   _____ Other (please specify)

5. What is your approximate annual income range?

    _____ less than $10,000   _____ $10,000–$24,999

    _____ $25,000–$49,999   _____ $50,000–$74,999

    _____ $75,000–$100,000   _____ over $100,000

6. With which political party are your views most closely aligned?

    _____ Democratic   _____ Republican   _____ Neither (Independent)

7. Please check the box below that most closely matches your religious affiliation:

    _____ Buddhist   _____ Christian

    _____ Hindu   _____ Jewish

    _____ Muslim   _____ Not religious   _____ Other (please specify)

8. How would you characterize your religious involvement?

    _____ Very religious   _____ Somewhat religious   _____ Not very religious

9. How would you characterize your political position?

    _____ Liberal   _____ Conservative   _____ Moderate

Part II: Analysis of Attitudes, Values, and Beliefs on a Specific Topic

Indicate your answers to the following questions about stem cell research by checking the appropriate blank.

10. It is unethical and immoral to permit any use of stem cells for medical research.

_____ Strongly agree   _____ Agree   _____ Undecided

_____ Disagree   _____ Strongly disagree

11. Do you think the government should or should not fund stem cell research?:

_____ Should   _____ Should not   _____ Neutral

12. Rather than destroy stem cells left over from in vitro fertilization, medical researchers should be allowed to use them to develop treatments for diseases.

_____ Strongly agree   _____ Agree   _____ Undecided

_____ Disagree   _____ Strongly disagree

13. What kind of cells come to mind when you think of stem cell therapy?

_____

14. Which of the following has had the biggest influence on your thinking about stem cell research?

_____ Media reports   _____ Opinions of friends and family

_____ Your religious beliefs   _____ Personal experience

Consult Published Sources

Yet another way to learn about audience members is through published sources. Organizations of all kinds, from social and professional groups to businesses and educational institutions, publish information describing their missions, goals, operations, and achievements. Sources include websites and related online articles, brochures, newspaper and magazine articles, and annual reports.

Although *published opinion polls* won't specifically reflect your particular listeners' responses, they can provide valuable insight into how a representative state, national, or international sample feels about the issue in question. (Polls also provide an excellent source of supporting material for your speech.) Consider consulting these and other polling organizations:

• Pew Research Center for the People and the Press: people-press.org

• National Opinion Research Center (NORC): www.norc.uchicago.edu

• Roper Center for Public Opinion Research: ropercenter.uconn.edu

• Gallup: www.gallup.com

■ Analyze the Speech Setting and Context

As important as analyzing the audience is assessing (and then preparing for) the setting in which you will give your speech—size of audience; location, time, and length of speech; and rhetorical situation. Planning for these factors will help you further adjust your speech to the actual circumstances in which it will occur.

Size of Audience and Physical Setting

The size of the audience and the physical setting in which a speech occurs can have a significant impact on the outcome of the speech. Some settings are formal, others less so. The atmosphere of a classroom is different from that of a banquet room, an outdoor amphitheater, or a large auditorium. A virtual audience requires unique considerations (see **CHAPTER 32** on online presentations). The larger the group, the less you are likely to interact with the audience—an important factor to consider when planning your delivery (see **CHAPTERS 12–14**). You will also need to plan how to position yourself and adjust your voice, with or without a microphone.

Time and Length of Speech

Both the time at which your speech is scheduled and its length will affect listeners' receptivity to it. People gathered at breakfast, lunch, or dinner meetings, for example, come to the speech occasion with more than one agenda. They may wish to hear you, but they will also want time to eat and converse with other people. Your boss or fellow employees may expect to receive information quickly so that they can proceed to other business.

In any speaking situation, always find out how long you are expected to speak. Bear in mind that few matters of speech etiquette are as annoying to an audience as a speaker's apparent disregard for time. Start on time and end well within the time allotted to you. **TABLE 5.2** includes typical lengths for various presentations.

The Rhetorical Situation

Any speech or presentation you deliver will always occur in a particular circumstance and for a particular reason, defined as the "rhetorical situation." You may be the third of six speakers on a panel, for instance. You might precede or follow a speaker who is more dynamic or well known than you are. Listeners may be anxious to hear certain information early in the speech, because it addresses matters vital to them. They may be preoccupied with unusual circumstances—a local sports team just won a championship, extreme weather conditions have disrupted everyday life, the president of the company just resigned, and so forth. By being alert to any of these contingencies, you can address them in your speech.

Table 5.2 Typical Length of Presentation

KIND OF PRESENTATION	LENGTH
In-depth speech	15–20 minutes
Presentation to boss	1–10 min
Toast	1–2 minutes
Award acceptance speech	3–5 minutes

CHECKLIST
Analyzing the Speech Situation
_____1. Where will the speech take place?
_____2. How long am I expected to speak?
_____3. How many people will attend?
_____4. Will I need a microphone?
_____5. How will any projecting equipment I plan to use in my speech, such as an LCD projector, function in the space?
_____6. Where will I stand or sit in relation to the audience?
_____7. Will I be able to interact with listeners?
_____8. Who else will be speaking?
_____9. What special events or circumstances of concern to my audience should I acknowledge?

Chapter 6

Organizing the Body of the Speech

- Beyond the Speech: Organizing as a Life Skill
- Parts of a Speech
- Use Supporting Points to Substantiate Your Claims
- Pay Close Attention to Coordination and Subordination
- Strive for a Unified, Coherent, and Balanced Outline
- Use Transitions to Give Direction to the Speech

This chapter is taken from Dan O'Hair, Rob Stewart, and Hannah Rubenstein, *A Speaker's Guidebook*, Sixth Edition, pp. 171–183 (Chapter 11).

Audience members quickly note the difference between a well-organized speech and one that has been put together haphazardly, with decidedly negative results when the speech is disorganized. The reason for this is simple: Our understanding of information is directly linked to how well it is organized.[1] Apparently, a little bit of disorganization won't ruin a speech for us if the topic and speaker are otherwise engaging, but we quickly lose interest, and even become irritated, when the speech is very disorganized.[2] On the other hand, we find speakers whose speeches are well organized more understandable, more believable, and more trustworthy than those who present poorly organized ones.[3] Given all this, you won't want to skip the crucial steps of arranging and outlining speech points.

As in written composition, organizing a speech—a stage in speech development classical speakers called **arrangement**—is the process of devising a logical and convincing structure for your message. Organizing occurs in stages, in which you decide upon the main points of the speech, select one of several formal patterns or designs for the speech's structure, and, using that design, complete the outline with subpoints. In an **outline**, you determine how to order your ideas and evidence into larger and smaller logical categories, or divisions and subdivisions. Your main points are the larger divisions, and your subpoints are the subdivisions or subcategories of these main points. Rather than making the job of drafting a speech harder, an outline lets you check for logical inconsistencies in the placement of speech points and pinpoint weaknesses in the amount and kind of support for them. **Outlining** your speech provides a vivid snapshot of its strengths and weaknesses and clearly points to how you can fix the flaws. Although a few famous speakers have managed to deliver successful speeches without first arranging and outlining them, for the vast majority of us, the success or failure of a speech will depend on doing so.

■ Beyond the Speech: Organizing as a Life Skill

As well as being of immense practical value in fashioning better speeches, skill in arranging and outlining information can have far-reaching positive effects on many aspects of your academic and professional life. Written and verbal skill in communication rank first in employers' "wish list" for employees. Employers seek workers who can communicate ideas logically and convincingly. Nearly all professional-level jobs, for example, require you to prepare well-organized written/oral reports and visual presentations, to both internal and external audiences. Similarly, written assignments in the classroom depend upon how convincingly and logically you present your viewpoint. Learning how to arrange ideas compellingly and gaining proficiency with outlining—a skill that depends on the logical coordination and subordination of ideas (see **p. 130**)—will serve you well as a public speaker and in these other arenas (see **TABLES 6.1 AND 6.2**).

CHAPTER 9 illustrates the three types of outline formats speakers use to prepare and deliver speeches. In this chapter we examine the elements of the speech body—main points, supporting points, and transitions—and their function and placement within an outline.

TABLE 6.1 Sample Outline Format

EXTENDED OUTLINE FORMAT
I.   Main point
A.   Subordinate to main point I
B.   Coordinate with subpoint A
1.   Subordinate to subpoint B
2.   Coordinate with sub-subpoint 1
a.   Subordinate to sub-subpoint 2
b.   Coordinate with sub-sub-subpoint a
(1)   Subordinate to sub-sub-subpoint b
(2)   Coordinate with sub-sub-sub-subpoint (1)
II.   Main point: Coordinate with main point I

■ Parts of a Speech

A speech structure is simple, composed of just three general parts: an introduction, a body, and a conclusion. The *introduction* establishes the purpose of the speech and shows its relevance to the audience (see **CHAPTER 7**). It lets listeners know where the speaker is taking them. The **body** of the speech presents main points that are intended to fulfill the speech purpose. Main points are developed with various kinds of supporting material to fulfill this purpose. The **conclusion** ties the purpose and the main points together (see **CHAPTER 8**). It brings closure to the speech by restating the purpose and reiterating why it is relevant to the audience, and by leaving audience members with something to think about. In essence, the introduction tells listeners where they are going, the body takes them there, and the conclusion lets them know that they have arrived.

Main points express the key ideas and major themes of the speech. Their function is to represent each of the main elements or claims being made in support of the speech thesis. The first step in creating main points is to identify the central ideas and themes of the speech. What are the most important ideas you want to convey? What is the thesis? What key ideas emerge from your research? What ideas can you demonstrate with supporting material? Each of these ideas or claims should be expressed as a main point.

Use the Purpose and Thesis Statements as Guides

You can use the specific purpose and thesis statements as reference points to help generate main points. As discussed in Chapter 4, the *specific purpose statement* expresses what you want the audience to learn or do as a result of your speech. Formulating it in your mind allows you to articulate precisely what you want the speech to accomplish (without stating it directly in the speech itself). The *thesis statement* (which *is* stated in the speech, in your introduction) expresses the central idea of the speech, concisely laying out what it is about. Main points should flow directly from your speech purpose and thesis, as in the following example:

Specific Purpose: (what you want the audience to learn or do as a result of your speech; not stated in speech itself): To show my audience, through a series of easy steps, how to perform meditation.

Thesis: (the central idea of the speech; thesis is expressed in speech): When performed correctly, meditation is an effective and easy way to reduce stress.

Main Points

I.   The first step of meditation is "positioning."

II.   The second step of meditation is "breathing."

III. The third step of meditation is "relaxation."

SELF-ASSESSMENT CHECKLIST
Do the Speech Points Illustrate or Prove the Thesis?
_____1. Are the most important ideas in your speech expressed in the main points?
_____2. Are any key ideas implied by your thesis not addressed by main points?
_____3. Does each supporting point offer sufficient evidence for the corresponding main point?
_____4. Do your supporting points reflect a variety of appropriate supporting material, such as examples, narratives, testimony, and facts and statistics?

Restrict the Number of Main Points

Research has shown that many audiences can comfortably take in only between two and seven main points. For most speeches, and especially those delivered in the classroom, between two and five main points should be sufficient.[4] As a rule, the fewer main points in a speech, the greater are the odds that you will keep your listeners' attention. Importantly, listeners have the best recall of points made at the beginning of a speech, a phenomenon termed the **primacy effect**, and at the end of a speech (the **recency effect**) than of those made in between (unless the ideas made in between are far more striking than the others).[5] Thus, if it is especially important that listeners remember certain ideas, introduce those ideas near the beginning of the speech and reiterate them at the conclusion.

If you find you have too many main points while organizing your speech, consider whether your topic is sufficiently narrow (see **CHAPTER 4**). If the problem does not lie in an overly broad topic, review your main and supporting points for proper subordination (see **p. 131** for a discussion on these topics).

Restrict Each Main Point to a Single Idea

A main point should not introduce more than one idea. If it does, split it into two (or more) main points:

Incorrect

I.   West Texas has its own Grand Canyon, and South Texas has its own desert.

Correct

I.   West Texas boasts its own Grand Canyon.

II. South Texas boasts its own desert.

The main points should be mutually exclusive of one another. If they are not, consider whether a main point more properly serves as a subpoint.

Express each main point as a *declarative sentence* (one that states a fact or argument). This emphasizes the point and alerts audience members to the main thrusts of your speech. For example, if one of your main points is that children need more vitamin D, you should clearly state, "According to the nation's leading pediatricians, children from infants to teens should consume more vitamin D." In addition, as shown in the following example, state your main points (and supporting points, see p. ??) in parallel form—that is, in similar grammatical form and style. This strategy helps listeners understand and retain the points (by providing consistency) and lends power and elegance to your words.

Thesis Statement: The Group of Eight (G8) of the world's leading industrial nations should take stronger steps at its next summit to reduce carbon dioxide emissions linked to global warming.

Incorrect

I.   The United States must adopt new stricter policies to reduce carbon dioxide emissions.

II. Canada failed to adopt a sound global-warming policy.

III. Switzerland didn't do anything either.

Correct

I. The United States must adopt stricter policies to reduce carbon dioxide emissions.

II. Canada must readdress the question of carbon dioxide emissions in its next session of parliament.

III. Switzerland must reevaluate its position on carbon dioxide emissions in its next plenary session.

■ Use Supporting Points to Substantiate Your Claims

Supporting points represent the supporting material or evidence you have collected to explain (in an informative speech) or justify (in a persuasive speech) the main points. It is here that you substantiate or prove your thesis with the examples, narratives, testimony, and facts and statistics discovered in your research.

In an outline, supporting points appear in a subordinate position to main points. This is indicated by **indentation**. As with main points, supporting points should be arranged in order of their importance or relevance to the main point. The most common format is the **roman numeral outline**. Main points are enumerated with uppercase roman numerals (I, II, III,...), supporting points are enumerated with capital letters (A, B, C,...), third-level points are enumerated with Arabic numerals (1, 2, 3,...), and fourth-level points are enumerated with lowercase letters (a, b, c,...), as seen in the following:

I. Main point

    A. Supporting point

        1. Subsupporting point

            a. Sub-subsupporting point

            b. Sub-subsupporting point

        2. Subsupporting point

            a. Sub-subsupporting point

            b. Sub-subsupporting point

    B. Supporting point

II. Main point

Here is an example (in phrase outline form, see p. 157) from a speech about using effective subject lines in business-related e-mails:

I. Subject line most important, yet neglected, part of e-mail.

    A. Determines if recipient reads message

        1. Needs to specify point of message

        2. Needs to distinguish from spam

        B. Determines if recipient ignores message

            1. May ignore e-mail with missing subject line

            2. May ignore e-mail with unclear subject line

  II.   Use proven techniques for effective subject lines.

        A. Make them informative

            1. Give specific details

            2. Match central idea of e-mail

            3. Be current

        B. Check for sense

            1. Convey correct meaning

            2. Reflect content of message

        C. Avoid continuing subject line in text

            1. May annoy the reader

            2. May be unclear

                a. Could be confused with spam

                b. Could be misinterpreted

Note that different levels of points are also distinguished by different levels of indentation. These differences clearly indicate the direction of your speech. They also enhance your recollection of points and make it easy for you to follow the outline as you speak.

▪ Pay Close Attention to Coordination and Subordination

Outlines are based on the principles of **coordination and subordination**—the logical placement of ideas relative to their importance to one another. Ideas that are *coordinate* are given equal weight; **coordinate points** are indicated by their parallel alignment. An idea that is *subordinate* to another is given relatively less weight; **subordinate points** are indicated by their indentation below the more important points. For an example, see the outline above on using effective subject lines in business-related e-mails: Coordinate points are aligned with one another, while subordinate points are indented below the points that they substantiate. Thus Main Point II is coordinate with Main Point I, Subpoint A is subordinate to Main Point I, Subpoint B is coordinate with Subpoint A, and so forth.

Recheck Division of Main and Subpoints

As you review your outline, evaluate whether any of your main points more properly belong as subpoints to other main points. In a speech draft about interviewing and etiquette training, University of Oklahoma student Amber Pointer found this to be the case when she saw that she had created six main points:

I.   Interviewing is competitive and requires preparation.

II.   As in sports, interviewing requires training to compete well against others.

III.   When you sell yourself in an interview, you want to make your best impression.

IV.   When you take a course on interviewing, you become more competitive.

V.   Dressing appropriately is critical to making a good impression.

VI.   Proper table manners are key to making a positive impression during a luncheon interview.

Upon examination, Amber realized that main points II and IV are actually subpoints of point I:

I.   Interviewing is competitive and requires preparation.

~~II.~~   A. As in sports, interviewing requires training to compete well against others.

~~IV.~~   B. When you take a course on interviewing, you become more competitive.

Similarly, points V and VI are subpoints of point III (which now becomes main point II):

II.   When you sell yourself in an interview, you want to make your best impression.

~~V.~~   A. Dressing appropriately is critical to making a good impression.

~~VI.~~   B. Proper table manners are key to making a positive impression during a luncheon interview.

As she examined her outline, Amber realized that she had introduced ideas later in her speech that properly supported the first main point and presented other material that was actually subordinate to her second main point. Rather than six main points, Amber's speech in fact consists of just two.

■ Strive for a Unified, Coherent, and Balanced Outline

A well-organized speech is characterized by unity, coherence, and balance. Try to adhere to these principles as you arrange your speech points.

TABLE 6.2

PRINCIPLES OF COORDINATION AND SUBORDINATION
• Assign equal weight to ideas that are coordinate.
• Assign relatively less weight to ideas that are subordinate.
• Indicate coordinate points by their parallel alignment.
• Indicate subordinate points by their indentation below the more important points.
• Every point must be supported by at least two points or none at all (consider how to address one "dangling" point in the point above it).

A speech exhibits *unity* when it contains only those points that are implied by the purpose and thesis statements. Each main point supports the thesis, and each supporting point provides evidence for the main points. Each subsupporting point supports each supporting point. Finally, each point should focus on a single idea.

A speech exhibits *coherence* when it is organized clearly and logically, using the principles of coordination and subordination to align speech points in logical progression (see TABLE 6.2). In addition, the speech body should follow logically from the introduction, and the conclusion should follow logically from the body. Within the body of the speech itself, main points should follow logically from the thesis statement, and supporting points should follow logically from the main points. Transitions (see p. 134) serve as logical bridges that help establish coherence.

Inexperienced public speakers may give overly lengthy coverage to one point and insufficient attention to others, or they might provide scanty evidence in the body of the speech after presenting an impressive introduction. The principle of *balance* suggests that appropriate emphasis or weight be given to each part of the speech relative to the other parts and to the thesis. The body of a speech should always be the longest part, and the introduction and the conclusion should be of roughly the same length. Stating the main points in parallel form is one aspect of balance. *Assigning each main point at least two supporting points is another.* If you have only one subpoint, consider how you might incorporate it into the superior point. *Think of a main point as a tabletop and supporting points as table legs; without at least two legs, the table cannot stand.*

CHECKLIST
Do the Speech Points Reflect Unity, Coherence, and Balance?
_____1. Does each main point refer directly to your specific purpose or thesis statement?
_____2. Does each point focus on a single idea?
_____3. Do your main points follow logically from your thesis statement?
_____4. Do your supporting points follow logically from the main points?
_____5. Do you spend roughly the same amount of time on each main point?
_____6. Is each main point substantiated by at least two supporting points?
_____7. Are speech points stated in parallel form?

■ Use Transitions to Give Direction to the Speech

Transitions are words, phrases, or sentences that tie the speech ideas together and enable the listener to follow the speaker as he or she moves from one point to the next. Considered the "neurosystem" of speeches, transitions (also called **connectives**) are especially important in speeches because listeners cannot go back and re-read what they might have missed. As you develop your speech, think about creating transitions to move listeners from one main point to the next, from main points to supporting points, and from one supporting point to another supporting point. Transitions are also used to move from the introduction to the body of the speech, and from the body to the conclusion. Transitions can take the form of full sentences, phrases, or single words (see TABLE 6.3).

Use Transitions between Speech Points

Use transitions to move between speech points: from one main point to the next, and from one subpoint to another.

Use Transitions between Supporting Points

Transitions between supporting points can be handled using single words, phrases, or full sentences as in the following:

> Next,...
>
> First,...(second, third, and so forth)
>
> Similarly,...
>
> We now turn...
>
> Finally, let's consider...
>
> If you think that's shocking, consider this...

Using a full-sentence transition to move from supporting point A ("Sales personnel will be motivated by competition") to supporting point B ("Contests are relatively inexpensive"), the speaker might state the following:

Another way that sales competitions will benefit us is by their relative cost effectiveness.

TABLE 6.3 Transitional Words and Phrases

FUNCTION	EXAMPLE
To show comparisons	Similarly; In the same way; Likewise; In comparison; Just as
To contrast ideas	On the other hand; And yet; At the same time; In spite of; However; In contrast
To illustrate cause and effect	As a result, Hence; Because; Thus; Consequently
To illustrate sequence of time or events	First, second, third,...; Following this; Before; After; Later; Earlier; At present; In the past
To indicate explanation	For example; To illustrate; In other words; To simplify; To clarify
To indicate additional examples	Not only; In addition to; Let's look at
To emphasize significance	Most importantly; Above all; Remember; Keep in mind
To summarize	As we have seen; In summary; Finally; In conclusion; Let me conclude by saying

Use Transitions between Main Points

When moving from one main point to another, full-sentence transitions are especially effective. For example, to move from main point I in a speech about sales contests ("Top management should sponsor sales contests to halt the decline in sales over the past two years") to main point II ("Sales contests will lead to better sales presentations"), the speaker might use the following transition:

> Next, let's look at exactly what sales contests can do for us.

Another full-sentence transition is the **rhetorical question**. Rather than inviting actual responses, rhetorical questions make the audience think (see also **CHAPTER 7**):

> Could there really be a way to use radiation without side effects, and to treat more types of cancer with it?

> How do the costs of contests stack up against the expense of training new people?

Don't be afraid to get creative with your use of transitions. In a speech on mountain biking, student Zachary Dominique used metaphoric language in this transition to lend color to the speech:

> Now, let's do a hopturn—a turn in reverse—and learn about the sport's colorful history.

Very frequently speakers will use internal previews and internal summaries as transitions, described next.

Use Previews and Summaries as Transitions

Previews briefly introduce audience members to the ideas that the speaker will address. As described in **CHAPTER 7**, in a speech introduction, the **preview** briefly describes what will be covered in the body of the speech. Within the body itself, an **internal preview** briefly introduces listeners to the ensuing discussion. Speakers use internal previews at various points throughout a speech both to introduce audience members to ideas the speaker will develop and to signal a shift from one main point or idea to another:

> Victoria Woodhull was a pioneer in many respects. Not only was she the first woman to run her own brokerage firm, but she was also the first to run for the presidency of the United States, though few people know this. Let's see how she accomplished these feats....

Similar to the internal preview, the **internal summary** draws together ideas before the speaker proceeds to another speech point. Internal summaries help listeners review and evaluate the thread of the theme thus far:

> It should be clear that the kind of violence we've witnessed in the schools and in our communities has a deeper root cause than the availability of handguns. Our young children are crying out for a sense of community, of relatedness and meaning, that they just aren't finding in the institutions that are meant to serve them.

Often, a speaker will transition from one major idea or main point to the next by using an internal summary and internal preview together:

> We've seen that mountain bikes differ from road bikes in the design of the tires, the seat, the gears, the suspension systems, and the handlebars. Now let's take a look at the different types of mountain bikes themselves. As you will see, mountain bikes vary according to the type of riding they're designed to handle—downhill, trails, and cross-country. Let's begin with cross-country.

SELF-ASSESSMENT CHECKLIST
Using Transitions
_____1.   Do you include enough transitions to adequately guide your listeners through your speech?
_____2.   Do you use transitions to signal comparisons, cause and effect, sequences in time, contrasting ideas, summaries, and so forth?
_____3.   Do you use transitions when moving from one main point to the next?
_____4.   Do you use internal previews and summaries where appropriate?
_____5.   Do you use transitions between the introduction and the body and between the body and the conclusion of the speech?

FROM POINT TO POINT

Using Transitions to Guide Your Listeners

Transitions direct your listeners from one point to another in your speech, leading them forward along a logical path while reinforcing key ideas along the way. At a bare minimum, plan on using transitions to move between:

- The introduction and the body of the speech

- The main points

- The subpoints, whenever appropriate

- The body of the speech and the conclusion

Introduction

I.   Today I'll explore the steps you can take to create a greener campus...

(**Transition:** Let's begin by considering what "going green" actually means.)

Body

I.   "Going green" means taking action to promote and maintain a healthy environment.

(**Transition:** So how do you go green?)

    A.   Get informed—understand what is physically happening to your planet

(**Transition:** Understanding the issues is only part of going green, however. Perhaps most important,...)

    B.   Recognize that change starts here, on campus, with you....

While transitions help guide your listeners from point to point, they can also do a lot more, including:

1.   Introduce main points

2.   Illustrate cause and effect

3.   Signal explanations and examples

4.   Emphasize, repeat, compare, or contrast ideas

5.   Summarize and preview information

6.   Suggest conclusions from evidence

Following is an excerpt from a working outline on a speech about campuses going green. Note how the student edits himself to ensure that he (1) uses transitions to help listeners follow along and retain his speech points and (2) uses transitions strategically to achieve his goal of persuading the audience.

1. Student inserts a transition (**rhetorical question**) to introduce a new point.

(Transition: Why are environmentalists targeting college campuses?)

I.   College campuses generate the waste equivalent of many large towns…

2. Student uses this transitional phrase to signal a **cause-effect relationship**.

(Transition: As a result…)

A.   Colleges face disposal issues, especially of electronics…

B.   Administrators face decisions about mounting energy costs…

1. Student uses a transition to **move to the next point.**

(**Transition:** Following are some ideas to create a greener campus. First…)

II.   Promote a campus-wide recycling program

3. This transitional **phrase introduces additional examples.**

(**Transition:** For example…)

A.   Decrease the availability of bottled water and disposable…

B.   Insist on recycling bins at all residence halls…

C.   Encourage computer centers to recycle…

4 & 5. Student inserts an **internal summary** to help listeners retain information and transition to the next main point.

(Transition: Recycling is a critical part of going green. Decreasing the consumption of plastic and paper, installing recycling bins, and responsibly disposing of print cartridges will make a huge difference. Another aspect of going green is using sustainable energy…)

III.   Lobby administrators to investigate solar, wind, and geothermal…

A.   Make an argument for "eco-dorms…"

B.   Explore alternative heating…

5. Student inserts an **internal preview** to move to the next main point.

(Transition: So far, we've talked about practical actions we can take to encourage a greener lifestyle on campus, but what about beyond the campus?)

IV.   Get involved at the town government level

A.   Town-grown committees…

B.   Speak up and voice your concerns…

6. Student inserts a transition to **signal a shift to the conclusion.**

(Transition: As you can see, we have work to do…)

Conclusion

I.   If we want our children and our children's children to live to see a healthy earth, we must take action now…

Chapter 7

Developing the Introduction

- Functions of the Introduction

- Motivate the Audience to Accept Your Goals

This chapter is taken from Dan O'Hair, Rob Stewart, and Hannah Rubenstein, *A Speaker's Guidebook*, Sixth Edition, pp. 219–226 (Chapter 14).

The introduction and conclusion, although not more important than the body of the speech, are essential to its overall success. Introductions set the tone and prepare the audience to hear the speech. A good opening previews what's to come in a way that engages audiences in the topic and establishes a tone of goodwill. An effective conclusion ensures that the audience remembers the key points of the speech and reacts in a way that the speaker intends.

This chapter describes the essential components of the speech introduction. Chapter 8 addresses the conclusion.

■ Functions of the Introduction

The choices you make about the introduction can affect the outcome of the entire speech. In the first several minutes (one speaker pegs it at ninety seconds), audience members will decide whether they are interested in the topic of your speech, whether they will believe what you say, and whether they will give you their full attention.

A good introduction serves to:

- Arouse your audience's attention and willingness to listen.

- Introduce the topic and purpose.

- Establish your credibility to speak on the topic.

- Preview the main points.

- Motivate the audience to accept your speech goals.

The introduction comes first in a speech, but plan on preparing it after you've completed the speech body. This way, you will know exactly what material you need to preview. Keep the introduction brief—as a rule, it should occupy no more than 10 to 15 percent of the entire speech.

Gain Audience Attention

The first challenge faced by any speaker is to win the audience's attention. Some time-honored techniques for doing this include sharing a compelling quotation or story, posing a question, providing unusual information, using humor, acknowledging the audience and establishing common ground, and referring to the occasion.

CHECKLIST
Guidelines for Preparing the Introduction
• Prepare the introduction after you've completed the speech body so you will know exactly what you need to preview.
• Keep the introduction brief—as a rule, no more than 10 to 15 percent of the entire speech.
• Plan the introduction word for word.
• Practice delivering your introduction until you feel confident you've got it right.

Use a Quotation

A Czech proverb says, "Do not protect yourself by a fence but rather by your friends." A good quotation, one that elegantly and succinctly expresses an idea relevant to your topic, is a very effective way to draw the audience's attention. Quotations can be culled from literature, poetry, film, the Internet, or directly from people you know. Clever sayings of any kind, whether spoken by a three-year-old child or by a wise friend, may express precisely the idea you are looking for.

Tell a Story

Noted speechwriter and language expert William Safire once remarked that stories are "surefire attention getters."[1] Speakers like to use stories, or *narratives,* to illustrate points, and audiences like to hear them, because they make ideas concrete and colorful. Stories personalize issues by encouraging audience identification and making ideas relevant. And they are, importantly, entertaining.

Anecdotes—brief stories of meaningful and entertaining incidents based on real life, often the speaker's own—can serve as a powerful tool to command the audience's attention. Dutch researchers discovered this when audience members they studied rated speeches introduced with anecdotes as more interesting and understandable than those that were not. The anecdotes also boosted speaker credibility and helped the subjects retain more of the speech.[2] Scientific studies aside, the key to successfully introducing a speech with any anecdote is choosing one that strikes a chord with the audience and which, like a good joke, can stand on its own without explanation.

Pose Questions

"Are you concerned about student loans?" Posing questions such as this can be an effective way to draw the audience's attention to what you are about to say. Questions can be real or rhetorical. **Rhetorical questions** do not invite actual responses. Instead, they make the audience think.

Whenever you use a rhetorical question in an introduction, always let the audience know that your speech will attempt to answer it:

> Are you concerned about whether you'll be able to find a job when you graduate? Are you worried that unemployment will remain high? If so, we are in this together. Today I'm going to talk about some steps you can take in college that will help you enter the job market sooner once you graduate.

Posing questions that seek an actual response, either in a show of hands or by verbal reply, also sparks interest. Here is an example of how a speech about trends in technology usage might be introduced by using real, or "polling," questions:

> How many of you have gone 24 hours without using any mobile devices? *(Speaker waits for a show of hands.)* How many of you think you'd enjoy doing so? *(Speaker waits for show of hands.)* Do you think you'd be comfortable not using a cell phone, iPad, Droid, laptop, or whatever other devices you own, for a week? *(Speaker waits for a show of hands.)* A month? *(Speaker waits for a show of hands.)* As you can see by looking around this room, not

many of us can visualize being particularly comfortable without our electronic devices. Today I'm going to describe trends in technology usage and our dependence on these modern devices....

Polling audience members is an effective way to gain their attention if your questions are thought-provoking and novel, but it has drawbacks. Bear in mind when using this attention-gaining technique that it is possible that no one will respond, or that the responses will be unexpected. Analyzing your audience will be helpful in designing effective rhetorical questions (see **CHAPTER 5**).

Offer Unusual Information

"In the United States, a woman is physically abused every nine seconds." Surprising audience members with startling or unusual information is one of the surest ways to get their attention. Such statements stimulate your listeners' curiosity and make them want to hear more about your topic.

Speakers frequently base their startling statements on statistics, a powerful means of illustrating consequences and relationships and of quickly bringing things into focus. In the following example, a student introducing a speech on domestic violence uses statistics to gain the audience's attention:

> Thirty percent of female homicide victims are murdered by their intimate partners compared with 5 percent of male homicide victims.... Today we will see.....[3]

Use Humor—Perhaps

Handled well, humor can build rapport and set a positive tone for a speech. Humor can also enliven a speech about a topic that is dry, difficult, or complex. Using humor can be a challenge, however, and it can backfire easily. Include humor in your speech with caution. Simply telling a series of unrelated jokes without making a relevant point will likely detract from your purpose. And few things turn an audience off more quickly than tasteless or inappropriate humor. In any speech, you should strictly avoid humor or sarcasm that belittles others—whether on the basis of race, sex, ability, or otherwise. A good rule of thumb is that speech humor should always match the audience, topic, purpose, and occasion.

SELF-ASSESSMENT CHECKLIST
Using Humor Appropriately
_____1. Is your humor appropriate to the audience and occasion?
_____2. Does your humor help you make a point about your topic or the occasion?
_____3. Have you avoided any potentially offensive issues such as race or religion?
_____4. Is your humor likely to insult or demean anyone?
_____5. Will the audience understand your humor?
_____6. Have you given your humor a trial run?
_____7. Is your use of humor likely to translate well to the cultural composition of the audience?

Refer to the Audience and Establish Common Ground

Just as friendships are formed by showing interest in others, audiences are won over when speakers express interest in them and show that they share in the audiences' concerns and goals. This creates goodwill and a feeling of common ground (or *identification;* see also **CHAPTER 5**). Finding common ground helps overcome the natural human divisions that separate people.

When the late Nelson Mandela, an anti-apartheid leader in South Africa who later became the country's president, was first released from prison after twenty-seven years, he addressed a huge crowd of supporters beginning this way:

> Friends, comrades, and fellow South Africans. I greet you all in the name of peace, democracy, and freedom for all. I stand here before you not as a prophet but as a humble servant of you, the people. Your tireless and heroic sacrifices have made it possible for me to be here today. I therefore place the remaining years of my life in your hands.[4]

Although Mandela had just tasted his first hours of freedom after more than two decades in prison, he chose to express goodwill toward the audience rather than focus on himself. In response, Mandela's listeners could not help but hold him in even higher esteem.

A CULTURAL PERSPECTIVE

Humor and Culture: When the Jokes Fall Flat

While humor can be a highly effective tool for introducing speeches, it can also be the cause of communication breakdowns. As one scholar notes:

> Although humor is present in all human groups, its content varies significantly across cultures. Many jokes don't translate well—or at all—because of differences in social structure and cultural norms. There is no universally appreciated joke; what is funny in one culture may not be amusing in another.[1]

Humor assumes shared understanding. When that understanding is absent, the jokes fall flat. Humor breakdowns can occur any time audience members do not share the same cultural assumptions as the speaker. These assumptions may be based on gender, social class, educational background, ethnicity, or nationality.[2] A new employee may not get a joke told by a presenter with a long history in the corporate culture. Or a non-native speaker may not be familiar with an idiom used to express humor or may not share the underlying belief on which the humor is based.

How can you avoid using humor that your audience won't understand? The obvious answer is to carefully consider your audience and, if possible, learn about audience members' cultures. Be as confident as possible that your material will make sense and be humorous to your listeners. Be particularly alert to nonverbal feedback. If you receive puzzled stares, consider clarifying your meaning. You might even acknowledge the cultural assumptions that your humor tacitly expresses.

1.   Lawrence T. White and Steven B. Jackson, "Culture Conscious," *Psychology Today*, May 2012, www.psychologytoday.com/blog/culture-conscious/201205/whats-funny.

2.   William Lee, "Communication about Humor as Procedural Competence in Intercultural Encounters," in *Intercultural Communication: A Reader*, eds. Larry A. Samovar and Richard E. Porter, 7th ed. (Belmont, CA: Wadsworth, 1994), 373.

Charles Taylor/Shutterstock

Refer to the Occasion

Introductions that include references to the speech occasion and to any relevant facts about the audience make listeners feel recognized as individuals. People appreciate a direct reference to the event, and they are interested in the meaning the speaker assigns to it. In her introduction to a ceremony honoring the fiftieth anniversary of Martin Luther King Jr.'s "I Have a Dream" speech, Oprah Winfrey began this way:

> On this date, in this place, at this time, 50 years ago today, Dr. Martin Luther King shared his dream for America with America.... Dr. King was the passionate voice that awakened the conscience of a nation and inspired people all over the world. The power of his words resonated because they were spoken out of an unwavering belief in freedom and justice, equality and opportunity for all. "Let Freedom Ring" was Dr. King's closing call for a better and more just America.[5]

Preview the Purpose and Topic

Once you've gained the audience's attention, use the introduction to alert listeners to the speech topic and purpose. You may already have alluded to your topic in the attention-getting phase of the introduction. If not, declare what your speech is about and what you hope to accomplish. Note an exception to this rule: When your purpose is to persuade, and the audience is not yet aware of this purpose, "forewarning" may predispose listeners in the opposite direction and thwart your persuasive goal. However, when the audience knows of your persuasive intent, previewing the topic and purpose can enhance understanding.[6]

Topic and purpose are clearly explained in this introduction to a speech by Marvin Runyon, postmaster general of the United States:

> This afternoon, I want to examine the truth of that statement—"Nothing moves people like the mail, and no one moves the mail like the U.S. Postal Service." I want to look at where we are today as a communications industry, and where we intend to be in the days and years ahead.[7]

Establish Your Credibility as a Speaker

During the introduction, audience members make a decision about whether they are interested not just in your topic but also in you. They want to know why they should believe in you. Most important of all, they want to feel that they can trust what you have to say—that they can believe in your *ethos*, or good character. Thus another function of the introduction is to establish your credibility to speak.

You signal positive ethos by demonstrating a solid grasp of your topic, an honest presentation of the material, and respect and concern for the audience's best interests. To get started, you might offer a simple statement of your qualifications for speaking on the topic at the particular occasion and to the specific audience. Briefly emphasize some experience, knowledge, or perspective you have that is different from or more extensive than that of your audience. If your goal, for example, was to persuade your audience to be more conscientious about protecting city parks, you might state, "I have felt passionate about conservation issues ever since I started volunteering with the city's local chapter of the Nature Conservancy four summers ago."

Although it is always important to establish your credibility in the introduction, it is particularly so when the audience does not know you well and you must clearly establish your expertise.[8] In these situations, be sure to stress the reasons why audience members should trust you and believe what you have to say.

Preview the Main Points

Once you've revealed the topic and purpose and established your credibility, use the introduction to briefly preview each of the main points of the speech. Previewing main points helps audience members mentally organize the speech and helps you keep their attention; it's an important step in orienting your listeners to what's to come. An introductory **preview statement** is straightforward. You simply tell the audience what the main points will be and in what order you will address them. Save your in-depth discussion of each one for the body of your speech. For example, you might state, "First, I'll start with a look at…" followed by "Next, I'll consider the causes of…." In a speech titled "U.S. Roads and Bridges: Highway Funding at a Crossroads," the president of the American Automobile Association, Robert L. Darbelnet, effectively introduces his topic, purpose, and main points:

> Good morning. When I received this invitation, I didn't hesitate to accept. I realized that in this room I would find a powerful coalition: the American Automobile Association and the National Asphalt Pavement Association. Where our two groups come together, no pun intended, is where the rubber meets the road.
>
> Unfortunately, the road needs repair.
>
> My remarks today are intended to give you a sense of AAA's ongoing efforts to improve America's roads. Our hope is that you will join your voices to ours as we call on the federal government to do three things:
>
> Number one: Perhaps the most important, provide adequate funding for highway maintenance and improvements.
>
> Number two: Play a strong, responsible, yet flexible role in transportation programs.
>
> And number three: Invest in highway safety.
>
> Let's see what our strengths are, what the issues are, and what we can do about them.[9]

When previewing your main points, simply mention those points, saving your in-depth discussion of each one for the body of your speech.

■ Motivate the Audience to Accept Your Goals

A final, and critical, function of the introduction is to motivate the audience to care about your topic and believe that it is relevant to them. One way to do this is to address its practical implications and what the audience stands to gain by listening to you. Another is to convince audience members that your speech purpose is consistent with their motives and values. A student speech about the value of interview training shows how this can be accomplished:

> Let me start by telling you why you need interview training. It all boils down to competition. As in sports, when you're not training, someone else is out there training to beat you. All things being equal, the person who has the best interviewing skills has got the edge.

SELF-ASSESSMENT CHECKLIST
How Effective Is Your Introduction?
Does your introduction…
_____1. Capture the audience's attention?
_____2. Stimulate their interest in what's to come?
_____3. Establish a positive bond with listeners?
_____4. Alert listeners to the speech purpose and topic?
_____5. Establish your credibility?
_____6. Preview the main points of the speech?
_____7. Motivate listeners to accept your speech goals?

Chapter 8
Developing the Conclusion

This chapter is taken from Dan O'Hair, Rob Stewart, and Hannah Rubenstein, *A Speaker's Guidebook*, Sixth Edition, pp. 227–231 (Chapter 15).

Just as a well-crafted introduction gets your speech effectively out of the starting gate, a well-constructed conclusion ensures that you go out with a bang and not a whimper. Conclusions give you the opportunity to drive home your purpose, and they offer you a final chance to make the kind of impression that will accomplish the goals of your speech. Conclusions also provide the audience with a sense of logical and emotional closure and give you a final opportunity to create a relationship with them.

■ Functions of Conclusions

Like introductions, conclusions consist of several elements that work together to make the end of a speech as memorable as the beginning. Conclusions serve to:

- Signal to the audience that the speech is coming to an end and provide closure.

- Summarize the key points.

- Reiterate the thesis or central idea of the speech.

- Challenge the audience to respond.

- End the speech memorably.

As with the introduction, prepare the conclusion after you've completed the speech body. Keep it brief—as a rule, no more than 10 to 15 percent, or about one-sixth, of the overall speech. And, just as you should outline the introduction in full-sentence and then key-word form (see **CHAPTER 7**), do so for the conclusion. Carefully consider your use of language in the conclusion. More than other parts of the speech, the conclusion can contain words that inspire and motivate.

CHECKLIST
Guidelines for Preparing the Conclusion
• During the research phase, be on the lookout for material that you can use in the conclusion.
• Do not leave the conclusion to chance. Prepare both a full-sentence outline and a key-word outline.
• Keep the length of the conclusion to no more than 10 to 15 percent or about one-sixth of the overall speech.
• Conclude soon after you signal you are about to end.

Signal the Close of a Speech and Provide Closure

People who listen to speeches are taking a journey of sorts, and they want and need the speaker to acknowledge the journey's end. The more emotional the journey, as in speeches designed to touch hearts and minds, the greater is the need for logical and emotional closure.

One way to alert the audience that a speech is about to end is by using a transitional word or phrase to signal closure: *in sum, finally, looking back, in conclusion, as I bring this to a close,* or *let me close by saying* (see **CHAPTER 6**). You can also signal closure by adjusting your manner of delivery; for example, you can vary your tone, pitch, rhythm, and rate of speech to indicate that the speech is winding down (see CHAPTER 13).

Few things annoy listeners more than hearing a speaker say "in conclusion," and then having to sit through another twenty minutes of the speech. Once you've signaled the end of your speech, conclude in short order (though not abruptly).

Summarize the Key Points

One bit of age-old advice for giving a speech is "Tell them what you are going to tell them (in the introduction), tell them (in the body), and tell them what you told them (in the conclusion)." The idea is that emphasizing the main points three times will help the audience to remember them.

Summarizing the main points in the conclusion accomplishes the last step of "telling them what you've told them." However, the summary or review should be more than a rote recounting. Consider how Holger Kluge, in a speech titled "Reflections on Diversity," summarizes his main points:

> I have covered a lot of ground here today. But as I draw to a close, I'd like to stress three things.
>
> First, diversity is more than equity....
>
> Second, weaving diversity into the very fabric of your organization takes time....
>
> Third, diversity will deliver bottom line results to your businesses and those results will be substantial....[1]

As the speaker reiterates each point, audience members are able to mentally check off what they've heard during the speech. Did they get all the key points? A restatement of points like the one above brings the speech full circle and helps give the audience a sense of completion.

Reiterate the Topic and Speech Purpose

Another function of the conclusion is to reinforce your message by reiterating the topic and speech purpose—to imprint them in the audience's memory. In the conclusion to a persuasive speech about the U.S. immigration debate, Elpidio Villarreal reminds his listeners of his central idea:

> Two paths are open to us. One path would keep us true to our fundamental values as a nation and a people. The other would lead us down a dark trail; one marked by 700-mile-long fences, emergency detention centers and vigilante border patrols. Because I really am an American, heart and soul, and because that means never being without hope, I still believe we will ultimately choose the right path. We have to.[2]

Reminding listeners of your speech purpose links their frame of reference to yours, thus allowing your audience to determine how well they've comprehended your central idea.

Challenge the Audience to Respond

A strong conclusion challenges audience members to put to use what the speaker has taught them. In an *informative speech,* the speaker challenges audience members to use what they've learned in a way that benefits them. In a *persuasive speech,* the challenge usually comes in the form of a **call to action**. Here the speaker challenges listeners to act in response to the speech, see the problem in a new way, change their beliefs about the problem, or change both their actions and their beliefs about the problem.

A concluding challenge is important because it shows audience members that the problem or issue being addressed is real and personally relevant to them. In the introduction, part of the goal is to show audience members how the topic is relevant to them; the call to action is a necessary part of completing that goal in the conclusion.

Hillary Rodham Clinton makes a strong call to action in her conclusion to an address presented to the United Nations World Conference on Women:

> We have seen peace prevail in most places for a half century. We have avoided another world war. But we have not solved older, deeply rooted problems that continue to diminish the potential of half the world's population. *Now it is time to act on behalf of women everywhere.* If we take bold steps to better the lives of women, we will be taking bold steps to better the lives of children and families too…. Let this conference be our—and the world's—call to action.[3]

■ Make the Conclusion Memorable

Beyond summarizing and providing closure, a key function of the conclusion is to make the speech memorable—to increase the odds that the speaker's message will linger after the speech is over. A speech that makes a lasting impression is one that listeners are most likely to remember and act on.

Strong conclusions contain vivid language that captures the audience's attention. Conclusions rely on (but are not limited to) the same devices for capturing attention as introductions (e.g., quotations, stories, startling statements, humor, and rhetorical questions; see **CHAPTER 7**). Following are examples of speakers who have created compelling conclusions using quotations, stories, rhetorical questions, and material first mentioned in the introduction of the speech (a technique known as "bookending").

Use Quotations

As with introductions, using a quotation that captures the essence of the speech can be a very effective way to close a speech. Note how Sue Suter quotes a character in *Star Trek* to conclude her speech on discrimination and the disabled:

> That brings us to the final lesson from *Star Trek.* I'd like to leave you with two quotations from Captain Picard that define what it means to be human. In *The Next Generation,* Picard confronts discrimination by agreeing that, yes, we may be different in appearance. Then he adds, "But we are both living beings. We are born, we grow, we live, and we die. In all the ways that matter, we are alike."[4]

Quoting from poetry is also a highly effective way to conclude a speech, as seen in this commencement address given by Oprah Winfrey to graduates of Wellesley College:

> I want to leave you with a poem that I say to myself sometimes…. Maya Angelou wrote a poem and I don't know a poem more fitting than "Phenomenal Woman" for this crowd, because you are and these words are for you.
>
> She says, "Pretty women, honey, they wonder just where my secret lies 'cause I'm not cuter, built to suit a fashion model size, but when I start to tell them, they say, Girl, you're telling lies and I said, no, honey, it's in the reach of my arms, it's in the span of my hips, it's in the stride of my stepping, it's in the curl of my lips, 'cause I'm a woman, honey, phenomenally, phenomenal, phenomenal woman."[5]

Tell a Story

A short concluding story, or *anecdote,* can bring the entire speech into focus very effectively. It helps the audience to visualize the speech:

> I would conclude with a story that applies to all of us in this industry. In ancient times there was a philosopher who had many disciples….

Another technique is to pick up on a story or an idea that you mentioned in the introduction, bringing the speech full circle. James May does this by reminding his audience of the story of Apollo 13 that started his speech:

> If I may draw one final lesson from the crippled spacecraft that made it back to earth on an empty fuel tank, it is that one should never underestimate the human capacity for doing "impossible" things. All through history, enterprising people have surprised themselves—and others around them—by finding ingenious solutions to the most complex problems. We can do that here.[6]

Pose a Rhetorical Question

Another effective way to make a speech memorable is to leave the audience with a *rhetorical question.* Just as such questions focus attention in the introduction, they can drive home the speech theme in the conclusion. President Barack Obama concluded his remarks on the Trayvon Martin shooting with a poignant rhetorical question. This served both to leave a lasting, emotional impression and to reiterate key speech points.

> If we're sending a message as a society in our communities that someone who is armed potentially has the right to use those firearms, even if there's a way for them to exit from a situation, is that really going to be contributing to the kind of peace and security and order that we'd like to see?[7]

Bring Your Speech Full Circle

Picking up on a story or idea you mentioned in the introduction—a technique known as "bookending"—can be a memorable way to close a speech and bring the entire presentation full circle. You can provide the resolution of the story ("what happened next?") or reiterate the link between the moral (lesson) of the story and the speech theme. You might also repeat lines from a poem you cited, or repeat a quotation you mentioned.

SELF-ASSESSMENT CHECKLIST
How Effective Is Your Conclusion?
Does your conclusion…
_____1. Alert the audience that the speech is ending?
_____2. Actually come to an end soon after you say you will finish?
_____3. Last no more than about one-sixth of the time spent on the body of the speech?
_____4. Reiterate the main points?
_____5. Remind listeners of the speech topic and purpose?
_____6. Challenge the audience to respond to your ideas or appeals?
_____7. Provide a sense of closure and make a lasting impression?
_____8. Add emotional appeal if the speech is intended to persuade the audience?

Chapter 9

Outlining the Speech

- Plan on Creating Two Outlines
- Create a Working Outline First
- Preparc a Speaking Outline for Delivery

This chapter is taken from Dan O'Hair, Rob Stewart, and Hannah Rubenstein, *A Speaker's Guidebook*, Sixth Edition, pp. 192–212 (Chapter 13).

Outlines are enormously helpful in putting together a speech, providing a framework for your speech materials and a blueprint for your presentation. In an **outline** you separate the main and supporting points—the major speech claims and the evidence to support them—into larger and smaller divisions and subdivisions. By plotting ideas into hierarchical fashion based on their relative importance to one another, and by using indentation to visually represent this hierarchy, you can't help but examine the underlying logic of the speech and the relationship of ideas to one another.[1]

Outlines rely on *coordination* and *subordination*. **Coordination** refers to assigning points of equal significance or weight the same level of numbering (e.g., *I, II, III, A, B, C, 1, 2, 3,* and so on). **Subordination** is the arrangement of points in order of their significance to one another, descending from general to specific or abstract to concrete. (For a review of the principles of coordination and subordination and the mechanics of outlining, see **CHAPTER 6**.)

■ Plan on Creating Two Outlines

As you develop a speech, you will actually create two outlines: a working outline (also called a *preparation* or *rough* outline) and a speaking, or delivery outline. The purpose of the **working outline** is to organize and firm up main points and, using the research you've gathered, to develop supporting points to substantiate them. Completed, the working outline should contain your entire speech, organized and supported to your satisfaction.

The **speaking outline** is the one you will use when you are practicing and actually presenting the speech. Speaking outlines, which contain your ideas in condensed form, are much briefer than working outlines. **FIGURE 9.1** provides an overview of the steps involved in outlining a speech.

Before taking a closer look at the working outline, consider the three types of wording formats speakers use to outline speeches.

Use Sentences, Phrases, or Key Words

Speeches can be outlined in complete sentences, phrases, or key words.

The Sentence Outline Format

In the **sentence outline** format, each main and supporting point is stated in sentence form as a declarative sentence (e.g., one that makes a statement or assertion about something). Often, these sentences are stated in much the same way the speaker wants to express the idea during delivery. Working outlines typically contain sentences, reflecting much if not all of the text of the speech. The following is an excerpt in sentence format from a speech by Mark B. McClellan on keeping prescription drugs safe:[2]

I.   The prescription drug supply is under unprecedented attack from a variety of increasingly sophisticated threats.

   A.   Technologies for counterfeiting—ranging from pill molding to dyes—have improved across the board.

   B.   Inadequately regulated Internet sites have become major portals for unsafe and illegal drugs.

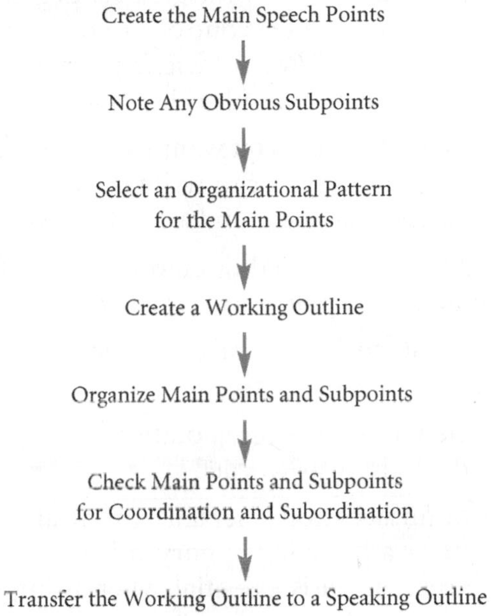

Create the Main Speech Points

↓

Note Any Obvious Subpoints

↓

Select an Organizational Pattern
for the Main Points

↓

Create a Working Outline

↓

Organize Main Points and Subpoints

↓

Check Main Points and Subpoints
for Coordination and Subordination

↓

Transfer the Working Outline to a Speaking Outline

FIGURE 9.1 Steps in Organizing and Outlining the Speech

The Phrase Outline Format

A **phrase outline** uses partial construction of the sentence form of each point. Phrase outlines encourage you to become so familiar with the speech that a glance at a few words is enough to remind you of exactly what to say. McClellan's sentence outline would appear as follows in phrase form:

I.   Drug supply under attack

   A.   Counterfeiting technologies more sophisticated

   B.   Unregulated Internet sites

The Key-Word Outline Format

The **key-word outline** uses the smallest possible units of understanding to outline the main and supporting points. In this format, each speech point contains just a few cue words to spur your memory.

A section of McClellan's outline would appear as follows in key-word outline form:

I.   Threats

   A.   Counterfeiting

   B.   Internet

Use a Key-Word Outline for Optimal Eye Contact

The type of outline you select will affect how well you deliver the speech. The less you rely on your outline notes, the more eye contact you can have with audience members, and eye contact is an essential aspect of a successful speech. For this reason, many speaking experts recommend using key-word or phrase outlines over sentence outlines for delivery, with the more succinct key-word outline often being the preferred format. Key-word outlines permit not only the greatest degree of eye contact but also greater freedom of movement and better control of your thoughts and actions than either sentence or phrase outlines. With sufficient practice, the key words will jog your memory so that the delivery of your ideas becomes more natural.

If there are points in your speech where you want to note exact quotations or precisely state complicated facts or figures, you can write those out in full sentences within the key-word outline. Sentences may help under the following conditions:

1. When the issue is highly controversial or emotion-laden for listeners and precise wording is needed to make the point as clear as possible

2. When the material is highly technical and exact sentence structure is critical to an accurate representation of the material

3. When a good deal of material relies on quotations and facts from another source that must be conveyed precisely as worded

Even with the inclusion of an occasional sentence, if at any time during the speech you experience stage fright or a lapse in memory, a key-word outline may not be of much help. This is why preparation is essential when using one. You must be confident in knowing the topic and the speech arrangement well enough to deliver the speech extemporaneously. An extemporaneous speech is carefully planned and practiced in advance and then delivered from a key-word or phrase outline (see **CHAPTER 12**). (Remember that outlining requirements differ among instructors. Be sure to understand your instructor's specific outlining and formatting requirements before you begin outlining your speech.)

■ Create a Working Outline First

Unless otherwise instructed, begin drafting your speech with a working outline using the sentence format before transferring its ideas to a speaking outline that uses key words or phrases. Working outlines are meant to be changed as you work through the mass of information you've collected. As you progress, you will no doubt rearrange points and add or omit material before you are satisfied that you have adequately demonstrated your speech thesis.

The completed working outline will give you confidence that you've satisfactorily fleshed out your ideas. Instead of worrying about whether you will have enough to say, or whether your speech will be well organized, you'll have an accurate picture of what you'll be able to communicate and how long it will take. Use the working outline to create a well-supported document containing all of your claims and research.

Separate the Introduction and Conclusion from the Body

Whether you are drafting a working or speaking outline, prepare the body of the speech before the introduction and the conclusion, and keep the introduction and conclusion *separate from* the main points. The introduction is the preface; the conclusion is the epilogue.

Introductions serve to gain the audience's attention and stir their interest; introduce the topic and thesis; establish the speaker's credibility, or ethos; and preview main points (see **CHAPTER 7** for more on developing the introduction). In outlines, treatments of these functions in the introduction can vary. As in this text, you can use such labels as *Attention Getter, Thesis, Credibility Statement,* and *Preview* to indicate how you will address these elements, as is done in the sample speech outlines on **pp. 160–165**. Alternatively, your instructor may prefer that you assign the introduction its own numbering system or simply write it out in paragraph format.

Similarly, in the conclusion you can indicate where you signal the close of the speech, summarize main points, reiterate the thesis and purpose, and leave the audience with something to think about or offer a call to action—or, again, assign it its own numbering system or write it out. (See **CHAPTER 8** for more on developing the conclusion.)

Indicate Your Sources

As you work on the outline, clearly indicate to yourself where speech points require source credit. Directly after the point, either insert a footnote *or* enclose in parentheses enough of the reference to be able to retrieve it in full (see sample outlines in this chapter). Once you complete the outline, prepare a bibliography per your instructor's directions. Instructors may prefer that you order the references alphabetically and place them on a sheet titled "Works Cited"; or that you create a "Works Consulted" list, including all sources consulted rather than just those cited in the speech.

CHECKLIST
Steps in Creating a Working Outline
_____1. On separate lines, label and write out your topic, general purpose, specific speech purpose, and thesis.
_____2. Establish your main points (optimally two to five).
_____3. Flesh out supporting points.
_____4. Check for correct subordination and coordination; follow the numbering system shown in **TABLE 6.1** (p. 127)
_____5. Label each speech part (i.e., "Introduction," "Body," and "Conclusion")
_____6. Write out each speech point in sentence format.
_____7. Label and write out transitions.
_____8. Note sources for the bibliography.
_____9. Assign the speech a title.

Create a Title

As the last step, assign the speech a title, one that informs the audience of its subject in a way that invites them to listen to or read it. Thoughtfully crafted titles communicate the essence of a speech. At times, you might even refer to the title during your speech, as a means of previewing or emphasizing your perspective on the topic.

Sample Working Outline

The following outline is from a speech delivered by public speaking student Zachary Dominique. It uses the sentence format and includes labeled transitions as well as the wording Zachary will use to cite his sources. Brief source references appear in parentheses (e.g., *ABC of Mountain Biking*) for ease in assembling a required bibliography.

The History and Sport of Mountain Biking

Zachary Dominque
St. Edwards University

Topic:	Mountain Biking
Specific Purpose:	To inform my listeners about the sport of mountain biking
Thesis Statement:	Mountain biking is a relatively new, exciting, and diverse sport

Introduction

(Attention getter:)

I. Imagine that you're on a bike, plunging down a steep, rock-strewn mountain, yet fully in control.

II. Adrenaline courses through your body as you hurtle through the air, touch down on glistening pebbled streams and tangled grasses, and rocket upward again.

III. You should be scared, but you're not; in fact, you're having the time of your life.

IV. Like we say, Nirvana.

V. How many of you like to bike—ride to campus, bike for fitness, or cycle just for fun?

VI. You might own a bike with a lightweight frame and thin wheels, and use it to log some serious mileage—or possibly a comfort bike, with a nice soft seat and solid tires.

(Credibility Statement:)

VII. Good morning, folks. My name is Zachary Dominque, and I'm a mountain biker.

VIII.   I've been racing since I was eight years old and won state champion three years ago, so this topic is close to my heart.

(Preview:)

IX.   Today, I'm going to take you on a tour of the exciting sport of mountain biking: I'll be your engine—your driver—in mountain bike–speak.

X.   Our ride begins with a brief overview of mountain biking; then we'll do a hopturn—a turn in reverse—to learn about the sport's colorful history.

XI.   Pedalling ahead in this beautiful autumn air, we'll chat about the various differences in design and function between mountain bikes and road bikes.

XII.   We'll conclude our tour at a local bike shop, where you can compare downhill, trail, and cross-country mountain bikes.

XIII.   These are the three main types of mountain bikes, designed for the three major types of mountain biking.

XIV.   I hope by then that you'll catch a little bit of mountain biking fever and see why I find it such an exciting, intense, and physically challenging sport.

Transition: Mountain biking is a sport that can be extreme, recreational, or somewhere in between. But no matter what kind of rider you are, it's always a great way to get out in the natural world and get the adrenaline going. To start, let me briefly define mountain biking.

Body

I.   The website ABC of Mountain Biking offers a good basic definition: "Mountain biking is a form of cycling on off-road or unpaved surfaces such as mountain trails and dirt roads; the biker uses a bicycle with a sturdy frame and fat tires." (ABC of Mountain Biking)

A.   The idea behind mountain biking is to go where other bikes won't take you.

1.   Mountain bikers ride on backcountry roads and on single-track trails winding through fields or forests.

2.   They climb up steep, rock-strewn hills and race down over them.

3.   The focus is on self-reliance, because these bikers often venture miles from help.

B.   According to the National Bicycle Dealers Association website, in 2013 mountain bikes accounted for 25 percent of all bikes sold in the United States.

1. If you factor in sales of the comfort bike, which is actually a mountain bike modified for purely recreational riders, sales jump to nearly 38 percent of all bikes sold.

2. Some 50 million Americans love riding their mountain bikes, according to data collected by the New England Mountain Bike Association.

Transition: So you see that mountain biking is popular with a lot of people. But the sport itself is fairly new.

II.   The history of mountain biking is less than 50 years old, and its founders are still around.

A. The man in this picture is Gary Fisher, one of the founders of mountain biking.

B. According to *The Original Mountain Bike Book,* written in 1998 by pioneering mountain bikers Rob van der Plas and Charles Kelly, they, along with Fisher, Joe Breeze, and other members of the founding posse from the Marin County, California, area, were instrumental in founding the modern sport of mountain biking in the early 1970s. *(Original MB Book)*

C. Mountain bikes—called MTBs or ATBs (for all-terrain bikes)—didn't exist then as we now know them, so as you can see, in this picture of Gary Fisher, he's riding a modified one-speed Schwinn cruiser.

1. Cruisers, or "ballooners," aren't made to go off road at all.

2. Nothing equips them to navigate trails, and their brakes aren't remotely equipped to handle stops on steep descents.

3. But this is the type of bike Fisher and others started out with.

D. By the mid-1970s, growing numbers of bikers in California got into using modified cruisers to race downhill on rocky trails.

1. They'd meet at the bottom of Mount Tamalpais, in Corte Madera, California.

2. They'd walk their bikes a mile or two up its steep slopes, and hurl on down.

E. As even more people got involved, Charles Kelly and others organized the famed Repack Downhill Race on Mt. Tam.

1. Held from 1976 to 1979, the Repack race became a magnet for enthusiasts and put the sport on the map, according to *The Original Mountain Bike Book. (Original MTB Book)*

Transition: The reason why the race was called "Repack" is a story in itself.

2. The trail in the Repack race plummeted 1,300 feet in less than 2 miles, according to Joe Breeze in an article posted on the Mountain Biking Hall of Fame website. (MTB Hall of Fame)

    a. Such a steep drop meant constant braking, which in turn required riders to replace, or "repack," their bikes' grease after nearly each run.

    b. As Breeze recounts in his own words: "The bikes' antiquated hub coaster brake would get so hot that the grease would vaporize, and after a run or two, the hub had to be repacked with new grease."

Transition: As you might imagine, these early enthusiasts eventually tired of the routine.

F. The bikers had tinkered with their bikes from the start, adding gearing, drum brakes, and suspension systems.

G. In 1979, Joe Breeze designed a new frame—called the "Breezer"—which became the first actual mountain bike.

H. By 1982, as van der Plas and Kelly write in *The Original Mountain Bike Book,* standardized production of mountain bikes finally took off.

Transition: Now that you've learned a bit of the history of mountain biking, let's look at what today's mountain bike can do. To make things clearer, I'll compare them to road bikes. Road bikes are the class of bikes that cyclists who compete in the Tour de France use.

III. Mountain bikes and road bikes are built for different purposes.

A. Mountain bikes are built to tackle rough ground, while road bikes are designed to ride fast on paved, smooth surfaces.

1. To accomplish their task, mountain bikes feature wide tires with tough tread.

2. In contrast, road bike tires are ultrathin and their frames extremely lightweight.

    a. If you take a road bike off-road, chances are you'll destroy it.

    b. Without the knobby tread and thickness found on mountain bike tires, road bike tires can't grip onto the rocks and other obstacles that cover off-road courses.

B. The handlebars on the bikes also differ.

1. Mountain bikes feature flat handlebars; these keep us in an upright stance, so that we don't flip over when we hit something.

2. The drop handlebars on road bikes require the cyclist to lean far forward; this position suits road cycling, which prizes speed.

    C. The gears and suspension systems also differentiate mountain bikes from road bikes.

        1. Mountain bikes use lower gears than road bikes and are more widely spaced, giving them more control to ride difficult terrain.

        2. As for suspension, road bikes generally don't have any kind of suspension system that can absorb power.

            a. That is, they don't have shock absorbers because they're not supposed to hit anything.

            b. Imagine riding over rocks and roots without shocks; it wouldn't be pretty.

        3. Many mountain bikes have at least a great front shock-absorbing suspension system.

            a. Some have rear-suspension systems.

            b. Some bikes have dual systems.

Transition:: I hope by now you have a sense of the mountain bike design. But there are finer distinctions to draw.

IV. There are actually three different types of mountain bikes, designed to accommodate the three major kinds of mountain biking—downhill, trails, and cross-country.

Transition: Let's start with downhill.

    A. Downhill bikes have the fewest gears of the three types of mountain bikes and weigh the most.

        1. That's because downhill biking is a daredevil sport—these bikers are crazy!

        2. They slide down hills at insane speeds, and they go off jumps.

        3. Lots of what they call *gravity checks,* or falls.

    B. As described on the website Trails.com, downhill racers catch a shuttle going up the mountain, then speed downhill while chewing up obstacles.

    C. Think of downhill racing as skiing with a bike.

Transition: Now let's swing by trails biking.

    D. Trails bikes look quite different than either downhill or cross-country bikes.

        1. They have very small wheels, measuring either 20, 24, or 26 inches, and smaller frames.

        2. These differences in design help trail bikers do what they do best: jump over obstacles—cars, rocks, and large logs.

E. The trail biker's goal is to not put a foot down on the ground.

F. Trail bike racing is one of the few types of biking that's done by time, not all at a mass start.

Transition: The third major type of mountain biking, cross-country, or XC cycling, is my sport.

G. Cross-country biking is also the most common type of mountain biking—and the one sponsored by the Olympics.

   1. That's right. In 1996, mountain biking became an Olympic sport.

   2. This was just two decades after its inception.

H. With cross-country, you get the best of all worlds, at least in my humble opinion.

   1. The courses are creative, incorporating hills and valleys and rough to not-so-rough terrain.

   2. If done competitively, cross-country biking is like competing in a marathon.

   3. Done recreationally, it offers you the chance to see the great outdoors while getting, or staying, in great shape.

I. Cross-country bikes come in two forms.

   1. XC bikes are very lightweight, with either full or partial suspension.

   2. The Trails/Marathon XC hybrid bikes are a bit heavier, with full suspension; XC bikes are designed for seriously long rides.

Transition: Well, it has been quite a tour, folks. *(Signals close of speech)*

Conclusion

   I. Our course began with an overview of mountain biking and a hopturn into a brief history of the sport.

   II. We also learned about the differences between mountain bikes and road bikes, and the three major categories of mountain bikes. *(Summarizes main points)*

   III. To me, mountain biking, and especially cross-country, is the perfect sport—fulfilling physical, spiritual, and social needs.

   IV. It's a great sport to take up recreationally. *(Leaves audience with something to think about)*

   V. And if you decide to mountain bike competitively, just remember: ride fast, drive hard, and leave your blood on every trail. *(Memorable close)*

■ Prepare a Speaking Outline for Delivery

Once you complete a full-sentence working outline, it is time to transfer your ideas to a speaking outline. Using the same numbering system as the working outline, condense the material in it into key words or phrases, using just enough words to jog your memory. Note that even though the delivery outline should contain key words or phrases almost exclusively, when exact wording is critical to an accurate representation of your speech material (as in conveying quotations verbatim or when the issue is highly controversial or emotional and precise wording is needed to make the point as clear as possible), you may want to write it out in full sentences.

Indicate Delivery Cues

Include in the speaking outline any **delivery cues** that will be part of the speech (see TABLE 9.1). To ensure visibility, capitalize the cues, place them in parentheses, and/or highlight them.

Place the outline on 4 × 6-inch notecards or 8.5 × 11-inch sheets of paper. Some speakers dislike notecards, finding them too small to contain enough material and too easily dropped. Others find notecards small enough to be handled unobtrusively but large enough to accommodate key words (assuming about one main point and supporting points per card). Whichever you use, be sure to print large and bold enough so that your words will be easily seen at a glance.

Practice the Speech

The key to the successful delivery of any speech, particularly one using a key-word outline, is practice. The more you rehearse your speech, the more comfortable you will become when you speak. For more information on practicing the speech, see CHAPTER 14.

TABLE 9.1 Common Delivery Cues in a Speaking Outline

DELIVERY CUE	EXAMPLE
Transitions	(TRANSITION)
Timing	(PAUSE) (SLOW DOWN)
Speaking Rate/Volume	(SLOWLY) (LOUDER)
Presentation Aids	(SHOW MODEL) (SLIDE 3)
Source	(ATLANTA CONSTITUTION, August 2, 2014)
Statistic	(2014, boys to girls = 94,232; U.S. Department of Health and Human Services)
Quotation	Eubie Blake, 100: "If I'd known I was gonna live this long, I'd have taken better care of myself."
Difficult-to-Pronounce or -Remember Names or Words	Eowyn (A-OH-win)

CHECKLIST	
Tips on Using Notecards or Sheets of Paper	
_____1.	Leave some blank space at the margins to find your place as you glance at the cards.
_____2.	Number the notecards or sheets so that you can follow them with ease.
_____3.	Instead of turning the cards or sheets, slide them under one another.
_____4.	Do not staple notes or sheets together.
_____5.	If you use a lectern, place the notes or sheets near eye level.
_____6.	Do not use the cards or sheets in hand gestures, as they become distracting pointers or flags.

Sample Speaking Outline

The History and Sport of Mountain Biking

Zachary Dominque
St. Edwards University

Introduction
(Attention getter:)

I.   Imagine on bike, plunging rock-strewn, yet control.

II.   Adrenaline, hurtle, touch downstream, rocket.

III.   Be scared, but not—time of life.

IV.   Nirvana.

V.   How many bike, fitness, fun?

VI.   Might own lightweight, thin wheels, serious mileage—or comfort, soft seat, solid tires.

(Credibility Statement:)

VII.   Morning, Zachary, MTBer

VIII.   Eight; champion, heart.

(Preview:)

IX.   Today, tour, exciting sport of...engine, driver, MTB-speak.

X.   Ride begins brief overview; do hopturn—colorful history.

XI.   Pedalling ahead autumn, chat differences between mountain, road.

XII.   Conclude shop, compare MTBs.

XIII.   Three types bikes, designed for three...

XIV.   Hope catch fever, exciting, intense, and physically.

Transition: MTB sport extreme...in-between. But no matter, always great way natural world, adrenaline. Start, define.

Body

I.   *ABC/MB def*: "MTB is a form of cycling on off-road or unpaved surfaces such as mountain trails and dirt roads; the biker uses a bicycle with a sturdy frame and fat tires." *(ABC of Mountain Biking)*

    A.   The idea—go where others.

        1.   MTBs ride backcountry, single-track winding fields, forests.

        2.   Climb steep, rock-strewn, race down.

        3.   Self-reliance, miles from help.

    B.   National Bicycle Dealers Assoc., 2013 MTBs 25 percent sold.

        1.   Factor comfort, actually MTB modified recreational, sales 38%.

        2.   50 million love riding, data gathered NE MTB Assn.

Transition: So MTB popular people. But fairly new.

II.   History MTB less 50, founders.

    A.   Gary Fisher, founders MTB. (SHOW PICTURE)

    B.   *Original Mountain Bike Book,* written 1998 by van der Plas, Kelly; they, along with Fisher, Breeze, other members posse Marin, instrumental founding modern sport early 1970s. *(Original MTB Book)*

    C.   MTBs or ATBs (terrain)—didn't exist, so picture Fisher, modified Schwinn cruiser. (SHOW PICTURE)

        1.   Cruisers, "ballooners," off-road.

        2.   Nothing equips navigate, brakes equipped stops descents.

        3.   But bike Fisher, others started.

    D.   Mid-1970s, growing numbers using modified race downhill.

        1.   Meet bottom Tamalpais, CA.

        2.   Walk bikes mile up steep, hurl.

    E.   Even involved, Kelly, others organized Repack.

        1.   1976–1979, magnet enthusiasts, on map, *Original MTB.* *(Original MTB Book)*

Transition: Reason called "Repack" story itself.

        2.   Trail plummeted 1,300 feet 2 miles, according Breeze article posted MTB Fame website.

            a.   Such drop constant braking, required riders replace, "repack," grease each run.

b. Breeze recounts: "The bikes' antiquated hub coaster brake would get so hot that the grease would vaporize, and after a run or two, the hub had to be repacked with new grease."

Transition: Might imagine, early enthusiasts tired.

F. Bikers tinkered, gearing, drum, suspension.

G. 1979, Breeze new frame—"Breezer"—first actual MTB.

H. 1982, as van der Plas, Kelly write in *Original MTB,* standardized took off.

Transition: Now learned history, let's look today's can do. Clearer, compare road. Class cyclists Tour de France use.

III.   MTB, road built different purposes.

A. MTB tackle rough, road designed fast, paved, smooth.

1. Accomplish task, wide tire, tough tread.

2. In contrast, road ultrathin, frames lightweight.

a. Take off-road, destroy.

b. Without knobby tread, thickness MTB tires, road can't grip rocks, obstacles.

B. Handlebars differ.

1. MTB flat; upright stance, don't flip.

2. Drop handlebars require lean forward; suits road cycling, prizes speed.

C. Gears, suspension also differentiate.

1. MTB lower gears, widely spaced—more control difficult terrain.

2. As for suspension, road don't, absorb power.

a. That is, don't have shock, not supposed to.

b. Imagine without shocks; wouldn't pretty.

3. Many MTBs at least a great front.

a. Some rear.

b. Some dual.

Transition: Hope sense MTB design. But finer distinctions to draw.

IV.   Actually three types MTB, accommodate three kinds.

Transition: Let's start with downhill.

A. Downhill fewest gears, weigh most.

   1. Because downhill daredevil—crazy!

   2. Slide insane, off jumps.

   3. Lots *gravity checks*.

B. Trails.com, downhill racers catch shuttle going up, speed downhill chewing up.

C. Think racing skiing bike.

Transition: Now let's swing by trails biking.

D. Trails bikes look different than either.

   1. Small wheels, 20, 24, or 26", smaller frames.

   2. Differences design help trail do best—jump obstacles—cars, rocks, large logs.

E. Trail goal not foot on ground.

F. Trail racing few types done by time, not mass.

Transition: Third major type MTB, cross-country, or XC.

G. Cross-country most common—Olympics.

   1. That's right. In 1996…

   2. Just two decades inception.

H. With XC, best all worlds, humble.

   1. Courses creative, incorporating hills, valleys, rough, not-so-.

   2. Competitively, XC like marathon.

   3. Recreationally, chance see outdoors, shape.

I. XC two forms.

   1. Lightweight, full or partial.

   2. Trails/Marathon XC hybrids heavier, full suspension; designed seriously long.

Transition: Quite tour. *(Signals close of speech)*

Conclusion

  I.   Course began overview, hopturn history sport.

  II.   Also learned differences mountain, road, three major categories of MTB, three types MTB accommodate fans. (***Summarizes main points***)

  III. To me, MTB, especially XC, perfect—fulfilling physical, spiritual, social needs.

  IV. Great take up recreationally. (***Leaves audience with something to think about***)

V.   Decide bike competitively, remember: ride fast, drive hard, leave blood. (***Memorable close***)

Full-Text Speech

Following is the full text of the speech outlined in this chapter. Zachary's assignment was to deliver a ten-minute informative speech citing at least four authoritative sources, incorporating at least two presentation aids, and including a list of references in either APA or MLA style.[3]

CHECKLIST
Steps in Creating a Speaking Outline
_____1.   Create the outline on sheets of paper or large notecards..
_____2.   Write large and legibly using at least a 14-point font or easy-to-read ink and large letters.
_____3.   For each main and subpoint, choose a key word or phrase that will jog your memory accurately.
_____4.   Include delivery cues.
_____5.   Write out full quotations or other critical information.
_____6.   Using the speaking outline, practice the speech at least five times

SAMPLE INFORMATIVE SPEECH

The History and Sport of Mountain Biking

Zachary Dominque
St. Edwards University

1. By asking the audience to visualize racing down a mountain, Zachary effectively captures the audience's attention.

Imagine that you're on a bike, plunging down a steep, rock-strewn mountain, yet fully in control. Adrenaline courses through your body as you hurtle through the air, touch down on glistening pebbled streams and tangled grasses, and rocket upward again. You should be scared, but you're not. In fact, you're having the time of your life. Like we say, Nirvana. [1]

How many of you like to bike? Perhaps you ride to campus, bike for fitness, or cycle just for fun. You might own a bike with a lightweight frame and thin wheels, and use it to log some serious mileage. Or possibly you ride a comfort bike, with a nice soft seat and solid tires.

2. Pointing to his lengthy experience with the sport lends Zachary credibility to address the topic.

Good morning, folks. My name is Zachary Dominque, and I'm a mountain biker. I've been racing since I was eight years old and won state champion three years ago, so this topic is close to my heart.[2]

3. Zachary previews the speech using metaphoric language in which the speech becomes a tour with courses.

Today, I'm going to take you on a tour of this exciting sport. I'll be your "engine"—your driver—in mountain bike–speak. Our ride begins with a brief overview of mountain biking; then we'll do a hopturn—a turn in reverse—to learn about the sport's colorful history. [3] Pedalling ahead in this beautiful autumn air, we'll chat about the differences between mountain bikes and road bikes. We'll conclude our tour at a local bike shop, where you can compare downhill, trail, and cross-country mountain bikes. These are the three main types of mountain bikes, designed for the three major types of mountain biking. I hope by then that you'll catch a little bit of mountain biking fever and see why I find it such an exciting, intense, and physically challenging sport.

4. Zachary transitions into the speech body.

To start, let me briefly define mountain biking. [4]

5. Zachary is careful to define his topic for the audience.

Mountain biking is a sport that can be extreme, recreational, or somewhere in-between. The website *ABC of Mountain Biking* offers a good basic definition: "Mountain biking is a form of cycling on off-road or unpaved surfaces such as mountain trails and dirt roads; the biker uses a bicycle with a sturdy frame and fat tires." [5]

The idea behind mountain biking is to go where other bikes won't take you. Mountain bikers ride on backcountry roads and on single-track trails winding through fields or forests. They climb up steep, rock-strewn hills and race down over them. The focus is on self-reliance, because these bikers often venture miles from help.

6. Zachary uses reputable sources and informs the audience of where the information can be located.

According to the National Bicycle Dealers Association website, in 2013 mountain bikes accounted for 25 percent of all bikes sold in the United States. If you factor in sales of the comfort bike, which is actually a mountain bike modified for purely recreational riders, sales jump to nearly 38 percent of all bikes sold. Some 50 million Americans love riding their mountain bikes, according to data published by the New England Mountain Bike Association (NEMBA). [6] According to NEMBA, that's 1-1/3 times the population of Canada. And that's one and one-half times the number of golfers in the U.S.

So you see that mountain biking is popular with a lot of people. But the sport itself is fairly new. [7]

The history of mountain biking is less than 50 years old. The man in this picture is Gary Fisher, one of the founders of mountain biking. [8] According to *The Original Mountain Bike Book,* written in 1998 by pioneering mountain bikers Rob van der Plas and Charles Kelly, they, along with Fisher, Joe Breeze, and other members of the founding posse from the Marin County, California, area, were instrumental in founding the modern sport of mountain biking in the early 1970s.

Mountain bikes—called MTBs or ATBs (for all terrain bikes)—didn't exist then as we now know them, so as you can see, in this picture [9] of Gary Fisher, he's riding a modified one-speed Schwinn cruiser. Cruisers, or "ballooners," aren't made to go off road at all. Nothing equips them to navigate trails, and their brakes aren't remotely equipped to handle stops on steep descents. But this is the type of bike Fisher and others started out with.

By the mid-1970s, growing numbers of bikers in California got into using modified cruisers to race downhill on rocky trails. They'd meet at the bottom of Mount Tamalpais, in Corte Madera, California, walk their bikes a mile or two up its steep slopes, and hurl on down. As even more people got involved, Charles Kelly and others organized the famed Repack Downhill Race on Mt. Tam. Held from 1976 to 1979, the Repack race became a magnet for enthusiasts and put the sport on the map, according to *The Original Mountain Bike Book.*

The reason why the race was called "Repack" is a story in itself.

The trail in the Repack race plummeted 1300 feet in less than 2 miles, according to Joe Breeze in an article posted on the Mountain Biking Hall of Fame website. Such a steep drop meant constant braking, which in turn required riders to replace, or "repack," their bikes' grease after nearly each run. As Breeze recounts in his own words: "The bikes' antiquated hub coaster brake would get so hot that the grease would vaporize, and after a run or two, the hub had to be repacked with new grease."

As you might imagine, these early enthusiasts eventually tired of the routine: The bikers had tinkered with their bikes from the start, adding gearing, drum brakes, and a suspension system. In 1979, Joe Breeze designed a new frame—called the "Breezer"—which became the first actual mountain bike. By 1982, as van der Plas and Kelly write in *The Original Mountain Bike Book,* [10] standardized production of mountain bikes finally took off.

Now that you've learned a bit of the history of mountain biking, let's look at what today's mountain bike can do. To make things clearer, I'll compare them to road bikes. Road bikes are the class of bikes that cyclists who compete in the Tour de France use. [11]

Mountain bikes and road bikes are built for different purposes. Mountain bikes are built to tackle rough ground, while road bikes are designed to ride fast on paved, smooth surfaces. To accomplish their task, mountain bikes feature wide tires with tough tread. In contrast, road bike tires are ultrathin and their frames extremely lightweight. If you take a road bike off-road, chances are you'll destroy it. Without the knobby tread and

---

7. Zachary uses a transition to signal a change in focus.

8. To add interest and involvement, Zachary supplements his description with photographs.

9. Zachary again supplements his verbal description with a visual aid.

10. Rather than relying solely on Internet sources, a practice that lessens speaker credibility, Zachary cites a key book on the topic, written by two founders of the sport.

11. To help foster understanding, Zachary compares and contrasts the mountain bike with the more familiar road bike.

thickness found on mountain bike tires, road bike tires can't grip onto the rocks or other obstacles that cover off-road courses.

The handlebars on the bikes also differ. Mountain bikes feature flat handlebars; these keep us in an upright stance, so that we don't flip over when we hit something. The drop handlebars on road bikes require the cyclist to lean far forward; this position suits road cycling, which prizes speed.

The gears and suspension systems also differentiate mountain bikes from road bikes.

Mountain bikes use lower gears than road bikes and the gears are more widely spaced. This gives them more control to ride difficult terrain.

As for suspension, road bikes generally don't have any kind of suspension system that can absorb power. That is, they don't have shock absorbers because they're not supposed to hit anything. Imagine riding over rocks and roots without shocks. It wouldn't be pretty. Many mountain bikes have at least a great front shock-absorbing suspension system; some have rear-suspension systems, and some bikes have dual systems. [12]

12. Zachary internally summarizes the speech points he's covered thus far and previews what he'll discuss next. Note his use of biking jargon to draw the audience in.

I hope by now you have a sense of the mountain bike design. But there are finer distinctions to draw. These are actually three different types of mountain bikes, designed to accommodate the three major kinds of mountain biking—downhill, trails, and cross-country.

Let's start with downhill. Downhill bikes have the fewest gears of the three types of mountain bikes and weigh the most. That's because downhill biking is a daredevil sport—these bikers are crazy! They slide down hills at insane speeds, and they go off jumps. Lots of what they call *gravity checks*, or falls. As described on the website Trails. com, downhill racers catch a shuttle going up the mountain, then speed downhill while chewing up obstacles. Think of downhill racing as skiing with a bike.

13. In this transition, Zachary extends the metaphor of his speech as a tour.

Now let's swing by trails biking. [13]

Trails bikes look quite different than either downhill or cross-country bikes. They have very small wheels, measuring either 20, 24, or 26 inches, and smaller frames. These differences in design help trail bikers do what they do best—jump over obstacles—cars, rocks, and large logs. The trail biker's goal is not to put a foot down on the ground. In trails biking, the course is set right there in front of you. Trail bike racing is one of the few types of biking that's done by time, not all at a mass start.

The third major type of mountain biking, cross-country, or XC cycling, is my sport.

Cross-country biking is also the most common type of mountain biking—and the one sponsored by the Olympics. That's right. In 1996, mountain biking became an Olympic sport—just two decades after its inception.

With cross-country, you get the best of all worlds, at least in my humble opinion. The courses are creative, incorporating hills and valleys and rough to not-so-rough terrain. If done competitively, cross-country biking is like competing in a marathon. Done recreationally, it offers you the chance to see the great outdoors while getting, or staying, in great shape.

Cross-country bikes come in two forms: XC bikes are very lightweight, with either full or partial suspension. The Trails/Marathon XC hybrid bikes are a bit heavier, with full suspension; XC bikes are designed for seriously long rides.

Well, it has been quite a tour, folks. [14] Our course began with an overview of mountain biking and a hopturn into a brief history of the sport. We also learned about the differences between mountain bikes and road bikes, the three major categories of mountain biking, and the three types of mountain bikes made to accommodate fans of each type.

To me, mountain biking, and especially cross-country, is the perfect sport—fulfilling physical, spiritual, and social needs. It's a great sport to take up recreationally. And if you decide to mountain bike competitively, just remember: ride fast, drive hard, and leave your blood on every trail. [15]

14. Zachary signals the close of the speech by reiterating his opening analogy in which he compares the speech to a tour.

15. Zachary's use of vivid language makes the conclusion memorable and leaves the audience with something to think about.

Works Cited

"Cycling, Mountain Biking." London 2012 Olympics website. Accessed November 9, 2010. www.london2012.com/games/olympic-sports/cycling-mountain-bike.php.

National Bicycle Dealers Association. "Industry Overview, 2012." Accessed October 13, 2013. nbda.com/articles/industry-overview-2012-pg34.htm

"Types of Mountain Bikes," Trails.com.

"The Economics and Benefits of Mountain Biking." Accessed November 1, 2013. www.nemba.org/

Van der Plas, Rob, and Charles Kelly. *The Original Mountain Bike Book.* Minneapolis: Motorbooks, 1998.

"What Is Mountain Biking?" ABC of Mountain Biking website. Accessed November 23, 2010. www.abc-of-mountainbiking.com/mountain-biking-basics/whatis-mountain-biking.asp.

Chapter 10

The Informative Speech

- Focus on Sharing Knowledge
- Categories of Informative Speeches
- Decide How to Convey the Information
- Take Steps to Reduce Confusion
- Arrange Speech Points in a Pattern

This chapter is taken from Dan O'Hair, Rob Stewart, and Hannah Rubenstein, *A Speaker's Guidebook*, Sixth Edition, pp. 322–343 (Chapter 23).

Ever wondered about the satellite technology behind Google Earth? Or which careers will be most financially rewarding in the next decade? How can you protect your reputation when using social networking sites?

To *inform* is to communicate knowledge. The goal of informative speaking is to increase the audience's awareness of some phenomenon and/or deepen understanding of it by imparting knowledge.[1] **Informative speeches** bring new topics to light, offer new insights on subjects with which we are familiar, provide novel ways of thinking about a topic, or demonstrate how to do things. Some speeches do all of this in a single speech; others remain focused in one or another direction.

■ Focus on Sharing Knowledge

With information available today in so many forms, electronic and otherwise, it might appear that we have little need for informative speeches. Yet it is precisely because of this glut of gathered facts that we thirst for thoughtful perspectives, and informative speeches can answer this need. Your speech might be an in-depth analysis of a complex subject, a report of an event, or a physical demonstration of how something works. As long as your audience learns something, the options are nearly limitless.

Enlighten Rather Than Advocate

The goal of an informative speech stands in contrast to that of the persuasive speech, which explicitly attempts to influence people's attitudes, values, beliefs, or behavior about an issue. Whereas a persuasive speech would seek to modify attitudes or ask the audience to adopt a specific position, an informative speech stops short of this. Yet scholars of public speaking point out that there is no such thing as a purely informative or persuasive speech; that is, there are always elements of persuasion in an informative speech, and vice versa. Rarely are we entirely dispassionate about a subject, especially one that tends to elicit strong reactions. Nevertheless, if you keep in mind the general informative speaking goal, you will be able to deliver an informative speech whose primary function is to enlighten rather than to advocate.

Use Audience Analysis

Audience members must be able to identify with the informative topic and see how they can use and benefit from the information you give them. You therefore will need to gauge what your listeners already know about your informative topic as well as what they want and need to know about it. Then adapt your speech accordingly. If speaking about collecting violins to a general audience, for example, you might describe the parts of a violin, the sounds it produces, and the names of the Italian families who made the most prized instruments. Only a specialized audience of musicians will want or need to hear about staccato bowings, sforzando marks, or other technical information.[2]

The importance of giving listeners a reason to care about your topic cannot be overstated. Early on in your speech (in your **preview statement,** for example) tell audience members why they should listen to you. Demonstrate the topic's relevance to the audience by pointing out how some aspect of it relates directly to listeners' lives.

Present New and Interesting Information

Audiences want to learn something new when they listen to a speaker. To satisfy this drive, try to uncover information that is fresh and compelling. Seek out unusual sources (but make certain they are credible), novel (but sound) interpretations, startling facts, compelling examples, and moving stories. As professional speaker Vickie K. Sullivan notes:

> The first point that transforms an ordinary speaker into an industry beacon is a new perspective on a major problem.... If the speech does not convey provocative information, audience members feel their time has been wasted (and rightfully will feel offended). They expect their thinking to be challenged.[3]

As important as offering new information, however, is not overwhelming listeners with too much of it. Most people will recall less than half of the information you tell them, so focus on what you most want to convey and trim material that does not strongly support your central idea.[4]

One way to discover new information is via the Web. The following sites provide search trends, hot topics, popular issues, and ideas that are trending now[5]:

- **Google Trends:** www.google.com/trends/ (you may also try either Hot Searches or Google Zeitgeist [www.google.com/zeitgeist/2012/#the-world])

- **Yahoo Buzz Log:** news.yahoo.com/blogs/trending-now/

- **Bing Trends:** www.bing.com/blogs/site_blogs/b/search/archive/2012/11/26/year-end.aspx

- **Bing Webmaster Keyword Research Beta:** www.bing.com/toolbox/keywords

- **AOL Search Trends:** search.aol.com/aol/trends

- **Twitter Search:** twitter.com/search-home

- **YouTube Trends:** youtube-trends.blogspot.com/

Look for Ways to Increase Understanding

People are not simply empty vessels into which you can pour facts and figures and expect them to recognize and remember all that information. Before we can retain information, we must be motivated to listen to it and be able to recognize and comprehend it.[6] Flesh out speech points with compelling supporting materials, such as examples, stories, opinions, and facts. Rhetorical devices such as *repetition* and *parallelism* can reinforce information and drive home key themes. Other necessary ingredients for an effective informative speech include:

- *A well-organized introduction that previews the main points* and a conclusion that concisely summarizes them will help listeners anticipate and remember information (see **CHAPTER 8**).

- *Clear transitions.* Signal words, phrases, and sentences that tie speech ideas together are especially important when listeners are learning new information.

- *An appropriate organizational pattern* can help listeners mentally organize ideas and see relationships among them.[7]

- *Presentation aids.* People process and retain information best when they hear it *and* see related (but not duplicated) information, as, for instance, in charts and diagrams (see **CHAPTERS 15–17**).

CHECKLIST
Help Listeners Follow Along
Audience members cannot put the speaker on "pause" in order to digest information, so help them stay on track:
• Preview main points in the introduction, and state what you hope listeners will gain from the speech.
• Use *internal previews* to forecast key points and *internal summaries* to reinforce them.
• Use transitions to help the audience follow the logical flow of ideas.
• Use repetition and parallel structure to help listeners grasp and retain key ideas and concepts.
• Choose an organizational pattern that suits the material.
• Reinforce your message with effective presentation aids.

■ Categories of Informative Speeches

Informative speeches are sometimes categorized according to the types of subject matter they address. Thus an informative speech may be about objects or phenomena, people, events, processes, issues, or concepts. These are not hard-and-fast divisions—a speech can be about both the *process* of dance and the *people* who perform it, for example—but they show the range of informative subjects and can point to a logical organizational pattern.

Speeches about Objects or Phenomena

Speeches about objects or phenomena explore anything that isn't human; it can be animate, as in the animal kingdom, or inanimate, as in electronic devices or sports equipment. Topics for such speeches run the gamut from ribbons used to raise awareness about diseases to therapy dogs and the making of a musical score. Phenomena such as new inventions, the history of graphic novels, and the evolution of "Texas English" belong to this broad category.

Speeches about People

Speeches about people inform audiences about individuals and groups who have made contributions to society (both positive and negative) or those who for one reason or another we simply find compelling. For example, what inspired Reshma Saujani to found Girls Who Code, and motivate more women to pursue careers in computing and engineering fields?

Speeches about people may also be autobiographical. Each of us has stories to tell, and if they express common themes—love, loss, growth, the overcoming of obstacles—audience members will be drawn in. The key to delivering an effective speech about yourself or another person is to provide a "lesson" that audience members can take away from the speech. How did the person face and overcome obstacles? What steps did the person take on the road to achievement? What human qualities harmed or helped the person? What turning points were noteworthy?

Speeches about Events

Speeches about events focus on noteworthy occurrences, past and present. What was the time line of the 2011 Egyptian opposition protests, and what is the state of freedom today in Egypt? Speeches about events rely on **reportage**—an account of the who, what, where, when, and why of the facts. The key to a speech about an event is to offer new insights and information about the event, and to shed light on its meaning. For example, what was the **backstory**—the story that leads up to the event that listeners might find interesting—that led to the online posting of NSA secrets by Edward Snowden involving thousands of classified U.S. military intelligence documents? Giving audience members "behind the scenes" information is a guaranteed way of catching their attention.

Speeches about Processes

Speeches about processes refer to a series of steps that lead to a finished product or end result. In this type of speech, you can talk about how something is done, how it is made, or how it works. How do hybrid cars operate? What steps are involved in interviewing for a job?

When discussing a process, you can either explain how something works or develops (*How do baby penguins develop?*) or actually teach audience members to perform the process (*how to make a quilt*). When describing how to do something, you might perform the actual task during the speech, demonstrating each step as you describe it, or use presentation aids to illustrate the steps involved. Presentation aids, from slides to models to the actual thing being demonstrated, often accompany speeches about processes (see **CHAPTER 15**, "Speaking with Presentation Aids").

Speeches about Issues

An *issue* is a problem or a matter in dispute, one that people seek to bring to a conclusion. Informative *speeches about issues* provide an overview or a report of problems in order to raise awareness and deepen understanding. The high cost of college, and the obesity epidemic in the United States are examples of issues that might be addressed in an informative speech.

Of the various types of informative speeches, speeches about issues have the greatest potential of "crossing the line" into the persuasive realm. Yet as long as your goal is to inform rather than to advocate, you can legitimately address issues in an informative speech. Thus, in a speech on immigration law, you might describe current immigration laws at the state and federal levels and discuss Supreme Court rulings. On the other hand, you would refrain from advocating for or against reforms to existing immigration policy.

Speeches about Concepts

A final category, *speeches about concepts,* focuses on abstract or complex ideas, theories, or beliefs and attempt to make them concrete and understandable to an audience. What is chaos theory? What do Hindus believe? We've heard the term *hate speech,* but we're confused because it seems to encompass everything from racist expressions to racist actions. Because they address abstract or complex ideas, speeches about concepts have the potential to confuse audience members. To ensure that this does not occur, follow the guidelines in "Take Steps to Reduce Confusion" later in this chapter (**p. 185**).

■ Decide How to Convey the Information

Whether in conversation, writing, or speeches, typically we communicate information by *defining, describing, demonstrating,* and/or *explaining* it. Some informative speeches rely almost exclusively on a single approach (e.g., their main purpose is to *demonstrate* how something works or to *explain* what something means). Many speeches, however, combine strategies within a presentation (see **TABLE 10.1**). As you prepare your speech, ask yourself, "How much emphasis should I give to defining my topic, demonstrating it, describing it, or explaining its meaning?"

Definition

Some informative topics clearly require more definition than others. When you *define* information, you identify the essential qualities and meaning of something. Consider, for example, these speech topics: What is cholesterol? What is a fractal? What is the Americans with Disabilities Act?

When your topic is new to the audience or is a complex concept (*"What is a fractal?"*), pay particular attention to providing clear definitions. Definition can also be necessary when clarifying a controversial idea or issue. For example, many of us are aware that affirmative action is a strategy to provide special opportunities for underrepresented groups, but how many people know about the *Fisher* decision that ruled it unlawful for colleges to use affirmative action as an admissions criteria?

Defining information may sound straightforward, but there are in fact a number of ways to define something, including the following:

- Defining the topic by explaining what it does (**operational definition**); for example, *A computer is something that processes information.*

- Defining the topic by describing what it is not (**definition by negation**); for example, *Courage is not the absence of fear.*

- Defining the topic by providing several concrete examples (**definition by example**); for example, *Health professionals include doctors, nurses, EMTs, and ambulance drivers.*

- Defining the topic by comparing it to something with which it is synonymous (**definition by synonym**); for example, *A friend is a comrade or a buddy.*

- Defining the topic by illustrating the root meaning of the word in question (**definition by etymology [word origin]**); for example, *The word* rival *derives from the Latin word* rivalis, *"one living near or using the same stream."*[8]

TABLE 10.1 Types of Informative Speeches and Sample Topics

SUBJECT MATTER	SAMPLE TOPICS
Objects or phenomena Define and describe object or phenomenon Demonstrate properties and functions	• MRI-based lie detectors • e-book readers • Liquid-filled eyeglasses • El Niño wind patterns in the western United States
People Vividly describe person's compelling characteristics and explain person's significance Offer stories about overcoming obstacles and lessons to be drawn from person's actions	• Athletes • Authors • Inventors • Political leaders • Soldiers • War or hurricane refugees
Current or historical events Use description to paint a vivid picture Use reporting and analysis Tell the backstory	• The Affordable Care Act • National College Cheerleading Finals • Battle of Britain • Violence along U.S./Mexico border
Speeches about processes If physically showing a process, rely on demonstration Use presentation aids	• Isolation of DNA in cells • Visualization in sports • Production of algae-based biofuels • Power Yoga routine
Speeches about issues Focus on explanation Avoid advocating for one position versus another	• Impact of long-term unemployment • Managing your reputation on social networking sites • Legalizing and taxing nonmedical marijuana
Speeches about concepts Offer multiple definitions Use analogies Discuss underlying processes/causes	• Chaos theory • Free speech • Responsible knowledge • Nanotechnology

Description

Some speech topics, such as an overview of postwar architecture in Rotterdam, call for a good deal of description. When you *describe* information, you provide an array of details that paint a mental picture of your topic. For example, you might offer your audience a "virtual tour" of the top of Mount Everest, or describe the physical ravages wrought by drug abuse. The point of speeches, or sections of speeches, relying on description is to offer a vivid portrayal of the topic.

Demonstration

Yet another approach to presenting information is to explain how something works or to actually *demonstrate* it. The many "how-to" television shows and podcasts on the Web, ranging from step-by-step guides to home remodeling to using software programs, rely on demonstration. A speech may not include an actual physical demonstration, but the speaker will nevertheless verbally demonstrate the steps involved. Speeches that rely on demonstration often work with the actual object, representations or models of it, or visual aids that diagram it. TABLE 10.2 contains sample topics for a speech using demonstration.

Explanation

A final, and very common, tool for conveying information is *explanation*. Certain informative speech topics are built on explanation—providing reasons or causes, demonstrating relationships, and offering interpretation and analysis. The classroom lecture is a classic example of using explanation in an informative context. But many kinds of speeches rely on explanation, from those that address difficult or confusing theories and processes such as *What is the relationship between the glycemic index and glycemic load?* to topics that challenge conventional thinking (*Why do researchers say that sometimes emotion makes us more rather than less logical?*)

See the checklist on p. 186 for strategies for explaining complex processes.

TABLE 10.2

SAMPLE TOPICS FOR A SPEECH USING DEMONSTRATION
• Treating a burn
• Posting videos on YouTube
• How muscles work
• How clouds are formed
• Programming an iPhone
• Performing the Heimlich maneuver on infants
• Performing an emergency tracheotomy
• Organizing topics on Pinterest
• Doing genealogy on the Web

■ Take Steps to Reduce Confusion

New information can be hard to grasp, especially when it addresses a difficult concept or term (such as *equilibrium* in engineering), a difficult-to-envision process (such as *cash-flow management* in business), or a counterintuitive idea—one that challenges commonsense thinking (such as *drinking a glass of red wine a day can be healthy*).[9]

Useful for most any speech, the following strategies for communicating information are especially helpful when attempting to clarify complex ideas.

Use Analogies to Build on Prior Knowledge

Audience members will understand a new concept more easily if the speaker uses an **analogy** to relate it to something that they already know. Indeed, the process of learning itself is sometimes defined as constructing new knowledge from prior knowledge.[10] By linking the unfamiliar with the familiar through an analogy, you will give your listeners an easier way to venture into new territory. For example, to explain the unpredictable paths that satellites often take when they fall to Earth, you can liken the effect to dropping a penny into water: "Sometimes it goes straight down, and sometimes it turns end over end and changes direction. The same thing happens when an object hits the atmosphere."[11]

You can organize part or even all of a speech around an analogy. When explaining how the thyroid functions, for instance, you could liken it to a conductor directing a symphony (the body).[12] Bear in mind, however, that no analogy can exactly represent another concept; at a certain point, the similarities will end.[13] Therefore, you may need to alert listeners to the limits of the comparison. The statement "The heart is like a pump, *except that the heart actually changes size as it pushes blood out*" demonstrates that, though similar, a heart and a pump are not the same.[14]

In the following excerpt from a speech about nanotechnology, Wolfgang Porod explains the size of a nanometer by comparing it to the diameter of the moon. Note how he attempts to reduce confusion by first defining the root *nano* and then comparing it to the size of the moon:

> What is a nano and what is special about a nano? *Nano* is a prefix derived from the Greek word for dwarf and it means one billionth of something. So a nanosecond is a billionth of a second. A nanometer is a billionth of a meter. Now, just saying that doesn't really tell you that much. So what does it mean to have the length scale of a billionth of a meter? Well, imagine the diameter of the moon. It just happens to be, roughly...a billion meters. So take that and shrink it down to the length scale of a meter, which is what it means to go a billion size scales. So a nanometer is a billionth of a meter.[15]

Demonstrate Underlying Causes

Listeners may fail to understand a process because they believe that something "obviously" works a certain way when in fact it does not. To counter faulty assumptions, first acknowledge common misperceptions and then offer an accurate explanation of underlying causes.[16]

CHECKLIST
Strategies for Explaining Complex Information
To explain a concept or term:
• Build on prior knowledge.
• Use analogies that link concepts to something familiar.
• Define terms in several ways (e.g., by example, by what it is not).
• Simplify terminology wherever possible.
• Check for understanding.
To explain a complex process or structure:
• All of the above, and:
• Make ample use of visual aids, including models and drawings.
• Make the topic fun.
To explain a counterintuitive idea:
• All of the above, and:
• Address the commonly held assumption first, acknowledge its plausibility, and then demonstrate its limitations using familiar examples.

Appeal to Different Learning Styles

Audience members are more likely to follow your points if you reinforce them with other media. The reason for this is that people have different learning styles, or preferred ways of processing information. One learning theory model suggests four such preferences: visual, aural, read/write, and kinesthetic.[17] *Visual learners* will most quickly grasp ideas by viewing visual explanations of them, either through pictures, diagrams, slides, or videos. Understanding for *aural learners* comes most easily through the spoken word, by hearing and speaking. *Read/write learners* are most comfortable processing information that is text-based. *Kinesthetic learners* learn best by experiencing information directly, through real-life demonstrations, simulations, and hands-on experience. Some of us are *multimodal learners,* in that we combine two or more preferences.

Audience analysis can sometimes give you a sense of the types of learners in an audience. For example, mechanics of all types have strong spatial visualization abilities and thus would be classified as visual learners; they may also be kinesthetic learners who want to "test" things for themselves. Often, however, you may not have enough information to determine your listeners' learning style, so *plan on conveying and reinforcing information in a variety of modes.* In your speech, use charts, diagrams, and other visual representations of ideas to appeal to visual learners. Use colorful and concrete language and strong examples and stories that will engage aural listeners.

Prepare text-based slides containing main ideas (but beware of crowding; see **p. 251**) and, if appropriate, consider distributing handouts at the end of your speech. Use demonstration to appeal to kinesthetic learners. TABLE 10.3 offers guidelines for presenting information to different types of learners.

Arrange Speech Points in a Pattern

Informative speeches can be organized using topical, chronological, spatial, cause-effect, comparative advantage, and narrative patterns. (Note that although the problem-solution pattern may be used in informative speeches, it often is a more logical candidate for persuasive speeches.)

TABLE 10.3 **Communicating Information to Different Types of Learners**

TYPE	ADVICE FOR COMMUNICATING INFORMATION
Visual	Will most easily grasp ideas communicated through pictures, diagrams, charts, graphs, flowcharts, or maps.
Aural	Will most easily grasp ideas communicated through the spoken word, whether in live lectures, tapes, group discussions, or podcasts.
Read/Write	Will most easily grasp ideas communicated through text-based delivery, handouts, or PowerPoint with text-based slides.
Kinesthetic	Will most easily grasp ideas communicated through real-life demonstrations, simulations, movies, and hands-on applications.

There are any number of ways to organize the various types of informative speeches. A speech about the Impressionist movement in painting, for example, could be organized *chronologically,* in which main points are arranged in sequence from the movement's early period to its later falling out of favor (subpoints can assume a different pattern than that of main points). It could be organized *causally* (cause-effect), by demonstrating that it came about as a reaction to the art movement that preceded it. It could also be organized *topically* (by categories), by focusing on the major figures associated with the movement, famous paintings linked to it, and notable contemporary artists who painted in the style.

Following are some possible pairings of speech types and organizational patterns:

> Objects—spatial, topical
>
> People—topical, narrative, chronological
>
> Events—topical, chronological, causal, narrative
>
> Processes—chronological, spatial, causal
>
> Concepts—topical, causal
>
> Issues—topical, chronological, causal

In a speech describing how to buy a guitar, Richard Garza organizes his main points chronologically:

Thesis Statement:	Buying and caring for a guitar involves knowing what to look for when purchasing it and understanding how to maintain it once you own it.
Main Points:	I. Decide what kind of guitar you need.
	II. Inspect the guitar for potential flaws.
	III. Maintain the guitar.

In a student speech on using radiofrequency waves to cure cancer, David Kruckenberg organizes his main points topically, dividing his points by categories:

Thesis Statement:	An engineer outside of the medical establishment discovers how to refine a medical procedure called radiofrequency ablation, potentially making it a critical tool in the fight against certain kinds of cancer.
Main Points:	I. Radiofrequency ablation, as currently practiced to treat cancer, poses risks to patients.
	II. Kanzius's invention uses nanoparticles to improve upon ablation.
	III. Kanzius's discovery is currently being tested in several large medical research centers.

CHECKLIST
Guidelines for Clearly Communicating Your Informative Message
In your introduction, tell audience members what you hope they will learn by listening to you.
•   Stress the topic's relevance to your listeners.
•   Use definition, description, explanation, and demonstration to convey your ideas.
•   Use analogies to make your examples familiar to the audience.
•   Choose an organizational pattern based on your communication goals, the nature of your topic, and the needs of your audience.
•   Use presentation aids to reinforce your points.

SAMPLE VISUALLY ANNOTATED
INFORMATIVE SPEECH

Freeganism: More Than a Free Lunch

DJ McCabe

This informative speech by DJ McCabe describes a movement or cause that might be unfamiliar to his audience. To ensure understanding, he is careful to define any potentially confusing or unknown terms, including, of course, the topic term freeganism. DJ provides a short but effective preview of his thesis and main points, which serves both to create interest in the topic and to signal how the speech will be organized—in this case topically. With strong supporting material in the form of examples and statistics and a compelling conclusion based on a story of a real-life freegan, DJ is able to convey a great deal of information in an engaging way.

DJ starts the speech by asking the audience a question.

How many people in this audience consider themselves—or know someone who is—vegetarian? How about vegan? [1] If you're not familiar with veganism, it's the form of strict vegetarianism in which individuals do not eat food containing any animal products, including dairy, eggs, or honey. Although some vegans choose this dietary lifestyle for health reasons, most do so for ideological reasons, ranging from a commitment to animal rights to concerns about pollution resulting from animal farming. [2]

Gestures help DJ define new terms.

To many of you, this may seem like an extreme lifestyle choice. However, there are people who take things a step beyond veganism. How many of you are familiar with the term *freegan*? According to the website Freegan.info, *freegan* is a combination of *free* and *vegan*. Freegans look for free products—from food to furniture—to minimize the impact of human consumerism on both the planet and other people. In fact, not all freegans are vegan; it is the "free" part that is key. Freegans oppose our consumer culture, in which we buy things we don't need and throw away things that are still usable.

Animated facial expressions help DJ connect with the audience.

During this presentation, I will introduce you to the freegan lifestyle—what the Freegan.info website defines as "living based on limited participation in" capitalism and "minimal consumption of resources." [3] I will first describe a few of the ways that freegans try to minimize their use of resources, then discuss the reasons why some people choose to live this way, and finally explore some legitimate criticisms of the freegan lifestyle.

First, the heart of freeganism is a commitment to using fewer resources, and one way to do that is to throw away less trash. [4] As reported in a 2007 article in the *New York Times* by Steven Kurutz, the Environmental Protection Agency found that we throw away nearly 250 million tons of trash per year, which translates to over 4 pounds on average, per person, every single day. Two freegan practices—waste minimization and waste reclamation—specifically deal with trash and seek to reduce the amount of garbage Americans produce every year.

Many of us already support one of the tenets of freeganism—*waste minimization*—through recycling; hopefully everyone in this room today will take the time to throw their empty plastic

1. Beginning the speech with a rhetorical question is an effective attention-getter, especially since most people do know someone who is vegetarian.

2. DJ takes care to define terms that may not be familiar to the audience, or about which they have an incomplete understanding.

3. Here is DJ's preview statement, in which he states the thesis and main points. He also signals how he will organize the speech—in this case topically, or by focusing on different categories of his topic.

4. DJ uses the signal word "first" to transition into the body of the speech.

5. Even though this is an informative speech, it contains elements of persuasion, just as persuasive speeches also inform.

6. DJ provides plenty of concrete examples that both enlarge understanding and add color and interest.

7. DJ encourages engagement in his topic by showing the topic's relevance to the audience members' own lives.

8. DJ continues to directly engage listeners, this time by acknowledging that most in the audience probably wouldn't engage in the more radical practices of freeganism.

9. When citing this finding DJ should have mentioned the name of the publication, which is the journal *Agricultural Research*.

10. DJ offers trustworthy sources throughout the speech.

11. This rhetorical question serves as an effective transition to the next point.

water bottles and soda cans into a recycling container. [5] But minimizing waste isn't just about recycling. Freegans also reuse everything they can, like using that old mayonnaise jar to hold pens and pencils instead of buying a specially designed pencil holder; this option reduces the demand for resources to make the specialty item and also eliminates the need for energy consumed during recycling. [6]

DJ's warm demeanor sparks interest in the topic.

Waste reclamation is just a formal term for what many of us know affectionately as "Dumpster diving." You've engaged in this truly free acquisition of items that other people have thrown away if you furnished your dorm or apartment with a chair or a bookcase that someone left on the curb or in a Dumpster. [7] But would you consider making your meals out of what other people throw away? Freegans do.[8] In his article on food waste, Robert Fireovid notes a U.S. Department of Agriculture finding: In 2008, the amount of food wasted by restaurants and stores averaged 275 pounds per American, not including what we throw away at home. [9] For freegans, this is unnecessary waste, and so they will reclaim any still-edible food along with other household items.

DJ checks his note cards when citing data

If you think it sounds gross to eat food that has been thrown away by someone else, there are certainly legitimate worries about illness from spoiled food. At the same time, recent research shows that a lot of the food thrown away by grocery stores, for example, is perfectly safe to eat. A 2013 report published by the Natural Resources Defense Council and the Harvard Law School Food Law and Policy Clinic noted that $900 million in food was thrown away by retailers in 2001 because the date listed on the product had expired. [10] Those date labels often refer to the date until which the product will retain its highest quality, not necessarily the date after which the food is no longer safe to eat. That same report confirms that "the FDA's Center for Food Safety and Applied Nutrition has noted that most foods, when kept in optimal storage conditions, are safe to eat and of acceptable quality for periods of time past the label date."

Yet even if freegans reclaim wasted food safely and are mindful of their health, *why* would people who could afford to buy food *choose* to dig it out of the trash? [11]

As defined at the beginning of my presentation, freegans try to avoid participating in capitalism, which they believe to be inherently exploitative. As the Freegan.info website puts it, "Instead of avoiding the purchase of products from one bad company only to support another, we avoid buying anything to the greatest degree we are able." Although many health- and environmentally conscious people choose to shop at certain stores so that they can buy organic or fair-trade goods, freegans see even those efforts as problematic choices. Organic and fair-trade products still need to be shipped to stores, consuming fossil fuels and producing exhaust emissions in the process. And given the amount of food wasted unnecessarily in the United States, freegans feel an ethical obligation not to contribute to increased consumer demand when so much of the existing supply is already unused.

DJ uses slides with graphics.

Despite their noble commitment to environmentalism and advocacy of a more humane economic system, freegans are not without critics. In some cities, Dumpster diving is

Maintaining strong eye contact, DJ explains his points.

illegal under municipal codes against trespassing and vandalism, although those laws are not often enforced against people "reclaiming" waste from Dumpsters unless the divers create a mess or property owners actively seek to have anti-trespassing laws applied. Harsher objections come from critics who argue that the freegan lifestyle does little to help the truly impoverished and may literally take food out of their mouths. In the words of Jerry Adler in a 2007 *Newsweek* article, "The freegans, most of whom are educated and capable of contributing to the economy, aren't sharing the surplus wealth of the West with those who are destitute by circumstance rather than choice. They are competing with them for it." Given both the small number of Americans who choose to live as freegans and the enormous amount of food wasted in this country, freegans are not very likely to consume all of the still-edible food thrown away by stores and restaurants. But their small numbers also mean they are not likely to have a significant impact on the environmental and economic problems their freegan lifestyle hopes to combat.

During this speech, I have introduced you to the subculture of freegans in the United States. [12] Through their practices of waste minimization and waste reclamation, freegans hope to avoid the negative impacts of capitalist consumption on both the environment and people. Whether freegans are prophets of a better world or naive idealists living on other people's trash remains an open question, but I hope that the next time you see someone exploring a Dumpster behind a supermarket, you remember that some people do so by choice rather than because it is their only option. And so I want to close by introducing you to one woman who made that choice.

12. DJ signals the conclusion of the speech.

DJ closes the speech with a quotation.

As described in the 2007 *New York Times* article by Steven Kurutz, Madeline Nelson lived a life to which many of us aspire, making over $100,000 per year as a communications director for Barnes & Noble bookstores. Frustrated that her job and daily life continued to reinforce the rat race of buying "stuff" only to throw it away before buying more, in 2005 Ms. Nelson sold her posh Manhattan apartment in favor of a small place in Brooklyn and quit her corporate job so she could live as a freegan. When asked if she misses the extravagances that once filled her life, she responds, "Most people work 40-plus hours a week at jobs they don't like to buy things they don't need." We might not wish to become freegans ourselves, but Madeline's life is quite literally food for thought. [13]

13. Concluding the speech with a real-life story of a freegan gives the topic even more relevance and leaves the audience with something to think about.

References

Adler, J. (2007, October). The noble scavenger on the living-room couch. *Newsweek, 150*(14), 48.

Fireovid, Robert L. (2013). Wasted food: What we are doing to prevent costly losses. *Agricultural Research, 61*(3), 2.

Kurutz, Steven. (2007, June 21). Not buying it. *The New York Times.* Retrieved from www.lexis-nexis.com

Leib, E. B., Gunders, D., Ferro, J., Nielsen, A., Nosek, G., & Qu, J. (2013, September). *The dating game: How confusing food date labels lead to food waste in America.* Retrieved from www.nrdc.org/food/files/dating-game-report.pdf

What is a freegan? (n.d.). Retrieved from http://freegan.info

SAMPLE VISUALLY ANNOTATED INFORMATIVE SPEECH

Social Media, Social Identity, and Social Causes

Anna Davis

The following informative speech by student Anna Davis may be characterized as a speech about both a concept and a phenomenon (see pp. 180, 182). The concept is social identity theory, which Anna uses to explain the contemporary phenomenon of promoting social causes on the Internet.

Anna makes ample use of definition and explanation to ensure her audience understands the theory and the terms used in her speech. She also offers analogies to make her explanations easier to understand. Note too her frequent use of transitions to help listeners follow along and her careful citation of sources. Anna's speech is organized topically, in which she focuses on different subsets or categories of the topic. Topical arrangements give you the greatest freedom to structure main points according to the way you wish to present your information.

1. This attention-getter works because it references something familiar to nearly everyone in a college-age audience.

Just before my first year of college, I was excited and nervous about meeting other new students on campus.

As soon as dorm assignments were announced, we all began "friending" each other on Facebook and following each other on Twitter. [1] This is how I found out that my roommate was an obsessive soccer fan and had seen all of Quentin Tarantino's movies. The school also sponsored online forums, allowing me to learn about different student groups and to find like-minded people across campus. For example, I connected immediately with students who share my interest in animal rescue and adoption. [2] These online connections and groups helped my college friendships develop quickly and meaningfully, and gave me a sense of belonging on campus before I even arrived.

2. A personal example can help establish the speaker's ethos, or credibility. This particular example also relates to the main theme of the speech, which deals with social identity and the answer to the question "Who am I?"

3. A preview statement, with brief mention of each main point, helps listeners mentally organize and anticipate the entire speech.

Today I'd like to share with you how social media is being used, not only to help students connect but also as a powerful tool to advance social causes and motivate us to act on their behalf. We'll start by looking at a compelling theory of why social media is so uniquely suited to forging connections. Next, I'll review some data on social media's meteoric rise. Finally, we'll see how today's activists are harnessing social media to support an array of social causes to make life better for us all. [3]

Anna begins her speech enthusiastically with a personal story.

4. Anna clearly signals her transition into the body of the speech with the signal phrase "Let's begin" and a rhetorical question.

Let's begin our conversation about these intriguing developments in communication by considering the underlying reasons why we want to use social media in the first place. What is it that drives us to connect through social media with like-minded people and groups? [4]

5. Anna defines technical terms used within the speech; she can then refer to them later with the assurance that the audience will understand precisely what she means.

Social identity theory offers a compelling answer to this question. First, let me define the concept of social identity. *Social identity* refers to how you understand yourself in relation to your group memberships. [5] Michael Hogg, a professor of social psychology at Claremont University, focuses on social identity research. In his 2006 book on contemporary social psychological

Using animated facial expressions, Anna keeps the audience engaged.

theories, Hogg explains that group affiliations provide us with an important source of identity, and we therefore want our groups to be valued positively in relation to other groups. [6] By "affiliations" I simply mean the groups that we join and perhaps link to online. [7]

Social psychologist Henry Tajfel—one of the founders of social identity theory—spent years considering how we form our social identities. Tajfel believes that the groups to which we attach ourselves, both online and off, help answer the very important question, Who am I? According to Tajfel's 1979 book *The Social Psychology of Intergroup Relations,* we associate with certain groups to help resolve the anxiety brought about by this fundamental question of identity. By selecting certain groups and not others, we define who we are and develop a sense of belonging in the social world. Social media sites such as Facebook provide a platform for this type of social identity formation by offering participants certain tools, such as the ability to "friend" people, groups, and even brands, and to "like" certain posts. The simple act of friending, for example, promotes social affiliation between two individuals, and our Facebook friends are collectively a source of social identity. Because we are proclaiming something important to our groups, announcing that we are in a serious relationship takes on great social significance. [8] As we all know, it's not official until it's "Facebook official." [9]

Gesturing at her slides, Anna explains the graph.

As you can see, social identity theory gives us insight into the reasons behind the popularity of social media sites: They let us proclaim to ourselves and the world, "This is who I am." Even so, the near miraculous rate of growth of these sites over the past decade is surprising. [10]

According to Marcia Clemmit's 2010 *CQ Researcher* article on social networking, Facebook had over one million members in 2005—just one year after its launch. This growth from zero to a million in one year was quite an impressive feat. Today, according to a May 2013 article on the number of active Facebook users published by the Associated Press, Facebook harbors over 1.16 billion members. That's almost four times the population of the United States. [11] Like Facebook, Twitter's growth has also been astronomical. Shea Bennett, editor of the Mediabistro-sponsored blog *AllTwitter,* reports in an October 2013 article that Twitter had 218 million active users at the end of June 2013. Like Facebook, its success can be largely attributed to the demand for virtual communities that enable users to connect with one another.

Anna uses strong eye contact while making her point.

As the data clearly show, people around the world are defining themselves socially and answering the question, "Who am I?" through the use of social media sites. [12] And social movement organizations have taken note. Organizations of all kinds are using social media to get their messages across to global consumers and spur their members into action.

Anna checks her notecards when relaying facts.

Social movements, defined by Princeton.edu as "a group of people with a common ideology who try together to achieve certain general goals," range across the political and social spectrum. Consider Occupy Wall Street and

6. Offering explanations from an expert on the topic helps establish credibility for your speech.

7. Anna remembers to define an ambiguous term.

8. Applying the key terms of the theory, Anna offers concrete explanations of how we create social identity online. This gives the listener a deeper understanding of the social media phenomena being discussed.

9. Taking a common phrase used by your peers, such as "Facebook official," encourages identification with the topic and speaker.

10. Anna offers a helpful internal summary of her points thus far and signals that she will transition to her next point.

11. It's important to present statistics in ways that make sense for listeners—for example, using analogies and comparison. Here, Anna compares the large number of Facebook users to the population of the United States, making the abstract figure "1.16 billion" concrete.

12. The subtle repetition of "Who am I?" reinforces the thesis of the speech.

13. An informative speech calls for balanced and unbiased examples.

the Tea Party. [13] Both of these organizations communicate their messages and build support through social media sites. For example they use Facebook to announce events and link to petitions. In fact, a nonprofit organization called Social Movement Technologies created a Facebook page to help individual social movement organizations get out their message.

14. Here, Anna uses an internal summary to review her points thus far and an internal preview for her next main point.

But social media is not just being used as a platform for informing the public of a group's mission and activities, or even merely to get people to sign petitions. Increasingly, activists are deploying social media to motivate like-minded people to get into the fight. To get a sense of what this means, consider the recent efforts of a seventeen-year-old skateboarder from St. Cloud, Minnesota. [14]

Using a real-life story, Anna connects to the audience.

For three years, Austin Lee found himself struggling to get support for a skate park in his local community. But when he decided to use Facebook for his cause, things changed nearly overnight. Lee's posting attracted 1,085 members, and even drew a portion of those members to city council meetings on behalf of his cause. David Unze of *USA Today* reported that Lee won the approval—and $500,000—for his skate park (2010). And it all happened within one day of Lee's original posting on Facebook.

So as you can see, if you can use social media to convince people to identify with what you want to accomplish, success is possible. Lee's accomplishment shows us that we not only identify and affiliate ourselves with groups, but also are willing to actively work toward accomplishing their goals.

15. Anna signals the close of the speech with the phrase, "Today I hope I've shown…"

[15] Today I hope I've shown that the skyrocketing use of social media sites over the past decade is no accident. The human desire to develop a positive sense of social identity through group affiliation is one reason for this phenomenon. Capitalizing on this universal psychological drive, social movement organizations are harnessing these technologies to accomplish their goals. Social media sites allow us to communicate, express, and identify with one another in ways that encourage affiliation as well as action. Whether it's a major political movement or a teenager's desire for a local skate park, social media technologies are powerful. [16]

16. Anna concludes by briefly summarizing the main points.

Concluding her speech, Anna ends on a warm note.

17. Finishing on a strong note, Anna leaves the audience with something to think about.

So as you tweet about new groups or see the next "Facebook official" status update, think about what groups you like, whom you have friended, and what those affiliations may be able to do for you. See you online! [17]

References

Associated Press. (2013, May 1). Number of active users at Facebook over the years. *Yahoo! News.* Retrieved from http://news.yahoo.com/number-active-users-facebook-over-230449748.html

Bennett, S. (2013, October 4). How many active users does Twitter have, and how fast is it growing? [Web log post]. Retrieved October 16, 2013, from www.mediabistro.com/alltwitter/tag/twitter-active-users

Brenner, J., & Smith, A. (2013, August 5). 72% of online adults are social networking site users. *Pew Internet and American Life Project.* Retrieved from www.pewinternet.org/~/media//Files/Reports/2013/PIP_Social_networking_sites_update.pdf

Clemmitt, M. (2010, September 17). Social networking. *CQ Researcher, 20*(32). Retrieved August 17, 2013, from www.cqpress.com/product/Researcher-Social-Networking-v20-32.html

Constine, J. (2012, February 12). Pinterest hits 10 million U.S. monthly uniques faster than any standalone site ever. [Web log post]. Retrieved August 17, 2013, from http://techcrunch.com/2012/02/07/pinterest-monthly-uniques

Hogg, M. (2006). Social identity theory. In P. J. Burke (Ed.), *Contemporary social psychological theories* (pp. 111–136). Palo Alto, CA: Stanford University Press.

Lipsman, A. (2011, August 30). Tumblr defies its name as user growth accelerates. [Web log post]. Retrieved August 17, 2013, from www.comscore.com/Insights/Blog/Tumblr_Defies_its_Name_as_User_Growth_Accelerates

Madden, M., Lenhart, A., Cortesi, S., Gasser, U., Duggan, M., Smith, A., & Beaton, M. (2013, May 21). Teens, social media, and privacy. *Pew Internet and American Life Project.* Retrieved from www.pewinternet.org/Reports/2013/Teens-Social-Media-And-Privacy.aspx

Occupy Wall Street. (n.d.). In *Facebook* [Group page]. Retrieved August 17, 2013, from www.facebook.com/OccupyWallSt Social movement. (n.d.). *Wordnetweb.Princeton.edu.* Retrieved from http://wordnetweb.princeton.edu/perl/webwn?s=social%20movement

Social Movement Technologies. (n.d.). In *Facebook* [Group page]. Retrieved August 17, 2013, from www.facebook.com/SocialMovementTechnologies

Tajfel, H., & Turner, J. C. (1979). An integrative theory of intergroup conflict. *The social psychology of intergroup relations*, v. 33, p. 47.

The Tea Party (n.d.). In *Facebook* [Group page]. Retrieved August 17, 2013, from www.facebook.com/TheTeaParty.net

Twitter. (2011, March 14). #numbers. [Web log post]. Retrieved from https://blog.twitter.com/2011/numbers

Unze, D. (2010, March 26). Facebook helps spark movements. *USA Today.* Retrieved from http://usatoday30.usatoday.com/news/nation/2010-03-25-facebook_N.htm

Chapter 11

Citing Sources in Your Speech

This chapter is taken from Dan O'Hair, Rob Stewart, and Hannah Rubenstein, *A Speaker's Guidebook*, Sixth Edition, pp. 153–163 (Chapter 10).

If you've ever challenged a speeding ticket in traffic court, you may not be surprised to learn that people rarely win their appeals without offering strong evidence to support their case.[1] Much the same can be said of convincing audience members to accept your speech points. Research confirms that when you back up your claims with evidence, audience members are more likely to process and accept them than if you make unsupported assertions.[2] Alerting the audience to the sources you use, as well as offering ones that they will find authoritative, is thus a critical aspect of delivering a speech or presentation. When you credit speech sources, you:

- Increase the odds that audience members will believe in your message.

- Demonstrate the quality and range of your research to listeners.

- Demonstrate that reliable sources support your position.

- Avoid plagiarism and gain credibility as an ethical speaker who acknowledges the work of others.

- Enhance your own authority.

- Enable listeners to locate your sources and pursue their own research on the topic.

Ethically you are bound to attribute any information drawn from other people's ideas, opinions, and theories—as well as any facts and statistics gathered by others—to their original sources. Remember, you need not credit sources for ideas that are *common knowledge*— established information likely to be known by many people and described in multiple places.

■ Alert Listeners to Key Source Information

An **oral citation** credits the source of speech material that is derived from other people's ideas. During your speech, always cite your sources at the same time as you present the information derived from them, rather than waiting until the end of the speech to disclose them to the audience. For each source, plan on briefly alerting the audience to the following:

1. The *author* or *origin of the source* ("documentary filmmaker Morgan Spurlock..." or "On the *National Science Foundation website...*")

2. The *type of source* (journal article, book, personal interview, website, blog, online video, etc.)

3. The *title* or a *description of the source* ("In the book *Endangered Minds...*" or "In *an article on sharks...*")

4. The *date of the source* ("The article, published in the *October 10th, 2014*, issue..." or "According to a report on financing student loans, posted online on September 28, 2014, on the *Daily Beast...*")

Of course, spoken citations need not include a complete bibliographic reference (exact titles, full names of all authors, volume and page numbers); doing so will interrupt the flow of your presentation and distract listeners' attention. However, do keep a running list of source details for a bibliography to appear at the end of your speech draft or outline. (For guidelines on creating a written bibliography for your speeches, see Appendices B, C and G–I). In place of bibliographic details, focus on presenting your sources in a rhetorically effective manner—that is, in a way that will encourage audience members to process and believe in the source material.

■ Establish the Source's Trustworthiness

Too often, inexperienced speakers credit their sources in bare-bones fashion, offering a rote recitation of citation elements. For example, they might cite the publication name and date but leave out key details, such that the source is a leading authority in his or her field, that could convince the audience to accept the source as reliable and its conclusions as true. Discerning listeners will accept as legitimate the supporting materials you offer for your claims—examples, stories, testimony, facts, and statistics—only if they believe that the sources are reliable and accurate, or credible.

Source reliability refers to our level of trust in a source's credentials and track record for providing accurate information. If you support a scientific claim by crediting it to an unknown student's personal blog, for example, listeners won't find it nearly as reliable as if you credited it to a scientist affiliated with a reputable institution.

While a source that is reliable is usually accurate, this is not always so.[3] Sometimes we have information that contradicts what we are told by a reliable source. For example, a soldier might read a news article in the *Washington Post* newspaper about a conflict in which he or she participated. The soldier knows the story contains inaccuracies because the soldier was there. In general, however, the soldier finds the *Washington Post* a reliable source. Since even the most reliable source can sometimes be wrong, it is always better to offer a variety of sources, rather than a single source, to support a major point. This is especially the case when your claims are controversial.

CHECKLIST
Offering Key Source Information
_____1. Have I identified the author or origin of the source?
_____2. Have I indicated the type of source?
_____3. Have I offered the title or description of the source?
_____4. Have I noted the date of the source?
_____5. Have I qualified the source to establish its reliability and credibility?

A simple and straightforward way to demonstrate a source's trustworthiness is to include a brief description of the source's qualifications to address the topic (a "**source qualifier**"), along with your oral citation (e.g., "researcher at the Salk Institute," columnist for *The Economist*). A brief mention of the source's relevant affiliations and credentials will allow the audience to put the source in perspective and establish the source's credibility, or *ethos*. And when offering your own insights or experience, don't forget to mention your own qualifications. Whoever the source, audience members will want to know why they should accept them. The "Overview of Source Types with Sample Oral Citations" below in this chapter and the From Source to Speech guide "Demonstrating Your Sources' Reliability and Credibility" on **p. 203** illustrate how you can orally cite your sources in a way that listeners will accept them.

■ Avoid a Mechanical Delivery

Acknowledging sources need not interrupt the flow of your speech. On the contrary, audience members will welcome information that adds backing to your assertions. The key is to avoid a formulaic, or mechanical, delivery. Audience members expect a natural style of delivery of your speech, and this includes delivery of speech sources.

Vary the Wording

One way to avoid a rote delivery of sources is to vary your wording. For example, if you introduce one source with the phrase "According to…," switch to another construction ("As reported by…,") for the next. Alternating introductory phrases, such as "In the words of…," "*Baltimore Sun* reporter Jonathan X writes that…," and so forth contributes to a natural delivery and provides the necessary variety listeners need.

Lead with the Claim

Another means of introducing variety in how you cite sources is to discuss the issue and present the evidence first and then reveal the source(s). For example, you might state the claim, "Caffeine can cause actual intoxication" and provide evidence to back it up before revealing the source(s) of it. For example, "A chief source for this argument is a report in the July 5th, 2014, issue of the *New England Journal of Medicine*…"

■ Overview of Source Types with Sample Oral Citations

Following is an overview of common types of sources cited in a speech, the specific citation elements to mention, and examples of how you might refer to these elements in a presentation. Note that each example includes a source qualifier describing the source's qualifications to address the topic ("director of undergraduate studies for four years"), ("pioneering researcher"). Including a source qualifier can make the difference between winning or losing acceptance for your supporting material.

Book

If a book has *two* or *fewer* authors, state first and last names, source qualifier, title, and date of publication. If *three or more* authors, state first and last name of first author and "coauthors."

Example: In the book *1948: The First Arab-Israeli War*, published in 2008, noted *Israeli historian* Benny Morris claims that...

Example: In *The Civic Potential of Video Games*, published in 2009, Joseph Kahne, *noted professor of education and director of the Civic Education Research Group at Mills College*, and his *two coauthors, both educators*, wrote that...

Reference Work

For a reference work (e.g., atlas, directory, encyclopedia, almanac), note title, date of publication, author or sponsoring organization, and source qualifier.

Example: According to the *2014 Literary Marketplace, the foremost guide to the U.S. book publishing industry, Karen Hallard and her coeditors* report that...

Print Article

When citing from a print article, use the same guidelines as you do for a book.

Example: In an article entitled *"How Junk Food Can End Obesity,"* published in the *July 2013* edition of *Atlantic Monthly* magazine, *David H. Freedman, a journalist and author* of the book *Wrong: Why the Experts Keep Failing Us*, argues that fast food chains such as McDonald's can offer lower-cost healthy foods than higher-priced health food stores...

Online-Only Magazine, Newspaper, Journal

Follow the same guidelines as for a book, and identify the publication as an "online magazine," "online newspaper," or "online journal."

Example: In an *article on massive online open courses (MOOCs)* posted on *July 23, 2013*, on *Slate, Gabriel Kahn, a professor at the University of Southern California and director of the Future of Journalism at Annenberg Innovation Lab*...

Organization Website

Name the website, source qualifier, section of website cited (if applicable), and last update.

Example: On its website, *last updated July 8, 2014*, the *Society of Interventional Radiology* explains that radio waves are harmless to healthy cells...

If website content is undated or not regularly updated, review the site for credibility before use, using the criteria listed on **p. 203**.

Blog

Name the blogger, source qualifier, affiliated website (if applicable), and date of posting.

> *Example:* In a *July 8, 2014,* posting on *Talking Points Memo, a news blog that specializes in original reporting on government and politics,* editor *Josh Marshall* notes that...

Television or Radio Program

If you are citing a television or radio program, name the program, segment, reporter, source qualifier, and date aired.

> *Example: Judy Woodruff, PBS Newshour cohost,* described in a *segment on immigration reform,* aired on *November 2, 2014...*

Online Video

For online videos, name the online video source, program, segment, source qualifier, and date aired (if applicable).

> *Example:* In *a session on "What's Next for Mindfulness"* delivered at the *University of California–Berkeley's Greater Good Science Center* on *April 20, 2010,* and broadcast on *YouTube, Jon Kabat-Zinn, scientist, author, and founding director of the Stress Reduction Clinic...*

Testimony

If you are citing testimony, name the person, source qualifier, context in which information was offered, and date information was offered.

> *Example:* On *June 6, 2013,* in *congressional testimony before the U.S. Senate Foreign Relations Committee, Robert O. Blake Jr., Assistant Secretary, Bureau of South and Central Asian Affairs,* revealed that labor conditions in Bangladesh...

Interview and Other Personal Communication

Name the person, source qualifier, and date of interview.

> *Example:* In an interview I conducted *last week, Tim Zeutenhorst, chairman of the Orange City Area Health System Board,* at Orange City Hospital in Iowa, said...

> *Example:* In a *June 23* e-mail/twitter post/letter/memorandum from *Ron Jones, a researcher at the Cleveland Clinic...*

FROM SOURCE TO SPEECH

Demonstrating Your Sources' Reliability and Credibility

How Can I Lead the Audience to Accept My Sources as Reliable and Credible?

- If the source is affiliated with a respected institution, identify that affiliation.

- If citing a study linked to a reputable institution, identify the institution.

- If a source has relevant credentials, note the credentials.

- If the source has relevant real-life experience, mention that experience.

In the following excerpt from a speech about becoming a socially conscious consumer, the speaker omits information about key sources that would help convince the audience that his evidence and sources are trustworthy:

> The force behind this new kind of partnership is called "cause marketing." According to the *Financial Times*, cause marketing is when a company and a consumer group—or a charity—tackle a social or environmental problem and create business value for the company at the same time. A survey on consumer responses to cause marketing was conducted by Nielsen. The poll found that two-thirds of consumers around the world would say they prefer to buy products and services from companies that have programs that give back to society. And over 46 percent of consumers were willing to pay more for goods and services from companies that are giving back.

Below we see a much more convincing use of the same sources.

> The force behind this new kind of partnership is called "cause marketing." According to the *Financial Times* Lexicon, an online dictionary found at the publication's website, in *cause marketing* a company and a consumer group—or a charity— tackle a social or environmental problem and create business value for the company at the same time. In March of 2012, the global marketing firm Nielson, which studies consumer behavior in more than one hundred countries, conducted a worldwide study on cause marketing. It found that two-thirds of consumers around the world say they prefer to buy products and services from companies that have programs that give back to society. And over 46 percent said that they were, and I'm quoting here from the survey question, "willing to pay more for goods and services from companies that are giving back."

1.

2.

4.

3.

1. The speaker states the date of the study.

2. Rather than merely mentioning the source's name (Nielsen), the speaker identifies the source as a reputable global marketing firm. Listeners are more likely to trust the source if it is connected to a trusted entity.

1. ───▶ GLOBAL | 03.27.2012

THE GLOBAL, SOCIALLY CONSCIOUS CONSUMER

Around the world, companies have invested time, talent, and treasure in social and environmental efforts for a range of complementary reasons. For many companies, cause marketing—the use of social and environmental efforts to build a brand and increase profits—has been a secondary if not primary motivation.

Cause marketing won't work with all customer segments—some simply don't care—but research suggests that there is a segment of socially conscious consumers that cause marketers should pay attention to. But who are these socially conscious consumers? What causes are most important to them? What's the best way to reach them?

New findings from a Nielsen survey of more than 28,000 online respondents from 56 countries around the world provide fresh insights to help businesses better understand the right audience for cause marketers, which programs resonate most strongly with this audience, and what marketing methods may be most effective in reaching these consumers.

4. ───▶ In the study, respondents were asked if they prefer to buy products and services from companies that implement programs that give back to society. Anticipating a positive response bias, respondents were also asked whether they would be willing to pay extra for those services. For the purposes of this study, Nielsen defines the "socially conscious consumer" as those who say they would be willing to pay the extra.

Two thirds (66%) of consumers around the world say they prefer to buy products and services from companies that have implemented programs to give back to society. That preference extends to other matters, too: they prefer to work for these companies (62%), and invest in these companies (59%). A smaller share, but still nearly half (46%) say they are willing to pay extra for products and services from these companies. These are the "socially conscious consumers," as defined by and focused upon in this report.

The Nielsen Company

Two thirds (66%) of consumers around the world say they prefer to buy products and services from companies that have implemented programs to give back to society. That preference extends to other matters, too: they prefer to work for these companies (62%), and invest in these companies (59%). A smaller share, but still nearly half (46%) say they are willing to pay extra for products and services from these companies. These are the "socially conscious consumers," as defined by and focused upon in this report.

3. The speaker directly quotes from the source instead of paraphrasing; this adds to the credibility of the evidence and strengthens the argument.

4. The speaker describes enough detail about the scope of the study ("worldwide"; "28,000 survey participants from 56 countries") to convince the audience of its credibility and reliability.

FROM SOURCE TO SPEECH

Recording and Citing Web Sources

When using a Web document as a source, locate and record the following citation elements:

1. Author of the Work
2. Title of the Work
3. Title of the Website
4. Date of Publication/Last Update
5. Site Address (URL)

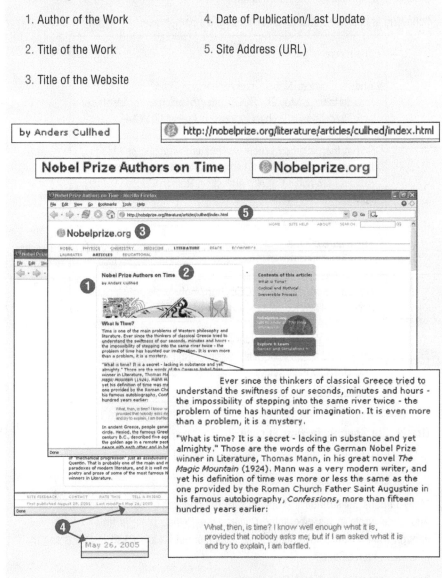

by Anders Cullhed

http://nobelprize.org/literature/articles/cullhed/index.html

Nobel Prize Authors on Time

Nobelprize.org

Ever since the thinkers of classical Greece tried to understand the swiftness of our seconds, minutes and hours - the impossibility of stepping into the same river twice - the problem of time has haunted our imagination. It is even more than a problem, it is a mystery.

"What is time? It is a secret - lacking in substance and yet almighty." Those are the words of the German Nobel Prize winner in Literature, Thomas Mann, in his great novel *The Magic Mountain* (1924). Mann was a very modern writer, and yet his definition of time was more or less the same as the one provided by the Roman Church Father Saint Augustine in his famous autobiography, *Confessions*, more than fifteen hundred years earlier:

What, then, is time? I know well enough what it is, provided that nobody asks me; but if I am asked what it is and try to explain, I am baffled.

May 26, 2005

Record Note

When taking notes, create a separate heading for each idea and record the citation elements from your source. Indicate whether the material is a direct quotation, a paraphrase, or a summary of the information.

Following are sample notes for a quotation and a paraphrase.

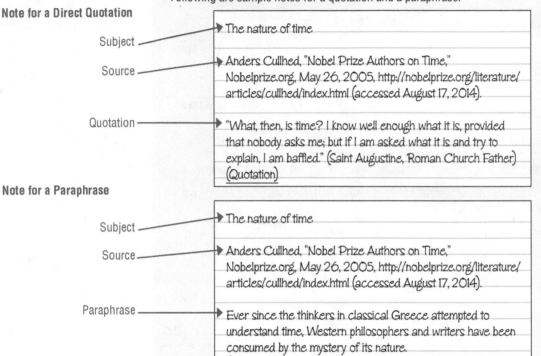

Note for a Direct Quotation

Subject →

Source →

Quotation →

The nature of time

Anders Cullhed, "Nobel Prize Authors on Time," Nobelprize.org, May 26, 2005, http://nobelprize.org/literature/articles/cullhed/index.html (accessed August 17, 2014).

"What, then, is time? I know well enough what it is, provided that nobody asks me; but if I am asked what it is and try to explain, I am baffled." (Saint Augustine, Roman Church Father) (Quotation)

Note for a Paraphrase

Subject →

Source →

Paraphrase →

The nature of time

Anders Cullhed, "Nobel Prize Authors on Time," Nobelprize.org, May 26, 2005, http://nobelprize.org/literature/articles/cullhed/index.html (accessed August 17, 2014).

Ever since the thinkers in classical Greece attempted to understand time, Western philosophers and writers have been consumed by the mystery of its nature. (Paraphrase)

Orally Cite Sources in Your Speech

In your speech, alert the audience to the source of any ideas not your own.

Speech Excerpt Indicating A Direct Quotation

Many famous thinkers have grappled with the concept of time. For example, Saint Augustine wrote in his biography, *Confessions*, "What, then, is time? I know well enough what it is, provided that nobody asks me; but if I am asked what it is and try to explain, I am baffled."

Speech Excerpt Indicating A Paraphrase

In an article on the nature of time posted on the website Nobelprize.org, professor of comparative literature Anders Cullhed notes that beginning with thinkers in ancient Greece, Western philosophers and writers have tried to understand the nature of time.

■ Credit Sources in Presentation Aids

Just as you acknowledge the ideas of others in the verbal portion of your speech, be sure to credit such material used in any accompanying presentation aids. When reproducing copyrighted material, such as a table or photograph, clearly label it with a copyright symbol (©) and the source information. Even if it is not copyrighted, supporting material listed on a visual aid requires citation. You may cite this material orally, print the citation unobtrusively on the aid, or both.

■ Properly Citing Facts and Statistics

Facts that are widely disseminated and commonly known require no attribution. Otherwise, credit the source of the fact in your speech:

> *According to the Galileo Project website* (name), *a project supported by Rice University* (source qualifier), *Galileo was appointed professor of mathematics at the University of Padua in 1592* (fact).

Statistics adds credibility to speech claims and can make your arguments more persuasive, if you tell listeners what the numbers actually mean, use terms that describe them accurately, and reveal the methods and scope of the research:

> According to *a nationally representative sample of males ages 15 and older, selected by a random digit sample of telephone numbers* (methods and scope of research) conducted by the Pew Research Center, *a major nonpartisan "fact tank" that provides information on the issues shaping America and the world* (source qualifier), a record 8 percent of households with children are now headed by single fathers, *up from just over 1 percent in 1960* (what the numbers actually mean).[4]

Courtesy of the USDA

FIGURE 11.1 PowerPoint that includes the source ("Courtesy of the USDA").

■ Properly Citing Summarized, Paraphrased, and Quoted Information

Information not your own may be cited in the form of a *summary* (a brief overview of someone else's ideas, opinions, or theories), *paraphrase* (a restatement of someone else's ideas, opinions, or theories in the speaker's own words), or *direct quotation* (statements made verbatim by someone else).

For examples of how to cite different types of supporting materials, including facts and statistics, see TABLE 11.1.

TABLE 11.1 Types of Supporting Materials and Sample Oral Citations

TYPE OF SUPPORTING MATERIAL	SAMPLE ORAL CITATION
Examples (real or hypothetical)	"One example of a website that evaluates charities is GiveWell. Founded by hedge fund employees, GiveWell conducts research into how much good various charities achieve and then publishes their research…"
Stories (extended or anecdotal)	"In J. R. R. Tolkien's classic trilogy, *The Lord of the Rings,* a young Hobbit boy named Frodo…"
Testimony (expert or lay)	"Dr. Mary Klein, a stem-cell researcher from the Brown University School of Medicine, echoed this sentiment when she spoke last Monday at the Public Health Committee meeting…"
Facts	"According to the *Farmer's Almanac*, published every year since 1818, originally the phrase 'blue moon' referred to the second of two full moons appea–ring in a single month."
Statistics	"Data from the U.S. Census Bureau, which produces national population estimates annually using the latest available data on births, deaths, and international migration, indicates that in 2009, there was one birth every eight seconds and one death every twelve seconds in the United States."

Chapter 12

Methods of Delivery

Qualities of Effective Delivery

Select a Method of Delivery

This chapter is taken from Dan O'Hair, Rob Stewart, and Hannah Rubenstein, *A Speaker's Guidebook*, Sixth Edition, pp. 249–255 (Chapter 17).

I wish you to see that public speaking is a perfectly normal act, which calls for no strange, artificial methods, but only for an extension and development of that most familiar act, conversation.

—James Albert Winans, *Public Speaking*[1]

The process of putting together a speech may be challenging, but what often creates the bigger challenge for most of us is contemplating or actually getting up in front of an audience and speaking. Many communication scholars have noted that *anticipating* giving a speech creates as much anxiety as giving one. Added to this uneasiness is the unfounded idea that speech delivery should be formulaic, mechanical, and exaggerated—that it is, in a way, unnatural or artificial. But as the early public speaking scholar James Albert Winans noted, a speech is really just an enlarged conversation, "quite the natural thing."

Natural, however, does not mean unplanned and unrehearsed. Each component of your speech "conversation," from the quality of your voice to your facial expressions, gestures, and manner of dress, affects how your listeners respond to you. As audience members listen to your words, they are simultaneously reacting to you on a nonverbal level—how you look, how you sound, and how you respond to them. If your verbal and nonverbal cues violate audience members' expectations, they will lose confidence in your credibility as a speaker.[2] Developing effective delivery skills is therefore a critical aspect of the speechmaking process.

■ Qualities of Effective Delivery

Effective delivery is the controlled use of voice and body to express the qualities of naturalness, enthusiasm, confidence, and directness. As Winans has noted, effective delivery is characterized by "a style at once simple and effective."[3] Thus an effective delivery style rests on the same natural foundation as everyday conversation, except that it is more rehearsed and purposeful.

Strive for Naturalness

Contemporary audiences expect naturalness from a speaker. Had you been a student in the early 1900s, during the heyday of the **elocutionary movement,** the opposite would have been true. The elocutionists regarded speechmaking as a type of performance, much like acting.[4] Students were given a rigid set of rules on how to use their eyes, faces, gestures, and voices to drive home certain points in the speech and to manipulate audience members' moods. Instructors emphasized delivery to such an extent that it often assumed more importance than the content of the speech.

Today, the content or message itself, rather than the delivery, is seen as being most important. Audience members expect speakers to be without artifice, to be genuine.

Conveying these qualities, however, requires practice. Perhaps ironically, it is only by thoroughly rehearsing the message that you gain the confidence to deliver it in a natural manner.

Show Enthusiasm

Enthusiasm is contagious, and is seldom criticized. When you talk about something that excites you, you talk more rapidly, use more gestures, look at your listeners more frequently, use more pronounced facial expressions, and probably stand closer to your listeners and perhaps even touch them more. Your enthusiasm spills over to your listeners, drawing them into your message. As their own enthusiasm grows, they listen more attentively because they want to know more about the thing that excites you. In turn, you sense their interest and responsiveness and realize that you are truly connecting with them. The value of enthusiastic delivery is thus accomplished: It focuses your audience's attention on the message.

Project a Sense of Confidence

Speeches delivered with confidence and composure inspire the audience's confidence in you and in your message. Your focus is on the ideas that you want to convey, not on memorized words and sentences and not on yourself. Instead of thinking about how you look and sound, think about the idea you're trying to convey and how well your listeners are grasping it. Confident delivery directs the audience's attention to the message and away from the speaker's behavior.

Be Direct

To truly communicate with an audience, you must build rapport with your listeners. You need to show that you care about them and their reasons for listening to you. This is generally done in two ways: by making your message relevant to the interests and attitudes of audience members, and by demonstrating your interest and concern for them in your delivery. The best way to do the latter is by being direct: Maintain eye contact; use a friendly tone of voice; animate your facial expressions, especially positive ones such as smiling and nodding; and position yourself so that you are physically close to the audience. Of course, you don't want to go overboard by becoming annoying or overly familiar with the audience. But neither do you want to appear distant, aloof, or uncaring. Both extremes draw audience attention away from the message. **CHAPTERS 13** and **14** focus on techniques for using your voice and body, respectively, to achieve a natural, enthusiastic, confident, and direct delivery. In the following section, we consider the major methods of delivery.

■ Select a Method of Delivery

For virtually any type of speech or presentation, you can choose from four basic methods of delivery: speaking from manuscript, speaking from memory, speaking impromptu, and speaking extemporaneously. Each method is distinguished by the expressive voice and body behaviors it uses or restricts, and by the qualities of delivery it promotes or impedes (see **TABLE 12.1**).

Speaking from Manuscript

When **speaking from manuscript,** you read a speech verbatim—that is, from prepared written text (either on paper or on a **TelePrompTer**) that contains the entire speech, word for word. As a rule, speaking from manuscript restricts eye contact and body movement, and may also limit expressiveness in vocal variety and quality. Watching a speaker read a speech can be monotonous and boring for the audience. Quite obviously, the natural, relaxed, enthusiastic, and direct qualities of delivery are all limited by this method. Commenting on the dangers of reading from a TelePrompTer, for instance, columnist and former speechwriter William Safire notes that it can make the speaker appear "shifty and untrustworthy."[5]

At certain times, however, it is advisable or necessary to read a speech, such as when you must convey a very precise message. As with politicians and business leaders, you may know that you will be quoted and must avoid misinterpretation. Or perhaps it is your responsibility to explain an emergency, so you will need to convey exact descriptions and directions (see **CHAPTER 29** on crisis communication). In some speech circumstances, such as when an award is being presented, tradition may dictate that your remarks be read from a manuscript.

TABLE 12.1 Methods of Delivery and Their Probable Uses

WHEN	METHOD OF DELIVERY
Precise wording is called for; for instance, when you want to avoid being misquoted or misconstrued, or you need to communicate exact descriptions and directions…	**Consider** *speaking from manuscript* (reading part or all of your speech from fully prepared text).
You must deliver a short special-occasion speech, such as a toast or introduction, or you plan on using direct quotations…	**Consider** *speaking from memory* (memorizing part or all of your speech).
You are called upon to speak without prior planning or preparation…	**Consider** *speaking impromptu* (organizing your thoughts with little or no lead time).
You have time to prepare and practice developing a speech or presentation that achieves a natural conversational style…	**Consider** *speaking extemporaneously* (developing your speech in working outline and then practicing and delivering it with a phrase or key-word outline).

If you must read from a prepared text, do what you can to deliver the speech naturally:

- Vary the rhythm of your words (see **CHAPTER 13**).

- Become familiar enough with the speech so that you can establish some eye contact.

- Use a large font and double- or triple-space the manuscript so that you can read without straining.

- Consider using some compelling presentation aids (see **CHAPTER 15**).

- Paginate your sheets in case the speech is dropped or shuffled.

Speaking from Memory

The formal name for **speaking from memory** is **oratory**. In oratorical style, you put the entire speech, word for word, into writing and then commit it to memory. In the United States, speaking from memory rarely occurs anymore, though this form of delivery is common in other parts of the world.[6]

Memorization is not a natural way to present a message. True eye contact with the audience is unlikely, and memorization invites potential disaster during a speech because there is always the possibility of a mental lapse or block. Some kinds of brief speeches, however, such as toasts and introductions, can be well served by memorization. Sometimes it's helpful to memorize a part of the speech, especially when you use direct quotations as a form of support. If you do find an occasion to use memorization, learn that portion of your speech so completely that in actual delivery you can convey enthusiasm and directness.

ESL SPEAKER'S NOTES

Avoiding the Pitfalls of Manuscript Delivery

Speaking from a manuscript may be difficult and perhaps even ill-advised for some ESL speakers. Reading a speech aloud, word for word, is likely to exaggerate existing problems with pronunciation and *word stress*, or the emphasis given to words in a sentence. These emphasized words or syllables are pronounced more loudly and with a higher pitch. Robbin Crabtree and Robert Weissberg note:

One of the most characteristic features of spoken English is the tendency of native speakers to take one word in every sentence and give it a stronger push than the others. This feature is called *primary stress*. If you try out a couple of sample sentences, you'll note that the primary stress normally falls at the end, or very close to the end, of the sentence: "That was one of the best speeches I've ever heard." "Let me know if you have trouble; and I'll be glad to help."[1]

If you have difficulty with word and sentence stress and you find that you need to deliver a speech from manuscript, spend extra practice time reading your speech with the aim of ensuring that your word and sentence stress align with the meaning you intend.

1. Dan O'Hair, Rob Stewart, Hannah Rubenstein, Robbin Crabtree and Robert Weissberg, *ESL Students in the Public Speaking Classroom: A Guide for Teachers* (Boston: Bedford/St. Martin's, 2012).

NASA Goddard Space Flight Center

Speaking Impromptu

Speaking impromptu, a type of delivery that is unpracticed, spontaneous, or improvised, involves speaking on relatively short notice with little time to prepare. Many occasions require that you make some remarks on the spur of the moment. An instructor may ask you to summarize key points from an assignment, for example, or a fellow employee who was scheduled to speak on a new project may be sick and your boss has invited you to take his or her place.

Try to anticipate situations that may require you to speak impromptu, and prepare some remarks beforehand. Otherwise, maximize the time you do have to prepare on the spot:

- *Think first about your listeners.* Consider their interests and needs, and try to shape your remarks accordingly. For example, who are the people present, and what are their views on the topic?

- *Listen to what others around you are saying.* Take notes in a key-word or phrase format and arrange them into ideas or main points from which you can speak.

- If your speech follows someone else's, acknowledge that person's statements. Then make your own points.

- Stay on the topic. Don't wander off track.

- Use transitions such as "first," "second," and "third," both to organize your points and to help listeners follow them.

As much as possible, try to organize your points into a discernible pattern. If addressing a problem, for example, such as a project failure or glitch, consider the problem-solution pattern—state problem(s), then offer solution(s); or the cause-effect pattern of organizational arrangement—state cause(s) first, then address effect(s). If called upon to defend one proposal as superior to another, consider using the comparative advantage pattern to illustrate various advantages of your favored proposal over the other options.

Taking steps like these will enhance your effectiveness because you will maintain the qualities of natural, enthusiastic, and direct delivery. And having even a hastily prepared plan can give you greater confidence than having no plan at all.

ETHICALLY SPEAKING

A Tool for Good and Evil

The philosopher Plato believed that the art of public speaking—or rhetoric, as the ancients referred to it—was too often corrupt.[1] Plato's cynicism toward public speaking was the result of unethical practices that he witnessed among his peers and other leaders in ancient Greece. From his perspective, rhetoric (at least as practiced) too often distorted the truth. Today, few people condemn public speaking per se as a dishonest form of communication. But many are aware of the power of delivery to corrupt. If history is any guide, these fears are well founded: one has only to think of such dictators as Mao Tse-tung, Joseph Stalin, Adolf Hitler, and Saddam Hussein, all of whom deliberately used delivery as a means of manipulation. Hitler's forceful delivery—a scorching stare, gestures, and a staccato voice—so mesmerized his listeners that millions accepted the horrific idea that an entire people should be annihilated. Historians note how Hitler spent countless hours practicing his vocal delivery and body language to achieve maximum hypnotic effect. As he did this, he would have himself photographed so that he could hone individual gestures to perfection.[2]

Like any tool, delivery can be used for both ethical and unethical purposes. Countless speakers, from Abraham Lincoln to Martin Luther King Jr. to Steve Jobs, have used their flair for delivery to uplift and inspire people. Yet there will always be those who try to camouflage weak or false arguments with an overpowering delivery. You can ensure that your own delivery is ethical by reminding yourself of the ground rules for ethical speaking: trustworthiness, respect, responsibility, and fairness. Always reveal your true purpose to the audience, review your evidence and reasoning for soundness, and grant your audience the power of rational choice.

1.   Thomas M. Conley, *Rhetoric in the European Tradition* (New York: Longman, 1990).
2.   Ian Kershaw, "The Hitler Myth," *History Today* 35, no. 11 (1985): 23.

Radu Bercan/Shutterstock

Speaking Extemporaneously

Speaking extemporaneously falls somewhere between impromptu and written or memorized deliveries. In an extemporaneous speech, you prepare well and practice in advance, giving full attention to all facets of the speech—content, arrangement, and delivery alike. Instead of memorizing or writing the speech word for word, you speak from an outline of key words and phrases (see CHAPTER 9), having concentrated throughout your preparation and practice on the ideas you want to communicate.

More speeches are delivered by extemporaneous delivery than by any other method. Many, if not most, PowerPoint presentations are extemporaneous. Because this technique is most conducive to achieving a natural, conversational quality of delivery, many speakers consider it to be the preferred method of the four types of delivery. Knowing your idea well enough to present it without memorization or manuscript gives you greater flexibility in adapting to the specific speaking situation. You can modify wording, rearrange your points, change examples, or omit information in keeping with the audience and the setting. You can have more eye contact, more direct body orientation, greater freedom of movement, and generally better control of your thoughts and actions than any of the other delivery methods allow.

Speaking extemporaneously does present several possible drawbacks. Because you aren't speaking from specifically written or memorized text, you may become repetitive and wordy. Fresh examples or points may come to mind that you want to share, so the speech may take longer than anticipated. Occasionally, even a glance at your speaking notes may fail to jog your memory on a point you wanted to cover, and you momentarily find yourself searching for what to say next. The remedy for these potential pitfalls is frequent practice using a speaking outline.

CHECKLIST
Ready for the Call: Preparing for the Extemporaneous Speech
_____1. Focus your topic as assigned or as appropriate to the audience and occasion.
_____2. Prepare a thesis statement that will serve as the central point or idea of your speech.
_____3. Research your topic in a variety of sources to gather support for your thesis and add credibility to your points.
_____4. Outline main and subordinate points.
_____5. Practice the speech at least six times.

Chapter 13

The Voice in Delivery

- Adjust Your Speaking Volume
- Vary Your Intonation
- Adjust Your Speaking Rate
- Use Strategic Pauses
- Strive for Vocal Variety
- Carefully Pronounce and Articulate Words

This chapter is taken from Dan O'Hair, Rob Stewart, and Hannah Rubenstein, *A Speaker's Guidebook*, Sixth Edition, pp. 256–261 (Chapter 18).

Used properly in the delivery of a speech, your voice is a powerful instrument of expression that should convey who you are and deliver your message in a way that engages listeners. Your voice also indicates your confidence and affects whether the audience perceives you to be in control of the situation.[1] If you have inadequate mastery of your voice, you may lose your audience's attention and fail to deliver a successful speech. Fortunately, as you practice your speech, you can learn to control each of the elements of vocal delivery. These include volume, pitch, rate, pauses, vocal variety, and pronunciation and articulation.

■ Adjust Your Speaking Volume

Volume, the relative loudness of a speaker's voice while giving a speech, is usually the most obvious and frequently cited vocal element in speechmaking, and with good reason. We need to hear the speaker at a comfortable level. *The proper volume for delivering a speech is somewhat louder than that of normal conversation.* Just how much louder depends on three factors: (1) the size of the room and of the audience, (2) whether or not you use a microphone, and (3) the level of background noise. Speaking at the appropriate volume is critical to how credible your listeners will perceive you to be. Audience members view speakers whose volume is too low less positively than those who project their voices at a pleasing volume.

Be alert to signals that your volume is slipping or is too loud and make the necessary adjustments. If your tendency is to speak softly, initially you will need to project more than seems necessary. To project your voice so that it is loud enough to be heard by everyone in the audience, breathe deeply from your diaphragm rather than more shallowly from your vocal cords. The strength of our voices depends on the amount of air the diaphragm—a large, dome-shaped muscle encasing the inner rib cage—pushes from the lungs to the vocal cords.

■ Vary Your Intonation

Imagine the variation in sound between the leftmost and the rightmost keys of a piano. This variation represents the instrument's **pitch**, or range of sounds from high to low (or vice versa). Pitch is determined by the number of vibrations per unit of time; technically, the more vibrations per unit (also called *frequency*), the higher the pitch, and vice versa.[2] The classic warm-up singing exercise "Do re mi fa so la ti do" is an exercise in pitch.

Vocal pitch is important in speechmaking—indeed, in talk of any kind—because it powerfully affects the meaning associated with spoken words. For example, say "Stop." Now, say "*Stop!*" Hear the difference? The rising and falling of vocal pitch across phrases and sentences, termed **intonation**,[3] conveys two very distinct meanings. Intonation, or pitch, is what distinguishes a question from a statement:

It's time to study already.

It's time to study al*ready*?

As you speak, pitch conveys your mood, level of enthusiasm, concern for the audience, and overall commitment to the occasion. When there is no variety in pitch, speaking becomes monotonous. A monotone voice is the death knell to any speech. Speakers who are vocally monotone rapidly lose the audience's attention and goodwill. The famous comedian Ben Stein is just about the only speaker we know who uses monotone effectively—and that is because his content is so sharp. The best way to avoid speaking in monotone is to practice and listen to your speeches with a recording device. If you have a recording device on your smart phone, you can use it to test your voice. You will readily identify instances that require better intonation.

CHECKLIST
Tips on Using a Microphone
_____ 1. Perform a sound check with the microphone at least several hours before delivering your speech.
_____ 2. When you first speak into the microphone, ask your listeners if they can hear you clearly.
_____ 3. Speak directly into the microphone; if you turn your head or body, you won't be heard.
_____ 4. To avoid broadcasting private statements, beware of "open" mikes.
_____ 5. When wearing a lavalier microphone attached to your lapel or collar, speak as if you were addressing a small group. The amplifier will do the rest.
_____ 6. When using a handheld or fixed microphone, beware of popping, which occurs when you use sharp consonants, such as p, t, and d, and the air hits the mike. To prevent popping, move the microphone slightly below your mouth and about six inches away.

Source: Susan Berkley, "Microphone Tips," *Great Speaking* 4, no. 7 (2002), accessed July 16, 2005, www.antion. com/ezine/v4n7.txt.

■ Adjust Your Speaking Rate

Speaking rate is the pace at which you convey speech. The normal rate of speech for adults is between 120 and 150 words per minute. A typical speech occurs at a rate slightly below 120 words per minute, but there is no standard, ideal, or most effective rate. If the rate is too slow, it may lull the audience to sleep. If your speech is too fast, listeners may see you as unsure about your control of the speech.[4]

Being alert to the audience's reactions is the best way to know whether your rate of speech is too fast or too slow. Some serious topics benefit from a slower speech rate; a lively pace generally corresponds with a lighter tone. An audience will get fidgety, bored, listless, perhaps even sleepy if you speak too slowly. If you speak too rapidly, listeners will appear irritated and confused, as though they can't catch what you're saying. Both slow and fast speaking rates can signal nervousness to your audience. We know from research that a slower speaking style is perceived as less credible than moderate or fast speaking rates.

To control your speaking rate, choose 150 words from your speech and time yourself for one minute as you read them aloud. If you fall very short of finishing, increase your pace. If you finish well before the minute is up, slow down. Practice until you achieve a comfortable speaking rate.

■ Use Strategic Pauses

Many novice speakers are uncomfortable with pauses. It's as if some social stigma is attached to any silence in a speech. We often react the same way in conversation, covering pauses with unnecessary and undesirable **vocal fillers**, such as "uh," "hmm," "you know," "I mean," and "it's like." Like pitch, however, pauses can be important strategic elements of a speech. **Pauses** enhance meaning by providing a type of punctuation, emphasizing a point, drawing attention to a key thought, or just allowing listeners a moment to contemplate what is being said. They make a speech far more effective than it might otherwise be. Both the speaker and the audience need pauses.

In his well-known "I Have a Dream" speech, Martin Luther King Jr. exhibits masterful use of strategic pauses. In what is now the most memorable segment of the speech, King pauses, just momentarily, to secure the audience's attention to the next words that are about to be spoken:

> I have a dream [*pause*] that one day on the red hills of Georgia....

> I have a dream [*pause*] that one day even the great state of Mississippi....[5]

Imagine how diminished the impact of this speech would have been if King had uttered "uh" or "you know" at each of these pauses! Unnecessary filled pauses can adversely affect your ability to convince your audience of your message.

■ Strive for Vocal Variety

Rather than operating separately, all the vocal elements described so far—volume, pitch, rate, and pauses—work together to create an effective delivery. Indeed, the real key to effective vocal delivery is to vary all these elements with a tone of enthusiasm, thereby producing **vocal variety**. For example, as King speaks the words "I have a dream," the pauses are immediately preceded by a combination of reduced speech rate and increased volume and pitch—a crescendo, you might say. The impact of this variety leaves an indelible impression on anyone who has heard his speech.

■ Carefully Pronounce and Articulate Words

Few things distract an audience more than improper pronunciation or unclear articulation of words. **Pronunciation** is the correct formation of word sounds. **Articulation** is the clarity or forcefulness with which the sounds are made, regardless of whether they are pronounced correctly. Incorrect pronunciation and poor articulation are largely a matter of habit. It is important to pay attention to and work on both areas.

Consider these words that are routinely mispronounced:

- effect *(ee-fect)* is stated as *uh-fect*.

- anyway *(any-way)* is said as *any-ways*.

- mobile *(mo-bile)* is said as *mo-bull* or *mo-bill*.

- leaves *(leevz)* is stated as *leephs*.

ESL SPEAKER'S NOTES

Vocal Variety and the Non-Native Speaker

Learning to deliver a speech with the vocal variety that English-speaking people in the United States expect can be particularly challenging for non-native speakers. In addition to having concerns about pronunciation and articulation, the non-native speaker may also be accustomed to patterns of vocal variety—volume, pitch, rate, and pauses—that are different from those discussed in this chapter.

The pronunciation of English depends on learning how to combine a series of about forty basic sounds (fifteen vowels and twenty-five consonants) that together serve to distinguish English words from one another. Correct pronunciation also requires that the speaker learn proper word stress, rhythm, and intonation or pitch.[1] As you practice your speeches, pay particular attention to these facets of delivery. Seek feedback from others to ensure that your goal of shared meaning will be met whenever you deliver speeches.

1.   Maryann Cunningham Florez, "Improving Adult ESL Learners' Pronunciation Skills," National Clearinghouse for ESL Literacy Education, 1998, accessed October 27, 2013, resources.marshalladulteducation.org/pdf/briefs/ImprovingPronun.Florez.pdf.

NASA Goddard Space Flight Center

SELF-ASSESSMENT CHECKLIST
Practice Check for Vocal Effectiveness
_____1.   As you practice, does your voice project authority?
_____2.   Is your voice too loud? Too soft?
_____3.   Do you avoid speaking in a monotone? Do you vary the stress or emphasis you place on words to clearly express your meaning?
_____4.   Is your rate of speech comfortable for listeners?
_____5.   Do you avoid unnecessary vocal fillers, such as "uh," "hmm," "you know," and "I mean"?
_____6.   Do you use silent pauses for strategic effect?
_____7.   Does your voice reflect a variety of emotional expressions? Do you convey enthusiasm?

Incorrect pronunciations are a matter of habit. Normally you may not know that you are mispronouncing a word because most people you talk with probably say the word much the same way you do. This habit may be associated with a regional accent or dialect. In that case, speaking to an audience of local origin may pose few problems if you pronounce words in regionally customary ways.

But if you are speaking to members of an audience for whom your accent and pronunciation patterns are not the norm, practice using correct pronunciation becomes especially important. In fact, the better your pronunciation all around, the more enhanced will be the audience's perceptions of your competence, and the greater will be the potential impact of your speech. (See TABLE 13.1 for lists of commonly mispronounced words.)

Articulation problems are also a matter of habit. A very common pattern of poor articulation is **mumbling**—slurring words together at a very low level of volume and pitch so that they are barely audible. Sometimes the problem is **lazy speech**. Common examples include saying "wanna" instead of "want to" and "theez 'er" instead of "these are."

Like any habit, poor articulation can be overcome by unlearning the problem behavior:

- If you mumble, practice speaking more loudly and with emphatic pronunciation.

- If you tend toward lazy speech, put more effort into your articulation.

- Consciously try to say each word clearly and correctly.

- Practice clear and precise enunciation of proper word sounds. Say *articulation* several times until it rolls off your tongue naturally.

- Do the same for these words: *want to, going to, riding, walking, Atlanta, chocolate, sophomore, California, affect.*

TABLE 13.1 Thirteen Commonly Mispronounced Words

CORRECT SPELLING	WRONG PRONUNCIATION	RIGHT PRONUNCIATION
ac*ts*	*aks*	*Akts*
a*sked*	*aks*	*Askt*
et *c*etera	*ek set er uh*	*et set er uh*
fa*ct*s	*faks*	*Fakts*
fi*fth*	*fith* or *fif*	*Fifth*
gen*ui*ne	*jen yu wine*	*jen yu in*
hund*red*	*hun dert*	*hun dred*
in*t*ernational	*innernashunal*	*in ter na shuh nal*
in*trod*uce	*innerdoos*	*in tro dyoos*
nu*cl*ear	*nookyouluhr*	*nook klee uhr*
pi*ct*ure	*pi chur*	*pik chur*
products	*prah duks*	*prah dukts*
reco*gn*i*zed*	*rekunized*	*re kug nized*

Source: Lilyan Wilder, *Seven Steps to Fearless Speaking* (New York: Wiley, 1999), 210–11. Reprinted with permission.

A CULTURAL PERSPECTIVE

Using Dialect (Language Variation) with Care

Every culture has subcultural variations on the preferred pronunciation and articulation of its languages. These variations represent **dialects** of the language. In the United States, for example, there is so-called Standard English, Ebonics (African American English), Tex-Mex (a combination of Spanish and English spoken with a distinct Texas drawl or accent), and such regional variations as those found in the South, New England, and along the border with Canada. In parts of Texas, for example, a common usage is to say "fixin' to" instead of "about to," as in "We're fixin' to go to a movie."

Your own dialect may be a factor in the effectiveness of your delivery when speaking to an audience of people whose dialect is different. Your dialect might call attention to itself and be a distraction to the audience. One strategy you can use is to determine which words in your usual vocabulary are spoken dialectically and practice articulating them in General American (GA) English pronunciation.

Charles Taylor Shutterstock

Chapter 14

The Body in Delivery

Enhance Your Credibility Through Nonverbal Cues

Pay Attention to Body Language

Practice the Delivery

This chapter is taken from Dan O'Hair, Rob Stewart, and Hannah Rubenstein, *A Speaker's Guidebook*, Sixth Edition, pp. 262–268 (Chapter 19).

Beyond the actual words that you say, audiences receive information from a speech through two nonverbal channels of communication: the aural and the visual. The *aural channel* consists of the vocalizations that form and accompany spoken words. These vocalizations, or **paralanguage**, include the qualities of volume, pitch, rate, variety, and pronunciation and articulation described in Chapter 13. Paralanguage refers to *how* something is said, not to *what* is said. Audience members simultaneously use their eyes (the *visual channel*) to evaluate messages sent by the speaker's physical appearance and **body language**—facial expressions, eye behavior, gestures, and general body movement.

Research confirms the importance of paying attention to aural and visual cues both during delivery of a speech and when listening to one. One study suggests that when speakers talk about their feelings and attitudes, the audience derives a mere *7 percent* of the speaker's meaning from the words they utter. The balance comes from the speaker's **nonverbal communication**: 38 percent from the speaker's voice, and 55 percent from the speaker's body language and appearance.[1]

■ Enhance Your Credibility Through Nonverbal Cues

Nonverbal communication behaviors play a key part in the audience's perception of your competence, trustworthiness, and character.[2] Research shows, for example, that audiences are more readily persuaded by speakers who emphasize vocal variety, eye contact, nodding at listeners, and standing with an open body position than by those who minimize these nonverbal cues.[3] Instructors, for instance, are judged as more credible when they demonstrate nonverbal behaviors such as direct eye contact, open gestures, and smiling. Audience members also respond more positively to speakers whom they perceive to be well dressed and attractive. They are apt to take them more seriously and are more objective in their responses than they are to speakers whom they do not find attractive.

■ Pay Attention to Body Language

As much as focusing on your words—the vocal channel—audience members will observe your body language to decode meaning visually.

Animate Your Facial Expressions

From our facial expressions, audiences can gauge whether we are excited about, disenchanted by, or indifferent to our speech—and the audience to whom we are presenting it.

Universally, few behaviors are more effective for building rapport with an audience than *smiling*.[4] A smile is a sign of mutual welcome at the start of a speech, of mutual comfort and interest during the speech, and of mutual goodwill at the close of a speech. In addition, smiling when you feel nervous or otherwise uncomfortable can help you relax and gain heightened composure. Of course, facial expressions need to correspond to the tenor of the speech. Doing what is natural and normal for the occasion should be the rule.

Maintain Eye Contact

If smiling is an effective way to build rapport, maintaining eye contact is mandatory in establishing a positive relationship with your listeners. Having eye contact with the audience is one of the most, if not *the* most, important physical actions in public speaking. Eye contact does the following:

- Maintains the quality of directness in speech delivery.

- Lets people know they are recognized.

- Indicates acknowledgment and respect.

- Signals to audience members that you see them as unique human beings.

With an audience of a hundred to more than a thousand members, it's impossible to look at every listener. But in most speaking situations you are likely to experience, you should be able to make the audience feel recognized by using a technique called scanning. When you scan an audience, you move your gaze from one listener to another and from one section to another, pausing to gaze at one person long enough to complete one thought before removing your gaze and shifting it to another listener. One speaking professional suggests following the "rule of three": Pick three audience members to focus on—one in the middle, one on the right, and one on the left of the room; these audience members will be your anchors as you scan the room.[5]

SELF-ASSESSMENT CHECKLIST
Tips for Using Effective Facial Expressions
_____1. Use animated expressions that feel natural and express your meaning.
_____2. Avoid a deadpan expression.
_____3. Never use expressions that are out of character for you or inappropriate to the speech occasion.
_____4. In practice sessions, loosen your facial features with exercises such as widening the eyes and moving the mouth.
_____5. Establish rapport with the audience by smiling naturally when appropriate.

Use Gestures That Feel Natural

Words alone seldom suffice to convey what we want to express. Physical gestures fill in the gaps, as in illustrating the size or shape of an object (e.g., by showing the size of it by extending two hands, palms facing each other) or expressing the depth of an emotion (e.g., by pounding a fist on a podium).[6] Gestures should arise from genuine emotions and should conform to your personality (see the checklist below for tips on gesturing effectively).

Create a Feeling of Immediacy

In most Western cultures, listeners learn more from and respond most positively to speakers who create a perception of physical and psychological closeness, called nonverbal immediacy, between themselves and audience members.[7]

Audience members soon tire of listening to a **talking head** who remains steadily positioned in one place behind a microphone or podium. As space and time allow, use your physical position vis-à-vis audience members to adjust your relationship with them, establishing a level of familiarity and closeness that is appropriate to the topic, purpose, and occasion. Movement toward listeners stimulates a sense of informality and closeness; remaining behind the podium fosters a more formal relationship of speaker to audience.

CHECKLIST
Tips for Effective Gesturing
_____1. Use natural, spontaneous gestures.
_____2. Avoid exaggerated gestures, but use gestures that are broad enough to be seen by each audience member.
_____3. Eliminate distracting gestures, such as fidgeting with pens or pencils or brushing back hair from your eyes.
_____4. Analyze your gestures for effectiveness in practice sessions.
_____5. Practice movements that feel natural to you.

CHECKLIST
Broad Dress Code Guidelines
_____1. For a "power" look, wear a dark-colored suit.
_____2. Medium-blue or navy paired with white can enhance your credibility.
_____3. Yellow and orange color tones convey friendliness.
_____4. The color red focuses attention on you.
_____5. Flashy jewelry distracts listeners.

Maintain Good Posture

A speaker's posture sends a definite message to the audience. Listeners perceive speakers who slouch as being sloppy, unfocused, and even weak. Strive to stand erect, but not ramrod straight. The goal is to appear authoritative, not rigid.

Dress Appropriately

Superficial as it may sound, the first thing an audience is likely to notice about you as you approach the speaker's position is your clothing. The critical criteria in determining appropriate dress for a speech are audience expectations and the nature of the speech occasion. If you are speaking as a representative of your business, for example, you will want to complement your company's image.[8] Consider the late Apple co-founder Steve Jobs, who invariably wore jeans and a black shirt when he rolled out a new product line. Jobs's attire conveyed a signature style that was casual and "cool," personifying the Apple products he represented.[9]

Although some speaking occasions permit casual dress, take care not to confuse casual with sloppy or unkempt. Even casual attire should be professional in the sense that it conveys a responsible, credible, and confident image. Your attire reveals an attitude about what you are doing and the amount of effort you seem willing to put into it. The more professional you look, the more professional you will feel, and the more positive the attitude you will convey to audience members. This advice is no less important for your classroom speeches than it is for speeches given elsewhere. You should dress for your speeches in class just as you would if you were delivering them to a business or professional group that you wanted to impress. At the very least, it's good practice, and it's likely to benefit your speech by showing your respect for both the occasion and the audience.

An extension of dress is having various objects on or around your person while giving a speech—pencil and pen, a briefcase, a glass of water, or papers with notes on them. Always ask yourself if these objects are really necessary. A sure way to distract an audience from what you're saying is to drag a briefcase or backpack to the speaker's stand and open it while speaking, or to fumble with a pen or other object.

A CULTURAL PERSPECTIVE

Nonverbal Communication Patterns in Different Cultures

As a speaker, it's important to remember that, like verbal communication, nonverbal communication is also profoundly influenced by culture. Gestures, for example, have entirely different meanings in different cultures, and many an unsuspecting speaker has inadvertently made a rude gesture in his or her host's culture. In the late 1950s, for instance, Vice President Richard Nixon made a goodwill tour of Latin America, where there were feelings of hostility toward the United States. On one of his stops, Nixon stepped off his plane and, smiling, gestured with the A-OK sign to the waiting crowd. The crowd booed. In that culture, Nixon's gesture meant "Screw you." Days of delicate diplomacy were undone by two seconds of nonverbal behavior.[1] This same gesture, incidentally, means "zero" in French and "money" in Japan. Roger Axtell catalogs a variety of gestures in his book *Gestures: The Do's and Taboos of Body Language around the World*. This eye-opening account demonstrates how something in one culture can mean literally the opposite in another (e.g., nodding means "yes" in the United States but can mean "no" in the former Yugoslavia and Iran).

The display of emotions is also guided by the social rules of the culture. The Japanese are conditioned to mask emotion, whereas Americans express emotion more freely. Speakers in different cultures thus use different facial expressions to convey emotions. Eye behavior also takes quite different forms; people in the United States and Canada use eye contact as a form of acknowledgment or politeness in greeting, but in other cultures—such as in Southeast Asia, Nigeria, and Puerto Rico, among other places—this is often considered disrespectful. Finally, appearance preferences also change from one culture to another.

No speaker should feel obliged to adopt nonverbal behaviors that are not his or her own. At the same time, a successful speech depends on shared meaning. As such, a thorough audience analysis is needed to anticipate potential misunderstandings that might occur nonverbally.

1. Roger Axtell, Gestures: *The Do's and Taboos of Body Language around the World* (New York: Wiley, 1991).

Source: Adapted from Dan O'Hair, Gustav Friedrich, and Lynda Dixon, *Strategic Communication in Business and the Professions* (Boston: Allyn Bacon, 2011), Chapter 3.

Charles Taylor/Shutterstock

■ Practice the Delivery

One of the most cited recommendations from public speaking experts—whether they appear in books, blogs, or websites—is the importance of practice. Practice is essential to effective delivery. The more you practice, the greater your comfort level will be when you actually deliver the speech. More than anything, it is uncertainty that breeds anxiety. By practicing your speech using a fully developed speaking outline (see **CHAPTER 9**), you will know what to expect when you actually stand in front of the audience.

Focus on the Message

The primary purpose of any speech is to get a message across, not to display extraordinary delivery skills. Keep this goal foremost in your mind. Psychologically, too, focusing on your message is likely to make your delivery more natural and more confident.

Record the Speech

Once you've practiced your speech several times, talk it out into an audio recorder. At a later stage in the practice process, you can place the recorder across the room from you and practice projecting your voice to the back row of the audience. To accurately gauge how you sound, use a good-quality recording device.

Videorecording two practice sessions can provide valuable feedback. As you watch your initial recording, make notes of the things you'd like to change. Before rerecording, practice several more times until you are comfortable with the changes you've incorporated. Note that no one is ever entirely thrilled with his or her image on video, so try to avoid unnecessary self-criticism. Videorecord your speech a second time, paying close attention to the areas of speech delivery that you want to improve.

Be Prepared to Revise Your Speaking Notes

As you practice, be prepared to revise your speech as needed. If your introduction or conclusion isn't as effective as you would like, rework it. Make other adjustments as necessary to improve your speech and make the outline easier to follow.

Practice under Realistic Conditions

Try to simulate the actual speech setting as you practice. Keep the seating arrangement in mind as you speak, picturing the audience as you go along. Turn various objects in the room into imaginary audience members, and project your voice in their direction. Practice scanning for eye contact. Practice with a podium of some kind (unless you know that you won't be using one). Stack some boxes to form a makeshift podium if you have to. Practice working with your speaking notes until you are confident that you can refer to them without overly relying on them. Practice placing your notes on a podium and moving around the podium for effective delivery.

At some point, practice your speech in front of at least one other person. Ask your volunteer(s) to identify the purpose and key points of your speech. Question them about what they did or did not understand. Seek detailed feedback about the quality of your delivery.

Time Your Speech

As you practice, time each part of the speech (introduction, body, and conclusion) so that if you exceed your time limit you can adjust these sections accordingly. Recall that, as a general rule, the introduction or the conclusion should make up no more than 10 or 15 percent of your entire speech (see **CHAPTERS 7** and **8**). If the speech is too long, look for extraneous material that can be cut. Consider your rate of speech. If it is too slow, practice speaking more concisely. If the speech is too short, review your evidence and make certain that you adequately support your main points. If your rate of speech is too fast, practice slowing your tempo.

Plan Ahead and Practice Often

If possible, begin practicing your speech at least several days before you are scheduled to deliver it. Many expert speakers recommend practicing your speech about five times in its final form. Since few speeches are longer than twenty minutes, and most are shorter, this represents a maximum of two hours of practice time—two hours well spent.

- Practice with your speaking notes, revising those parts of the speech that aren't satisfactory, and altering the notes as you go.

- Focus on your speech ideas rather than on yourself.

- Time each part of your speech—introduction, body, and conclusion.

- Practice with any presentation aids you plan to use.

- Practice your speech several times, and then record it.

- If possible, videotape yourself twice—once after several practice sessions, and again after you've worked to incorporated any changes into your speech.

- Visualize the setting in which you will speak, and practice the speech under realistic conditions, paying particular attention to projecting your voice to fill the room.

- Practice in front of at least one volunteer, and seek constructive criticism.

- Schedule your practice sessions early in the process so that you have time to prepare.

Chapter 15

Speaking with Presentation Aids

This chapter is taken from Dan O'Hair, Rob Stewart, and Hannah Rubenstein, *A Speaker's Guidebook,* Sixth Edition, pp. 275–287 (Chapter 20).

An old cliché states, "A picture is worth a thousand words." To modernize the cliché we should say, "A picture plus sound plus motion and other special effects are worth a thousand words"—that is, of course, when they are used in a context that is appropriate to the topic, the audience, and the occasion (i.e., the rhetorical situation).

Presentation aids include objects, models, pictures, graphs, charts, video, audio, and multimedia. Each of these elements, used alone and in combination, helps the audience see relationships among concepts and elements. Aids also help audience members store and remember material and critically examine key ideas. As valuable as they can be, however, the strength of any particular presentation aid lies in the context in which it is used. No matter how powerful a photograph or chart or video may be, the audience will be less interested in merely gazing at it than in discovering how you will relate it to a specific point. Emphasis should be on using those aids that help audience members process and retain key speech points most efficiently.[1]

■ Functions of Presentation Aids

Used judiciously, presentation aids can help listeners process and retain information, spark interest, convey information in a time-saving fashion, and enhance an image of professionalism.

Help Listeners Process and Retain Information

Most people process and retain information best when they receive it both verbally and visually. That is, they learn better from words and pictures than from words alone, a principle called the **multimedia effect**.[2] However, when speakers simply read text from slides, or when graphics contain too much text, audience members will become distracted and actually retain less information than they would receiving information in one format alone.[3]

Promote Interest and Motivation

Effective presentation aids draw audience members into a speech and stimulate their interest through **visual rhetoric**—the conveyance of meaning by integrating the visual with the verbal message.[4] Literally seeing the facts of an argument laid out in front of them, for example, can make a significant difference in how listeners respond to a persuasive appeal. In a call for donations for the homeless, for instance, a good argument coupled with a photograph that portrays homeless conditions, or a chart that illustrates high rates of homelessness, can more eloquently convey the speaker's message than can the verbal argument alone.[5]

Convey Information Concisely

Presentation aids can concisely communicate ideas that might otherwise be difficult or time-consuming to express. Visual images, such as a child running to her mother who has just returned from military service, can vividly represent an idea or a feeling instantaneously. Complex ideas and abstract or difficult concepts can also be more clearly explained with presentation aids. For example, graphs and charts efficiently summarize statistical relationships, and different styles of jewelry are shown in close-up photographs.

Lend a Professional Image

By using quality visual aids, you show your listeners that you are approaching the presentation professionally and motivate them to approach it in the same way. Presenting your company's official "brand" on each slide of a PowerPoint presentation, for example, increases your credibility, which further helps get your message across. But moderation is important. Emphasis, again, should be on using the aids to fulfill the speech purpose and not on the aids themselves.

■ Types of Presentation Aids

A variety of presentation aids are at your disposal. Base your choices on which aid will most effectively convey the information visually (or aurally, or both). Here we move from least to most high-tech. (See **CHAPTER 17** for a discussion on using presentation software.)

Props and Models

A **prop** can be any object, inanimate or live. Sometimes, the prop *is* the subject of the speech, as when a student brings a snake to class for a speech about snakes. A **model** is a three-dimensional, scale-size representation of an object. Presentations in engineering, architecture, medicine, the visual arts, and many other disciplines often make use of models. When using a prop or model:

- In most cases, keep the prop or model hidden until you are ready to use it.

- Make sure it is big enough for everyone to see (and read, if applicable).

- Practice your speech using the prop or model.

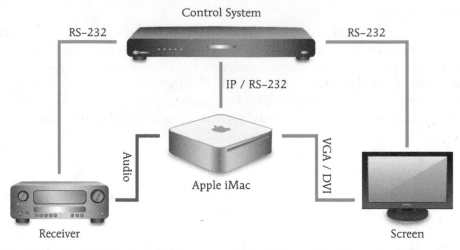

Source: "Inline Control: Control Solutions for the Mac," accessed July 10, 2010, www.inlinecontrol.com.

FIGURE 15.1 Diagram or Schematic Drawing of Media Center Connections

Pictures

Pictures are *two-dimensional representations* and include photographs, line drawings, diagrams, maps, and posters of people, places, ideas, or objects.

A *diagram* or *schematic drawing* explains how something works or how it is constructed or operated, and is well suited to clarifying precise procedures and operations. **FIGURE 15.1** is a diagram that shows how to connect a computer and other elements of a home media center.

Maps help audience members visualize geographic areas and understand various relationships among them: They also illustrate the proportion of one thing to something else in different areas.

A *poster* is a large, bold, two-dimensional design incorporating words, shapes, and (if desired) color, placed on an opaque backing. Because posters are economical and easy to use, they are a good choice for speakers who give the same presentation many times.

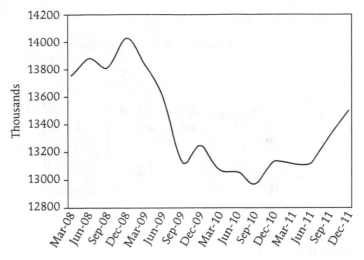

Source: Accessed November 17, 2013, www.sec.gov.

FIGURE 15.2 Line Graph Depicting South Africa Total Employment, 2008–2011

Graphs and Charts

A **graph** represents relationships among two or more things. Four types of graphs are line graphs, bar graphs, pie graphs, and pictograms. A *line graph* uses points connected by lines to demonstrate how something changes or fluctuates in value. For example, FIGURE 15.2 represents fluctuations in the South African employment rate for the years 2008–2011. Line graphs are the most versatile and extensively used family of graphs[6] because they are easier to read at a glance than more complicated tables and charts of data.

A *bar graph* uses bars of varying lengths to compare quantities or magnitudes. Bars may be arranged either vertically (column graphs) or horizontally (true bar graphs). *Multidimensional bar graphs*—bar graphs distinguished by different colors or markings—compare two or more different kinds of information or quantities in one chart (see FIGURE 15.3). A *pie graph* depicts the division of a whole with portions or segments called slices. Each slice constitutes a percentage of the whole (see FIGURE 15.4). A **picto-gram** uses picture symbols (icons) to illustrate relationships and trends. FIGURE 15.5 is a pictogram that demonstrates an increase in the number of college students.

A **chart** visually organizes complex information into compact form. Several different types of charts are helpful for speakers. A **flowchart** is a diagram that shows step-by-step progression through a procedure, a relationship, or a process. A flowchart is the visual aid of choice to show a sequence of activities or the directional flow in a process (see FIGURE 15.6).

Vertical Bar Graph

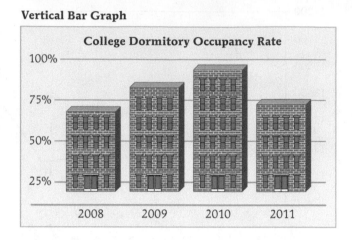

Horizontal Bar Graph

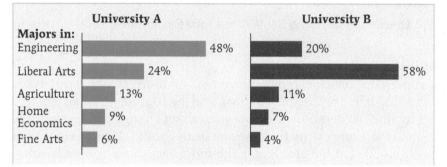

FIGURE 15.3 Bar Graphs of Quantities and Magnitudes

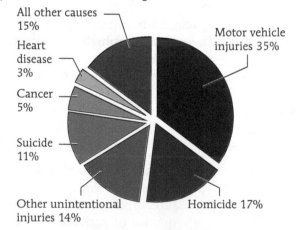

Source: Centers for Disease Control and Prevention, accessed November 17, 2013, www.cdc.gov/motorvehiclesafety/teenbrief/.

FIGURE 15.4 Pie Graph Showing Various Causes of Teen Deaths

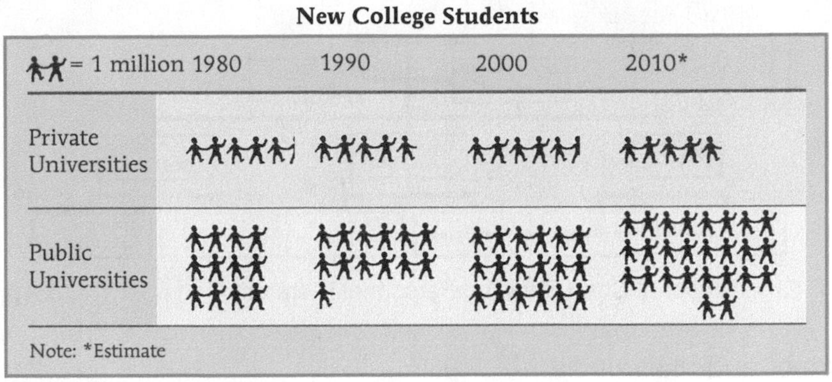

New College Students

♟♟ = 1 million	1980	1990	2000	2010*
Private Universities	♟♟♟♟♟	♟♟♟♟♟	♟♟♟♟♟	♟♟♟♟♟
Public Universities	♟♟♟♟ ♟♟♟♟ ♟♟♟♟	♟♟♟♟♟♟ ♟♟♟♟♟ ♟	♟♟♟♟♟♟ ♟♟♟♟♟ ♟♟♟♟♟♟	♟♟♟♟♟♟♟♟ ♟♟♟♟♟♟♟ ♟♟♟♟♟♟♟♟ ♟♟

Note: *Estimate

FIGURE 15.5 Pictogram Showing Increase in College Students

An *organizational chart* illustrates the organizational structure or chain of command in an organization. It shows the interrelationship of the different positions, divisions, departments, and personnel (see FIGURE 15.7). A **table** (tabular chart) systematically arranges data in column form, allowing viewers to examine and make comparisons about information quickly. TABLE 15.1 on the following page, for example, summarizes the best uses of different types of graphs and charts.

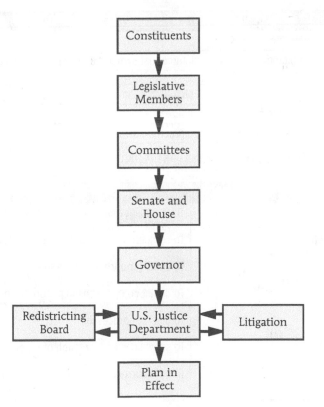

Source: ESRI, accessed July 10, 2010, proceedings.esri.com/library/userconf/.

FIGURE 15.6 Flowchart Showing Decision Process for a State's Political Redistricting

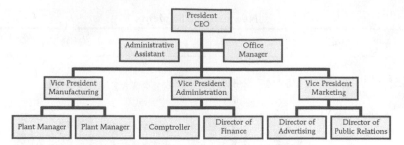

FIGURE 15.7 Organizational Chart Showing Personnel Hierarchy

Audio, Video, and Multimedia

Introducing an *audio clip*—a short recording of sounds, music, or speech—can enliven certain presentations. Similarly, *video*—including clips from movies, television, and other recording sources—can serve to motivate attention by helping to introduce, transition into, and clarify points in a speech.[7] Because audio and video clips can be linked to PowerPoint slides, are easily stored on personal digital devices, and are transportable to a variety of playback devices, both are generally a safe choice as presentation aids. (See the checklist below for incorporating tips on various media into your presentation.)

CHECKLIST
Tips for Creating Effective Pictograms
_____1. When creating pictograms, choose pictures that symbolize the subject being represented to a broad spectrum of viewers.
_____2. To avoid confusing the eye, make all pictograms the same size.
_____3. Clearly label what the pictogram symbolizes.
_____4. Clearly label the axes of the pictogram graph.

Table 15.1 Best Use of Different Types of Graphs and Charts

TYPE OF GRAPH OR CHART	BEST USE
Line Graph	To represent trends or information that changes over time
Bar and column graph	To compare magnitude or volume among categories
Pie graph	To show proportions of the total
Pictogram	To depict comparisons in picture form
Flowchart	To diagram processes
Organizational chart	To show lines and direction of reporting in a hierarchy
Table	To summarize information or data in an easily viewable form

CHECKLIST
Tips for Creating Effective Line, Bar, and Pie Graphs
_____1. Label both axes of the line or bar graph appropriately.
_____2. Start the numerical axis of the line or bar graph at zero.
_____3. Compare only like variables.
_____4. Put no more than two lines of data on one graph.
_____5. Assign a clear title to the graph..
_____6. Clearly label all relevant points of information in the graph.
_____7. When creating multidimensional bar graphs, do not compare more than three kinds of information.
_____8. When creating a pie graph, restrict the number of pie slices to seven.
_____9. When creating a pie graph, identify the value or percentage of each pie slice, and check that each slice of the pie accurately represents the value or percentage (e.g., use half of the pie to show 50 percent).
_____10. When creating a pie graph, consider using color or background markings to distinguish the different slices of the pie.

Multimedia combines several media (stills, sound, video, text, and data) into a single production. This rich variety of information cues can potentially boost audience attention, comprehension, and retention.[8] But multimedia does require more planning and time commitment than other forms of presentation aids. To produce multimedia, you need to become familiar with presentation software programs such as Windows Movie Maker and Apple iMovie (see CHAPTER 17).

CHECKLIST
Tips on Incorporating Audio and Video into Your Presentation
_____1. Use the audio or video clip in a manner consistent with copyright.
_____2. Cue the audio or video clip to the appropriate segment before the presentation.
_____3. Alert audience members to what they will be hearing or viewing before you play it back.
_____4. Reiterate the relevance of the audio or video clip to your key points once it is over.

■ Options for Displaying the Presentation Aid

Once you've selected the presentation aids that are best suited for communicating your ideas, you have a variety of options for displaying them during your speech. Many presenters create computer-generated aids shown with digital projectors or LCD displays (see CHAPTER 17). On the more traditional side, options include overhead transparencies, flip charts, chalkboards, posters, and handouts.

Computer-Generated Aids and Displays

With software programs such as Microsoft PowerPoint and Apple Keynote, speakers can create slides to project using LCD (liquid crystal display) panels and projectors or the newer DLP (digital light processing) projectors. (See CHAPTER 17 for a discussion of how to use presentation software.) Dual screens, when available, help listeners retain comparative information, with one set of information on one screen and the other set on the other screen.[9]

Flip Charts

A **flip chart** is simply a large (27–34 inches) pad of paper on which a speaker can write or draw. They are often prepared in advance; then, as you progress through the speech, you simply flip through the pad to the next exhibit. You can also write and draw on the pad as you speak.

Chalkboards and Whiteboards

On the lowest-tech end of the spectrum lies the *writing board* on which you can write with chalk (on a *chalkboard*) or with nonpermanent markers (on a *whiteboard*). Writing boards are useful for impromptu explanations, as when someone asks a question for which you do not have an aid but feel you can clarify with words or drawings. In general, try to reserve the writing board for quick explanations, such as presenting simple processes that are done in steps, or for engaging the audience in short brainstorming sessions. If you have the time to prepare a speech properly, however, don't rely on a writing board. They force the speaker to turn his or her back to the audience, they make listeners wait while you write on the board, and they require legible handwriting that will be clear to all viewers.

Handouts

A **handout** conveys information that either is impractical to give to the audience in another manner or is intended to be kept by audience members after the presentation. Handouts can effectively and inexpensively give an audience more information than can be covered in the presentation. They can also be useful when it is best to have audience members follow along with you while you go over information. Sometimes handouts have blanks to be filled in by the listeners as the speaker covers key points. This approach has been shown to enhance recall and retention, especially when the handouts contain relevant graphics.[10]

To avoid distracting listeners, unless you specifically want listeners to read the information or fill in blanks as you speak, *wait until you are done before you distribute the handout.* If you do want the audience to view a handout during the speech, distribute it only when you are ready to talk about it. Avoid distributing too many or too lengthy handouts because audience members will find them tiresome and may lose interest.

CHECKLIST
Incorporating Presentation Aids into Your Speech
_____1. Practice your speech with the aids until you are confident that you can handle them without causing undue distractions.
_____2. Talk to your audience rather than to the screen or object—avoid turning your back to the audience.
_____3. Maintain eye contact with the audience.
_____4. Reiterate the relevance of the audio or video clip to your key points once it is over.
_____5. Place the aid to one side rather than behind you, so that the entire audience can see it and you can move away from it and still face the audience.
_____6. Display the aid only when you are ready to discuss it.
_____7. If you decide to use a pointer, once you've indicated the point, put it down.
_____8. In case problems arise, be prepared to give your presentation without the aids.

FROM IDEA TO IMAGE

Using Presentation Aids

As you select each aid for your presentation, ask yourself:

> Is the *type* of aid the *best choice* to convey the information?

> Is my *timing* of the aid optimal?

> Will the aid help me achieve my *desired effect*?

Following are examples of one student's effective use of presentation aids in her speech about plastic bags and the environment.

The Plastic Bag Plague

Introduction

I.   Picture a swirling, plastic-laden gyre of ocean waters, twice the size of Texas…
     (Attention getter)

The notion of such large garbage patches in the middle of the ocean is difficult to fathom without a visual, so to build credibility, the student decides to show a map.

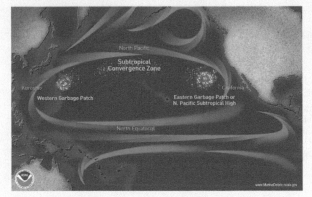

NOAA(NEW)

Body

I.   Plastic bags choke the land and water…

  A.   Americans throw out 30 million tons of plastic annually, or nearly 12 percent of all solid waste, and recycle only 6 percent of it.

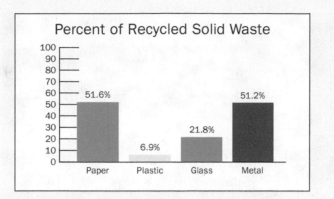

Comparing recycling rates of solid wastes, the student uses a bar graph to show how plastic is the least biodegradable.

B.   100,000 marine animals are killed annually…

Dave McAleavy/Shuttershock

To appeal to the audience's emotions, or pathos, the student shows a video of marine life suffering the consequences of plastic bag pollution. She hyperlinks the image to the video URL. On the day of her presentation, she makes sure the presentation room has an Internet connection and that her hyperlinked video works.

C.   200,000 plastic bags get deposited in landfills every hour and take 1,000 years to decompose…

Sami Sarkis/Photodisc/Getty Images

The student illustrates this dramatic statistic with a photograph of a landfill teeming with plastic.

Conclusion

I.   Prevent major impact on our world...

Stop Plastic Bag Waste

> Take plastic bags to recycle bin at local grocery store.
> Use reusable bags when shopping.
> Encourage stores to offer paper bags instead of plastic bags.
> E-mail your senator or representative in support of government regulation on plastics.

Stressing the need to act, the student concludes with a text slide listing actions students can take. Note that she selects a font color that contrasts well with the background color.

II.   Use environmentally friendly bags...

David McNew/Getty Images News/Getty Images

The student shows this reusable bag from Whole Foods as a prop to demonstrate her point.

III.   Hold up your reusable bag and say, "No thank you, I brought my own…"

Once again, the student holds up a reusable shopping bag to reiterate one of her speech's primary points: Decrease plastic bag consumption.

Chapter 16

Designing Presentation Aids

- Keep the Design Simple
- Use Design Elements Consistently
- Select Appropriate Typeface Styles and Fonts
- Use Color Carefully

This chapter is taken from Dan O'Hair, Rob Stewart, and Hannah Rubenstein, *A Speaker's Guidebook*, Sixth Edition, pp. 288–293 (Chapter 21).

Whether you create your presentation aids by hand or generate them using software, certain principles of rhetorical communication and graphic design apply. Keep in mind that the purpose of a presentation aid is to support your ideas, not to repeat verbatim what you are saying in your speech. Any presentation aid, even those that are expertly designed, can hurt your effectiveness as a speaker if the audience's attention is drawn more to the aids than to the message itself.[1] Thus you should focus on creating aids that will truly clarify information, taking care not to overweight the speech with slides.

■ Keep the Design Simple

Presentation aids that contain too much information or appear overly complex will quickly overwhelm the audience. On average, audience members have thirty seconds or less to view an aid, so focus on designing the aids simply and using text sparingly.

Assign Each Point a Separate Slide

Present one major idea per slide, and use a sequential layout of separate slides to cover a series of points or ideas. Follow the **six-by-six rule** to minimize the number of words you use in each presentation aid—use no more than six words in a line and six lines on one slide. This way the audience will spend less time reading the aid and more time listening to you.

Word Slides in the Active Voice

Word your text in active verb form and parallel grammatical structure. For example, an informative speech on the process of registering to vote could include a slide labeled "Gather Necessary Documents." Note in **FIGURE 16.1** the differences between a first draft and a final slide. The first slide shows a lack of parallel structure, with dissimilar grammatical and stylistic construction, the wordy use of full sentences, and the passive construction in point 3 ("It is recommended that..."). In the final slide, the speaker poses each point in the active rather than passive form ("Shop around" instead of "It is recommended that..."). All points are short, crisp phrases containing no more than six lines on a slide.

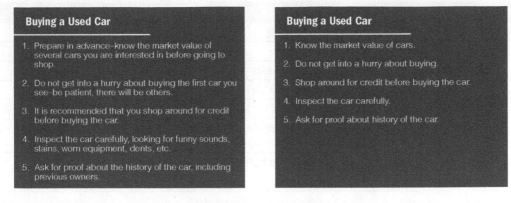

FIGURE 16.1 Cluttered versus Easy-to-Read Presentation Aid

Avoid Clutter

Use graphics and text sparingly. Certain kinds of information—especially statistical data and sequences of action—are best understood through visual reasoning. However, try to avoid what design expert Edward Tufte coined "chartjunk"—slides jammed with too many graphs, charts, and other meaningless design elements that obscure rather than illuminate information. Tufte advises using as few slides as possible and only those design elements that truly enhance meaning.[2]

■ Use Design Elements Consistently

The principle of continuity dictates that you apply the same design decisions you make for one aid to all of the aids you display in a speech. Businesses, agencies, and your college or university apply this principle to their websites and publications. Doing so maintains a consistent professional image and ensures that viewers don't become distracted by a jumble of unrelated visual elements. Carry your choice of design elements—colors, fonts, uppercase and lowercase letters, styling (boldface, underlining, italics), general page layout, and repeating elements such as titles and logos—through each slide.

■ Select Appropriate Typeface Styles and Fonts

A **typeface** is a specific style of lettering, such as Arial, Times Roman, or Courier. Typefaces come in a variety of **fonts**, or sets of sizes (called the point size) and uppercases and lowercases.

CHECKLIST
Applying the Principles of Simplicity and Continuity
_____1.   Restrict your coverage to one idea per aid.
_____2.   Create concise titles that reinforce your message.
_____3.   Use phrases or single words to display the points clearly.
_____4.   Use the six-by-six rule—no more than six words per line and six lines per aid.
_____5.   Apply design decisions consistently to each aid. Use the same combinations of fonts, uppercase and lowercase lettering, styling (boldface, underlining, italics), and spacing.
_____6.   Use colors consistently across all slides to highlight key ideas and enhance readability.
_____7.   Carry through any repeating elements such as logos or pictograms across all aids.

Designers divide the thousands of typefaces available today into two categories: serif and sans serif. **Serif typefaces** include small flourishes, or strokes, at the tops and bottoms of each letter. **Sans serif typefaces** are more blocklike and linear; they are designed without the tiny strokes. Some studies show that small amounts of text, such as headings, are best viewed in sans serif type (see FIGURE 16.2), whereas blocks of text, such as paragraphs, are better viewed in serif typefaces. Consider these guidelines when selecting type sizes for presentation aids:

1. Whether you are using a hand-drawn poster board or a slide, check your lettering for legibility, taking into consideration the audience's distance from the presentation. Text for on-screen projection should be 18 points or larger. Generally, major headings should be displayed in 36-point type, subheadings in 24-point type, and body text in 18-point type (see FIGURE 16.3).

2. Lettering should stand apart from the background. Use either light lettering on dark background, or dark lettering on light background.

3. Use a typeface that is simple and easy to read, not distracting.

4. Use standard uppercase and lowercase type rather than all capitals.

5. Use **boldface**, underlining, or *italics* sparingly to emphasize only the most important points.

FIGURE 16.2 Serif and Sans Serif Typefaces

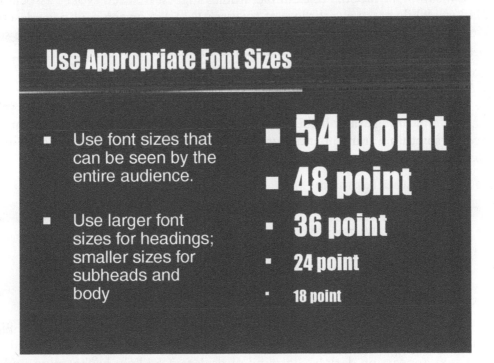

FIGURE 16.3 Use Appropriate Font Sizes

CHECKLIST
Tips for Using Typefaces, Fonts, and Sizes Effectively
_____1. For on-screen projection, use a minimum 18-point font for body text, perhaps 24-point in large rooms.
_____2. Avoid ornate typefaces—they are difficult to read.
_____3. Use a sans serif typeface for titles and major headings.
_____4. Consider a serif typeface when the body of the text is only a few lines.
_____5. Experiment with 36-point type for major headings and 24-point type for subheads.
_____6. As a rule, use no more than two different typefaces in a single visual aid.
_____7. Use uppercase and lowercase type rather than all capitals.
_____8. Use boldface, underlining, or italics sparingly.

■ Use Color Carefully

Skillful use of color can draw attention to key points, set the mood of a presentation, and make things easier to see. Conversely, poor color combinations will set the wrong mood, render an image unattractive, or make it just plain unreadable. **TABLE 16.1** below describes the effects of several color combinations.

Because colors evoke distinct associations in people, take care not to summon an unintended meaning or mood. For example, studies suggest that red evokes associations with failure, while green elicits those of success.[3] **TABLE 16.2** on the next page describes some of the subjective interpretations attached to several colors. Following are some tips for using color effectively in your presentation aids.

- Keep the *background color* of your presentation constant across all slides.

- Use *bold, bright colors* to emphasize important points. Warm colors such as yellow, red, and orange rank highest in visibility, so use these colors to highlight text or objects within a frame. But be careful: These colors can be difficult to see from a distance.

TABLE 16.1 Effects of Color Combinations

COLOR	EFFECT IN COMBINATION
Yellow	Warm on white, harsh on black, fiery on red, soothing on light blue
Blue	Warm on white, hard to see on black
Red	Bright on white, warm or difficult to see on black

Source: Cheryl Currid, *Make Your Point: The Complete Guide to Successful Business Presentations Using Today's Technology* (Rocklin, CA: Prima Publishing, 1995), 75.

- For typeface and graphics, use colors that contrast rather than clash with or blend into the background color. Audiences will remember information just as easily if white text appears on dark background or dark text on light background, so long as the design is appealing.[4]

- Limit the number of colors you use in a graphic to three, and certainly no more than four. More color choices can be used in complex and detailed aids.

TABLE 16.2 Subjective Interpretations of Color

COOL COLORS	MOOD, EMOTION	MEANINGS
Blue	calm, cool	reassurance, mystery, peace, importance, confidence, intelligence, stability
Green	life, renewal	restfulness, calmness, balance, harmony, stability
Gray	elegant, neutral	conservative, mourning, formality, strength, mystery
White	light, brilliance	purity, cleanliness, innocence, softness

NEUTRAL COLORS	MOOD, EMOTION	MEANINGS
Ivory	relaxation, quiet	earthiness, pleasantness, purity, elegance
Brown	down-to-earth	wholesomeness, earthiness, dullness, steadfastness, friendliness
Beige	dependable, flexible	calmness, crispness, conventionality, simplicity

WARM COLORS	MOOD, EMOTION	MEANINGS
Red	love, hot	conflict, anger, exertion, power, danger, war
Yellow	warm, happiness	conflict, caution, hope, cowardice
Orange	flamboyant, energetic	vibrancy, energy, autumn, citrus
Black	dark, absence	conservative, seriousness, conventionality, mystery, sophistication

Source: Adapted from Jacci H. Bear, "The Meaning of Color," About.com, accessed July 17, 2010, desktoppub.about.com/od/choosingcolors/p/color_meanings.htm.

Chapter 17

Using Presentation Software

This chapter is taken from Dan O'Hair, Rob Stewart, and Hannah Rubenstein, *A Speaker's Guidebook*, Sixth Edition, pp. 294–308 (Chapter 22).

Public speakers can use a variety of powerful software tools for creating and displaying high-quality visual aids. These programs include the familiar Microsoft PowerPoint and its Apple counterpart, Keynote. In addition to these desktop applications, several Web-based presentation programs, such as Prezi (www.prezi.com), SlideRocket (www.sliderocket.com), and Zoho Show (www.zoho.com), provide some of the same basic features. Preloaded *templates* provide expert guidelines for font, color, and background combinations, or you can compose customized designs. Multimedia displays may be produced by importing photos, audio, and video into your displays.

■ Give a Speech, Not a Slide Show

Frequently we hear someone say, "I'm giving a PowerPoint today," instead of "I'm giving a speech today." Some speakers hide behind their visual displays, focusing their attention on the slide show rather than on the audience. They might erroneously believe that the computerized display itself is the presentation, or that it will somehow save an otherwise poorly planned speech.[1] Other speakers become so enamored of generating graphics or creating glitzy multimedia presentations that they forget their primary mission: to communicate through the spoken word[2] and their physical presence. These behaviors usually signal inadequate preparation on the speaker's part.[3] As with all presentation aids, software tools such as PowerPoint, Keynote, and Prezi can sometimes help listeners process information and enhance a speech, but only as long as you truly work to engage the audience and achieve your speech goal.

■ Avoid Technical Glitches

Technical errors are always a hazard with computerized slides. Common risks include incompatibility of a PowerPoint or Keynote file with an operating system, an Internet connection failing while using Prezi, a display screen malfunction, or a computer drive freezing when a media file is clicked to play. (See the checklist on preventive maintenance on P. 259 to review steps you can take to avoid these problems.)

CHECKLIST
Avoid Technical Glitches
• Check that the operating system of the computer you will use during your speech (e.g., Windows XP, Mac OS X) is compatible with the operating system used to create the aids.
• Confirm that the version of the presentation software used to create the aids corresponds to the software on the computer you will use in the presentation; this will prevent distortions in your graphics, sound, and video.
• Save all the files associated with your presentation (i.e., images, sound files, videos) into the same folder you will use in your presentation.
• Verify that you've saved the files to a source—a flash drive, CD, DVD, website, or e-mail—that will be recognized by the presentation computer.
• Familiarize yourself with the layout and functioning of the presentation computer *before the speech* to facilitate smooth operation during the presentation.
• Prepare a digital backup of your presentation in case of technical challenges.

A Brief Guide to Using PowerPoint, Keynote, and Prezi

Presentation software can be used to display text, artwork, photos, charts, graphs, tables, clip art, videos, and sound. You can upload PowerPoint and Keynote presentations onto the Web for viewing elsewhere, and with additional software you can stream your presentation online in real time. Because Prezi is a Web-based platform, your presentation will be available to you wherever you have an Internet connection. And Web versions of PowerPoint and Keynote provide the general functionality of these platforms online.

Developing a Plan

Often the best place to begin planning your slides is with your speaking outline. Think through which points in your speech might be better explained to your audience with some kind of visual: decide what the content of your slides should be, how many slides you'll need, and how to arrange your slides. Usually, a speaking outline will contain up to five main points. Each main point has at least two subpoints. Consider whether some points are more suited for visual display than others. What features should be used for each slide?

Following is a brief overview of common features and uses of the PowerPoint, Keynote, and Prezi platforms. (For more detailed guidance, consult the online support site for each platform.)

Compose a Presentation in Microsoft PowerPoint

PowerPoint provides three options for composing a set of presentation slides. Begin by familiarizing yourself with the toolbars and icons at the top and bottom of the main screen (see **FIGURE 17.1**).

The *Home tab* presents menus for inserting new slides after the first one, choosing layouts and themes for your slides, and manipulating fonts and styles. Use *Slide Lay-*

out to choose the format you want to display a title page and section pages, headings, body text, pictures, and captions. This layout will apply to all slides. In the left pane, you can view slides as you create them.

The *Design tab* includes about forty-eight predesigned templates, called *Themes.* Templates allow you to apply a consistent layout and color scheme to each slide in the presentation. Each template is designed to convey a certain look or feel. With *Blank* slide layout, you customize every aspect of the presentation: color, font, type and size, organization of content, and graphics. This option allows the greatest degree of flexibility. The challenge is that each slide essentially starts from scratch, but once you have designed a slide with the features you want, you can set it as a template so all slides share the same features.

View Options

PowerPoint offers three different ways to view slides as you create them: *normal view, slide-sorter view,* and *slide-show view.*

- *Normal view* allows you to view and edit the individual slides (see **FIGURE 17.1**). Below each slide is a space to add notes. The left pane of the normal view screen shows the thumbnail and outline views of the slides as they are created. You can enter and edit slide text in the outline pane.

- *Slide-sorter view* provides a graphical representation of all the slides in the presentation, in the order they were created. In this view you can click and drag slides to reorganize the presentation sequence or to delete slides (see **FIGURE 17.2**).

- *Slide-show view* is the actual view to use for projecting the presentation to an audience. Each slide appears in its proper sequence and fills the entire screen.

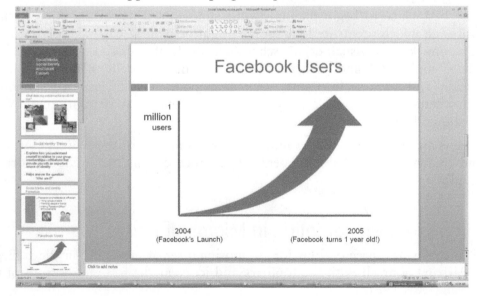

Microsoft

FIGURE 17.1 Normal View in PowerPoint

Masters

For each presentation you create using a design template, PowerPoint creates a *Slide Master*. Slide Masters contain any unique elements (font, background, colors, and so forth) that you want to appear on every slide. For example, if you want a logo, an image, or a line of text to appear on each slide, add that item to the Slide Master, and it will automatically appear on all the slides in your presentation. The *Handout Master* is a page-size view depicting a number of slides per page. When printed, this view may serve as a handout useful for audience members to have as a record of the presentation. To display a Master, click the *View tab* and select *Slide Master.*

In any slide layout other than a blank layout, you replace the sample text in a textbox with your own text. (In a blank layout you insert a textbox where needed.) You can apply bold, italics, and other text modifications. When you finish entering text, deselect the placeholder by clicking a blank area of the slide.

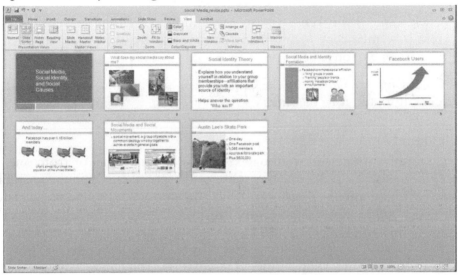

Microsoft

FIGURE 17.2 Slide-Sorter View in PowerPoint

Inserting Objects

You can easily import photos, graphs, clip art, and other objects into PowerPoint as *slide inserts* to supplement or illustrate your speech points. Some slide layouts display icons for each kind of object that can be inserted into the slide show. With a slide open in normal view, select the *Insert menu* at the top of your screen, and click on the type of object you want to insert: Picture, Clip Art, Shapes, Chart, Word Art, Equation, or even Sound or Video. Be careful not to overuse inserts; audience attention tends to lessen as slides appear more complex.[4]

Inserting Video

Video clips can be inserted into your PowerPoint presentation for added impact. PowerPoint presentations can include video clips and even portions of movies and television as supporting material for speeches. The availability of amateur video on websites such as YouTube (www.youtube.com) and the increasing ease of transferring video to computers from portable digital devices make embedding video even simpler. Though it's easy to add video to your presentation, you will need to practice running the video in your slideshow. To add video to a slide, follow these steps:

1. In *Normal view,* click the slide to which you want to add a video clip.

2. On the *Insert menu,* click the arrow under video.

3. Do one of the following:

   - Click *Video from File,* locate the folder that contains the file, and then double-click the file that you want to add. You will have to include this file in the same folder with your PowerPoint file if you display the presentation from a different computer.

   - Click *Video from Website,* paste the embed code from the website into the text box, then click Insert (an embed code is provided with each video on sites such as YouTube).

   - Click *Clip Art Video,* use the Clip Art task pane to find an image, and then click it to add it to the slide.

Transition and Animation Effect

When moving from one slide to the next in your presentation, or from one point to another within a single slide, you may wish to add special effects in the form of transitions and text animations. *Transition effects* add motion and sound as you click from one slide to another. For example, you can play a "swoosh" sound when the slide appears, or you can make the slides dissolve into black or red as you shift from one to another. *Animation effects*—sometimes referred to as *builds*—allow you to reveal text or graphics within a slide during a presentation. You can reveal one letter, word, or paragraph at a time as you discuss each item. Or you can make text or objects look dimmer or change color when you add another element.

Note that your PowerPoint presentation will be just as effective without transitions and animation effects. If you do decide to use them, however, use them sparingly and keep them consistent throughout the entire slide show or within different sections. Unnecessary effects can distract from your message and harm the presentation.

■ Compose a Presentation in Apple Keynote

You can create a Keynote presentation in a few easy steps. After opening the Keynote application, locate the task menu at the top of the page and pull down the *File menu* to choose *New.* A window will open showing you a variety of themes to choose from (see FIGURE 17.3). Select a theme by double-clicking it (or single-click it then click Choose at the bottom of the window). A new window will open showing the Navigator view—a central panel depicting an editable slide with formatting menus across the top and more down the right. Down the left pane is the thumbnail-size strip of slides in your presentation. You can view your slides in editable form in the Light Table view and the Outline view. The Light Table view shows the strip of slides in the central panel laid out in a matrix ordered left to right from top to bottom, as if laying photo negatives across an actual light table. This is a useful layout for rearranging your slides. The Outline view allows you to edit and arrange your slides.

Apple

FIGURE 17.3 Apple Keynote Design Themes

Formatting Text

You can format text easily as you create your Keynote slides. Formatting text in your Keynote slides is essentially the same as with PowerPoint slides. In the Navigator view of a selected template are preset placeholders for entering text. Use these placeholders to maintain the layouts and fonts set for your selected template. You can also modify these features by clicking on the *Text formatting* button at the top of the screen (denoted by the large capital T) to open the text formatting menu pane on the right, referred to as the Inspector. With the Inspector you are able to select a font style, size, and emphasis (e.g., bold or italic), set the alignment and spacing of text within its field on the slide, and arrange text in bullet or list formats. You can also change the locations, sizes, and shapes of text boxes in your slides. Click on or near the text on a slide to view the borders of the text box. Click and hold a border to manipulate it.

Adding Slides

Adding more slides in Keynote is simple. Click the plus (+) sign at the bottom of the left side pane to reveal several options, whether slides for text only or for also displaying images. Whichever style of slide you select, you will be able to modify text and image placement to your preferences using the formatting pane on the right (see **FIGURE 17.4**).

Inserting Objects

Keynote enables you to easily embed objects such as images, charts, tables, and media into your presentation slides. Each of these objects has its own formatting options that appear in the Inspector pane when a particular object is selected. Select an object type from the toolbar at top of the Navigator window. Options are *Table, Chart, Text, Shape,* and *Media.* Clicking one of these options will reveal a menu of object types within that category. For example, by clicking *Table* you will see several different table layouts to choose from. The one you select will immediately load onto your draft slide in the Navigator, and the Inspector pane will show a set of tools for modifying the table to fit your needs. The tools include setting colors, borders, shadows, and reflection styles for both cells of the table and formatting the text within cells. Similar options are available when you select objects such as charts and shapes to place in your slides. Note that preset colors, borders, and shadows are available by default to match the theme selected for your presentation, so seldom will you have to actually make adjustments to these features of objects in your slides.

You can add media such as images and audio to your Keynote slides. Click *Media* in the toolbar at the top of the Navigator window; select *Photo, Music,* or *Movies;* then select the media file of choice stored elsewhere on your computer. An embedded audio or video clip will play when that slide is showing in your presentation.

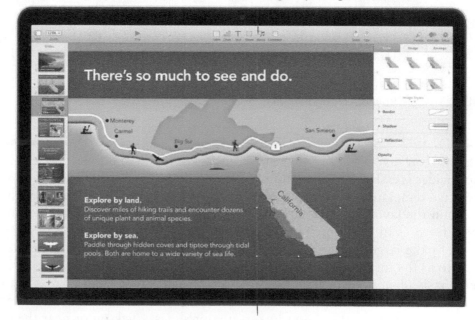

Apple

FIGURE 17.4 Sample Apple Keynote Presentation

Transition and Animation Effects

In Keynote as in PowerPoint, once you have drafted the full set of slides for your presentation you can apply animations to your slides. Set transitions to move from slide to slide. Set object animations to apply movement among objects within slides. To set a transition between slides, select a slide from the left side pane in the Navigator view. In the Inspector pane on the right side of the window, click *Add an Effect* and select a type of transition. You will immediately see a preview of the effect. Use other controls in the Transitions pane to set the direction (e.g., left to right) and duration (e.g., three seconds) of the transition. Somewhat different controls appear depending on the transition type.

In Keynote, animation effects are referred to as *build effects*. Objects such as images, shapes, text, tables, and charts can be made to move onto or off of a slide. Moving an object onto a slide is referred to as *building in*. Moving an object off of a slide is called *building out*. To apply these effects, open a slide for editing. Select the object you want to animate and then select the *Animate tab* in the Inspector pane. In the *Build In* option, click *Add an Effect* and choose an animation effect. Make a similar selection in the *Build Out* option to animate an object off the slide. Additional controls enable you to set the duration and other aspects of the animation. As discussed in the section on PowerPoint, it's best to use build effects sparingly for a professional presentation.

Navigation

To run the Keynote presentation, first select the slide you want to start with, normally the first slide—most likely formatted as a title slide. Next, click the *Play* arrow button at the top of the window. The first slide will appear in full screen. To advance to each successive slide, press the right arrow key on your keyboard or tap the left side of the mouse or a corresponding button on a handheld remote device. Jump ahead to a slide by typing the number of the slide and pressing return. When your presentation has completed, press the Esc key to exit. As you review the slide presentation, you can return to the Navigator window at any time to make adjustments or edits to slides by tapping the Esc key while on that slide. Resume by clicking the *Play* arrow.

■ Compose a Presentation in Prezi

In contrast to applications like PowerPoint and Keynote that operate from software on a desktop, laptop, or tablet computer, Prezi is a Web-based application that requires only an Internet connection. Another key difference is that instead of the "slide" format of PowerPoint and Keynote, Prezi utilizes a "canvas" format. Whereas the slide format provides a relatively lockstep or linear sequence moving from one slide to the next, the canvas format follows a continuous path, presenting a stream-like flow from one *path point* to another, zooming in or out, scrolling up or down, and panning across the canvas to provide transitions among points.

Getting Started

To begin composing a Prezi presentation, go to www.prezi.com. Press the *Get Started* button. You can sign up with a free account, or click the *Student and Teacher Licenses* button to register a student account. Once logged in, you will see a screen labeled All Prezis. Click the *New Prezi* button to open a new presentation. On the next page you can select a template similar to those in PowerPoint and Keynote, or opt to start with a blank format (see **FIGURE 17.5**). Beginning with one of the dozens of available templates will familiarize you with how Prezi operates before trying a blank canvas.

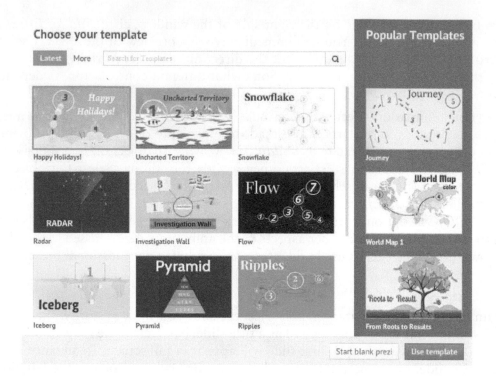

Prezi

FIGURE 17.5 Prezi Templates

Menus

Upon opening a template you should see in the main panel of the window an overview of the elements of the template. At the top center of the window are three pulldown menus giving you options to modify frames and arrows (see **FIGURE 17.6**); insert objects such as media, pictures, and hyperlinks; and select from various themes to change colors to preset formats. The *Present* button at the top left of the window is to put your Prezi into presentation mode, as your audience will see it. Next to it are a button to undo the last action taken in composing your Prezi and a button to save your work. At the top right of the screen is a help and support menu (the one with three short horizontal lines), a menu for selecting different ways to share your Prezi, and a button to close out of the current Prezi session. Place your cursor over the center of the right-hand margin of the screen to see a set of zoom buttons. These are useful to move in and out of different parts of your presentation.

Click to add Title

Prezi

FIGURE 17.6 Frames and Arrows in Prezi

Path Points

In PowerPoint and Keynote, the left-hand pane in the slide editing view shows the thumbnail images of the series of slides comprising the presentation. In Prezi, the left-hand pane shows thumbnail images of the *path points* in the presentation. Path points serve the same purpose as slides—presenting the key and supporting points of information constituting the body of your speech. The first thumbnail, path point 1, is the overview of the entire canvas, highlighting each path point with a number corresponding to its position in the sequence pane on the left-side pane. Clicking on either the thumbnail images or on the numbered path points in the overview activates a zoom-in view of that path point. This view allows you to edit the text and other objects for that portion of your speech content.

Inserting Objects

As with PowerPoint and Keynote slides, a Prezi template has labeled fields where you can add text and other objects. To add a shape, image, or media file to a Prezi presentation, click the *Insert* menu at the top of the window and select the type of object—*Image, Symbols & Shapes, Diagram, YouTube video, Background Music, Document or Media file,* or even *PowerPoint file.* To insert a picture from your own digital photo file, for example, select *Image* in the *Insert* menu. A task pane will open on the right-hand side of the window. You have options to select files, search for images on the Web, or use images already provided by Prezi. Click *Select files* if you are using your own picture. This will open the Explorer (on Windows) or Finder (on Macs) on your computer where you can access your photo files. Select the preferred file and click *Open.* The image will appear in a new frame in the path point you are editing. Follow similar steps to add other objects as support material in your Prezi presentation.

Navigation

In the overview (path point 1), click any object to reveal the Navigation tool, consisting of three buttons—a plus (+) sign, a hand icon, and a minus (–) sign—arranged in a vertical rectangle, hovering over or in the object selected. Clicking the plus sign zooms into or enlarges the object, and the minus sign zooms out of or reduces the object. Clicking the home button reverts to the full overview of the canvas. Clicking and holding down the frame surrounding the object will enable resizing the object. Similar functions are accessible in the *Frames & Arrows* menu at the top of the window.

Clicking on an object frame brings up another part of the Navigation tool containing a *Zoom* button, an icon that activates a shape selection menu, and a *Delete* button. This is the Transformation tool. It enables the selection, sizing, and moving of the frame and the text or objects in it. The frame shape can be changed from rectangular to circular, for example. The *Zoom* button will bring the object to nearly full screen to view space for other elements and objects that can be used as path points in the presentation. Other editing functions can be activated when clicking on the object in close view. For example, a text editing tool will appear when you click anywhere inside the frame so that text can be added to the object.

You can also navigate the canvas and frames with mouse gestures. Scroll forward or backward with your index finger to zoom in and out. Click and hold, then move the mouse left or right, up or down to pan across the canvas.

To view your Prezi as your audience will see it, click the *Present* button at top left of the screen. The Prezi will open in full screen, with a dialog box asking whether you want to stay in the full screen mode, which also gives you keyboard control of the presentation. Click *Allow*. Your presentation will begin with the path point you were on when you clicked *Present*. Be sure to begin with path point 1, the overview (you can easily zoom out to the overview using mouse gestures as noted earlier). Two directional arrows are located at the footer of the screen. Click the right arrow to proceed forward through your path points. Click the left arrow to back up or repeat. As you proceed through your speech, click to the path point in your Prezi that corresponds to where you are in your speech. You will notice the more stream-like movement among points as compared to PowerPoint and Keynote.

■ Finding Media for Presentations

You can import still images, clip art, video, or sound directly into your computer-generated displays by downloading the files from the Internet.

For downloadable digital images, try the following websites:

- Corbis.com (www.corbisimages.com): Contains more than 2 million photographs, prints, and paintings, 35,000 of which you can download for your personal use (for a fee).

- Google (www.google.com), Yahoo! (www.yahoo.com), and Bing (www.bing.com): Popular search engines that offer extensive image searches.

The following sites contain free photographs and other still images:

- www.flickr.com/creativecommons: Access to thousands of photographs shared by amateur and hobbyist photographers.

- www.exalead.com/search/image: An innovative image search engine with over 2 billion images.

- memory.loc.gov/ammem/index/html: Free access to still and moving images depicting the history of the American experience.

The following sites offer downloadable music files and audio clips:

- www.mp3.com

- www.soundclick.com

- www.archive.org/details/audio

- www.dailywav.com

- www.freeaudioclips.com

The following sites contain useful video clips:

- CNN Video (www.cnn.com/video) and ABC News Video (abcnews.go.com/video): Especially useful for speech topics on current events or timely social issues.

- video.search.yahoo.com

- www.bing.com/videos/browse

- video.google.com

Avoiding Copyright Infringement

Be certain to abide by copyright restrictions when using visual and audio materials from the Internet or other sources. Recognize when material is available under fair-use provisions. Even if fair use applies, cite the source of the material in your presentation. Consult your school's information technology (IT) office for statements of policy pertaining to copyrighted and fair-use materials, especially from undocumented sources such as peer-to-peer (P2P) sharing. Improper acquisition or use of a copyrighted object could lead to loss of privileges on your campus computer network or, worse, to legal consequences.

CHECKLIST
Tips for Successfully Using Presentation Software in Your Speech
• Don't let the technology get in the way of relating to your audience.
• Talk to your audience rather than to the screen. Maintain eye contact as much as possible.
• Have a backup plan in case of technical errors.
• If you use a pointer (laser or otherwise), turn it off and put it down as soon as you have made your point.
• Never shine a laser pointer into anyone's eyes. It will burn them!
• Incorporate the aids into your practice sessions until you are confident that they strengthen, rather than detract from, your core message.

CHECKLIST
Ensuring Legal Use of Media Acquired Electronically
• Cite the source of all copyrighted material in your presentation. For example, include a bibliographic footnote on the slide containing the material.
• Be wary of sites purporting to offer "royalty free" media objects; there might actually be other costs associated with the materials.
• When time, resources, and ability allow, create and use your own pictures, video, or audio for your presentation slides.

FROM SLIDE SHOW TO PRESENTATION

Getting Ready to Deliver a PowerPoint, Keynote, or Prezi Presentation

Your software-generated displays can help listeners visually process information (especially complex statistical data; see **From Idea to Image: Using Presentation Aids, P. 244**). Following good preparation practices with these resources can help you avoid distracting technical glitches and take full advantage of this powerful medium.

Check the Venue

Before your speech, take stock of the available presentation technology and the venue layout. It's worthwhile to perform this step even if the speech venue is your usual classroom—you may discover that you didn't know as much about the room as you thought, and familiarizing yourself with its layout and technology will also help you combat any speaking anxiety. See the annotated photo below for important considerations that can help you master a smooth delivery, especially if you are planning to use a computer and the Internet during your presentation.

(clockwise) Jeff Presnail/Getty Images; Purestock/Getty Images; Caspar Benson/Getty Images; iStockphoto

1. **Power sources.** Locate plugs and power strips and ensure that cords can reach the presentation equipment. Consider taping power cords to the floor to keep them from getting in the way.

2. **Computer needs and compatibility.** Figure out which computer you'll be using during the speech and check that all your files, from the slide show to audio and video clips, load successfully to this computer. If possible, you should practice at least once on the presentation computer.

3. **Internet access.** Especially if you use Prezi or if your PowerPoint or Keynote displays require Internet access, check the venue's Internet connections before the speech. Make sure you know any pertinent wireless log-in information or that you have a cable that reaches the Internet jack.

4. **Backup plan.** Create a contingency plan that covers you in case of computer failure. If an overhead projector is available, you might print overhead transparencies from your slide show. Or you might be prepared to put pertinent information on the board. Paper handouts generated from the slide show are another solid backup plan.

5. **Audio.** Determine how you will broadcast any audio aids, and always make sure speaker volume is appropriate before your speech.

Pick Speaker Placement Carefully

Before your speech, choose a place to stand that gives the audience clear sight lines to you and your slide show. When picking your placement, keep in mind that you should be able to face forward at all times, even when changing slides or gesturing toward your aids. This helps you connect with your audience and project clearly, and it prevents you from reading off your slides.

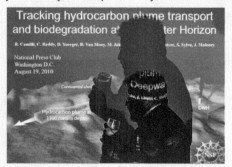

Mark Wilson/Getty Images News/Getty Images

Needs improvement: As this speaker pauses to sip some water, he blocks the slide image with his shadow. His sideways stance discourages eye contact with the audience and indicates that he may be reading off his slides.

Good placement: This speaker's body placement leaves the audience with a clear view of the presentation screen. She can easily access the presentation computer and can also gesture toward the slides without blocking them.

CIS 111
Persuade

In Composition and Communication, just like anything else, there are foundational skills upon which you will continue to build as you develop and articulate more sophisticated messages. In CIS 110, the focus was on developing a strong foundation and mastering basic skills in both written and oral communication. In CIS 110, you also learned how to locate and evaluate information and sources in order to support your informative messages. You have probably heard the saying that "you have to learn to walk before you can run." Well, in Composition and Communication, you have to learn to inform before you can persuade. Working to inform yourself through solid research, and then to develop effective communication messages to inform others has helped you form a strong foundation as you move forward into CIS 111...

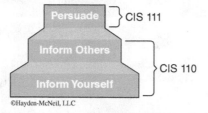

©Hayden-McNeil, LLC

CIS 111 picks up where 110 left off. In this course, you will build on your informative communication skills in order to produce arguments meant to persuade various audiences. You will learn to research, construct, analyze, and critique persuasive messages in a variety of modes including essays, speeches, group projects, and video projects. To communicate confidently on the issues important to your world, you must first cultivate a fundamental understanding of argument. Let's get to it.

Chapter 18

Structuring Arguments

The Classical Oration

Rogerian and Invitational Arguments

Toulmin Argument

This chapter is taken from Dan O'Hair, Rob Stewart, and Hannah Rubenstein, *A Speaker's Guidebook*, Sixth Edition, pp. 121–150 (Chapter 7).

I get hives after eating ice cream. My mouth swells up when I eat cheese. Yogurt triggers my asthma.	Dairy products make me sick. Ice cream is a dairy product.
↓	↓
Dairy products make me sick.	Ice cream makes me sick.

These two sets of statements illustrate the most basic ways in which Western culture structures logical arguments. The first piles up specific examples and draws a conclusion from them: that's **inductive reasoning** and structure. The second sets out a general principle (the major premise of a syllogism) and applies it to a specific case (the minor premise) in order to reach a conclusion: that's **deductive reasoning** and structure. In everyday reasoning, we often omit the middle statement, resulting in what Aristotle called an *enthymeme*: "Since dairy products make me sick, I better leave that ice cream alone." (See p. 379 for more on enthymemes.)

But the arguments you will write in college call for more than just the careful critical thinking offered within inductive and deductive reasoning. You will also need to define claims, explain the contexts in which you are offering them, consider counterarguments fairly and carefully, defend your assumptions, offer convincing evidence, appeal to particular audiences, and more. And you will have to do so using a clear structure that moves your argument forward. This chapter introduces you to three helpful ways to structure arguments. Feel free to borrow from all of them!

■ The Classical Oration

The authors of this book once examined a series of engineering reports and found that—to their great surprise—these reports were generally structured in ways similar to those used by Greek and Roman rhetors two thousand years ago. Thus, this ancient structuring system is alive and well in twenty-first-century culture. The classical oration has six parts, most of which will be familiar to you, despite their Latin names:

Exordium: You try to win the attention and goodwill of an audience while introducing a topic or problem.

Narratio: You present the facts of the case, explaining what happened when, who is involved, and so on. The *narratio* puts an argument in context.

Partitio: You divide up the topic, explaining what the claim is, what the key issues are, and in what order they will be treated.

Confirmatio: You offer detailed support for the claim, using both logical reasoning and factual evidence.

Refutatio: You carefully consider and respond to opposing claims or evidence.

Peroratio: You summarize the case and move the audience to action.

This structure is powerful because it covers all the bases: readers or listeners want to know what your topic is, how you intend to cover it, and what evidence you have to offer. And you probably need a reminder to present a pleasing *ethos* when beginning a presentation and to conclude with enough *pathos* to win an audience over completely. Here, in outline form, is a five-part updated version of the classical pattern, which you may find useful on many occasions:

Introduction

- gains readers' interest and willingness to listen

- establishes your qualifications to write about your topic

- establishes some common ground with your audience

- demonstrates that you're fair and even-handed

- states your claim

Background

- presents information, including personal stories or anecdotes that are important to your argument

Lines of Argument

- presents good reasons, including logical and emotional appeals, in support of your claim

Alternative Arguments

- carefully considers alternative points of view and opposing arguments

- notes the advantages and disadvantages of these views

- explains why your view is preferable to others

Conclusion

- summarizes the argument

- elaborates on the implications of your claim

- makes clear what you want the audience to think or do

- reinforces your credibility and perhaps offers an emotional appeal

Not every piece of rhetoric, past or present, follows the structure of the oration or includes all its components. But you can identify some of its elements in successful arguments if you pay attention to their design. Here are the words of the 1776 Declaration of Independence:

Opens with a brief *exordium* explaining why the document is necessary, invoking a broad audience in acknowledging a need to show "a decent respect to the opinions of mankind." Important in this case, the lines that follow explain the assumptions on which the document rests.

When in the Course of human events, it becomes necessary for one people to dissolve the political bands which have connected them with another, and to assume among the powers of the earth, the separate and equal station to which the Laws of Nature and of Nature's God entitle them, a decent respect to the opin- ions of mankind requires that they should declare the causes which impel them to the separation.

We hold these truths to be self-evident, that all men are created equal, that they are endowed by their Creator with certain unalienable Rights, that among these are Life, Liberty, and the pursuit of Happiness—that to secure these rights, Governments are instituted among Men, deriving their just powers from the consent of the governed—That whenever any Form of Government becomes destructive to these ends, it is the Right of the People to alter or to abolish it and to institute new Government, laying its Foundation on such principles and organizing its powers in such form, as to them shall seem most likely to effect their Safety and Happiness. Prudence, indeed, will dictate that Governments long established should not be changed for light and transient causes; and accordingly all experience hath shewn that mankind are more disposed to suffer, while evils are sufferable, than to right themselves by abolishing the forms to which they are accustomed. But when a long train of abuses and usurpations, pursuing invariably the same Object evinces a design to reduce them under absolute Despotism, it is their right, it is their duty, to throw off such Government and to provide new Guards for their future security.—Such has been the patient sufferance of these Colonies; and such is now the necessity which constrains them to alter their former Systems of Government. The history of the present King of Great Britain is a history of repeated injuries and usurpations, all having in direct object the establishment of an absolute Tyranny over these States. To prove this, let Facts be submitted to a candid world.

A *narratio* follows, offering background on the situation: because the government of George III has become destructive, the framers of the Declaration are obligated to abolish their allegiance to him.

—Declaration of Independence, July 4, 1776

Arguably, the partitio begins here, followed by the longest part of the document (not reprinted here), a *confirmatio* that lists the "long train of abuses and usurpations" by George III.

The authors might have structured this argument by beginning with the last two sentences of the excerpt and then listing the facts intended to prove the king's abuse and tyranny. But by choosing first to explain the purpose and "self-evident" assumptions behind their argument and only then moving on to demonstrate how these "truths" have been denied by the British, the authors forge an immediate connection with readers and build up to the memorable conclusion. The structure is both familiar and inventive—as your own use of key elements of the oration should be in the arguments you compose.

National Archives

FIGURE 18.1 The Declaration of Independence

■ Rogerian and Invitational Arguments

In trying to find an alternative to confrontational and angry arguments like those that so often erupt in legislative bodies around the world, scholars and teachers of rhetoric have adapted the nonconfrontational principles employed by psychologist Carl Rogers in personal therapy sessions. In simple terms, Rogers argued that people involved in disputes should not respond to each other until they could fully, fairly, and even sympathetically state the other person's position. Scholars of rhetoric Richard E. Young, Alton L. Becker, and Kenneth L. Pike developed a four-part structure that is now known as Rogerian argument:

1. **Introduction:** You describe an issue, a problem, or a conflict in terms rich enough to show that you fully understand and respect any alternative position or positions.

2. **Contexts:** You describe the contexts in which alternative positions may be valid.

3. **Writer's position:** You state your position on the issue and present the circumstances in which that opinion would be valid.

4. **Benefits to opponent:** You explain to opponents how they would benefit from adopting your position.

The key to Rogerian argumentation is a willingness to think about opposing positions and to describe them fairly. In a Rogerian structure, you have to acknowledge that alternatives to your claims exist and that they might be reasonable under certain circumstances. In tone, Rogerian arguments steer clear of heated and stereotypical language, emphasizing instead how all parties in a dispute might gain from working together.

In the same vein, feminist scholars Sonja Foss and Cindy Griffin have outlined a form of argument they label "invitational," one that begins with careful attention to and respect for the person or the audience you are in conversation with. Foss and Griffin show that such listening—in effect, walking in the other person's shoes—helps you see that person's points of view more clearly and thoroughly and thus offers a basis for moving together toward new understandings. The kind of argument they describe is what another rhetorician, Krista Ratcliffe, calls "rhetorical listening," which helps to establish productive connections between people and thus helps enable effective cross-cultural communications.

Invitational rhetoric has as its goal not winning over opponents but getting people and groups to work together and identify with each other; it strives for connection, collaboration, and the mutually informed creation of knowledge. As feminist scholar Sally Miller Gearhart puts it, invitational argument offers a way to disagree without hurting one another, to disagree with respect. This kind of argument is especially important in a society that increasingly depends on successful collaboration to get things done. In college, you may have opportunities to practice invitational rhetoric in peer-review sessions, when each member of a group listens carefully in order to work through problems and issues. You may also practice invitational rhetoric looking at any contested issue from other people's points of view, taking them into account, and engaging them fairly and respectfully in your own argument. Students we know who are working in high-tech industries also tell us how much such arguments are valued, since they fuel innovation and "out of the box" thinking.

Invitational arguments, then, call up structures that more resemble good two-way conversations or free-ranging dialogues than straight-line marches from thesis to conclusion. Even conventional arguments benefit from invitational strategies by giving space early on to a full range of perspectives, making sure to present them thoroughly and clearly. Remember that in such arguments your goal is enhanced understanding so that you can open up a space for new perceptions and fresh ideas.

Consider how Frederick Douglass tried to broaden the outlook of his audiences when he delivered a Fourth of July oration in 1852. Most nineteenth-century Fourth of July speeches followed a pattern of praising the Revolutionary War heroes and emphasizing freedom, democracy, and justice. Douglass, a former slave, had that tradition in mind as he delivered his address, acknowledging the "great principles" that the "glorious anniversary" celebrates. But he also asked his (white) listeners to see the occasion from another point of view:

Fellow-citizens, pardon me, allow me to ask, why am I called upon to speak here today? What have I, or those I represent, to do with your national independence? Are the great principles of political freedom and natural justice, embodied in the Declaration of Independence, extended to us? And am I, therefore, called upon to bring our humble offering to the national altar, and to confess the benefits and express devout gratitude for the blessings resulting from your independence to us?...I say it with a sad sense of the disparity between us. I am not included within the pale of this glorious anniversary! Your high independence only reveals the immeasurable distance between us. The blessings in which you, this day, rejoice, are not enjoyed in common. The rich inheritance of justice, liberty, prosperity and independence, bequeathed by your fathers, is shared by you, not by me. The sunlight that brought life and healing to you, has brought stripes and death to me. This Fourth of July is yours, not mine. You may rejoice, I must mourn.

—Frederick Douglass, "What to the Slave is the Fourth of July?"

© World History Archive/Alamy

FIGURE 18.2 Frederick Douglass

Although his speech is in some ways confrontational, Douglass is also inviting his audience to see a version of reality that they could have discovered on their own had they dared to imagine the lives of African Americans living in the shadows of American liberty. Issuing that invitation, and highlighting its consequences, points a way forward in the conflict between slavery and freedom, black and white, oppression and justice, although response to Douglass's invitation was a long time in coming.

In May 2014, First Lady Michelle Obama used elements of invitational argument in delivering a speech to high school graduates from several high schools in Topeka, Kansas. Since the speech occurred on the sixtieth anniversary of the Supreme Court's decision to disallow "separate but equal" schools in the landmark *Brown v. Board of Education* case, which was initiated in Topeka, Mrs. Obama invited the audience to experience the ups and downs of students before and after the decision, putting themselves in the places of the young African Americans who, in 1954, desperately wanted the freedom to attend well-funded schools open to white students. So she tells the stories of some of these young people, inviting those there to walk a while in their shoes. And she concludes her speech with a call for understanding and cooperation:

> Every day, you have the same power to choose our better history—by opening your hearts and minds, by speaking up for what you know is right, by sharing the lessons of *Brown v. Board of Education*, the lessons you learned right here in Topeka, wherever you go for the rest of our lives. I know you all can do it. I am so proud of all of you, and I cannot wait to see everything you achieve in the years ahead.

AP Photo/Orlin Wagner

FIGURE 18.3 Michelle Obama speaking in Topeka, Kansas

In this speech, Mrs. Obama did not castigate audience members for failing to live up to the ideals of *Brown v. Board of Education* (though she could have done so), nor does she dwell on current ills in Topeka. Rather, she invokes "our better history" and focuses on the ways those in Topeka have helped to write that history. She identifies with her audience and asks them to identify with her—and she aims to inspire the young graduates to follow her example.

The use of invitational argument and careful listening in contemporary political life are rare, but in spite of much evidence to the contrary (think of the repeatedly demonstrated effectiveness of political attack ads), the public claims to prefer nonpartisan and invitational rhetoric to one-on-one, winner-take-all battles, suggesting that such an approach strikes a chord in many people, especially in a world that is increasingly open to issues of diversity. The lesson to take from Rogerian or invitational argument is that it makes good sense in structuring your own arguments to learn opposing positions well enough to state them accurately and honestly, to strive to understand the points of view of your opponents, to acknowledge those views fairly in your own work, and to look for solutions that benefit as many people as possible.

RESPOND

Choose a controversial topic that is frequently in the news, and decide how you might structure an argument on the subject, using the general principles of the classical oration. Then look at the same subject from a Rogerian or invitational perspective. How might your argument differ? Which approach would work better for your topic? For the audiences you might want to address?

■ Toulmin Argument

In *The Uses of Argument* (1958), British philosopher Stephen Toulmin presented structures to describe the way that ordinary people make reasonable arguments. Because Toulmin's system acknowledges the complications of life—situations when we qualify our thoughts with words such as *sometimes, often, presumably, unless,* and *almost*—his method isn't as airtight as formal logic that uses syllogisms (see p. 278 in this chapter). But for that reason, Toulmin logic has become a powerful and, for the most part, practical tool for understanding and shaping arguments in the real world.

Toulmin argument will help you come up with and test ideas and also figure out what goes where in many kinds of arguments. Let's take a look at the basic elements of Toulmin's structure:

Claim	the argument you wish to prove
Qualifiers	any limits you place on your claim
Reason(s)/Evidence	support for your claim
Warrants	underlying assumptions that support your claim
Backing	evidence for warrant

If you wanted to state the relationship between them in a sentence, you might say:

> My claim is true, to a qualified degree, because of the following reasons, which make sense if you consider the warrant, backed by these additional reasons.

These terms—claim, evidence, warrants, backing, and qualifiers—are the building blocks of the Toulmin argument structure. Let's take them one at a time.

Making Claims

Toulmin arguments begin with claims, debatable and controversial statements or assertions you hope to prove.

A claim answers the question *So what's your point?* or *Where do you stand on that?* Some writers might like to ignore these questions and avoid stating a position. But when you make a claim worth writing about, then it's worth standing up and owning it.

Is there a danger that you might oversimplify an issue by making too bold a claim? Of course. But making that sweeping claim is a logical first step toward eventually saying something more reasonable and subtle. Here are some fairly simple, undeveloped claims:

> Congress should enact legislation that establishes a path to citizenship for illegal immigrants.

> It's time for the World Health Organization (WHO) to exert leadership in coordinating efforts to stem the Ebola epidemic in West Africa.

> NASA should launch a human expedition to Mars.

> Veganism is the most responsible choice of diet.

> Military insurance should not cover the cost of sex change surgery for service men and women.

Good claims often spring from personal experiences. You may have relevant work or military or athletic experience—or you may know a lot about music, film, sustainable agriculture, social networking, inequities in government services—all fertile ground for authoritative, debatable, and personally relevant claims.

RESPOND

Claims aren't always easy to find. Sometimes they're buried deep within an argument, and sometimes they're not present at all. An important skill in reading and writing arguments is the ability to identify claims, even when they aren't obvious.

Collect a sample of six to eight letters to the editor of a daily newspaper (or a similar number of argumentative postings from a political blog). Read each item, and then identify every claim that the writer makes. When you've compiled your list of claims, look carefully at the words that the writer or writers use when stating their positions. Is there a common vocabulary? Can you find words or phrases that signal an impending claim? Which of these seem most effective? Which ones seem least effective? Why?

Offering Evidence and Good Reasons

You can begin developing a claim by drawing up a list of reasons to support it or finding **evidence** that backs up the point.

| EVIDENCE AND REASON(S) | → | SO CLAIM |

One student writer wanted to gather good reasons in support of an assertion that his college campus needed more official spaces for parking bicycles. He did some research, gathering statistics about parking-space allocation, numbers of people using particular designated slots, and numbers of bicycles registered on campus. Before he went any further, however, he listed his primary reasons for wanting to increase bicycle parking:

- **Personal experience:** At least twice a week for two terms, he was unable to find a designated parking space for his bike.

- **Anecdotes:** Several of his friends told similar stories. One even sold her bike as a result.

- **Facts:** He found out that the ratio of car to bike parking spaces was 100 to 1, whereas the ratio of cars to bikes registered on campus was 25 to 1.

- **Authorities:** The campus police chief told the college newspaper that she believed a problem existed for students who tried to park bicycles legally.

On the basis of his preliminary listing of possible reasons in support of the claim, this student decided that his subject was worth more research. He was on the way to amassing a set of good reasons and evidence that were sufficient to support his claim.

In shaping your own arguments, try putting claims and reasons together early in the writing process to create enthymemes. Think of these enthymemes as test cases or even as topic sentences:

> Bicycle parking spaces should be expanded because the number of bikes on campus far exceeds the available spots.

It's time to lower the driving age because I've been driving since I was fourteen and it hasn't hurt me.

National legalization of marijuana is long overdue since it is already legal in over twenty states, has shown to be less harmful than alcohol, and provides effective relief from pain associated with cancer.

Violent video games should be carefully evaluated and their use monitored by the industry, the government, and parents because these games cause addiction and psychological harm to players.

As you can see, attaching a reason to a claim often spells out the major terms of an argument.

"I know your type, you're the type who'll make me prove every claim I make."

FIGURE 18.4 Anticipate challenges to your claims.

© 2009 Charles Barsotti/The New Yorker Collection/The Cartoon Bank

But your work is just beginning when you've put a claim together with its supporting reasons and evidence—because readers are certain to begin questioning your statement. They might ask whether the reasons and evidence that you're offering really do support the claim: should the driving age really be changed just because you've managed to drive since you were fourteen? They might ask pointed questions about your evidence: exactly how do you know that the number of bikes on campus far exceeds the number of spaces available? Eventually, you've got to address potential questions about the quality of your assumptions and the quality of your evidence. The connection between claim and reason(s) is a concern at the next level in Toulmin argument.

Determining Warrants

Crucial to Toulmin argument is appreciating that there must be a logical and persuasive connection between a claim and the reasons and data supporting it. Toulmin calls this connection the **warrant**. It answers the question *How exactly do I get from the data to the claim?* Like the warrant in legal situations (a search warrant, for example), a sound warrant in an argument gives you authority to proceed with your case.

The warrant tells readers what your (often unstated) assumptions are—for example, that any practice that causes serious disease should be banned by the government. If readers accept your warrant, you can then present specific evidence to develop your claim. But if readers dispute your warrant, you'll have to defend it before you can move on to the claim itself.

Stating warrants can be tricky because they can be phrased in various ways. What you're looking for is the general principle that enables you to justify the move from a reason to a specific claim—the bridge connecting them. The warrant is the assumption that makes the claim seem believable. It's often a value or principle that you share with your readers. Here's an easy example:

> Don't eat that mushroom: it's poisonous.

The warrant supporting this enthymeme can be stated in several ways, always moving from the reason (*it's poisonous*) to the claim (*Don't eat that mushroom*):

> Anything that is poisonous shouldn't be eaten.

> If something is poisonous, it's dangerous to eat.

Here's the relationship, diagrammed:

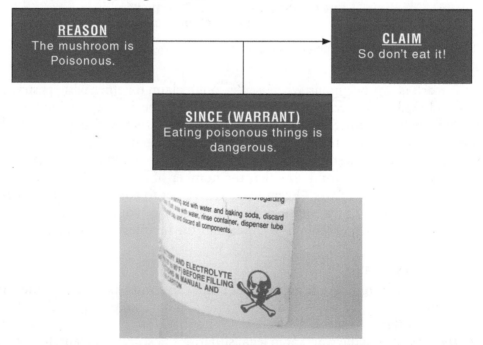

FIGURE 18.5 A simple icon—a skull and crossbones—can make a visual argument that implies a claim, a reason, and a warrant.

PhotoLink/Getty Images

Perfectly obvious, you say? Exactly—and that's why the statement is so convincing. If the mushroom in question is a death cap or destroying angel (and you might still need expert testimony to prove that it is), the warrant does the rest of the work, making the claim that it supports seem logical and persuasive.

Let's look at a similar example, beginning with the argument in its basic form:

> We'd better stop for gas because the gauge has been reading empty for more than thirty miles.

In this case, you have evidence that is so clear (a gas gauge reading empty) that the reason for getting gas doesn't even have to be stated: the tank is almost empty. The warrant connecting the evidence to the claim is also pretty obvious:

> If the fuel gauge of a car has been reading empty for more than thirty miles, then that car is about to run out of gas.

Since most readers would accept this warrant as reasonable, they would also likely accept the statement the warrant supports.

Naturally, factual information might undermine the whole argument: the fuel gauge might be broken, or the driver might know that the car will go another fifty miles even though the fuel gauge reads empty. But in most cases, readers would accept the warrant.

Now let's consider how stating and then examining a warrant can help you determine the grounds on which you want to make a case. Here's a political enthymeme of a familiar sort:

> Flat taxes are fairer than progressive taxes because they treat all taxpayers in the same way.

Warrants that follow from this enthymeme have power because they appeal to a core American value—equal treatment under the law:

> Treating people equitably is the American way.

> All people should be treated in the same way.

You certainly could make an argument on these grounds. But stating the warrant should also raise a flag if you know anything about tax policy. If the principle is obvious and universal, then why do federal and many progressive state income taxes require people at higher levels of income to pay at higher tax rates than people at lower income levels? Could the warrant not be as universally popular as it seems at first glance? To explore the argument further, try stating the contrary claim and warrants:

> Progressive taxes are fairer than flat taxes because people with more income can afford to pay more, benefit more from government, and shelter more of their income from taxes.

> People should be taxed according to their ability to pay.

> People who benefit more from government and can shelter more of their income from taxes should be taxed at higher rates.

Now you see how different the assumptions behind opposing positions really are. If you decided to argue in favor of flat taxes, you'd be smart to recognize that some members of your audience might have fundamental reservations about your position. Or you might even decide to shift your entire argument to an alternative rationale for flat taxes:

> Flat taxes are preferable to progressive taxes because they simplify the tax code and reduce the likelihood of fraud.

Here, you have two stated reasons that are supported by two new warrants:

> Taxes that simplify the tax code are desirable.

> Taxes that reduce the likelihood of fraud are preferable.

Whenever possible, you'll choose your warrant knowing your audience, the context of your argument, and your own feelings.

Be careful, though, not to suggest that you'll appeal to any old warrant that works to your advantage. If readers suspect that your argument for progressive taxes really amounts to *I want to stick it to people who work harder than I*, your credibility may suffer a fatal blow.

Examples of Claims, Reasons, and Warrants

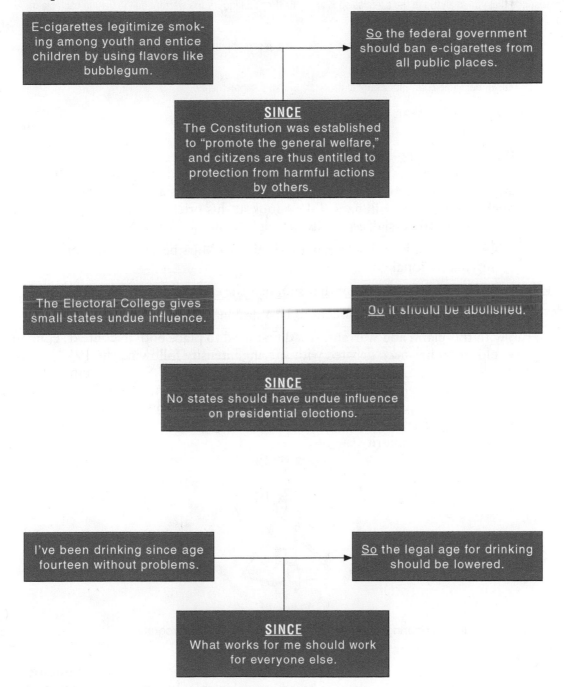

E-cigarettes legitimize smoking among youth and entice children by using flavors like bubblegum.

So the federal government should ban e-cigarettes from all public places.

SINCE
The Constitution was established to "promote the general welfare," and citizens are thus entitled to protection from harmful actions by others.

The Electoral College gives small states undue influence.

So it should be abolished.

SINCE
No states should have undue influence on presidential elections.

I've been drinking since age fourteen without problems.

So the legal age for drinking should be lowered.

SINCE
What works for me should work for everyone else.

Offering Evidence: Backing

The richest, most interesting part of a writer's work—backing—remains to be done after the argument has been outlined. Clearly stated claims and warrants show you how much evidence you will need. Take a look at this brief argument, which is both debatable and controversial, especially in tough economic times:

> NASA should launch a human expedition to Mars because Americans need a unifying national goal.

Here's one version of the warrant that supports the enthymeme:

> What unifies the nation ought to be a national priority.

To run with this claim and warrant, you'd first need to place both in context. Human space exploration has been debated with varying intensity following the 1957 launch of the Soviet Union's *Sputnik* satellite, after the losses of the U.S. space shuttles *Challenger* (1986) and *Columbia* (2003), and after the retirement of the Space Shuttle program in 2011. Acquiring such background knowledge through reading, conversation, and inquiry of all kinds will be necessary for making your case. (See **CHAPTER 22** for more on gaining authority.)

FIGURE 18.6 Sticker honoring the retirement of the Space Shuttle program

© Steven Barrymore

There's no point in defending any claim until you've satisfied readers that questionable warrants on which the claim is based are defensible. In Toulmin argument, evidence you offer to support a warrant is called **backing.**

Warrant

> What unifies the nation ought to be a national priority.

Backing

> Americans want to be part of something bigger than themselves. (Emotional appeal as evidence)

> In a country as diverse as the United States, common purposes and values help make the nation stronger. (Ethical appeal as evidence)

> In the past, government investments such as the Hoover Dam and the *Apollo* moon program enabled many—though not all—Americans to work toward common goals. (Logical appeal as evidence)

In addition to evidence to support your warrant (backing), you'll need evidence to support your claim:

Argument in Brief (Enthymeme/Claim)

> NASA should launch a human expedition to Mars because Americans now need a unifying national goal.

Evidence

> The American people are politically divided along lines of race, ethnicity, religion, gender, and class. (Fact as evidence)

> A common challenge or problem often unites people to accomplish great things. (Emotional appeal as evidence)

> A successful Mars mission would require the cooperation of the entire nation—and generate tens of thousands of jobs. (Logical appeal as evidence)

> A human expedition to Mars would be a valuable scientific project for the nation to pursue. (Appeal to values as evidence)

As these examples show, appeals to values and emotions can be just as appropriate as appeals to logic and facts, and all such claims will be stronger if a writer presents a convincing ethos. In most arguments, appeals work together rather than separately, reinforcing each other. (See CHAPTER 22 for more on ethos.)

Using Qualifiers

Experienced writers know that qualifying expressions make writing more precise and honest. Toulmin logic encourages you to acknowledge limitations to your argument through the effective use of **qualifiers**. You can save time if you qualify a claim early in the writing process. But you might not figure out how to limit a claim effectively until after you've explored your subject or discussed it with others.

Qualifiers

few	more or less	often
it is possible	in some cases	perhaps
rarely	many	under these conditions
it seems	typically	possibly
some	routinely	for the most part
it may be	most	if it were so
sometimes	one might argue	in general

Never assume that readers understand the limits you have in mind. Rather, spell them out as precisely as possible, as in the following examples:

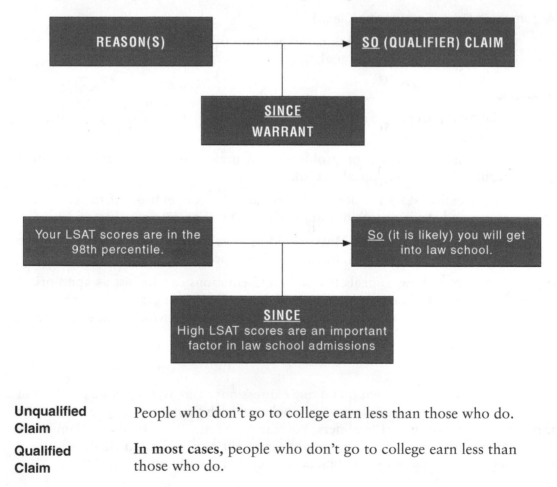

Unqualified Claim	People who don't go to college earn less than those who do.
Qualified Claim	**In most cases,** people who don't go to college earn less than those who do.

Understanding Conditions of Rebuttal

In the Toulmin system, potential objections to an argument are called **conditions of rebuttal**. Understanding and reacting to these conditions are essential to support your own claims where they're weak and also to recognize and understand the reasonable objections of people who see the world differently. For example, you may be a big fan of the Public Broadcasting Service (PBS) and the National Endowment for the Arts (NEA) and prefer that federal tax dollars be spent on these programs. So you offer the following claim:

Claim	The federal government should support the arts.

You need reasons to support this thesis, so you decide to present the issue as a matter of values:

Argument in Brief	The federal government should support the arts because it also supports the military.

Now you've got an enthymeme and can test the warrant, or the premises of your claim:

Warrant	If the federal government can support the military, then it can also support other programs.

But the warrant seems frail: you can hear a voice over your shoulder saying, "In essence, you're saying that *Because we pay for a military, we should pay for everything!*" So you decide to revise your claim:

Revised Argument	If the federal government can spend huge amounts of money on the military, then it can afford to spend moderate amounts on arts programs.

Now you've got a new warrant, too:

Revised Warrant	A country that can fund expensive programs can also afford less expensive programs.

This is a premise that you can defend, since you believe strongly that the arts are just as essential as a strong military is to the well-being of the country. Although the warrant now seems solid, you still have to offer strong grounds to support your specific and controversial claim. So you cite statistics from reputable sources, this time comparing the federal budgets for the military and the arts. You break them down in ways that readers can visualize, demonstrating that much less than a penny of every tax dollar goes to support the arts.

FIGURE 18.7 The new NEA logo

But then you hear those voices again, saying that the "common defense" is a federal mandate; the government is constitutionally obligated to support a military, and support for the arts is hardly in the same league! Looks like you need to add a paragraph explaining all the benefits the arts provide for very few dollars spent, and maybe you should suggest that such funding falls under the constitutional mandate to "promoe the general welfare." Though not all readers will accept these grounds, they'll appreciate that you haven't ignored their point of view: you've gained credibility by anticipating a reasonable objection.

Dealing with conditions of rebuttal is an essential part of argument. But it's important to understand rebuttal as more than mere opposition. Anticipating objections broadens your horizons, makes you more open to alternative viewpoints, and helps you understand what you need to do to support your claim.

Within Toulmin argument, conditions of rebuttal remind us that we're part of global conversations: Internet newsgroups and blogs provide potent responses to positions offered by participants in discussions; instant messaging and social networking let you respond to and challenge others; links on Web sites form networks that are infinitely variable and open. In cyberspace, conditions of rebuttal are as close as your screen.

RESPOND

Using an essay or a project you are composing, do a Toulmin analysis of the argument. When you're done, see which elements of the Toulmin scheme are represented. Are you short of evidence to support the warrant? Have you considered the conditions of rebuttal? Have you qualified your claim adequately? Next, write a brief revision plan: How will you buttress the argument in the places where it is weakest? What additional evidence will you offer for the warrant? How can you qualify your claim to meet the conditions of rebuttal? Then show your paper to a classmate and have him/her do a Toulmin analysis: a new reader will probably see your argument in different ways and suggest revisions that may not have occurred to you.

Outline of a Toulmin Argument

Consider the claim that was mentioned on **p. 291**:

Claim	The federal government should ban e-cigarettes.
Qualifier	The ban would be limited to public spaces.
Good Reasons	E-cigarettes have not been proven to be harmless.
	E-cigarettes legitimize smoking and also are aimed at recruiting teens and children with flavors like bubblegum and cotton candy.
Warrants	The Constitution promises to "promote the general welfare."
	Citizens are entitled to protection from harmful actions by others.
Backing	The United States is based on a political system that is supposed to serve the basic needs of its people, including their health.

Evidence	Analysis of advertising campaigns that reveal direct appeals to children
	Lawsuits recently won against e-cigarette companies, citing the link between e-cigarettes and a return to regular smoking
	Examples of bans on e-cigarettes already imposed in many public places
Authority	Cite the FDA and medical groups on effect of e-cigarette smoking.
Conditions of Rebuttal	E-cigarette smokers have rights, too.
	Smoking laws should be left to the states.
	Such a ban could not be enforced.
Responses	The ban applies to public places; smokers can smoke in private.

A Toulmin Analysis

You might wonder how Toulmin's method holds up when applied to an argument that is longer than a few sentences. Do such arguments really work the way that Toulmin predicts? In the following short argument, well-known linguist and author Deborah Tannen explores the consequences of a shift in the meaning of one crucial word: *compromise*. Tannen's essay, which originally appeared as a posting on Politico.com on June 15, 2011, offers a series of interrelated claims based on reasons, evidence, and warrants that culminate in the last sentence of the essay. She begins by showing that the word *compromise* is now rejected by both the political right and the political left and offers good reasons and evidence to support that claim. She then moves back to a time when "a compromise really was considered great," and offers three powerful pieces of evidence in support of that claim. The argument then comes back to the present, with a claim that the compromise and politeness of the nineteenth century have been replaced by "growing enmity." That claim is supported with reasoning and evidence that rest on an underlying warrant that "vituperation and seeing opponents as enemies is corrosive to the human spirit." The claims in the argument—that *compromise* has become a dirty word and that enmity and an adversarial spirit are on the rise— lead to Tannen's conclusion: rejecting compromise breaks the trust necessary for a democracy and thus undermines the very foundation of our society. While she does not use traditional qualifying words, she does say that the situation she describes is a "threat" to our nation, which qualifies the claim to some extent: the situation is not the "death" of our nation but rather a "threat." Tannen's annotated essay follows.

WHY IS "COMPROMISE" NOW A DIRTY WORD?

DEBORAH TANNEN

Photo: Stephen Voss, courtesy of Deborah Tannen

When did the word "compromise" get compromised?

When did the negative connotations of "He was caught in a compromising position" or "She compromised her ethics" replace the positive connotations of "They reached a compromise"?

Contextual information leading up to initial claim

House Speaker John Boehner said it outright on *60 Minutes* last year. When talking about "compromise," Boehner said, "I reject the word."

Contextual information leading up to initial claim

"When you say the word 'compromise,'" he explained, "...a lot of Americans look up and go, 'Uh-oh, they're gonna sell me out.'" His position is common right now.

In the same spirit, Tony Perkins wrote in a recent CNN.com op-ed piece, "When it comes to conservative principles, compromise is the companion of losers."

The political right is particularly vehement when it comes to compromise. Conservatives are now strongly swayed by the tea party movement, whose clarion call is a refusal to compromise, regardless of the practical consequences.

But the rejection of compromise is more widespread than that. The left regularly savages President Barack Obama for compromising too soon, too much or on the wrong issues. Many who fervently sought universal health coverage, for example, could not celebrate its near accomplishment because the president gave up the public option.

Initial claim

Reason

The death of compromise has become a threat to our nation as we confront crucial issues such as the debt ceiling and that most basic of legislative responsibilities: a federal budget. At stake is the very meaning of what had once seemed unshakable: "the full faith and credit" of the U.S. government.

Evidence

Back when the powerful nineteenth-century senator Henry Clay was called "the great compromiser," achieving a compromise really was considered great. On three occasions, the Kentucky statesman helped the Senate preserve the Union by crafting compromises between the deadlocked slave-holding South and the Northern free states. In 1820, his Missouri Compromise stemmed the spread of slavery. In 1833, when the South was poised to defy federal tariff laws favored by the North and the federal government was about to authorize military action, Clay found a last-minute compromise. And his Compromise of 1850 averted civil war for at least a decade.

It was during an 1850 Senate debate that Clay stated his conviction: "I go for honorable compromise whenever it can be made." Something else he said then holds a key to how the dwindling respect for compromise is related to larger and more dangerous developments in our nation today.

"All legislation, all government, all society," Clay said, "is formed upon the principle of mutual concession, politeness, comity, courtesy; upon these, everything is based."

Warrant

Concession, politeness, comity, courtesy—none of these words could be uttered now with the assurance of listeners' approval. The word "comity" is rarely heard; "concession" sounds weak; "politeness" and "courtesy" sound quaint—much like the contemporary equivalent, "civility."

Claim

Reason

That Clay lauded both compromise and civil discourse in the same speech reveals the link between, on the one hand, the word "compromise" falling into disrepute, and, on the other, the glorification of aggression that I wrote about in my book, *The Argument Culture: Stopping America's War of Words*.

Evidence

Today we have an increasing tendency to approach every task—and each other—in an ever more adversarial spirit. Nowhere is this more evident, or more destructive, than in the Senate.

Claim

Though the two-party system is oppositional by nature, there is plenty of evidence that a certain (yes) comity has been replaced by growing enmity. We don't have to look as far back as Clay for evidence. In 1996, for example, an unprecedented fourteen incumbent senators announced that they would not seek reelection. And many, in farewell essays, described an increase in vituperation and partisanship that made it impossible to do the work of the Senate.

Rebuttal

Evidence

"The bipartisanship that is so crucial to the operation of Congress," Howell Heflin of Alabama wrote, "especially the Senate, has been abandoned." J. James Exon of Nebraska described an "ever-increasing vicious polarization of the electorate" that had "all but swept aside the former preponderance of reasonable discussion."

Evidence

But this is not happening only in the Senate. There is a rising adversarial spirit among the people and the press. It isn't only the obvious invective on TV and radio. A newspaper story that criticizes its subject is praised as "tough"; one that refrains from criticism is scorned as a "puff piece."

Claim

The notion of "balance" today often leads to a search for the most extreme opposing views—so they can be presented as "both sides," leaving no forum for subtlety, multiple perspectives or the middle ground, where most people stand. Framing issues in this polarizing way reinforces the impression that Boehner voiced: that compromising is selling out.

Reason

Evidence

Being surrounded by vituperation and seeing opponents as enemies is corrosive to the human spirit. It's also dangerous to our democracy. The great anthropologist Margaret Mead explained this in a 1962 speech.

Warrant

Claim

"We are essentially a society which must be more committed to a two-party system than to either party," Mead said. "The only way you can have a two-party system is to belong to a party formally and to fight to the death..." not for your party to win but "for the right of the other party to be there too."

Reason

Today, this sounds almost as quaint as "comity" in political discourse.

Reason

Mead traced our two-party system to our unique revolution: "We didn't kill a king and we didn't execute a large number of our people, and we came into our own without the stained hands that have been associated with most revolutions."

With this noble heritage, Mead said, comes "the obligation to keep the kind of government we set up"—where members of each party may "disagree mightily" but still "trust in each other and trust in our political opponents."

Conclusion

Losing that trust, Mead concluded, undermines the foundation of our democracy. That trust is exactly what is threatened when the very notion of compromise is rejected.

What Toulmin Teaches

As Tannen's essay demonstrates, few arguments you read have perfectly sequenced claims or clear warrants, so you might not think of Toulmin's terms in building your own arguments. Once you're into your subject, it's easy to forget about qualifying a claim or finessing a warrant. But remembering what Toulmin teaches will always help you strengthen your arguments:

- Claims should be clear, reasonable, and carefully qualified.

- Claims should be supported with good reasons and evidence. Remember that a Toulmin structure provides the framework of an argument, which you fill out with all kinds of data, including facts, statistics, precedents, photographs, and even stories.

- Claims and reasons should be based on assumptions your audience will likely accept. Toulmin's focus on warrants can be confusing because it asks us to look at the assumptions that underlie our arguments—something many would rather not do. Toulmin pushes us to probe the values that support any argument and to think of how those values relate to particular audiences.

- Effective arguments respectfully anticipate objections readers might offer. Toulmin argument acknowledges that any claim can crumble under certain conditions, so it encourages a complex view that doesn't demand absolute or unqualified positions.

It takes considerable experience to write arguments that meet all these conditions. Using Toulmin's framework brings them into play automatically. If you learn it well enough, constructing good arguments can become a habit.

CULTURAL CONTEXTS FOR ARGUMENT

Organization

As you think about organizing your argument, remember that cultural factors are at work: patterns that you find persuasive are probably ones that are deeply embedded in your culture. In the United States, many people expect a writer to "get to the point" as directly as possible and to articulate that point efficiently and unambiguously. The organizational patterns favored by many in business hold similarities to the classical oration—a highly explicit pattern that leaves little or nothing unexplained—introduction and thesis, background, overview of the parts that follow, evidence, other viewpoints, and conclusion. If a piece of writing follows this pattern, American readers ordinarily find it "well organized."

So it's no surprise that student writers in the United States are expected to make their structures direct and their claims explicit, leaving little unspoken. Their claims usually appear early in an argument, often in the first paragraph.

But not all cultures take such an approach. Some expect any claim or thesis to be introduced subtly, indirectly, and perhaps at the end of a work, assuming that audiences will "read between the lines" to understand what's being said. Consequently, the preferred structure of arguments (and face-to-face negotiations, as well) may be elaborate, repetitive, and full of digressions. Those accustomed to such writing may find more direct Western styles overly simple, childish, or even rude.

When arguing across cultures, look for cues to determine how to structure your presentations effectively. Here are several points to consider:

- Do members of your audience tend to be very direct, saying explicitly what they mean? Or are they restrained, less likely to call a spade a spade? Consider adjusting your work to the expectations of the audience.

- Do members of your audience tend to respect authority and the opinions of groups? They may find blunt approaches disrespectful or contrary to their expectations.

- Consider when to state your thesis: At the beginning? At the end? Somewhere else? Not at all?

- Consider whether digressions are a good idea, a requirement, or an element to avoid.

Chapter 19

PROPOSALS

This chapter is taken from Andrea A. Lunsford and John J. Ruszkiewicz, *Everything's An Argument*, Seventh Edition, pp. 272–304 (Chapter 12).

Left to right: © Florian Kopp/agefotostock.com; spaxiax/Shutterstock; AP Photo/Eric Gay

A student looking forward to spring break proposes to two friends that they join a group that will spend the vacation helping to build a school in a Haitian village.

The members of a club for undergrad business majors talk about their common need to create informative, appealing, interactive résumés. After much talk, three members suggest that the club develop a résumé app especially for business majors looking for a first job.

A project team at a large architectural firm works for three months developing a response to an RFP (request for proposal) to convert a university library into a digital learning center.

■ Understanding and Categorizing Proposals

We live in an era of big proposals—complex programs for health care reform, bold dreams to privatize space exploration, multibillion-dollar designs for high-speed rail systems, ceaseless calls to improve education, and so many other such ideas brought down to earth by sobering proposals for budget reform and deficit reduction. As a result, there's often more talk than action because persuading people (or legislatures) to do something—or *anything*!—is always hard. But that's what *proposal arguments* do: they provide thoughtful reasons for supporting or sometimes resisting change.

Such arguments, whether national or local, formal or casual, are important not only on the national scene but also in all of our lives. How many proposals do you make or respond to in one day? A neighbor might suggest that you volunteer to help clean up an urban creek bed; a campus group might demand that students get better seats at football games; a supervisor might ask for ideas to improve customer satisfaction at a restaurant; you might offer an ad agency reasons to hire you as a summer intern—or propose to a friend that you take in the latest zombie film. In each case, the proposal implies that some action should take place and suggests that there are sound reasons why it should.

By permission of Steve Breen and Creators Syndicate, Inc.

FIGURE 19.1 This cartoon, by Steve Breen, suggests that high-speed rail proposals are going to run into a major obstacle in California.

In their simplest form, proposal arguments look something like this:

A should do B because of C.

```
┌──────── A ────────┐┌──────────── B ────────────┐
```
Our student government should endorse the Academic Bill of Rights

```
┌──────────────────── C ────────────────────┐
```
because students should not be punished in their courses for their personal political views.

Proposals come at us so routinely that it's not surprising that they cover a dizzyingly wide range of possibilities. So it may help to think of proposal arguments as divided roughly into two kinds—those that focus on specific practices and those that focus on broad matters of policy. Here are several examples of each kind:

Proposals about Practices

- The college should allow students to pay tuition on a month-by-month basis.

- Commercial hotels should stop opposing competitors like Airbnb.

- College athletes should be paid for the services they provide.

Proposals about Policies

- The college should adopt a policy guaranteeing that students in all majors can graduate in four years.

- The United Nations should make saving the oceans from pollution a global priority.

- Major Silicon Valley firms should routinely reveal the demographic makeup of their workforces.

■ Characterizing Proposals

Proposals have three main characteristics:

1. They call for change, often in response to a problem.

2. They focus on the future.

3. They center on the audience.

Proposals always call for some kind of action. They aim at getting something done— or sometimes at *preventing* something from being done. Proposals marshal evidence and arguments to persuade people to choose a course of action: *Let's build a completely green house. Let's oppose the latest Supreme Court ruling on Internet privacy. Let's create a campus organization for first-generation college students. Let's ban drones from campus airspace, especially at sporting events.* But you know the old saying, "You can lead a horse to water, but you can't make it drink." It's usually easier to *convince* audiences what a good course of action is than to *persuade* them to take it (or pay for it). Even if you present a cogent proposal, you may still have work to do.

Proposal arguments must appeal to more than good sense. Ethos matters, too. It helps if a writer suggesting a change carries a certain gravitas earned by experience or supported by knowledge and research. If your word and credentials carry weight, then an audience is more likely to listen to your proposal. So when the commanders of three *Apollo* moon missions, Neil Armstrong, James Lovell, and Eugene Cernan, wrote an open letter to President Obama expressing their dismay at his administration's decision to cancel NASA's plans for advanced spacecraft and new lunar missions, they won a wide audience:

> For The United States, the leading space faring nation for nearly half a century, to be without carriage to low Earth orbit and with no human exploration capability to go beyond Earth orbit for an indeterminate time into the future, destines our nation to become one of second or even third rate stature. While the President's plan envisages humans traveling away from Earth and perhaps toward Mars at some time in the future, the lack of developed rockets and spacecraft will assure that ability will not be available for many years.

> Without the skill and experience that actual spacecraft operation provides, the USA is far too likely to be on a long downhill slide to mediocrity. America must decide if it wishes to remain a leader in space. If it does, we should institute a program which will give us the very best chance of achieving that goal.

But even their considerable ethos was not enough to carry the day with the space agency and the man who made the decision.

Michael Williamson/The Washington Post/Getty Images

FIGURE 19.2 All that remains of the American space program?

Yet, as the space program example obviously demonstrates, proposal arguments focus on the future—what people, institutions, or governments should do over the upcoming weeks, months, or, in the NASA moon-mission example, decades. This orientation toward the future presents special challenges, since few of us have crystal balls. Proposal arguments must therefore offer the best evidence available to suggest that actions we recommend will achieve what they promise.

In May 2014, Senator Elizabeth Warren introduced legislation aimed at reducing student loan debt, in part by allowing for refinancing. In an interview in *Rolling Stone*, Senator Warren explained:

> Homeowners refinance their loans when interest rates go down. Businesses refinance their loans. But right now, there's no way for students to be able to do that. I've proposed that we reduce the interest rate on the outstanding loan debt to the same rate Republicans and Democrats came together last year to set on new loans [3.86 percent]. For millions of borrowers, that would cut interest rates in half or more.

Yet Warren's proposal soon came under fire, particularly from senators who argued that the proposed bill did little to reduce borrowing or lower the cost of higher education. So despite the concerns of bankers and economists that the $1.1 trillion student loan debt is dampening the national economy, the bill was turned aside on June 11, 2014.

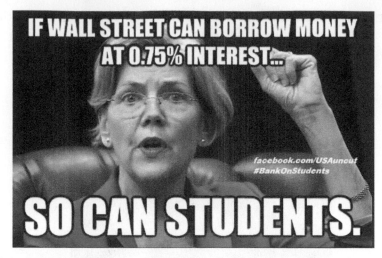

IF WALL STREET CAN BORROW MONEY AT 0.75% INTEREST...

facebook.com/USAuncut
#BankOnStudents

SO CAN STUDENTS.

http://www.ClassWarfareExists.com

FIGURE 19.3

Which raises the matter of audiences, and we are left asking whether Senator Warren's bill spoke equally well to students, parents, bankers, and members of Congress. Some of those audiences failed to be convinced.

Some proposals are tailored to general audiences; consequently, they avoid technical language, make straightforward and relatively simple points, and sometimes use charts, graphs, and tables to make data comprehensible. You can find such arguments, for example, in newspaper editorials, letters to the editor, and political documents like Senator Warren's proposed legislation. And such appeals to a broad group make sense when a proposal—say, to finance new toll roads or build an art museum—must surf on waves of community support and financing.

But often proposals need to win the approval of specific groups or individuals (such as financiers, developers, public officials, and legislators) who have the power to make change actually happen. Such arguments will usually be more technical, detailed, and comprehensive than those aimed at the general public because people directly involved with an issue have a stake in it. They may be affected by it themselves and thus have in-depth knowledge of the subject. Or they may be responsible for implementing the proposal. You can expect them to have specific questions about it and, possibly, formidable objections. So identifying your potential audiences is critical to the success of any proposal. On your own campus, for example, a plan to alter admissions policies might be directed both to students in general and (perhaps in a different form) to the university president, members of the faculty council, and admissions officers.

Ron Sanford/Science Source®/Photo Researchers

FIGURE 19.4 Proposals have to take audience values into account. Shooting deer, even when they're munching on garden flowers, is unacceptable to most suburbanites.

An effective proposal also has to be compatible with the values of the audience. Some ideas may make good sense but cannot be enacted. For example, many American towns and cities have a problem with expanding deer populations. Without natural predators, the deer are moving closer to homes, dining on gardens and shrubbery, and endangering traffic. Yet one obvious and feasible solution—culling the herds through hunting—is usually not saleable to communities (perhaps too many people remember *Bambi*).

RESPOND

Work in a group to identify about half a dozen problems on your campus or in the local community, looking for a wide range of issues. (Don't focus on problems in individual classes.) Once you have settled on these issues, then use various resources—the Web, the phone book (if you can find one), a campus directory—to locate specific people, groups, or offices whom you might address or influence to deal with the issues you have identified.

■ Developing Proposals

In developing a proposal, you will have to do some or all of the following:

- Define a problem that needs a solution or describe a need that is not currently addressed.

- Make a strong claim that addresses the problem or need. Your solution should be an action directed at the future.

- Show why your proposal will fix the problem or address the need.

- Demonstrate that your proposal is feasible.

This might sound easy, but writing a proposal argument can be a process of discovery. At the outset, you think you know exactly what ought to be done, but by the end, you may see (and even recommend) other options.

Defining a Need or Problem

To make a proposal, first establish that a need or problem exists. You'll typically dramatize the problem that you intend to fix at the beginning of your project and then lead up to a specific claim. But in some cases, you could put the need or problem right after your claim as the major reason for adopting the proposal:

> Let's ban cell phones on campus now. Why? Because we've become a school of walking zombies. No one speaks to or even acknowledges the people they meet or pass on campus. Half of our students are so busy chattering to people that they don't participate in the community around them.

How can you make readers care about the problem you hope to address? Following are some strategies:

- Paint a vivid picture of the need or problem.

- Show how the need or problem affects people, both those in the immediate audience and the general public as well.

- Underscore why the need or problem is significant and pressing.

- Explain why previous attempts to address the issue may have failed.

For example, in proposing that the military draft be restored in the United States or that all young men and women give two years to national service (a tough sell!), you might begin by drawing a picture of a younger generation that is self-absorbed, demands instant gratification, and doesn't understand what it means to participate as a full member of society. Or you might note how many young people today fail to develop the life skills they need to strike out on their own. Or like congressional representative Charles Rangel (D-New York), who regularly proposes a Universal National Service Act, you could define the issue as a matter of fairness, arguing that the current all-volunteer army shifts the burden of national service to a small and unrepresentative sample of the American population. Speaking on CNN on January 26, 2013, Rangel said:

> Since we replaced the compulsory military draft with an all-volunteer force in 1973, our nation has been making decisions about wars without worry over who fights them. I sincerely believe that reinstating the draft would compel the American public to have a stake in the wars we fight as a nation. That is why I wrote the Universal National Service Act, known as the "draft" bill, which requires all men and women between ages 18 and 25 to give two years of service in any capacity that promotes our national defense.

Of course, you would want to cite authorities and statistics to prove that any problem you're diagnosing is real and that it touches your likely audience. Then readers *may* be ready to hear your proposal.

© Mike Keefe/Cagle Cartoons, Inc.

FIGURE 19.5 File this cartoon under "anticipate objections to your proposal."

In describing a problem that your proposal argument intends to solve, be sure to review earlier attempts to fix it. Many issues have a long history that you can't afford to ignore (or be ignorant of). Understand too that some problems seem to grow worse every time someone tinkers with them. You might pause before proposing any new attempt to reform the current system of financing federal election campaigns when you discover that previous reforms have resulted in more bureaucracy, more restrictions on political expression, and more unregulated money flowing into the system. *"Enough is enough"* can be a potent argument when faced with such a mess.

RESPOND

If you review "Let's Charge Politicians for Wasting Our Time" at the end of this chapter, a brief proposal by political and culture writer/blogger Virginia Postrel, you'll see that she spends quite a bit of time pointing out the irritation caused by unwanted political robocalls to her landline, even though she recognizes that such calls are illegal on cell phones. Does this focus on the landline take away from her proposal that the politicians should have to pay a fee for such calls as well as for unsolicited email messages they send, a proposal also put forward by technology guru Esther Dyson? Would you advise her to revise her argument—and if so, how?

Making a Strong and Clear Claim

After you've described and analyzed a problem, you're prepared to offer a fix. Begin with your claim (a proposal of what X or Y should do), followed by the reason(s) that X or Y should act and the effects of adopting the proposal:

Claim   Communities should encourage the development of charter schools.

Reason   Charter schools are not burdened by the bureaucracy that is associated with most public schooling.

Effects   Instituting such schools will bring more effective education to communities and offer an incentive to the public schools to improve their programs.

Having established a claim, you can explore its implications by drawing out the reasons, warrants, and evidence that can support it most effectively:

Claim   In light of a recent U.S. Supreme Court decision that ruled that federal drug laws cannot be used to prosecute doctors who prescribe drugs for use in suicide, our state should immediately pass a bill legalizing physician-assisted suicide for patients who are terminally ill.

Reason   Physician-assisted suicide can relieve the suffering of those who are terminally ill and will die soon.

Warrant   The relief of suffering is desirable.

Evidence Oregon voters have twice approved the state's Death with Dignity Act, which has been in effect since 1997, and to date the suicide rate has not risen sharply, nor have doctors given out a large number of prescriptions for death-inducing drugs. Several other states are considering ballot initiatives in favor of doctor-assisted suicide.

The *reason* sets up the need for the proposal, whereas the *warrant* and *evidence* demonstrate that the proposal is just and could meet its objective. Your actual argument would develop each point in detail.

RESPOND

For each problem and solution below, make a list of readers' likely objections to the solution offered. Then propose a solution of your own, and explain why you think it's more workable than the original.

Problem   Future deficits in the Social Security system
Solution Raise the age of retirement to seventy-two.

Problem   Severe grade inflation in college courses
Solution Require a prescribed distribution of grades in every class: 10% A; 20% B; 40% C; 20% D; 10% F.

Problem   Increasing rates of obesity in the general population
Solution Ban the sale of high-fat sandwiches and entrees in fast-food restaurants.

Problem   Inattentive driving because drivers are texting
Solution Institute a one-year mandatory prison sentence for the first offense.

Problem   Increase in sexual assaults on and around campus
Solution Establish a 10:00 p.m. curfew on weekends.

FIGURE 19.6 A proposal argument in four panels.

Showing That the Proposal Addresses the Need or Problem

An important but tricky part of making a successful proposal lies in relating the claim to the need or problem that it addresses. Facts and probability are your best allies. Take the time to show precisely how your solution will fix a problem or at least improve upon the current situation. Sometimes an emotional appeal is fair play, too. Here's former NBA player John Amaechi using that approach when he asks superstar Kobe Bryant of the L.A. Lakers not to appeal a $100,000 penalty he received for hurling an antigay slur at a referee:

> Kobe, stop fighting the fine. You spoke ill-advised words that shot out like bullets, and if the emails I received from straight and gay young people and sports fans in Los Angeles alone are anything to go by, you did serious damage with your outburst.
>
> A young man from a Los Angeles public school emailed me. You are his idol. He is playing up, on the varsity team, he has your posters all over his room, and he hopes one day to play in college and then in the NBA with you. He used to fall asleep with images of passing you the ball to sink a game-winning shot. He watched every game you played this season on television, but this week he feels less safe and less positive about himself because he stared adoringly into your face as you said the word that haunts him in school every single day.

Kobe, stop fighting the fine. Use that money and your influence to set a new tone that tells sports fans, boys, men, and the society that looks up to you that the word you said in anger is not OK, not ever. Too many athletes take the trappings of their hard-earned success and leave no tangible legacy apart from "that shot" or "that special game."

—John Amaechi, "A Gay Former NBA Player
Responds to Kobe Bryant"

Left: Chris Goodney/Bloomberg News/Getty Images; right: © Lucy Nicholson/Reuters/LANDOV

FIGURE 19.7 Left: John Amaechi; right: Kobe Bryant.

The paragraph describing the reaction of the schoolboy provides just the tie that Amaechi needs between his proposal and the problem it would address. The story also gives his argument more power.

Alternatively, if you oppose an idea, these strategies work just as well in reverse: if a proposal doesn't fix a problem, you have to show exactly why. Here are a few paragraphs from an editorial posting by Doug Bandow for *Forbes* in which he refutes a proposal for reinstating military conscription:

> All told, shifting to conscription would significantly weaken the military. New "accessions," as the military calls them, would be less bright, less well educated, and less positively motivated. They would be less likely to stay in uniform, resulting in a less experienced force. The armed forces would be less effective in combat, thereby costing America more lives while achieving fewer foreign policy objectives.
>
> Why take such a step?
>
> One argument, most recently articulated by Thomas Ricks of the Center for a New American Security, is that a draft would save "the government money." That's a poor reason to impress people into service.
>
> First, conscription doesn't save much cash. It costs money to manage and enforce a draft—history demonstrates that not every inductee would go quietly. Conscripts serve shorter terms and reenlist less frequently, increasing turnover, which is expensive. And unless the government instituted a Czarist lifetime draft, everyone beyond the first ranks would continue to expect to be paid.

Second, conscription shifts rather than reduces costs. Ricks suggested that draftees should "perform tasks currently outsourced at great cost to the Pentagon: paperwork, painting barracks, mowing lawns, driving generals around." Better to make people do grunt work than to pay them to do it? Force poorer young people into uniform in order to save richer old people tax dollars. Ricks believes that is a good reason to jail people for refusing to do as the government demands?

The government could save money in the same way by drafting FBI agents, postal workers, Medicare doctors, and congressmen. Nothing warrants letting old politicians force young adults to pay for Washington's profligacy. Moreover, by keeping some people who want to serve out while forcing others who don't want to serve in—creating a veritable evasion industry along the way—conscription would raise total social costs. It would be a bad bargain by any measure.

—Doug Bandow, "A New Military Draft Would Revive
a Very Bad Old Idea"

Finally, if your own experience backs up your claim or demonstrates the need or problem that your proposal aims to address, then consider using it to develop your proposal (as John Amaechi does in addressing his proposal to Kobe Bryant). Consider the following questions in deciding when to include your own experiences in showing that a proposal is needed or will in fact do what it claims:

- Is your experience directly related to the need or problem that you seek to address or to your proposal about it?

- Will your experience be appropriate and speak convincingly to the audience? Will the audience immediately understand its significance, or will it require explanation?

- Does your personal experience fit logically with the other reasons that you're using to support your claim?

Be careful. If a proposal seems crafted to serve mainly your own interests, you won't get far.

Showing That the Proposal Is Feasible

To be effective, proposals must be *feasible*—that is, the action proposed can be carried out in a reasonable way. Demonstrating feasibility calls on you to present evidence—from similar cases, from personal experience, from observational data, from interview or survey data, from Internet research, or from any other sources—showing that what you propose can indeed be done with the resources available. "Resources available" is key: if the proposal calls for funds, personnel, or skills beyond reach or reason, your audience is unlikely to accept it. When that's the case, it's time to reassess your proposal, modify it, and test any new ideas against these revised criteria. This is also when you can reconsider proposals that others might suggest are better, more effective, or more workable than yours. There's no shame in admitting that you may have been wrong. When drafting a proposal, ask friends to think of counterproposals. If your own proposal can stand up to such challenges, it's likely a strong one.

Considering Design and Visuals

Because proposals often address specific audiences, they can take a number of forms—a letter, a memo, a Web page, a feasibility report, an infographic, a brochure, a prospectus, or even an editorial cartoon (see Andy Singer's "No Exit" item on **P. 313**). Each form has different design requirements. Indeed, the design may add powerfully to—or detract significantly from—the effectiveness of the proposal. Typically, though, proposals are heavy in photographs, tables, graphs, comparison charts, and maps, all designed to help readers understand the nature of a problem and how to solve it. Needless to say, any visual items should be handsomely presented: they contribute to your ethos.

Lengthy reports also usually need headings—or, in an oral report, slides—that clearly identify the various stages of the presentation. Those headings, which will vary, would include items such as Introduction, Nature of the Problem, Current Approaches or Previous Solutions, Proposal/Recommendations, Advantages, Counterarguments, Feasibility, Implementation, and so on. So before you produce a final copy of any proposal, be sure its design enhances its persuasiveness.

A related issue to consider is whether a graphic image might help readers understand key elements of the proposal—what the challenge is, why it demands action, and what exactly you're suggesting—and help make the idea more attractive. That strategy is routinely used in professional proposals by architects, engineers, and government agencies.

For example, the artist rendering below shows the Bionic Arch, a proposed skyscraper in Taiwan designed by architect Vincent Callebaut. As a proposal, this one stands out because it not only suggests an addition to the city skyline, but it also offers architectural innovations to make the structure more environmentally friendly. If you look closely, you'll notice that each floor of the building includes suspended "sky gardens" that, according to the proposal, will help solve the problem of city smog by siphoning away toxic fumes. According to Callebaut, "The skyscraper reduces our ecological footprint in the urban area. It respects the environment and gives a new symbiotic ecosystem for the biodiversity of Taiwan. The Bionic Arch is the new icon of sustainable development." Who wouldn't support a building that looked great *and* helped clean the air?

FIGURE 19.8 The Bionic Arch proposes to do more than add retail and office space.

GUIDE TO WRITING A PROPOSAL

Finding a Topic or Identifying a Problem

You're entering a proposal argument when you:

- make a claim that supports a change in practice: *Bottled water should carry a warning label describing the environmental impact of plastic.*

- make a claim that supports a change in policy: *Government workers, especially legislators and administrative officials, should never be exempt from laws or programs imposed on other citizens.*

- make a claim that resists suggested changes in practice or policy: *The surest way to guarantee that HOV lanes on freeways improve traffic flow is not to build any.*

- explore options for addressing existing issues or investigate opportunities for change: *Urban planners need to examine the long-term impact digital technologies may have on transportation, work habits, housing patterns, power usage, and entertainment opportunities in cities of the future.*

Since your everyday experience often calls on you to consider problems and to make proposals, begin your brainstorming for topics with practical topics related to your life, education, major, or job. Or make an informal list of proposals that you would like to explore in broader academic or cultural areas—problems you see in your field or in the society around you. Or do some freewriting on a subject of political concern, and see if it leads to a call for action.

Researching Your Topic

For many proposals, you can begin your research by consulting the following types of sources:

- newspapers, magazines, reviews, and journals (online and print)

- television or radio news reports

- online databases

- government documents and reports

- Web sites, blogs, social networking sites, listservs, or newsgroups

- books

- experts in the field, some of whom might be right on your campus

Consider doing some field research, if appropriate—a survey of student opinions on Internet accessibility, for example, or interviews with people who have experienced the problem you are trying to fix.

Finally, remember that your proposal's success can depend on the credibility of the sources you use to support it, so evaluate each source carefully (see **CHAPTER 25**).

Formulating a Claim

As you think about and explore your topic, begin formulating a claim about it. To do so, come up with a clear thesis that makes a proposal and states the reasons that this proposal should be adopted. To start formulating a claim, explore and respond to the following questions:

- What do I know about the proposal that I'm making?

- What reasons can I offer to support my proposal?

- What evidence do I have that implementing my proposal will lead to the results I want?

Rather than make a specific proposal, you may sometimes want to explore the range of possibilities for addressing a particular situation or circumstance. In that case, a set of open-ended questions might be a more productive starting point than a focused thesis, suggesting, for instance, what goals any plausible proposal might have to meet.

Examples of Proposal Claims

- Because lowering the amount of fuel required to be blended with ethanol would lower greenhouse gas emissions by millions of tons and decrease land use that is releasing unhealthy amounts of carbon into the atmosphere, the EPA proposal to reduce ethanol produced from corn should be adopted.

- Every home should be equipped with a well-stocked emergency kit that can sustain inhabitants for at least three days in a natural disaster.

- Congress should repeal the Copyright Extension Act, since it disrupts the balance between incentives for creators and the right of the public to information as set forth in the U.S. Constitution.

- To simplify the lives of consumers and eliminate redundant products, industries that manufacture rechargeable batteries should agree on a design for a universal power adapter.

- People from different economic classes, age groups, political philosophies, and power groups (government, Main Street, Wall Street) all have a stake in reforming current budget and tax policies. But how do we get them to speak and to listen to each other? That is the challenge we face if we hope to solve our national economic problems.

Preparing a Proposal

If your instructor asks you to prepare a proposal for your project, here's a format that may help:

State the thesis of your proposal completely. If you're having trouble doing so, try outlining it in Toulmin terms:

Claim:

Reason(s):

Warrant(s):

Alternatively, you might describe your intention to explore a particular problem in your project, with the actual proposal (and thesis) coming later.

- Explain why this issue deserves attention. What's at stake?

- Identify and describe those readers whom you hope to reach with your proposal. Why is this group of readers appropriate? Can you identify individuals who can actually fix a problem?

- Briefly discuss the major difficulties that you foresee for your proposal. How will you demonstrate that the action you propose is necessary and workable? Persuade the audience to act? Pay for the proposal?

- Determine what research strategies you'll use. What sources do you expect to consult?

Considering Format and Media

Your instructor may specify that you use a particular format and/or medium. If not, ask yourself these questions to help you make a good choice:

- What format is most appropriate for your proposal? Does it call for an academic essay, a report, an infographic, a brochure, or something else?

- What medium is most appropriate for your argument? Would it be best delivered orally to a live audience? Presented as an audio essay or podcast? Presented in print only or in print with illustrations?

- Will you need visuals, such as moving or still images, maps, graphs, charts—and what function will they play in your argument? Make sure they are not just "added on" but are necessary components of the argument.

Thinking about Organization

Proposals can take many different forms but generally include the following elements:

- a description of the problem you intend to address or the state of affairs that leads you to propose the action

- a strong and specific proposal, identifying the key reasons for taking the proposed action and the effects that taking this action will have

- a clear connection between the proposal and a significant need or problem

- a demonstration of ways in which the proposal addresses the need

- evidence that the proposal will achieve the desired outcome

- a consideration of alternative ways to achieve the desired outcome and a discussion of why these may not be feasible

- a demonstration that the proposal is feasible and an explanation of how it may be implemented

Getting and Giving Response: Questions for Peer Response

Your instructor may assign you to a group for the purpose of reading and responding to each other's drafts. If not, ask for responses from serious readers or consultants at a writing center. Use the following questions to evaluate a colleague's draft. Since specific comments help more than general observations, be sure to illustrate your comments with examples. Some of the questions below assume a conventional, thesis-driven project, but more exploratory, open-ended proposal arguments also need to be clearly phrased, organized, and supported with evidence.

The Claim

- Does the claim clearly call for action? Is the proposal as clear and specific as possible? Is it realistic or possible to accomplish?

- Is the proposal too sweeping? Does it need to be qualified? If so, how?

- Does the proposal clearly address the problem that it intends to solve? If not, how could the connection be strengthened?

- Is the claim likely to get the audience to act rather than just to agree? If not, how could it be revised to do so?

Evidence for the Claim

- Is enough evidence furnished to get the audience to support the proposal? If not, what kind of additional evidence is needed? Does any of the evidence provided seem inappropriate or otherwise ineffective? Why?

- Is the evidence in support of the claim simply announced, or are its significance and appropriateness analyzed? Is a more detailed discussion needed?

- Are objections that readers might have to the claim or evidence adequately and fairly addressed?

- What kinds of sources are cited? How credible and persuasive will they be to readers? What other kinds of sources might work better?

- Are all quotations introduced with appropriate signal phrases (such as "As Tyson argues,...") and blended smoothly into the writer's sentences?

- Are all visual sources labeled, introduced, and commented upon?

Organization and Style

- How are the parts of the argument organized? Is this organization effective?

- Will readers understand the relationships among the claims, supporting reasons, warrants, and evidence? If not, how might those connections be clearer? Is the function of every visual clear? Are more transitions needed? Would headings or graphic devices help?

- Are the transitions or links from point to point, sentence to sentence, and paragraph to paragraph clear and effective? If not, how could they be improved?

- Are all visuals carefully integrated into the text? Is each visual introduced and commented on to point out its significance? Is each visual labeled as a figure or a table and given a caption as well as a citation?

- Is the style suited to the subject? Is it too formal, casual, or technical? Can it be improved?

- Which sentences seem effective? Which ones seem weaker, and how could they be improved? Should short sentences be combined, and any longer ones be broken up?

- How effective are the paragraphs? Too short or too long? How can they be improved?

- Which words or phrases seem effective? Do any seem vague or inappropriate for the audience or the writer's purpose? Are technical or unfamiliar terms defined?

Spelling, Punctuation, Mechanics, Documentation, and Format

- Are there any errors in spelling, punctuation, capitalization, and the like?

- Is the documentation appropriate and consistent?

- Does the paper or project follow an appropriate format? Is it appropriately designed and attractively presented?

PROJECTS

1. Identify a proposal currently in the news or one advocated unrelentingly by the media that you really don't like. It may be a political initiative, a cultural innovation, a transportation alternative, or a lifestyle change. Spend time studying the idea more carefully than you have before. And then compose a proposal argument based on your deeper understanding of the proposal. You may still explain why you think it's a bad idea. Or you may endorse it, using your new information and your interesting perspective as a former dissenter.

2. The uses and abuses of technology and media—from smartphones and smartwatches to social networks—seem to be on everyone's mind. Write a proposal argument about some pressing dilemma caused by the digital screens that are changing (ruining?) our lives. You might want to explain how to bring traditional instructors into the digital age or establish etiquette for people who walk in traffic using handheld electronic devices. Or maybe you want to keep parents off of social networks. Or maybe you have a great idea for separating professional and private lives online. Make your proposal in some pertinent medium: print op-ed, cartoon, photo essay, infographic, set of PowerPoint or Prezi slides, podcast.

3. Write a proposal to yourself diagnosing some minor issue you would like to address, odd behavior you'd like to change, or obsession you'd like to curb. Explore the reasons behind your mania and the problems it causes you and others. Then come up with a plausible proposal to resolve the issue and prove that you can do it. Make the paper hilarious.

4. Working in a group initially, come up with a list of problems—local, national, or international—that seem just about insoluble, from persuading nations to cut down on their CO_2 emissions to figuring out how to keep tuition costs in check. After some discussion, focus on just one or two of these matters and then discuss not the issues themselves but the general reasons that the problems have proven intractable. What exactly keeps people from agreeing on solutions? Are some people content with the status quo? Do some groups profit from the current arrangements? Are alternatives to the status quo just too costly or not feasible for other reasons? Do people find *change* uncomfortable? Following the discussion, work alone or collaboratively on an argument that examines the general issue of change: What makes it possible in any given case? What makes it difficult? Use the problems you have discussed as examples to illustrate your argument. Your challenge as a writer may be to make such an open-ended discussion interesting to general readers.

TWO SAMPLE PROPOSALS

A Call to Improve Campus Accessibility

Manasi Deshpande[1]

Courtesy of Manasi Deshpande

The paper opens with a personal example and dramatizes the issue of campus accessibility.

INTRODUCTION

Wes Holloway, a sophomore at the University of Texas at Austin (UT), never considered the issue of campus accessibility during his first year on campus. But when an injury his freshman year left him wheelchair-bound, he was astonished to realize that he faced an unexpected challenge: maneuvering around the UT campus. Hills that he had effortlessly traversed became mountains; doors that he had easily opened became anvils; and streets that he had mindlessly crossed became treacherous terrain. Says Wes: "I didn't think about accessibility until I had to deal with it, and I think most people are the same way."

Both problem and solution are previewed here, with more details provided in subsequent sections of the paper.

For the ambulatory individual, access for the mobility impaired on the UT campus is easy to overlook. Automatic door entrances and bathrooms with the universal handicapped symbol make the campus seem sufficiently accessible. But for many students and faculty at UT, including me, maneuvering the UT campus in a wheelchair is a daily experience of stress and frustration. Although the University has made a concerted and continuing effort to improve access, students and faculty with physical disabilities still suffer from discriminatory hardship, unequal opportunity to succeed, and lack of independence.

The introduction's final paragraph summarizes the argument.

The University must make campus accessibility a higher priority and take more seriously the hardship that the campus at present imposes on people with mobility impairments. Better accessibility would also benefit the numerous students and faculty with temporary disabilities and help the University recruit a more diverse body of students and faculty.

The author's fieldwork (mainly interviews) enhances her authority and credibility.

ASSESSMENT OF CURRENT EFFORTS

The current state of campus accessibility leaves substantial room for improvement. There are approximately 150 academic and administrative buildings on campus (Grant). Eduardo Gardea, intern architect at the Physical Plant, estimates that only about nineteen buildings comply fully with the Americans with Disabilities Act (ADA). According to Penny Seay, PhD, director of the Center for Disability Studies at UT Austin, the ADA in theory "requires every building on campus to be accessible." However, as Bill Throop,

---

1 Manasi Deshpande wrote a longer version of this essay for a course preparing her to work as a consultant in the writing center at the University of Texas at Austin. We have edited it to emphasize the structure of her complex proposal. Note, too, how she reaches out to a general audience to make an argument that might seem to have a narrow constituency. This essay is documented using MLA style.

associate director of the Physical Plant, explains, there is "no legal deadline to make the entire campus accessible"; neither the ADA nor any other law mandates that certain buildings be made compliant by a certain time. Though not bound by specific legal obligation, the University should strive to fulfill the spirit of the law and recognize campus accessibility as a pressing moral obligation.

THE BENEFITS OF CHANGE

Benefits for People with Permanent Mobility Impairments

Improving campus accessibility would significantly enhance the quality of life of students and faculty with mobility impairments. The campus at present poses discriminatory hardship on these individuals by making daily activities such as getting to class and using the bathroom unreasonably difficult. Before Wes Holloway leaves home, he must plan his route carefully to avoid hills, use ramps that are easy to maneuver, and enter the side of the building with the accessible entrance. As he goes to class, Wes must go out of his way to avoid poorly paved sidewalks and roads. Sometimes he cannot avoid them and must take an uncomfortable and bumpy ride across potholes and uneven pavement. If his destination does not have an automatic door, he must wait for someone to open the door for him because it is too heavy for him to open himself. To get into Burdine Hall, he has to ask a stranger to push him through the heavy narrow doors because his fingers would get crushed if he pushed himself. Once in the classroom, Wes must find a suitable place to sit, often far away from his classmates because stairs block him from the center of the room.

Other members of the UT community with mobility impairments suffer the same daily hardships as Wes. According to Mike Gerhardt, student affairs administrator of Services for Students with Disabilities (SSD), approximately eighty students with physical disabilities, including twenty to twenty-five students using wheelchairs, are registered with SSD. However, the actual number of students with mobility impairments is probably higher because some students choose not to seek services from SSD. The current state of campus accessibility discriminates against all individuals with physical disabilities in the unnecessary hardship it imposes and in the ways it denies them independence.

Benefits for People with Temporary Mobility Impairments

In addition to helping the few members of the UT campus with permanent mobility impairments, a faster rate of accessibility improvement would also benefit the much larger population of people with temporary physical disabilities. Many students and faculty will become temporarily disabled from injury at some point during their time at the University. They will encounter difficulties similar to those facing people with permanent disabilities, including finding accessible entrances, opening doors without automatic entrances, and finding convenient classroom seating. And, according to Dr. Jennifer Maedgen, assistant dean of students and director of SSD, about 5 to 10 percent of the approximately one thousand students registered with SSD at any given time have temporary disabilities. By improving campus accessibility, the University would in fact reach out to all of its members, even those who have never considered the possibility of mobility impairment or the state of campus accessibility.

The paper uses several layers of headings to organize its diverse materials.

The author outlines the challenges faced by a student with mobility impairment.

Accessibility issues are given a human face with examples of the problems that mobility-impaired people face on campus.

The author broadens the appeal of her proposal by showing how improved accessibility will benefit everyone on campus.

Numbers provide hard evidence for an important claim.

The author offers a new but related argument: enhanced accessibility could bolster recruitment efforts.

Benefits for the University

Better accessibility would also benefit the University as a whole by increasing recruitment of handicapped individuals and thus promoting a more diverse campus. When prospective students and faculty with disabilities visit the University, they might decide not to join the UT community because of poor access. On average, about one thousand students, or 2 percent of the student population, are registered with SSD. Mike Gerhardt reports that SSD would have about 1,500 to 3,000 registered students if the University reflected the community at large with respect to disability. These numbers suggest that the University can recruit more students with disabilities by taking steps to ensure that they have an equal opportunity to succeed.

The paper briefly notes possible objections to the proposal.

Counterarguments

Arguments against devoting more effort and resources to campus accessibility have some validity but ultimately prove inadequate. Some argue that accelerating the rate of accessibility improvements and creating more efficient services require too much spending on too few people. However, this spending actually enhances the expected quality of life of all UT community members rather than just the few with permanent physical disabilities. Unforeseen injury can leave anyone with a permanent or temporary disability at any time. In making decisions about campus accessibility, administrators must realize that having a disability is not a choice and that bad luck does not discriminate. They should consider how their decisions would affect their campus experience if they became disabled. Despite the additional cost, the University should make accessibility a priority and accommodate more accessibility projects in its budget.

RECOMMENDATIONS

Foster Empathy and Understanding for Long-Term Planning

The University should make campus accessibility a higher priority and work toward a campus that not only fulfills legal requirements but also provides a user-friendly environment for the mobility impaired. It is difficult for the ambulatory person to empathize with the difficulties faced by these individuals. Recognizing this problem, the University should require the administrators who allocate money to ADA projects to use wheelchairs around the campus once a year. Administrators must realize that people with physical disabilities are not a small, distant, irrelevant group; anyone can join their ranks at any time. Administrators should ask themselves if they would find the current state of campus accessibility acceptable if an injury forced them to use a wheelchair on a permanent basis.

After establishing a case for enhanced campus accessibility, the author offers specific suggestions for action.

In addition, the University should actively seek student input for long-term improvements to accessibility. The University is in the process of creating the ADA Accessibility Committee, which, according to the office of the Dean of Students' Web site, will "address institutionwide, systemic issues that fall under the scope of the Americans with Disabilities Act." Students should play a prominent and powerful role in this new ADA Accessibility Committee. The Committee should select its student representatives carefully to make sure that they are driven individuals committed to working for progress and representing the interests of students with disabilities. The

University should consider making Committee positions paid so that student representatives can devote sufficient time to their responsibilities.

Improve Services for the Mobility Impaired

The University should also work toward creating more useful, transparent, and approachable services for its members with physical disabilities by making better use of online technology and helping students take control of their own experiences.

First, SSD can make its Web site more useful by updating it frequently with detailed information on construction sites that will affect accessible routes. The site should delineate alternative accessible routes and approximate the extra time required to use the detour. This information would help people with mobility impairments to plan ahead and avoid delays, mitigating the stress of maneuvering around construction sites.

The University should also develop software for an interactive campus map. The software would work like MapQuest or Google Maps but would provide detailed descriptions of accessible routes on campus from one building to another. It would be updated frequently with new ADA improvements and information on construction sites that impede accessible routes.

Since usefulness of services is most important for students during their first encounters with the campus, SSD should hold one-on-one orientations for new students with mobility impairments. SSD should inform students in both oral and written format of their rights and responsibilities and make them aware of problems that they will encounter on the campus. Beyond making services more useful, these orientations would give students the impression of University services as open and responsive, encouraging students to report problems that they encounter and assume the responsibility of self-advocacy.

As a continuing resource for people with physical disabilities, the SSD Web site should include an anonymous forum for both general questions and specific complaints and needs. Many times, students notice problems but do not report them because they find visiting or calling SSD time-consuming or because they do not wish to be a burden. The anonymity and immediate feedback provided by the forum would allow for more freedom of expression and provide students an easier way to solve the problems they face.

Services for the mobility impaired should also increase their transparency by advertising current accessibility projects on their Web sites. The University should give its members with mobility impairments a clearer idea of its efforts to improve campus accessibility. Detailed online descriptions of ADA projects, including the cost of each project, would affirm its resolve to create a better environment for its members with physical disabilities.

The writer reiterates her full proposal.

CONCLUSION

Although the University has made progress in accessibility improvements on an old campus, it must take bolder steps to improve the experience of its members with mobility impairments. At present, people with permanent mobility impairments face unreasonable hardship, unequal opportunity to succeed, and lack of independence. To enhance the quality of life of all of its members and increase recruitment of disabled individuals, the University should focus its resources on increasing the rate of accessibility improvements and improving the quality of its services for the mobility impaired.

As a public institution, the University has an obligation to make the campus more inclusive and serve as an example for disability rights. With careful planning and a genuine desire to respond to special needs, practical and cost-effective changes to the University campus can significantly improve the quality of life of many of its members and prove beneficial to the future of the University as a whole.

Works Cited

Gardea, Eduardo. Personal interview. 24 Mar. 2005.

Gerhardt, Michael. Personal interview. 8 Apr. 2005.

Grant, Angela. "Making Campus More Accessible." *Daily Texan Online*. 14 Oct. 2003. Web. 1 Mar. 2005.

Holloway, Wesley Reed. Personal interview. 5 Mar. 2005.

Maedgen, Jennifer. Personal interview. 25 Mar. 2005.

Office of the Dean of Students, University of Texas at Austin. "ADA Student Forum." 6 Apr. 2005. Web. 23 Apr. 2005.

Seay, Penny. Personal interview. 11 Mar. 2005.

Throop, William. Personal interview. 6 Apr. 2005.

LET'S CHARGE POLITICIANS FOR WASTING OUR TIME

Virginia Postrel

There's an election today here in California, and that means my landline at home is ringing constantly with robocalls from assorted public figures whose recorded voices urge me to get out and vote for their favorite candidates. One called the other day while I was conducting an interview on the mobile phone I use for most purposes. I didn't answer, but it interrupted the flow of the conversation. Yesterday I picked up the receiver to find five voice mails, all from recorded political voices (including two identical messages from the same sheriff candidate).

Our phone number is on the National Do Not Call Registry, but those rules for telemarketers don't apply to political campaigns. The folks who make the laws aren't about to do away with a technique that works.

Political robocalls are illegal to mobile phones but OK to most landlines, as long as they meet disclosure requirements. Everyone I know hates such calls, and even political consultants know they're a problem. "Some voters get turned off by too many robocalls," cautions a political-strategy website. The cumulative annoyance, it warns, means that voters may resent yours even if they're rare. Yep.

Recorded, automatically dialed messages arguably constitute a legitimate and potentially important form of political speech. If I weren't so annoyed, I might actually like to know who's endorsing whom for sheriff. But it's ridiculous that the only way to limit the onslaught is to pay someone $24.99 to tell organizations, who may or may not listen, that I don't want them bothering me.

Here's a better idea: You should be able to set a charge for calling you. Every number that isn't on your "free" list would automatically be assessed a fee. The phone company would get a percentage of the revenue, and you'd be able to adjust the fee to different levels at different times of the day or for different seasons. (The nearer the election, the higher I'd make my charge.) If candidates really think it's valuable to call me, they should be willing to pay. Otherwise, they're just forcing me to subsidize their political efforts with my time and attention.

Technology investor Esther Dyson has for years been pushing a similar idea for e-mail. Unsolicited phone calls are much more annoying, and the technological challenges of "reversing the charges" should be much easier. Although you can't track down the true scamsters who break the do-not-call law and peddle fraudulent schemes from phony numbers, the politicians and charities that pester us for support aren't trying to hide. They're just trying to get something scarce and precious—our time and attention—for free.

Virginia Postrel posted this column on the *Bloomberg View* on June 3, 2014. She has also written for Forbes, the *Wall Street Journal*, the *New York Times*, and the *Atlantic*.

Chapter 20

Fallacies of Argument

Fallacies of Emotional Argument

Fallacies of Ethical Argument

Fallacies of Logical Argument

This chapter is taken from Andrea A. Lunsford and John J. Ruszkiewicz, *Everything's an Argument*, Seventh Edition, pp. 71–86, (Chapter 5).

"Doing tricks is a slippery slope."

THE COOKIE CUTTER

Left to right: Roy Delgado/www.Cartoonstock.com; © Bish/Cagle Cartoons, Inc.; © Eric Allie/Cagle Cartoons, Inc.

Do these editorial cartoons strike a chord with you? All three are complicated. The first panel pokes fun at slippery slope arguments, which aim to thwart action by predicting dire consequences: chase that Frisbee and you'll soon be pulling milk carts. The second item uses a scare tactic (a potential fallacy of argument) to raise opposition to the educational reform called "Common Core," suggesting ominously that the program's cookie-cutter approach will produce children who all think alike. And the third cartoon points to a fallacy of argument that a prominent politician has perhaps slipped into— the sentimental appeal; it alludes to Hillary Clinton's comment in a 2014 interview with Diane Sawyer that she and husband Bill "came out of the White House not only dead broke but in debt."

Fallacies are argumentative moves flawed by their very nature or structure. Because such tactics can make productive principled argument more difficult, they potentially hurt everyone involved, including the people responsible for them. The worst sorts of fallacies muck up the frank but civil conversations that people should be able to have, regardless of their differences.

Yet it's hard to deny the power in offering audiences a compelling either/or choice or a vulnerable straw man in an argument. For exactly that reason, it's important that you can recognize and point out fallacies in the work of others—and avoid them in your own writing. This chapter aims to help you meet these goals: here we'll introduce you to fallacies of argument classified according to the emotional, ethical, and logical appeals we've discussed earlier (see **CHAPTERS 21, 22**, and **23**).

■ Fallacies of Emotional Argument

Emotional arguments can be powerful and suitable in many circumstances, and most writers use them frequently. However, writers who pull on their readers' heartstrings or raise their blood pressure too often can violate the good faith on which legitimate argument depends.

Scare Tactics

Politicians, advertisers, and public figures sometimes peddle their ideas by frightening people and exaggerating possible dangers well beyond their statistical likelihood. Such ploys work because it's easier to imagine something terrible happening than to appreciate its rarity.

Scare tactics can also be used to stampede legitimate fears into panic or prejudice. Laborers who genuinely worry about losing their jobs can be persuaded to fear immigrants who might work for less money. Seniors living on fixed incomes can be convinced that minor changes to entitlement programs represent dire threats to their well-being. Such tactics have the effect of closing off thinking because people who are scared often act irrationally. Even well-intended fear campaigns—like those directed against smoking, unprotected sex, or the use of illegal drugs—can misfire if their warnings prove too shrill. People just stop listening.

Either/Or Choices

Either/or choices can be well-intentioned strategies to get something accomplished. Parents use them all the time ("Eat your broccoli, or you won't get dessert"). But they become fallacious arguments when they reduce a complicated issue to excessively simple terms or when they're designed to obscure legitimate alternatives. Here, for example, is Riyad Mansour, the Palestinian representative to the United Nations, offering the nation of Israel just such a choice in an interview with Charlie Rose in January 2014:

> It is up to them [the Israelis] to decide what kind of a state they want to be. Do they want to be a democratic state where Israel will be the state for all of its citizens? Or do they want to be a state for the Jewish people, therefore excluding 1.6 million Palestinian Arabs who are Israelis from their society? That debate is not our debate. That debate is their debate.

But Joel B. Pollak, writing for Breitbart News Network, describes Mansour's claim as a "false choice" since Israel already is a Jewish state that nonetheless allows Muslims to be full citizens. The either/or argument Mansour presents, according to Pollack, does not describe the realities of this complex political situation.

© Adam Zyglis/Cagle Cartoons, Inc.

FIGURE 20.1 A false choice?

Slippery Slope

The **slippery slope** fallacy portrays today's tiny misstep as tomorrow's slide into disaster. Some arguments that aim at preventing dire consequences do not take the slippery slope approach (for example, the parent who corrects a child for misbehavior now is acting sensibly to prevent more serious problems as the child grows older). A slippery slope argument becomes wrongheaded when a writer exaggerates the likely consequences of an action, usually to frighten readers. As such, slippery slope arguments are also scare tactics. In recent years, the issue of gun ownership in America has evoked many slippery slope arguments. Here's one perspective on the tactic:

> The leadership of the NRA is exceptionally fond of the Slippery Slope argument. "Universal background checks will inevitably be followed by a national registry of gun-owners which will inevitably be followed by confiscation of all their guns." Or, "A ban on assault-style weapons and thirty+ round magazines will inevitably be followed by a ban on hand guns with ten-round magazines, that will inevitably be followed by bans on all guns, including antique dueling pistols inherited from our Founding Fathers."
>
> Problem number one with this slide down the fearsome slope is how much weaponry has changed since the days of militias with muskets. Even the NRA agrees that lines have to be drawn somewhere. They do not favor legalization of civilian use of rocket-propelled grenades, bazookas or stinger missiles. If there is a slippery slope we are starting approximately half-way down.
>
> —Michael Wolkowitz, "Slippery Slopes, Imagined and Real"

Social and political ideas and proposals do have consequences, but they aren't always as dire as writers fond of slippery slope tactics would have you believe.

Overly Sentimental Appeals

Overly **sentimental appeals** use tender emotions excessively to distract readers from facts. Often, such appeals are highly personal and individual and focus attention on heartwarming or heartrending situations that make readers feel guilty if they challenge an idea, a policy, or a proposal. Emotions become an impediment to civil discourse when they keep people from thinking clearly.

Such sentimental appeals are a major vehicle of television news, where tugging at viewers' heartstrings can mean high ratings. For example, when a camera documents the day-to-day sacrifices of a single parent trying to meet mortgage payments and keep her kids in college, the woman's on-screen struggles can seem to represent the plight of an entire class of people threatened by callous bankers and college administrators. But while such human interest stories stir genuine emotions, they seldom give a complete picture of complex social or economic issues.

Tim Boyle/Getty Images

FIGURE 20.2 This image, taken from a gun control protest, is designed to elicit sympathy by causing the viewer to think about the dangers guns pose to innocent children and, thus, support the cause.

Bandwagon Appeals

Bandwagon appeals urge people to follow the same path everyone else is taking. Such arguments can be relatively benign and seem harmless. But they do push people to take the easier path rather than think independently about what choices to make or where to go.

Many American parents seem to have an innate ability to refute bandwagon appeals. When their kids whine, *Everyone else is going camping without chaperones*, the parents reply, *And if everyone else jumps off a cliff (or a railroad bridge or the Empire State Building), you will too?* The children groan—and then try a different line of argument.

Unfortunately, not all bandwagon approaches are so transparent. In recent decades, bandwagon issues have included a war on drugs, the nuclear freeze movement, campaigns against drunk driving, campaigns for immigration reform, bailouts for banks and businesses, and *many* fads in education from high-stakes testing to MOOCs. All these issues are too complex to permit the suspension of judgment that bandwagon tactics require.

FIGURE 20.3 Some bandwagon appeals work better than others.

■ Fallacies of Ethical Argument

Because readers give their closest attention to authors they respect or trust, writers usually want to present themselves as honest, well-informed, likable, or sympathetic. But not all the devices that writers use to gain the attention and confidence of readers are admirable. (For more on appeals based on character, see **CHAPTER 22**.)

Appeals to False Authority

Many academic research papers find and reflect on the work of reputable authorities and introduce these authorities through direct quotations or citations as credible evidence. (For more on assessing the reliability of sources, see **CHAPTER 25**.) **False authority**, however, occurs when writers offer themselves or other authorities as sufficient warrant for believing a claim:

Claim	X is true because I say so.
Warrant	What I say must be true.
Claim	X is true because Y says so.
Warrant	What Y says must be true.

Though they are seldom stated so baldly, claims of authority drive many political campaigns. American pundits and politicians are fond of citing the U.S. Constitution and its Bill of Rights (Canadians have their Charter of Rights and Freedoms) as ultimate authorities, a reasonable practice when the documents are interpreted respectfully. However, the rights claimed sometimes aren't in the texts themselves or don't mean what the speakers think they do. And most constitutional matters are debatable—as volumes of court records prove. Likewise, religious believers often base arguments on books or traditions that wield great authority in a particular religious community. But the power of such texts is usually limited to that group and less capable of persuading others solely on the grounds of authority.

In short, you should pay serious attention to claims supported by respected authorities, such as the Centers for Disease Control, the National Science Foundation, or the *Globe and Mail*. But don't accept information simply because it is put forth by such offices and agencies. To quote a Russian proverb made famous by Ronald Reagan, "Trust, but verify."

Dogmatism

A writer who asserts or assumes that a particular position is the *only one* that is conceivably acceptable is expressing **dogmatism**, a fallacy of character that undermines the trust that must exist between those who make and listen to arguments. When people or organizations write dogmatically, they imply that no arguments are necessary: the truth is self-evident and needs no support. Here is an extreme example of such an appeal, quoted in an *Atlantic* story by Tracy Brown Hamilton and describing an anti-smoking appeal made by the Third Reich:

> "Brother national socialist, do you know that your Fuhrer is against smoking and thinks that every German is responsible to the whole people for all his deeds and omissions, and does not have the right to damage his body with drugs?"
>
> —From Tracy Brown Hamilton, "The Nazis' Forgotten
> Anti-Smoking Campaign"

Subjects or ideas that can be defended with facts, testimony, and good reasons ought not to be off the table in a free society. In general, whenever someone suggests that even raising an issue for debate is totally unacceptable—whether on the grounds that it's racist, sexist, unpatriotic, blasphemous, insensitive, or offensive in some other way—you should be suspicious.

Ad Hominem Arguments

Ad hominem (Latin for "to the man") **arguments** attack the character of a person rather than the claims he or she makes: when you destroy the credibility of your opponents, you either destroy their ability to present reasonable appeals or distract from the successful arguments they may be offering. Such attacks, of course, aren't aimed at men only, as columnist Jamie Stiehm proved when she criticized Supreme Court Justice Sonia Sotomayor for delaying an Obamacare mandate objected to by the Little Sisters of the Poor, a Catholic religious order. Stiehm directly targets Sotomayor's religious beliefs:

> Et tu, Justice Sonia Sotomayor? Really, we can't trust you on women's health and human rights? The lady from the Bronx just dropped the ball on American women and girls as surely as she did the sparkling ball at midnight on New Year's Eve in Times Square. Or maybe she's just a good Catholic girl.

> —Jamie Stiehm, "The Catholic Supreme Court's War on Women"

Stiehm then widens her *ad hominem* assault to include Catholics in general:

> Sotomayor's blow brings us to confront an uncomfortable reality. More than WASPs, Methodists, Jews, Quakers or Baptists, Catholics often try to impose their beliefs on you, me, public discourse and institutions. Especially if "you" are female.

Arguably, *ad hominem* tactics like this turn arguments into two-sided affairs with good guys and bad guys (or gals), and that's unfortunate, since character often really *does* matter in argument. People expect the proponent of peace to be civil, a secretary of the treasury to pay his or her taxes, and the champion of family values to be a faithful spouse. But it's fallacious to attack an idea by uncovering the foibles of its advocates or by attacking their motives, backgrounds, or unchangeable traits.

Stacking the Deck

Just as gamblers try to stack the deck by arranging cards so they are sure to win, writers **stack the deck** when they show only one side of the story—the one in their favor. In a Facebook forum on the documentary film *Super Size Me* (which followed a 32-year-old man who ate three meals a day at McDonald's for thirty days with drastic health consequences), one student points out an example of stacking the deck:

> One of the fallacies was stacking the deck. Spurlock stated many facts and gave plenty of evidence of what can happen if you eat fast food in abundance. Weight gain, decline in health, habit forming, and a toll on your daily life. But he failed to show what could happen if you ate the fast food and participated in daily exercise and took vitamins. The fallacy is that he does not show us both sides of what can happen. Possibly you could eat McDonald's for three meals a day for thirty days and if you engaged in daily exercise and took vitamins maybe your health would be just fine. But we were not ever shown that side of the experiment.

> —Heather Tew Alleman, on a Facebook forum

In the same way, reviewers have been critical of documentaries by Michael Moore and Dinesh D'Souza that resolutely show only one side of a story or prove highly selective in their coverage. When you stack the deck, you take a big chance that your readers will react like Alleman and decide not to trust you: that's one reason it's so important to show that you have considered alternatives in making any argument.

■ Fallacies of Logical Argument

You'll encounter a problem in any argument when the claims, warrants, or proofs in it are invalid, insufficient, or disconnected. In theory, such problems seem easy enough to spot, but in practice, they can be camouflaged by a skillful use of words or images. Indeed, logical fallacies pose a challenge to civil argument because they often seem reasonable and natural, especially when they appeal to people's self-interests.

Hasty Generalization

A **hasty generalization** is an inference drawn from insufficient evidence: because *my* Fiat broke down, then *all* Fiats must be junk. It also forms the basis for most stereotypes about people or institutions: because *a few* people in a large group are observed to act in a certain way, *all* members of that group are inferred to behave similarly. The resulting conclusions are usually sweeping claims of little merit: *women are bad drivers*; *men are slobs*; *English teachers are nitpicky*; *computer jocks are . . .* , and on and on.

To draw valid inferences, you must always have sufficient evidence and you must qualify your claims appropriately. After all, people do need generalizations to make reasonable decisions in life. Such claims can be offered legitimately if placed in context and tagged with sensible qualifiers—*some, a few, many, most, occasionally, rarely, possibly, in some cases, under certain circumstances, in my limited experience.*

Faulty Causality

In Latin, **faulty causality** is known as *post hoc, ergo propter hoc*, which translates as "after this, therefore because of this"—the faulty assumption that because one event or action follows another, the first causes the second. Consider a lawsuit commented on in the *Wall Street Journal* in which a writer sued Coors (unsuccessfully), claiming that drinking copious amounts of the company's beer had kept him from writing a novel.

Some actions do produce reactions. Step on the brake pedal in your car, and you move hydraulic fluid that pushes calipers against disks to create friction that stops the vehicle. In other cases, however, a supposed connection between cause and effect turns out to be completely wrong. For example, doctors now believe that when an elderly person falls and breaks a hip or leg, the injury usually caused the fall rather than the other way around.

That's why overly simple causal claims should always be subject to scrutiny. In summer 2008, writer Nicholas Carr posed a simple causal question in a cover story for the *Atlantic*: "Is Google Making Us Stupid?" Carr essentially answered yes, arguing that "as we come to rely on computers to mediate our understanding of the world, it is our own intelligence that flattens" and that the more one is online the less he or she is able to concentrate or read deeply.

But others, like Jamais Cascio (senior fellow at the Institute for Ethics and Emerging Technologies), soon challenged that causal connection: rather than making us stupid, Cascio argues, Internet tools like Google will lead to the development of "'fluid intelligence'—the ability to find meaning in confusion and to solve new problems, independent of acquired knowledge." The final word on this contentious causal relationship—the effects on the human brain caused by new technology—has yet to be written, and will probably be available only after decades of complicated research.

Begging the Question

Most teachers have heard some version of the following argument: *You can't give me a C in this course; I'm an A student.* A member of Congress accused of taking kickbacks can make much the same argument: *I can't be guilty of accepting such bribes; I'm an honest person.* In both cases, the claim is made on grounds that can't be accepted as true because those grounds themselves are in question. How can the accused bribe-taker defend herself on grounds of honesty when that honesty is in doubt? Looking at the arguments in Toulmin terms helps to see the fallacy:

Claim	You can't give me a C in this course...
Reason	...because I'm an A student.
Warrant	An A student is someone who can't receive Cs.
Claim	Representative X can't be guilty of accepting bribes...
Reason	...because she's an honest person.
Warrant	An honest person cannot be guilty of accepting bribes.

With the warrants stated, you can see why **begging the question**—assuming as true the very claim that's disputed—is a form of circular argument that goes nowhere. (For more on Toulmin argument, see **CHAPTER 18.**)

FIGURE 20.4

Equivocation

Equivocations—half truths or arguments that give lies an honest appearance—are usually based on tricks of language. Consider the plagiarist who copies a paper word for word from a source and then declares that "I wrote the entire paper myself"— meaning that she physically copied the piece on her own. But the plagiarist is using *wrote* equivocally and knows that most people understand the word to mean composing and not merely copying words.

Parsing words carefully can sometimes look like equivocation or be the thing itself. For example, early in 2014 Internal Revenue Service Commissioner John Koskinen promised to turn over to a committee of the House of Representatives all the relevant emails in a scandal involving the agency. Subsequently, the agency revealed that some of those requested emails had been destroyed by the failure of a computer's hard drive. But Koskinen defended his earlier promise by telling the chair of the committee, "I never said I would provide you emails we didn't have." A simple statement of fact or a slick equivocation?

Non Sequitur

A **non sequitur** is an argument whose claims, reasons, or warrants don't connect logically. You've probably detected a non sequitur when you react to an argument with a puzzled, "Wait, that doesn't follow." Children are adept at framing non sequiturs like this one: *You don't love me or you'd buy me a new bicycle!* It doesn't take a parental genius to realize that love has little connection with buying children toys.

Non sequiturs often occur when writers omit steps in an otherwise logical chain of reasoning. For example, it might be a non sequitur to argue that since postsecondary education now costs so much, it's time to move colleges and university instruction online. Such a suggestion *may* have merit, but a leap from brick-and-mortar schools to virtual ones is extreme. Numerous issues and questions must be addressed step-by-step before the proposal can be taken seriously.

Politicians sometimes resort to non sequiturs to evade thorny issues or questions. Here for example is presidential candidate Mitt Romney in a 2011 CNBC Republican primary debate turning moderator John Harwood's question about changing political positions into one about demonstrating personal integrity:

> *Harwood:* …Your opponents have said you switched positions on many issues…. What can you say to Republicans to persuade them that the things you say in the campaign are rooted in something deeper than the fact that you are running for office?

> *Romney:* John, I think people know me pretty well…. I think people understand that I'm a man of steadiness and constancy. I don't think you are going to find somebody who has more of those attributes than I do. I have been married to the same woman for…42 years…. I have been in the same church my entire life.

Conservative writer Matt K. Lewis took Romney to task for this move, pointing out that a steady personal life is no guarantor of a consistent political philosophy:

> This, of course, is not to say that values and character do not matter—they *do*—but it is to say that Romney's answer was a non sequitur. Everyone knows Mitt Romney is a decent, respectable person. The question is whether or not he can be trusted to advance conservatism as president.

Straw Man

Those who resort to the **straw man** fallacy attack arguments that no one is really making or portray opponents' positions as more extreme or far less coherent than they actually are. The speaker or writer thus sets up an argument that is conveniently easy to knock down (like a man of straw), proceeds to do so, and then claims victory over an opponent who may not even exist.

Straw men are especially convenient devices for politicians who want to characterize the positions of their opponents as more extreme than they actually are: consider obvious memes such as "war on women" and "war on Christmas." But straw man arguments are often more subtle. For instance, Steven Novella of Yale University argues that political commentator Charles Krauthammer slips into the fallacy when he misconstrues the meaning of "settled science" in a column on climate change. Novella rebuts Krauthammer's assertion that "There is nothing more anti-scientific than the very idea that science is settled, static, impervious to challenge" by explaining why such a claim is deceptive:

> Calling something an established scientific fact means that it is reasonable to proceed with that fact as a premise, for further research or for policy. It does not mean "static, impervious to challenge." That is the straw man. Both evolution deniers and climate change deniers use this tactic to misinterpret scientific confidence as an anti-scientific resistance to new evidence or arguments. It isn't. It does mean that the burden of proof has shifted to those opposing the theory that is now well-established (because it has already met a significant burden of proof).
>
> —Steven Novella, *NeuroLogica Blog*, February 25, 2014

In other words, Krauthammer's definition of *science* is not one that most scientists use.

Red Herring

This fallacy gets its name from the old British hunting practice of dragging a dried herring across the path of the fox in order to throw the hounds off the trail. A **red herring** fallacy does just that: it changes the subject abruptly or introduces an irrelevant claim or fact to throw readers or listeners off the trail. For example, people skeptical about climate change will routinely note that weather is always changing and point to the fact that Vikings settled in Greenland one thousand years ago before harsher conditions drove them away. True, scientists will say, but the point is irrelevant to arguments about worldwide global warming caused by human activity.

The red herring is not only a device writers and speakers use in the arguments they create, but it's also a charge used frequently to undermine someone else's arguments. Couple the term "red herring" in a Web search to just about any political or social cause and you'll come up with numerous articles complaining of someone's use of the device.

> climate change + red herring
>
> common core + red herring
>
> immigration reform + red herring

"Red herring" has become a convenient way of saying "I disagree with your argument" or "your point is irrelevant." And perhaps making a too-easy rebuttal like that can itself be a fallacy?

Faulty Analogy

Comparisons can help to clarify one concept by measuring it against another that is more familiar. Consider the power and humor of this comparison attributed to Mark Twain, an implicit argument for term limits in politics:

> Politicians and diapers must be changed often, and for the same reason.

When comparisons such as this one are extended, they become *analogies*—ways of understanding unfamiliar ideas by comparing them with something that's better known (see p. 382). But useful as such comparisons are, they may prove false if either taken on their own and pushed too far, or taken too seriously. At this point, they turn into **faulty analogies**—inaccurate or inconsequential comparisons between objects or concepts. Economist Paul Krugman provides an eye-opening analysis of a familiar but, as he sees it, false analogy between personal and government debt:

> Deficit-worriers portray a future in which we're impoverished by the need to pay back money we've been borrowing. They see America as being like a family that took out too large a mortgage, and will have a hard time making the monthly payments.
>
> This is, however, a really bad analogy in at least two ways.
>
> First, families have to pay back their debt. Governments don't—all they need to do is ensure that debt grows more slowly than their tax base. The debt from World War II was never repaid; it just became increasingly irrelevant as the U.S. economy grew, and with it the income subject to taxation.
>
> Second—and this is the point almost nobody seems to get—an overborrowed family owes money to someone else; U.S. debt is, to a large extent, money we owe to ourselves.

Whether you agree with the Nobel laureate or not, his explanation offers insight into how analogies work (or fail) and how to think about them critically.

RESPOND

1.   Examine each of the following political slogans or phrases for logical fallacies.

"Resistance is futile." (Borg message on *Star Trek: The Next Generation*)

"It's the economy, stupid." (sign on the wall at Bill Clinton's campaign headquarters)

"Make love, not war." (antiwar slogan popularized during the Vietnam War)

"A chicken in every pot." (campaign slogan)

"Guns don't kill, people do." (NRA slogan)

"Dog Fighters Are Cowardly Scum." (PETA T-shirt)

"If you can't stand the heat, get out of the kitchen." (attributed to Harry S Truman)

2.   Choose a paper you've written for a college class and analyze it for signs of fallacious reasoning. Then find an editorial, a syndicated column, and a news report on the same topic and look for fallacies in them. Which has the most fallacies—and what kind? What may be the role of the audience in determining when a statement is fallacious?

3.   Find a Web site that is sponsored by an organization (the Future of Music Coalition, perhaps), a business (Coca-Cola, Pepsi), or another group (the Democratic or Republican National Committee), and analyze the site for fallacious reasoning. Among other considerations, look at the relationship between text and graphics and between individual pages and the pages that surround or are linked to them.

4.   Political blogs such as *Mother Jones* and *InstaPundit* typically provide quick responses to daily events and detailed critiques of material in other media sites, including national newspapers. Study one such blog for a few days to see whether and how the site critiques the articles, political commentary, or writers it links to. Does the blog ever point out fallacies of argument? If so, does it explain the problems with such reasoning or just assume readers will understand the fallacies? Summarize your findings in a brief oral report to your class.

Chapter 21

Arguments Based on Emotion: Pathos

This chapter is taken from Andrea A. Lunsford and John J. Ruszkiewicz, *Everything's an Argument,* Seventh Edition, pp. 28–39 (Chapter 2).

Center: PRNews Photo/Wide World/AP Photo; right: Used with permission of Gary Varvel and Creators Syndicate. All rights reserved.

Emotional appeals (*appeals to pathos*) are powerful tools for influencing what people think and believe. We all make decisions—even including the most important ones—based on our feelings. That's what the Food and Drug Administration hoped to capitalize on when it introduced nine tough warning labels for cigarettes, one of which you see above. One look at the stained, rotting teeth and the lip sore may arouse emotions of fear strong enough to convince people not to smoke.

In the second panel, Bob Dorigo Jones, an opponent of lawsuit abuse, takes concerns about product liability in a different direction, publishing a book entitled *Remove Child before Folding: The 101 Stupidest, Silliest, and Wackiest Warning Labels Ever* to make us laugh and thereby, perhaps, to wonder why common sense seems in such short supply. In the third panel, editorial cartoonist for the *Indianapolis Star* Gary Varvel uses the anti-smoking meme to point out a potent irony in burgeoning campaigns to legalize marijuana.

The arguments packed into these three images all appeal to emotion, and research has shown us that we often make decisions based on just such appeals. So when you hear that formal or academic arguments should rely solely on facts to convince us, remember that facts alone often won't carry the day, even for a worthy cause. The largely successful case made this decade for same-sex marriage provides a notable example of a movement that persuaded people equally by virtue of the reasonableness and the passion of its claims. Like many political and social debates, though, the issue provoked powerful emotions on every side—feelings that sometimes led to extreme words and tactics.

Of course, we don't have to look hard for arguments fueled with emotions such as hatred, envy, and greed, or for campaigns intended to drive wedges between economic or social groups, making them fearful or resentful. For that reason alone, writers should not use emotional appeals rashly or casually. (For more about emotional fallacies, see **"FALLACIES OF ARGUMENT."**)

■ Reading Critically for Pathos

On February 24, 2014, Senator Tom Harkin of Iowa, fresh from two "fact-finding" trips to Cuba, described his experiences on the Senate floor in a rambling, forty-minute speech, praising that island nation's accomplishments in health care and education and urging a normalization of Cuban–American relationships. Later that day, Florida senator Marco Rubio, expecting to speak about growing repression in Venezuela, found it impossible to ignore Harkin's rosy view of the "fascinating" socialist experiment ninety miles from the coast of the United States. Seizing a kairotic moment, the first-term senator delivered a passionate fifteen-minute rejoinder to Harkin without a script or teleprompter—though Rubio did use posters prepared originally for the Venezuelan talk. After a sarcastic taunt ("Sounded like he had a wonderful trip visiting what he described as a real paradise"), Rubio quickly turned serious, even angry, as he offered his take on the country Harkin had toured:

> I heard him also talk about these great doctors that they have in Cuba. I have no doubt they're very talented. I've met a bunch of them. You know where I met them? In the United States because they defected. Because in Cuba, doctors would rather drive a taxi cab or work in a hotel than be a doctor. I wonder if they spoke to him about the outbreak of cholera that they've been unable to control, or about the three-tiered system of health care that exists where foreigners and government officials get health care much better than that that's available to the general population.

The speech thereafter settles into a rhythm of patterned inquiries designed to raise doubts about what Senator Harkin had seen, Rubio's informal language rippling with contempt for his colleague's naïveté:

> I heard about their [the Cubans'] wonderful literacy rate, how everyone in Cuba knows how to read. That's fantastic. Here's the problem: they can only read censored stuff. They're not allowed access to the Internet. The only newspapers they're allowed to read are *Granma* or the ones produced by the government....

> He talked about these great baseball players that are coming from Cuba—and they are. But I wonder if they informed him [that] every single one of those guys playing in the Major Leagues defected. They left Cuba to play here....

> So it's great to have literacy, but if you don't have access to the information, what's the point of it? So I wish somebody would have asked about that on that trip....

> I wonder if anybody asked about terrorism, because Cuba is a state sponsor of terrorism....

Language this heated and pointed has risks, especially when a young legislator is taking on a genial and far more experienced colleague. But Rubio, the son of Cuban immigrants, isn't shy about allowing his feelings to show. Segueing to his original topic—growing political repression in socialist Venezuela—he uses the kind of verbal repetition common in oratory to drive home his major concern about Cuba, its influence on other nations:

CIS 111

Let me tell you what the Cubans are really good at, because they don't know how to run their economy, they don't know how to build, they don't know how to govern a people. What they are really good at is repression. What they are really good at is shutting off information to the Internet and to radio and television and social media. That's what they're really good at. And they're not just good at it domestically, they're good exporters of these things.

Rubio's actual audience in the U.S. Senate was very small, but today all speeches from that chamber are carried nationwide and archived by C-SPAN, and in the age of You-Tube, bits and pieces of political addresses reach many listeners. Former speechwriter and *Wall Street Journal* columnist Peggy Noonan was among those who caught Rubio's remarks and blogged about them: "We have pressed in these parts for American political figures to speak clearly and with moral confidence about American sympathies in various international disputes. Rubio's speech is honest political indignation successfully deployed." You can watch the entire speech on C-SPAN's Web site (listed as "Rubio Speech on Venezuela") to see if you agree. And though Cuba and the United States did re-establish diplomatic relationships roughly ten months after the Harkin/Rubio exchange, issues raised by both senators—from health care to the immigration status of Cuban baseball players—will likely be argued for years to come.

As originally aired on C-SPAN2 on February 24 2014

FIGURE 21.1

Respond

Working with a classmate, make a list of reasons why speakers in highly charged situations might need to use emotional appeals cautiously, even sparingly. What consequences might heightened emotional appeals lead to? What is at stake for the speaker in such situations, in terms of credibility and ethos? What are the advantages of evoking emotions in support of your claims or ideas?

■ Using Emotions to Build Bridges

You may sometimes want to use emotions to connect with readers to assure them that you understand their experiences or "feel their pain," to borrow a sentiment popularized by President Bill Clinton. Such a bridge is especially important when you're writing about matters that readers regard as sensitive. Before they'll trust you, they'll want assurances that you understand the issues in depth. If you strike the right emotional note, you'll establish an important connection. That's what Apple founder Steve Jobs does in a much-admired 2005 commencement address in which he tells the audience that he doesn't have a fancy speech, just three stories from his life:

> My second story is about love and loss. I was lucky. I found what I loved to do early in life. Woz [Steve Wozniak] and I started Apple in my parents' garage when I was twenty. We worked hard and in ten years, Apple had grown from just the two of us in a garage into a $2 billion company with over four thousand employees. We'd just released our finest creation, the Macintosh, a year earlier, and I'd just turned thirty, and then I got fired. How can you get fired from a company you started? Well, as Apple grew, we hired someone who I thought was very talented to run the company with me, and for the first year or so, things went well. But then our visions of the future began to diverge, and eventually we had a falling out. When we did, our board of directors sided with him, and so at thirty, I was out, and very publicly out....
>
> I didn't see it then, but it turned out that getting fired from Apple was the best thing that could have ever happened to me. The heaviness of being successful was replaced by the lightness of being a beginner again, less sure about everything. It freed me to enter one of the most creative periods in my life. During the next five years I started a company named NeXT, another company named Pixar and fell in love with an amazing woman who would become my wife. Pixar went on to create the world's first computer-animated feature film, *Toy Story*, and is now the most successful animation studio in the world.
>
> —Steve Jobs, "You've Got to Find What You Love, Jobs Says"

In no obvious way is Jobs's recollection a formal argument. But it prepares his audience to accept the advice he'll give later in his speech, at least partly because he's speaking from meaningful personal experiences.

A more obvious way to build an emotional tie is simply to help readers identify with your experiences. If, like Georgina Kleege, you were blind and wanted to argue for more sensible attitudes toward blind people, you might ask readers in the first paragraph of your argument to confront their prejudices. Here Kleege, a writer and college instructor, makes an emotional point by telling a story:

> I tell the class, "I am legally blind." There is a pause, a collective intake of breath. I feel them look away uncertainly and then look back. After all, I just said I couldn't see. Or did I? I had managed to get there on my own—no cane, no dog, none of the usual trappings of blindness. Eyeing me askance now, they might detect that my gaze is not quite focused.... They watch me glance down, or towards the door where someone's coming in late. I'm just like anyone else.
>
> —Georgina Kleege, "Call It Blindness"

Given the way she narrates the first day of class, readers are as likely to identify with the students as with Kleege, imagining themselves sitting in a classroom, facing a sightless instructor, confronting their own prejudices about the blind. Kleege wants to put her audience on the edge emotionally.

CIS 111

Let's consider another rhetorical situation: how do you win over an audience when the logical claims that you're making are likely to go against what many in the audience believe? Once again, a slightly risky appeal to emotions on a personal level may work. That's the tack that Michael Pollan takes in bringing readers to consider that "the great moral struggle of our time will be for the rights of animals." In introducing his lengthy exploratory argument, Pollan uses personal experience to appeal to his audience:

> The first time I opened Peter Singer's *Animal Liberation*, I was dining alone at the Palm, trying to enjoy a rib-eye steak cooked medium-rare. If this sounds like a good recipe for cognitive dissonance (if not indigestion), that was sort of the idea. Preposterous as it might seem to supporters of animal rights, what I was doing was tantamount to reading *Uncle Tom's Cabin* on a plantation in the Deep South in 1852.
>
> —Michael Pollan, "An Animal's Place"

In creating a vivid image of his first encounter with Singer's book, Pollan's opening builds a bridge between himself as a person trying to enter into the animal rights debate in a fair and open-minded, if still skeptical, way and readers who might be passionate about either side of this argument.

THE BIRTH OF A VEGETARIAN   @

© Robert Mankoff/The New Yorker Collection/The Cartoon Bank

FIGURE 21.2 A visual version of Michael Pollan's rhetorical situation.

■ Using Emotions to Sustain an Argument

You can also use emotional appeals to make logical claims stronger or more memorable. That is the way that photographs and other images add power to arguments. In a TV attack ad, the scowling cell phone video of a disheveled political opponent may do as much damage as the insinuation that he bought his home on the cheap from a financier convicted of fraud. In contrast, a human face smiling or showing honest emotion can sell just about any product—that's why indicted political figures now routinely smile for their mug shots. Using emotion is tricky, however. Lay on too much feeling—especially sentiments like outrage, pity, or shame, which make people uncomfortable—and you may offend the very audiences you hoped to convince.

Still, strong emotions can add energy to a passage or an entire argument, as they do when Walter Russell Mead, editor-at-large of the *American Interest*, argues about what *really* motivates Americans to donate lavishly to many colleges and universities. As you read the following excerpt, notice how the author paints vivid pictures of people at college sporting events, describes the emotions at those games, and then argues what schools really need to do to win contributions:

> But if you want to understand why so many generations of Americans have sent so much dough back to the campuses where they wasted some of the happiest years of their lives, watch the intensity of the tens of thousands of fans who attend these events. Look at the shirtless boys with faces and torsos painted in the school colors; look at the cheerleaders on the fields, the "waves" surging through the stands.
>
> American universities, those temples of reason (at their best), are tribes. The kids bond to each other and to their schools in the heat of the intense emotions that these contests generate. Those shirtless kids covered in paint, shivering in the November weather as they cheer their team on, will be prosperous, middle-aged alumni one day—and when they are, they will still be stirred by the memory of the emotions and the loyalty that brought them out to the field.
>
> If you want your alumni to give, you first have to make them fall in love with your school. This is not about having better chemistry programs or more faculty with higher name recognition than the school up the road. It is not about scoring higher on world indices of university quality. It is about competition, drama, intensity, about hope and fear, collective celebrations or collective disasters, seared into young and impressionable hearts where they will never be forgotten—and where they will be annually renewed as each sport in its season produces new highs and lows, new hopes and fears. Alumni watching their schools' games on TV, or celebrating or mourning their schools' results each week with friends, family and colleagues, are renewing their ties with their alma maters affirming that being an "Aggie" or a "Tar Heel" is an *identity*, not a line on the resume.
>
> This is why most of them give. It is irrational and tribal love. It is intense emotion, not a vague sense of obligation or philanthropy. They want to beat State.
>
> —Walter Russell Mead and *The American Interest* staff,
> "It All Begins with Football"

Mead's claim, emotional in itself, may not be exactly what college and university administrators and faculty want to hear. But in using language this evocative, he makes his argument memorable, hoping perhaps to make general readers admit how they have felt and acted themselves.

Kevin C. Cox/Getty Images

FIGURE 21.3

It's difficult to gauge how much emotion will work in a given argument. Some issues—such as racism, immigration, abortion, and gun control—provoke strong feelings and, as a result, are often argued on emotional terms. But even issues that seem deadly dull—such as reform of federal student loan programs—can be argued passionately when proposed changes in these programs are set in human terms: reduce support for college loans and Kai, Riley, and Jayden end up in dead-end, low-paying jobs; don't reform the program and we're looking at another Wall Street–sized loan bailout and subsequent recession. Both alternatives might scare people into paying enough attention to take political action.

■ Using Humor

Humor has always played an important role in argument, sometimes as the sugar that makes the medicine go down. You can slip humor into an argument to put readers at ease, thereby making them more open to a proposal you have to offer. It's hard to say *no* when you're laughing. Humor also makes otherwise sober people suspend their judgment and even their prejudices, perhaps because the surprise and naughtiness of wit are combustive: they provoke laughter or smiles, not reflection. Who can resist a no-holds-barred attack on a famous personality, such as this assessment of *Twilight* star Kristen Stewart:

> The original scoffing, scowling, stammering, stuttering, gaping open mouth, temper-tantrum throwing, lip-biting, hair-flipping, plank of wood moody actress… A tape recorder in a mannequin could do her job.

Humor deployed cleverly may be why TV shows like *South Park* and *Modern Family* became popular with mainstream audiences, despite their willingness to explore controversial themes. Similarly, it's possible to make a point through humor that might not work in more sober writing. People argue endlessly about eating the right foods, typically defined by diet gurus who favor locally sourced, organically grown, and profoundly dull vegetables. *Wall Street Journal* columnist Ron Rosenbaum will have none of that. With new research suggesting that fatty diets may have unanticipated health benefits, Rosenbaum deploys some high-calorie humor to argue for the pleasures of dining lavishly:

Preventing obesity is a laudable goal, but it has become the rationale for indiscriminate fat hunters. It can shade into a kind of bullying of the overweight, a badgering of anyone who likes butter or heavy cream. To the antifat crusaders, I say: Attack fatty junk food all you want. I'm with you. But you can deny me my roasted marrow bones when you pry them from my cold, dead hands.

I'm not suggesting that we embrace these life-changing food experiences just on grounds of pure pleasure (though there's much to be said for pure pleasure). As it turns out, the science on the matter is changing as well. We are discovering that fatty delights can actually be good for you: They allow Spaniards, Italians and Greeks to live longer, and they make us satisfied with eating less. I'm speaking up not for obesity-generating fat, then, but for the kind of fatty food that leads to swooning sensual satiety.

Roast goose, for instance, is a supremely succulent, mind-alteringly flavorful fatty food. In most of America, roast goose would be viewed as the raven of cardiac mortality, hoarsely honking "never more." And listening to the doctors on cable TV, you might think that it's better to cook up a batch of meth than to cook with butter.

Eating fatty foods has become the culinary version of *Breaking Bad*: a dangerous walk on the wild side for the otherwise timid consumers of tasteless butter substitutes and Lean Cuisine.

—Ron Rosenbaum, "Let Them Eat Fat"

Our laughter testifies to what some people have thought all along: people who want us to eat tofu are the real problem. Note the pleasure Rosenbaum takes in the emotive power of words themselves: *swooning sensual satiety*; *the raven of cardiac mortality, hoarsely honking "never more."*

A writer or speaker can even use humor to deal with sensitive issues. For example, sports commentator Bob Costas, given the honor of eulogizing the great baseball player Mickey Mantle, couldn't ignore problems in Mantle's life. So he argues for Mantle's greatness by admitting the man's weaknesses indirectly through humor:

It brings to mind a story Mickey liked to tell on himself and maybe some of you have heard it. He pictured himself at the pearly gates, met by St. Peter, who shook his head and said, "Mick, we checked the record. We know some of what went on. Sorry, we can't let you in. But before you go, God wants to know if you'd sign these six dozen baseballs."

—Bob Costas, "Eulogy for Mickey Mantle"

Similarly, politicians may use humor to deal with issues they couldn't acknowledge in any other way. Here, for example, is former president George W. Bush at the 2004 Radio and TV Correspondents' Dinner discussing his much-mocked intellect:

Those stories about my intellectual capacity do get under my skin. You know, for a while I even thought my staff believed it. There on my schedule first thing every morning it said, "Intelligence briefing."

—George W. Bush

Not all humor is well-intentioned or barb-free. In fact, among the most powerful forms of emotional argument is ridicule—humor aimed at a particular target. Eighteenth-century poet and critic Samuel Johnson was known for his stinging and humorous put-downs, such as this comment to an aspiring writer: "Your manuscript is both good and original, but the part that is good is not original and the part that is original is not good." (Expect your own writing teachers to be kinder.) In our own time, the *Onion* has earned a reputation for its mastery of both ridicule and satire, the art of using over-the-top humor to making a serious point.

But because ridicule is a double-edged sword, it requires a deft hand to wield it. Humor that reflects bad taste discredits a writer completely, as does satire that misses its mark. Unless your target deserves riposte and you can be very funny, it's usually better to steer clear of such humor.

■ Using Arguments Based on Emotion

You don't want to play puppet master with people's emotions when you write arguments, but it's a good idea to spend some time early in your work thinking about how you want readers to feel as they consider your persuasive claims. For example, would readers of your editorial about campus traffic policies be more inclined to agree with you if you made them envy faculty privileges, or would arousing their sense of fairness work better? What emotional appeals might persuade meat eaters to consider a vegan diet—or vice versa? Would sketches of stage props on a Web site persuade people to buy a season ticket to the theater, or would you spark more interest by featuring pictures of costumed performers?

Consider, too, the effect that a story can have on readers. Writers and journalists routinely use what are called *human-interest stories* to give presence to issues or arguments. You can do the same, using a particular incident to evoke sympathy, understanding, outrage, or amusement. Take care, though, to tell an honest story.

Respond

1. To what specific emotions do the following slogans, sales pitches, and maxims appeal?

   "Just do it." (ad for Nike)

   "Think different." (ad for Apple computers)

   "Reach out and touch someone." (ad for AT&T)

   "By any means necessary." (rallying cry from Malcolm X)

   "Have it your way." (slogan for Burger King)

   "The ultimate driving machine." (slogan for BMW)

   "It's everywhere you want to be." (slogan for Visa)

   "Know what comes between me and my Calvins? Nothing!" (tag line for Calvin Klein jeans)

   "Don't mess with Texas!" (anti-litter campaign slogan)

   "American by Birth. Rebel by Choice." (slogan for Harley-Davidson)

2. Bring a magazine to class, and analyze the emotional appeals in as many full-page ads as you can. Then classify those ads by types of emotional appeal, and see whether you can connect the appeals to the subject or target audience of the magazine. Compare your results with those of your classmates, and discuss your findings. For instance, how exactly are the ads in publications such as *Cosmopolitan*, *Wired*, *Sports Illustrated*, *Motor Trend*, and *Smithsonian* adapted to their specific audiences?

3. How do arguments based on emotion work in different media? Are such arguments more or less effective in books, articles, television (both news and entertainment shows), films, brochures, magazines, email, Web sites, the theater, street protests, and so on? You might explore how a single medium handles emotional appeals or compare different media. For example, why do the comments pages of blogs seem to encourage angry outbursts? Are newspapers an emotionally colder source of information than television news programs? If so, why?

4. Spend some time looking for arguments that use ridicule or humor to make their point: check out your favorite Twitter feeds or blogs; watch for bumper stickers, posters, or advertisements; and listen to popular song lyrics. Bring one or two examples to class, and be ready to explain how the humor makes an emotional appeal and whether it's effective.

Chapter 22

Arguments Based on Character: Ethos

- Thinking Critically about Arguments Based on Character
- Establishing Trustworthiness and Credibility
- Claiming Authority
- Coming Clean about Motives

This chapter is taken from Andrea A. Lunsford and John J. Ruszkiewicz, *Everything's an Argument*, Seventh Edition, pp. 40–50 (Chapter 3).

Left to right: © Jon Arnold Images Ltd./Alamy; © Bernhard Classen/age fotostock; Richard Shotwell/Invision/AP

Whenever you read anything—whether it's a news article, an advertisement, a speech, or a text message—you no doubt subconsciously analyze the message for a sense of the character and credibility of the sender: *Is this someone I know and trust? Does the PBS reporter seem biased? Why should I believe an IRS official? Is this scholar really an authority on the subject?* Our culture teaches us to be skeptical of most messages, especially those that bombard us with slogans, and such reasonable doubt is a crucial skill in reading and evaluating arguments.

For that reason, people and institutions that hope to influence us do everything they can to establish their character and credibility, what ancient rhetors referred to as *ethos*. And sometimes slogans such as "All the News That's Fit to Print," "Fair & Balanced," or "Lean Forward" can be effective. At the very least, if a phrase is repeated often enough, it begins to sound plausible. Maybe CNN *is* the most trusted name in news!

But establishing character usually takes more than repetition, as marketers of all kinds know. It arises from credentials actually earned in some way. In the auto industry, for instance, companies such as Toyota, General Motors, and Nissan are hustling to present themselves as environmentally responsible producers of fuel-efficient, low-emission cars—the Prius, Volt, and Leaf. BMW, maker of "the ultimate driving machine," points to its fuel-sipping i3 and i8 cars as evidence of its commitment to "sustainable mobility." And Elon Musk (who builds rockets as well as Tesla cars) polishes his good-citizenship bona fides by sharing his electric vehicle patents with other manufacturers. All of these companies realize that their future success is linked to an ability to project a convincing ethos for themselves and their products.

If corporations and institutions can establish an ethos, consider how much character matters when we think about people in the public arena. Perhaps no individual managed a more exceptional assertion of personal ethos than Jorge Mario Bergoglio did after he became Pope Francis on March 13, 2013, following the abdication of Benedict XVI—a man many found scholarly, cold, and out of touch with the modern world. James Carroll, writing for the *New Yorker*, identifies the precise moment when the world realized that it was dealing with a new sort of pope:

"Who am I to judge?" With those five words, spoken in late July [2013] in reply to a reporter's question about the status of gay priests in the Church, Pope Francis stepped away from the disapproving tone, the explicit moralizing typical of popes and bishops.

—James Carroll, "Who Am I to Judge?"

Carroll goes on to explain that Francis quickly established his ethos with a series of specific actions, decisions, and moments of identification with ordinary people, marking him as someone even nonbelievers might listen to and respect:

As pope, Francis has simplified the Renaissance regalia of the papacy by abandoning fur-trimmed velvet capes, choosing to live in a two-room apartment instead of the Apostolic Palace, and replacing the papal Mercedes with a Ford Focus. Instead of the traditional red slip-ons, Francis wears ordinary black shoes. …Yet Francis didn't criticize the choices of other prelates. "He makes changes without attacking people," a Jesuit official told me. In his interview with *La Civiltà Cattolica*, Francis said, "My choices, including those related to the day-to-day aspects of life, like the use of a modest car, are related to a spiritual discernment that responds to a need that arises from looking at things, at people, and from reading the signs of the times."

In that last sentence, Francis acknowledges that ethos is gained, in part, through identification with one's audience and era. And this man, movingly photographed embracing the sick and disfigured, also posed for selfies!

AP Photo/L'Osservatore Romano, Riccardo Aguiari

FIGURE 22.1

You can see, then, why Aristotle treats ethos as a powerful argumentative appeal. Ethos creates quick and sometimes almost irresistible connections between readers and arguments. We observe people, groups, or institutions making and defending claims all the time and inevitably ask ourselves, *Should we pay attention to them? Can we rely on them? Do we dare to trust them?* Consider, though, that the same questions will be asked about you and your work, especially in academic settings.

■ Thinking Critically about Arguments Based on Character

Put simply, arguments based on character (ethos) depend on *trust*. We tend to accept arguments from those we trust, and we trust them (whether individuals, groups, or institutions) in good part because of their reputations. Three main elements—credibility, authority, and unselfish or clear motives—add up to *ethos*.

To answer serious and important questions, we often turn to professionals (doctors, lawyers, engineers, teachers, pastors) or to experts (those with knowledge and experience) for good advice. Based on their backgrounds, such people come with their ethos already established. Thus, appeals or arguments about character often turn on claims like these:

- A person (or group or institution) is or is not trustworthy or credible on this issue.

- A person (or group or institution) does or does not have the authority to speak to this issue.

- A person (or group or institution) does or does not have unselfish or clear motives for addressing this subject.

■ Establishing Trustworthiness and Credibility

Trustworthiness and credibility speak to a writer's honesty, respect for an audience and its values, and plain old likability. Sometimes a sense of humor can play an important role in getting an audience to listen to or "like" you. It's no accident that all but the most serious speeches begin with a joke or funny story: the humor puts listeners at ease and helps them identify with the speaker. Writer J. K. Rowling, for example, puts her audience (and herself) at ease early in the commencement address she delivered at Harvard in 2008 by getting real about such speeches:

> Delivering a commencement address is a great responsibility; or so I thought until I cast my mind back to my own graduation. The commencement speaker that day was the distinguished British philosopher Baroness Mary Warnock. Reflecting on her speech has helped me enormously in writing this one, because it turns out that I can't remember a single word she said. This liberating discovery enables me to proceed without any fear that I might inadvertently influence you to abandon promising careers in business, the law, or politics for the giddy delights of becoming a gay wizard.
>
> You see? If all you remember in years to come is the "gay wizard" joke, I've come out ahead of Baroness Mary Warnock. Achievable goals: the first step to self improvement.
>
> —J. K. Rowling, "The Fringe Benefits of Failure, and the Importance of Imagination"

In just a few sentences, Rowling pokes fun at herself, undercuts the expectation that graduation addresses change people's lives, slides in an allusion from her Harry Potter series, and then even offers a smidgen of advice. For an audience well disposed toward her already, Rowling has likely lived up to expectations.

But using humor to enhance your credibility may be more common in oratory than in the kind of writing you'll do in school. Fortunately, you have many options, one being simply to make plausible claims and then back them up with evidence. Academic audiences appreciate a reasonable disposition; we will discuss this approach at greater length in the next chapter.

You can also establish trustworthiness by connecting your own beliefs to core principles that are well established and widely respected. This strategy is particularly effective when your position seems to be—at first glance, at least—a threat to traditional values. For example, when former Smith College president Ruth J. Simmons describes her professional self to a commencement audience she is addressing, she presents her acquired reputation in terms that align perfectly with contemporary values:

> For my part, I was cast as a troublemaker in my early career and accepted the disapproval that accompanies the expression of unpopular views: unpopular views about disparate pay for women and minorities; unpopular views about sexual harassment; unpopular views about exclusionary practices in our universities.
>
> —Ruth J. Simmons

It's fine to be a rebel when you are on the right side of history.

Writers who establish their credibility seem trustworthy. But sometimes, to be credible, you have to admit limitations, too, as *New York Times* columnist David Brooks does as he wrestles with a problem common in our time, an inability to focus on things that matter:

> Like everyone else, I am losing the attention war. I toggle over to my emails when I should be working. I text when I should be paying attention to the people in front of me. I spend hours looking at mildly diverting stuff on YouTube. ("Look, there's a bunch of guys who can play 'Billie Jean' on beer bottles!")
>
> And, like everyone else, I've nodded along with the prohibition sermons imploring me to limit my information diet. Stop multitasking! Turn off the devices at least once a week!
>
> And, like everyone else, these sermons have had no effect. Many of us lead lives of distraction, unable to focus on what we know we should focus on.
>
> —David Brooks, "The Art of Focus"

Making such concessions to readers sends a strong signal that you've looked critically at your own position and can therefore be trusted when you turn to arguing its merits. Speaking to readers directly, using *I* or *you* or *us*, can also help you connect with them, as can using contractions and everyday or colloquial language—both strategies employed by Brooks. In other situations, you may find that a more formal tone gives your claims greater credibility. You'll be making such choices as you search for the ethos that represents you best.

In fact, whenever you write a paper or present an idea, you are sending signals about your credibility, whether you intend to or not. If your ideas are reasonable, your sources are reliable, and your language is appropriate to the project, you suggest to academic readers that you're someone whose ideas *might* deserve attention. Details matter: helpful graphs, tables, charts, or illustrations may carry weight with readers, as will the visual attractiveness of your text, whether in print or digital form. Obviously, correct spelling, grammar, and mechanics are important too. And though you might not worry about it now, at some point you may need letters of recommendation from instructors or supervisors. How will they remember you? Often chiefly from the ethos you have established in your work. Think about that.

■ Claiming Authority

When you read or listen to an argument, you have every right to ask about the writer's authority: *What does he know about the subject? What experiences does she have that make her especially knowledgeable? Why should I pay attention to this person?* When you offer an argument yourself, you have to anticipate and be prepared to answer questions like these, either directly or indirectly.

How does someone construct an authoritative ethos? In examining what he describes as "the fundamental problem with President Obama's communications ethos," Ron Fournier, editorial director of *National Journal*, explains that authority cannot be taken for granted:

> He and his advisers are so certain about their moral and political standing that they believe it's enough to make a declaration. *If we say it, the public should believe it.*
>
> That's not how it works. A president must earn the public's trust. He must teach and persuade; speak clearly, and follow word with action; show empathy toward his rivals, and acknowledge the merits of a critique. A successful president pays careful attention to how his image is projected both to U.S. voters and to the people of the world. He knows that to be strong, a leader must look strong. Image matters, especially in an era so dominated by them.
>
> —Ron Fournier, "Is the White House Lying, or
> Just Bad at Crisis Communications?"

Of course, writers establish their authority in various ways. Sometimes the assertion of ethos will be bold and personal, as it is when writer and activist Terry Tempest Williams attacks those who poisoned the Utah deserts with nuclear radiation. What gives her the right to speak on this subject? Not scientific expertise, but gut-wrenching personal experience:

> I belong to the Clan of One-Breasted Women. My mother, my grandmothers, and six aunts have all had mastectomies. Seven are dead. The two who survive have just completed rounds of chemotherapy and radiation.

> I've had my own problems: two biopsies for breast cancer and a small tumor between my ribs diagnosed as a "borderline malignancy."
>
> —Terry Tempest Williams, "The Clan of One-Breasted Women"

We are willing to listen to Williams because she has lived with the nuclear peril she will deal with in the remainder of her essay.

Other means of claiming authority are less dramatic. By simply attaching titles to their names, writers assert that they hold medical or legal or engineering degrees, or some other important credentials. Or they may mention the number of years they've worked in a given field or the distinguished positions they have held. As a reader, you'll pay more attention to an argument about global warming offered by a professor of atmospheric and oceanic science at the University of Minnesota than one by your Uncle Sid, who sells tools. But you'll prefer your uncle to the professor when you need advice about a reliable rotary saw.

When readers might be skeptical of both you and your claims, you may have to be even more specific about your credentials. That's exactly the strategy Richard Bernstein uses to establish his right to speak on the subject of "Asian culture." What gives a New York writer named Bernstein the authority to write about Asian peoples? Bernstein tells us in a sparkling example of an argument based on character:

> The Asian culture, as it happens, is something I know a bit about, having spent five years at Harvard striving for a Ph.D. in a joint program called History and East Asian Languages and, after that, living either as a student (for one year) or a journalist (six years) in China and Southeast Asia. At least I know enough to know there is no such thing as the "Asian culture."
>
> —Richard Bernstein, *Dictatorship of Virtue*

When you write for readers who trust you and your work, you may not have to make such an open claim to authority. But making this type of appeal is always an option.

■ Coming Clean about Motives

When people are trying to convince you of something, it's important (and natural) to ask: *Whose interests are they serving? How will they profit from their proposal?* Such suspicions go to the heart of ethical arguments.

In a hugely controversial essay published in the *Princeton Tory*, Tal Fortgang, a first-year student at the Ivy League school, argues that those on campus who used the phrase "Check your privilege" to berate white male students like him for the advantages they enjoy are, in fact, judging him according to gender and race, and not for "all the hard work I have done in my life." To challenge stereotypical assumptions about the "racist patriarchy" that supposedly paved his way to Princeton, Fortgang writes about the experiences of his ancestors, opening the paragraphs with a striking parallel structure:

> Perhaps it's the privilege my grandfather and his brother had to flee their home as teenagers when the Nazis invaded Poland, leaving their mother and five younger siblings behind, running and running....
>
> Or maybe it's the privilege my grandmother had of spending weeks upon weeks on a death march through Polish forests in subzero temperatures, one of just a handful to survive....
>
> Perhaps my privilege is that those two resilient individuals came to America with no money and no English, obtained citizenship, learned the language and met each other....
>
> Perhaps it was my privilege that my own father worked hard enough in City College to earn a spot at a top graduate school, got a good job, and for 25 years got up well before the crack of dawn, sacrificing precious time he wanted to spend with those he valued most—his wife and kids—to earn that living.
>
> —Tal Fortgang, "Checking My Privilege:
> Character as the Basis of Privilege"

Fortgang thus attempts to establish his own ethos and win the argument against those who make assumptions about his roots by dramatizing the ethos of his ancestors:

> That's the problem with calling someone out for the "privilege" which you assume has defined their narrative. You don't know what their struggles have been, what they may have gone through to be where they are. Assuming they've benefitted from "power systems" or other conspiratorial imaginary institutions denies them credit for all they've done, things of which you may not even conceive. You don't know whose father died defending your freedom. You don't know whose mother escaped oppression. You don't know who conquered their demons, or may still [be] conquering them now.

As you might imagine, the pushback to "Checking My Privilege" was enormous, some of the hundreds of comments posted to an online version accusing Fortgang himself of assuming the very ethos of victimhood against which he inveighs. Peter Finocchiaro, a reviewer on *Slate*, is especially brutal: "Only a few short months ago he was living at home with his parents. His life experience, one presumes, is fairly limited. So in that sense, he doesn't really know any better.... He is an ignorant 19-year-old white guy from Westchester." You can see in this debate how ethos quickly raises issues of knowledge and motives. Fortgang tries to resist the stereotype others would impose on his character, but others regard the very ethos he fashions in his essay as evidence of his naïveté about race, discrimination, and, yes, privilege.

We all, of course, have connections and interests that bind us to other human beings. It makes sense that a young man would explore his social identity, that a woman might be concerned with women's issues, that members of minority groups might define social and cultural conditions on their own terms—or even that investors might look out for their investments. It's simply good strategy to let your audiences know where your loyalties lie when such information does, in fact, shape your work.

Using Ethos in Your Own Writing

- Establish your credibility by acknowledging your audience's values, showing respect for them, and establishing common ground where (and if) possible. How will you convince your audience you are trustworthy? What will you admit about your own limitations?

- Establish your authority by showing you have done your homework and know your topic well. How will you show that you know your topic well? What appropriate personal experience can you draw on?

- Examine your motives for writing. What, if anything, do you stand to gain from your argument? How can you explain those advantages to your audience?

CULTURAL CONTEXTS FOR ARGUMENT

Ethos

In the United States, students are often asked to establish authority by drawing on personal experiences, by reporting on research they or others have conducted, and by taking a position for which they can offer strong evidence. But this expectation about student authority is by no means universal.

Some cultures regard student writers as novices who can most effectively make arguments by reflecting on what they've learned from their teachers and elders—those who hold the most important knowledge and, hence, authority. When you're arguing a point with people from cultures other than your own, ask questions like:

- Whom are you addressing, and what is your relationship with that person?

- What knowledge are you expected to have? Is it appropriate or expected for you to demonstrate that knowledge—and if so, how?

- What tone is appropriate? And remember: politeness is rarely, if ever, inappropriate.

RESPOND

1.   Consider the ethos of these public figures. Then describe one or two products that might benefit from their endorsements as well as several that would not.

Edward Snowden—whistleblower

Kaley Cuoco-Sweeting—actress

James Earl Jones—actor

Michael Sam—athlete

Megyn Kelly—TV news commentator

Miley Cyrus—singer

Seth Meyers—late-night TV host

Cristiano Ronaldo—soccer player

2.   Opponents of Richard Nixon, the thirty-seventh president of the United States, once raised doubts about his integrity by asking a single ruinous question: *Would you buy a used car from this man?* Create your own version of the argument of character. Begin by choosing an intriguing or controversial person or group and finding an image online. Then download the image into a word-processing file. Create a caption for the photo that is modeled after the question asked about Nixon: *Would you give this woman your email password? Would you share a campsite with this couple? Would you eat lasagna that this guy fixed?* Finally, write a serious 300-word argument that explores the character flaws or strengths of your subject(s).

3.   Take a close look at your Facebook page (or your page on any other social media site). What are some aspects of your character, true or not, that might be conveyed by the photos, videos, and messages you have posted online? Analyze the ethos or character you see projected there, using the advice in this chapter to guide your analysis.

Chapter 23

Arguments Based on Facts and Reason: Logos

- Thinking Critically about Hard Evidence
- Using Reason and Common Sense
- Providing Logical Structures for Argument

This chapter is taken from Andrea A. Lunsford and John J. Ruszkiewicz, *Everything's an Argument*, Seventh Edition, pp. 51–70 (Chapter 4).

"And it's recommended by nine out of ten people we believe to be doctors."

Left to right: Yui Mok/Press Association via AP Images; © NBC/Photofest, Inc.; © Frank Cotham/The New Yorker/The Cartoon Bank

These three images say a lot about the use and place of logic (*logos*) in Western and American culture. The first shows Benedict Cumberbatch from the BBC TV series *Sherlock*, just one of many actors to play Arthur Conan Doyle's much-loved fictional detective Sherlock Holmes, who solves perplexing crimes by using precise observation and impeccable logic. The second refers to an equally popular TV (and film) series character, Spock, the Vulcan officer in *Star Trek* who tries to live a life guided by reason alone—his most predicable observation being some version of "that would not be logical." The third is a cartoon spoofing a pseudo-logical argument (nine out of ten prefer X) made so often in advertising that it has become something of a joke.

These images attest to the prominent place that logic holds for most people: like Holmes, we want to know the facts on the assumption that they will help us make sound judgments. We admire those whose logic is, like Spock's, impeccable. So when arguments begin, "Nine out of ten authorities recommend," we respond favorably: those are good odds. But the three images also challenge reliance on logic alone: Sherlock Holmes and Spock are characters drawn in broad and often parodic strokes; the "nine out of ten" cartoon itself spoofs abuses of reason. Given a choice, however, most of us profess to respect and even prefer *appeals to logos*—that is, claims based on facts, evidence, and reason—but we're also inclined to read factual arguments within the context of our feelings and the ethos of people making the appeals.

■ Thinking Critically about Hard Evidence

Aristotle helps us out in classifying arguments by distinguishing two kinds:

ARTISTIC PROOFS	Arguments the writer/ speaker creates	Constructed arguments	Appeals to reason; commonsense
INARTISTIC PROOFS	Arguments the writer/ speaker is given	Hard evidence	Facts, statistics, testimonies, witnesses, contracts, documents

We can see these different kinds of logical appeals at work in a single paragraph from President Barack Obama's 2014 State of the Union address. Typically in such speeches—nationally televised and closely reviewed—the president assesses the current condition of the United States and then lays out an agenda for the coming years, a laundry list of commitments and goals. One of those items mentioned about half-way through the 2014 address focuses on the admirable objective of improving the conditions of working women:

> Today, women make up about half our workforce. But they still make 77 cents for every dollar a man earns. That is wrong, and in 2014, it's an embarrassment. A woman deserves equal pay for equal work. She deserves to have a baby without sacrificing her job. A mother deserves a day off to care for a sick child or sick parent without running into hardship—and you know what, a father does, too. It's time to do away with workplace policies that belong in a *Mad Men* episode. This year, let's all come together—Congress, the White House, and businesses from Wall Street to Main Street—to give every woman the opportunity she deserves. Because I firmly believe when women succeed, America succeeds.
>
> —Barack Obama, State of the Union address

As you see, Obama opens the paragraph with an important "inartistic" proof, that ratio of just 77 cents to a dollar representing what women earn in the United States compared to men. Beginning with that fact, he then offers a series of reasonable "artistic" appeals phrased as applause lines: *that is wrong; a woman deserves equal pay; a mother deserves a day off...a father does, too.*" Obama then concludes the paragraph by stating the core principle behind all these claims, what we'll later describe as the *warrant* in an argument (see **CHAPTER 18**): *when women succeed, America succeeds.*

Note, then, the importance of that single number the president puts forward. It is evidence that, despite decades of political commitment to pay equity and even federal laws banning gender discrimination in employment and compensation, much work remains to be done. Who can be satisfied with the status quo in the face of that damning number? But where did that statistic come from, and *what if it is wrong*?

Now, no one expects footnotes and documentation in a presidential address. The ethos of the office itself makes the public (at least some portion of it) willing to accept a president's factual claims, if only because his remarks have surely been vetted by legions of staffers. Yet some statistics and claims assume a life of their own, repeated so often that most people—even presidents and their speechwriters—assume that they are true. Add the problem of "confirmation bias," the tendency of most people to believe evidence that confirms their views of the world, and you have numbers that will not die.

We live, however, in an age of critics and fact-checkers. Writing for the *Daily Beast*, Christina Hoff Sommers, a former professor of philosophy and no fan of contemporary feminism, complains that the president is perpetuating an error: "What is wrong and embarrassing is the President of the United States reciting a massively discredited factoid." And in case you won't believe Sommers (and most feminists and those in the president's camp wouldn't), she directs skeptics to a more objective source, the *Washington Post*, which routinely fact-checks the State of the Union and other major addresses.

Like Sommers, that paper does raise questions about the 77/100 earnings ratio, and its detailed analysis of that number suggests just how complicated evidential claims can be. Here's a shortened version of the *Post's* statement, which you'll note cites several government sources:

> There is clearly a wage gap, but differences in the life choices of men and women—such as women tending to leave the workforce when they have children—make it difficult to make simple comparisons.
>
> Obama is using a figure (annual wages, from the Census Bureau) that makes the disparity appear the greatest. The Bureau of Labor Statistics, for instance, shows that the gap is 19 cents when looking at weekly wages. The gap is even smaller when you look at hourly wages—it is 14 cents—but then not every wage earner is paid on an hourly basis, so that statistic excludes salaried workers....
>
> Economists at the Federal Reserve Bank of St. Louis surveyed economic literature and concluded that "research suggests that the actual gender wage gap (when female workers are compared with male workers who have similar characteristics) is much lower than the raw wage gap." They cited one survey, prepared for the Labor Department, which concluded that when such differences are accounted for, much of the hourly wage gap dwindled, to about 5 cents on the dollar.

Is the entire paragraph of the president's address discredited because his hard evidence seems overstated or oversimplified? Not if we accept the *constructed* arguments he makes on the general principle of fairness for offering women—and men—more support as laborers in the job force. But he might have been more convincing at this point in a very lengthy speech if someone in the White House had taken a moment to check the government's own numbers, as the *Washington Post* did. This ongoing controversy over wage equity does, however, illustrate how closely logical arguments—whether artistic or inartistic—will be read and criticized. And so the connections between them matter.

FIGURE 23.1 Factual arguments are often made or enhanced by charts, graphs, and infographics. Here PayScale, an online salary and wage information site, presents numbers to explain the pay equity issue: "Yes, men do earn more than women on average, but not that much more when they work the same job and they have similar experience and abilities." We reproduce here just a portion of the full infographic.

RESPOND

Discuss whether the following statements are examples of hard evidence or constructed arguments. Not all cases are clear-cut.

1. Drunk drivers are involved in more than 50 percent of traffic deaths.

2. DNA tests of skin found under the victim's fingernails suggest that the defendant was responsible for the assault.

3. A psychologist testified that teenage violence could not be blamed on video games.

4. An apple a day keeps the doctor away.

5. "The only thing we have to fear is fear itself."

6. Air bags ought to be removed from vehicles because they can kill young children and small-framed adults.

Facts

Gathering factual information and transmitting it faithfully practically define what we mean by professional journalism and scholarship. We'll even listen to people we don't agree with if their evidence is really good. Below, a reviewer for the conservative

National Review praises William Julius Wilson, a liberal sociologist, because of how well he presents his case:

> In his eagerly awaited new book, Wilson argues that ghetto blacks are worse off than ever, victimized by a near-total loss of low-skill jobs in and around inner-city neighborhoods. In support of this thesis, he *musters mountains of data, plus excerpts from some of the thousands of surveys and face-to-face interviews that he and his research team conducted among inner-city Chicagoans.* It is a book that deserves a wide audience among thinking conservatives.

> —John J. DiIulio Jr., "When Decency Disappears" (emphasis added)

When your facts are compelling, they may stand on their own in a low-stakes argument, supported by little more than saying where they come from. Consider the power of phrases such as "reported by the *Wall Street Journal*" or "according to FactCheck.org." Such sources gain credibility if they have reported facts accurately and reliably over time. Using such credible sources in an argument can also reflect positively on you.

In scholarly arguments, which have higher expectations for accuracy, what counts is drawing sober conclusions from the evidence turned up through detailed research or empirical studies. The language of such material may seem dryly factual to you, even when the content is inherently interesting. But presenting new knowledge dispassionately is (ideally at least) the whole point of scholarly writing, marking a contrast between it and the kind of intellectual warfare that occurs in many media forums, especially news programs and blogs. Here for example is a portion of a lengthy opening paragraph in the "Discussion and Conclusions" section of a scholarly paper arguing that people who spend a great deal of time on Facebook often frame their lives by what they observe there:

> The results of this research support the argument that using Facebook affects people's perceptions of others. For those that have used Facebook longer, it is easier to remember positive messages and happy pictures posted on Facebook; these readily available examples give users an impression that others are happier. As expected in the first hypothesis, the results show that the longer people have used Facebook, the stronger was their belief that others were happier than themselves, and the less they agreed that life is fair. Furthermore, as predicted in the second hypothesis, this research found that the more "friends" people included on their Facebook whom they did not know personally, the stronger they believed that others had better lives than themselves. In other words, looking at happy pictures of others on Facebook gives people an impression that others are "always" happy and having good lives, as evident from these pictures of happy moments. In contrast to their own experiences of life events, which are not always positive, people are very likely to conclude that others have better lives than themselves and that life is not fair.

> —Hui-Tzu Grace Chou, PhD, and Nicholas Edge, BS, "'They Are Happier and Having Better Lives Than I Am': The Impact of Using Facebook on Perceptions of Others' Lives"

There are no fireworks in this conclusion, no slanted or hot language, no unfair or selective reporting of data, just a faithful attention to the facts and behaviors uncovered by the study. But one can easily imagine these facts being subsequently used to support overdramatized claims about the dangers of social networks. That's often what happens to scholarly studies when they are read and interpreted in the popular media.

Of course, arguing with facts can involve challenging even the most reputable sources if they lead to unfair or selective reporting or if the stories are presented or "framed" unfairly.

In an ideal world, good information—no matter where it comes from—would always drive out bad. But you already know that we don't live in an ideal world, so sometimes bad information gets repeated in an echo chamber that amplifies the errors.

Statistics

You've probably heard the old saying "There are three kinds of lies: lies, damned lies, and statistics," and, to be sure, it is possible to lie with numbers, even those that are accurate, because numbers rarely speak for themselves. They need to be interpreted by writers—and writers almost always have agendas that shape the interpretations.

Of course, just because they are often misused doesn't mean that statistics are meaningless, but it does suggest that you need to use them carefully and to remember that your careful reading of numbers is essential. Consider the attention-grabbing map on the next page that went viral in June 2014. Created by Mark Gongloff of the *Huffington Post* in the wake of a school shooting in Oregon, it plotted the location of all seventy-four school shootings that had occurred in the United States since the Sandy Hook tragedy in December 2012, when twenty elementary school children and six adults were gunned down by a rifle-wielding killer. For the graphic, Gongloff drew on a list assembled by the group Everytown for Gun Safety, an organization formed by former New York City mayor and billionaire Michael Bloomberg to counter the influence of the National Rifle Association (NRA). Both the map and Everytown's sobering list of shootings received wide attention in the media, given the startling number of incidents it recorded.

Everytown for Gun Safety Action

FIGURE 23.2

It didn't take long before questions were raised about their accuracy. Were American elementary and secondary school children under such frequent assault as the map based on Everytown's list suggested? Well, yes and no. Guns were going off on and around school campuses, but the firearms weren't always aimed at children. The *Washington Post*, CNN, and other news outlets soon found themselves pulling back on their initial reporting, offering a more nuanced view of the controversial number. To do that, the *Washington Post* began by posing an important question:

What constitutes a school shooting?

That five-word question has no simple answer, a fact underscored by the backlash to an advocacy group's recent list of school shootings. The list, maintained by Everytown, a group that backs policies to limit gun violence, was updated last week to reflect what it identified as the 74 school shootings since the massacre in Newtown, Conn., a massacre that sparked a national debate over gun control.

Multiple news outlets, including this one, reported on Everytown's data, prompting a backlash over the broad methodology used. As we wrote in our original post, the group considered any instance of a firearm discharging on school property as a shooting—thus casting a broad net that includes homicides, suicides, accidental discharges and, in a handful of cases, shootings that had no relation to the schools themselves and occurred with no students apparently present.

—Niraj Chokshi, "Fight over School Shooting ListUnderscores Difficulty in Quantifying Gun Violence"

CNN followed the same path, re-evaluating its original reporting in light of criticism from groups not on the same page as Everytown for Gun Safety:

Without a doubt, that number is startling.

So…CNN took a closer look at the list, delving into the circumstances of each incident Everytown included….

CNN determined that 15 of the incidents Everytown included were situations similar to the violence in Newtown or Oregon—a minor or adult actively shooting inside or near a school. That works out to about one such shooting every five weeks, a startling figure in its own right.

Some of the other incidents on Everytown's list included personal arguments, accidents and alleged gang activities and drug deals.

—Ashley Fantz, Lindsey Knight, and Kevin Wang, "A Closer Look: How Many Newtown-like School Shootings since Sandy Hook?"

Other news organizations came up with their own revised numbers, but clearly the interpretation of a number can be as important as the statistic itself. And what were Mark Gongloff's Twitter reactions to these reassessments? They made an argument as well:

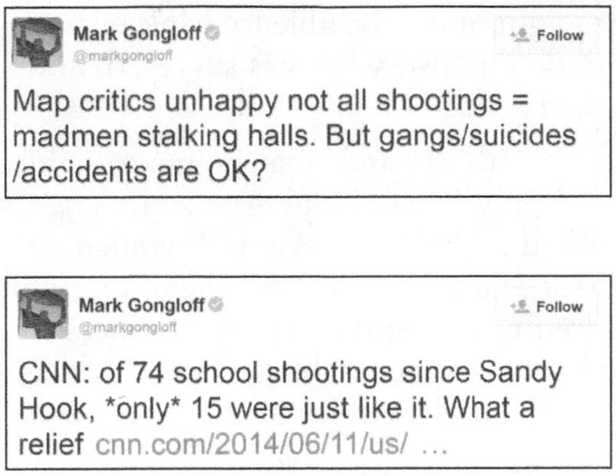

> **Mark Gongloff** ✔
> @markgongloff
> ⬩ Follow
>
> Map critics unhappy not all shootings = madmen stalking halls. But gangs/suicides /accidents are OK?

> **Mark Gongloff** ✔
> @markgongloff
> ⬩ Follow
>
> CNN: of 74 school shootings since Sandy Hook, *only* 15 were just like it. What a relief cnn.com/2014/06/11/us/ …

FIGURE 23.3

One lesson, surely, is that when you rely on statistics in your arguments, make sure you understand where they come from, what they mean, and what their limitations might be. Check and double-check them or get help in doing so: you don't want to be accused of using fictitious data based on questionable assumptions.

RESPOND

Statistical evidence becomes useful only when interpreted fairly and reasonably. Go to the *USA Today* Web site and look for the daily graph, chart, or table called the "USA Today Snapshot." Pick a snapshot, and use the information in it to support three different claims, at least two of which make very different points. Share your claims with classmates. (The point is not to learn to use data dishonestly but to see firsthand how the same statistics can serve a variety of arguments.)

Surveys and Polls

When they verify the popularity of an idea or a proposal, surveys and polls provide strong persuasive appeals because they come as close to expressing the will of the people as anything short of an election—the most decisive poll of all. However, surveys and polls can do much more than help politicians make decisions. They can be important elements in scientific research, documenting the complexities of human behavior. They can also provide persuasive reasons for action or intervention. When surveys show, for example, that most American sixth-graders can't locate France or Wyoming on a map—not to mention Ukraine or Afghanistan—that's an appeal for better instruction in geography. It always makes sense, however, to question poll numbers, especially when they support your own point of view. Ask who commissioned the poll, who is publishing its outcome, who was surveyed (and in what proportions), and what stakes these parties might have in its outcome.

Are we being too suspicious? No. In fact, this sort of scrutiny is exactly what you might anticipate from your readers whenever you use (or create) surveys to explore an issue. You should be confident that enough subjects have been surveyed to be accurate, that the people chosen for the study were representative of the selected population as a whole, and that they were chosen randomly—not selected because of what they are likely to say. In a splendid article on how women can make research-based choices during their pregnancy, economist Emily Oster explores, for example, whether an expectant mother might in fact be able to drink responsibly. She researches not only the results of the data, but also who was surveyed, and how their participation might have influenced the results:

> It is possible to unearth research that points to light drinking as a problem, but this work is deeply flawed. One frequently cited study from the journal *Pediatrics*, published in 2001, interviewed women about their drinking while they were pregnant and then contacted them for a child behavior assessment when their children were about 6. The researchers found some evidence that lighter drinking had an impact on behavior and concluded that even one drink a day could cause behavior problems.

> So what's wrong with this finding?

> In the study, 18% of the women who didn't drink at all and 45% of the women who had one drink a day reported using cocaine during pregnancy. Presumably your first thought is, really? Cocaine? Perhaps the problem is that cocaine, not the occasional glass of Chardonnay, makes your child more likely to have behavior problems.

> —Emily Oster, "Take Back Your Pregnancy"

Clearly, polls, surveys, and studies need to be examined critically. You can't take even academic research at face value until you have explored its details.

The meaning of polls and surveys is also affected by the way that questions are posed. In the recent past, research revealed, for example, that polling about same-sex unions got differing responses according to how questions are worded. When people were asked whether gay and lesbian couples should be eligible for the same inheritance and partner health benefits that heterosexual couples receive, a majority of those polled said yes—unless the word *marriage* appeared in the question; then the responses are primarily negative. If anything, the differences here reveal how conflicted people may have been about the issue and how quickly opinions might shift—as they did. Remember, then, to be very careful in reviewing the wording of survey or poll questions.

Finally, always keep in mind that the date of a poll may strongly affect the results—and their usefulness in an argument. In 2010, for example, nearly 50 percent of California voters supported building more nuclear power plants. Less than a year later, that percentage had dropped to 37 percent after the meltdown of Japanese nuclear power plants in the wake of the March 2011 earthquake and tsunami. On public and political issues, you need to be sure that you are using timely information.

RESPOND

Choose an important issue and design a series of questions to evoke a range of responses in a poll. Try to design a question that would make people strongly inclined to agree, another question that would lead them to oppose the same proposition, and a third that tries to be more neutral. Then try out your questions on your classmates.

Testimonies and Narratives

Writers can support arguments by presenting human experiences in the form of narrative or testimony—particularly if those experiences are their own. In courts, judges and juries often take into consideration detailed descriptions and narratives of exactly what occurred. Look at this reporter's account of a court case in which a panel of judges decided, based on the testimony presented, that a man had been sexually harassed by another man. The narrative, in this case, supplies the evidence:

> The Seventh Circuit, in a 1997 case known as *Doe v. City of Belleville*, drew a sweeping conclusion allowing for same-sex harassment cases of many kinds. …This case, for example, centered on teenage twin brothers working a summer job cutting grass in the city cemetery of Belleville, Ill. One boy wore an earring, which caused him no end of grief that particular summer—including a lot of menacing talk among his coworkers about sexually assaulting him in the woods and sending him "back to San Francisco." One of his harassers, identified in court documents as a large former marine, culminated a verbal campaign by backing the earring-wearer against a wall and grabbing him by the testicles to see "if he was a girl or a guy." The teenager had been "singled out for this abuse," the court ruled, "because the way in which he projected the sexual aspect of his personality"—meaning his gender—"did not conform to his coworkers' view of appropriate masculine behavior."

> —Margaret Talbot, "Men Behaving Badly"

Personal perspectives can support a claim convincingly and logically, especially if a writer has earned the trust of readers. In arguing that Tea Party supporters of a government shutdown in 2011 had no business being offended when some opponents described them as "terrorists," Froma Harrop, one of the writers who used the term, argued logically and from experience why the characterization was appropriate:

> [T]he hurt the tea party writers most complained of was to their feelings. I had engaged in name-calling, they kept saying. One professing to want more civility in our national conversation, as I do, should not be flinging around the *terrorist* word.

> May I presume to disagree? Civility is a subjective concept, to be sure, but hurting people's feelings in the course of making solid arguments is fair and square. The decline in the quality of our public discourse results not so much from an excess of spleen, but a deficit of well-constructed arguments. Few things upset partisans more than when the other side makes a case that bats home.

> "Most of us know that effectively scoring on a point of argument opens us to the accusation of mean-spiritedness," writes Frank Partsch, who leads the National Conference of Editorial Writers' Civility Project. "It comes with the territory, and a commitment to civility should not suggest that punches will be pulled in order to avoid such accusations."

> —Froma Harrop, "Hurt Feelings Can Be a Consequence of
> Strong Arguments"

This narrative introduction gives a rationale for supporting the claim Harrop is making: we can expect consequences when we argue ineffectively. (For more on establishing credibility with readers, see **CHAPTER 22**.)

RESPOND

Bring to class a full review of a recent film that you either enjoyed or did not enjoy. Using testimony from that review, write a brief argument to your classmates explaining why they should see that movie (or why they should avoid it), being sure to use evidence from the review fairly and reasonably. Then exchange arguments with a classmate, and decide whether the evidence in your peer's argument helps to change your opinion about the movie. What's convincing about the evidence? If it doesn't convince you, why doesn't it?

■ Using Reason and Common Sense

If you don't have "hard facts," you can turn to those arguments Aristotle describes as "constructed" from reason and common sense. The formal study of such reasoning is called *logic*, and you probably recognize a famous example of deductive reasoning, called a **syllogism**:

> All human beings are mortal.
>
> Socrates is a human being.
>
> Therefore, Socrates is mortal.

In valid syllogisms, the conclusion follows logically—and technically—from the premises that lead up to it. Many have criticized syllogistic reasoning for being limited, and others have poked fun at it, as in the cartoon below.

Logic: another thing that penguins aren't very good at.

© Randy Glasbergen/glasbergen.com
FIGURE 23.4

But we routinely see something like syllogistic reasoning operating in public arguments, particularly when writers take the time to explain key principles. Consider the step-by-step reasoning Michael Gerson uses to explain why exactly it was wrong for the Internal Revenue Service in 2010–2011 to target specific political groups, making it more difficult for them to organize politically:

> Why does this matter deserve heightened scrutiny from the rest of us? Because crimes against democracy are particularly insidious. Representative government involves a type of trade. As citizens, we cede power to public officials for important purposes that require centralized power: defending the country, imposing order, collecting taxes to promote the common good. In exchange, we expect public institutions to be evenhanded and disinterested. When the stewards of power—biased judges or corrupt policemen or politically motivated IRS officials—act unfairly, it undermines trust in the whole system.
>
> —Michael Gerson, "An Arrogant and Lawless IRS"

Gerson's criticism of the IRS actions might be mapped out by the following sequence of statements.

> Crimes against democracy undermine trust in the system.
>
> Treating taxpayers differently because of their political beliefs is a crime against democracy.
>
> Therefore, IRS actions that target political groups undermine the American system.

Few writers, of course, think about formal deductive reasoning when they support their claims. Even Aristotle recognized that most people argue perfectly well using informal logic. To do so, they rely mostly on habits of mind and assumptions that they share with their readers or listeners—as Gerson essentially does in his paragraph.

In **CHAPTER 18**, we describe a system of informal logic that you may find useful in shaping credible appeals to reason—Toulmin argument. Here, we briefly examine some ways that people use informal logic in their everyday lives. Once again, we begin with Aristotle, who used the term **enthymeme** to describe an ordinary kind of sentence that includes both a claim and a reason but depends on the audience's agreement with an assumption that is left implicit rather than spelled out. Enthymemes can be very persuasive when most people agree with the assumptions they rest on. The following sentences are all enthymemes:

> We'd better cancel the picnic because it's going to rain.
>
> Flat taxes are fair because they treat everyone the same.
>
> I'll buy a PC instead of a Mac because it's cheaper.

Sometimes enthymemes seem so obvious that readers don't realize that they're drawing inferences when they agree with them. Consider the first example:

> We'd better cancel the picnic because it's going to rain.

Let's expand the enthymeme a bit to say more of what the speaker may mean:

> We'd better cancel the picnic this afternoon because the weather bureau is predicting a 70 percent chance of rain for the remainder of the day.

Embedded in this brief argument are all sorts of assumptions and fragments of cultural information that are left implicit but that help to make it persuasive:

> Picnics are ordinarily held outdoors.
>
> When the weather is bad, it's best to cancel picnics.
>
> Rain is bad weather for picnics.
>
> A 70 percent chance of rain means that rain is more likely to occur than not.
>
> When rain is more likely to occur than not, it makes sense to cancel picnics.

For most people, the original statement carries all this information on its own; the enthymeme is a compressed argument, based on what audiences know and will accept.

But sometimes enthymemes aren't self-evident:

> Be wary of environmentalism because it's religion disguised as science.
>
> iPhones are undermining civil society by making us even more focused on ourselves.
>
> It's time to make all public toilets unisex because to do otherwise is discriminatory.

In these cases, you'll have to work much harder to defend both the claim and the implicit assumptions that it's based on by drawing out the inferences that seem self-evident in other enthymemes. And you'll likely also have to supply credible evidence; a simple declaration of fact won't suffice.

CULTURAL CONTEXTS FOR ARGUMENT

Logos

In the United States, student writers are expected to draw on "hard facts" and evidence as often as possible in supporting their claims: while ethical and emotional appeals are important, logical appeals tend to hold sway in academic writing. So statistics and facts speak volumes, as does reasoning based on time-honored values such as fairness and equity. In writing to global audiences, you need to remember that not all cultures value the same kinds of appeals. If you want to write to audiences across cultures, you need to know about the norms and values in those cultures. Chinese culture, for example, values authority and often indirect allusion over "facts" alone. Some African cultures value cooperation and community over individualism, and still other cultures value religious texts as providing compelling evidence. So think carefully about what you consider strong evidence, and pay attention to what counts as evidence to others. You can begin by asking yourself questions like:

- What evidence is most valued by your audience: Facts? Concrete examples? Firsthand experience? Religious or philosophical texts? Something else?

- Will analogies count as support? How about precedents?

- Will the testimony of experts count? If so, what kinds of experts are valued most?

■ Providing Logical Structures for Argument

Some arguments depend on particular logical structures to make their points. In the following pages, we identify a few of these logical structures.

Degree

Arguments based on degree are so common that people barely notice them, nor do they pay much attention to how they work because they seem self-evident. Most audiences will readily accept that *more of a good thing* or *less of a bad thing* is good. In her novel *The Fountainhead*, Ayn Rand asks: "If physical slavery is repulsive, how much more repulsive is the concept of servility of the spirit?" Most readers immediately comprehend the point Rand intends to make about slavery of the spirit because they already know that physical slavery is cruel and would reject any forms of slavery that were even crueler on the principle that *more of a bad thing is bad*. Rand still needs to offer evidence that "servility of the spirit" is, in fact, worse than bodily servitude, but she has begun with a logical structure readers can grasp. Here are other arguments that work similarly:

> If I can get a ten-year warranty on an inexpensive Kia, shouldn't I get the same or better warranty from a more expensive Lexus?

> The health benefits from using stem cells in research will surely outweigh the ethical risks.

> Better a conventional war now than a nuclear confrontation later.

AP Photo/Seth Wenig

FIGURE 23.5 A demonstrator at an immigrants' rights rally in New York City in 2007. Arguments based on values that are widely shared within a society—such as the idea of equal rights in American culture—have an automatic advantage with audiences.

Analogies

Analogies, typically complex or extended comparisons, explain one idea or concept by comparing it to something else.

Here, writer and founder of literacy project 826 Valencia, Dave Eggers, uses an analogy in arguing that we do not value teachers as much as we should:

> When we don't get the results we want in our military endeavors, we don't blame the soldiers. We don't say, "It's these lazy soldiers and their bloated benefits plans! That's why we haven't done better in Afghanistan!" No, if the results aren't there, we blame the planners. . . . No one contemplates blaming the men and women fighting every day in the trenches for little pay and scant recognition. And yet in education we do just that. When we don't like the way our students score on international standardized tests, we blame the teachers.
>
> —Dave Eggers and Nínive Calegari,
> "The HighCost of Low Teacher Salaries"

Precedent

Arguments from **precedent** and arguments of analogy both involve comparisons. Consider an assertion like this one, which uses a comparison as a precedent:

> If motorists in most other states can pump their own gas safely, surely the state of Oregon can trust its own drivers to be as capable. It's time for Oregon to permit self-service gas stations.

You could tease out several inferences from this claim to explain its reasonableness: people in Oregon are as capable as people in other states; people with equivalent capabilities can do the same thing; pumping gas is not hard; and so forth. But you don't have to because most readers get the argument simply because of the way it is put together.

Here is an excerpt from an extended argument by blogger Abby Phillip, in which she argues that the Ebola outbreak that began in 2014 may not follow the same pattern as past outbreaks:

> An idea long viewed as an unlikely possibility is now becoming increasingly real: Ebola might not go away for a very long time.
>
> It has never happened before in the thirty-eight-year history of the virus. Every other time Ebola has made the unlikely jump from the animal world to the human one, it has been snuffed out within days, weeks or, at most, months.
>
> This time, though, in Guinea, Sierra Leone and Liberia, the Ebola virus is raging like a forest fire, in the words of several public health officials. And some of them are raising the possibility that the outbreak-turned-full-fledged-epidemic could become fundamentally different from any other Ebola outbreak on record, in that it might stick around.
>
> "What's always worked before—contact tracing, isolation and quarantine—is not going to work, and it's not working now," said Daniel Lucey, a professor of microbiology and immunology at Georgetown University Medical Center, who spent three weeks treating Ebola patients in Sierra Leone and will soon travel to the Liberian capital of Monrovia for another five-week stint.
>
> "In my opinion," Lucey added, "a year from now, we won't have one or two cases; we'll have many cases of Ebola."
>
> Unlike past outbreaks, in which Ebola emerged in the sparsely populated countryside of central Africa, this outbreak has become an exponentially spreading urban menace.
>
> —Abby Phillip, "This Ebola Outbreak Could Be Here to Stay"

Unfortunately, the prediction proved to be more accurate than Phillip might have preferred.

You'll encounter additional kinds of logical structures as you create your own arguments. You'll find some of them in **CHAPTER 20**, "Fallacies of Argument," and still more in **CHAPTER 18** on Toulmin argument.

Chapter 24

Rhetorical Analysis

This chapter is taken from Andrea A. Lunsford and John J. Ruszkiewicz, *Everything's an Argument*, Seventh Edition, pp. 87–118 (Chapter 6).

All images © Andy Anderson, Lone River Productions

If you watched the 2013 Super Bowl between the Baltimore Ravens and the San Francisco 49ers, you may remember the commercial. For two solemn minutes, still photographs of rural America and the people who work there moved across the screen accompanied by the unmistakable voice of the late Paul Harvey reading words he had first delivered in 1978. Maria Godoy of NPR described it this way: "It may not have been as dramatic as the stadium blackout that halted play for more than a half-hour, or as extravagant as Beyonce's halftime show. But for many viewers of Super Bowl XLVII, one of the standout moments was a deceptively simple ad for the Dodge Ram called 'God Made a Farmer.'" It was a fourth quarter interrupted by cattle, churches, snowy farmyards, bales of hay, plowed fields, hardworking men, and a few sturdy women. Occasionally, a slide discreetly showed a Ram truck, sponsor of the video; but there were no overt sales pitches—only a product logo in the final frame. Yet visits to the Ram Web site spiked immediately, and sales of Ram pickups did too. (The official video has been viewed on YouTube more than 17 million times.)

So how to account for the appeal of such an unconventional and unexpected commercial? That would be the work of a **rhetorical analysis,** the close reading of a text or, in this case, a video commercial, to figure out exactly how it functions. Certainly, the creators of "God Made a Farmer" counted on the strong emotional appeal of the photographs they'd commissioned, guessing perhaps that the expert images and Harvey's spellbinding words would contrast powerfully with the frivolity and emptiness of much Super Bowl ad fare:

> God said, "I need somebody willing to sit up all night with a newborn colt. And watch it die. Then dry his eyes and say, 'Maybe next year.'"

They pushed convention, too, by the length of the spot and the muted product connection, doubtless hoping to win the goodwill of a huge audience suddenly all teary-eyed in the midst of a football game. And they surely gained the respect of a great many truck-buying farmers.

Rhetorical analyses can also probe the contexts that surround any argument or text—its impact on a society, its deeper implications, or even what it lacks or whom it excludes. Predictably, the widely admired Ram commercial (selected #1 Super Bowl XLVII spot by *Adweek*) acquired its share of critics, some attacking it for romanticizing farm life, others for ignoring the realities of industrial agriculture. And not a few writers noted what they regarded as glaring absences in its representation of farmers. Here, for instance, is copywriter and blogger Edye Deloch-Hughes, offering a highly personal and conflicted view of the spot in what amounts to an informal rhetorical analysis:

> ...I was riveted by the still photography and stirring thirty-five-year-old delivery of legendary radio broadcaster Paul Harvey. But as I sat mesmerized, I waited to see an image that spoke to my heritage. What flashed before me were close-ups of stoic white men whose faces drowned out the obligatory medium shots of a minority token or two; their images minimized against the amber waves of grain.
>
> God made a Black farmer too. Where was my Grandpa, Grandma and Great Granny? My Auntie and Uncle Bolden? And didn't God make Hispanic and Native American farmers? They too were under represented.
>
> I am the offspring of a century and a half of African-American caretakers of the land, from Arkansas, Mississippi and Louisiana, who experienced their toils and troubles, their sun ups and sun downs. Their injustices and beatdowns. I wrestled with my mixed emotions; loving the commercial and feeling dejected at the same time.
>
> ...Minimizing positive Black imagery and accomplishments is as American as wrestling cattle. We're often footnotes or accessories in history books, TV shows, movies and magazines as well as TV commercials. When content is exceptional, the omission is harder to recognize or criticize. Some friends of mine saw—or rather **felt**—the omission as I did. Others did not. I say be aware and vocal about how you are represented—if represented at all, otherwise your importance and relevance will be lost.
>
> —Edye Deloch-Hughes, "So God Made a Black Farmer Too"

As this example suggests, whenever you undertake a rhetorical analysis, follow your instincts and look closely. Why does an ad for a cell phone or breakfast sandwich make people want one immediately? How does an op-ed piece in the *Washington Post* suddenly change your long-held position on immigration? A rhetorical analysis might help you understand. Dig as deep as you can into the context of the item you are analyzing, especially when you encounter puzzling, troubling, or unusually successful appeals—ethical, emotional, or logical. Ask yourself what strategies a speech, editorial, opinion column, film, or ad spot employs to move your heart, win your trust, and change your mind—or why, maybe, it fails to do so.

■ Composing a Rhetorical Analysis

You perform a rhetorical analysis by analyzing how well the components of an argument work together to persuade or move an audience. You can study arguments of any kind—advertisements (as we've seen), editorials, political cartoons, and even songs, movies, or photographs. In every case, you'll need to focus your rhetorical analysis on elements that stand out or make the piece intriguing or problematic. You could begin by exploring *some* of the following issues:

- What is the purpose of this argument? What does it hope to achieve?

- Who is the audience for this argument? Who is ignored or excluded?

- What appeals or techniques does the argument use—emotional, logical, ethical?

- What type of argument is it, and how does the genre affect the argument? (You might challenge the lack of evidence in editorials, but you wouldn't make the same complaint about bumper stickers.)

- Who is making the argument? What ethos does it create, and how does it do so? What values does the ethos evoke? How does it make the writer or creator seem trustworthy?

- What authorities does the argument rely on or appeal to?

- What facts, reasoning, and evidence are used in the argument? How are they presented?

- What claims does the argument make? What issues are raised—or ignored or evaded?

- What are the contexts—social, political, historical, cultural—for this argument? Whose interests does it serve? Who gains or loses by it?

- How is the argument organized or arranged? What media does the argument use and how effectively?

- How does the language or style of the argument persuade an audience?

In answering questions like these, try to show *how* the key devices in an argument actually make it succeed or fail. Quote freely from a written piece, or describe the elements in a visual argument. (Annotating a visual text is one option.) Let readers know where and why an argument makes sense and where it falls apart. If you believe that an argument startles, challenges, insults, or lulls audiences, explain why that is the case and provide evidence. Don't be surprised when your rhetorical analysis itself becomes an argument. That's what it should be.

■ Understanding the Purpose of Arguments You Are Analyzing

To understand how well any argument works, begin with its purpose: Is it to sell running shoes? To advocate for limits to college tuition? To push a political agenda? In many cases, that purpose may be obvious. A conservative blog will likely advance right-wing causes; ads from a baby food company will likely show happy infants delighted with stewed prunes.

But some projects may hide their persuasive intentions. Perhaps you've responded to a mail survey or telephone poll only to discover that the questions are leading you to switch your cable service or buy apartment insurance. Do such stealthy arguments succeed? Do consumers resent the intrusion? Answering questions like these provides material for useful rhetorical analyses that assess the strengths, risks, and ethics of such strategies.

■ Understanding Who Makes an Argument

Knowing *who* is claiming *what* is key to any rhetorical analysis. That's why persuasive appeals usually have a name attached to them. Remember the statements included in TV ads during the last federal election: "Hello, I'm X—and I approve this ad"? Federal law requires such statements so we can tell the difference between ads a candidate endorses and ones sponsored by groups not even affiliated with the campaigns. Their interests and motives might be very different.

But knowing a name is just a starting place for analysis. You need to dig deeper, and you could do worse than to Google such people or groups to discover more about them. What else have they produced? Who publishes them: the *Wall Street Journal*, the blog *The Daily Kos*, or even a LiveJournal celebrity gossip site such as *Oh No They Didn't*? Check out related Web sites for information about goals, policies, contributors, and funding.

© Chris Maddaloni/CQ Roll Call

FIGURE 24.1 Funny, offensive, or both?

RESPOND

Describe a persuasive moment that you can recall from a speech, an editorial, an advertisement, a YouTube clip, or a blog posting. Or research one of the following famous persuasive moments and describe the circumstances—the historical situation, the issues at stake, the purpose of the argument—that make it so memorable.

Abraham Lincoln's Gettysburg Address (1863)

Elizabeth Cady Stanton's Declaration of Sentiments at the Seneca Falls Convention (1848)

Chief Tecumseh's address to General William Henry Harrison (1810)

Winston Churchill's radio addresses to the British people during World War II (1940)

Martin Luther King Jr.'s "Letter from Birmingham Jail" (1963)

Ronald Reagan's tribute to the *Challenger* astronauts (1986)

Toni Morrison's speech accepting the Nobel Prize (1993)

Will.i.am's "Yes We Can" song/collage on YouTube (2008)

■ Identifying and Appealing to Audiences

Most arguments are composed with specific audiences in mind, and their success depends, in part, on how well their strategies, content, tone, and language meet the expectations of that audience. So your rhetorical analysis of an argumentative piece should identify its target readers or viewers if possible, or make an educated guess about the audience, since most arguments suggest whom they intend to reach and in what ways.

Both a flyer stapled to a bulletin board in a college dorm ("Why you shouldn't drink and drive") and a forty-foot billboard for Bud Light might be aimed at the same general population—college students. But each will adjust its appeals for the different moods of that group in different moments. For starters, the flyer will appeal to students in a serious vein, while the beer ad will probably be visually stunning and virtually text-free.

You might also examine how a writer or an argument establishes credibility with an audience. One effective means of building credibility is to show respect for your readers or viewers, especially if they may not agree with you. In introducing an article on problems facing African American women in the workplace, editor in chief of *Essence* Diane Weathers considers the problems that she faced with respecting all her potential readers:

> We spent more than a minute agonizing over the provocative cover line for our feature "White Women at Work." The countless stories we had heard from women across the country told us that this was a workplace issue we had to address. From my own experience at several major magazines, it was painfully obvious to me that Black and White women are not on the same track. Sure, we might all start out in the same place. But early in the game, most sisters I know become stuck—and the reasons have little to do with intelligence or drive. At some point we bump our heads against that ceiling. And while White women may complain of a glass ceiling, for us, the ceiling is concrete.
>
> So how do we tell this story without sounding whiny and paranoid, or turning off our White-female readers, staff members, advertisers and girlfriends? Our solution: Bring together real women (several of them highly successful senior corporate executives), put them in a room, promise them anonymity and let them speak their truth.

—Diane Weathers, "Speaking Our Truth"

Beth Hall/Bloomberg News/Getty Images

FIGURE 24.2 Retailers like Walmart build their credibility by simple "straight talk" to shoppers: our low prices make your life better.

Both paragraphs affirm Weathers's determination to treat audiences fairly *and* to deal honestly with a difficult subject. The strategy would merit attention in any rhetorical analysis.

Look, too, for signals that writers share values with readers or at least understand an audience. In the following passage, writer Jack Solomon is clear about one value that he hopes readers have in common—a preference for "straight talk":

> There are some signs in the advertising world that Americans are getting fed up with fantasy advertisements and want to hear some straight talk. Weary of extravagant product claims..., consumers trained by years of advertising to distrust what they hear seem to be developing an immunity to commercials.

> —Jack Solomon, "Masters of Desire:
> The Culture of American Advertising"

But straight talk still requires common sense. If ever a major television ad seriously misread its audience, it may have been a spot that ran during the 2014 Winter Olympics for Cadillac's pricey new plug-in hybrid, the ELR. The company seemed to go out of its way to offend a great many people, foreign and domestic. As is typical strategy in rhetorical analyses, *Huffington Post*'s Carolyn Gregoire takes care to describe in detail the item she finds offensive:

> The opening shot shows a middle-aged man, played by the actor Neal Mc-Donough, looking out over his backyard pool, asking the question: "Why do we work so hard? For this? For stuff?"

> As the ad continues, it becomes clear that the answer to this rhetorical question is actually a big fat YES. And it gets worse. "Other countries, they work," he says. "They stroll home. They stop by the cafe. They take August off. Off."

> Then he reveals just what it is that makes Americans better than all those lazy, espresso-sipping foreigners.

> "Why aren't you like that?" he says. "Why aren't we like that? Because we're crazy, driven, hard-working believers, that's why."

> —Carolyn Gregoire, "Cadillac Made a Commercial
> about the American Dream, and It's a Nightmare"

Her conclusion then is blistering, showing how readily a rhetorical analysis becomes an argument—and subject to criticism itself:

> Cadillacs have long been a quintessentially American symbol of wealth and status. But as this commercial proves, no amount of wealth or status is a guarantee of good taste. Now, the luxury car company is selling a vision of the American Dream at its worst: Work yourself into the ground, take as little time off as possible, and buy expensive sh*t (specifically, a 2014 Cadillac ELR).

■ Examining Arguments Based on Emotion: Pathos

Some emotional appeals are just ploys to win over readers with a pretty face, figurative or real. You've seen ads promising an exciting life and attractive friends if only you drink the right soda or wear a particular brand of clothes. Are you fooled by such claims? Probably not, if you pause to think about them. But that's the strategy—to distract you from thought just long enough to make a bad choice. It's a move worth commenting on in a rhetorical analysis.

FIGURE 24.3 How well does the emotional appeal here work?

Yet emotions can add real muscle to arguments, too, and that's worth noting. For example, persuading people not to drink and drive by making them fear death, injury, or arrest seems like a fair use of an emotional appeal. The public service announcement above uses an emotion-laden image to remind drivers to think of the consequences.

In a rhetorical analysis, you might note the juxtaposition of image with text, leading readers to connect casual notes left on windshields with the very serious consequences of drunk driving.

In analyzing emotional appeals, judge whether the emotions raised—anger, sympathy, fear, envy, joy, love, lust—advance the claims offered. Consider how columnist Ron Rosenbaum (whom we met in **CHAPTER 21**) makes the reasonable argument he offers for fatty foods all the more attractive by larding it with voluptuous language:

> The foods that best hit that sweet spot and "overwhelm the brain" with pleasure are high-quality fatty foods. They discourage us from overeating. A modest serving of short ribs or Peking duck will be both deeply pleasurable and self-limiting. As the brain swoons into insensate delight, you won't have to gorge a still-craving cortex with mediocre sensations. "Sensory-specific satiety" makes a slam-dunk case (it's science!) for eating reasonable servings of superbly satisfying fatty foods.
>
> —Ron Rosenbaum, "Let Them Eat Fat"

Does the use of evocative language ("swoons," "insensate delight," "superbly satisfying," "slam-dunk") convince you, or does it distract from considering the scientific case for "sensory-specific satiety"? Your task in a rhetorical analysis is to study an author's words, the emotions they evoke, and the claims they support and then to make this kind of judgment.

Kittipojn Pravalpatkul/Shutterstock

FIGURE 24.4 Health food?

RESPOND

Browse YouTube or another Web site to find an example of a powerful emotional argument that's made visually, either alone or using words as well. In a paragraph, defend a claim about how the argument works. For example, does an image itself make a claim, or does it draw you in to consider a verbal claim? What emotion does the argument generate? How does that emotion work to persuade you?

■ Examining Arguments Based on Character: Ethos

It should come as no surprise: readers believe writers who seem honest, wise, and trustworthy. So in analyzing the effectiveness of an argument, look for evidence of these traits. Does the writer have the experience or authority to write on this subject? Are all claims qualified reasonably? Is evidence presented in full, not tailored to the writer's agenda? Are important objections to the author's position acknowledged and addressed? Are sources documented? Above all, does the writer sound trustworthy?

When a Norwegian anti-immigration extremist killed seventy-six innocent people in July 2011, Prime Minister Jens Stoltenberg addressed the citizens of Norway (and the world), and in doing so evoked the character or ethos of the entire nation:

> We will not let fear break us! The warmth of response from people in Norway and from the whole world makes me sure of this one thing: evil can kill a single person, but never defeat a whole people. The strongest weapon in the world—that is freedom of expression and democracy.

In analyzing this speech, you would do well to look at the way this passage deploys the deepest values of Norway—freedom of expression and democracy—to serve as a response to fear of terrorism. In doing so, Stoltenberg evokes ethical ideals to hold onto in a time of tragedy.

Or take a look at the following paragraph from a blog posting by Timothy Burke, a teacher at Swarthmore College and parent of a preschool child who is trying to think through the issue of homework for elementary school kids:

So I've been reading a bit about homework and comparing notes with parents. There is a lot of variation across districts, not just in the amount of homework that kids are being asked to do, but in the kind of homework. Some districts give kids a lot of time-consuming busywork; other districts try to concentrate on having homework assignments be substantive work that is best accomplished independently. Some give a lot from a very early point in K-12 education; some give relatively little. As both a professional educator and an individual with personal convictions, I'd tend to argue against excessive amounts of homework and against assigning busywork. But what has ultimately interested me more about reading various discussions of homework is how intense the feelings are swirling around the topic and how much that intensity strikes me as a problem in and of itself. Not just as a symptom of a kind of civic illness, an inability to collectively and democratically work through complex issues, but also in some cases as evidence of an educational failure in its own right.

Burke establishes his ethos by citing his reading and his talks with other parents.

He underscores his right to address the matter.

He expresses concern about immoderate arguments and implies that he will demonstrate an opposite approach.

In considering the role of ethos in rhetorical analyses, pay attention to the details right down to the choice of words or, in an image, the shapes and colors. The modest, tentative tone that Burke uses in his blog is an example of the kind of choice that can shape an audience's perception of ethos. But these details need your interpretation. Language that's hot and extreme can mark a writer as either passionate or loony. Work that's sober and carefully organized can paint an institution as competent or overly cautious. Technical terms and abstract phrases can make a writer seem either knowledgeable or pompous.

■ Examining Arguments Based on Facts and Reason: Logos

In analyzing most arguments, you'll have to decide whether an argument makes a plausible claim and offers good reasons for you to believe it. Not all arguments will package such claims in a single neat sentence, or **thesis**—nor should they. A writer may tell a story from which you have to infer the claim. Visual arguments may work the same way: viewers have to assemble the parts and draw inferences in order to get the point.

Some conventional arguments (like those on an editorial page) may be perfectly obvious: writers stake out a claim and then present reasons that you should consider, or they may first present reasons and lay out a case that leads you to accept a claim in the conclusion. Consider the following example. In a tough opinion piece in *Time*, political commentator John McWhorter argues that filmmaker Spike Lee is being racist when he rails against hipsters moving into Fort Greene, a formerly all-black neighborhood in Brooklyn, New York. Lee fears that the whites are raising housing prices, pushing out old-time residents and diminishing the African American character of Fort Greene. McWhorter, an African American like Lee, sees matters differently:

> Basically, black people are getting paid more money than they've ever seen in their lives for their houses, and a once sketchy neighborhood is now quiet and pleasant. And this is a bad thing...why?

Lee seems to think it's somehow an injustice whenever black people pick up stakes. But I doubt many of the blacks now set to pass fat inheritances on to their kids feel that way. This is not the old story of poor blacks being pushed out of neighborhoods razed down for highway construction. Lee isn't making sense.

—John McWhorter, "Spike Lee's Racism Isn't Cute"

When you encounter explicit charges like these, you analyze whether and how the claims are supported by good reasons and reliable evidence. A lengthy essay may, in fact, contain a series of claims, each developed to support an even larger point. Here's McWhorter, for instance, expanding his argument by suggesting that Lee's attitudes toward whites are irreconcilable.

"Respect the culture" when you move in, Lee growls. But again, he isn't making sense. We can be quite sure that if whites "respected" the culture by trying to participate in it, Lee would be one of the first in line to call it "appropriation." So, no whites better open up barbecue joints or spoken word cafes or try to be rappers. Yet if whites walk on by the culture in "respectful" silence, then the word on the street becomes that they want to keep blacks at a distance.

© Charles Platiau/Reuters/Corbis

FIGURE 24.5 An anti-fur protestor in London makes a rather specific claim.

Indeed, every paragraph in an argument may develop a specific and related idea. In a rhetorical analysis, you need to identify all these separate propositions and examine the relationships among them: Are they solidly linked? Are there inconsistencies that the writer should acknowledge? Does the end of the piece support what the writer said (and promised) at the beginning?

You'll also need to examine the quality of the information presented in an argument, assessing how accurately such information is reported, how conveniently it's displayed (in charts or graphs, for example), and how well the sources cited represent a range of *respected* opinions on a topic. (For more information on the use of evidence, see **CHAPTER 23**.)

Knowing how to judge the quality of sources is more important now than ever before because the digital universe is full of junk. In some ways, the computer terminal has become the equivalent of a library reference room, but the sources available online vary widely in quality and have not been evaluated by a library professional. As a consequence, you must know the difference between reliable, firsthand, or fully documented sources and those that don't meet such standards. (For using and documenting sources, see **CHAPTERS 25** and **26**.)

■ Examining the Arrangement and Media of Arguments

Aristotle carved the structure of logical argument to its bare bones when he observed that it had only two parts:

- statement

- proof

You could do worse, in examining an argument, than to make sure that every claim a writer makes is backed by sufficient evidence. Some arguments are written on the fly in the heat of the moment. Most arguments that you read and write, however, will be more than mere statements followed by proofs. Some writers will lay their cards on the table immediately; others may lead you carefully through a chain of claims toward a conclusion. Writers may even interrupt their arguments to offer background information or cultural contexts for readers. Sometimes they'll tell stories or provide anecdotes that make an argumentative point. They'll qualify the arguments they make, too, and often pause to admit that other points of view are plausible.

In other words, there are no formulas or acceptable patterns that fit all successful arguments. In writing a rhetorical analysis, you'll have to assess the organization of a persuasive text on its own merits.

It's fair, however, to complain about what may be *absent* from an argument. Most arguments of proposal (see **CHAPTER 19**), for example, include a section that defends the feasibility of a new idea, explaining how it might be funded or managed. In a rhetorical analysis, you might fault an editorial that supports a new stadium for a city without addressing feasibility issues. Similarly, analyzing a movie review that reads like an off-the-top-of-the-head opinion, you might legitimately ask what criteria of evaluation are in play.

Rhetorical analysis also calls for you to look carefully at an argument's transitions, headings and subheadings, documentation of sources, and overall tone or voice. Don't take such details for granted, since all of them contribute to the strength—or weakness—of an argument.

Nor should you ignore the way a writer or an institution uses media. Would an argument originally made in a print editorial, for instance, work better as a digital presentation (or vice versa)? Would a lengthy paper have more power if it included more images? Or do these images distract from a written argument's substance?

Finally, be open to the possibility of new or nontraditional structures of arguments. The visual arguments that you analyze may defy conventional principles of logic or arrangement—for example, making juxtapositions rather than logical transitions between elements or using quick cuts, fades, or other devices to link ideas. Quite often, these nontraditional structures will also resist the neatness of a thesis, leaving readers to construct at least a part of the argument in their heads. As we saw with the "God Made a Farmer" spot at the beginning of this chapter, advertisers are growing fond of soft-sell multimedia productions that can seem like something other than what they really are—product pitches. We may be asked not just to buy a product but also to live its lifestyle or embrace its ethos. Is that a reasonable or workable strategy for an argument? Your analysis might entertain such possibilities.

■ Looking at Style

Even a coherent argument full of sound evidence may not connect with readers if it's dull, off-key, or offensive. Readers naturally judge the credibility of arguments in part by how stylishly the case is made—even when they don't know exactly what style is. Consider how these simple, blunt sentences from the opening of an argument shape your image of the author and probably determine whether you're willing to continue to read the whole piece:

> We are young, urban, and professional. We are literate, respectable, intelligent, and charming. But foremost and above all, we are unemployed.
>
> —Julia Carlisle, "Young, Privileged, and Unemployed"

The strong, straightforward tone and the stark juxtaposition of being "intelligent" with "unemployed" set the style for this letter to the editor.

Now consider the brutally sarcastic tone of Nathaniel Stein's hilarious parody of the Harvard grading policy, a piece he wrote following up on a professor's complaint of out-of-control grade inflation at the school. Stein borrows the formal language of a typical "grading standards" sheet to mock the decline in rigor that the professor has lamented:

> The A+ grade is used only in very rare instances for the recognition of truly exceptional achievement.
>
> For example: A term paper receiving the A+ is virtually indistinguishable from the work of a professional, both in its choice of paper stock and its font. The student's command of the topic is expert, or at the very least intermediate, or beginner. Nearly every single word in the paper is spelled correctly; those that are not can be reasoned out phonetically within minutes. Content from Wikipedia is integrated with precision. The paper contains few, if any, death threats....

An overall course grade of A+ is reserved for those students who have not only demonstrated outstanding achievement in coursework but have also asked very nicely.

Finally, the A+ grade is awarded to all collages, dioramas and other art projects.

—Nathaniel Stein, "Leaked! Harvard's Grading Rubric"

Both styles probably work, but they signal that the writers are about to make very different kinds of cases. Here, style alone tells readers what to expect.

Manipulating style also enables writers to shape readers' responses to their ideas. Devices as simple as repetition, parallelism, or even paragraph length can give sentences remarkable power. Consider this passage from an essay by Sherman Alexie in which he explores the complex reaction of straight men to the announcement of NBA star Jason Collins that he is gay:

Homophobic basketball fans will disparage his skills, somehow equating his NBA benchwarmer status with his sexuality. But let's not forget that Collins is still one of the best 1,000 basketball players in the world. He has always been better than his modest statistics would indicate, and his teams have been dramatically more efficient with him on the court. He is better at hoops than 99.9 percent of you are at anything you do. He might not be a demigod, but he's certainly a semi-demigod. Moreover, his basketball colleagues universally praise him as a physically and mentally tough player. In his prime, he ably battled that behemoth known as Shaquille O'Neal. Most of all, Collins is widely regarded as one of the finest gentlemen to ever play the game. Generous, wise, and supportive, he's a natural leader. And he has a degree from Stanford University.

In other words, he's a highly attractive dude.

—Sherman Alexie, "Jason Collins Is the Envy of Straight Men Everywhere"

In this passage, Alexie uses a sequence of short, direct, and roughly parallel sentences ("He is...He might...He ably battled...He has") to present evidence justifying the playful point he makes in a pointedly emphatic, one-sentence paragraph. The remainder of his short essay then amplifies that point.

© Gary A. Vasquez/USA Today Sports Images

FIGURE 24.6 Jason Collins

In a rhetorical analysis, you can explore such stylistic choices. Why does a formal style work for discussing one type of subject matter but not another? How does a writer use humor or irony to underscore an important point or to manage a difficult concession? Do stylistic choices, even something as simple as the use of contractions or personal pronouns, bring readers close to a writer, or do technical words and an impersonal voice signal that an argument is for experts only?

To describe the stylistic effects of visual arguments, you may use a different vocabulary and talk about colors, camera angles, editing, balance, proportion, fonts, perspective, and so on. But the basic principle is this: the look of an item—whether a poster, an editorial cartoon, or a film documentary—can support the message that it carries, undermine it, or muddle it. In some cases, the look will *be* the message. In a rhetorical analysis, you can't ignore style.

Foto Presseamt Münster, City of Münster, Press Office

FIGURE 24.7 This poster, promoting travel to the bicycle-friendly city of Münster, Germany, demonstrates visually the amount of space needed to transport the same number of people by car, bicycle, and bus.

■ Examining a Rhetorical Analysis

On the following pages, well-known political commentator and columnist for the *New York Times* David Brooks argues that today's college graduates have been poorly prepared for life after school because of what he sees as a radical excess of supervision. Responding to his argument with a detailed analysis is Rachel Kolb, a student at Stanford University.

IT'S NOT ABOUT YOU

David Brooks

© David Levene/eyevine/Redux Pictures

Over the past few weeks, America's colleges have sent another class of graduates off into the world. These graduates possess something of inestimable value. Nearly every sensible middle-aged person would give away all their money to be able to go back to age 22 and begin adulthood anew.

But, especially this year, one is conscious of the many ways in which this year's graduating class has been ill served by their elders. They enter a bad job market, the hangover from decades of excessive borrowing. They inherit a ruinous federal debt.

More important, their lives have been perversely structured. This year's graduates are members of the most supervised generation in American history. Through their childhoods and teenage years, they have been monitored, tutored, coached and honed to an unprecedented degree.

Yet upon graduation they will enter a world that is unprecedentedly wide open and unstructured. Most of them will not quickly get married, buy a home and have kids, as previous generations did. Instead, they will confront amazingly diverse job markets, social landscapes and lifestyle niches. Most will spend a decade wandering from job to job and clique to clique, searching for a role.

No one would design a system of extreme supervision to prepare people for a decade of extreme openness. But this is exactly what has emerged in modern America. College students are raised in an environment that demands one set of navigational skills, and they are then cast out into a different environment requiring a different set of skills, which they have to figure out on their own.

Worst of all, they are sent off into this world with the whole baby-boomer theology ringing in their ears. If you sample some of the commencement addresses being broadcast on C-Span these days, you see that many graduates are told to: Follow *your* passion, chart *your* own course, march to the beat of *your* own drummer, follow *your* dreams and find *your*self. This is the litany of expressive individualism, which is still the dominant note in American culture.

But, of course, this mantra misleads on nearly every front.

College grads are often sent out into the world amid rapturous talk of limitless possibilities. But this talk is of no help to the central business of adulthood, finding serious things to tie yourself down to. The successful young adult is beginning to make sacred commitments—to a spouse, a community and calling—yet mostly hears about freedom and autonomy.

Today's graduates are also told to find their passion and then pursue their dreams. The implication is that they should find themselves first and then go off and live their quest. But, of course, very few people at age 22 or 24 can take an inward journey and come out having discovered a developed self.

Most successful young people don't look inside and then plan a life. They look outside and find a problem, which summons their life. A relative suffers from Alzheimer's and a young woman feels called to help cure that disease. A young man works under a miserable boss and must develop management skills so his department can function. Another young woman finds herself confronted by an opportunity she never thought of in a job category she never imagined. This wasn't in her plans, but this is where she can make her contribution.

Most people don't form a self and then lead a life. They are called by a problem, and the self is constructed gradually by their calling.

The graduates are also told to pursue happiness and joy. But, of course, when you read a biography of someone you admire, it's rarely the things that made them happy that compel your admiration. It's the things they did to court unhappiness—the things they did that were arduous and miserable, which sometimes cost them friends and aroused hatred. It's excellence, not happiness, that we admire most.

Finally, graduates are told to be independent-minded and to express their inner spirit. But, of course, doing your job well often means suppressing yourself. As Atul Gawande mentioned during his countercultural address...at Harvard Medical School, being a good doctor often means being part of a team, following the rules of an institution, going down a regimented checklist.

Today's grads enter a cultural climate that preaches the self as the center of a life. But, of course, as they age, they'll discover that the tasks of a life are at the center. Fulfillment is a byproduct of how people engage their tasks, and can't be pursued directly. Most of us are egotistical and most are self-concerned most of the time, but it's nonetheless true that life comes to a point only in those moments when the self dissolves into some task. The purpose in life is not to find yourself. It's to lose yourself.

UNDERSTANDING BROOKS'S BINARIES

Rachel Kolb

Courtesy of Rachel Kolb

Connects article to personal experience to create an ethical appeal.

As a high school and college student, I was given an incredible range of educational and extracurricular options, from interdisciplinary studies to summer institutes to student-organized clubs. Although today's students have more opportunities to adapt their educations to their specific personal goals, as I did, David Brooks argues that the structure of the modern educational system nevertheless leaves young people ill-prepared to meet the challenges of the real world. In his *New York Times* editorial "It's Not about You," Brooks illustrates excessive supervision and uncontrolled individualistic rhetoric as opposing problems that complicate young people's entry into adult life, which then becomes less of a natural progression than an outright paradigm shift. Brooks's argument itself mimics the pattern of moving from "perversely structured" youth to "unprecedentedly wide open" adulthood: it operates on the basis of binary oppositions, raising familiar notions about how to live one's life and then dismantling them. Throughout, the piece relies less on factual evidence than on Brooks's own authoritative tone and skill in using rhetorical devices.

Provides brief overview of Brooks's argument. States Brooks's central claim.

Transition sentence.

In his editorial, Brooks objects to mainstream cultural messages that sell students on individuality, but bases his conclusions more on general observations than on specific facts. His argument is, in itself, a loose form of rhetorical analysis. It opens by telling us to "sample some of the commencement addresses being broadcast on C-Span these days," where we will find messages such as: "Follow *your* passion, chart *your* own course, march to the beat of *your* own drummer, follow *your* dreams and find *your*self." As though moving down a checklist, it then scrutinizes the problems with this rhetoric of "expressive individualism." Finally, it turns to Atul Gawande's "countercultural address" about working collectively, en route to confronting the individualism of modern America. C-Span and Harvard Medical School aside, however, Brooks's argument is astonishingly short on external sources. He cites no basis for claims such as "this year's graduates are members of the most supervised generation in American history" or "most successful young people don't look inside and then plan a life," despite the fact that these claims are fundamental to his observations. Instead, his argument persuades through painting a picture—first of "limitless possibilities," then of young men and women called into action by problems that "summon their life"—and hoping that we will find the illustration familiar.

Comments critically on author's use of evidence.

Instead of relying on the logos of his argument, Brooks assumes that his position as a baby boomer and *New York Times* columnist will provide a sufficient enough ethos to validate his claims. If this impression of age and social status did not enter our minds along with his bespectacled portrait, Brooks reminds us of it. Although he refers to the theology of the baby boomer generation as the "worst of all," from the beginning of his editorial he allots himself as another "sensible middle-aged person" and distances himself from college graduates by referring to them as "they" or as "today's grads," contrasting with his more inclusive reader-directed "you." Combined with his repeated use of passive sentence constructions that create a confusing sense of responsibility ("The graduates are sent off into the world"; "graduates are told"), this sense of distance could be alienating to the younger audiences for which this editorial seems intended. Granted, Brooks compensates for it by embracing themes of "excellence" and "fulfillment" and by opening up his message to "most of us" in his final paragraph, but nevertheless his self-defined persona has its limitations. Besides dividing his audience, Brooks risks reminding us that, just as his observations belong only to this persona, his arguments apply only to a subset of American society. More specifically, they apply only to the well-educated middle to upper class who might be more likely to fret after the implications of "supervision" and "possibilities," or the readers who would be most likely to flip through the *New York Times*.

Analyzes author's intended audience.

Brooks overcomes his limitations in logos and ethos through his piece's greatest strength: its style. He effectively frames cultural messages in binaries in order to reinforce the disconnect that exists between what students are told and what they will face as full members of society. Throughout his piece, he states one assumption after another, then prompts us to consider its opposite. "Serious things" immediately take the place of "rapturous talk"; "look[ing] inside" replaces "look[ing] outside"; "suppressing yourself" becomes an alternative to being "independent-minded." Brooks's argument is consumed with dichotomies, culminating with his statement "It's excellence, not happiness, that we admire most." He frames his ideas within a tight framework of repetition and parallel structure, creating muscular prose intended to engage his readers. His repeated use of the phrase "but, of course" serves as a metronomic reminder, at once echoing his earlier assertions and referring back to his air of authority.

Closely analyzes Brooks's style.

Brooks illustrates the power of words in swaying an audience, and in his final paragraph his argument shifts beyond commentary. Having tested our way of thinking, he now challenges us to change. His editorial closes with one final binary, the claim that "The purpose in life is not to find yourself" but "to lose yourself." And, although some of Brooks's previous binaries have clanged with oversimplification, this one rings truer. In accordance with his adoption of the general "you," his concluding message need not apply only to college graduates. By unfettering its restrictions at its climax, Brooks liberates his argument. After all, only we readers bear the responsibility of reflecting, of justifying, and ultimately of determining how to live our lives.

Analyzes author's conclusion.

Work Cited

Brooks, David. "It's Not about You." *Everything's an Argument.* By Andrea A. Lunsford and John J. Ruszkiewicz. 7th ed. Boston: Bedford, 2016. 106–8. Print. Rpt. of "It's Not about You." *New York Times* 30 May 2011.

GUIDE TO WRITING A RHETORICAL ANALYSIS

Finding a Topic

A rhetorical analysis is usually assigned: you're asked to show how an argument works and to assess its effectiveness. When you can choose your own subject for analysis, look for one or more of the following qualities:

- a complex verbal or visual argument that challenges you—or disturbs or pleases you

- a text that raises current or enduring issues of substance

- a text that you believe should be taken more seriously

Look for arguments to analyze in the editorial and op-ed pages of any newspaper, political magazines such as the *Nation* or *National Review*, Web sites of organizations and interest groups, political blogs such as *Huffington Post* or *Power Line*, corporate Web sites that post their TV ad spots, videos and statements posted to YouTube, and so on.

Researching Your Topic

Once you've got a text to analyze, find out all you can about it. Use library or Web resources to explore:

- who the author is and what his or her credentials are

- if the author is an institution, what it does, what its sources of funding are, who its members are, and so on

- who is publishing or sponsoring the piece, and what the organization typically publishes

- what the leanings or biases of the author and publisher might be

- what the context of the argument is—what preceded or provoked it and how others have responded to it

Formulating a Claim

Begin with a hypothesis. A full thesis might not become evident until you're well into your analysis, but your final thesis should reflect the complexity of the piece that you're studying. In developing a thesis, consider questions such as the following:

- How can I describe what this argument achieves?

- What is the purpose, and is it accomplished?

- What audiences does the argument address and what audiences does it ignore, and why?

- Which of its rhetorical features will likely influence readers most: ethos of the author? emotional appeals? logical progression? style?

- What aspects of the argument work better than others?

- How do the rhetorical elements interact?

Here's the hardest part for most writers of rhetorical analyses: whether you agree or disagree with an argument usually doesn't matter in a rhetorical analysis. You've got to stay out of the fray and pay attention only to how—and to how well—the argument works.

Examples of Possible Claims for a Rhetorical Analysis

- Some people admire the directness and confidence of Hillary Clinton; others are put off by her bland and sometimes tone-deaf rhetoric. A close look at several of her speeches and public appearances will illuminate both sides of this debate.

- Today's editorial in the Daily Collegian about campus crimes may scare first-year students, but its anecdotal reporting doesn't get down to hard numbers—and for a good reason. Those statistics don't back the position taken by the editors.

- The imageboard 4chan has been called an "Internet hate machine," yet others claim it as a great boon to creativity. A close analysis of its homepage can help to settle this debate.

- The original design of New York's Freedom Tower, with its torqued surfaces and evocative spire, made a stronger argument about American values than its replacement, a fortress-like skyscraper stripped of imagination and unable to make any statement except "I'm 1,776 feet tall."

Preparing a Proposal

If your instructor asks you to prepare a proposal for your rhetorical analysis, here's a format you might use:

- Provide a copy of the work you're analyzing, whether it's a print text, a photograph, a digital image, or a URL, for instance.

- Offer a working hypothesis or tentative thesis.

- Indicate which rhetorical components seem especially compelling and worthy of detailed study and any connections between elements. For example, does the piece seem to emphasize facts and logic so much that it becomes disconnected from potential audiences? If so, hint at that possibility in your proposal.

- Indicate background information you intend to research about the author, institution, and contexts (political, economic, social, and religious) of the argument.

- Define the audience you'd like to reach. If you're responding to an assignment, you may be writing primarily for a teacher and classmates. But they make up a complex audience in themselves. If you can do so within the spirit of the assignment, imagine that your analysis will be published in a local newspaper, Web site, or blog.

- Conclude by briefly discussing the key challenges you anticipate in preparing a rhetorical analysis.

Considering Format and Media

Your instructor may specify that you use a particular format and/or medium. If not, ask yourself these questions to help you make a good choice:

- What format is most appropriate for your rhetorical analysis? Does it call for an academic essay, a report, an infographic, a brochure, or something else?

- What medium is most appropriate for your analysis? Would it be best delivered orally to a live audience? Presented as an audio essay or podcast? Presented in print only or in print with illustrations?

- Will you need visuals, such as moving or still images, maps, graphs, charts—and what function will they play in your analysis? Make sure they are not just "added on" but are necessary components of the analysis.

Thinking about Organization

Your rhetorical analysis is likely to include the following:

- Facts about the text you're analyzing: Provide the author's name; the title or name of the work; its place of publication or its location; the date it was published or viewed.

- Contexts for the argument: Readers need to know where the text is coming from, to what it may be responding, in what controversies it might be embroiled, and so on. Don't assume that they can infer the important contextual elements.

- A synopsis of the text that you're analyzing: If you can't attach the original argument, you must summarize it in enough detail so that a reader can imagine it. Even if you attach a copy of the piece, the analysis should include a summary.

- Some claim about the work's rhetorical effectiveness: It might be a simple evaluative claim or something more complex. The claim can come early in the paper, or you might build up to it, providing the evidence that leads toward the conclusion you've reached.

- A detailed analysis of how the argument works: Although you'll probably analyze rhetorical components separately, don't let your analysis become a dull roster of emotional, ethical, and logical appeals. Your rhetorical analysis should be an argument itself that supports a claim; a simple list of rhetorical appeals won't make much of a point.

- Evidence for every part of the analysis.

- An assessment of alternative views and counterarguments to your own analysis.

Getting and Giving Response: Questions for Peer Response

If you have access to a writing center, discuss the text that you intend to analyze with a writing consultant before you write the paper. Try to find people who agree with the argument and others who disagree, and take notes on their observations. Your instructor may assign you to a peer group for the purpose of reading and responding to one another's drafts; if not, share your draft with someone on your own. You can use the following questions to evaluate a draft. If you're evaluating someone else's draft, be sure to illustrate your points with examples. Specific comments are always more helpful than general observations.

The Claim

- Does the claim address the rhetorical effectiveness of the argument itself rather than the opinion or position that it takes?

- Is the claim significant enough to interest readers?

- Does the claim indicate important relationships between various rhetorical components?

- Would the claim be one that the creator of the piece would regard as serious criticism?

Evidence for the Claim

- Is enough evidence given to support all your claims? What evidence do you still need?

- Is the evidence in support of the claim simply announced, or are its significance and appropriateness analyzed? Is a more detailed discussion needed?

- Do you use appropriate evidence, drawn from the argument itself or from other materials?

- Do you address objections readers might have to the claim, criteria, or evidence?

- What kinds of sources might you use to explain the context of the argument? Do you need to use sources to check factual claims made in the argument?

- Are all quotations introduced with appropriate signal phrases (for instance, "As Áida Álvarez points out"), and do they merge smoothly into your sentences?

Organization and Style

- How are the parts of the argument organized? How effective is this organization? Would some other structure work better?

- Will readers understand the relationships among the original text, your claims, your supporting reasons, and the evidence you've gathered (from the original text and any other sources you've used)? If not, what could be done to make those connections clearer? Are more transitional words and phrases needed? Would headings or graphic devices help?

- Are the transitions or links from point to point, sentence to sentence, and paragraph to paragraph clear and effective? If not, how could they be improved?

- Is the style suited to the subject and appropriate to your audience? Is it too formal? Too casual? Too technical? Too bland or boring?

- Which sentences seem particularly effective? Which ones seem weakest, and how could they be improved? Should some short sentences be combined, or should any long ones be separated into two or more sentences?

- How effective are the paragraphs? Do any seem too skimpy or too long? Do they break the analysis at strategic points?

- Which words or phrases seem particularly effective, accurate, and powerful? Do any seem dull, vague, unclear, or inappropriate for the audience or your purpose? Are definitions provided for technical or other terms that readers might not know?

Spelling, Punctuation, Mechanics, Documentation, and Format
- Check the spelling of the author's name, and make sure that the name of any institution involved with the work is correct. Note that the names of many corporations and institutions use distinctive spelling and punctuation.

- Get the title of the text you're analyzing right.

- Are there any errors in spelling, punctuation, capitalization, and the like?

- Does the assignment require a specific format? Check the original assignment sheet to be sure.

RESPOND

Find an argument on the editorial page or op-ed page in a recent newspaper. Then analyze it rhetorically, using principles discussed in this chapter. Show how it succeeds, fails, or does something else entirely. Perhaps you can show that the author is unusually successful in connecting with readers but then has nothing to say. Or perhaps you discover that the strong logical appeal is undercut by a contradictory emotional argument. Be sure that the analysis includes a summary of the original essay and basic publication information about it (its author, place of publication, and publisher).

Chapter 25

Evaluating Sources

- Assessing Print Sources
- Assessing Electronic Sources
- Assessing Field Research

This chapter is taken from Andrea A. Lunsford and John J. Ruszkiewicz, *Everything's an Argument*, Seventh Edition, pp. 427–435 (Chapter 19).

Left to right: © Bartomeu Amengual/age fotostock; © Terry Harris/Alamy; © Zoonar/pzAxe/age fotostock

As many examples in this text have shown, the effectiveness of an argument often depends on the quality of the sources that support or prove it. You'll need to carefully evaluate and assess all your sources, including those that you gather in libraries, from other print sources, in online searches, or in your own field research.

Remember that different sources can contribute in different ways to your work. In most cases, you'll be looking for reliable sources that provide accurate information or that clearly and persuasively express opinions that might serve as evidence for a case you're making. At other times, you may be seeking material that expresses ideas or attitudes—how people are thinking and feeling at a given time. You might need to use a graphic image, a sample of avant-garde music, or a controversial YouTube clip that doesn't fit neatly into categories such as "reliable" or "accurate" yet is central to your argument. With any and all such sources and evidence, your goals are to be as knowledgeable about them and as responsible in their use as you can be and to share honestly what you learn about them with readers.

"I'm *not* being a tattle-tale! —
I'm being a reliable source!"

www.Cartoonstock.com

FIGURE 25.1 Might a tattle-tale ever be a reliable source?

No writer wants to be naïve in the use of source material, especially since most of the evidence that is used in arguments on public issues—even material from influential and well-known sources—comes with considerable baggage. Scientists and humanists alike have axes to grind, corporations have products to sell, politicians have issues to promote, journalists have reputations to make, publishers and media companies have readers, listeners, viewers, and advertisers to attract and to avoid offending. All of these groups produce and use information to their own benefit, and it's not (usually) a bad thing that they do so. You just have to be aware that when you take information from a given source, it will almost inevitably carry with it at least some of the preferences, assumptions, and biases—conscious or not—of the people who produce and disseminate it. Teachers and librarians are not exempted from this caution: even when we make every effort to be clear and comprehensive in reporting information, we cannot possibly see that information from every single angle. So even the most honest and open observer can deliver only a partial account of an event.

To correct for these biases, draw on as many reliable sources as you can handle when you're preparing to write. You shouldn't assume that all arguments are equally good or that all the sides in a controversy can be supported by the same weight of evidence and good reasons. But you want to avoid choosing sources so selectively that you miss essential issues and perspectives. That's easy to do when you read only sources that agree with you or when the sources that you read all seem to carry the same message. In addition, make sure that you read each source thoroughly enough that you understand its overall points: national research conducted for the Citation Project indicates that student writers often draw from the first paragraph or page of a source and then simply drop it, without seeing what the rest of the source has to say about the topic at hand.

© Adam Zyglis/Cagel Cartoons, Inc.

FIGURE 25.2 When might a blogger actually be a reliable source—and how would you know?

Especially when writing on political subjects, be aware that the sources you're reading or citing almost always support particular beliefs and goals. That fact has been made apparent in recent years by bloggers—from all parts of the political spectrum—who put the traditional news media under daily scrutiny, exposing errors, biases, and omissions. Even so, these political bloggers (mostly amateur journalists, although many are professionals in their own fields) have their own agendas and so must be read with caution themselves.

■ Assessing Print Sources

Since you want information to be reliable and persuasive, it pays to evaluate each potential source thoroughly. The following principles can help you evaluate print sources:

- **Relevance.** Begin by asking what a particular source will add to your argument and how closely the source is related to your argumentative claim. For a book, the table of contents and the index may help you decide. For an article, look for an abstract that summarizes its content. If you can't think of a good reason for using the source, set it aside. You can almost certainly find something better.

- **Credentials of the author.** Sometimes the author's credentials are set forth in an article, in a book, or on a Web site, so be sure to look for them. Is the author an expert on the topic? To find out, you can gather information about the person on the Internet using a search engine like Yahoo! or Ask.com. Another way to learn about the credibility of an author is to search Google Groups for postings that mention the author or to check the Citation Index to find out how others refer to this author. If you see your source cited by other sources you're using, look at how they cite it and what they say about it, which could provide clues to the author's credibility.

- **Stance of the author.** What's the author's position on the issue(s) involved, and how does this stance influence the information in the source? Does the author's stance support or challenge your own views?

- **Credentials of the publisher or sponsor.** If your source is from a newspaper, is it a major one (such as the *Wall Street Journal* or the *Washington Post*) that has historical credentials in reporting, or is it a tabloid? Is it a popular magazine like *O: The Oprah Magazine* or a journal sponsored by a professional group, such as the *Journal of the American Medical Association*? If your source is a book, is the publisher one you recognize or that has its own Web site? When you don't know the reputation of a source, ask several people with more expertise: a librarian, an instructor, or a professional in the field.

- **Stance of the publisher or sponsor.** Sometimes this stance will be obvious: a magazine called *Save the Planet!* will take a pro-environmental position, whereas one called *America First!* will probably take a conservative stance. But other times, you need to read carefully between the lines to identify particular positions and see how the stance affects the message the source presents. Start by asking what the source's goals are: what does the publisher or sponsoring group want to make happen?

- **Currency.** Check the date of publication of every book and article. Recent sources are often more useful than older ones, particularly in the sciences. However, in some fields (such as history and literature), the most authoritative works may well be the older ones.

- **Accuracy.** Check to see whether the author cites any sources for the information or opinions in the article and, if so, how credible and current they are.

- **Level of specialization.** General sources can be helpful as you begin your research, but later in the project you may need the authority or currency of more specialized sources. Keep in mind that highly specialized works on your topic may be difficult for your audience to understand.

- **Audience.** Was the source written for a general readership? For specialists? For advocates or opponents?

FIGURE 25.3 Note the differences between the cover of the *Journal of Abnormal Psychology* and *The How of Happiness*, a book about psychology.

- **Length.** Is the source long enough to provide adequate details in support of your claim?

- **Availability.** Do you have access to the source? If it isn't readily accessible, your time might be better spent looking elsewhere.

- **Omissions.** What's missing or omitted from the source? Might such exclusions affect whether or how you can use the source as evidence?

■ Assessing Electronic Sources

You'll probably find working with digital media both exciting and frustrating, for even though these tools (the Web, social networks, Twitter, and so on) are enormously useful, they offer information of widely varying quality—and mountains and mountains of it. Because Web sources are mostly open and unregulated, careful researchers look for corroboration before accepting evidence they find online, especially if it comes from a site whose sponsor's identity is unclear.

Alfred Eisenstadt/The Life Picture Collection/Getty Images

FIGURE 25.4 *Every man [and woman] should have a built-in automatic crap detector operating inside him.* —Ernest Hemingway, during a 1954 interview with Robert Manning

Practicing Crap Detection

In such an environment, you must be the judge of the accuracy and trustworthiness of particular electronic sources. This is a problem all researchers face, and one that led media critic Howard Rheingold to develop a system for detecting "crap," that is, "information tainted by ignorance, inept communication, or deliberate deception." To avoid such "crap," Rheingold recommends a method of triangulation, which means finding three separate credible online sources that corroborate the point you want to make. But how do you ensure that these sources are credible? One tip Rheingold gives is to use sites like FactCheck.org to verify information, or to use the search term "whois" to find out about the author or sponsor of a site. Try googling Martin Luther King Jr., he says, and somewhere in the top ten "hits" you'll see something called "Martin Luther King, Jr.—a True Historical Examination," which sounds like it should be credible. Check by typing "whois" and the URL of the True Historical Examination, however, and you will find that it is sponsored by a group called Stormfront. Check out *that* site and you'll find that it is a white supremacist group. Hardly a fair, unbiased, and credible source.

In making judgments about online sources, then, you need to be especially mindful and to rely on the same criteria and careful thinking that you use to assess print sources. In addition, you may find the following questions helpful in evaluating online sources:

- Who has posted the document or message or created the site/medium? An individual? An interest group? A company? A government agency? For Web sites, does the URL offer any clues? Note especially the final suffix in a domain name—*.com* (commercial), *.org* (nonprofit organization), *.edu* (educational institution), *.gov* (government agency), *.mil* (military), or *.net* (network). Also note the geographical domains that indicate country of origin—as in *.ca* (Canada) or *.ar*

(Argentina). Click on some links of a Web site to see if they lead to legitimate and helpful sources or organizations.

- What can you determine about the credibility of the author or sponsor? Can the information in the document or site be verified in other sources? How accurate and complete is it? On a blog, for example, look for a link that identifies the creator of the site (some blogs are managed by multiple authors).

- Who can be held accountable for the information in the document or site? How well and thoroughly does it credit its own sources? On a wiki, for example, check its editorial policies: who can add to or edit its materials?

- How current is the document or site? Be especially cautious of undated materials. Most reliable sites are refreshed or edited regularly and should list the date.

- What perspectives are represented? If only one perspective is represented, how can you balance or expand this point of view? Is it a straightforward presentation, or could it be a parody or satire?

Left: Discovery Communications, Inc.; right: NOAA

FIGURE 25.5 What are the kinds and levels of information available on these Web sites—a commercial site about the TV show *Stormchasers* and a federal site on tornadoes and severe weather?

■ Assessing Field Research

If you've conducted experiments, surveys, interviews, observations, or any other field research in developing and supporting an argument, make sure to review your results with a critical eye. The following questions can help you evaluate your own field research:

- Have you rechecked all data and all conclusions to make sure they're accurate and warranted?

- Have you identified the exact time, place, and participants in all your field research?

- Have you made clear what part you played in the research and how, if at all, your role could have influenced the results or findings?

- If your research involved other people, have you gotten their permission to use their words or other materials in your argument? Have you asked whether you can use their names or whether the names should be kept confidential?

- If your research involved interviews, have you thanked the person or persons you interviewed and asked them to verify the words you have attributed to them?

RESPOND

1. The chapter claims that "most of the evidence that is used in arguments on public issues…comes with considerable baggage" (**p. 413**). Find an article in a journal, newspaper, or magazine that uses evidence to support a claim of some public interest. It might be a piece about new treatments for malaria, Internet privacy, dietary recommendations for schoolchildren, proposals for air-quality regulation, the rise in numbers of campus sexual assaults, and so on. Identify several specific pieces of evidence, information, or data presented in the article and then evaluate the degree to which you would accept, trust, or believe those statements. Be prepared to explain specifically why you would be inclined to trust or mistrust any claims based on the data.

2. Check out Goodreads (you can set up an account for free) and see what people there are recommending—or search for "common reading programs" or "common reading lists." Then choose one of the recommended books, preferably a work of nonfiction, and analyze it by using as many of the principles of evaluation for printed books listed in this chapter as you can without actually reading the book: Who is the author, and what are his/her credentials? Who is the publisher, and what is its reputation? What can you find out about the book's relevance and popularity: why might the book be on the list? Who is the primary audience for the book? How lengthy is it? How difficult? Finally, consider how likely it is that the book you have selected would be used in an academic paper. If you do choose a work of fiction, might the work be studied in a literature course?

3. Choose a news or information Web site that you visit routinely. Then, using the guidelines discussed in this chapter, spend some time evaluating its credibility. You might begin by comparing it with Google News or Arts & Letters Daily, two sites that have a reputation for being reliable.

Chapter 26

Using Sources

- Practicing Infotention
- Building a Critical Mass
- Synthesizing Information

This chapter is taken from Andrea A. Lunsford and John J. Ruszkiewicz, *Everything's an Argument*, Seventh Edition, pp. 436–454 (Chapter 20).

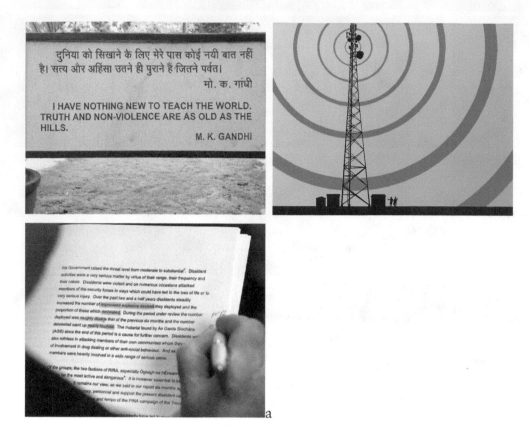

Top left: © imageBROKER/age fotostock; top right: kstudija/Shutterstock; bottom: Paul Faith/PA Wire URN:9724483 (Press Association via AP Images)

You may gather an impressive amount of evidence on your topic—from firsthand interviews, from careful observations, and from intensive library and online research. But until that evidence is thoroughly understood and then woven into the fabric of your own argument, it's just a stack of details. You still have to turn that data into credible information that will be persuasive to your intended audiences.

■ Practicing Infotention

Today it's a truism to say that we are all drowning in information, that it is pouring out at us like water from a never-ending fire hose. Such a situation has its advantages: it's never been easier to locate information on any imaginable topic. But it also has distinct disadvantages: how do you identify useful and credible sources among the millions available to you, and how do you use them well once you've found them? Finding good sources is only the first step. Experts on technology and information like professors Richard Lanham and Howard Rheingold point to the next challenge: managing *attention*. Lanham points out that our age of information calls on us to resist the allure of every single thing vying for our attention and to discriminate among what deserves notice and what doesn't. Building on this insight, Rheingold has coined the term "infotention," which he says "is a word I came up with to describe a mind-machine combination of brain-powered attention skills and computer-powered information filters" (Howard Rheingold, "Infotention," http://www.rheingold.com).

Practicing infotention calls for synthesizing and thinking critically about the enormous amount of information available to us from the "collective intelligence" of the Web. And while some of us can learn to be mindful while multitasking (a fighter pilot is an example Rheingold gives of those who must learn to do so), most of us are not good at it and need to train ourselves, literally, to pay attention to attention (and intention as well), to be aware of what we are doing and thinking, to take a deep breath and notice where we are directing our focus. In short, writers today need to learn to focus their attention, especially online, and learn to avoid distractions. So just how do you put all these skills together to practice infotention?

■ Building a Critical Mass

We've stressed the need to discover as much evidence as possible in support of your claim and to read and understand it as thoroughly as you can. If you can find only one or two pieces of evidence—only one or two reasons or illustrations to back up your thesis—then you may be on unsteady ground. Although there's no definite way of saying just how much evidence is enough, you should build toward a critical mass by having several pieces of evidence all pulling in the direction of your claim. Begin by putting Rheingold's triangulation into practice: find at least three credible sources that support your point.

And remember that **circumstantial evidence** (that is, indirect evidence that *suggests* that something occurred but doesn't prove it directly) may not be enough if it is the only evidence that you have. In the infamous case of Jack the Ripper, the murderer who plagued London's East End in 1888, nothing but circumstantial evidence ever surfaced and hence no one was charged with or convicted of the crimes. In 2007, however, amateur detective Russell Edwards bought a shawl at auction—a shawl found at one of the murder sites. After consulting with a number of scientific experts and using DNA evidence, Edwards identified Jack the Ripper as Aaron Kosminski, who eventually died in an asylum.

© Cog Design, Ltd.

FIGURE 26.1

If your evidence for a claim relies solely on circumstantial evidence, on personal experience, or on one major example, you should extend your search for additional sources and good reasons to back up your claim—or modify the argument. Your initial position may simply have been wrong.

■ Synthesizing Information

As you gather information, you must find a way to make all the facts, ideas, points of view, and quotations you have encountered work with and for you. The process involves not only reading information and recording data carefully (paying "infotention"), but also pondering and synthesizing it—that is, figuring out how the sources you've examined come together to support your specific claims. Synthesis, a form of critical thinking highly valued by business, industry, and other institutions—especially those that reward innovation and creative thinking—is hard work. It almost always involves immersing yourself in your information or data until it feels familiar and natural to you.

At that point, you can begin to look for patterns, themes, and commonalities or striking differences among your sources. Many students use highlighters to help with this process: mark in blue all the parts of sources that mention point A; mark in green those that have to do with issue B; and so on. You are looking for connections among your sources, bringing together what they have to say about your topic in ways you can organize to help support the claim you are making.

You typically begin this process by paraphrasing or summarizing sources so that you understand exactly what they offer and which ideas are essential to your project. You also decide which, if any, sources offer materials you want to quote directly or reproduce (such as an important graph or table). Then you work to introduce such borrowed materials so that readers grasp their significance, and organize them to highlight important relationships. Throughout this review process, use "infotention" strategies by asking questions such as the following:

- Which sources help to set the context for your argument? In particular, which items present new information or give audiences an incentive for reading your work?

- Which items provide background information that is essential for anyone trying to understand your argument?

- Which items help to define, clarify, or explain key concepts of your case? How can these sources be presented or sequenced so that readers appreciate your claims as valid or, at a minimum, reasonable?

- Which of your sources might be used to illustrate technical or difficult aspects of your subject? Would it be best to summarize such technical information to make it more accessible, or would direct quotations be more authoritative and convincing?

- Which sources (or passages within sources) furnish the best support or evidence for each claim or sub-claim within your argument? Now is the time to group these together so you can decide how to arrange them most effectively.

- Which materials do the best job outlining conflicts or offering counterarguments to claims within a project? Which sources might help you address any important objections or rebuttals?

Remember that yours should be the dominant and controlling voice in an argument. You are like the conductor of an orchestra, calling upon separate instruments to work together to create a rich and coherent sound. The least effective academic papers are those that mechanically walk through a string of sources—often just one item per paragraph—without ever getting all these authorities to talk to each other or with the author. Such papers go through the motions but don't get anywhere. You can do better.

Paraphrasing Sources You Will Use Extensively

In a **paraphrase,** you put an author's ideas—including major and minor points—into your own words and sentence structures, following the order the author has given them in the original piece. You usually paraphrase sources that you expect to use heavily in a project. But if you compose your notes well, you may be able to use much of the paraphrased material directly in your paper (with proper citation) because all of the language is your own. A competent paraphrase proves you have read material or data carefully: you demonstrate not only that you know what a source contains but also that you appreciate what it means. There's an important difference.

Here are guidelines to help you paraphrase accurately and effectively in an academic argument:

- Identify the source of the paraphrase, and comment on its significance or the authority of its author.

- Respect your sources. When paraphrasing an entire work or any lengthy section of it, cover all its main points and any essential details, following the same order the author uses. If you distort the shape of the material, your notes will be less valuable, especially if you return to them later.

*"Who is the fairest one of all,
and state your sources!"*

FIGURE 26.2 Backing up your claims with well-chosen sources makes almost any argument more credible.

- If you're paraphrasing material that extends over more than one page in the original source, note the placement of page breaks since it is highly likely that you will use only part of the paraphrase in your argument. You will need the page number to cite the specific page of material you want to cite.

- Make sure that the paraphrase is in your own words and sentence structures. If you want to include especially memorable or powerful language from the original source, enclose it in quotation marks. (See "Using Quotations Selectively and Strategically" on **p. 428**.)

- Keep your own comments, elaborations, or reactions separate from the paraphrase itself. Your report on the source should be clear, objective, and free of connotative language.

- Collect all the information necessary to create an in-text citation as well as an item in your works cited list or references list. For online materials, be sure you know how to recover the source later.

- Label the paraphrase with a note suggesting where and how you intend to use it in your argument.

- Recheck to make sure that the words and sentence structures are your own and that they express the author's meaning accurately.

Here is a passage from linguist David Crystal's book *Language Play,* followed by a student's paraphrase of the passage.

> Language play, the arguments suggest, will help the development of pronunciation ability through its focus on the properties of sounds and sound contrasts, such as rhyming. Playing with word endings and decoding the syntax of riddles will help the acquisition of grammar. Readiness to play with words and names, to exchange puns and to engage in nonsense talk, promotes links with semantic development. The kinds of dialogue interaction illustrated above are likely to have consequences for the development of conversational skills. And language play, by its nature, also contributes greatly to what in recent years has been called metalinguistic awareness, which is turning out to be of critical importance to the development of language skills in general and literacy skills in particular (180).

Paraphrase of the Passage from Crystal's Book

> In *Language Play*, David Crystal argues that playing with language—creating rhymes, figuring out riddles, making puns, playing with names, using inverted words, and so on—helps children figure out a great deal, from the basics of pronunciation and grammar to how to carry on a conversation. This kind of play allows children to understand the overall concept of how language works, a concept that is key to learning to use—and read—language effectively (180).

Summarizing Sources

Unlike a paraphrase, a **summary** records just the gist of a source or a key idea—that is, only enough information to identify a point you want to emphasize. Once again, this much-shortened version of a source puts any borrowed ideas into your own words. At the research stage, summaries help you identify key points you want to make and, just as important, provide a record of what you have read. In a project itself, a summary helps readers understand the sources you are using.

Here are some guidelines to help you prepare accurate and helpful summaries:

- Identify the thesis or main point in a source and make it the heart of your summary. In a few detailed phrases or sentences, explain to yourself (and readers) what the source accomplishes.

- If your summary includes a comment on the source (as it might in the summaries used for annotated bibliographies), be sure that you won't later confuse your comments with what the source itself asserts.

- When using a summary in an argument, identify the source, state its point, and add your own comments about why the material is significant for the argument that you're making.

- Include just enough information to recount the main points you want to cite. A summary is usually much shorter than the original. When you need more information or specific details, you can return to the source itself or prepare a paraphrase.

- Use your own words in a summary and keep the language objective and denotative. If you include any language from the original source, enclose it in quotation marks.

- Collect all the information necessary to create an in-text citation as well as an item in your works cited list or references list. For online sources without page numbers, record the paragraph, screen, or section number(s) if available.

- Label the summary with a note that suggests where and how you intend to use it in your argument.

- Recheck the summary to make sure that you've captured the author's meaning accurately and that the wording is entirely your own.

Following is a summary of the David Crystal passage:

> In *Language Play*, David Crystal argues that playing with language helps children figure out how language works, a concept that is key to learning to use—and read—language effectively (180).

Notice that the summary is shorter than the paraphrase shown on p. 427.

Using Quotations Selectively and Strategically

To support your argumentative claims, you'll want to quote (that is, to reproduce an author's precise words) in at least three kinds of situations:

1. when the wording expresses a point so well that you cannot improve it or shorten it without weakening it,

2. when the author is a respected authority whose opinion supports your own ideas powerfully, and/or

3. when an author or authority challenges or seriously disagrees with others in the field.

Consider, too, that charts, graphs, and images may also function like direct quotations, providing convincing evidence for your academic argument.

In an argument, quotations from respected authorities will establish your ethos as someone who has sought out experts in the field. Just as important sometimes, direct quotations (such as a memorable phrase in your introduction or a detailed eyewitness account) may capture your readers' attention. Finally, carefully chosen quotations can broaden the appeal of your argument by drawing on emotion as well as logic, appealing to the reader's mind and heart. A student who is writing on the ethical issues of bullfighting, for example, might introduce an argument that bullfighting is not a sport by quoting Ernest Hemingway's comment that "the formal bull-fight is a tragedy, not a sport, and the bull is certain to be killed" and then accompany the quotation with an image such as the one on the next page.

The following guidelines can help you quote sources accurately and effectively:

- Quote or reproduce materials that readers will find especially convincing, purposeful, and interesting. You should have a specific reason for every quotation.

Juan Castillo/AFP/Getty Images

FIGURE 26.3 A tragedy, not a sport?

- Don't forget the double quotation marks [" "] that must surround a direct quotation in American usage. If there's a quote within a quote, it is surrounded by a pair of single quotation marks [' ']. British usage does just the opposite, and foreign languages often handle direct quotations much differently.

- When using a quotation in your argument, introduce its author(s) and follow the quotation with commentary of your own that points out its significance.

- Keep quoted material relatively brief. Quote only as much of a passage as is necessary to make your point while still accurately representing what the source actually said.

- If the quotation extends over more than one page in the original source, note the placement of page breaks in case you decide to use only part of the quotation in your argument.

- In your notes, label a quotation you intend to use with a note that tells you where you think you'll use it.

- Make sure you have all the information necessary to create an in-text citation as well as an item in your works cited list or references list.

- Copy quotations carefully, reproducing the punctuation, capitalization, and spelling exactly as they are in the original. If possible, copy the quotation from a reliable text and paste it directly into your project.

- Make sure that quoted phrases, sentences, or passages fit smoothly into your own language. Consider where to begin the quotation to make it work effectively within its surroundings or modify the words you write to work with the quoted material.

- Use square brackets if you introduce words of your own into the quotation or make changes to it ("And [more] brain research isn't going to define further the matter of 'mind'").

- Use ellipsis marks if you omit material ("And brain research isn't going to define...the matter of 'mind'").

- If you're quoting a short passage (four lines or less in MLA style; forty words or less in APA style), it should be worked into your text, enclosed by quotation marks. Longer quotations should be set off from the regular text. Begin such a quotation on a new line, indenting every line one inch or ten spaces (MLA) or a half inch or five to seven spaces (APA). Set-off quotations do not need to be enclosed in quotation marks.

- Never distort your sources or present them out of context when you quote from them. Misusing sources is a major offense in academic arguments.

Framing Materials You Borrow with Signal Words and Introductions

Because source materials are crucial to the success of arguments, you need to introduce borrowed words and ideas carefully to your readers. Doing so usually calls for using a signal phrase of some kind in the sentence to introduce or frame the source. Often, a signal phrase will precede a quotation. But you need such a marker whenever you introduce borrowed material, as in the following examples:

> According to noted primatologist Jane Goodall, the more we learn about the nature of nonhuman animals, the more ethical questions we face about their use in the service of humans.

> The more we learn about the nature of nonhuman animals, the more ethical questions we face about their use in the service of humans, according to noted primatologist Jane Goodall.

> The more we learn about the nature of nonhuman animals, according to noted primatologist Jane Goodall, the more ethical questions we face about their use in the service of humans.

In each of these sentences, the signal phrase tells readers that you're drawing on the work of a person named Jane Goodall and that this person is a "noted primatologist."

Now look at an example that uses a quotation from a source in more than one sentence:

In *Job Shift*, consultant William Bridges worries about "dejobbing and about what a future shaped by it is going to be like." Even more worrisome, Bridges argues, is the possibility that "the sense of craft and of professional vocation...will break down under the need to earn a fee" (228).

The signal verbs *worries* and *argues* add a sense of urgency to the message Bridges offers. They also suggest that the writer either agrees with—or is neutral about—Bridges's points. Other signal verbs can have a more negative slant, indicating that the point being introduced by the quotation is open to debate and that others (including the writer) might disagree with it. If the writer of the passage above had said, for instance, that Bridges *unreasonably contends* or that he *fantasizes,* these signal verbs would carry quite different connotations from those associated with *argues*.

In some cases, a signal verb may require more complex phrasing to get the writer's full meaning across:

Bridges recognizes the dangers of changes in work yet refuses to be overcome by them: "The real issue is not how to stop the change but how to provide the necessary knowledge and skills to equip people to operate successfully in this New World" (229).

As these examples illustrate, the signal verb is important because it allows you to characterize the author's or source's viewpoint as well as your own—so choose these verbs with care.

Some Frequently Used Signal Verbs

acknowledges	claims	emphasizes	remarks
admits	concludes	expresses	replies
advises	concurs	hypothesizes	reports
agrees	confirms	interprets	responds
allows	criticizes	lists	reveals
argues	declares	objects	states
asserts	disagrees	observes	suggests
believes	discusses	offers	thinks
charges	disputes	opposes	writes

Note that in APA style, these signal verbs should be in a past tense: *Blau (1992) claimed; Clark (2001) has concluded.*

Using Sources to Clarify and Support Your Own Argument

The best academic arguments often have the flavor of a hearty but focused intellectual conversation. Scholars and scientists create this impression by handling research materials strategically and selectively. Here's how some college writers use sources to achieve their own specific goals within an academic argument.

Establish context. Taylor Pearson, in his essay "Why You Should Fear Your Toaster More Than Nuclear Power," sets the context for his argument in the first two sentences, in which he cites a newspaper source ("Japan Nuclear Disaster Tops Scale") as representative of "headlines everywhere" warning of nuclear crises and the danger of existing nuclear plants. Assuming that these sentences will remind readers of other warnings and hence indicate that this is a highly fraught argument with high emotional stakes, Pearson connects those fears to his own argument by shifting, in the third sentence, into a direct rebuttal of the sources (such fears are "nothing more than media sensationalism") before stating his thesis: "We need nuclear energy. It's clean, it's efficient, it's economic, and it's probably the only thing that will enable us to quickly phase out fossil fuels." It will be up to Pearson in the rest of the essay to explain how, even in a context of public fear, his thesis is defensible:

For the past month or so, headlines everywhere have been warning us of the horrible crises caused by the damaged Japanese nuclear reactors. Titles like "Japan Nuclear Disaster Tops Scale" have fueled a new wave of protests against anything nuclear—namely, the construction of new nuclear plants or even the continued operation of existing plants. However, all this reignited fear of nuclear energy is nothing more than media sensationalism. We need nuclear energy. It's clean, it's efficient, it's economic, and it's probably the only thing that will enable us to quickly phase out fossil fuels.

FIGURE 26.4 When using Web sources such as blogs, take special care to check authors' backgrounds and credentials.

Review the literature on a subject. You will often need to tell readers what authorities have already written about your topic, thus connecting them to your own argument. So, in a paper on the effectiveness of peer editing, Susan Wilcox does a very brief "review of the literature" on her subject, pointing to three authorities who support using the method in writing courses. She quotes from the authors and also puts some of their ideas in her own words:

Bostock cites one advantage of peer review as "giving a sense of ownership of the assessment process" (1). Topping expands this view, stating that "peer assessment also involves increased time on task: thinking, comparing, contrasting, and communicating" (254). The extra time spent thinking over the assignment, especially in terms of helping someone else, can draw in the reviewer and lend greater importance to taking the process seriously, especially since the reviewer knows that the classmate is relying on his advice. This also adds an extra layer of accountability for the student; his hard work—or lack thereof—will be seen by peers, not just the instructor. Cassidy notes, "[S]tudents work harder with the knowledge that they will be assessed by their peers" (509): perhaps the knowledge that peer review is coming leads to a better-quality draft to begin with.

The paragraph is straightforward and useful, giving readers an efficient overview of the subject. If they want more information, they can find it by consulting Wilcox's works cited page.

Introduce a term or define a concept. Quite often in an academic argument, you may need to define a term or explain a concept. Relying on a source may make your job easier *and* enhance your credibility. That is what Laura Pena achieves in the following paragraph, drawing upon two authorities to explain what teachers mean by a "rubric" when it comes to grading student work:

To understand the controversy surrounding rubrics, it is best to know what a rubric is. According to Heidi Andrade, a professor at SUNY-Albany, a rubric can be defined as "a document that lists criteria and describes varying levels of quality, from excellent to poor, for a specific assignment" ("Self-Assessment" 61). Traditionally, rubrics have been used primarily as grading and evaluation tools (Kohn 12), meaning that a rubric was not used until after students handed their papers in to their teacher. The teacher would then use a rubric to evaluate the students' papers according to the criteria listed on the rubric.

Note that the first source provides the core definition while information from the second offers a detail important to understanding when and how rubrics are used—a major issue in Pena's paper. Her selection of sources here serves her thesis while also providing readers with necessary information.

Present technical material. Sources can be especially helpful, too, when material becomes technical or difficult to understand. Writing on your own, you might lack the confidence to handle the complexities of some subjects. While you should challenge yourself to learn a subject well enough to explain it in your own words, there will be times when a quotation from an expert serves both you and your readers. Here is Natalie San Luis dealing with some of the technical differences between mainstream and Black English:

The grammatical rules of mainstream English are more concrete than those of Black English; high school students can't check out an MLA handbook on Ebonics from their school library. As with all dialects, though, there are certain characteristics of the language that most Black English scholars agree upon. According to Samy Alim, author of *Roc the Mic Right*, these character-istics are the "[h]abitual be [which] indicates actions that are continuing or ongoing…. Copula absence….. Stressed been….. Gon [indicating] the future tense….. They for possessive….. Postvocalic -r….. [and] Ank and ang for 'ink' and 'ing'" (115). Other scholars have identified "[a]bsence of third-person singular present-tense s….. Absence of possessive 's," repetition of pronouns, and double negatives (Rickford 111–24).

Note that using ellipses enables San Luis to cover a great deal of ground. Readers not familiar with linguistic terms may have trouble following the quotation, but remember that academic arguments often address audiences comfortable with some degree of complexity.

> **Develop or support a claim.** Even academic audiences expect to be convinced, and one of the most important strategies for a writer is to use sources to amplify or support a claim.

Here is Manasi Deshpande, whose proposal argument appears in **CHAPTER 19 (pp. 324–328)**, making the following claim: "Although the University has made a concerted and continuing effort to improve access, students and faculty with physical disabilities still suffer from discriminatory hardship, unequal opportunity to succeed, and lack of independence." See how she weaves sources together in the following paragraph to help support that claim:

> The current state of campus accessibility leaves substantial room for improvement. There are approximately 150 academic and administrative buildings on campus (Grant). Eduardo Gardea, intern architect at the Physical Plant, estimates that only about nineteen buildings comply fully with the Americans with Disabilities Act (ADA). According to Penny Seay, PhD, director of the Center for Disability Studies at UT Austin, the ADA in theory "requires every building on campus to be accessible."

Highlight differences or counterarguments. The sources you encounter in developing a project won't always agree with each other or you. In academic arguments, you don't want to hide such differences, but instead point them out honestly and let readers make judgments based upon actual claims. Here is a paragraph in which Laura Pena again presents two views on the use of rubrics as grading tools:

> Some naysayers, such as Alfie Kohn, assert that "any form of assessment that encourages students to keep asking, 'How am I doing?' is likely to change how they look at themselves and what they're learning, usually for the worse."

> Kohn cites a study that found that students who pay too much attention to the quality of their performance are more likely to chalk up the outcome of an assignment to factors beyond their control, such as innate ability, and are also more likely to give up quickly in the face of a difficult task (14). However, Ross and Rolheiser have found that when students are taught how to properly implement self-assessment tools in the writing process, they are more likely to put more effort and persistence into completing a difficult assignment and may develop higher self-confidence in their writing ability (sec. 2). Building

self-confidence in elementary-age writers can be extremely helpful when they tackle more complicated writing endeavors in the future.

In describing Kohn as a "naysayer," Pena may tip her hand and lose some degree of objectivity. But her thesis has already signaled her support for rubrics as a grading tool, so academic readers will probably not find the connotations of the term inappropriate.

These examples suggest only a few of the ways that sources, either summarized or quoted directly, can be incorporated into an academic argument to support or enhance a writer's goals. Like these writers, you should think of sources as your copartners in developing and expressing ideas. But you are still in charge.

Avoiding "Patchwriting"

When using sources in an argument, writers—and especially those new to research-based writing—may be tempted to do what Professor Rebecca Moore Howard terms "**patchwriting**": stitching together material from Web or other sources without properly paraphrasing or summarizing and with little or no documentation. Here, for example, is a patchwork paragraph about the dangers wind turbines pose to wildlife:

> Scientists are discovering that technology with low carbon impact does not mean low environmental or social impacts. That is the case especially with wind turbines, whose long, massive fiberglass blades have been chopping up tens of thousands of birds that fly into them, including golden eagles, red-tailed hawks, burrowing owls, and other raptors in California. Turbines are also killing bats in great numbers. The 420 wind turbines now in use across Pennsylvania killed more than 10,000 bats last year—mostly in the late summer months, according to the State Game Commission. That's an average of 25 bats per turbine per year, and the Nature Conservancy predicts as many as 2,900 turbines will be set up across the state by 2030. It's not the spinning blades that kill the bats; instead, their lungs effectively blow up from the rapid pressure drop that occurs as air flows over the turbine blades. But there's hope we may figure out solutions to these problems because, since we haven't had too many wind turbines heretofore in the country, we are learning how to manage this new technology as we go.

The paragraph reads well and is full of details. But it would be considered plagiarized because it fails to identify its sources and because most of the material has simply been lifted directly from the Web. How much is actually copied? We've highlighted the borrowed material:

> Scientists are discovering that technology with low carbon impact does not mean low environmental or social impacts. That is the case especially with wind turbines, whose long, massive fiberglass blades have been chopping up tens of thousands of birds that fly into them, including golden eagles, red-tailed hawks, burrowing owls, and other raptors in California. Turbines are also killing bats in great numbers. The 420 wind turbines now in use across Pennsylvania killed more than 10,000 bats last year—mostly in the late sum-

mer months, according to the State Game Commission. That's an average of 25 bats per turbine per year, and the Nature Conservancy predicts as many as 2,900 turbines will be set up across the state by 2030. It's not the spinning blades that kill the bats; instead, their lungs effectively blow up from the rapid pressure drop that occurs as air flows over the turbine blades. But there's hope we may figure out solutions to these problems because, since we haven't had too many wind turbines heretofore in the country, we are learning how to manage this new technology as we go.

But here's the point: an academic writer who has gone to the trouble of finding so much information will gain more credit and credibility just by properly identifying, paraphrasing, and quoting the sources used. The resulting paragraph is actually more impressive because it demonstrates how much reading and synthesizing the writer has actually done:

> Scientists like George Ledec of the World Bank are discovering that technology with low carbon impact "does not mean low environmental or social impacts" (Tracy). That is the case especially with wind turbines. Their massive blades spinning to create pollution-free electricity are also killing thousands of valuable birds of prey, including eagles, hawks, and owls in California (Rittier). Turbines are also killing bats in great numbers (Thibodeaux). The *Pittsburgh Post-Gazette* reports that 10,000 bats a year are killed by the 420 turbines currently in Pennsylvania. According to the state game commissioner, "That's an average of 25 bats per turbine per year, and the Nature Conservancy predicts as many as 2,900 turbines will be set up across the state by 2030" (Schwartzel). It's not the spinning blades that kill the animals; instead, *DiscoveryNews* explains, "the bats' lungs effectively blow up from the rapid pressure drop that occurs as air flows over the turbine blades" (Marshall). But there's hope that scientists can develop turbines less dangerous to animals of all kinds. "We haven't had too many wind turbines heretofore in the country," David Cottingham of the Fish and Wildlife Service points out, "so we are learning about it as we go" (Tracy).

Works Cited

Marshall, Jessica. "Wind Turbines Kill Bats without Impact." *DiscoveryNews.com*. Discovery Communications, 25 Aug. 2008. Web. 11 Dec. 2011.

Rittier, John. "Wind Turbines Taking Toll on Birds of Prey." *USA Today*. Gannett, 4 Jan. 2005. Web. 10 Dec. 2011.

Schwartzel, Erich. "Pa. Wind Turbines Deadly to Bats, Costly to Farmers." *Post-Gazette.com*. PG Publishing, 17 July 2011. Web. 12 Dec. 2011.

Thibodeaux, Julie. "Bats Getting Caught in Texas Wind Turbines." *Pegasus-News.com*. PanLocal Media, 9 Nov. 2011. Web. 10 Dec. 2011.

Tracy, Ryan. "Wildlife Slows Wind Power." *WallStreetJournal.com*. Dow Jones, 10 Dec. 2011. Web. 10 Dec. 2011.

RESPOND

1. Select one of the essays from **CHAPTER 19**, or another essay of your own chooing. Following the guidelines in this chapter, write a paraphrase of the essay that you might use subsequently in an academic argument. Be careful to describe the essay accurately and to note on what pages specific ideas or claims are located. The language of the paraphrase should be entirely your own—though you may include direct quotations of phrases, sentences, or longer passages you would likely use in a paper. Be sure these quotations are introduced and cited in your paraphrase: *Pearson claims that nuclear power is safe, even asserting that "your toaster is far more likely to kill you than any nuclear power plant" (175).* When you are done, trade your paraphrase with a partner to get feedback on its clarity and accuracy.

2. Summarize three readings or fairly lengthy passages from this book, following the guidelines in this chapter. Open the item with a correct MLA or APA citation for the piece. Then provide the summary itself. Follow up with a one- or two-sentence evaluation of the work describing its potential value as a source in an academic argument. In effect, you will be preparing three items that might appear in an annotated bibliography. Here's an example:

    > Pearson, Taylor. "Why You Should Fear Your Toaster More Than Nuclear Power." *Everything's an Argument.* By Andrea A. Lunsford and John J. Ruszkiewicz. 7th ed. Boston: Bedford, 2016. 174-79. Print. Argues that since the dangers of nuclear power (death, radiation, waste) are actually less than those of energy sources we rely on today, nuclear plants represent the only practical way to generate the power we need and still reduce greenhouse gases. The journalistic piece provides many interesting facts about nuclear energy, but is informally documented and so does not identify its sources in detail or include a bibliography.

3. Working with a partner, agree upon an essay that you will both read either one of the essays from **CHAPTER 19** or one of your own choosing, examining it as a potential source for a research argument. As you read it, choose about a half-dozen words, phrases, or short passages that you would likely quote if you used the essay in a paper and attach a frame or signal phrase to each quotation. Then compare the passages you selected to quote with those your partner culled from the same essay. How do your choices of quoted material create an image or ethos for the original author that differs from the one your partner has created? How do the signal phrases shape a reader's sense of the author's position? Which set of quotations best represents the author's argument? Why?

4. Select either one of the essays from **CHAPTER 19** or one of your own choosing, to examine the different ways an author uses source materials to support claims. Begin by highlighting the signal phrases you find attached to borrowed ideas or direct quotations. How well do they introduce or frame this material? Then categorize the various ways the author actually uses particular sources. For example, look for sources that provide context for the topic, review the scholarly literature, define key concepts or terms, explain technical details, furnish evidence, or lay out contrary opinions. When you are done, write a paragraph assessing the author's handling of sources in the piece. Are the borrowed materials integrated well with the author's own thoughts? Do the sources represent an effective synthesis of ideas?

Chapter 27

Visual Rhetoric

The Power of Visual Arguments

Using Visuals in Your Own Arguments

This chapter is taken from Andrea A. Lunsford and John J. Ruszkiewicz, *Everything's an Argument*, Seventh Edition, pp. 330–343 (Chapter 14).

To commemorate the two hundredth anniversary of "The Star-Spangled Banner," its lyrics composed by Francis Scott Key in September 1814 following the failed British bombardment of Fort McHenry outside Baltimore, the Smithsonian Institution asked a group of artists to reflect on what the American flag means today. Most of the artists expressed their ideas and opinions visually, through paintings, photographs, montages, sculptures, films, even a graphic "fantasy." Three of their items are reproduced above: left to right, a steel-and-aluminum flag by architect Daniel Libeskind; a figure in acrylic and watercolor by Anita Kunz; and a photo collage by graphic designer David Carson. Even so small a sampling of visual rhetoric underscores what you doubtless already know: images tease our imaginations, provoke responses from viewers, and, yes, make arguments. They have clout.

■ The Power of Visual Arguments

Even in everyday situations, images—from T-shirts to billboards to animated films and computer screens—influence us. Media analyst Kevin Kelly ponders the role screens and their images now play in our lives:

> Everywhere we look, we see screens. The other day I watched clips from a movie as I pumped gas into my car. The other night I saw a movie on the backseat of a plane. We will watch anywhere. Screens playing video pop up in the most unexpected places—like ATM machines and supermarket checkout lines and tiny phones; some movie fans watch entire films in between calls. These ever-present screens have created an audience for very short moving pictures, as brief as three minutes, while cheap digital creation tools have empowered a new generation of filmmakers, who are rapidly filling up those screens. We are headed toward screen ubiquity.

> —Kevin Kelly, "Becoming Screen Literate"

Of course, visual arguments weren't invented by YouTube, and their power isn't novel either. The pharaohs of Egypt lined the banks of the Nile River with statues of themselves to assert their authority, and there is no shortage of monumental effigies in Washington, D.C., today.

© Mel Longhurst/Photoshot

FIGURE 27.1 Not only the high and mighty: sculpture of a Great Depression—era breadline at the Franklin Delano Roosevelt Memorial in Washington, D.C.

Still, the ease with which all of us make and share images *is* unprecedented: people are uploading a billion shots a *day* to Snapchat, a photo-messaging application that deletes items after only a brief viewing. And most of us have easily adjusted to instantaneous multichannel, multimedia connectivity. We expect it to be seamless too. The prophet of this era was Marshall McLuhan, who nearly fifty years ago proclaimed that "the medium is the massage," with the play on *message* and *massage* intentional. As McLuhan says, "We shape our tools and afterwards our tools shape us. . . . All media works us over completely."

RESPOND

Find an advertisement, either print or digital, that uses both verbal and visual elements. Analyze its argument first by pointing out the claims the ad makes (or implies) and then by identifying the ways it supports them verbally and/or visually. Then switch ads with a classmate and discuss his/her analysis. Compare your responses to the two ads. If they're different—and they probably will be—how might you account for the differences?

■ Using Visuals in Your Own Arguments

Given the power of images, it's only natural that you would use them in your own composing. In fact, many college instructors now expect papers for their courses to be posted to the Web, where digital photos, videos, and design elements are native. Other instructors invite or even require students to do multimedia reports or to use videos, photo collages, cartoons, or other media to make arguments—an assignment not unlike that given to the artists in the Smithsonian's "Star-Spangled Banner" project. If using visual media still strikes you as odd in academic settings, just consider that such arguments can have all the reach and versatility of more conventional verbal appeals to pathos, ethos, and logos. Often even more.

Using Images and Visual Design to Create Pathos

Many advertisements, YouTube videos, political posters, rallies, marches, and even church services use visual images to trigger emotions. You can't flip through a magazine, watch a video, or browse the Web without being cajoled or seduced by figures or design elements of all kinds—most of them fashioned in some way to attract your eye and attention.

Technology has also made it incredibly easy for you to create on-the-spot photographs and videos that you can use for making arguments of your own. With a GoPro camera strapped to your head, you could document transportation problems in and around campus and then present your visual evidence in a paper or an oral report. You don't have to be a professional these days to produce poignant, stirring, or even satirical visual texts.

Yet just because images are powerful doesn't mean they always work. When you compose visually, you have to be certain to generate impressions that support your arguments, not weigh against them.

Shape Visuals to Convey Appropriate Feelings

To appeal visually to your readers' emotions, think first of the goal of your writing: you want every image or use of multimedia to advance that purpose. Consider, for a moment, the iconic *Apollo 8* "earthrise" photograph of our planet hanging above the horizon of the moon. You could adapt this image to introduce an appeal for additional investment in the space program. Or it might become part of an argument about the need to preserve frail natural environments, or a stirring appeal against nationalism: *From space, we are one world.* Any of these claims might be supported successfully without the image, but the photograph—like most visuals—will probably touch members of your audience more strongly than words alone could.

NASA

FIGURE 27.2 Still striking almost fifty years later, this 1968 *Apollo 8* photograph of the earth shining over the moon can support many kinds of arguments.

Consider Emotional Responses to Color

As the "earthrise" photo demonstrates, color can have great power too: the beautiful blue earth floating in deep black space carries a message of its own. Indeed, our response to color is part of our biological and cultural makeup. So it makes sense to consider what shades are especially effective with the kinds of arguments you're making, whether they occur in images themselves or in elements such as headings, fonts, backgrounds, screens, banners and so on. And remember that a black-and-white image can also be a memorable design choice.

In most situations, let your selection of colors be guided by your own good taste, by designs you admire, or by the advice of friends or helpful professionals. Some design and presentation software will even help you choose colors by offering dependable "default" shades or an array of pre-existing designs and compatible colors (for example, of presentation slides). To be emotionally effective, the colors you choose for a design should follow certain commonsense principles. If you're using background colors on a political poster, Web site, or slide, the contrast between words and background should be vivid enough to make reading easy. For example, white letters on a yellow background are not usually legible. Similarly, bright background colors should be avoided for long documents because reading is easiest with dark letters against a light or white background. Avoid complex patterns; even though they might look interesting and be easy to create, they often interfere with other more important elements of a presentation.

When you use visuals in your college projects, test them on prospective readers. That's what professionals do because they appreciate how delicate the choices of visual and multimedia texts can be. These responses will help you analyze your own arguments and improve your success with them.

© Eve Arnold/Magnum Photos

FIGURE 27.3 Eve Arnold took this powerful black-and-white photograph in 1958 at a party in Virginia for students being introduced to mixed-race schools. How might a full-color image have changed the impact of the scene?

Using Images to Establish Ethos

If you are on Facebook, LinkedIn, or other social networking sites, you no doubt chose photographs for those sites with an eye to creating a sense of who you are, what you value, and how you wish to be perceived. You fashioned a self-image. So it shouldn't come as a surprise that you can boost your credibility as a writer by using visual design strategically: we know one person whose Facebook presentation of images and media so impressed a prospective employer that she got a job on the spot. So whether you are using photographs, videos, or other media on your personal pages or in your college work, it pays to attend to how they construct your ethos.

Understand How Images Enhance Credibility and Authority

You might have noticed that just about every company, organization, institution, government agency, or club now sports a logo or an emblem. Whether it's the Red Cross, the Canadian Olympic Committee, or perhaps the school you attend, such groups use carefully crafted images to signal their authority and trustworthiness. An emblem or a logo can also carry a wealth of cultural and historical implications. That's why university Web sites typically include the seal of the institution somewhere on the homepage (and always on its letterhead) or why the president of the United States travels with a presidential seal to hang on the speaker's podium.

© Bruce Davidson/Magnum Photos

FIGURE 27.4 How does a photograph like this 1999 Bruce Davidson shot of President Bill Clinton shape your sense of Clinton's ethos? Based on this image alone, what words might you use to describe Clinton as a *politician*?

Though you probably don't have a personal logo or trademark, your personal ethos functions the same way when you make an argument. You can establish it by offering visual evidence of your knowledge or competence. In an essay on safety issues in competitive biking, you might include a photo of yourself in a key race, embed a video showing how often serious accidents occur, or include an audio file of an interview with an injured biker. The photo proves that you have personal experience with biking, while the video and audio files show that you have done research and know your subject well, thus helping to affirm your credibility.

Predictably, your choice of *medium* also says something important about you. Making an appeal on a Web site sends signals about your technical skills, contemporary orientation, and personality. So if you direct people to a Facebook or Flickr page, be sure that any materials there present you favorably. Be just as careful in a classroom that any handouts or slides you use for an oral report demonstrate your competence. And remember that you don't always have to be high-tech to be effective: when reporting on a children's story that you're writing, the most sensible medium of presentation might be cardboard and paper made into an oversized book and illustrated by hand.

Left to right: NASA; Courtesy Internal Revenue Service; Courtesy Environmental Protection Agency

FIGURE 27.5 Take a look at these three government logos, each of which intends to convey credibility, authority, and maybe more. Do they accomplish their goals? Why or why not?

You demonstrate your ethos simply by showing an awareness of the basic design conventions for any kind of writing you're doing. It's no accident that lab reports for science courses are sober and unembellished. Visually, they reinforce the professional ethos of scientific work. The same is true of a college research paper. So whether you're composing a term paper, a résumé, a film, an animated comic, or a Web site, look for successful models and follow their design cues.

Consider How Details of Design Reflect Your Ethos

As we have just suggested, almost every design element you use in a paper or project sends signals about character and ethos. You might resent the tediousness of placing page numbers in the appropriate corner, aligning long quotations just so, and putting footnotes in the right place, but these details prove that you are paying attention. Gestures as simple as writing on official stationery (if, for example, you are representing a club or campus organization) or dressing up for an oral presentation matter too: suddenly you seem more mature and competent.

Even the type fonts that you select for a document can mark you as warm and inviting or as efficient and contemporary. The warm and inviting fonts often belong to a family called *serif*. The serifs are those little flourishes at the ends of the strokes that make the fonts seem handcrafted and artful:

> warm and inviting (Bookman Old Style)
>
> warm and inviting (Times New Roman)
>
> warm and inviting (Georgia)

Cleaner, modern fonts go without those little flourishes and are called *sans serif*. These fonts are cooler, simpler, and, some argue, more readable on a computer screen (depending on screen resolution):

> efficient and contemporary (Helvetica)
>
> efficient and contemporary (Verdana)
>
> efficient and contemporary (Comic Sans MS)

Other typographic elements send messages as well. The size of type can make a difference. If your text or headings are in boldface and too large, you'll seem to be shouting:

LOSE WEIGHT! PAY NOTHING!*

Tiny type, on the other hand, might make you seem evasive:

*Excludes the costs of enrollment and required meal purchases. Minimum contract: 12 months.

Finally, don't ignore the signals you send through your choice of *illustrations* and *photographs* themselves. Images communicate your preferences, sensitivities, and inclusiveness—sometimes inadvertently. Conference planners, for example, are careful to create brochures that represent all participants, and they make sure that the brochure photos don't show only women, only men, or only members of one racial or ethnic group.

RESPOND

Choose a project or an essay you have written recently and examine it for how well *visually* it establishes your credibility and how well it is designed. Ask a classmate or friend to look at it and describe the ethos you convey through the item. Then go back to the drawing board with a memo to yourself about how you might use images or media to improve it.

The White House, photo by Pete Souza

FIGURE 27.6 Who's missing in this picture of senior advisers to the president taken in December 2012? The *New York Times*, which published the item, pointed out that, if you looked very closely, you could see Valerie Jarrett's leg.

Using Visual Images to Support Logos

Not that long ago, media critics ridiculed the colorful charts and graphs in newspapers like *USA Today*. Now, comparable features appear in even the most traditional publications because they work: they convey information efficiently *and* persuasively. We now expect evidence to be presented graphically and have learned to use and interact with multiple streams of data and information.

Organize Information Visually

Graphic presentation calls for design that enables readers and viewers to look at an item and understand what it does. A brilliant, much-copied example of such an intuitive design is a seat adjuster invented many years ago by Mercedes-Benz (see photo at left). It's shaped like a tiny seat. Push any element of the control, and the real seat moves in that direction—back and forth, up and down. No instructions are necessary.

© Ron Kimball/Kimball Stock

FIGURE 27.7 Mercedes-Benz's seat adjuster

Good visual design can work the same way in an argument by conveying evidence, data, and other information without elaborate instructions. Titles, headings, subheadings, enlarged quotations, running heads, and boxes are some common visual signals:

- Use headings to guide your readers through your print or electronic document. For long and complex pieces, use subheadings as well, and make sure they are parallel.

- Use type font, size, and color to show related information among headings.

- Arrange headings or text on a page to enforce relationships among comparable items, ideas, or bits of evidence.

- Use a list or a box to set off material for emphasis or to show that it differs from the rest of the presentation. You can also use shading, color, and typography for emphasis.

- Place your images and illustrations strategically. What you position front and center will appear more important than items in less conspicuous places. Images of comparable size will be treated as equally important.

Remember, too, that design principles evolve and change from medium to medium. A printed text or presentation slide, for example, ordinarily works best when its elements are easy to read, simply organized, and surrounded by restful white space. But some electronic texts thrive on visual clutter, packing a grab bag of data into a limited space (See the "infographic of Infographics" on p. 449.) Look closely, though, and you'll probably find the logic in these designs.

Use Visuals to Convey Data Efficiently

Words are capable of great precision and subtlety, but some information is conveyed far more effectively by charts, graphs, drawings, maps, or photos—as several items in CHAPTER 23 illustrate. When making an argument, especially to a large group, consider what information might be more persuasive and memorable in nonverbal form.

A *pie chart* is an effective way of comparing parts to the whole. You might use a pie chart to illustrate the ethnic composition of your school, the percentage of taxes paid by people at different income levels, or the consumption of energy by different nations. Pie charts depict such information memorably.

A *graph* is an efficient device for comparing items over time or according to other variables. You could use a graph to trace the rise and fall of test scores over several decades, to show college enrollment by sex, race, and Hispanic origin, or to track bicycle usage in the United States, as in the bar graph on p. 449.

Diagrams or *drawings* are useful for attracting attention to details. Use drawings to illustrate complex physical processes or designs of all sorts. After the 2001 attack on the World Trade Center, for example, engineers prepared drawings and diagrams to help citizens understand precisely what led to the total collapse of the buildings.

You can use *maps* to illustrate location and spatial relationships—something as simple as the distribution of office space in your student union or as complex as poverty in the United States, as in the map on p. 450. In fact, scholars in many fields now use geographic information system (GIS) technology to merge maps with databases in all fields to offer new kinds of arguments about everything from traffic patterns and health care trends to character movements in literary works. Plotting data this way yields information far different from what might be offered in words alone. You can find more about GIS applications online.

Timelines allow you to represent the passage of time graphically, and online tools like Dipity can help you create them for insertion into your documents. Similarly, Web pages can make for valuable illustrations. Programs like ShrinkTheWeb let you create snapshots of Web sites that can then be inserted easily into your writing. And when you want to combine a variety of graphs, charts, and other texts into a single visual argument, you might create an *infographic* using software such as Google Public Data Explorer, Many Eyes, StatPlanet, and Wordle.

Follow Professional Guidelines for Presenting Visuals

Charts, graphs, tables, illustrations, timelines, snapshots of Web sites, and video clips play such an important role in many fields that professional groups have come up with guidelines for labeling and formatting these items. You need to become familiar with those conventions as you advance in a field. A guide such as the *Publication Manual of the American Psychological Association* (6th edition) or the *MLA Handbook for Writers of Research Papers* (7th edition) describes these rules in detail.

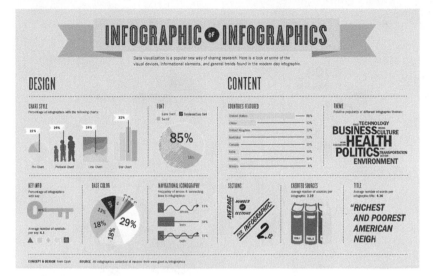

© Ivan Cash, CashStudios.com

FIGURE 27.8

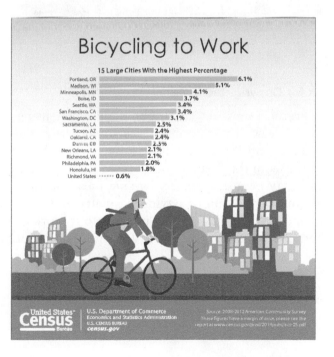

U.S. Census Bureau

FIGURE 27.9

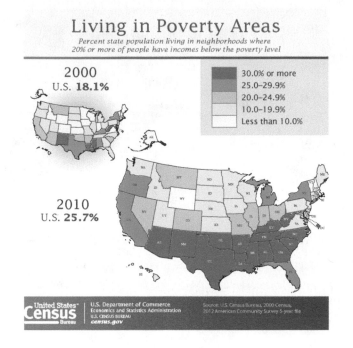

U.S. Census Bureau

FIGURE 27.10

Remember to Check for Copyrighted Material

You also must be careful to respect copyright rules when using visual items that were created by someone else. If you do introduce any borrowed items into academic work, be careful to document them fully. It's relatively easy these days to download visual texts of all kinds from the Web. Some of these items—such as clip art or government documents—may be in the *public domain*, meaning that you're free to use them without requesting permission or paying a royalty. But other visual texts may require permission, especially if you intend to publish your work or use the item commercially. Remember: anything you place on a Web site is considered "published."

Chapter 28

Communicating in Groups

- Understanding Groups
- Complexity of Group Communication
- Understanding Group Roles
- Group Climate

chapter outcomes

After you have finished reading this chapter, you will be able to

- List the characteristics and types of groups and explain how groups develop

- Describe ways in which group size, social relationships, and communication networks affect group communication

- Define the roles individuals play in a group

- Explain how a group's cohesion, norms, and individual differences affect group processes and outcomes

This chapter is taken from Dan O'Hair, Mary Wiemann, Dorothy Imric Mullin, and Jason Teven, *Real Communication*, Third Edition, pp. 242–270 (Chapter 9).

When a 7.0-magnitude earthquake devastated Haiti on January 10, 2010, Jacob Wood and William McNulty didn't just watch television in horror. They didn't just say a prayer or make donations to the Red Cross. Instead, they made some phone calls and a couple of Facebook posts, and within three days, they and a small team of fellow veterans were on the ground in Port-au-Prince. As Marine Corp veterans who had served in both Iraq and Afghanistan and who had volunteered in New Orleans after Hurricane Katrina, it was clear to Wood and McNulty that disasters and war zones had a lot in common: limited resources, collapsed infrastructure, a lack of information or communication, populations in chaos, and horrific sights and situations that can grind even the most earnest volunteer to a halt. It was also clear that the skills they honed during their deployments—medical triage, decisive leadership, the ability to quickly assess and respond to a situation, and focus intently on the task at hand—were invaluable, especially during the first few days after a disaster. The group refers to its role as "bridging the gap" between disasters and the arrival of conventional aid (Team Rubicon, 2014).

In the years since, Team Rubicon, the veteran's service/disaster response organization founded by Wood and McNulty, has provided intense, immediate relief in the aftermaths of floods, earthquakes, hurricanes, tornadoes, and other disasters around the world and around the United States. The organization consists of more than fourteen thousand members, most of them military veterans, who mobilize quickly and deploy to disaster-stricken areas and regions on a moment's notice (Team Rubicon, 2014). But in the process of providing relief, Wood and McNulty found yet another gap they needed to bridge. Returning veterans often find it difficult to adjust to civilian life, a reality that was brought into sharp relief when close friend and founding member of Team Rubicon, Clay Hunt, took his own life in March 2012. Once again proving that adaptability and focus are crucial to "bridging the gap," Team Rubicon adjusted its mission to include veteran's services, including suicide prevention, career training, and leadership opportunities.

When three or more people come together, their interactions and relationships—and their communication—take on new characteristics. As you can see in our discussion of Team Rubicon, groups can have a tremendous impact, both on individual members and on those with whom the groups interact. In this chapter, we'll learn more about group communication, how groups operate, and the factors that influence their communication.

■ Understanding Groups

Your family sitting down to dinner. A group of coworkers having a drink together at the end of a shift. Six exasperated parents sitting in a doctor's office with sick kids. Each of these examples involves multiple people engaged in some activity—and most of us would probably say that these are examples of "groups of people." But are they really groups? We'll explore what it actually means to be in a group, in addition to understanding what types of groups exist and how those groups develop in the first place.

Characteristics of Groups

We consider a collection of individuals a **group** when there are more than two people who share some kind of relationship, communicate in an interdependent fashion, and collaborate toward some shared purpose. When we break that definition down, we can identify three key characteristics:

- *A shared identity.* Members of a group perceive themselves as a group. That is, they share a sense of identity: they recognize other members of the group, have specific feelings toward those individuals, and experience a sense of belonging. People may identify themselves, for example, as members of the student council, a park cleanup crew, a baseball team, or a string quartet.

- *Common goals.* Members of a group usually identify with one another because they have one or more goals in common. Goals may be very specific—coming up with an ad campaign for a new project or organizing a fund-raiser for your soccer team—or they might be more general, such as socializing. In either case, a shared sense of purpose helps define a group, even when there is some disagreement about specific goals or ways of achieving them.

- *Interdependent relationships.* Members of a group are connected to one another and communicate in an interdependent way. Simply put, the behavior of each member affects the behavior of every other member. This interdependence is fostered by the way that group members adopt specific roles and collaborate to accomplish their goals.

Looking back at the examples at the beginning of this section, you can probably guess that your family or a group of coworkers constitutes a group. You share an identity with the other members and have feelings about them (for better or worse); you likely have common goals, and you are interdependent—that is, you rely on them, and they on you, for love, friendship, or professional accomplishments. This is not the case with the strangers in a pediatrician's office. They might share a goal (seeing the doctor), but they do not interact with each other interdependently, and they do not share an identity. Note that it is not the number of people involved or their location that determines whether people are communicating in groups. Four friends chatting over coffee at your local Starbucks constitute a group; so do twenty mothers who've never met but who contribute regularly to an online parenting forum. In both cases, the individuals are joined by shared goals, shared identity, and interdependence.

Tim Mosenfelder/Getty Images

FIGURE 28.1 Bandmates such as the members of Vampire Weekend must share a sense of identity, communicate interdependently, and collaborate to achieve their shared goal of creating music.

Types of Groups

Groups can take many forms. The most common among them are called **primary groups**—long-lasting groups that form around the relationships that mean the most to their members. Your family constitutes one primary group to which you belong; your friends are another.

In addition to primary groups, there are groups defined by their specific functions (for instance, support groups, study groups, and social groups). However, any one of these groups can perform multiple functions. Alcoholics Anonymous (AA), for example, is primarily a **support group**—a set of individuals who come together to address personal problems while benefiting from the support of others with similar issues. But AA is also a **social group**, as membership in the group offers opportunities to form relationships with others. And finally, as a group with a specific mission—to help members manage their struggles with alcohol and addiction—AA is also a **problem-solving group**.

Although all groups are to some degree social, some groups are more task-oriented than others. **Study groups,** for example, are formed for the specific purpose of helping students prepare for exams. Perhaps the most task-oriented and goal-driven type of group is the **team**—a group that works together to carry out a project or to compete against other teams. Sports teams are an obvious example, but teams are also common in large organizations or as subsets of other groups: an Army unit might select a few members to form a reconnaissance team; a community group might nominate a team of individuals to take charge of its annual fund-raiser.

> AND YOU?
> Think about your family as a group. What are the family's common goals? What do the members of your family see as the family's defining traits? How can a change in behavior by one family member affect other members?

One of the more noteworthy and common types of teams in today's organizations is the **self-directed work team** (**SDWT**), a group of skilled workers who take responsibility themselves for producing high-quality finished work (Colvin, 2012; Douglas, 2002). In self-directed work teams, members control their own management functions, such as arranging their schedules, buying equipment, and setting standards for productivity, quality, and costs. They also conduct their own peer evaluations and coordinate their future plans with management. Their complementary skills and experiences enable the team to accomplish more together than any individual member could achieve independently (Katzenbach & Smith, 1993).

WIRED FOR COMMUNICATION

Smart Mobs: What Flash Mobs and Political Protests Have in Common

In 2014, more than four thousand straphangers in New York City—and countless others in twenty-five countries around the world—boarded mass-transit trains in their boxers, briefs, or bloomers for a coordinated "no pants subway ride" (Improv Everywhere, 2014). A seemingly spontaneous dance performance also erupted in 2014 among passengers at a train station in Shanghai—it was to celebrate the Chinese new year and renew interest in Chinese folk traditions. In 2011, Occupy Wall Street demonstrators converged on New York's Zuccotti Park to protest economic policies that they felt were deepening the divide between rich and poor.

What do these stories have in common? They're all examples of smart mobs: large groups of individuals who act in concert, even though they don't know each other, and who connect and cooperate with one another, at least initially, via electronically mediated means (Rheingold, 2002). But smart mobs have two important additional characteristics that a generic social network lacks: a shared goal and a finite time frame (Harmon & Metaxas, 2010). Like all electronic social networks, smart mobs are grounded in a shared desire for communication and rely on affordable devices that offer instantaneous communication. Simply communicating is not enough to make a smart mob—there must be a tangible goal that is organized via mediated communication and achieved quickly and effectively.

There's a difference, of course, between a social movement and an absurd, pants-free subway ride. The latter is what has come to be called a flash mob—a form of smart mob in which people come together for a brief public act that may seem pointless or ridiculous. Even if the goal, often entertainment or artistic expression, seems not-so-smart, flash mobs are still smart mobs: through technology the participants are organized and quickly mobilized to carry out their collective act. Political protests, on the other hand, are largely comprised of activists who may already be connected and organized but use technology—including smart mob demonstrations—as tools for making their political or social goals more visible (Conover et al., 2013). In fact, the term *smart mob* was first identified in 2001, when calls for protest in the Philippines spread via text message, gathering more than a million people to a nonviolent demonstration in Manila within four days. Largely hailed as the world's first "e-revolution," the Manila protests quickly and peacefully brought about the resignation of President Joseph Estrada.

In the years since, social media–fueled revolutions in Tunisia, Egypt, and other Middle Eastern nations—sometimes referred to as "Twitter Revolutions" by media pundits—have bolstered the notion that electronic communications are somehow responsible for modern social movements. This is, most likely, an oversimplification: social movements are usually the culmination of frustrations that have been building for many years, which come to a pinnacle when activists begin to organize. Malcom Gladwell points out that one of the most dramatic political demonstrations in American history started with just four African American college students asking for service at a "whites only" lunch counter in Greensboro, North Carolina, on February 1, 1960; within a month, the sit-ins had spread throughout the South—all without a single text or tweet (Gladwell, 2010). But, even then, the existing media played an important role: newspaper photos of those first four students printed in the Greensboro *Record* inspired others to join them.

Think About This

1. Many social movements benefit from social networks, but is it fair to credit electronic communication with bringing about social change? How did groups like the American civil rights movem ent organize demonstrations? If these groups relied on technology, does that make them smart mobs?

2. In an effort to quell uprisings in Egypt in 2011, the Egyptian government blocked citizens' access to the Internet, yet protests continued. What does this say about the pervasive nature of electronic communication? What does it say about the role of electronic communication in causing and fueling action?

3. What is the social value of a flash mob? Is it just something fun that technology makes possible, or might there be important effects for the participants or the audiences?

4. Is a smart mob really a group, as defined in this chapter? If not, what is it?

Perhaps the most dramatic impact of self-directed teams is the improved performance and cooperation of employees throughout the organization. Organizations are shifting their structural power and decision making from upper levels to lower levels of management in efforts to implement change and growth and empower employees (Douglas, Martin, & Krapels, 2006). Federal Express and Minnesota-based 3M are among an increasing number of companies that involve employees through work teams. (See Table 28.1 for tips on working in a self-directed work team.).

(top left) David Furst/AFP/Getty Images; (top right) © 20th Century Fox Film Corp. All rights reserved. Courtesy Everett Collection; (bottom left) AP Photo/Vail Daily, Shane Macomber; (bottom right) ABC/Photofest

FIGURE 28.2 Groups come in all shapes and sizes. Although the design team from *Extreme Makeover: Home Edition* and a hip-hop dance crew might vary in size and purpose, both are considered groups.

AND YOU?

In your first job out of college, do you think you would prefer to work as part of a self-directed work team or in a more traditionally arranged team where a manager takes control? What would be the advantages of each?

Models of Group Development

If you've ever become wrapped up in a reality TV show such as *Survivor*, *The Biggest Loser*, or *The Amazing Race*, you know how fascinating and dramatic group interactions can be. In each of these shows, a season typically opens with the forming of a group: cast members start off as strangers but are quickly thrust into a group situation—sharing a living space and working together to accomplish certain tasks. As the season progresses, the group members bond, conflicts erupt, and alliances are forged. In fact, much of the drama in reality television stems from the tensions that arise between cast members as they struggle to work with—or against—one another (and, of course, editing can heighten the drama even more). Research shows that as a group progresses, it goes through several specific stages. Let's look at two different research perspectives on the stages of group development.

Table 28.1 Self-Directed Work Teams: Tips for Working Collaboratively

ACTION	CONSIDERATIONS
Define a clear purpose for the team	What are the team's goals—short term *and* long term?
Foster team spirit	Build a sense of energy, excitement, and commitment in your team by engaging in team-building activities and events, rewarding members who demonstrate commitment, and identifying new challenges for the team to take on.
Train	Working on a self-directed team may be a new experience for some members. See if your organization can provide training to help members understand and implement the defining practices of self-directed teams.
Clarify expectations	Make sure all members of the team understand what's expected of them in terms of their roles and performance. For example, what functions will each member serve? How, specifically, will the team define "success"?
Set boundaries	Articulate where the team's responsibilities begin and end. If necessary, remind members that they are working in the service of the organization and that they need to stay focused on their specific purpose.

Sources: Capozzoli (2002); Nelson (2002); Rosenthal (2001).

CONNECT

Developing a relationship with a group isn't so different from starting a new interpersonal relationship. In both contexts, we reduce uncertainty about our relational partners so that we feel secure and confident about roles, interactions, and so on.

Tuckman's Model of Group Development

Tuckman's model states that as groups develop, they progress through five stages: forming, storming, norming, performing, and adjourning. The model proposes that these stages are linear—that is, groups go through them in order over time. Although the model was originally proposed for face-to-face groups, recent research has also applied these stages to how "virtual" teams develop online (Johnson, Suriya, Yoon, Berrett, & Fleur, 2002). Let's look more closely at each particular stage:

- *Forming.* When a group first comes together, its members are unsure how to act around one another, nervous about how others perceive them, and unclear on their roles and the group's task. In this **forming** stage, group members try to figure out who will be in charge and what the group's goals will be. The primary purpose of this stage is for group members to learn more about one another and the group's objectives. Once individuals feel accepted, they can begin to identify with the group (Moreland & Levine, 1994).

- *Storming.* After forming, group members move into the **storming** stage, in which they inevitably begin experiencing conflicts over issues such as who will lead the group and what roles members will play. Group members also begin to disagree on goals, tasks, and cliques, and other competitive divisions may even begin to form (Wheelan, 2012; Wheelan & Burchill, 1999). The group members must work on mending these differences and resolve conflicts if the group is to continue to function effectively.

- *Norming.* During the **norming** stage, group members move beyond their conflicts, and norms emerge among members that govern expected behavior. **Norms** are recurring patterns of behavior or thinking that come to be accepted in a group as the "usual" way of doing things (Scheerhorn & Geist, 1997). During this stage, group roles also solidify based on individual member strengths, and a leader may emerge. In addition, group identity grows stronger as members realize the importance of their roles within the group and the need to cooperate to accomplish goals.

- *Performing.* Once the group has established norms, the action shifts to accomplishing their tasks. During the **performing** stage, members combine their skills and knowledge to work toward the group's goals and overcome hurdles. This stage is characterized by high levels of interdependence, motivation, and clarity in delegation of team member tasks.

- *Adjourning.* Many groups—though clearly not all—eventually disband. For groups whose project or task has come to an end, there is an **adjourning** stage (Tuckman & Jensen, 1977). The group members reflect on their accomplishments and failures as well as determine whether the group will disassemble or take on another project. Some groups choose to celebrate their achievements with a final get-together, what Keyton (1993) calls a **termination ritual**. Members may also opt to maintain friendships even if they will no longer be working together.

AND YOU?
Think about your experience as part of a group to which you no longer belong—an old job, your high school class, or a club that you're not a part of anymore. Did the group go through all five phases described here?

Gersick's Punctuated Equilibrium Model

Although Tuckman's model represents a linear view of group development, other scholars have argued that groups do not necessarily follow sequential "stages" of development. Gersick (1988), for example, argues instead that groups progress in a **punctuated equilibrium** process. This means that groups experience a period of inertia or inactivity until they become aware of time, pressure, and looming deadlines, which then compel group members to take action.

As a student, a pattern of procrastination followed by bursts of activity may sound familiar to you. Research confirms that it is common to procrastinate on class assignments, especially when working in groups when there is a perceived diffusion or share of responsibilities (Karau & Williams, 2001). Gersick (1988) suggests that groups often procrastinate (and, in reality, waste time) until the critical halfway point of a project. Then, when they hit this midpoint transition and realize that their original plan isn't coming together, they focus their energy on completing the project and mobilizing their efforts. Gersick argues that groups go through this in a cyclical fashion, with long periods of inactivity followed by spurts of intense activity and change (Chidambaram & Bostrom, 1996), and that this pattern almost becomes a habit or routine (Gersick & Hackman, 1990).

FIGURE 28.3 Bill and Ted procrastinate until they need the help of a time machine to finish their report in cult classic *Bill and Ted's Excellent Adventure*.

We should point out, however, that not all groups experience the critical transition that gets them to mobilize and adapt their behavior successfully (Okhuysen & Eisenhardt, 2002; Okhuysen & Waller, 2002). Thus, it might be wise from the beginning of a group project to take note of the inactivity or procrastination your group is experiencing so that you can help spur action earlier and avoid a stressful rush or failure to finish the project by the deadline.

REAL COMMUNICATOR

NAME: Jack MacKenzie

OCCUPATION: Media Research Professional

As executive vice president of a national media research consulting firm, I know the importance of understanding group dynamics. Our office is made up of teams that work together to provide valuable information about marketing and design for a diverse client base. These clients include broadcast networks, cable channels, Internet start-ups, and video game producers, as well as product providers of everything from apple juice to mobile phone features.

Our research is conducted by two teams of highly qualified people. The quantitative team crunches the data and the qualitative team focuses on the majority of the in-person interaction with consumers (meaning interviews and focus groups). These groups work together as an even larger team to generate the feedback we give clients. Obviously, it is important that they work together smoothly.

Our teams are mainly self-directed, meaning that they take the responsibility for producing high-quality work without a lot of supervision. My part in encouraging this outcome is to hire independent, efficient, and responsible employees. If I'm successful in picking the right candidates, then I don't need to step in and supervise too closely. Some of the skills I would say are most important for self-directed work teams are flexibility, ability to process and analyze information, mindfulness of fair treatment of others, and a sense of what responses are appropriate in any given situation.

Another important aspect of self-directed teams is that teammates are able to figure out their roles and arrange their workflow based on work style and intellectual or emotional compatibility. As team members work together, they negotiate responsibilities, demonstrate their strengths, and rely on one another to get the job done in the most efficient way possible. If you've ever worked in groups at school, work, or in your community, you may have experienced some frustrating behavior: group members not listening, hogging the floor, or not doing their share of the work. I remind my teams that a lot of people pay more attention to what comes out of their mouths than what comes into their ears and that they should be doing the opposite. *Listening* is what makes a good consultant—and a good team member.

Research consulting is a fast-paced business that requires the ability to listen, acquire information, and share that information with clients—all within a team setting. One of the most rewarding parts of my job is hearing that a client has found one of our teams so helpful that the client has requested to work with the same group for further research and analysis. When this happens, I know the team has functioned very well.

I've studied generational groups at length: Millennials, GenXers, Baby Boomers, and the emerging Pluralist Generation. I enjoy opening the eyes of our clients to seeing the world through a generational lens—how to understand generational transition and how it affects program development and revenue streams. On a personal note, the results of this research are comforting to me. I have confidence in the young adults who are going to lead us in the future; I understand where they are coming from and where they will lead us. Perhaps because of this, society makes more sense to me than it does to other people.

My job does not get old. Conducting research on human behavior and attitudes necessarily means the information is changing every day. Sharing that information with our clients and helping them make smart business decisions with our information is very rewarding.

■ Complexity of Group Communication

When you chat with an instructor in her office, you probably speak freely and informally. The two of you may exchange questions and comments rapidly, interrupt one another, and prompt each other for more information. But when you sit with that same professor in a classroom full of other students, the nature of your communication changes; you might be expected to raise your hand, defer to other students who are already speaking, or not ask questions at all.

What has changed? Why is the nature of your communication so different in the classroom from the way you converse in her office? In this section, we'll take a look at how complex group communication can be, depending on the number of individuals involved, their relationships, and their patterns of interaction.

> AND YOU?
> When you work independently, do you work in a linear fashion or does your pattern of activity resemble the punctuated equilibrium model? Does that behavior change when you work in a group?

Size and Complexity of Groups

Dyadic communication refers to interactions between just two people (a dyad). When a third person joins the interaction, the dyad becomes a small group. Scholars generally agree that small group communication involves at least three members (Bormann, 1990), with a maximum of fifteen to twenty-five members (Sosha, 1997). Some communication scholars argue that in order to effectively perform tasks within classrooms or work projects, five to seven members may be optimum (Cragan, Wright, & Kasch, 2008). The basic logistics of communication—the need to take turns speaking and listening, for example—grow more complex the larger a group gets, creating the need for more structured exchanges among members.

(left) © Bob Mahoney/The Image Works; (right) AP Photo/Damian Dovarganes

FIGURE 28.4 When you're chatting with a professor during office hours, you are the focus of your professor's attention. However, in the classroom, you have to respect that other students want to speak as well!

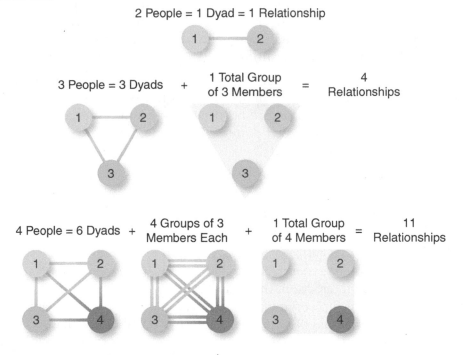

FIGURE 28.5 Complexity of Group Relationships
Each time a person is added to a group, the number of relationships increases substantially.

Specifically, the bigger the group, the more its communication takes on the following characteristics:

- *Interaction is more formal.* Group communication simply cannot work in the same kind of informal way that dyadic communication occurs, due to the need to include more communicators in the discourse. Individuals participating in a group may feel the need to obtain permission to speak, and they may also be reluctant to interrupt a speaker.

- *Each member has limited opportunities to contribute.* Participants may want or be required by a leader to share "floor time" with other group members. Such time constraints can inhibit the quality and quantity of their contributions. Even without a formal leader, in larger groups a few members tend to dominate much of the talk, while the less assertive members tend to remain quiet.

- *The communication becomes less intimate.* The greater the number of participants is, the less comfortable participants feel self-disclosing or voicing controversial opinions.

- *The interaction consumes more time.* As more participants are invited to contribute or debate, and there are more opinions possible, the interaction takes longer to complete.

- *Relationships become more complex.* As more participants are added, the relationships become more complex. In the dyad, of course, there is only one relationship—that between person 1 and person 2. But as shown in FIGURE 28.4, add another person, and you now have four potential relationships—between persons 1 and 2, 1 and 3, 2 and 3, and all three together. The number of relationships multiplies further with each additional participant!

The Formation of Cliques

In the comedy series *The Big Bang Theory*, geniuses Leonard and Sheldon are roommates and close friends. Sheldon, the quirky theoretical physicist, is extremely socially awkward and rarely takes kindly to new people or situations. Inevitably, when Leonard starts dating their neighbor, Penny, Sheldon has a difficult time adapting to his friend's new time commitments. In fact, he even winds up trying to trail along on Leonard and Penny's dates and frequently interrupts them when they wish to enjoy time alone. Even if you've never behaved quite like Sheldon, perhaps you've felt like he does—you love hanging out with your best friend, but whenever her boyfriend is around, you feel like you might as well be invisible. That's because your presence has changed the nature of the communication from dyadic to group communication, but the other two people haven't adjusted their communication behavior. They've remained a dyad that leaves you the lone outsider.

CONNECT

We define ourselves by our group memberships, with a tendency toward favoring our *ingroup* members and comparing ourselves to (and sometimes excluding) *outgroup* members. Although it may be a natural tendency to form cliques with those who share our affiliations, competent communicators must remember to be inclusive of various groups and co-cultures—particularly in team and organizational settings.

As a group's size increases, small subgroups of individuals often begin to bond together within the group, forming **cliques** (or coalitions) (Wilmot, 1987). Cliques are a common part of group life—they're a fixture in middle school and high school. You have your marching band kids, your football players, the art students, and so on. Many people think that they will escape cliques once high school ends, but this is rarely the case. In college, you might form cliques with others in your major, your dorm, or a particular organization. In office settings, members of cliques or coalitions typically sit next to each other in meetings, eat lunch together, share similar opinions, and support one another's positions.

When cliques take shape in a group, communication becomes more challenging because members are no longer dealing only with other individual members. Rather, they must navigate relationships and figure out how to communicate with entire subgroups. In addition, **countercoalitions**, in which one subgroup positions itself against another on an issue, can leave anyone who isn't affiliated with a subgroup in a very awkward position.

This tendency for members of groups to organize themselves into coalitions or cliques can have consequences for those who find themselves left out. **Social ostracism** is the exclusion of a particular group member (or members)—for example, when one clique or coalition limits the amount of information they share with a particular member and exclude him or her from group activities and the decision-making process (Kameda, Ohtsubo, & Takezawa, 1997). Ostracism can also occur in virtual groups, such as online work teams or Facebook friendship networks. In online environments, exclusion may occur through more subtle signals, such as reduced message frequency or an overall lack of responsive communication (Cramton, 1997; Williams, Govan, Croker, Tynan, Cruickshank, & Lam, 2002).

MONTY BRINTON/CBS/Landov

FIGURE 28.6 Stuart from *The Big Bang Theory* wants to be part of the gang, but often ends up feeling ostracized.

Rejection by one's peers can lead to anxiety, anger, and sadness, as targets of ostracism feel a decrease in belonging, control, and self-esteem (Williams, 2001; Wittenbaum, Shulman, & Braz, 2010). However, responses to social ostracism vary. Research on gender differences (Williams & Sommer, 1997), for example, has found that females who are ostracized are more likely to compensate, that is, work harder to be part of the group. Males, on the other hand, tend to engage in a practice called **social loafing**, which we discuss next.

AND YOU?

If you've ever been bullied or witnessed bullying, you know that social ostracism can be a powerful—and hurtful—force. But is excluding someone from communication always aggressive or malevolent? Consider situations in which you may have excluded a group member from communication, either in person or online. What were your motives, and how did it affect communication in the group?

Social Loafing

On many education and learning blogs, you can find students and instructors complaining about one of the most dreaded assignments of all time: the group project. At first glance, doesn't it seem that group projects should be easier than working solo? There are more minds with whom to try out ideas and share in the work. But what we all dread is having group members who don't pull their own weight. The fact is, in a group, people may become prone to social loafing—failing to invest the same level of effort in the group that they'd put in if they were working alone or with one other person (Karau & Williams, 1993). In almost every group situation, from your high school yearbook committee to cut-throat competitions like *Survivor*, there are always a few individuals who manage to make it through to the end simply by keeping their heads low and letting their teammates do most of the work. Clearly, social loafing affects both participation and communication in groups (Comer, 1998; Shultz, 1999).

Despite the negative connotation of the word *loafing*, it's not always due to laziness. When a person fails to speak up because he or she feels shy around a lot of people, the person is engaging in social loafing. Social loafing also results from the feelings of anonymity that can occur in larger groups, where it is more difficult for an individual member's contributions to be evaluated. Thus a member may put in less effort, believing that nobody will notice that he or she is slacking or, conversely, that he or she is working hard. If group members perceive an inequality in individual effort, conflict can and often does emerge, harming team morale. Social loafing even occurs in online groups and teams (Piezon & Ferree, 2008): members of an online discussion group, for example, may post messages or photos that are unrelated to the group's topic or they may not respond at all to a request for everyone's opinion on an idea.

Scholars argue that there are several practices that can help to manage your group's productivity and prevent or reduce social loafing (Cox & Brobrowski, 2000; Latane, Williams, & Harkins, 1979; Van Dick, Tissington, & Hertel, 2009):

- *Establish objectives and performance goals.* Make the schedule clear to all team members so everyone is aware of deadlines. Clarify what each member's individual responsibility is. You may even consider putting everything in writing, akin to a contract, so that there's no confusion about who should be taking care of what.

- *Establish individual accountability.* At the beginning of a project, be sure that all team members understand that they are expected to carry out their duties responsibly. This will establish the importance of each person's future performance. Also discuss how members will be evaluated and the consequences of social loafing or poor performance (Cox & Brobrowski, 2000).

- *Encourage team identity and ownership.* Early on in the process, promote team unity by coming up with a group name or symbol. Take the time to get to know each other and build social bonds and trust. This will help foster more team loyalty. Encourage team members to take pride and ownership in their work—which will also promote dedication to the cause.

- *Stay in contact.* If a miscommunication occurs between members, be sure to discuss it right away. Ambiguity and confusion will only encourage members to become less connected with the group and more likely to engage in social loafing.

AND YOU?

Have you ever been excessively quiet or shy in a group? Do you consider this behavior social loafing or do you feel that the situational or relational context is primarily to blame? Why?

■ What About You?

Are You a "Social Loafer"?

Do you exert less effort on a task when participating in a group than you would if you were performing it alone? If so, you may be a social loafer. A major complaint about group work involves dealing with free-riding behavior: resentment about group members who don't do their fair share or who even undermine the overall group goal. With your last group experience in mind, use the following five-point scale to determine if you were a social loafer: 5 = extremely like me; 4 = somewhat like me; 3 = neither like nor unlike me; 2 = somewhat unlike me; and 1 = extremely unlike me.

	1. I arrived on time for group meetings and stayed until the end.
	2. I showed enthusiasm about group activities.
	3. I showed a positive attitude toward fellow group members.
	4. I participated in planning the project/activity.
	5. I volunteered for tasks appropriate to my expertise.
	6. I contributed regularly to group discussion.
	7. I put forth effort equal to or greater than that of my group members.
	8. I delivered my contributions in a complete fashion.
	9. My fellow group members perceived me as agreeable.
	10. My fellow group members perceived me as thorough.
	11. My fellow group members perceived me as dependable.
	12. My fellow group members perceived me as conscientious.
	13. I met all deadlines.
	14. I asked for help from others when needed.
	15. I supported the contributions of other group members.
	16. I was open to suggestions from others.
	17. I gave credit to others for their suggestions and contributions.
	18. I made positive adaptations to the differences of group members.
	19. I tried my absolute best.
	20. I shared credit/blame for the outcome of our group.
	Add your scores together to get an informal assessment of social loafing.

74–100: You are NOT a social loafer. You carry your weight in a group and reinforce the contributions of others. People value you and your contributions.

47–73: You may be a social loafer in certain group situations. With your last group experience, you were probably frustrated but not sure how to make it better. In the future, be sure you are communicating support and involvement, and show respect for others so that each person feels that he or she has a useful role to play.

20–46: Social loafer! In group situations, people are likely to see you as apathetic and may even resent you. Whenever you join a group in the future, you should work harder to do your fair share and show support for all your group members.

Source: Adapted from Maiden & Perry (2011).

Group Networks

Just as a group's size and social relationships influence the complexity of communication within the group, so do networks. **Networks** are patterns of interaction governing who speaks with whom in a group and about what. To understand the nature of networks, you must first consider two main positions within them. The first is *centrality*, or the degree to which an individual sends and receives messages from others in the group. The most central person in the group receives and sends the highest number of messages in a given time period. At the other end of the spectrum is *isolation*—a position from which a group member sends and receives fewer messages than other members.

A team leader or manager typically has the highest level of centrality in a formal group, but centrality is not necessarily related to status or power. The CEO of a company, for example, may be the end recipient of all information generated by teams below her, but in fact only a limited number of individuals within the organization are able to communicate directly with her. Her assistant, in fact, may have a higher degree of centrality in the network, because she must interact with so many people in the organization. As you might imagine, networks play a powerful role in any group's communication, whether the group is a family, a sports team, a civic organization, or a large corporation.

In some groups, all members speak with all others regularly about a wide range of topics. In others, perhaps only a few members are "allowed" to speak directly with the group's leader or longest-standing member about serious issues. In still other groups, some members may work alongside one another without communicating at all. There are several types of networks, including chain networks, all-channel networks, and wheel networks (see **FIGURE 28.7**) (Bavelous, 1950).

AND YOU?

What group are you spending most of your time in these days? What type of communication network exists in the group? Is that network helping the group achieve its goals? If not, what changes might the group make to operate more effectively?

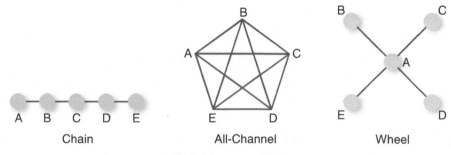

Chain   All-Channel   Wheel

Source: Adapted with permission from Scott (1981, p. 8).

FIGURE 28.7 Group Communication Networks

Chain Networks

In a **chain network,** information is passed from one member to the next in a sequential pattern. Such networks can be practical for sharing written information: an e-mail, forwarded from person to person along a chain, for example, allows each person to read the original information from other prior recipients. But this form of group communication can lead to frustration and miscommunication when information is spoken, as the messages can easily get distorted as they are passed along. Person A tells person B that their boss, Luis, had a fender bender on the way to work and will miss the 10:00 A.M. meeting. Person B tells person C that Luis was in an accident and will not be in the office today. Person C tells person D that Luis was injured in an accident; no one knows when he'll be in. You can imagine that Luis will be in a full-body cast by the time the message reaches person G!

All-Channel Networks

In an **all-channel network,** all members interact with each other equally. When people talk about roundtable discussions, they're talking about all-channel groups: there is no leader, and all members operate at the same level of centrality. Such networks can be useful for collaborative projects and for brainstorming ideas, but the lack of order can make it difficult for such groups to complete tasks efficiently. Imagine, for example, that you're trying to arrange to meet up with a group of friends. You send out a mass e-mail to all of them, to determine days that will work, and you ask for suggestions about where to meet. The recipients each hit "reply all" and share their responses with the whole group. By using an all-channel network, the entire group may learn that Friday is not good for anyone, but Saturday is. However, only a few people have suggested favorite spots, and there's no consensus on where to go. That's where wheel networks come in.

Wheel Networks

Wheel networks are a sensible alternative for situations in which individual members' activities and contributions must be culled and tracked in order to avoid duplicating efforts and to ensure that all tasks are being completed. In a **wheel network,** one individual acts as a touchstone for all the others in the group; all group members share their information with that one individual, who then shares the information with the rest of the group. Consider the preceding example: as the sender of the initial e-mail, you might take on a leadership role and ask everyone just to reply to you. Then you could follow up with a decision about time and place to meet and send that out to everyone else. Wheel networks have the lowest shared centrality but are very efficient (Leavitt, 1951).

AP Photo/Herbert Knosowski

FIGURE 28.8 The copyediting team in a newsroom works as a wheel network. All of the copy editors report to one copy chief, who regulates the copyediting style.

■ Understanding Group Roles

When we communicate in groups, we tend to fall into particular roles, much like playing different parts in a play. These roles influence the process and outcomes of group interaction. Let's look closely at three types of roles—task, social, and antigroup.

Task Roles

In some cases, a role is defined by a task that needs doing, and a person is asked or appointed to fill it (or he or she volunteers). Such **task roles** are concerned with the accomplishment of the group's goals—specifically, the activities that need to be carried out for the group to achieve its objectives. For example, your role on a committee charged with organizing a campus Zumba party might be to post advertisements for the event in key locations around campus, in the student newspaper, and on the university Web site.

Task roles can also be specifically related to the group's communication; for instance:

- An *information giver* offers facts, beliefs, personal experience, or other input during group discussions ("When the College Republicans posted their ad in the student lounge, they had good attendance at their event").

- An *information seeker* asks for input or clarification of ideas or opinions that members have presented ("Jeff, are you saying you don't think we would get good attendance on a Thursday night?").

- An *elaborator* provides further clarification of points, often adding to what others have said ("I agree with Ellie about getting Spike to DJ the event—he has a huge following in town").

- An *initiator* helps the group move toward its objective by proposing solutions, presenting new ideas, or suggesting new ways of looking at an issue the group is discussing ("How essential is it that we schedule our event for the last Thursday of the month? If we moved it a week later, we wouldn't have to compete with the Homecoming festivities").

- An *administrator* keeps the conversation on track ("OK, let's get back to the subject of when to schedule the event") and ensures that meetings begin and end on time ("We've got five minutes left; should we wind up?"). This role appears in online groups, too, where forum administrators (also known as moderators or masters) coordinate and sometimes screen the members' comments.

Social Roles

Some roles evolve to manage how people in the group are feeling and getting along with each other; such roles are called **social roles**. For example, in a college dormitory, one student might unofficially fill the role of "hall parent"—mentoring freshmen, listening compassionately to people's problems, and making everyone feel secure. Consider these additional examples of social roles (Anderson, Riddle, & Martin, 1999; Benne & Sheats, 1948; Salazar, 1996):

- A *harmonizer* seeks to smooth over tension in the group by settling differences among members and working out compromises when conflict arises ("There is only one communal TV lounge per floor, so can we plan on reserving the first-floor lounge for people who want to watch the football game on Sunday, and leaving the second floor free for people who want to watch the Golden Globe Awards?").

- A *gatekeeper* works to ensure that each member of the group gets a chance to voice their opinions or otherwise contribute to discussions. ("Tonya, we haven't heard from you yet on the issue of overnight guests in our dorm. What are your thoughts?").

- A *sensor* expresses group feelings, moods, or relationships in an effort to recognize the climate and capitalize on it or modify it for the better ("I feel like tempers are getting a little short right now—maybe we ought to break for dinner, and meet back here in an hour to continue this discussion when we're all feeling less hungry?").

Each member in a group can play task and social roles, and the roles can be official or unofficial. For example, Evelyn is the dorm's resident advisor, officially tasked with maintaining harmony among the students who live there. But Mike is also an unofficial harmonizer because he has a knack for mitigating tensions between people. Mike also has a lot of ideas for events, so he frequently finds himself acting as an initiator during meetings. Members like Mike can move into or out of such personal or task roles depending on whether the role is needed and whether others in the group are willing to fill it.

Antigroup Roles

Unlike task and social roles, **antigroup roles** create problems because they serve individual members' priorities at the expense of group needs. You've probably seen evidence of these antigroup roles in the groups you belong to:

- A *blocker* indulges in destructive communication, including opposing or criticizing all ideas and stubbornly reintroducing an idea after the group has already rejected or bypassed it ("None of the dates any of you proposed will work for the party. It really needs to be five weeks from today, as I said earlier").

- An *avoider* refuses to engage in the group's proceedings by expressing cynicism or nonchalance toward ideas presented or by joking or changing the subject ("Well, whatever, I'm guessing it's not a big deal if this party doesn't even happen, right?").

- A *recognition seeker* calls attention to himself or herself by boasting or by going on and on about his or her qualifications or personal achievements ("I planned a gathering for a women's studies group last year, and it went really well. People still talk about it! So trust me on this one").

- A *distractor* goes off on tangents or tells irrelevant stories ("Does anyone know what happened on *Game of Thrones* last night? I missed it").

These antigroup roles are not limited to face-to-face group communication—you've no doubt run into a few distractors, blockers, or recognition seekers in online forums. Online groups are also often disrupted by *trolls*—individuals who intentionally insert irrelevant and inflammatory comments into the discussion in order to stir up controversy.

Antigroup roles obviously add to the dysfunction of a group (Wilson & Hanna, 1993). For instance, a *blocker* who acts superior to other team members and criticizes the members' ideas may harm group morale and productivity. To mitigate the impact of these antigroup roles, members can revisit the norms the group has established and make the changes needed to improve group communication (for example, "All ideas get a fair hearing"). People fulfilling certain task or social roles can also help. For instance, if you're a gatekeeper, you can prompt an avoider to contribute her opinion on a proposal that the group has been considering. Research also indicates that positive and proactive responses to avoiders and blockers can help establish individuals as leaders in their organizations (Garner & Poole, 2009).

Role Conflict

Imagine that you work at a local retail store and you've been promoted to store manager. As part of your new role, you will have to manage staff members who are working as individual contributors at the store. In this new role, you'll be managing several close friends who you used to work alongside as regular staff. That's where things might get complicated: as manager, you'll have to evaluate staff members' performance, and how can you give a good friend a poor performance review and still remain friends?

Role conflict arises in a group whenever expectations for a member's behavior are incompatible (Baxter & Montgomery, 1996). Role conflict can make group communication profoundly challenging. For the manager who must evaluate a friend—especially a friend whose performance could be better—there is rarely a perfect option. You might give candid constructive feedback to your friend on his performance while trying to constrain the damage to your friendship by saying something like "I hope you know I'm offering this feedback as a way to help you improve. As your friend and manager, I want to see you do well here." A less ethical approach, of course, would be to defer to your friend's feelings instead of to your responsibility as manager—essentially, to spare his feelings by giving him a better review than he deserves.

> ### AND YOU?
> Have you ever been in a leadership role in a group of friends? Have you ever been subordinate to a friend in a group situation? Did any conflict arise and, if so, how did you resolve it?

Status

Groups also form around—or are defined by—status. Status is like a social currency, unequally distributed within groups, which gives some members more power than others. In some groups, status is formally defined by a clear hierarchy: the military, for example, operates on a hierarchy of leadership with officers outranking enlisted troops. But status is also informally conferred: a charismatic or especially competent military recruit may emerge as a leader and gain status among her peers even if she does not outrank them. That kind of perceived status—based not in any kind of formal rules but instead on peoples' perceptions of one another—can be potent.

A number of factors have been shown to increase perceptions of status. For example, status can be gained through having access to material resources or information that other group members do not have (Poole & Hollingshead, 2005). Similarly, physical attractiveness has been known to enhance a group member's status (Webster & Driskell, 1978, 1983). Gender may play a role, too, as males have traditionally had higher status and participation rates and greater access to resources and information than females (Carli, 1999; Ellyson, Dovidio, & Brown; Smith-Lovin, Skvortz, & Hudson, 1986). Of course, as mentioned in the foregoing military example, people can also *earn* status through their own competence or communicative effectiveness as they participate in the group.

Within groups, those with higher status are given more opportunities to make contributions toward completing the task, their suggestions are often evaluated more positively, and they exert greater influence over lower-status members (Berger, Wagner, & Zelditch, 1985). Perceptions of higher status can lead to those group members having greater influence even if they don't have any formal power. The "popular kids" at a high school, for example, may have more influence on school events than the elected student council. All of these vagaries are at play in the popular British period drama *Downton Abbey*, which depicts the goings-on at a stately manor house in the early twentieth century. The Granthams, the aristocratic family that lives in the home, have a high status conferred on them not only by wealth but also by noble title. Within the family, the men are afforded more status than the women, who cannot inherit the estate and are limited in their ability to make decisions. Status also separates the family from the "downstairs" staff, who lack fortune or title, but who consider their status superior to those who work in factories or on the local farms.

Joss Barratt/©PBS/Courtesy Everett Collection

FIGURE 28.9 When chauffeur Tom marries the youngest Grantham daughter, both family and staff struggle to figure out where he fits into the hierarchy of the estate.

CONNECT

Status is often pertinent in the workplace—especially between supervisors and supervisees. To settle well into a company's *organization culture,* it's necessary to carefully foster this relationship.

■ Group Climate

In addition to the complexity of group interaction and the roles that group members play, group communication is also strongly affected by the overall "climate" or collective atmosphere in the group. Specifically, group members are affected by the level of the group's cohesion, the norms that emerge for their behavior, clarity of goals, and their differences as individuals. In the sections that follow, we explore each of these factors in more detail.

Cohesion

Cohesion is the degree to which group members bond, like each other, and consider themselves to be one entity. A cohesive group identifies itself as a single unit rather than a collection of individuals, which helps hold the group together in the face of adversity. In fact, cohesion is an important factor in generating a positive group climate, in which members take pride in the group, treat each other with respect, develop trust, feel confident about their abilities, and achieve higher success in accomplishing goals. Such positive climates can also foster optimism and confidence in the face of obstacles. A self-confident, cohesive group tends to minimize problems, eliminate barriers, and cope well with crises (Folger, Poole, & Stutman, 2001). In general, cohesive groups perform better than noncohesive groups on decision-making tasks (for example, selecting a course of action more quickly and making more informed choices) (Carless & DePaola, 2000; Welch, Mossholder, Stell, & Bennett, 1998). Nonverbal communication is also influenced by group cohesion; Yasui (2009) found that cohesive group members often repeat and build on one another's gestures.

You can determine group cohesion in several ways. If you take a look at how the participants feel about their own membership in the group, you'll see that the more satisfaction and fulfillment members feel, the more cohesive they are. Members of a cohesive group are also enthusiastic, identify with the purposes of the group (Tekleab, Quigley, & Tesluk, 2009), and tell outsiders about its activities. Even positive, constructive argumentation (as opposed to verbal aggressiveness) can be a sign of group cohesion (Anderson & Martin, 1999). Finally, consider how well the group retains members. A cohesive group will retain more members than a noncohesive group.

Gouran (2003) offers several practical suggestions individuals can use for increasing cohesion and fostering a more positive group experience:

- Avoid dominating other group members.

- Stay focused on the tasks the group must accomplish.

- Be friendly.

- Show sensitivity to and respect for other members.

- Demonstrate that you value others' opinions.

- Cooperate with other members rather than compete with them.

Clearly, cohesion offers groups tremendous benefits, but unfortunately there is also a downside. Too much cohesion can actually cause the group to be unproductive. For example, if you and the other members of your study group enjoy each other's company so much that you talk and laugh together about everything *but* the course material, you'll never get your work done, which will hurt your goal of doing well on the exam! In addition, if your group members wish to maintain their cohesion at all costs, they may fail to question or criticize each other's knowledge or ideas, even if they are incorrect. In this scenario, you could all end up with the wrong understanding of some key concepts that will be on your exam. In the next chapter, we'll also see that excessive cohesion and the failure to express disagreement play a key part in groupthink, a serious problem in the group decision-making process. We now turn our attention to group norms.

CONNECT

In **CHAPTER 1**, we discuss *jargon*, vocabulary unique to a specific hobby or profession. Jargon helps build group cohesion because it connects members to one another. A group of police officers, for example, might speak about *perps* (perpetrators), *vics* (victims), *collars* (arrests), and *brass* (supervisors)—terms that their mechanic or physician friends would not use. This use of language helps officers bond as a group.

COMMUNICATION ACROSS CULTURES

The International American Pastime

The typical major league baseball team has a full roster of players and a substantial staff of coaches who work with players on specific skills. There's the general manager, a bullpen coach, a batting coach, a bench coach, and strength and conditioning coaches. There's a bevy of trainers and coordinators. And, sometimes, there's a language coach.

In 2012, more than a quarter of the players in Major League Baseball (MLB) were foreign-born (Associated Press, 2013). Many of them arrive in American locker rooms with much fanfare but with few or no English skills. In order to succeed as part of a team, however, it's crucial that they be able to communicate with their teammates and coaches, both on and off the field. The finite rules and language of the game, along with the formal nonverbal signals teams develop to communicate on the field, help to create a clear code of communication. For Asian players, most of whom are drafted straight out of the Japanese leagues, like Yu Darvish, Hiroki Kuroda, and Wei-Yin Chen, translators are essential. They have long accompanied players on the field during practices and assisted them in interviews, and in 2014, new MLB rules solidified translators' roles in their organizations by allowing them to accompany coaches onto the field during games for on-field conferences (Associated Press, 2014).

But the new rule may have limited impact on the many Latino players in the league. Because most Spanish speakers have at least a few bilingual teammates who can translate for them, and because most spend some time in the farm system, where they can pick up a somewhat functional, if limited, English vocabulary (what one reporter called "Baseball English"), most Spanish speakers do not have team-provided translators (Andriesen, 2007; Associated Press, 2014). It's unclear whether this less formal mode of communication is sufficient. Yankees closer Mariano Rivera admits that, early in his career, there were times when he was completely lost when "talking" with his coaches. "You nod your head yes, but you have no idea what they are saying" (Riviera, in Associated Press, 2014, para. 2).

The answer may be for the game to become more bilingual. The San Diego Padres, like many other organizations, offer English language classes to help players who are not fluent in English. But the team also takes the opposite approach: they teach basic Spanish to their staff. "It's something I thought was important to make us efficient when dealing with players when we're going to the Dominican [Republic] or with our players who are just coming here and don't have command of the English language yet," said Padres Director of Player Development Randy Smith (Brock, 2010). The next step might be targeting players long before they get to the big leagues: in 2013, Major League Baseball announced a pilot program that will provide English language classes and other educational support for prospects in the Dominican Republic (Sanchez, 2013).

THINK ABOUT THIS

1. How important is it to have all the players on a team speak the same language? Would having a single language policy increase group cohesion? What might the downsides of such a policy be?

2. Who is responsible for developing a shared code when coaches and players speak different languages? How might the rules of communication be worked out between individuals who speak different languages?

3. What other cultural differences might inhibit communication on a professional sports team? How does multiculturalism and globalization affect other sports?

4. Is it fair to provide translators for Asian players but not for Latinos? Why or why not? Should all members of the organization be tasked with learning a second language or just the ones who don't speak English?

Norms

As you saw earlier in the chapter, over time a group will develop norms. Norms emerge within the group and are imposed by members on themselves and each other; they may not be stated outwardly, but they direct the behavior of the group as a whole and affect the conduct of individual members. In a business environment, norms might dictate the kinds of topics that can be expressed in a meeting (Should non-task-related conversation be interjected? Are jokes appropriate?). In an online group, norms might evolve to govern the use of foul language, negative comments, or criticism. For example, a recent study showed that established members of an online anorexia support group allow new members to share pro-anorexic statements in order to establish that they are ill. In time, however, these members are initiated into the group norm that prohibits such unhealthy and negative statements (Stommel & Koole, 2010).

Some norms have a negative impact on communication. For example, suppose a group permits one member to dominate the conversation or allows members to dismiss an idea before discussing its pros and cons. A group with these norms will have difficulty generating enough diverse ideas to make informed decisions. If you find yourself in a group with unproductive norms like these, consider modifying them—this is possible if you approach the task diplomatically (Brilhart & Galanes, 1992). The following three-step process can help:

1. *Express your loyalty and dedication to the group, to show that you have the group's best interests at heart.* For instance, "I've been a member of this school committee for two years now and have hung in there during the tough times as well as the good times. I want to see us be the best we can be."

2. *Cite specific examples of the behavior you find harmful to the group's effectiveness.* To illustrate, "When we didn't take time to explore the pros and cons of the special-ed funding strategy that came up last month, we ended up making a decision that we regretted later."

3. *Ask other members for their opinions about the problem norm you've identified.* If others feel that the norm is still warranted, they may advocate keeping it ("Well, there are some situations where we don't have as much time as we'd like to consider the merits of an idea. During those moments, we need to be able to move ahead with a decision quickly").

With respectful, productive discussion, the group may decide to maintain the norm, change it under specific conditions ("We'll have someone play devil's advocate when time allows"), or abandon it entirely.

CONNECT

Goal achievement is an important function of communication in all contexts. Just remember that although it's important for a group to keep the end goal in sight, competent communicators are flexible—they try to maintain interdependence while being open to various ideas on achieving goals. They also recognize that the goal itself may change as group members share ideas and present solutions to problems.

Clarity of Goals

Think of the worst group meeting you've ever attended. How would you describe that meeting? Was the conversation disorganized? Unproductive? Confusing? Did you leave the meeting with a bad feeling about working with the group again in the future? Often such a poor communication climate is caused by the group's lack of a clear goal to begin with. To communicate productively and promote a positive atmosphere in any group, members need goal clarity: that is, they must understand what the group's purpose is, what goals will help the group achieve its purpose, how close the group is to achieving its goals, and whether the activities members are engaging in are helping the group move toward its goals.

Goals vary considerably from one group to another. For example, a team in one of your classes may have the simple goal of completing a fifteen-minute in-class exercise and reporting the results to the rest of the class. An urban beautification fund-raising committee may have the goal of collecting $4,000 for new landscaping at a neighborhood park.

One effective way to make sure your group has clear goals is to encourage the members to define them as a group. When members take part in establishing goals, they feel more committed to and excited about achieving those objectives. Research shows that a group is more likely to reach its goals when those goals are communicated in terms that are specific ("Raise $4,000 by the end of March"), inspiring ("Imagine our neighborhood becoming a community of choice for young families"), and prioritized ("We'll need to focus on this goal first and then this other one next") (O'Hair, Friedrich, & Dixon, 2007).

- *Enable group members to prepare.* Each group member should have a clear idea of what he or she is to be working on and should prepare accordingly. Send an agenda and any relevant assignments to team members in advance of any meetings.

- *Use time productively.* Avoid unnecessary meetings—don't meet just for the sake of meeting. In any meeting situation—be it a face-to-face, sit-down meeting or a telephone conference calls, be sure to establish clear goals in advance to keep the meeting on task.

Once your group begins working toward its goals, encourage yourself and your fellow members to talk regularly about the decisions you're making and the actions you're taking to ensure that these all support progress toward the goals.

© Matt Slocum/AP

FIGURE 28.10 Just as any Girl Scout troop sets personal and group goals for the cookie-selling season, your groups can productively divvy up responsibilities to make sure you achieve your aims.

Individual Differences

Members of a group may share norms, goals, and cohesion with their fellow members, but they also each bring personal differences that can strongly affect the communication climate. Let's examine how cultural factors and communication apprehension—which vary by individual—affect our ability to communicate in groups.

Cultural Factors

As you've learned throughout this book, culture has a big impact on how we communicate. Cultural diversity can have a particularly significant impact on group processes and outcomes (Thomas, Ravlin, & Wallace, 1996). When a group has culturally diverse members, that diversity can have benefits (such as enabling the group to produce a wide array of viewpoints) as well as challenges (including misunderstandings between members).

As we discussed in **CHAPTER 1**, cultures in English-speaking nations such as the United States, Great Britain, and Canada are largely individualist and low context, valuing personal accomplishment, self-esteem, and direct communication. As such, people in individualist cultures want their own opinions heard and appreciated, and they are likely to express them clearly and openly. In a collectivist and high-context culture, people value cooperation and group harmony, as well as indirect expression. They allow group norms (rather than their own personal goals) to have the largest influence on their behaviors and thoughts (Triandis, Brislin, & Hul, 1988). Not surprisingly, this difference can present a challenge when members of these cultures are working together in groups. People from individualist cultures will likely more openly vocalize their disagreement with the others and try to persuade each other, whereas the collectivists may feel "bulldozed" as they stifle their own objections for the good of the group. Conflict also occurs because of these differences in members' attitudes and basic orientations to problems (Tjosvold, 1992).

AND YOU?

Have you ever misunderstood another member of a group you were involved in because of cultural differences? If so, how did you and the other person deal with the misunderstanding?

Communication Apprehension

The next time you're sitting in your communication classroom or logging on to a discussion forum in your online course, take a peek around. Is there someone who never speaks up or raises a hand? Perhaps you're assuming that this person has nothing to say or that he or she is a social loafer. Maybe you're right. But it's also possible that this individual feels uncomfortable participating in group conversation even when his or her contribution would clearly help the group. People who are fearful or nervous about speaking up in groups are experiencing **communication apprehension** (CA). This anxiety is particularly common in public speaking situations, but it can affect collaboration in groups as well. Particularly in newly formed groups, individuals experiencing high levels of communication apprehension are less likely to participate; they produce and share fewer ideas with team members, make less significant contributions to the group discussions, and perceive group discussions as less positive than do members of the team with low levels of communication apprehension (Comadena, 1984; Jablin, Seibold, & Sorensen, 1977; Jablin & Sussman, 1978; Sorenson & Mc-Croskey, 1977). Team members experiencing communication apprehension are also less likely to be perceived as leaders (Hawkins & Stewart, 1991). Within the work environment, those with high levels of communication apprehension prefer to work independently, engage in more listening and observation than action during group interactions, and respond less favorably to change and evolving task demands (Russ, 2012).

What explains this communication apprehension? Scholars have identified several causes (Schullery & Gibson, 2001):

- *Lack of self-esteem.* When individuals doubt the worth of their contributions, they may decline to speak up in a group. Fear of being wrong, of being mocked, or of creating a bad impression can further lead to communication apprehension.

- *Status differences.* Group members who hold a relatively low position in the group's social or political hierarchy may avoid disagreeing with their superiors in the group because they fear retribution from the more powerful persons.

- *Unbalanced participation.* When a group member—or a small number of group members—dominates the conversation in a group, the less aggressive members may retreat from communicating. This strongly influences how decisions are made in the group.

Some simple techniques can help a group address communication apprehension among members. For example, to ease self-esteem problems, consider starting a group meeting by having each member tell the member to the left what he or she appreciates about that person. To neutralize status differences, have members sit in a circle and invite lower-status members to speak before higher-status ones. To rebalance participation, suggest a norm that calls for everyone to weigh in on ideas presented in the group. Or look for members who are holding back and invite them specifically to contribute their views.

You may be wondering how communication apprehension manifests or changes in the somewhat anonymous world of online groups. Indeed, the online environment affords those with high communication apprehension more anonymity and less social risk (Curtis, 1997; Ward & Tracey, 2004), and shy individuals tend to report less communication apprehension during discussions conducted online rather than face to face (Hammick & Lee, in press). However, research relating to the impact of communication apprehension in online contexts is mixed and has produced inconsistent findings (Flaherty, Pearce, & Rubin, 1998; Hunt, Atkin, & Krishnan; 2012; McKenna, 1998; Patterson & Gojdycz, 2000). Studies reveal that shy and apprehensive college students self-disclose much less on Facebook, are less self-expressive, and have fewer friends (Hunt et al., 2012; Sheldon, 2008). But regardless of the channel (traditional or online), communicatively apprehensive individuals are more reticent to participate in groups.

EVALUATING COMMUNICATION ETHICS

Sketchy Behavior

You have recently formed a comedy troupe with four other friends: Calvin, Eddie, Meredith, and Sylvia. Your first live show with the group is in just a few weeks, and your group has written and rehearsed five sketches. But you and Calvin have had doubts about one sketch, written by Eddie and Sylvia, since day one. Rather than voice your concerns, you and Calvin have been trying to come up with an alternative sketch. During a late-night session, the two of you come up with an idea for a sketch that in your opinion outclasses the one you've been having problems with.

It is now a few days before the show, and the two of you have decided, independent of the other members, that the weaker sketch needs to be changed in favor of the one you've written. You are concerned about how this will look and have a nagging feeling the other members are going to perceive your writing of this sketch as a selfish way to push your work over that of your teammates, but you feel strongly that the new sketch will make the show a greater success. Calvin suggests that you present your sketch to Meredith, since she was not involved in writing either sketch. "If we convince Meredith that our sketch is the stronger one," Calvin reasons, "we'll be able to point to her opinion as a truly objective opinion—she's got no agenda."

You're pretty certain that Meredith will prefer your sketch, not only because you feel it is better but also because it features a role that Meredith would love to play. And you know that if you talk to Meredith beforehand, you'll have a clear majority in favor of your sketch should the decision be put to a vote. But is this ethical?

THINK ABOUT THIS

1. What role did group communication play in this scenario? Might cliques have been involved? What were other communication options?

2. Is it unethical to attempt to gain Meredith's vote even if you honestly believe that it's in the best interest of the group?

3. What ethical implications arise from approaching Meredith with the new sketch? Should the sketch be presented to the entire team at the same time? Is it fair to tempt Meredith with a juicy role in exchange for her vote?

Assertiveness and Argumentativeness

Although people who experience communication apprehension are *less* likely to speak up in groups, there are also people whose traits make them *more* likely to speak up. Have you noticed when working on class projects that some members of your group always seem to voice their opinions boldly or never seem to be afraid to speak out when they disagree with group members? These are likely to be students with assertive and argumentative personalities. **Assertiveness** refers to the use of communication messages that demonstrate confidence, dominance, and forcefulness to achieve personal goals. For example, you are being assertive when you openly tell your group members, "I want an 'A' on this project, so I would like us all to work as hard as possible to make this happen." Some people have a greater tendency than others to use such assertive messages. **Argumentativeness** is a particular form of assertiveness, in which a person tends to express positions on controversial issues and verbally attack the positions that other people take (Infante & Rancer, 1982)—in other words, people who are argumentative tend, not surprisingly, to argue, and they often even enjoy it! But note that to be "argumentative" and not "aggressive" means that you refute the other people's *positions on issues*—you do not attack them personally!

What effect do assertive or argumentative people have on group interaction? Highly argumentative group members are likely to be more dominant and, hence, play a significant role in group decision making (Limon & La France, 2005). In meetings, for example, individuals who are more argumentative are perceived as more credible communicators (Infante, 1981), and within small groups they are more often perceived as leaders (Schultz, 1980, 1982). Interestingly, research has found that leadership appears to be most strongly associated with higher levels of argumentativeness *in combination with* lower levels of communication apprehension (Limon & La France, 2005).

You might think that group harmony would suffer when people openly assert or argue their positions, but argumentativeness can actually reinforce cohesion within a group (Anderson & Martin, 1999). This is because group members are advocating for the solutions that may be most helpful at accomplishing the group's tasks. Indeed, in most group situations, assertiveness and argumentativeness are perceived as constructive traits (Infante, 1987). It is important to remember, however, that we must distinguish these constructive forms of speaking up with the destructive tactic of "verbal aggressiveness"as a negative, hostile way of handling conflict.

Universal Pictures/Photofest

FIGURE 28.11 Initially In *Pitch Perfect,* Aubrey leads the Bellas with an overwhelming assertiveness that leaves little room for any of the other a capella girls' input. Ultimately, the key to the group's success lies in a more balanced participation that allows for shared ideas and cooperation.

Back To Team Rubicon

At the beginning of the chapter, we were introduced to Team Rubicon, a team of military veterans who provide disaster relief. Let's consider what we've learned in this chapter, and how it applies to the experience of these inspiring veterans.

- The name "Team Rubicon" sends two messages. "Team" speaks to the small, cohesive nature of military units. "Rubicon" is taken from the phrase "crossing the Rubicon," a military metaphor that dates back to classical Rome and refers to making a commitment to a difficult course of action from which there is no turning back. By establishing its goals right in the group's name, Team Rubicon makes both its goals and its means clear. Although the organization has many members, it consists of many small teams that are able to adjust plans and adapt tactics to administer immediate aid in the most dire of circumstances.

- The only people who can truly understand what combat veterans are going through are other veterans. Team Rubicon draws on this unique bond, as well as the specialized skills of veterans, and the group's impact comes in the form of small, platoonlike groups that share a goal and a purpose. That unity, identity, and cohesiveness mean a lot. "It is a brotherhood—or a sisterhood," explains Danielle Harrington, an Army reservist and Team Rubicon volunteer who joined hurricane relief efforts in New York in 2012. "It is nice to be around like-minded people, who have the same values and the same ethos" (Harrington, in Hameed, 2012, 2:30).

- In military organizations, roles are assigned to each group member with a clear hierarchy of leadership and designated task roles. These roles are easily adapted to emergency situations, when decisions must be made and actions taken quickly and effectively. That's a large part of Team Rubicon's success. But it is also true that the decisions involved in civilian jobs, higher education, and family life might seem unimportant or insignificant to men and women returning from life-and-death situations. This lack of purpose can be devastating for veterans, especially when coupled with depression or post-traumatic stress. Through career training programs like the Clay Hunt Fellowship, Team Rubicon hopes to help veterans adapt their very specific skills to nonemergent situations, while continuing to find purpose, community, and self-worth through service.

■ Things To Try

Activities

1. Consider a group to which you belong—your communication class, your family, your religious community, and so on. Draw a chart that depicts members of the group and the patterns of communication among them. What kind of network does the group most closely resemble?

2. Read up on the history of some influential but now defunct music group (such as the Beatles, Public Enemy, or Nirvana). Did the group go through all the stages of group development outlined in this chapter? How did the group determine roles and establish norms? How did members deal with conflict? How did the eventual disbanding of the group play out?

3. Consider the adjourning phase of group development for a group you were part of that disbanded—Scouts, a sports team, the school newspaper staff—and think about what aspects of the group made for the hardest good-bye from the group. Are high-performing groups hardest to leave? Groups with the clearest established norms? What sorts of closing rituals have you experienced?

4. The telephone game, passing a message from person to person, is fun simply because of the inevitable message distortion that gets revealed at the end. Can you think of a time when a message was passed to you from an indirect source that you discovered to be blatantly wrong? Maybe it was bungled homework instructions or a wrong meeting time or place. Given these sorts of problems, what type of workplace might function best with a chain network?

5. Analyze the group dynamics from five of your favorite television shows. See if you can identify the various social and antigroup role types in each of the groups.

6. Next time you work in a group, pay attention to how the group works. Does the activity follow a linear model, or is the activity punctuated by periods of inertia and periods of intense activity? How does the group activity pattern differ from your own behaviors when you work alone?

Chapter 29
Leadership and Decision Making in Groups

chapter outcomes

After you have finished reading this chapter, you will be able to

- Describe the types of power that effective leaders employ

- Describe how leadership styles should be adapted to the group situation

- Identify the qualities that make leaders effective at enacting change

- Identify how culture affects appropriate leadership behavior

- List the forces that shape a group's decisions

- Explain the six-step group decision process

- List behaviors to improve effective leadership in meetings

- Demonstrate aspects of assessing group performance

This chapter is taken from Dan O'Hair, Mary Wiemann, Dorothy Imric Mullin, and Jason Teven, *Real Communication*, Third Edition, pp. 272–302 (Chapter 10).

Captain Ray Holt is finally in charge: as the new commanding officer on Brooklyn Nine-Nine, he arrives at his post intent on making the precinct into one of the best in the NYPD. But the motley crew of detectives he inherits may not fit the bill. His two top detectives, the fiercely competitive Amy Santiago and the immature yet effective Jake Peralta, are continually at odds with each other. The mysterious Rosa Diaz doesn't even try to control her temper. Holt's old friend and new second-in-command, Sergeant Terry Jeffords, is on desk duty after, upon becoming a father, he found himself suddenly—and comically—risk-averse.

But Holt is undeterred. He advises his staff that he has high expectations: regulations are to be followed; paperwork is to be properly filed. With his no-nonsense style and an imposing presence, he does not seem like a man to be trifled with. But that doesn't stop the childish Peralta: when Holt insists he wear a necktie, Peralta responds by wearing one around his waist.

But before long, Peralta is wearing that tie, Jeffords is back in action, and Diaz is managing to smile at juries during testimony. Holt earns their respect, loyalty, and even obedience, not by laying down a hard line but by explaining himself. When Peralta asks why it took him so long to get his own command, Holt succinctly explains that it had to do with his coming out twenty-five years earlier. "The NYPD was not ready for an openly gay detective," Holt says. "But then, the old guard died out, and suddenly they couldn't wait to show off the fact that they had a high-ranking gay officer. I made captain. But they put me in a public affairs unit. I was a good soldier. I helped recruitment. But all I ever wanted was my own command. And now, I've finally got it, and I'm not going to screw it up" (*Brooklyn Nine-Nine*, 2013).

What makes a leader? Power? Experience? Decisiveness? In this chapter, we continue our discussion of group communication by examining two additional processes that often emerge in groups: leadership and decision making. These two processes are tightly interrelated: a group's leader affects how the group makes decisions, and the decisions a group makes affect how the leader operates. When leadership and decision making work together in a constructive way, a group stands the best possible chance of achieving its goals. To understand how these processes influence a group's effectiveness, let's begin by taking a closer look at group leadership.

■ Understanding Group Leadership

It's a word that's constantly tossed about in political campaigns, highlighted on ré-sumés, and used in book titles and biographies. But just what is *leadership*? Scholars have grappled with the task of defining leadership for many years.

Two key terms that show up in many definitions over the years have been *direction* and *influence*. That's because in its most essential form, **leadership** is the ability to direct or influence others' behaviors and thoughts toward a productive end (Nieren-berg, 2009). This capacity for influence may stem from a person's power or simply from group members' admiration or respect for the individual. Because influence involves power over others, let's take a look at power—what it is and where it comes from.

Five Sources of Power

If you've ever seen the classic Steven Spielberg film *Jaws*, you know that it is, on the surface, the tale of a small coastal town being terrorized by a nasty, man-eating shark. But at the heart of the tale is the interaction among a group of men, each of whom bears or takes some responsibility for ridding the waters of the treacherous animal. First, there's the town's mayor, whose main priority is protecting the local economy. Second, there's the town's new chief of police, who's thrust into the story when the first body washes ashore. Also playing a role are Matt Hooper, a young marine bi-ologist who studies sharks, and Quint, the war-scarred local shark hunter. Over the course of the film, each man demonstrates leadership that is firmly rooted in the na-ture of the power he possesses.

Researchers have identified five types of power—legitimate, coercive, reward, expert, and referent (French & Raven, 1959).

- **Legitimate power** comes from an individual's role or title. The president, the su-pervisor at work, and the coach of a team all possess legitimate power as elected or appointed leaders. In *Jaws*, the elected mayor of Amity Island, Larry Vaughn, has some degree of legitimate power, as does Martin Brody, the chief of police, though his power is subordinate to the mayor's authority.

- **Coercive power** stems from a person's ability to threaten or harm others. A harsh dictator who keeps his people under threat of violence or economic hardship holds such power, but so does a boss who threatens to dock or demote employees if they step out of line. In Jaws, the mayor—whose primary concern is protecting the town's tourist-dependent economy—uses this kind of power to influence or override decisions made by the police chief: he hired Chief Brody, and he can fire him.

© Universal Pictures/Courtesy Everett Collection

FIGURE 29.1 Quint, Chief Brody, and Matt Hooper each bring something different to the shark-hunting mission and derive their power from different sources.

- **Reward power** derives from an individual's capacity to provide rewards. For example, your boss might offer all the people in your department a paid day off if they work late three nights in a row on an important project. In the film, the mayor relies on reward power: hundreds of local fishermen set out to catch the shark in hopes of winning a monetary reward.

- **Expert power** comes from the information or knowledge that a leader possesses. Expert power is divided in *Jaws*. Faced with any other kind of homicide, Brody's credentials as a former New York City police officer might have given him a fair amount of expert power, but as a newcomer without fishing experience, he gets little respect from the islanders. Matt Hooper, who studies sharks, fares a little bit better. But Quint, who has decades of shark-hunting experience, quickly emerges as the true expert, garnering the respect of his crewmates.

- **Referent power** stems from the admiration, respect, or affection that followers have for a leader. The popular kids in your high school may have had the power to influence other students' style of dress or way of behaving simply because others admired them. In *Jaws*, Quint demonstrates this kind of power: when he relays his story as a survivor of the USS *Indianapolis*, which sank in shark-infested waters during World War II, Brody and Hooper gain a new sense of understanding of, and admiration for, Quint's obsession with killing sharks.

It's important to note that these types of power are not exclusive of one another; indeed, most leaders wield several, if not all, of these types of power. Consider the instructor for your course. He or she demonstrates legitimate power as your teacher but may also exercise reward and expert power, providing you with some extra credit and offering valuable information, respectively. As another example, Quint demonstrates legitimate power as captain of his own vessel as well as expert and referent power. Note also that individuals gain power only if others grant it to them. That's true to some degree even of coercive power: for example, Brody could have chosen to quit his job early on rather than to acquiesce to the mayor. Thus group members often decide to allow a particular individual to lead them.

COMMUNICATION ACROSS CULTURES

Leaning In versus Gender Judo

Making up 50 percent of the population and 47 percent of the workforce (U.S. Census Bureau, 2012), women are outperforming men in terms of earning college and advanced degrees (Associated Press, 2011; Perry, 2013). But when you look at the highest levels of corporate and public sector leadership, it's clearly still a man's world: in January 2014, a mere 23 of the CEOs of *Fortune* 500 companies were female and the United States Congress had only 99 women (79 out of 435 in the House of Representatives). Leaving aside the reasons for the underrepresentation of half the population in corner offices, consider the communication challenges that women working in male-dominated industries face. What's it like to be the lone woman at the boy's club? And how do women overcome preconceived notions of masculine versus feminine leadership styles?

Facebook CEO Sheryl Sandberg struck a chord with women when she suggested that females in leadership roles take a firmer stand in advocating for themselves—and, by extension, for all women. Her 2013 book *Lean In: Women, Work, and the Will to Lead* encouraged women to stop underestimating themselves and act like men, to stop worrying about appearing "bossy," and to simply be the boss. The phrase "lean in" took hold in the public imagination as stylistic shorthand for women to push themselves outside of their comfort zone and to make the same demands that men typically do. By "leaning in" instead of "pulling back," Sandberg argued, women would be playing by the same rules as men, allowing themselves to be as ambitious—and successful and well compensated—as their male colleagues. When outnumbered in the boardroom, Sandberg explained, it is even more crucial for women to demand their seat at the table.

But other women in similar situations have noted that it may be easier—and more effective—to use more traditional feminine communication techniques when dealing with an entrenched masculine culture. Joan C. Williams interviewed 127 highly successful women and found that adopting masculine communication styles often backfired. "If you're too feminine," Williams explains, "you're perceived as incompetent. But if you're too masculine, you're seen as difficult to work with." Williams suggests what she calls "gender judo" (judo being the Japanese martial art of the "gentle way," which involves overcoming your opponent by using his own momentum to overpower him). In practice, it means reminding men of traditional feminine roles (like that of a mother, daughter, or teacher) with which they are comfortable and using those roles to exert authority. "Be warm Ms. Mother 95 percent of the time," explained one executive "so that the 5 percent of the time when you need to be tough, you can be" (quoted in Williams, 2014).

THINK ABOUT THIS

1. Which of these tactics seems more ethical? If adopting a masculine style of leadership—for example, being "bossy"—has proven problematic for women, is it fair for them to rely on stereotypical, gendered leadership roles to communicate?

2. Don't men bear some of the responsibility for ensuring that they communicate competently and ethically with their female supervisors, colleagues, and staff? Do workplaces need to become, essentially, more feminine?

3. Sandberg's work is directed primarily at women in leadership roles. How does her advice affect women with less power? Is Williams's advice more or less salient to women lower on the organizational chart?

AND YOU?

Consider three groups to which you belong. Is there a clearly established leader for each group? If so, what type of power does this leader have? Do you find certain types of power more ethical or appropriate than others? Explain your answer.

Shared Leadership

With so many sources of power, it's not surprising that in some groups several individuals take on leadership roles, each drawing from different sources of power. Thus leadership can be shared by a few members of the group who divvy up the power and take control of specific tasks. For example, imagine that your sorority is planning a trip to Jazz Fest in New Orleans. As chair of the social committee, you take care of organizing the group for the event—publicizing the trip and recording the names of individuals who are interested in going. Another sorority sister, Eva, takes care of booking a block of hotel rooms in the French Quarter and negotiating a group rate. Lily, the chapter president, gets in touch with the sister chapter at Louisiana State University to arrange to meet up. Meanwhile, Keisha, your chapter's community outreach chair, organizes a fundraiser on campus in the hope of raising money for Habitat for Humanity in New Orleans so that your sorority may present the organization with a generous check during your visit.

When the talents and powers of each group member are leveraged through shared leadership, members feel more satisfied with the group process and more motivated to perform (Foels, Driskell, Mullen, & Salas, 2000; Kanter, 2009). As a result, the group is more likely to achieve its goals. Probably for these reasons, many businesses and professional organizations in the United States are moving toward a shared-leadership model, whereby people at lower levels of an organization carry out leadership and decision-making responsibilities (Krayer, 2010).

CONNECT

Shared leadership is at the heart of the self-directed work team we describe in **CHAPTER 28**, where sharing leadership goes beyond improving group member motivation to allow members to set standards for the group, conduct peer evaluations, bring in new members, and coordinate plans with management. The end result is often goal achievement and a sense of cooperation rather than divisive competition among members.

Group Leadership Styles

What is the best way to lead a group? Should you accept input from the members or rule with an iron fist? Do you focus mainly on the task at hand or help resolve relationship problems? It turns out that there is no one "best" style of leadership. Rather, scholars argue that effective group leaders, whether they're leading alone or sharing power with someone else in the group, adapt their leadership styles to the needs of the group or the situation at hand. Five possible styles are discussed here—directive, supportive, participative, laissez-faire, and achievement oriented—each of which works best under different conditions (Gouran, 2003; Pavitt, 1999).

Directive

A **directive leader** focuses on the group's tasks and controls the group's communication by conveying specific instructions to members. This style works best when members are unsure of what's expected of them or how to carry out their responsibilities. Directive leaders can move their group in the right direction by charting next steps in the group's tasks and clarifying the group's goals, plans, and desired outcomes. For example, the leader of a police squad—like Ray Holt, discussed in the chapter opener—would instruct his team specifically as to how they should handle their paperwork or follow complicated regulations.

©NBC/Photofest

FIGURE 29.2 Law and Order's Lieutenant Van Buren never leaves her detectives hanging; she gives them specific and thorough directions for every step of a case.

Supportive

A **supportive leader** attends to group members' emotional and relational needs. This style is especially helpful when members feel frustrated with their task or with each other. Supportive leaders might stress the importance of positive relationships in the group, reminding members of the group's importance, and expressing appreciation for members' talents and work ethic. Consider Tim Gunn of *Project Runway*. As a leader and mentor figure to the aspiring designers, he helps them not only visualize their designs and talk through their frustrations but also encourages team members to communicate with each other, listen to each other, and "make it work." He is always profuse in his praise, and even when a particular design doesn't impress him, he is encouraging and positive in his criticism.

Participative

A **participative leader** views group members as equals, welcomes their opinions, summarizes points that have been raised, and identifies problems that need discussion rather than dictating solutions. This style works well when group members are competent and motivated to take on their tasks but also benefit from their leader's involvement and feedback. Participative leaders do give some assistance and support to group members, but unlike directive or supportive leaders, they tend to guide and facilitate group discussion rather than giving direct instructions or motivational messages. Many online topic forums and blogs are moderated by participative leaders—they allow discussion among members of the group to take off in many directions, and they contribute right along with everyone else. But they also step in when needed to remind inappropriately contributing members of the purpose of the discussion or the accepted rules of discourse.

Laissez-Faire

The **laissez-faire leader**, whom some call a "hands-off" or delegating leader, is the leader who gives up some degree of power or control and gives that power to team members. This style is the absence of involved leadership—the leader trusts others to handle their own responsibilities, does not take part in the group's discussions or work efforts, and provides feedback only when asked. Parks Director Ron Swanson of *Parks and Recreation i*s a hilarious parody of this style of leadership—he is a die-hard libertarian who believes that his role as a government employee is to "do as little as possible." Although it may seem like a *lack* of leadership, the laissez-faire leader can actually be effective, particularly with mature or experienced groups, where just checking in occasionally and seeing if the group has questions is all that is warranted. Ron Swanson is able to remain hands off because he delegates responsibility to his supercompetent deputy director, Leslie Knope.

NBC/Photofest

FIGURE 29.3 Parks and Recreation's Ron Swanson and Leslie Knope strike a balance of leadership styles, with Ron's hands-off attitude complemented by Leslie's passionate commitment to getting things done.

Achievement Oriented

An **achievement-oriented leader** sets challenging goals and communicates high expectations and standards to members. This style works best when group members are highly skilled and are eager to produce great accomplishments. In addition to setting lofty goals, such leaders encourage outside-the-box thinking, compare the group with other high-performing groups, and keep members focused on tangible outcomes. *Parks and Recreation*'s Leslie Knope has an achievement-oriented style of leadership. She identifies an ambitious goal and then does everything in her power to make that goal happen. Her ambition is often initially at odds with her apathetic coworkers and reluctant community. But her commitment, enthusiasm, and optimism are infectious, and she usually ends up inspiring everyone around her to help pitch in to make it happen.

■ What About You?

What Type of Leader Are You?

Leadership is the ability to direct or influence others toward a productive end. Leadership behaviors can vary from person to situation. Use the following five-point scale to find out which style(s) of leadership you exhibit: 5 = extremely like me; 4 = somewhat like me; 3 = neither like nor unlike me; 2 = somewhat unlike me; and 1 = extremely unlike me.

	1. I ask a lot of questions to find out what others know.
	2. I usually know or find out the facts and delegate work to group members early on.
	3. I have high expectations and expect everyone to contribute positively.
	4. I watch the emotional reactions of group members to be sure I don't hurt anyone's feelings
	5. I think that my group members should be able to make their own decisions.
	6. I ask questions and encourage others to participate so they will contribute their ideas.
	7. I organize the group's notes and agenda, paying less attention to individuals.
	8. I figure everyone should share responsibility for making the group successful.
	9. If people aren't participating, I'll reach out to find out why.
	10. I don't give a lot of feedback to group members; they should know what they are doing.
	11. When a problem arises in a group, I present it and then sit back and listen to everyone's responses.
	12. I am comfortable explaining the overall project and then assigning others to specific tasks.
	13. I expect everyone to have high standards for success.
	14. I pay attention to personal problems that may affect the working environment.
	15. I find that group members will be more successful if I just check in on them occasionally.

Sum your answers for the question numbers that follow, noting the areas with the highest score:

_____ (#1, 6, 11) You are a participative leader.

_____ (#2, 7, 12) You are a directive leader.

_____ (#3, 8, 13) You are an achievement-oriented leader.

_____ (#4, 9, 14) You are a supportive leader.

_____ (#5, 10, 15) You are a delegating leader.

A mix of high numbers (12–15) indicates a diverse leadership style; as we point out in this chapter, adapting your leadership style to suit your group's needs is an essential leadership skill.

Leadership Qualities

When leaders are able to adapt their styles to the needs of the groups they guide, they can enhance the productivity and satisfaction of group members in their day-to-day activities. But there are also leaders who have unique qualities that enable them to effect change on a larger scale—be it reforming a school, turning a small company into a huge, multinational corporation, coaching a winning sports team, or inspiring a massive social movement. Let's examine some of these unique qualities.

- *Vision.* A principal at a failing high school might have an idea in her mind of what her school would look like if it were functioning more effectively. She might envision students who are engaged in cooperative projects, an active PTA organization, a new library or computer lab, or mentoring partnerships with members of the surrounding business community. **Visionary leaders** are able to picture a new or different reality from what currently exists and consider the bigger, long-range picture of the group's or organization's future (Sashkin & Burke, 1990). They do not just consider how best to reach certain goals, but they also question the very goals themselves and are able to empower group members to take some risks, explore possibilities, and develop creative ideas (Uhl-Bien, 2006). Of course, when leading groups on a day-to-day basis, such questioning may stall the ability to move forward on basic tasks. But when attempting major reforms or trying to get to the root of serious problems, having this kind of vision is a key ingredient of leadership effectiveness (Bennis & Nanus, 1985).

- *Charisma.* Although vision may be important for many kinds of leadership, other leaders may be effective because they have an engaging personality and dynamic speaking style. Charismatic leaders are vibrant, likable communicators who generate a positive image among their followers. Their charisma can motivate people and make them respond receptively to their leader's ideas (Bono & Ilies, 2006; Cherulnik, Donley, Wiewel, & Miller, 2001). The principal, for example, might at a town meeting speak enthusiastically about the school and her plans, compliment the community, and maybe even tell some tasteful jokes. Her dynamism could help motivate her faculty, her students, their parents, and community leaders to embrace and work toward her goals.

- *Initiative.* Our principal may have vision or charisma (or both), but to make major reforms at her school, she is also likely to need the initiative and energy to make these changes a real possibility. **Transformative leaders** see change, adaptation, and growth as the means for groups and organizations to survive. They spark change not only by *having* a new vision but also by conveying that vision clearly to others, showing real passion for the work ahead, and energizing the group toward meeting the goals set forth in the vision. If the principal is able to change her school from a failing one to a highly successful one (that is, to bring reality in line with her vision), she would have to ensure that things actually happen—for example, that her incentives or programs actually make students and teachers work harder and that the hard work results in higher levels of engagement and performance. As Northhouse (2012) explains, "transformational leadership involves an exceptional form of influence that moves followers to accomplish more than what is usually expected of them" (p. 169).

You have likely noticed that many of our most celebrated leaders, like Martin Luther King, Jr., Alice Paul, Winston Churchill, and Mahatma Ghandi, possess all three of these qualities. Dr. King, for example, had a clear vision for the United States and eloquently articulated his seminal "I Have a Dream" speech. He was also charismatic—a gifted writer and speaker with a magnetic personality and a presence that inspired Americans to join him in demanding equal rights for all citizens. And, finally, he was a transformative leader: he motivated those inside the movement to work hard for civil rights, while changing the way others thought about race, rights, and equality. In a similar vein, our effective high school principal may exhibit vision, charisma, and initiative as she successfully transforms her school.

CONNECT

All types of leaders—visionary, transformative, and charismatic—must have the ability to persuade others to their plan or way of thinking. They must be able to speak persuasively in a way that resonates with their audience.

JIM RUYMEN/UPI/Landov

FIGURE 29.4 Activist celebrities like environmentalist Leonardo DiCaprio use their charisma to bring about social change and awareness for causes.

EVALUATING COMMUNICATION ETHICS

Leading the Interns

You are currently working as an editorial assistant at a reputable music magazine, and among your responsibilities is leading a group of young, aspiring summer interns. You find this task especially rewarding because, as a college student, you suffered through a mind-numbing internship in order to get your foot in the door, so you hope that you can make this internship rewarding for the students in your department.

Back when you were an intern, you worked with an assistant named Bradley, who was in a position similar to the one you're in now. Bradley always seemed to pass off his boring, menial tasks—such as filing, answering his boss's e-mail, and setting up appointments—to the interns so that he could sit and listen to new records in an attempt to further his career in rock criticism. You and the other interns were willing to take on just about any task in order to get a good recommendation, but you always slightly resented Bradley, feeling that he had used you and others in your group.

Since you started working long hours at your assistant job, however, you've wondered if Bradley actually had the right idea. Like Bradley, you aspire to be a music critic, and the mundane tasks of your job are beginning to frustrate you. Such tasks are, however, part of your job description—they are what every assistant does.

You want to have time to talk to writers, to write or edit copy, and to be able to sit in on pitch meetings. Bradley kept you from such experiences as an intern because you were too busy fetching lattes for his boss. The problem is, now you need to get lattes for your own boss, and this is keeping you from gussying up your own portfolio. Yet here are new, young interns willing and eager to do anything to get ahead, perhaps even taking over those menial tasks. What should you do?

THINK ABOUT THIS

1. Was Bradley wrong, or was he just doing what any aspiring journalist would do to free up his time? Do you have a greater understanding for his struggle in light of your own position?

2. Is It OK to pawn your work off on unpaid college students, even if they're willing to do it?

3. As the group's leader, do you have a responsibility to these interns to ensure that they get the most from their internship experience?

4. Looking back at your own internship, is possible that it was more valuable than you think? What might you have learned about the business while answering the boss's e-mails or filing his completed work?

Unethical Leadership

Competent leadership requires more than the ability to adapt your leadership styles to your group or exhibit the effective qualities of vision, charisma, and initiative. Competent leaders also hold both themselves and the group accountable for achieving their results, and they treat all group members in an ethical manner.

However, some leaders use unethical tactics to try to acquire and keep control over an entire group or individual members within a group. Some people use verbal aggressiveness to try to get what they want or to "bully" others in online environments. Unfortunately, unethical leaders may also make use of such **bullying** tactics, which include harsh criticism, name-calling, gossip, slander, personal attacks, or threats to safety or job security (Smith, 2005). Bullying can also include offensive gestures, ignoring, withering looks, or even just a sarcastic tone of voice. In group situations, a leader might withhold needed information from group members, exclude them from meetings, or insist on unrealistic deadlines or expectations. Unfortunately, such unethical tactics can prove effective for some leaders. Take chef Gordon Ramsay on the reality TV series *Hell's Kitchen*. Aspiring chefs are split into two teams that are pitted against each other in challenges while also preparing and serving dinner to a roomful of diners. Ramsay is very particular about how he wants the food to taste and look. If something is not up to par, he often screams profanities at the contestant responsible for the mistake, showing no qualms about insulting contestants' appearance, ethnicity, or professional background. Although his anger and derogatory statements are usually met by a grim "Yes, chef," and although he may gain the respect of some of the contestants, some do tire of being abused on a regular basis and break down or walk out. And although Ramsay has been very successful with his aggressive, bullying style of leadership, few would consider his outbursts to be ethical.

Although Gordon Ramsay's bullying behavior is aggressive and potentially harmful, it is, at least, transparent. There is little guessing as to what he wants from his staff or why he punishes them. But some unethical leaders might use more sinister means to manipulate their subordinates. Consider, for example, a crime lord who speaks with sweetness and praise but who intimidates by hinting at violent consequences for those who would challenge his control in a particular community. On a smaller scale, a supervisor might manipulate employees by pretending to favor one employee's position while also making a "backroom" deal with an opposing employee. Such maneuvering reflects an unethical leadership style known as **Machiavellianism**, named for sixteenth-century philosopher Niccolò Machiavelli, who advised rulers to use deceit, flattery, and other exploitative measures strategically to achieve their desired ends (Becker & O'Hair, 2007; Christie & Geis, 1970). Machiavellian leaders in groups may, like bullies, have some success in exerting power and control but at a cost—they are liked less and have less credibility (Teven, McCroskey, & Richmond, 2006).

It's also important to be aware that the very talents and qualities mentioned earlier that make leaders effective can also be used for unethical purposes. Some leaders use their charisma or transformative power for self-serving purposes (O'Connor et al., 1995; Yukl, 1999) or in pursuit of a vision that is morally reprehensible. Consider, for example, Adolf Hitler and Osama Bin Laden. Both of these men held visions that were destructive and hateful, and they possessed the personal charisma to motivate others to work toward their vision—resulting in some of the most notorious acts of evil in human history.

CONNECT

In many organizational contexts, bullying behaviors can escalate to illegal harassment, communication that hurts and offends, creating a hostile environment.

The Everett Collection

FIGURE 29.5 Machiavellian mobster Don Corleone from *The Godfather* may outwardly seem like a calm family man, but consider the consequences of not taking him up on one of his "offers you can't refuse."

■ Culture and Group Leadership

As you'll recall from **CHAPTER 1**, culture can strongly shape the way people interact. Let's look at two issues—gender and cultural variations—that prove to be particularly powerful factors when leading a group.

Gender and Leadership

Would you vote for a female presidential candidate? A 2013 poll shows 86 percent of Americans think the country is ready to elect a woman president. And nearly 75 percent think the country will elect one in 2016 (Fox, 2013). But why the concern over a leader's biological sex? Is there really a difference between men and women as leaders?

With a few key exceptions, research has provided little support for the popular notion that men and women inherently lead differently, although the idea has nonetheless persisted. For example, we might assume that men would have a masculine style of leadership, emphasizing command and control, whereas women would have a feminine style of leadership, emphasizing more nurturing relationship environments. Some research has indeed suggested that feminine leaders think of organizations as webs of relationships, with leaders at the center of the web, in contrast to the more traditionally masculine view of organizations as pyramids with a leader at the top.

Feminine leaders may also view the boundaries between work and personal life as fluid and may communicate their understanding of employees' need to balance professional and personal obligations (Helgesen, 1990; Mumby, 2000; Rosener, 1990). However, meta-analyses (which examine the combined results from many different studies) have found that men and women do not differ in overall leadership effectiveness (Eagly, Karau, & Makhijani, 1995). In fact, one study (Rutherford, 2001) even notes that men and women's leadership styles are often dictated by factors *other* than sex and gender, such as the general communication style of the group or organization.

Cultural Variations

Two additional leadership factors are the variations we see among cultures, such as whether they are high or low context or value high or low power distance. You may recall that people from high-context cultures (such as Japan) tend to communicate in indirect ways, whereas those from low-context cultures (like the United States) communicate with more verbal directness (Hall, 1976). Imagine, for example, a manager tasked with keeping a team on target to meet a very tight deadline. A leader from a high-context culture might simply present a calendar noting due dates and filled with tasks and competing projects; she would rely on her team to get the point that the deadline is in trouble and expect team members to offer solutions. A leader from a low-context culture, on the other hand, would be more likely to clarify the situation directly: "I'm moving the deadline earlier by two weeks; that means you'll need to accelerate your work accordingly." The ways in which group members respond will also be influenced by culture: group members from a high-context culture might communicate in a similarly indirect way with their leader ("We have some concerns about the new deadline"), whereas those from a low-context culture would be more direct ("Sorry, we can't make the new deadline").

Power distance is another cultural difference that affects how groups may communicate with their leaders. As we learned in CHAPTER 1, *power distance* is the extent to which less powerful members of a group, be it a business organization or a family, accept that power is distributed unequally. In a high power distance culture, the members are not likely to challenge their leader's opinions or authority. This means that a leader who wants all members to offer their ideas at a meeting might need to make a special effort to encourage everyone to participate in the discussion. In contrast, in a culture with low power distance, members are likely to offer their opinions and disagree with the leader without much prodding.

(left) Image 100/Punchstock/Getty Images; (right) Blend Images/Punchstock/Getty Images

FIGURE 29.6 In a low power distance culture, meetings might feel like roundtable discussions, where everyone gets a chance to speak. In a high power distance culture, meetings are usually more hierarchical.

■ Decision Making in Groups

On January 28, 1986, the blue skies above Cape Canaveral in Florida seemed to be ripped open when the U.S. Space Shuttle *Challenger* suddenly exploded shortly after liftoff. One of the worst disasters in NASA history (the second being the explosion of the *Columbia* seventeen years later), it claimed the lives of seven astronauts. Investigation into the tragedy found that faulty fittings (called O-rings) had failed during takeoff, causing the explosion. But a large part of the blame for the disaster was laid on communication failures within NASA. Prior to launch, there had been some concern among NASA engineers that the O-rings might fail, but the shuttle launched in spite of these concerns.

How could a collection of such brilliant minds have committed such a grave error? Although some faulty leadership may have played a role, there were many people involved in the exchange of information as well as in the final decision making. Indeed, decision making in a group is more complex than decision making by one leader or between just two people, and thus it is important to examine the forces that influence the group decision-making process. In the following sections, we examine each of these topics in detail, looking at the *Challenger* disaster specifically as an example of what can go wrong in group decision making.

Groupthink

The *Challenger* disaster is often pointed to as a classic example of **groupthink**—a problem in which group members strive to maintain cohesiveness and minimize conflict by refusing to critically examine ideas, analyze proposals, or test solutions (Janis, 1982). After the disaster, NASA engineers testified that the climate at NASA made them reluctant to voice their concerns if they couldn't back them up with a full set of data (McConnell, 1987). Indeed, the Rogers Commission (1986), which investigated the disaster, noted that had safety concerns been more clearly articulated—and had NASA management been more receptive to concerns raised by engineers from various departments—it is unlikely that *Challenger* would have launched that day.

Engaging in productive conflict fosters healthy debate and leads to better decision making. Unity and cohesion are important for groups to operate effectively, but if these qualities are taken to an extreme—that is, if they become more powerful than members' desire to evaluate alternative courses of action—the group can't generate enough diverse ideas to make smart decisions (Miller & Morrison, 2009; Park, 2000). This appears to have been the case at NASA in the 1980s. In a more receptive group climate, a productive conflict over the O-rings might have revealed the problems that the engineers sensed but couldn't quite voice specifically. The following are some symptoms of groupthink that you should be aware of in your group interactions:

- Participants reach outward consensus and avoid expressing disagreement so as not to hurt each other's feelings or appear disloyal.

- Members who do express disagreement with the majority are pressured to conform to the majority view.

- Tough questions are ignored or discouraged.

- Members spend more effort justifying their decisions than testing them.

© Bettmann/Corbis

FIGURE 29.7 Sometimes voicing dissent is more important than group unity. If the engineers at NASA had shared their concerns, the *Challenger* disaster might not have happened.

One important way to prevent groupthink is to encourage dissent among members and manage it productively (Klocke, 2007). For example, frame conflicts as disagreements over issues or ideas, not as evidence of a weak character or some other personal shortcoming in particular members. To illustrate, when someone in the group expresses a dissenting viewpoint, don't say, "It's clear that you aren't as dedicated to our cause as I had hoped." Instead, say something like "It looks like we have some different ideas circulating about how to handle this new problem. Let's list these ideas and talk about the possible benefits and risks of each of them." A recent study by

Aakhus and Rumsey (2010) supports this point by noting that productive conflict can generate more supportive communication for members of an online cancer support community than simply expecting members to keep dissenting opinions private.

Forces That Shape Group Decision Making

Experts have identified three forces—cognitive, psychological, and social—that strongly affect how groups and their leaders discuss and arrive at decisions (Hirokawa, Gouran, & Martz, 1988). All of them appear to have played some role in the *Challenger* disaster.

Cognitive Forces

Cognitive forces consist of group members' thoughts, beliefs, and emotions. These affect how everyone in a particular group perceives, interprets, evaluates, stores, and retrieves information, which in turn influences the group's decisions. NASA officials who made the fateful decision to launch the *Challenger* shuttle apparently discounted the credibility of key information available to them at the time, and they drew incorrect conclusions from the data. They also wrongly believed that the shuttle system was sound, which made them overly confident in their ability to have a successful launch.

Psychological Forces

Psychological forces refer to group members' personal motives, emotions, attitudes, and values. In the *Challenger* disaster, lower-level NASA decision makers had initially recommended postponing the launch until the day warmed up. But when higher-ups pressured them to reverse their recommendation, they caved in—perhaps because they were worried about losing their jobs if they didn't go along.

The decision makers also changed their attitudes about which criteria to use for postponing a shuttle launch. Previously, NASA rules dictated that a launch wouldn't take place if anyone doubted its safety. But with the *Challenger*, the rule had changed: the launch would proceed unless someone presented conclusive evidence that it was unsafe. Engineers hesitated to express their inconclusive qualms, and so the launch proceeded.

Social Forces

Social forces are group standards for behavior that influence decision making. In the *Challenger* disaster, engineers were unable to persuade their own managers and higher NASA officials to postpone the launch. They tried to prove that it was *unsafe* to launch rather than take the opposite (and possibly more effective) tactic: showing that no data existed to prove that the launch was *safe*. Part of the difficulty may have been some loyalty to or pride in the NASA identity. With so many years of successes in the space program, many members may have felt that no project of NASA's could *be* unsafe.

AND YOU?
How do cognitive, psychological, and social forces affect decision making in the groups in which you're currently involved? Have these forces ever caused your group to make a poor decision? If so, how?

The Problem-Solving Process

As the *Challenger* disaster illustrates, group decision making is complicated and affected by social forces that can hamper communication—sometimes with tragic results. How can groups come to better decisions? To make decisions, groups and their leaders often go through a six-step process (Dewey, 1933). To illustrate these steps, consider EcoCrew, a group of sixteen environmentally active students at a West Coast community college who wish to resolve environmental problems in their community.

Identifying the Problem

The EcoCrew group has scheduled its first meeting in the student union lounge. Susan, the group's founder, is the designated leader. Deciding to adopt a participative leadership style, Susan invites each person to give his or her perception of the problem the group will set out to address before debates or questions occur. Members pipe up with a number of issues and activities they'd like the group to address. One suggests the elimination of plastic bags from campus shops; another wants to address littering on the beaches.

By inviting members to voice their concerns one at a time, Susan is providing an opportunity for the group to identify and define several problems. Once all the members have presented their views, Susan encourages the group to discuss the various proposed definitions of the problem and agree on one that EcoCrew can productively address. The group decides that litter, both on campus and on the nearby beach, is the most immediately troubling environmental issue.

Having defined the problem it wants to address, EcoCrew has gotten off to an effective start. According to researchers, many groups don't spend enough time identifying the problem they want to tackle (Gouran, 2003). Without a clear, agreed-on problem to address, a group can't work through the rest of the decision-making process in a focused way.

CONNECT

Brainstorming and clustering can help you in both public speaking and small group settings. When choosing a topic, both strategies allow you to generate ideas based on your interests, your audience's interests, and your time constraints. In a group, brainstorming and clustering allow you to identify and discuss solutions from a variety of perspectives to ensure that the solution meets the needs of the group.

Analyzing the Problem

Having decided to tackle litter cleanup as its primary mission, EcoCrew begins to analyze the problem. Susan suggests that members each carry a diary for a week and note how much litter they see and where. When the group meets again the following week, all members agree that the two biggest litter problems in the area are on the beaches and in the wooded areas surrounding the campus parking lots. Several members note that the trash cans on the beaches are not being emptied often enough by city sanitation workers, causing trash overflow to be blown onto the beach by the ocean wind.

Generating Solutions

Once the EcoCrew team has identified and analyzed the problem, the next step is to come up with a solution. Susan starts asking for ideas from the group and writes them down on a whiteboard to be evaluated later.

This technique, called **brainstorming**, encourages members of a group to come up with as many ideas as possible without judging the merits of those ideas at first. The intent is to prompt fresh thinking and to generate a larger number of potential solutions than a group might arrive at if members evaluated each idea as it came up. As the EcoCrew members throw out idea after idea, the whiteboard grows dense and colorful with possibilities (see **FIGURE 29.9**).

Once the members have run out of new ideas, they'll need to narrow down the list. To help them focus on the one or two strongest ideas, Susan invites them to define the criteria that eventual solutions will have to meet. First, Susan reminds them that the primary goal would be to reduce litter on the beach. Another member, Wade, then points out that at this point, the group has no budget, so it needs to limit its initial efforts to tasks that have little or no cost. Another member, Larissa, notes that because the group has a relatively small membership, it should focus on things either that the group can manage on its own or in which the group could encourage nonmembers to participate. The group concludes that an acceptable solution must meet these key criteria.

Punchstock/Getty Images

FIGURE 29.8 Writing down any ideas that your team has on a whiteboard can be a great way to get the creative juices flowing.

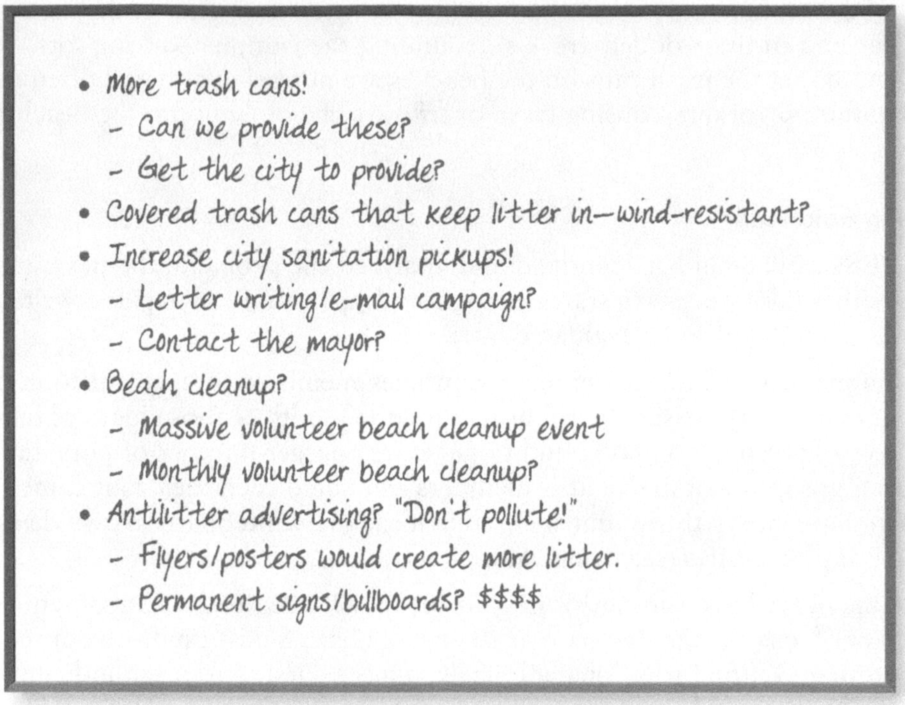

- More trash cans!
  - Can we provide these?
  - Get the city to provide?
- Covered trash cans that keep litter in—wind-resistant?
- Increase city sanitation pickups!
  - Letter writing/e-mail campaign?
  - Contact the mayor?
- Beach cleanup?
  - Massive volunteer beach cleanup event
  - Monthly volunteer beach cleanup?
- Antilitter advertising? "Don't pollute!"
  - Flyers/posters would create more litter.
  - Permanent signs/billboards? $$$$

FIGURE 29.9 Susan's Whiteboard

Evaluating and Choosing Solutions

Once EcoCrew has generated its list of possible solutions, group members have to evaluate the pros and cons of each idea to consider how well it meets the criteria the members have defined. For example, one member, Kathryn, points out that the lack of funding makes replacing the garbage cans out of the question and would make an antilitter advertising campaign difficult, if not impossible. Wade notes that organizing a beach cleanup would cost next to nothing: they could all volunteer to get together to pick up garbage and clean up the beach. Larissa adds that if they get the word out, they'd also be able to attract additional volunteers—and potential new members— from outside the group to participate. Thus the group decides to launch a monthly beach cleanup: a regular social event to raise awareness of the group, encourage nonmembers to participate and new members to join, and involve little to nothing in terms of cost.

Implementing the Solution

Implementing a solution means putting into action the decision that the group has made. For EcoCrew, this means making plans for the regular beach cleanup. The group focuses first on logistics—setting dates and times. One member, Allison, volunteers to act as a liaison with the county sanitation department to see if it can provide trash bags and picks for the volunteers and to arrange for the sanitation trucks to pick up the trash once it's been bagged.

Larissa adds that, with a bit of legwork, the group could turn the cleanup into a large community event; she volunteers to arrange for an end-of-day gathering and to see if she can get her mother's sandwich shop to donate food. Wade notes that he can probably get his roommate's band to entertain free of charge as well.

FIGURE 29.10 After their beach cleanup, the EcoCrew team needs to assess the results. The first question should be: "Was the beach cleaner after our event?"

Assessing the Results

Once a group has implemented its agreed-upon solution, members should evaluate the results. Evaluation can shed light on how effective the solution was and whether the group needs to make further decisions about the problem at hand. For EcoCrew, it will be helpful to assess the first event in terms of how well it met the three key criteria:

- Was the beach cleaner at the end of the day as a result of the group's efforts? Before-and-after photos of the beach reveal a very successful cleanup.

- Did the event wind up costing the members any money? Thanks to the donations of local restaurants and supplies provided by the county sanitation department, along with free advertising via social networks, the event cost the group absolutely nothing.

- Did the event attract volunteers from outside the group? Fifteen nonmembers participated in the cleanup, among them several schoolchildren who attended with their parents.

By revisiting these criteria, the group is able to tweak its plan for the following month's cleanup event. Larissa suggests that the members pitch in a few dollars to place an ad in the local paper thanking the volunteers and donors and announcing the date of the next cleanup. Wade follows up by suggesting that the group make a pitch at the nearby schools to get more local families involved. Kathryn volunteers to submit a brief story about the cleanup, along with photos of the event and the results, to the campus newspaper. And Susan suggests holding a raffle at the next event, with half the proceeds paid out in prizes and half retained by the group, to get a small budget started to cover future ads and expenses.

AND YOU?
Consider the six steps to problem solving we've just discussed. If Susan, the leader of EcoCrew, had chosen a different leadership style, would this have affected how the problem-solving steps were carried out? If so, how? What has your experience been in solving problems in groups with different types of leaders?

■ Leadership in Meetings

EcoCrew was able to identify a problem, create a solution, and implement it very successfully. Much of the planning and implementation took place in meetings. Group leader Susan was able to direct the discussion and manage the deliberations in ways that kept the group focused and invited input from all participants. Indeed, meetings—be they face to face, over the phone, online, or through a combination of media—are an integral part of many group activities. But they are not always successful, and the failure of a meeting often rests on the shoulders of the group leader.

Consider Julia, a freelance Web designer who works from a home office. On Friday, Julia received an e-mail from her biggest client, Jacob, asking her to phone in to a meeting with the sales team to discuss marketing materials related to the launch of the new Web site she's designing for his skateboard manufacturing company. Struggling with several competing deadlines, Julia dreaded spending an hour or two listening to a group of people she'd never met discuss parts of the project with which she had little to do. But she reluctantly confirmed that she could take part in the meeting the following Monday.

After spending the better part of Monday morning reviewing her design for the project and outlining a few ideas for ways it could be teased into the marketing campaign, Julia dutifully dialed in to the conference room at the designated time, only to find herself placed on hold for twenty minutes before the meeting began. What followed was equally frustrating: Jacob spent the better part of an hour describing all aspects of the site to the team of salespeople, who were entirely unfamiliar with the project. Julia—who was responsible only for creating the look and functionality of the Web site and had nothing to do with content or sales—sat miserably watching the clock, grateful that at least the team couldn't see her as she scribbled angry doodles and notes to herself.

Meetings can be integral to group decision making, but they can often be unproductive and frustrating. Ineffective meetings are one of the top time wasters cited by workers: one survey of more than thirty-eight thousand workers worldwide found that people spend more than five working hours per week in meetings, and about 70 percent of the respondents felt that most meetings weren't productive (Microsoft, 2005). In this section, we'll analyze meetings from a communication perspective and consider how they can be best used to arrive at better decisions and solutions. We'll discuss how technology has changed meetings—and how it hasn't. Most important, we'll show that effective leadership is crucial to conducting effective and productive meetings.

CONNECT

Planning a meeting can be similar to planning a speech, particularly regarding audience analysis. In both contexts, you must be aware of the expectations and goals of others involved (your audience or attendees): Why are they present? Why should they listen to you? How is the meeting or speech relevant to them? In addition, you need to consider the situational context for the event (location, room setup, and so on) in both contexts to ensure that it won't inhibit communication.

Planning Meetings Effectively

Let's consider all the reasons why Julia found the meeting we've just described so frustrating. First, it was a bad time: she was struggling to meet deadlines and really didn't want to stop working to sit in on a meeting. Worse, she probably didn't really have to be there either—the client was using the meeting to inform the sales team about the site as a whole, not to discuss Julia's design. Further complicating the issues were the meeting's late start, Julia's unfamiliarity with the sales force, and a medium—speakerphone—that limited Julia's communication with the team. Put simply, the meeting was poorly planned.

Proper planning is crucial for successful meetings. Making a few decisions beforehand and taking steps to clarify goals and logistics for the team can lead to more effective decision making during the meeting itself. There are several steps that group leaders can take to plan meetings more effectively.

> ### AND YOU?
>
> How do you feel about group meetings? Do you find them energizing, boring, or a waste of time? Consider an effective meeting and an ineffective meeting that you've attended. To what degree did the leaders plan appropriately, justify each meeting, and clarify the purpose?

Justify the Meeting

Before calling a meeting, a group leader should consider what he or she wants to accomplish and assess whether a meeting is even necessary to meet that goal. If there are no clear goals for a meeting, it's impossible for any goals to be met as a result of it. The leader also needs to ensure that only those whose presence is necessary in order to meet the goals or who would truly benefit from attending are included.

In many cases, meetings can be avoided altogether or made smaller and more efficient by asking team members to contribute information ahead of time or simply picking up the phone to ask someone a question when one arises (Conlin, 2006).

Clarify the Purpose and the Participants

If a meeting is necessary, it is the responsibility of the leader to clearly articulate the goals of the meeting and the roles of everyone who is to attend. Think back to Julia's situation. Her client, Jacob, wants to get his sales force interested and excited about the launch of the Web site. Getting the sales force together to view the beta version and get feedback on it might seem like a good way to brainstorm ideas for marketing. But Jacob failed to clarify what he wanted to accomplish at the meeting and what Julia's role would be. He might have made a more efficient use of Julia's time by discussing elements of the design with her prior to the meeting or asking her to outline a few key features for him to use in the meeting without her actually attending.

Set an Agenda

President Dwight D. Eisenhower noted, "I have often found that plans are useless, but planning is indispensable." Creating a plan is a valuable phase in decision making, even if the plan itself isn't followed to the letter in the end. Setting an agenda is crucial.

An **agenda** for a meeting should detail the meeting's subject, goal, logistics, and schedule. It should list or include any materials that participants would need to have read or reviewed in advance of the meeting so that everyone arrives with the appropriate background on the issue. Think of your agenda as a checklist—an essential component of meeting success (Gawande, 2009). A sample agenda for Jacob's meeting is provided in **FIGURE 29.11**.

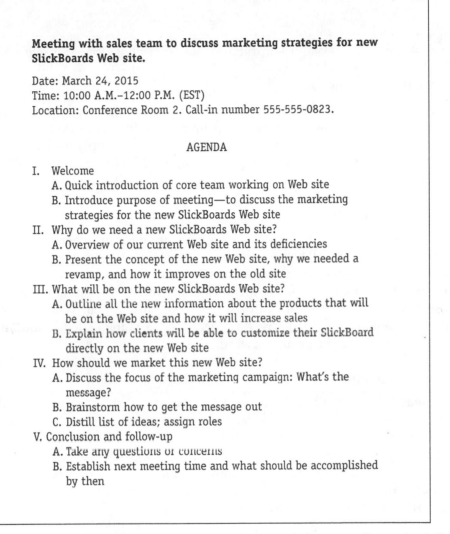

Meeting with sales team to discuss marketing strategies for new SlickBoards Web site.

Date: March 24, 2015
Time: 10:00 A.M.–12:00 P.M. (EST)
Location: Conference Room 2. Call-in number 555-555-0823.

AGENDA

I. Welcome
   A. Quick introduction of core team working on Web site
   B. Introduce purpose of meeting—to discuss the marketing strategies for the new SlickBoards Web site
II. Why do we need a new SlickBoards Web site?
   A. Overview of our current Web site and its deficiencies
   B. Present the concept of the new Web site, why we needed a revamp, and how it improves on the old site
III. What will be on the new SlickBoards Web site?
   A. Outline all the new information about the products that will be on the Web site and how it will increase sales
   B. Explain how clients will be able to customize their SlickBoard directly on the new Web site
IV. How should we market this new Web site?
   A. Discuss the focus of the marketing campaign: What's the message?
   B. Brainstorm how to get the message out
   C. Distill list of ideas; assign roles
V. Conclusion and follow-up
   A. Take any questions or concerns
   B. Establish next meeting time and what should be accomplished by then

FIGURE 29.11 Jacob's Agenda: Although Jacob's meeting agenda is very well organized, there is no indication that Julia needs to be present for it or that she plays a role in this meeting.

Managing Meetings Effectively

So you now see that meetings can go well—or they can go horribly off track. During a meeting, the leader is responsible for managing the discussion in ways that help the group communicate while remaining focused on the meeting's goal. The following steps can help.

Arrive Prepared

When running a meeting, it's crucial that the leader has done the preparation we described previously. As the leader, if you've planned properly, you are fully aware of your goals for the meeting and familiar with all the background information you'll need. If you can't articulate a goal for the meeting, you probably shouldn't call the meeting at all (*Business Week*, 2005).

CONNECT

To keep a group focused and productive, you must employ effective listening skills. You might think that leaders should talk more than listen, but without informational, critical, and empathic listening skills, they miss opportunities to learn new information from others or to analyze ideas that might help the group achieve goals.

Keep the Group Focused

Participants often contribute relevant information during meetings, but they also often get off track. When a member brings up a topic that's not on the agenda or goes off on a tangent, the leader should politely interrupt by simply noting, "We're getting off the subject here," which can bring the group back to the main focus of the meeting (*Business Week*, 2005).

Keep an Eye on the Time

Nobody likes wasting time sitting through a long meeting when a short one would do. Group leaders need to be aware of time constraints to keep their meetings running efficiently and to respect the time pressures on the other members. When large groups are involved or when the agenda includes many topics or issues, it can be helpful to impose *time limits* on certain components of the discussion. When a decision must be made, taking an informal vote on a decision—a tactic called a **nonbinding straw poll**—can help move the group forward.

Manage Distractions

Unfortunately, even the best of us can easily become distracted. In particular, the use of cell phones during meetings can really harm group productivity: checking e-mail or texts (or surfing the Web!) is totally inappropriate and often offensive to colleagues. Research shows that cell phone use impacts the way group members perceive individual communication competence (Tolman, 2012). Thus, it's essential that your group comes up with a policy regarding proper etiquette and behavior during its meetings, particularly in regard to cell phone use.

Jordin Althaus/©Fox/Courtesy Everett Collection

FIGURE 29.12 Although Dr. Mindy Lahiri and her colleagues often disagree about how best to run their practice, they're able to work through disputes to manage a well-respected office known for strong patient care.

Manage Conflict

The best decisions are usually those that have come from productive conflict (Kuhn & Poole, 2000; Nicotera, 1997). When group members deal with conflict productively, they ask clarifying questions, respectfully challenge one another's ideas, consider worst-case scenarios, and revise proposals as needed to reflect new information and insights. This process leads to sound decisions because it enables group members to generate the widest possible range of ideas as well as test each idea's pros and cons. An idea that survives this rigorous process has a better chance of succeeding in action.

The other advantage of productive conflict is that the group members who have a hand in exploring and arriving at a decision will feel a greater sense of ownership over the decision, which leads to greater commitment. Thus, decisions made through productive conflict have a greater chance of being implemented. That's a good thing, since even the most brilliant decision is useless unless a group puts it into action.

REAL COMMUNICATOR

NAME: Aaron Tolson

OCCUPATION: Dancer, Choreographer, Instructor

I jump feet first into my work. I am a tap dance instructor, performer, and choreographer, and—together with my voice—I use my feet to champion the art form, promote it worldwide, and share it with others.

Tap is my life. I choreograph, produce, and direct a number of programs and shows, as well as perform and teach around the United States and internationally. As a teacher, I take the role of directive leader, as students come to me from all over the world for instruction on how to learn the art of tap. This type of dance is very popular throughout Europe and also in Russia and in Japan, so I have the pleasure of working with a varied group of international students. Beyond my dance expertise, I also share my own stories of failings and successes in order to help my students navigate the complex (and sometimes difficult) world of professional dance.

I read my classes for their learning style, observe their nonverbal behavior, and adapt my leadership approach accordingly. The pace and tempo of the classes vary, as well as my leadership behaviors. For example, with older students I'm less sarcastic and with younger groups I use more humor.

I've been interested in dance since the age of ten. I also ran track and was able to get a track scholarship to college, where I earned an undergraduate degree in communication. During my time there, I also focused on looking for opportunities to dance wherever I could. By my senior year, I landed a place in the New York Shakespeare Festival tap program, Funk U!

After college, I became a company member in Manhattan Tap. My big break came when I was chosen for a featured role in *Riverdance*. I toured with *Riverdance* for six years as a soloist and dance captain of an extremely talented and motivated group. We performed at Radio City Music Hall, on Broadway, at NBA games, and on stages around the world.

Having become a leader in the tap community, I was made national spokesman for SóDança, a professional dancewear company. Since I was chosen for my expertise, I appreciate the opportunity to try out their tap shoes and offer ideas to make them even better. I've even gotten the chance to help design a pink shoe that represents my daughter. I met my wife when choreographing her tap number for the Miss America Pageant, so I have dance to thank for the two most important ladies in my life.

In an effort to enhance and develop tap opportunities for aspiring dancers, I helped to create Speaking in Taps, a preprofessional company designed to teach youth, as well as Tap2You, a program that offers classes and tap competitions (which I started with a business partner, Derick Grant). Through all these endeavors, I strive to emphasize the rhythm, musicality, and timing of tap with a strong focus on performance and education. I hope to inspire others to do what I did: jump feet first into a dancing career.

For this reason, making decisions by **consensus**—group solidarity in sentiment, belief, or decision—is often a better approach than making decisions by majority vote. According to the consensus approach, everyone must agree on the final decision before it can be implemented. It takes more time than deciding by majority vote, but it can be a powerful way to enhance feelings of ownership and commitment from group members. One caution, however, is to be careful to encourage *genuine* consensus, rather than allowing group members to silence their opposition in order to preserve group harmony!

AND YOU?
Do you have experience with group conflict as either a group member or leader? If so, how was this conflict handled? Did conflict strengthen or weaken the communication between group members?

Summarize Periodically

As a group explores and settles on decisions, it's important that someone (a leader or any member) regularly summarize what has happened. Summaries provide members with opportunities to confirm, correct, or clarify what has occurred so far during the conversation. Summaries thus help ensure agreement, formation of next steps, and how members are to carry out their designated tasks.

Follow Up

After the meeting has concluded, group members should implement their decisions and take stock of the results as well as the experience of working together. A simple follow-up e-mail that details the decisions reached at the meeting can ensure that everyone comes away with the same perceptions and is aware of what each person must do to keep the group moving toward its goal.

Using Meeting Technology Effectively

Technology has changed the nature of meetings in both positive and negative ways. Obviously, the ability to set up virtual meetings through teleconferencing and Internet videoconferencing makes it possible for groups to collaborate over long distances. That's how Julia, the freelance designer, is able to "attend" a meeting with her client and his sales staff without leaving home. Such virtual links can be beneficial for a team that needs to actively communicate about some issue or problem. But it also can be ineffective; the fact that everyone *can* be included doesn't necessarily mean that everyone *must* be included. Julia, for example, did not need to sit in on the meeting with the sales team; she had little to add and gained nothing by being there. Further, the ability to share information with team members quickly and efficiently via e-mail and file sharing has enabled teams to avoid some meetings altogether (Conlin, 2006). Julia and Jacob, for example, might have e-mailed a link to the beta version of the site to the entire sales team rather than having a meeting to discuss it in the abstract.

Busco/Getty Images

FIGURE 29.13 Research indicates that although group members work better face to face initially, individuals who are familiar with each other and established as a team also work productively with videoconferencing technology.

WIRED FOR COMMUNICATION

Leadership. With Lasers.

Hands-on managers usually like to make some kind of personal connection with all their employees. But how can they do it when employees are spread across several offices, in different cities, even in different countries?

Evernote CEO Phil Libin uses technology to bridge the gap. Huge video monitors, along with webcams, are installed in high traffic areas of both the corporate headquarters in Mountainview, California, and studio office in Austin, Texas. But the monitors are not there for videoconferencing. The idea was to create, essentially, a window from one office to the other to connect the two spaces in a way that would encourage casual chats between coworkers in different places. The connection, Libin explains, helps to foster a cohesive atmosphere between the main office and the satellite studio. "We very specifically wanted to avoid the feeling that if you're not working at headquarters, you're in a second-place office" (Libin, quoted in Bryant, 2012, para 26).

But encouraging interconnectedness between his scattered employees wasn't quite enough for Libin. He wanted a way to be in both offices, even when he couldn't be in either one. And so, enter the robots: Libin can log into "his anybot," a six-foot-tall, mobile "telepresence" (think of a Segway with an iPad on top) and take a virtual stroll around the office, carrying a live feed from his webcam. The robot serves as his eyes and ears and allows him to have casual conversations with employees he meets as he drives his robotic avatar around. Libin also points out that the robot has a laser pointer. "You can shoot lasers, which is just good design," he explains. "You shouldn't build a robot without a laser" (quoted in Bryant, 2012, para. 28).

As a programmer turned CEO, it's probably not surprising that Libin is so eager to embrace technology. But just as he's brought in some new electronic wizardry, he's also gotten rid of some conventional technology. Specifically, employees at Evernote do not have phones on their desks. Because the work they do generally does not involve phone calls, the company discourages chatter in the work space; employees can chat on their company-provided cell phones just by walking to a quiet area. "If you have a phone at your desk, it's just sitting there and you're kind of encouraging people to talk on it. . . . If you're at your desk, you should be working. And that's actually worked really well. I don't think anyone misses phones. Even though it's one big room, it's actually fairly quiet because no one is sitting there talking at their desk" (quoted in Bryant, 2012, para. 12).

THINK ABOUT THIS

1. What advantage does a mobile robot offer over a simple phone call or a video chat? Is it a tool or a toy?

2. What does the use of a robot say about Libin's leadership style? Do you think it's effective?

3. Does the idea of a constant live video stream between two offices seem inviting or invasive to you? Do you think such a channel would encourage competent communication?

4. What kinds of companies do you think are more likely to be early adopters of technology like robots or virtual windows? Do you think their employees would be more receptive than those in other sorts of businesses? Do the same factors affect the acceptability of removing former technology, like phones?

But is there a difference between face-to-face meetings and virtual meetings? Research indicates that face-to-face teams perform better initially. However, once the group is established, virtual teams actually do better at brainstorming, whereas face-to-face teams perform better on tasks that require negotiation or compromise (Alge, Wiethoff, & Klein, 2003; Salkever, 2003). Savvy team leaders, then, will bring their teams together for face time early in the process, if possible, so that team members can get to know one another and get a sense of the others' styles and personalities. But as the teams develop, electronically mediated communication—especially e-mail—can often take the place of face-to-face group meetings.

■ Evaluating Group Performance

Groups that intend to work together and meet on a regular basis should evaluate their decision-making performance periodically. By assessing how well the group makes decisions, achieves its goals, and solves problems, a group can identify and address areas needing improvement. Regular and consistent assessment helps ensure quality and improvement (Beebe, Mottet, & Roach, 2012). When evaluating your group's performance, it's helpful to assess the group's overall effectiveness as well as the performance of individual members and leaders.

Kowitz and Knutson (1980), scholars with extensive research on evaluating groups, recommend assessing three aspects of a group's performance: the informational, procedural, and interpersonal considerations.

Informational Considerations

Ask yourself whether your group is working on a task that requires everyone's expertise and insights. If not, the group doesn't actually need to be a group! In this case, it should select a different task or assign just one or two members to deal with the current task.

If the task does require contributions from all members, how well is the group doing on this front? For example, are members conducting needed research and inviting one another to share information during group gatherings? Does the group know when it needs to get more data before making a decision? Does the group analyze problems well? Come up with creative solutions? Offer opinions respectfully? Elaborate on problems, concerns, and solutions?

By regularly assessing these aspects of information management in your group, you can identify where the group is falling short and address the problem promptly. For instance, if you notice that the group rushes to make decisions without getting all the facts first, you could say something like "I think we need to find out more about the problem before we take action."

Jon Feingersh/Getty Images

FIGURE 29.14 Think about whether each group member's expertise is necessary to achieve a goal. If not, those members don't need to be present.

Procedural Effectiveness

How well does your group coordinate its activities and communication? Key things to evaluate on this front are how the group elicits contributions, delegates and directs action, summarizes decisions, handles conflict, and manages processes. For example, do some members talk too much while others give too little input? If so, the group needs someone to improve the balance of contributions. Simply saying something like "Allie, I think we should hear from some other people on this subject" can be very effective. Or does your group tend to revisit issues it has already decided on? If so, you can expect many members to express frustration with this time-wasting habit. A leader or another member can steer the group back toward its current task by saying something like "OK, what we've been talking about is..." or "I'm not sure revisiting this previous decision is helping us deal with our current problem."

Interpersonal Performance

How would you describe the relationships among the members of your group while everyone is working together to accomplish a task? If these relationships are strained, awkward, or prickly, the group probably won't function effectively. Observe how group members behave on the following four fronts:

- Do they provide *positive reinforcement* for one another—for instance, by showing appreciation for each other's contributions and hard work?

- Do members seem to feel a sense of *solidarity* with one another—for example, by sharing responsibility for both successes and failures?

- Do members *cooperate freely* with one another, fulfilling the responsibilities they've agreed to shoulder and pitching in when needed?

- Do members demonstrate *respect* for one another—for example, by keeping disagreements focused on the issues at hand rather than on personal character?

If you can answer yes to these four questions, your group scores high on interpersonal performance.

CONNECT

As you evaluate interpersonal performance, you are essentially determining what type of climate your group has developed. Supportive climates—in which individuals are open to and supportive of one another's ideas—often have an advantage in being effective and achieving goals.

Individual Performance

One of the most important assessments you can make is about yourself and what predispositions you bring to the group. According to Keyton and Frey (2002), **grouphate** is the extent to which you detest (or otherwise feel negatively about) working in groups. To assess grouphate, group members are asked a series of questions about the degree to which they like or dislike working in groups:

- I like working in groups.

- I would rather work alone.

- Group work is fun.

- Groups are terrible.

- I would prefer to work in an organization in which teams are used.

- My ideal job is one in which I can be interdependent with others.

To what extent to you agree or disagree with each of these questions? Your basic orientation to group interaction can influence your communication. It is not always easy to work with others but it is a fact of organizational (and academic) life. This process of self-introspection will foster personal growth and learning.

Conversely, your group can also benefit from systematic assessments of team members. Simple evaluation forms can be created and used to evaluate team members on a variety of qualities. For example, you can rate your team members on the quality of their contributions. Specific questions pertaining to a team member could include the following:

- Was the team member prepared for meetings and well informed?

- Did the team member meet individual responsibilities and deadlines?

- Was the team member respectful and tactful with fellow team members?

- Did the team member listen to, understand, and follow the group's discussions?

- Were the team member's comments relevant and well timed?

- Was the team member open-minded?

- Did the team member deal with conflict appropriately and effectively?

Both self-assessment and peer evaluations can provide information that can benefit the group by identifying areas of concern or deficiency and suggest specific areas for improvement. This information will only help improve the group process and decision making. In sum, assessment is healthy for the life and success of a group.

Back To *Brooklyn Nine-Nine*

At the beginning of this chapter, we took a look at Captain Ray Holt, the fictional commanding officer at a New York police precinct on the sitcom *Brooklyn Nine-Nine*. Let's take a look at Holt's leadership in light of what we've learned in this chapter.

- In the NYPD, there is a clear hierarchy of legitimate power. As commanding officer, Captain Holt has authority over all of his detectives, but even a captain must defer to the chiefs who outrank him. For Holt, that meant "being a good soldier" and working in the public affairs office for many years. Although that job did not align with Holt's career goals, it helped the department to meet other goals: having a gay (and African American) captain in a high-profile role helped the department to change its image and improve recruitment.

- Holt's power is rooted not only in his rank as captain (legitimate power) but also in his experience as a veteran officer who knows how to solve major cases (expert power). As commanding officer, he also has coercive and reward power—he can reward or punish his detectives based on their performance. His personal story, too, affords him an additional degree of referent power: over the course of his long career, Holt overcame prejudices within the department and played a central role in changing the face of the NYPD, something his young, diverse squad might have taken for granted.

- In a police squad room, there is an expectation of a directive style of leadership—supervisors lay out clear instructions, and officers are expected to follow those instructions. But Holt knows that, despite their hijinks, his detectives are capable and competent. For this reason, he can take a more achievement-oriented approach, setting goals and providing guidance for meeting those goals.

■ Things To Try

Activities

1. Arrange an interview with the chair, president, or director of an organization to determine how the various groups within the organization operate. How closely do these groups conform to the decision-making process discussed in this chapter? Report what you have learned to the class.

2. Create a chart that lists the four leadership styles described in this chapter (directive, participative, supportive, and achievement oriented). Evaluate the leaders of each of the different groups in which you participate—your boss at work, your professors, your resident assistant in the dorm—in terms of their leadership style. Where do they fall on your chart? Do some fit more than one category? Do some fit none of the categories?

3. Select a city, state, or campus problem that is relevant to the members of your class. Form a group to solve the problem using the six-step decision-making process described in this chapter.

Chapter 30

Organizing the Persuasive Speech

This chapter is taken from Dan O'Hair, Rob Stewart, and Hannah Rubenstein, *A Speakers' Guidebook*, Sixth Edition, pp. 371–389 (Chapter 26).

Once you've developed your persuasive speech claims, the next step is to structure speech points using one (or more) of the organizational patterns—problem-solution, topical/categorical, causal (cause-effect), narrative, chronological, and spatial—and three patterns introduced in this chapter designed specifically for persuasive speeches. There is no one "right" way to organize a persuasive speech—or any kind of speech—but only choices that will be more or less effective for your particular message, audience, and objective. Experimenting with the various patterns can help you to decide; often an effective choice will become apparent fairly quickly.

■ Factors to Consider When Choosing an Organizational Pattern

Beyond experimentation, what criteria should you consider when choosing an organizational pattern? Depending on (1) the nature of your claims (whether of fact, value, or policy), (2) audience members' attitudes toward the topic, and (3) the response you want to elicit from them, certain patterns can be more effective than others.

What Do the Claims and Evidence Suggest?

Some speech topics or claims clearly suggest a specific design. A speech that argues for limiting the sale of minimally nutritious, or "junk," foods in school cafeterias, for example, implies that unrestricted sales of these foods represent a *problem* and that limiting them represents a *solution*. Thus one obvious way to arrange main points is with the *problem-solution pattern*. Many such *claims of policy* (i.e., claims that recommend a specific course of action) fit naturally into the problem-solution pattern. However, another pattern may be equally or more effective for this argument. Perhaps your research has uncovered several advantages associated with limiting junk food and a number of disadvantages associated with not doing so. In this event, the *comparative advantage pattern of arrangement* (see **p. 537** in this chapter) might serve you well.

Similarly, consider a speech in which you argue that religious freedom dictates that people should be legally free to practice polygamy, or to marry multiple partners. One potentially effective way of ordering this *claim of value* (i.e., a claim that addresses issues of judgment) is with the *topical* (also called *categorical*) *pattern of arrangement*. Here, the speaker arranges main points to reflect a series of reasons in support of the claim. (Recall that a topical pattern arranges information according to different subtopics or categories of relatively equal importance within a larger topic.)

Finally, consider the *claim of fact* (i.e., claims addressing whether something is or is not true or will or will not happen) that "Deficits are projected to rise again as more baby boomers begin drawing from Medicare, Medicaid, and Social Security." The claim implies a cause-effect relationship in which a large aging population drawing on services (cause) leads to rising deficits (effect). Alternatively, you could argue this claim in a *problem-solution* or *problem-cause-solution pattern,* so that the first point establishes the problem (rising deficits) and subsequent points explain reasons for the problem (aging population/ need for more services) and provide a solution (raise taxes/lower benefits).

What Response Do You Seek?

All persuasive speeches seek to influence attitudes, but some speeches focus on passive agreement while others encourage action, such as donating to a cause or signing a petition. Thus yet another consideration in choosing how you will order speech points is your *specific speech purpose*—how you want your audience to react to your message. As noted below, one particularly effective pattern for getting people to act is *Monroe's motivated sequence*—a pattern that explicitly calls for audience members to act on the speaker's suggestions. (Remember that in any speech asking audience members to do something, be sure to include a **call to action** (see **p. 152** in **CHAPTER 8.**) **TABLE 30.1** summarizes the patterns discussed in this chapter.

What Is the Attitude of the Audience?

As you can see, examining your claims can help to identify a pattern for your persuasive speech. Another consideration you might consider when selecting an organizational arrangement is where your **target audience** stands in relation to your topic (see **CHAPTER 5**). How receptive to or critical of your claims are they likely to be? Persuasion scholar Herbert Simon describes four types of potential audiences, including the **hostile audience or one that strongly disagrees;** the **critical and conflicted audience;** the **sympathetic audience;** and the **uninformed, less educated, or apathetic audience.** As demonstrated in **TABLE 30.2,** depending on the audience's disposition, certain organizational patterns and persuasive strategies can be more effective than others.[1]

■ Problem-Solution Pattern of Arrangement

One commonly used design for persuasive speeches, especially (but not restricted to) those based on claims of policy, is the **problem-solution pattern of arrangement.** Here you organize speech points to demonstrate the nature and significance of a problem and then to provide justification for a proposed solution:

I.   Problem (define what it is)

II.   Solution (offer a way to overcome the problem)

But many problem-solution speeches require more than two points to adequately explain the problem and to substantiate the recommended solution. Thus a **problem-cause-solution pattern of arrangement** may be in order:

I.   The nature of the problem (define what it is)

II.   Reasons for the problem (explain why it's a problem, for whom, etc.)

III.   Unsatisfactory solutions (discuss those that have not worked) *(optional step)*

IV.   Proposed solution (explain why it's expected to work)

Table 30.1 Sample Organizational Formats

ORGANIZATIONAL FORMAT	DESCRIPTION
Topical/Categorical *(Used in both informative and persuasive speeches)*	Speech points arranged according to different subtopics within a larger topic
Chronological *(Used in both informative and persuasive speeches)*	Speech points arranged according to their occurrence in time relative to each other
Spatial *(Used in both informative and persuasive speeches)*	Speech points arranged in order of their physical proximity or direction relative to each other
Narrative *(Used in both informative and persuasive speeches)*	Speech points tell a story; they can use any design as long as together the points convey the story
Causal (cause-effect) *(Used in both informative and persuasive speeches)*	Speech points arranged to demonstrate that a particular set of circumstances (causes) leads to a specific result (effects) or, conversely, that various results (effects) follow from a particular set of circumstances (causes)
Problem-Solution *(Primarily used in persuasive speeches)*	Speech points arranged to demonstrate a problem and then to offer a solution
Problem-Cause-Solution *(Primarily used in persuasive speeches)*	Speech points arranged in order to demonstrate problem, reasons for problem, and solution to problem
Monroe's Motivated Sequence *(Used in persuasive speeches)*	Speech points arranged to motivate listeners to act on something or to shift their attitudes in direction of speaker's
Comparative Advantage *(Used in persuasive speeches)*	Speech points arranged to demonstrate that your viewpoint or proposal contrasts favorably with (is superior or preferable to) one or more alternative positions
Refutation *(Used in persuasive speeches)*	Speech points arranged to disprove opposing claims

Table 30.2 Persuading Different Types of Audiences

AUDIENCE DISPOSITION	POSSIBLE STRATEGIES
Hostile audience or one that strongly disagrees	• Stress areas of agreement; focus on focus on diffusing anger or suspicion by demonstrating respect
	• Address opposing views
	• Don't expect major changes in attitudes
	• Wait until the end before asking audience to act, if at all
	• Reason *inductively*—start with evidence, leaving conclusion until last ("tuition should be raised")
	• Consider the *refutation* pattern, in which you present both sides of the argument and demonstrate the strength of your position in contrast to the other side (see p. in this chapter).
Critical and conflicted audience	• Present strong arguments and audience evidence
	• Address opposing views, perhaps by using the *refutation* pattern (**see p.538**)
Sympathetic audience	• Use motivational stories and emotional appeals to reinforce positive attitudes
	• Stress your commonality with listeners
	• Clearly tell audience what you want them to think or do
	• Refutation isn't necessary; most patterns appropriate, including the *narrative* (storytelling) pattern
Uninformed, less-educated, or apathetic audience	• Focus on capturing their attention
	• Stress personal credibility and "likability"
	• Stress the topic's relevance to listeners
	• Consider Monroe's motivated sequence

When arguing a claim of policy, it may be important to demonstrate the proposal's feasibility. To do this, consider a four-point *problem-cause-solution-feasibility* pattern: (1) a need or a problem, (2) reasons for the problem, (3) a solution to the need or problem, and (4) evidence of the solution's feasibility.

First comes a *need* or a *problem*. The policy must speak to a real issue that the audience would like to have resolved. If your claim is that "to prevent the collapse of the Social Security system, we should change eligibility requirements," the *need* is for a lessening of financial challenges to funding Social Security. Second, the justification for a policy must provide *reasons for the problem*. One reason that the Social Security program faces financial shortfalls is that too many people are taking money out of the system and too few are putting money into it. (You can list multiple reasons.) Next, you must provide a *solution to the problem*, a specific way to address the need. The policy claim that Social Security should be changed must then offer an alternative policy, such as "The Social Security program needs to raise the normal retirement age from 65 to 70." Fourth, the justification for the policy claim should offer *evidence of the solution's feasibility*. In this case, the speaker could provide evidence showing that based on a retirement age of 70, budget analysts project X amount of savings over a 30-year period.

General Purpose:	To persuade
Specific Purpose:	To persuade my audience that the nation's Social Security program is in danger of collapse and needs a major overhaul.
Thesis Stated as Needed or Problem:	Serious financial challenges to our nation's Social Security program require that we take steps to ensure it will be able to meets its obligations to citizens.
Main Points:	I. To keep Social Security funded, we need to raise both the full benefits age and the early eligibility age. (*Need/problem*)
	II. People are living longer in retirement, which means they are collecting Social Security over a longer period. (*Reasons for the problem; you can offer single or multiple reasons*)
	III. Congress needs to raise the early eligibility age from 62 to 67 and the normal retirement age from 67 to 70. (*Solution to the problem*)
	IV. Social Security programs in countries X and Y have done this successfully. (*Evidence of the solution's feasibility*)

■ Monroe's Motivated Sequence

The **motivated sequence pattern of arrangement**, developed in the mid-1930s by Alan Monroe,[2] is a five-step process that begins with arousing listeners' attention and ends with calling for action. This time-tested variant of the problem-solution pattern of arrangement is particularly effective when you want the audience to do something—buy a product, donate to a cause, and so forth. Yet it is equally useful when you want listeners to reconsider their present way of thinking about something or continue to believe as they do but with greater commitment.

CHECKLIST
Organizing a Claim of Policy Using the Problem-Cause-Solution Pattern
• Describe the need or problem.
• Discuss reasons for the problem.
• Offer a solution to the need or problem.
• Offer evidence of the solution's feasibility..

Step 1: Attention

The *attention step* addresses listeners' core concerns, making the speech highly relevant to them. Here is an excerpt from a student speech by Ed Partlow on becoming an organ donor:

> Today I'm going to talk about a subject that can be both personal and emotional. I am going to talk about becoming an organ donor. Donating an organ is a simple step you can take that will literally give life to others—to your husband or wife, mother or father, son or daughter—or to a beautiful child whom you've never met.
>
> There is one thing I want to acknowledge from the start. Many of you may be uncomfortable with the idea of becoming an organ donor. I want to establish right off that it's OK if you don't want to become a donor.
>
> Many of us are willing to donate our organs, but because we haven't taken the action to properly become a donor, our organs go unused. As a result, an average of eighteen people die every day because of lack of available organs.

In this first step, the speaker makes the topic relevant to listeners by showing how their actions could help those closest to them. He further involves the audience by acknowledging the sensitive nature of his topic and assuring them that he respects their right to make up their own minds. The statistic he cites underscores the seriousness of his purpose.

Step 2: Need

The *need step* isolates the issue to be addressed. If you can show the members of an audience that they have an important need that must be satisfied or a problem that must be solved, they will have a reason to listen to your propositions. Continuing with the organ donor speech, here the speaker establishes the need for organ donors:

> According to statistics compiled by the U.S. Department of Health and Human Services, Organ Procurement and Transplantation Network, found on the OPTN website, there are over 121,000 people on the waiting list *today* for an organ transplant. Each day, about 79 people receive a transplant, but about 18 people die as a result of not getting one in time. According to the National Kidney Foundation, over 96,000 patients are waiting for kidney transplants alone, and the stakes are high: 90 percent of patients who receive a kidney from a living donor live at least ten years after the transplant. One of the people on the waiting list is Aidan Malony, who graduated from this college two years ago. Without a transplant, he will die. It is agonizing for his

family and friends to see him in this condition. And it is deeply frustrating to them that more people don't sign and carry organ donor cards. I have always carried my organ donor card with me, but I didn't realize the extreme importance of doing so before talking to Aidan.

Every ten minutes another name joins that of Aidan Malony and is added to the National Transplant Waiting List.

Step 3: Satisfaction

The *satisfaction step* identifies the solution. This step begins the crux of the speech, offering audience members a proposal to reinforce or change their attitudes, beliefs, and values regarding the need at hand. Here is an example from the speech on organ donation:

It takes only a few steps to become an organ donor.

First, sign up as an organ and tissue donor in your state's donor registry.

Second, designate your decision on your driver's license.

Tell your health care provider and family that you want to become an organ donor and ask them to honor your wishes when the time arrives. If possible, include a directive for organ donation in a living will.

Step 4: Visualization

The *visualization step* provides the audience with a vision of anticipated outcomes associated with the solution. The purpose of the step is to carry audience members beyond accepting the feasibility of your proposal to seeing how it will actually benefit them:

There are so many organs and such a variety of tissue that may be transplanted. One organ donor can help up to fifty people. Who can forget the story of 7-year-old American Nicholas Green, the innocent victim of a highway robbery in Italy that cost him his life? Stricken with grief, Nicholas's parents, Reg and Maggie Green, nevertheless immediately decided to donate Nicholas's organs. As a direct result of the donation, seven Italians thrive today, grateful recipients of Nicholas's heart, corneas, liver, pancreas cells, and kidneys. Today, organ donations in Italy are twice as high as they were in 1993, the year preceding Nicholas's death. The Italians called this phenomenon "The Nicholas Effect."

CHECKLIST
Steps in the Motivated Sequence
• Step 1: *Attention*—address listeners' core concerns, making the speech highly relevant to them.
• Step 2: *Need*—show listeners that they have an important need that must be satisfied or a problem that must be solved.
• Step 3: *Satisfaction*—introduce your proposed solution.
• Step 4: *Visualization*—provide listeners with a vision of anticipated outcomes associated with the solution.
• Step 5: *Action*—make a direct request of listeners that involves changing or strengthening their present way of thinking or acting.

Step 5: Action

Finally, in the *action step* the speaker asks audience members to act according to their acceptance of the message. This may involve reconsidering their present way of thinking about something, continuing to believe as they do but with greater commitment, or implementing a new set of behaviors. Here, the speaker makes an explicit call to action:

> It takes courage to become an organ donor.

> You have the courage to become an organ donor. According to the U.S. Department of Health and Human Services organdonor.gov website, 100 million people in the U.S. have signed up to be an organ donor.

> All you need to do is say yes to organ and tissue donation on your state's donor registry and discuss your decision with your family and health care provider.

> Be part of "The Nicholas Effect."

■ Comparative Advantage Pattern of Arrangement

Another way to organize speech points is to show how your viewpoint or proposal is superior to one or more alternative viewpoints or proposals. This design, called the **comparative advantage pattern of arrangement,** is most effective when your audience is already aware of the issue or problem and agrees that a need for a solution (or an alternative view) exists. Because listeners are alert to the issue, you don't have to spend time establishing its existence. Instead, you can proceed directly to favorably comparing your position with the alternatives.

In order to maintain your credibility, make sure to identify alternatives that your audience is familiar with and ones supported by opposing interests. If you omit familiar alternatives, your listeners will wonder if you are fully informed on the topic and become skeptical of your comparative alternative as well as your credibility. The final step in a comparative advantage speech is to drive home the unique advantages of your option relative to competing options with brief but compelling evidence.

Using the comparative advantage pattern, the main points in a speech addressing the best way to control the deer population might look like this:

Thesis: Rather than hunting, fencing, or contraception alone, the best way to reduce the deer population is by a dual strategy of hunting and contraception.

Main Point I: A combination strategy is superior to hunting alone because many areas are too densely populated by humans to permit hunting; in such cases contraceptive darts and vaccines can address the problem. (*Advantage over alternative No. 1*)

Main Point II: A combination strategy is superior to relying solely on fencing because fencing is far too expensive for widespread use. (*Advantage over alternative No. 2*)

Main Point III: A dual strategy is superior to relying only on contraception because only a limited number of deer are candidates for contraceptive darts and vaccines. (*Advantage over alternative No. 3*)

■ Refutation Pattern of Arrangement

Similar to debate, the **refutation pattern of arrangement** addresses each main point and then refutes (disproves) an opposing claim to your position. The aim here is to bolster your own position by disproving the opposing claim. This pattern can effectively address competing arguments. Refutation is a favorite tool of political candidates, who use it to strengthen their position on an issue and debunk the position taken by the opposing candidate.

If done well, refutation may influence audience members who either disagree with you or are conflicted about where they stand. Note that it is important to refute *strong* rather than *weak* objections to the claim, since refuting weak objections won't sway the audience.[3] Further, it is probably best to use this pattern when you are confident that the opposing argument is weak and vulnerable to attack.

Main points arranged in a refutation pattern follow a format similar to this:

Main Point I: State the opposing position.

Main Point II: Describe the implications or ramifications of the opposing claim.

Main Point III: Offer arguments and evidence for your position.

Main Point IV: Contrast your position with the opposing claim to drive home the superiority of your position.

Consider the speaker who argues for increased energy conservation versus a policy of drilling for oil in protected land in Alaska:

Thesis: Rather than drilling for oil in Alaska's Arctic National Wildlife Refuge (ANWR), we should focus on energy conservation measures as a way of protecting the environment.

Main Point I: Proponents claim that drilling in the Arctic refuge is necessary to decrease dependence on foreign oil sources and hold down fuel costs while adding jobs, and that modern drilling techniques along with certain environmental restrictions will result in little negative impact on the environment. (*Describes opposing claims*)

Main Point II: By calling for drilling, these proponents sidestep our need for stricter energy conservation policies, overlook the need to protect one of the last great pristine lands, and ignore the fact that the oil would make a negligible dent in oil imports—from 68 percent to 65 percent by 2025. (*Describes implications and ramifications of opposing claims*)

Main Point III: The massive construction needed to access the tundra will disturb the habitat of caribou, polar bear, and thousands of species of birds and shift the focus from energy conservation to increased energy consumption, when the focus should be the reverse. (*Offers arguments and evidence for the speaker's position, as developed in subpoints*)

Main Point IV: The proponents' plan would encourage consumption and endanger the environment; my plan would encourage energy conservation and protect one of the world's few remaining wildernesses. (*Contrasts the speaker's position with the opposition's to drive home the former's superiority*)

SAMPLE VISUALLY ANNOTATED PERSUASIVE SPEECH

Becoming a Socially Conscious Consumer

Jacob Hahn

*In this carefully planned persuasive speech, Jacob Hahn offers strong evidence and reasons for his claims in support of socially responsible consumerism. Jacob organizes the speech using Monroe's five-step motivated sequence. He begins with the attention step, making the speech relevant to listeners, and ends with the action step, demonstrating clearly what audience members can do. Note Jacob's persuasive use of language throughout, especially in the strong imagery that helps listeners visualize the tragedy that occurred in a factory in Bangladesh ("bodies, bricks, and garments left in the rubble") and use of personal pronouns to involve audience members personally ("The thousands of miles that separate **us** from tragedies like this can make them seem unrelated to **our** everyday lives. But what if…by purchasing the products these companies make, individuals such as **you** and **me** are also somewhat responsible for what happened?).*

1. Jacob starts the persuasive speech with a dramatic story line ("a few cracks…") that serves as an effective attention getter.

It started with a few cracks in the wall.[1] But then, on April 24, 2013, it became the worst disaster in the history of the garment industry. According to BBC News, on that day the Rana Plaza garment factory in Dhaka, Bangladesh, completely collapsed, leading to the deaths of over 1,100 people.

Jacob uses his own clothing as a visual to show the audience how his topic relates to everyday life.

2. Continuing with the "story" keeps the audience involved and wanting to know more.

Along with the bodies, bricks, and garments left in the rubble, questions remained about who was to blame for the tragedy. Sure, there were the obvious culprits—the plaza owner, the construction company. But, there were other suspects too. What about the companies whose goods were manufactured there? [2] As Emran Hossain and Dave Jamieson pointed out in their May 2, 2013, *Huffington Post* article, garment industry insiders partially blame Western retailers for the tragedy. They claim that it is retailer demand for low-priced labor that creates these poorly constructed and unsafe work factories, which then leads to disasters like the factory collapse.

Gesturing to the audience in an inviting way indicates that Jacob wants the audience to feel involved.

3. Step 1, the *attention* step of Monroe's sequence, demonstrates the topic's relevance to audience members.

The thousands of miles that separate us from tragedies like this can make them seem unrelated to our everyday lives. But what if they are not? What if, by purchasing the products these companies make, individuals such as you and me are also somewhat responsible for what happened? [3]

4. Jacob states his thesis.

As we'll see today, there is evidence to support the idea that consumers and companies share a responsibility to ensure safer conditions for factory workers. [4] This is why I encourage all of you to become socially conscious consumers and help convince companies to adopt ethical manufacturing standards. Being a socially conscious consumer means being aware of the issues communities face worldwide and actively trying to correct them.

Jacob is conscious to make eye contact with audience members in every area of the room.

Why would companies do business with factories that allow dangerous working conditions? It's actually quite simple: Corporations want bigger profit margins. The cheaper the production costs, the more money they make when the product sells. And since consumers show more interest in buying lower-priced products than in thinking about how such items are produced, the pressure is on to provide inexpensive goods. The only way to do this and still make money is to make the goods at the lowest cost possible.

But there is a way to break this cycle of cheap labor and deadly working conditions. You, me, all of us as consumers, must be willing to step up and take an active role in the system. [5]

We can do this in two ways: First, we can pressure companies to improve working conditions for factory laborers, and second, we can pay fairer prices. Some consumer groups are now signaling their willingness to do this, and corporations are responding. [6]

The force behind this new kind of partnership is called "cause-related marketing." According to the *Financial Times, cause-related marketing* is when a company and a charity (or a consumer group) tackle a social or an environmental problem and create business value for the company at the same time. [7]

Coordinating body movement with his speech drives home his main points.

In March 2012, the global marketing firm Nielsen conducted a worldwide study on consumer responses to cause marketing. The poll found that two-thirds of consumers around the world say they prefer to buy products and services from companies that give back to society. Nearly 50 percent of consumers said that they were, and I'm quoting here, "willing to pay more for goods and services from companies that are giving back." [8]

The fact that large numbers of consumers are concerned enough about fairness to pay more for products is key to solving the problems that surround the ethical manufacture of clothing. Corporations can appeal to this group of socially conscious consumers, as they are called, by addressing concerns about ethical manufacturing. What do corporations gain by meeting these concerns? It allows them to charge more for their products while also raising their profit margins and improving their brand image. This means that as socially conscious consumers, we can set the standards that corporations must meet if they wish to maximize their profit from our purchasing power.

You may find yourself asking, Can this actually work? The answer is a simple yes. [9] In both the food and apparel industries, calls for changes in working conditions led to the now widely known nonprofit organization Fair Trade USA. According to its website, Fair Trade USA is an organization that seeks "to inspire the rise of the [socially] Conscious Consumer and eliminate exploitation" worldwide. If products are stamped with the Fair Trade logo, it means the farmers and workers who created those products were fairly treated and justly compensated through an internationally established price.

5. Step 2, the *need* step, shows listeners why they should listen to the speaker's propositions—in this case, to help factory workers obtain safer working conditions.

6. Step 3, the *satisfaction* step, identifies how to meet the need.

7. Jacob clearly defines a potentially confusing term, offering an explanation from a credible source.

8. Jacob provides convincing evidence from a credible source.

9. Here is step 4: *visualization*. Jacob offers a vision of outcomes associated with the proposed solution.

10. Is this a claim of fact, value, or policy?

Fair Trade USA made its mark in the food industry through its relationship to coffee production in third-world nations. Its success helped major companies such as Starbucks and Whole Foods recognize the strength of cause marketing: If you appeal to the high ethical standards of socially conscious consumers, they will pay more for your product. [10]

Appealing to high ethical standards is often directly related to tragedies like the one that occurred in Bangladesh. After the factory collapsed, the major apparel sellers faced intense criticism over their lax labor practices. In response, these companies are now much more interested in establishing their products as Fair Trade to meet socially conscious consumer standards. For example, as Jason Burke, Saad Hammadi, and Simon Neville report in the May 13, 2013, edition of the *Guardian*, major fashion chains like H&M, Zara, C&A, Tesco, and Primark have pledged to help raise the standards for working conditions. According to the article, they will be helping to "finance fire safety and building improvements in the factories they use in Bangladesh." [11]

11. Note that Jacob provides evidence in support of his claim.

12. Here begins step 5 of Monroe's motivated sequence: the *action* step—a direct request of listeners to act on the speaker's suggestions and concrete directions for doing so.

Emotional facial expressions add to the seriousness of Jacob's topic.

So, what exactly can you do to help bring about ethical labor practices within the clothing industry? The two steps I encourage you to take are these: Become informed, and ask questions about what you're buying—whether it's shoes, a t-shirt, or any other type of apparel. [12]

To be informed, go to websites such as fairtradeusa.org, thirdworldtraveler.com, and tenthousandvillages.com, which list and sell products from clothing manufacturers who have worked to meet the Fair Trade conditions. This list grows monthly, and by supporting these companies through your purchases, you can become a socially conscious consumer.

Additionally, ask questions of other retailers. Whether you shop online or at local retail stores, ask direct questions before purchasing clothes—for example, Where are your products made? Do you have proof of fair-trade practices? Where can I find this information before I make my purchase? Such questions define the socially conscious consumer, and they ensure that you will not be directly contributing to unsafe and unfair labor practices.

13. Jacob concludes by reinforcing his call to action and leaves the audience with a new perspective to consider.

Although several factors contributed to the tragedy in Bangladesh, there is one clear way to help prevent future disasters: become a socially conscious consumer. By being informed and asking questions, you, too, can make a difference in the lives of workers around the world. [13]

SAMPLE VISUALLY ANNOTATED PERSUASIVE SPEECH

Preventing Cyberbullying

Elijah Lui

Elijah Lui gives an online speech that helps the audience recognize how problematic cyberbullying is and lets them know how they can address and prevent it. Organizationally, the speech is arranged along the lines of the problem-solution pattern. Note that Elijah uses a variety of sources, from books to scholarly articles to publications posted on reputable websites, to support his arguments. [1]

1. For guidelines on preparing an online presentation, see Chapter 32, Preparing Online Presentations.

On the evening of September 22, 2010, Rutgers University freshman Tyler Clementi updated his Facebook status: "Jumping off the gw [George Washington] Bridge sorry." According to Lisa Foderaro's report in the *New York Times*, a few hours later Clementi did just that. But what would cause Clementi, recognized as a bright student and talented musician with a promising future, to take his own life? The answer, unhappily, involves a bully with a Web cam.

According to a May 21, 2012, report on CNN, Clementi's roommate was sentenced to 30 days in jail, 3 years of probation, 300 hours of community service, and $11,000 in restitution for using a Web cam to view and transmit images of Clementi in an intimate encounter with another young man.

Tyler Clementi's story is tragic, but it's not an isolated event. On September 9, 2013, 12-year-old Rebecca Sedwick jumped to her death allegedly after being tormented by two girls on Facebook. And a few months earlier, Rehtaeh Parsons, a 17-year-old Canadian high school student, hanged herself after cell phone pictures of her being sexually assaulted were distributed by the alleged attackers. [2]

2. Elijah begins his speech with several dramatic examples that capture the audience's attention; these serve as appeals to pathos.

What is going on here? In a word—it's *cyberbullying*.

My name is Elijah and I'm here today to confront the growing problem of electronic harassment experienced by Tyler Clementi and so many others. I'll start with a look at the various forms cyberbullying takes and describe the scope of the problem. [3] But I'm not here just to talk about one more social ill. I want to show you how you and your loved ones can stay safe—both by scrupulously guarding your personal information and by actively thwarting cyberbullies.

3. Here, Elijah sets up the organizational pattern of the speech, indicating that he will describe a problem and offer solutions; he also previews the main points.

Elijah cleans up to provide an appropriate background for his online speech.

And should you or someone you know become a victim, I want you to be able to respond constructively.

As you can imagine from the heartbreaking story that I've shared about Tyler Clementi, cyberbullying poses serious mental health risks to the nation's children, teens, and young adults. The Cyberbullying Research Center, a leading resource on the topic, [4] defines *cyberbullying* as "willful and repeated harm inflicted through the use of computers, cell phones, and other electronic devices." [5] Cyberbullying can take many forms, including the following: posting or sending harassing messages via websites, blogs,

4. Elijah qualifies his source and demonstrates its credibility.

5. He begins the body of the speech by ensuring that the audience knows what cyberbullying means.

or text messages; posting embarrassing or private photos of someone without their permission; recording or videotaping someone and sharing it without permission; and creating fake websites or social networking profiles in someone else's name to humiliate them. Often these acts are done anonymously.

6. Words such as "chilling" strike an emotional chord (pathos) and serve to persuade.

Recent research paints a chilling picture of the frequency and harms of electronic harassment. [6] According to Hani Morgan, an Education Professor at the University of Southern Mississippi, the statistics vary widely, but 42% of teens in a 2011 study reported being the victims of cyberbullying. Although most of the research to date has focused on cyberbullying among middle and high school students, a 2012 study published in the *Journal of School Violence* confirmed that the problem of electronic harassment continues into college. Psychologists Allison Schenk and William Fremouw found that nearly 9% of university students reported having experienced cyberbullying; that means that at least 2 or 3 people listening to this speech know what I'm describing because they've felt it. [7]

7. Translating the statistic into something concretely related to audience members makes the evidence more persuasive.

Sitting a safe distance from the camera allows Elijah's body movements and gestures to be seen.

We have seen with Tyler, Rebecca, Rehtaeh, and too many others that cyberbullying has tragically cut short promising lives. But other consequences less dramatic than suicide take a serious toll on victims. The same study by Schenk and Fremouw reported more symptoms of depression and anxiety, as well as difficulty concentrating, among bullied college students.

8. Elijah now moves from describing the problem to offering solutions.

As Professor Morgan explains, the anonymity of unsigned messages and fake user names marks cyberbullying as a dangerous evolution of a long-standing face-to-face bullying problem, but you can take steps to protect yourself. [8] For one, you can be vigilant about safeguarding your personal information. Our school's Information Technology office lists the following advice on its website. First, never, ever, leave your laptops unattended. Second, keep your account passwords and Social Security numbers completely private. Third, use the most secure privacy settings on your social networking sites. Finally, think carefully about the types of pictures of yourself and your friends that you post online, and restrict views of them to "friends" only. Each of these steps can minimize opportunities for bullies to harm or embarrass you in some way. [9]

9. Elijah helps listeners follow along by using the signal words *first, second, third,* and *finally.*

Elijah maintains strong eye contact to evoke confidence and assurance in his speech.

In addition to zealously guarding your personal information, you can help combat cyberbullying by being a voice against it whenever you see it happening. Several organizations have websites that provide information you can use to be part of the solution. The Facebook Group "Don't Stand By, Stand Up!" is a student-led organization formed soon after Tyler Clementi's suicide. The group urges Internet users to take a stand against cyberbullying by recognizing that bullies—in all forms—rarely succeed in their harassment without the support and attention of bystanders. The National Crime Prevention Council website gives specific tips on how to thwart a bully's attempts. The first is to refuse to pass bullying messages along to others—whether via text or photo messaging, social networking, or e-mail—and to let the original sender know that you find the message offensive or stupid.

Despite your best efforts to keep your personal information private and speak out against cyberbullying, you may still become a victim. [10]

Online safety expert Parry Aftab's website, stopcyberbullying.org, advises victims to use the "Stop, Block, and Tell" method to respond to bullying behaviors directed against them. While often taught to younger children, this response makes sense in any case of cyberbullying. After receiving a bullying message you should first "Stop." In other words, do nothing. Take five minutes to cool down, take a walk, breathe deeply, or do whatever helps to calm down the understandable anger you are feeling. Then, "Block": Prevent the cyberbully from having any future communication with you. This may mean anything from removing him or her from your social networking sites' "friends" list to having your cell phone service provider block the bully from being able to call or text you. The third step is to "Tell" someone about the abuse without embarrassment or shame. For example, you might call campus security or confide in a counselor at the Health and Counseling Center—particularly if the abuse has been going on for a long time and you feel that your self-esteem or relationships have been affected. Similarly, parents of younger children should encourage their children to report any bullying to a trusted adult.

Today we've ventured into the very real—and very dangerous—world of cyberbullying. We've seen cyberbullying's negative impact on people of all ages. We've also seen how you can counter this potentially deadly problem by being vigilant about protecting your personal information and speaking out against cyberbullying. And if you or someone you know experiences cyberbullying, you can react constructively with the "Stop, Block, and Tell" method. [11]

Elijah's facial expressions exemplify the seriousness of the subject of his speech.

Cyberbullying isn't just someone else's problem. It's very likely something you need to guard against, now or in the future, as a student today or as a parent tomorrow. I urge each of you to make a personal commitment to do your part to combat the problem. [12] Refuse to stay silent in the face of cyberbullying. Resolve that you will never send nor pass along cyberbullying messages of any kind, no matter how harmless doing so might seem. This act alone can make a world of difference in the life of the intended victim. And wouldn't you want someone to take this simple step for you?

We must never forget Tyler Clementi, and the other young lives cut short by unnecessary bullying. Who knows? Your best friend, your younger brother, or your future son could just have easily been on that bridge that fateful September evening. [13]

10. Elijah transitions to his next point.

11. Elijah signals the conclusion of the speech with a summary of the main points.

12. Elijah issues a call to action.

13. By stressing the personal relevance of the topic to the audience, Elijah leaves them with something to think about.

Works Cited

Foderaro, Lisa W. "Private Moment Made Public, Then a Fatal Jump." *New York Times*, September 29, 2010. http://query.nytimes.com/gst/fullpage.html?res=9B07E6D-91638F933A0575AC0A9669D8B63

Hayes, Ashley. "Prosecutors to appeal 30-day sentence in Rutgers gay bullying case." *CNN*, May 21, 2012. www.cnn.com/2012/05/21/justice/new-jersey-rutgers-sentencing/index.html

Hinduja, Sameer, and Justin W. Patchin. "Cyberbullying: Identification, Prevention, and Response." Fact Sheet. Cyberbullying Research Center website. 2010. www.cyberbullying.us/Cyberbullying_Identification_Prevention_Response_Fact_Sheet.pdf

Martinez, Michael. "Charges in Rebecca Sedwick's suicide suggest 'tipping point' in bullying cases." CNN, October 28, 2013. www.cnn.com/2013/10/25/us/rebecca-sedwick-bullying-suicide-case/index.html

Morgan, Hani. "Malicious Use of Technology: What Schools, Parents, and Teachers Can Do to Prevent Cyberbullying." *Childhood Education* 89, no. 3 (May/June 2013): 146–151.

Newton, Paula. "Canadian teen commits suicide after alleged rape, bullying." *CNN*, April 10, 2013. www.cnn.com/2013/04/10/justice/canada-teen-suicide/index.html

Schenk, Allison M., and William J. Fremouw. "Prevalence, Psychological Impact, and Coping of Cyberbully Victims Among College Students." *Journal of School Violence* 11, no. 1 (January 2012): 21–37.

"Stop, Block, and Tell!" Stopcyberbullying.org Web site. Accessed November 1, 2013. http://www.stopcyberbullying.org/take_action/stop_block_and_tell.html

"Stop Cyberbullying before It Starts." National Crime Prevention Council website. Accessed February 9, 2011. www.ncpc.org/resources/files/pdf/bullying/cyberbullying.pdf

Chapter 31

Collaborating and Presenting in Groups

- Becoming an Effective Group Participant

- Adopting an Effective Leadership Style

- Making Presentations in Teams

This chapter is taken from Dan O'Hair, Rob Stewart, and Hannah Rubenstein, *A Speaker's Guidebook,* Sixth Edition, pp. 425–431.

Most of us will spend a substantial portion of our educational and professional lives communicating in **small groups** or teams (usually between three and twenty people) as opposed to a large public audience,[1] and many of the experiences we have as speakers—in the classroom, workforce, or in virtual groups online—occur in a group setting. In a **virtual group**, members who are geographically dispersed interact and exchange ideas through mediated communication such as e-mail, texting, and videoconferencing.[2] Whether they are virtual or face-to-face, groups often report on the results they've achieved, and some groups form solely for the purposes of coordinating oral presentations. Thus clear communication is vital to working cooperatively in groups and to getting to the point where you have something worthwhile to report.

■ Becoming an Effective Group Participant

How well or poorly you meet the objectives of the group—whether to coordinate a team presentation or meet some other purpose—is largely a function of how you keep sight of the group's goals and avoid behaviors that detract from these goals. The more you use the group's goals as a steadying guide, the less likely you are to be diverted from your real responsibilities as a participant. Setting an **agenda** can help participants stay on track by identifying the items to be accomplished during a meeting; often it will specify time limits for each item of business.[3] **FIGURE 31.1** offers an example of an agenda.

Plan on Assuming Dual Roles

In a group, you will generally assume dual roles: a task role and an interpersonal role. **Task roles** are the hands-on roles that directly relate to the group's accomplishment of its objectives. Examples include "recording secretary" (takes notes), "moderator" (facilitates discussion), "initiator" (helps the group get moving by generating new ideas, offering solutions), and "information seeker" (seeks clarification and input from the group).[4] Members also adopt various social or **interpersonal roles,** based on individual personality traits and how they relate in the group. These "relational" roles facilitate group interaction and include, for example, "harmonizer" (reduces tension) and "gatekeeper" (keeps the discussion moving and gets everyone moving).[5]

AGENDA

Staff meeting, June 4, 2015
Creative Communication Innovations
9 to 11 A.M.
Third Floor Conference Room

Participants: Lisa Gomez, Jonathan Halberstat, Juliann Chen,
Georgianna Walker, Carol Ludlow, Jerry Freely

1. Welcome and call to order
2. Opening remarks
3. Introduction of guests
4. Approval of minutes from previous meeting
5. Briefing from product line managers
6. Update from auditors
7. Report from consultants on new product line rollouts
8. Report on architecture designs for new assembly plant in Mexico
9. Summary
10. Adjournment

Source: Adapted from Dan O'Hair, Gustav Friedrich, and Lynda Dixon, Strategic Communication in Business and the Professions, 7th ed. (Boston: Allyn Bacon, 2011).

FIGURE 31.1 Sample Meeting Agenda

Task roles and interpersonal roles help the group maintain cohesion and achieve its mission. Sometimes, however, group members focus on individual needs irrelevant to the tasks on hand. **Antigroup roles**—such as "floor hogger" (not allowing others to speak), "blocker" (being overly negative about group ideas; raising issues that have been settled), and "recognition seeker" (acts to call attention to oneself rather than to group tasks)—do not further the group's goals and should be avoided.

Center Disagreement around Issues

Whenever people come together to consider an important issue, conflict is inevitable. But conflict doesn't have to be destructive. In fact, the best decisions are usually those that emerge from productive conflict.[6] In **productive conflict**, group members clarify questions, challenge ideas, present counterexamples, consider worst-case scenarios, and reformulate proposals. After a process like this, the group can be confident that its decision has been put to a good test. Productive conflict centers disagreements around issues rather than personalities. In *personal-based conflict*, members argue about one another instead of about the issues, wasting time and impairing motivation. In contrast, *issues-based conflict* allows members to test and debate ideas and potential solutions. It requires each member to ask tough questions, press for clarification, and present alternative views.[7]

Resist Groupthink

For groups to be truly effective, members eventually need to form a **collective mind**[8]— that is, engage in communication that is critical, careful, consistent, and conscientious.[9] Maintaining a collective mind obviously requires the careful management of issues-based and personal-based conflict, but at the same time group members must avoid the tendency to think too much alike. **Groupthink** is the tendency to accept information and ideas without subjecting them to critical analysis.[10]

Groups prone to groupthink typically exhibit these behaviors:

- Participants reach a consensus and avoid conflict in order not to hurt others' feelings, but without genuinely agreeing.

- Members who do not agree with the majority of the group feel pressured to conform.

- Disagreement, tough questions, and counterproposals are discouraged.

- More effort is spent justifying the decision than testing it.

Research suggests that groups can reach the best decisions by adopting two methods of argument: **devil's advocacy** (arguing for the sake of raising issues or concerns about the idea under discussion) or **dialectical inquiry** (devil's advocacy that goes a step further by proposing a countersolution to the idea).[11] Both approaches help expose underlying assumptions that may be preventing participants from making the best decision. As you lead a group, consider how you can encourage both methods of argument.

Leaders and group members can also be helpful by raising the following questions to open up the discussion:

- Do group members avoid examining new information from outside sources?

- Do group members avoid forming contingency plans for when their first (and only) decision fails?

- Does the leader dampen open discussion of ideas?

- Do members criticize others when new options are raised?[12]

■ Adopting an Effective Leadership Style

It is the group leader's task to set goals, to encourage active participation among group participants, and to assess a group's productivity and adapt accordingly.[13] When called upon to lead a group, bear in mind the four broad styles of leadership possible within groups, and select the *participative model*:

- *Autocratic* leader (makes decisions and announces them to the group)

- *Consultative* leader (makes decisions after discussing them with the group)

- *Delegative* leader (asks the group to make the decision)

- *Participative* leader (makes decisions with the group)

Research suggests that often the most effective leadership style is participative—that is, the leader facilitates a group's activities and interaction in ways that lead to a desired outcome. Following the steps below will help you become an effective participative leader.

Set Goals

Most negative experiences in groups result from a lack of a clear goal. Each member of a group should be able to clearly identify the purpose(s) of the group and the goals it is charged with reaching. The group leader should be a catalyst in setting these goals and ensuring that they are reached in collaboration with other group members. The accompanying checklist contains guidelines for setting group goals.

CHECKLIST
Guidelines for Setting Group Goals
_____1. Identify the problem.
_____2. Map out a strategy.
_____3. Set a performance goal.
_____4. Identify the resources necessary to achieving the goal.
_____5. Recognize contingencies that may arise.
_____6. Obtain feedback.

Encourage Active Participation

Group members tend to adopt solutions that receive the largest number of favorable comments, whether these comments emanate from one individual or many. If only one or two members participate, it is their input that sets the agenda, whether or not their solution is optimal.[14] When you lead a group, take these steps to encourage active participation:

- *Directly ask members to contribute.* Sometimes one person, or a few people, dominates the discussion. Encourage the others to contribute by redirecting the discussion in their direction ("Patrice, we haven't heard from you yet" or "Juan, what do you think about this?").

- *Set a positive tone.* Some people are reluctant to express their views because they fear ridicule or attack. Minimize such fears by setting a positive tone, stressing fairness, and encouraging politeness and active listening.

- *Make use of devil's advocacy and dialectical inquiry.* Raise pertinent issues or concerns, and entertain solutions other than the one under consideration.

Use Reflective Thinking

To reach a decision or solution that all participants understand and are committed to, guide participants through a six-step process of reflective thinking shown in FIGURE 31.2, which is based on the work of the educator John Dewey.[15] Dewey suggested that this sequence of steps encourages group members to "think reflectively" about their task. In this way, all the relevant facts and opinions can be discussed and evaluated, thereby ensuring a better decision.

Step 1   Identify the Problem
- What is being decided upon?
Group leader summarizes problem, ensures that all group members understand problem, and gains agreement from all members.

↓

Step 2   Conduct Research and Analysis
- What information is needed to solve the problem?
Conduct research to gather relevant information.
Ensure that all members have relevant information.

↓

Step 3   Establish Guidelines and Criteria
- Establish criteria by which proposed solutions will be judged.
Reach criteria through consensus and record criteria.

↓

Step 4   Generate Solutions
- Conduct brainstorming session.
Don't debate ideas; simply gather and record all ideas.

↓

Step 5   Select the Best Solution
- Weigh the relative merits of each idea against criteria. Select one alternative that can best fulfill criteria.
If more than one solution survives, select solution that best meets criteria.
Consider merging two solutions if both meet criteria.
If no solution survives, return to problem identification step.

↓

Step 6   Evaluate Solution
- Does the solution have any weaknesses or disadvantages?
- Does the solution resemble the criteria that were developed?
- What other criteria would have been helpful in arriving at a better solution?

FIGURE 31.2 Making Decisions in Groups: John Dewey's Six-Step Process of Reflective Thinking

■ Making Presentations in Teams

Once a group has achieved its goal or selected a solution, members face the task of communicating their results to others in the form of a written report, an oral presentation, or a combination of the two. Group or **team presentations** are oral presentations prepared and delivered by a group of three or more individuals. Team presentations have many of the same characteristics as presentations done individually, but there are differences; while in an individual presentation one person assumes all responsibility for presenting a topic, in a team presentation some or all of the group members share responsibility. Regularly assigned in the classroom and frequently delivered in the workplace, successful team presentations require close cooperation and planning.

Analyze the Audience and Set Goals

Even if the topic is assigned and the audience consists solely of the instructor and classmates (perhaps in an online setting; see **CHAPTER 32**), consider their interests and needs with respect to the topic and how you can meet them. Then, just as you would do during group work, establish goals for the presentation that you can all agree upon.

Assign Roles and Tasks

First, designate a *team leader* to help guide coordination among members, beginning with the selection of roles and tasks. Next, assign team members to various aspects of the research, perhaps selecting different team members to present the introduction, body of the presentation, and conclusion—or other responsibilities. Set firm time limits for each portion of the presentation.

Establish Transitions between Speakers

Work out transitions between speakers ahead of time—for example, whether one team member will introduce every speaker or whether each speaker will introduce the next speaker upon the close of his or her presentation. The quality of the presentation will depend in great part on smooth transitions between speakers.

Be Mindful of Your Nonverbal Behavior

During a team presentation, the audience's eyes will fall on everyone involved, not just the person speaking. Thus any signs of disinterest or boredom by a team member will be easily noticed. Give your full attention to the other speakers and project an attitude of interest toward audience members.

Consider the Presenters' Strengths

Audiences become distracted by marked disparities in style, such as hearing a captivating speaker followed by an extremely dull one. If you are concerned about an uneven delivery, consider choosing the person with the strongest presentation style and credibility level for the opening. Put the more cautious presenters in the middle of the presentation. Select another strong speaker to conclude the presentation.[16]

Coordinate the Presentation Aids

To ensure design consistency (see **CHAPTER 16**, "Designing Presentation Aids"), consider assigning one person the job of coordinating templates for slides, videos, and/or audio. The team can also assign a single individual the task of presenting the aids as the other team members speak. If this is done, be sure to position the person presenting the aids unobtrusively so as not to distract the audience from the speaker.

Rehearse the Presentation Several Times

Together with the whole group, members should practice their portions of the presentation, with any presentation aids they will use, in the order they will be given in the final form. Rehearse several times, until the presentation proceeds smoothly, using the techniques for rehearsal described in CHAPTER 14 in the section "Plan Ahead and Practice Often" on p. 232.

CHECKLIST
Team Presentation Tips
• Establish each team member's responsibilities regarding content and presentation aids.
• Determine how introductions will be made—all at once at the beginning or by having each speaker introduce the next one.
• Practice introductions and transitions to create a seamless presentation.
• Establish an agreed-upon set of hand signals to indicate when a speaker is speaking too loud or soft, too slow or fast.
• Assign someone to manage the question-and-answer session.
• Rehearse the presentation with presentation aids several times from start to finish.

Chapter 32
Preparing Online Presentations

Apply Your Knowledge of Face-to-Face Speaking

Plan for the Unique Demands of Online Delivery

Real-Time or Recorded? Plan for the Delivery Mode

Choose an Online Presentation Format

This chapter is taken from Dan O'Hair, Rob Stewart, and Hannah Rubenstein, *A Speaker's Guidebook*, Sixth Edition, pp. 418–424.

As virtual communication technologies gain in sophistication and costs of travel rise, the demand for people skilled in speaking to remote audiences continues to grow. Employees in certain sectors routinely prepare presentations for delivery online, and students enrolled in distance education courses likewise often are called upon to do the same. Even applicants to colleges and graduate schools may now supplement their written applications with digital video presentations that highlight their talents. So whether you plan to address classmates, co-workers, customers, potential employers, or even admissions officers, you'll want to feel confident in preparing for and delivering presentations for distribution online.

■ Apply Your Knowledge of Face-to-Face Speaking

Online presentations require the same basic elements of planning and delivery as in-person presentations. As in traditional public speaking, an online speaker will select among the three *general speech purposes* of informing, persuading, or marking a special occasion (see **CHAPTER 4**, "Identify the General Purpose of Your Speech" **p. 93**). Both online and in-person contexts call for careful audience analysis, credible supporting materials, a clear organizational structure, and a natural style of delivery. And whether presenting electronically or in-person, as a speaker you must continually engage the audience; when separated physically, this focus becomes all the more critical (see **FIGURE 32.1**).

■ Plan for the Unique Demands of Online Delivery

While much is similar, important differences exist between online and in-person speaking, in both the means of delivery and nature of the audience. These distinctive qualities pose some unique considerations in presenting an online speech. Thus, as you plan your online presentations, follow the fundamental techniques of public speaking you already know while making the necessary adjustments, as described below, to transmit your message effectively online.

Review the Equipment

Unlike in-person speeches, online presentations require at least some familiarity with digital communication tools. Well before the actual delivery time, be sure to review any equipment you'll be using, and rehearse your presentation several times with it (see **CHAPTER 14**, "Plan Ahead and Practice Often," **p.232**).

FIGURE 32.1 The first time that Elijah gives his online presentation, he delivers the speech in too-casual attire, and allows himself to get distracted.

Preparation may not always avert a technical failure, but it will almost always speed recovery time and allow you to continue your presentation more smoothly.

Following are the major tools used to produce and display online presentations:

- Broadband Internet connection
- Website or server for distribution to audience
- Hardware for recording audio and video (Webcam/video camera/microphone)
- Software for recording and editing audio and video (e.g., Adobe Audition)
- Video capture software (e.g., ScreenFlow, Camtasia)
- Web-based presentation software (e.g., Prezi, SlideRocket)
- Podcasting software (e.g., Propaganda, Audacity)
- Popular commercial websites (e.g., YouTube, Vimeo)
- Online conferencing tools (e.g., Glance, GoToMeeting, Yugma, Skype)

FIGURE 32.2 The second time that Elijah gives his speech online, he remembers to practice his speech, dresses for the occasion, neatly arranges the presentation area, and gives a confident presentation.

Focus on Vocal Variety

In an online presentation, the audience cannot interact with your physical presence, making your voice an even more critical conduit of communication. More than body movement, which online presentations tend to restrict, *vocal variety*—alternations in volume, pitch, speaking rate, pauses, and pronunciation and articulation—must hold audience interest. Especially important to eliminate are vocal fillers and repetitive phrases such as "umm," "aww," and "I mean." In place of these, focus on using strategic pauses to help audience members process information.

Focus on a Conversational Style of Speaking

Staring into a computer screen rather than listeners' eyes makes it difficult to infuse your voice with the enthusiasm and naturalness that eye contact encourages. But a conversational style is key for most online presentations (see **CHAPTER 13**). To circumvent the lack of actual persons to focus upon, consider delivering your first presentations with someone else in the room, talking to that person rather than to the screen. Alternatively, you might experiment with addressing your remarks to a picture, photograph, or even your own reflection in a mirror.[1]

Practice the Presentation

Practice is as critical for online presentations as for those delivered in person. As a final step, practice and then actually deliver your speech by looking directly into the camera, as if it were a person's face. One approach is to practice your introduction, body, and conclusion separately and in no particular order until you are comfortable with each part. Then practice them together until you are confident in your grasp of it. Think about any gestures you want to make and include those in your practice.

Provide Superior Visual Aids

The audience might not see you in person, but with presentation aids you can still provide them with a compelling visual experience. Consider how you can illustrate your talking points in eye-catching text form or with photos, animations, and video clips (see **CHAPTERS 15–17**). Carefully practice using your visual aids so you maintain a smooth flow throughout your presentation.

◼ Real-Time or Recorded? Plan for the Delivery Mode

Online presentations can be "streamed" in real time, or recorded for distribution later whenever an audience wants to access them. Understanding the advantages and limitations of both delivery modes can help you plan more effectively.

Real-Time Presentations

Real-time presentations connect presenter and audience live, in **synchronous communication**. Immediate interactivity—being able to interact with the audience in real time—is an advantage of this type of presentation: Speaker and audience can respond to one another even though they are not in the same location. As in traditional speaking situations, audience feedback allows you to adapt topic coverage according to (for example) real-time audience input and questions, or adjust technical issues as they occur.

A chief limitation of real-time presentations is scheduling them around conflicting time zones. The more geographically dispersed the audience, the greater the logistical challenge. As such, many speakers reserve real-time presentations for occasions when they are in time zones close to the audience.

Recorded Presentations

In a **recorded presentation**, transmission of the online presentation and reception of it occur at different times, in **asynchronous communication**. Viewers can access the presentation at their convenience, such as listening to a podcast at night.

Lack of direct interaction with the audience poses challenges with recorded presentations, however. Without immediate feedback from the audience to enliven the presentation, you must work harder to produce something polished and engaging, especially by providing compelling content, delivery style, and presentation aids.

◼ Choose an Online Presentation Format

Online presentation formats include videos, podcasts, vodcasts, Webinars, and graphical presentations, any of which may be streamed in real time or recorded for later delivery.

Video

Many people get their message out by presenting it via video: from individuals using a smartphone camera or Webcam, to professional companies sending out messages using high definition digital video cameras. With **video capture software**, such as Camtasia or Adobe Audition, you can seamlessly incorporate video clips into an online presentation.

You can also use dedicated software to create screencasts. A **screencast** captures whatever is displayed on your computer screen, from text to slides to streaming video. Screencasts can be streamed in real time or recorded for playback or export to a hosting website. The screencast format is especially useful for training purposes. For example, a presentation relying on screen captures can be used to demonstrate how to create a screencast using QuickTime Player on the Mac.

Podcasts and Vodcasts

A **podcast** is a digital audio recording of a speech or presentation captured and stored in a form that is accessible via the Web. A **vodcast** (also called *vidcast* and *video podcasting*) is a podcast containing video clips.

News sites, government information repositories such as the Library of Congress (www.loc.gov/podcasts/), and academic institutions offer countless examples of podcasts and vodcasts (see **FIGURE 32.3**). Commercial recording outlets such as iTunes also provide a wide selection of podcasts and vodcasts.

Recording, storing, and delivering a speech via podcast require a microphone attached to a computer; simple, cost-free digital audio recording software (e.g., Audacity); and a website to host the podcast and provide your audience with access to it. Using PowerPoint, you can use the *Record Narration* feature in the slide creation function to produce a podcast-like presentation file; the file can be used and distributed as you would any PowerPoint file, even via e-mail.

FIGURE 32.3 Podcast Offerings from Indiana University

CHECKLIST
Creating a Podcast
Most current models of desktop, laptop, and tablet computers include the basic equipment and software needed to create a podcast. The only other pieces you may need are an external microphone and audio recording software such as Audacity (audacity.sourceforge.net/). Then try these steps:
• Plan what you want to say.
• Seat yourself in an upright, direct position facing your computer, with the microphone no more than 8 inches from your mouth.
• Make sure that your external microphone is plugged into your computer, or that your built-in microphone is operational.
• Open your audio recording software. Be familiar with how to start, pause, and stop a recording.
• Activate the recording software and begin speaking into the microphone. You're now making your presentation.
• At the conclusion of your presentation, stop the recording.
• Save the new recording as an audio file, such as .mp3.
• Close your audio recording software and disengage the microphone.
• Go to the new audio file saved to your computer, and open and play it. Now you are listening to your recorded presentation.
• Transfer the saved file to a website, blog, or podcast hosting site.

Webinars

Webinars are real-time seminars, meetings, training sessions, or other presentations that connect presenters and audiences from their computers or mobile devices.[2] Webinars typically include video capture and screencasting, as well as interactive functions such as chat and polling.

As in any speech or presentation, planning a Webinar starts with considering the audience's needs and wants. Many Webinars are *team presentations,* so use the guidelines on **p. 552** in "Making Presentations in Teams" during the planning stages.[3]

1. Start with a title that indicates what the Webinar will do for the audience (e.g., "What an Increase in the Minimum Wage Would Mean for Our Company").

2. Time each aspect of the Webinar and distribute the following information to each presenter:

    Introduction of speaker(s) and purpose

    Length and order of each speaker's remarks

    Length of question-and-answer session, if separate

3. Rehearse the Webinar (remotely if necessary).

4. Check meeting room for noise and visual distractions; check equipment.

5. Create backup plans in case of technical problems.

Put a Face to the Speaker(s)

To encourage a feeling of connection between yourself and the audience during a Webinar, consider displaying a photographic headshot, captioned by your name and title. A second slide might announce start and finish times; a third, a list of speech objectives.[4] During the presentation, you can alternate displays of text and graphic slides with views of your photograph (and/or other presenters) or, in some cases, side-by-side with the aids.

CHECKLIST
Online Presentation Planning
Keeping in mind both the fundamental guidelines for preparing and presenting a face-to-face speech as well as those unique qualities of online presentations, here are some additional tips to follow.[1]
• *Be well organized*. Offer a clear statement of purpose and preview of main points. Proceed with a solid structure that the audience can easily follow. Conclude by restating your purpose, reviewing the main points, and encouraging the audience to watch or listen for more.
• *Have reasonable expectations*. Fit the amount of content to the allotted time. Don't pack too much into too little time.
• *Design powerful presentation aids*. For video and Webcasts, plan for meaningful graphics and images that properly convey your ideas.
• *Keep your audience engaged*. In real-time presentations, encourage audience interaction by incorporating chat, instant messaging, or polling features. In recorded presentations, offer an e-mail address, Weblog comment, URL, or Twitter address where audience members can submit comments and questions. Use these tools to acquire feedback from your audience, much the way you would use eye contact in a face-to-face speech or presentation.
• *Prepare a contingency plan in case of technology glitches*. For example, have a backup computer running simultaneously with the one used to deliver the presentation. Provide a list of FAQs or a Web page with instructions for audience members to manage technology problems.
• *Maintain ethical standards*. Use the same degree of decorum as you would in a face-to-face speech, bearing in mind that online presentations may be recorded and have the potential to go viral.
• *Get in plenty of practice time*. Rehearse, record, and listen to yourself as many times as needed.

1. Patricia Fripp, "15 Tips for Webinars: How to Add Impact When You Present Online," eLearn Magazine, July 7, 2009, elearnmag.org/featured.cfm?aid=1595445.

■ References

References taken from Dan O'Hair, Mary Wiemann, Dorothy Imric Mullin, and Jason Teven, *Real Communication*, Third Edition.

Aakhus, M., & Rumsey, E. (2010). Crafting supportive communication online: A communication design analysis of conflict in an online support group. *Journal of Applied Communication Research, 38*(1), 65–84.

ABC News. (2013, April). Anchor A.J. Clemente fired after profanity-laced debut. Retrieved from http://abcnews .go.com/blogs/entertain-ment/2013/04/anchor-a-j-clem-ente-fired-after-profanity-laced-de-but

ABC News. (2013, April 23). Worst first day ever. Retrieved from http://newsfeed.time.com/2013/04/23/worst-first-day-ever-rookie-tv-an-chor-fired-for-profanity-in-first-newscast

Abrams v. *United States*, 250 U.S. 616 (1919).

Acitelli, L. K. (2008). Knowing when to shut up: Do relationship reflections help or hurt relationship satisfaction. *Social Relationships: Cognitive, Affective, and Motivational Processes*, 115–129.

Action for Children's Television v. *Federal Communications Commission*, 932 F.2d 1504 (ACT II) (D.C. Cir. 1991).

Action for Children's Television v. *Federal Communications Commission*, 58 F.3d 654 (ACT III) (D.C. Cir. 1995).

Adalian, J. (2013, June). *Under the Dome* and TV's new ad-less ways to make cash. Vulture.com. Retrieved from http://www.vulture.com/2013/06/under-the-dome-tv-revenue-when-ads-fail.html

Adkins, M., & Brashers, D. E. (1995). The power of language in computer-mediated groups. *Management Communication Quarterly, 8*, 289–322.

Adkins, R. PhD. (2006). Elemental truths. Retrieved from http://ele-mentaltruths.blogspot.com/2006/11/conflict-management-quiz.html

Afifi, T., Afifi, W., Merrill, A. F., Denes, A. & Davis, S. (2013). "You Need to Stop Talking About This!": Verbal rumination and the costs of social support. *Human Communication Research, 39*(4), 395–421.

Afifi, T. D., McManus, T., Hutchinson, S., & Baker, B. (2007). Parental divorce disclosures, the factors that prompt them, and their impact on parents' and adolescents' well-being. *Communication Monographs, 74*, 78–103.

Afifi, T. D., McManus, T., Steuber, K., & Coho, A. (2009). Verbal avoidance and dissatisfaction in intimate conflict situations. *Human Communication Research, 35*(3), 357–383.

Ahlfeldt, S. L. (2009). Serving our communities with public speaking skills. *Communication Teacher, 23*(4), 158–161.

Albada, K. F., Knapp, M. L., & Theune, K. E. (2002). Interaction appearance theory: Changing perceptions of physical attractiveness through social interaction. *Communication Theory, 12,* 8–40.

Albert, N. M. Ph.D., R.N., Wocial, L. Ph.D, R.N., Meyer, K. H. M.S., Na, J. M.S., & Trochelman, K. M.S.N. (2008, November). Impact of nurses' uniforms on patient and family perceptions of nurse professionalism. *Applied Nursing Research, 21*(4), 181–190. Retrieved from http://dx.doi.org/10.1016/j.apnr.2007.04.008

Alexander, A. L. (2008). Relationship resources for coping with unfulfilled standards in dating relationships: Commitment, satisfaction, and closeness. *Journal of Social and Personal Relationships, 25*(5), 725–747.

Alge, B. J., Wiethoff, C., & Klein, H. J. (2003). When does the medium matter? Knowledge-building experiences and opportunities in decision-making teams. *Organizational Behavior and Human Decision Processes, 91,* 26–37.

Allan, T. (2004). *The troubles in Northern Ireland.* Chicago: Heinemann Library/Reed Elsevier Inc.

Allen, L. F., Babin, E. A., & McEwan, B. (2012). Emotional investment: An exploration of young adult friends' emotional experience and expression using an investment model framework. *Journal of Social and Personal Relationships, 29*(2), 206–227.

Allen, M. (1991). Comparing the persuasiveness of one-sided and two-sided messages using meta-analysis. *Western Journal of Speech Communication, 55,* 390–404.

Allen, R. R., & McKerrow, R. E. (1985). *The pragmatics of public communication* (3rd ed.). Dubuque, IA: Kendall/Hunt.

Allport, G. W. (1954). *The nature of prejudice.* Cambridge, MA: Addison-Wesley.

Alter, C. (2013, October 10). Miley Cyrus reels in best *Saturday Night Live* ratings since March. *Time.* Retrieved from http://entertainment.time.com/2013/10/10/miley-cyrus-reels-in-best-saturday-night-live-ratings-since-march

Altman, I., & Taylor, D. A. (1973). *Social penetration: The development of interpersonal relationships.* New York: Holt, Rinehart and Winston.

Alvarez, C., Salavati, S., Nussbaum, M., & Milrad, M. (2013). Collboard: Fostering new media literacies in the classroom through collaborative problem solving supported by digital pens and interactive whiteboards. *Computers and Education, 63,* 368–379.

Amadeo, K. (2013). Obama State of the Union 2013 Address: Summary and economic impact. Retrieved on May 9, 2014, from http://useconomy.about.com/od/Politics/p/2013-State-of-the-Union-Address.htm

American Psychological Association Zero Tolerance Task Force (2008). Are zero tolerance policies effective in the schools? *American Psychologist, 63*(9), 852–862.

Andersen, J. F. (1979). Teacher immediacy as a predictor of teaching effectiveness. In B. Ruben (Ed.), *Communication yearbook 3* (pp. 543–559). New Brunswick, NJ: Transaction Books.

Andersen, P. A. (1998). The cognitive valence theory of intimate communication. In M. Palmer & G. A. Barnett (Eds.), *Progress in communication sciences*: Vol. 14. Mutual influence in interpersonal communication theory and research in cognition, affect, and behavior (pp. 39–72). Norwood, NJ: Ablex.

Andersen, P. A., Guerrero, L. K., Buller, D. B., & Jorgensen, P. F. (1998). An empirical comparison of three theories of nonverbal immediacy exchange. *Human Communication Research, 24*, 501–535.

Andersen, P. A., Guerrero, L. K., & Jones, S. M. (2006). Nonverbal behavior in intimate interactions and intimate relationships. In V. Manusov & M. L. Patterson (Eds.), *The SAGE handbook of nonverbal communication* (pp. 259–278). Thousand Oaks, CA: Sage Publications.

Anderson, A. A., Brossard, D., Scheufele, D. A., Xenos, M. A., & Ladwig, P. (2013). The "nasty effect:" Online incivility and risk perceptions of emerging technologies. *Journal of Computer-Mediated Communication, 19*, 373–387.

Anderson, C. M., & Martin, M. M. (1999). The relationship of argumentativeness and verbal aggressiveness to cohesion, consensus, and satisfaction in small groups. *Communication Reports, 12*, 21–31.

Anderson, C. M., Riddle, B. L., & Martin, M. M. (1999). Socialization in groups. In L. Frey, D. Gouran, & M. Poole (Eds.), *Handbook of group communication theory and research* (pp. 139–163). Thousand Oaks, CA: Sage Publications.

Andreisen, D. (2007, March 29). "Baseball English" helps Mariners overcome various language barriers. *Seattle Post-Intelligencer*. Retrieved from http://www.seattlepi.com/sports/baseball/article/Baseball-English-helps-Mariners-overcome-1232513.php

Annino, J. (Executive producer). (2007, July 5). Cooking in cramped quarters [Television series episode]. In *The Rachael Ray Show*. Video retrieved from http://www.rachaelrayshow.com/show/segments/view/cooking-in-cramped-quarters

Antaki, C., Barnes, R., & Leudar, I. (2005). Self-disclosure as a situated interactional practice. *British Journal of Social Psychology, 44*(2), 181–199.

Antheunis, M. L., Valkenburg, P. M., & Peter, J. (2010). Getting acquainted through social network sites: Testing a model of online uncertainty reduction and social attraction. *Computers in Human Behavior, 26*(1), 100–109.

Antonijevic, S. (2008). From text to gesture online: A microethnographic analysis of nonverbal communication in the *Second Life* virtual environment. *Information, Communication & Society, 11*(2), 221–238.

Arasaratnam, L. (2007). Research in intercultural communication competence. *Journal of International Communication, 13*, 66–73.

Araton, H. (2010, April 26). The understated elegance of the Yankees' Rivera. *The New York Times*, p. D1.

Armstrong, B., & Kaplowitz, S. A. (2001). Sociolinguistic interference and intercultural coordination: A Bayesian model of communication competence in intercultural communication. *Human Communication Research, 27*, 350–381.

Asmuß, B. (2008). Performance appraisal interviews. *Journal of Business Communication, 45*(4), 408–429.

Asmuß, B. (2013). The emergence of symmetries and asymmetries in performance appraisal interviews: An interactional perspective. *Economic & Industrial Democracy, 34*(3), 553–570.

Assilaméhou, Y., & Testé, B. (2013). How you describe a group shows how biased you are: Language abstraction and inferences about a speaker's communicative intentions and attitudes toward a group. *Journal of Language & Social Psychology, 32*(2), 202–211.

Associated Press. (2011). In a first, women surpass men in college degrees. Reported in CBSNews.com. Retrieved from http://www.cbsnews.com/news/in-a-first-women-surpass-men-in-college-degrees

Associated Press. (2012, March 15). In *The Chicago Tribune Online*. Retrieved from http://triblive.com/sports/mlb/3670340-74/players-rule-baseball#axzz2qg4exWAI

Associated Press. (2013, November 6). Swedish cinemas test films' gender bias. *The Guardian*. Retrieved from http://www.theguardian.com/world/2013/nov/06/swedish-cinemas-bechdel-test-films-gender-bias

Associated Press. (2014, January 16). MLB tries to ease language barrier with new rule. In *Tribune Live*. Retrieved from http://triblive.com/sports/mlb/3670340-74/players-rule-baseball#axzz2qg4exWAI

Atkinson, J., & Dougherty, D. S. (2006). Alternative media and social justice movements: The development of a resistance performance paradigm of audience analysis. *Journal of Western Communication, 70*, 64–89.

Atlas, J. (2011, July 10). The art of the interview. *The New York Times*, p. SR7.

Atwood, J. D. (2012). Couples and money: The last taboo. *American Journal of Family Therapy, 40*(1), 1–19. doi: 10.1080/01926187.2011.600674

Aust, P. J. (2004). Communicated values as indicators of organizational identity: A method for organizational assessment and its application in a case study. *Communication Studies, 55*, 515–535.

Avtgis, T. A., & Rancer, A. S. (2003). Comparing touch apprehension and affective orientation between Asian-American and European-American siblings. *Journal of Intercultural Communication Research, 32*(2), 67–74.

Axtell, R. E. (1991). *Gestures: The do's and taboos of body language around the world*. Hoboken, NJ: Wiley.

Ayres, J. (2005). Performance visualization and behavioral disruption: A clarification. *Communication Reports, 18*, 55–63.

Ayres, J., & Hopf, T. (1993). *Coping with speech anxiety*. Norwood, NJ: Ablex.

Ayres, J., Keereetaweep, T., Chen, P., & Edwards, P. (1998). Communication apprehension and employment interviews. *Communication Education, 47,* 1–17.

Ayres, J., Wilcox, A. K., & Ayres, D. M. (1995). Receiver apprehension: An explanatory model and accompanying research. *Communication Education, 44,* 223–235.

Bachman, G. F., & Guerrero, L. K. (2006). Forgiveness, apology, and communicative responses to hurtful events. *Communication Reports, 19,* 45–56.

Back to twerk. (2013, September 10). *Sydney Morning Herald.* Retrieved from http://www.smh.com.au/entertainment/music/back-to-twerk-miley-cyrus-wrecking-ball-video-goes-ballistic-on-youtube-20130910-2tht6.html

Baez, J. (2013, August 28). Kate Middleton: No baby bump just 37 days after giving birth. Hollywoodlife.com. Retrieved from http://hollywoodlife.com/2013/08/28/kate-middleton-weight-loss-waitrose-pic-post-pregnancy

Baile, J., Steeves, V., Brukell, J., & Regan, P. (2013, April). Negotiating with gender stereotypes on social networking sites: From "Bicycle Face" to Facebook. *Journal of Communication Inquiry, 37*(2), 91–112.

Baker, H. G., & Spier, M. S. (1990). The employment interview: Guaranteed improvement in reliability. *Public Personnel Management, 19,* 85–90.

Baker, M. J., & Churchill, G. A. (1977). The impact of physically attractive models on advertising evaluations. *Journal of Marketing Research, 14,* 538–555.

Bakke, E. (2010). A model and measure of mobile communication competence. *Human Communication Research, 36*(3), 348–371.

Balaji, M., & Worawongs, T. (2010). The new Suzie Wong: Normative assumptions of white male and Asian female relationships. *Communication, Culture & Critique, 3*(2), 224–241.

Baldwin, M. W., & Keelan, J. P. R. (1999). Interpersonal expectations as a function of self-esteem and sex. *Journal of Social and Personal Relationships, 16,* 822–833.

Ball, K. (2010). Workplace surveillance: An overview. *Labor History, 51*(1), 87–106.

Ball-Rokeach, S. J. (1998). A theory of media power and a theory of media use: Different stories, questions, and ways of thinking. *Mass Communication and Society, 1,* 5–40.

Bandura, A. (1982). Self-efficacy mechanism in human agency. *American Psychologist, 37,* 122.

Bandura, A. (2001). Social cognitive theory of mass communication. *Media Psychology, 3,* 265–299.

Barker, L. L., & Watson, K. W. (2000). *Listen up: How to improve relationships, reduce stress, and be more productive by using the power of listening.* New York: St. Martin's Press.

Bartels, S., Kelly, J., Scott, J., Leaning, J., Mukwege, D., Joyce, N., & Vanrooyen, M. (2013). Militarized sexual violence in South Kivu, Democratic Republic of Congo. *Journal of Interpersonal Violence, 28*(2), 340–358.

Bartsch, R. A., & Coburn, K. M. (2003). Effectiveness of PowerPoint presentations in lectures. *Computers and Education, 41*, 77–86.

Bates, B. (1988). *Communication and the sexes.* New York: Harper & Row.

Bates, C. (2010). The nurse's cap and its rituals. *Dress, 36*, 21–40. Retrieved from http://www.ingentaconnect.com/content/maney/dre/2010/00000036/00000001/art00003

Bates, C. (2013). A cultural history of the nurse's uniform. Canadian Museum of Civilization. Gatineau, Quebec, Canada.

Bavelas, J. B., & Chovil, N. (2006). Nonverbal and verbal communication: Hand gestures and facial displays as part of language use in face-to-face dialogue. In V. Manusov & M. L. Patterson (Eds.), *The SAGE handbook of nonverbal communication* (pp. 97–117). Thousand Oaks, CA: Sage Publications.

Bavelous, A. (1950). Communication patterns in task-oriented groups. *Journal of the Acoustical Society of America, 22*, 725–730.

Baxter, L. A. (1990). Dialectical contradictions in relationship development. *Journal of Social and Personal Relationships, 7*, 69–88.

Baxter, L. A., Braithwaite, D. O., Bryant, L., & Wagner, A. (2004). Stepchildren's perceptions of the contradictions in communication with stepparents. *Journal of Social and Personal Relationships, 21*, 447–467.

Baxter, L. A,. & Bullis, C. (1986). Turning points in developing romantic relationships. *Human Communication Research, 12*, 469–493.

Baxter, L. A., & Montgomery, B. M. (1996). *Relating: Dialogues and dialectics.* New York: Guilford.

Baxter, L. A., & Simon, E. P. (1993). Relationship maintenance strategies and dialectical contradictions in personal relationships. *Journal of Social and Personal Relationships, 10*, 225–242.

Baxter, L. A., & Wilmot, W. W. (1985). Taboo topics in close relationships. *Journal of Social and Personal Relationships, 2*, 253–269.

Bayly, S. (1999). *Caste, society and politics in India from the eighteenth century to the modern age.* Cambridge: Cambridge University Press.

Bazelon, E. (2013). *Sticks and stones: Defeating the culture of bullying and rediscovering the power of character and empathy.* New York: Random House. Kindle Location 215.

Bazelon, E. (2013, March 11). Defining bullying down. *The New York Times.* Retrieved from http://www.nytimes.com/2013/03/12/opinion/defining-bullying-down.html

Bearak, B. (2010, September 6). Dead join the living in a family celebration. *The New York Times*, p. A7.

Beard, D. (2009). A broader understanding of the ethics of listening: Philosophy, cultural studies, media studies and the ethical listening subject. *International Journal of Listening, 23*(1), 7–20.

Becker, J. A., & O'Hair, D. (2007). Machiavellians' motives in organizational citizenship behavior. *Journal of Applied Communication Research, 35*(3), 246–267.

Beebe, S. A., Mottet, T. P., & Roach, K. D. (2012). *Training and development: Communicating for success* (2nd ed.). Boston: Pearson.

Behnke, R. R., & Sawyer, C. R. (1999). Milestones of anticipatory public speaking anxiety. *Communication Education, 48*, 164–172.

Behrendt, H., & Ben-Ari, R. (2012). The positive side of negative emotion: The role of guilt and shame in coping with interpersonal conflict. *Journal of Conflict Resolution, 56*(6), 1116–1138.

Beiser, V. (2013, May 21). Alone with everyone else. *Pacific Standard.* Retrieved from http://www.ps-mag.com/culture/pluralistic-ignorance-55562

Bélisle, J-F., & Onur Bodur, H. (August 2010). Avatars as information: Perception of consumers based on their avatars in virtual worlds. *Psychology & Marketing, 27*(8): 741–765. Published online in Wiley InterScience (www.interscience.wiley.com). Retrieved from http://jfbelisle.com/wp-content/uploads/2009/06/Belisle-and-Bodur-2010.pdf

Bellis, T. J., & Wilber, L. A. (2001). Effects of aging and gender on interhemispheric function. *Journal of Speech, Language,and Hearing Research, 44*, 246–264.

Benne, K. D., & Sheats, P. (1948). Functional roles in group members. *Journal of Social Issues, 4*, 41–49.

Bennett, J. M., & Bennett, M. J. (2004). Developing intercultural sensitivity: An integrative approach to global and domestic diversity. In D. Landis, J. M. Bennett, & M. J. Bennett (Eds.), *Handbook of intercultural training,* 3rd ed. (pp. 147–165). Thousand Oaks, CA: Sage Publications.

Bennis, W., & Nanus, B. (1985). *Leaders.* New York: Harper & Row.

Ben-Porath, E. (2010). Interview effects: Theory and evidence for the impact of televised political interviews on viewer attitudes. *Communication Theory, 20*(3), 323–347.

Bentley, S. C. (2000). Listening in the twenty-first century. *International Journal of Listening, 14*, 129–142.

Bercovici, J. (2013, October 30). Facebook admits it's seen a drop in usage among teens. Forbes.com. Retrieved from http://www.forbes.com/sites/jeffbercovici/2013/10/30/facebook-admits-its-seen-a-drop-in-usage-among-teens

Bergen, K. M. (2010). Accounting for difference: Commuter wives and the master narrative of marriage. *Journal of Applied Communication Research, 38*(1), 47–64.

Berger, A. (2007). *Media and society: A critical perspective.* Lanham, MD: Rowman & Littlefield.

Berger, C. R., & Bradac, J. J. (1982). *Language and social knowledge: Uncertainty in interpersonal relations.* London: Edward Arnold.

Berger, C. R., Roloff, M. E., & Roskos-Ewoldsen, D. R. (Eds.). (2010). *The handbook of communication science* (2nd ed.). Thousand Oaks, CA: Sage Publications.

Berger, J., Wagner, D. G., & Zelditch, M. Jr. (1985). Introduction: Expectation states theory: Review and assessment. In J. Berger & M. Zelditch Jr. (Eds.), *Theoretical research programs: Studies in the growth of theory* (pp. 1–72). Stanford, CA: Stanford University Press.

Berliet, M. (2013, July 3). The importance of kissing beyond the beginning. *Pacific Standard*. Retrieved from http://www.psmag.com/culture/the-importance-of-kissing-beyond-the-beginning-61780

Berrisford, S. (2006). How will you respond to the information crisis? *Strategic Communication Management, 10,* 26–29.

Berryman-Fink, C. (1993). Preventing sexual harassment through male–female communication training. In G. Kreps (Ed.), *Sexual harassment: Communication implications* (pp. 267–280). Cresskill, NJ: Hampton Press.

Berscheid, E., Dion, K., Walster, E., & Walster, G. M. (1971). Physical attractiveness and dating choice: A test of the matching hypothesis. *Journal of Experimental Social Psychology, 7,*173–189.

Bianca, A. (2013). The importance of public speaking skills within organizations. Retrieved on April 29, 2014, from http://smallbusiness.chron.com/importance-public-speaking-skills-within-organizations-12075.html

Biever, C. (2004, August). Language may shape human thought. *New Scientist*. Retrieved from http://www.newscientist.com

Bippus, A. M., & Daly, J. A. (1999). What do people think causes stage fright? Native attributions about the reasons for public speaking anxiety. *Communication Education, 48,* 63–72.

Birditt, K. S. (2013). Age differences in emotional reactions to daily negative social encounters. *The Journals of Gerontology Series B: Psychological Sciences and Social Sciences.* doi:10.1093/geronb/gbt045

Bishop, G. (2010, February 20). On and off the ice, Ohno is positioned for success. *The New York Times*, p. D3.

Bishop, R. (2000). More than meets the eye: An explanation of literature related to the mass media's role in encouraging changes in body image. In M. E. Roloff (Ed.), *Communication yearbook* (Vol. 23, pp. 271–304). Thousand Oaks, CA: Sage Publications.

Blanchard-Fields, F., Mienaltowski, A., & Seay, R. B. (2007). Age differences in everyday problem-solving effectiveness: Older adults select more effective strategies for interpersonal problems. *Journals of Gerontology, Series B: Psychological Sciences and Social Sciences, 62,* 61–64.

Bloch, J. (2011). Teaching job interviewing skills with the help of television shows. *Business Communication Quarterly, 74*(1), 7–21.

Blumenthal, M., & Edwards-Levy, A. (2014, February 4). HUFFPOLLSTER: Obamacare approval remains low. Huffingtonpost.com. Retrieved from http://www.huffingtonpost.com/2014/02/04/obamacare-approval_n_4726118.html

Blumler, J., & Katz, E. (1974). *The uses of mass communications*. Beverly Hills, CA: Sage Publications.

Blumstein, P., & Schwartz, P. (1983). *American couples: Money, work, sex*. New York: Morrow.

Bodie, G. D. (2010). A racing heart, rattling knees, and ruminative thoughts: Defining, explaining, and treating public speaking anxiety. *Communication Education, 59*(1), 70–105.

Bodie, G. D. (2013). Issues in the measurement of listening. *Communication Research Reports, 30*(1), 76–84.

Bodie, G. D., & Fitch-Hauser, M. (2010). Quantitative research in listening: Explication and overview. In A. D. Wolvin (Ed.), *Listening and human communication in the 21st century* (pp. 46–93). Oxford, England: Blackwell.

Bodie, G. D., & Jones, S.M. (2012). The nature of supportive listening II: The role of verbal person centeredness and nonverbal immediacy. *Western Journal of Communication 76*(3), 250–269.

Bodie, G. D., St. Cyr, K., Pence, M., Rold, M., & Honeycutt, J. (2012). Listening competence in initial interactions I: Distinguishing between what listening is and what listeners do. *International Journal of Listening, 26*(1), 1–28.

Bodie, G. D., Vickery, A. J., & Gearhart, C. C. (2013). The nature of supportive listening, I: Exploring the relation between supportive listeners and supportive people. *International Journal of Listening, 27*(1), 39–49.

Bodie, G. D., & Villaume, W. A. (2003). Aspects of receiving information: The relationship between listening preferences, communicator style, communication apprehension, and receiver apprehension. *International Journal of Listening, 17*, 47–67.

Bodie, G. D., Worthing, D., Imhof, M., & Cooper, L. O. (2008). What would a unified field of listening look like? A proposal linking past perspectives and future endeavors. *International Journal of Listening, 22*: 103–122.

Bodie, G. D., Worthington, D. L., & Gearhart, C. C. (2013, January). The listening styles profile-revised (LSP-R): A scale revision and evidence for validity. *Communication Quarterly, 61*(1), 72–90.

Boje, D. M. (1991). The storytelling organization: A study of story performance in an office-supply firm. *Administrative Science Quarterly, 36*, 106–126.

Bommelje, R., Houston, J. M., & Smither, R. (2003). Personality characteristics of effective listeners: A five factor perspective. *International Journal of Listening, 17*, 32–46.

Bono, J. E. & Ilies, R. (2006). Charisma, positive emotions and mood contagion. *The Leadership Quarterly, 17*, 317–334.

Bormann, E. G. (1990). *Small group communication* (3rd ed.). New York: Harper & Row.

Bosman, J. (2006). Retrieved from http://www.nytimes.com/2006/08/15/business/media/15adco.html?_r=0

Bosman, J. (2011, January 4). Publisher tinkers with Twain. *The New York Times*. Retrieved from http://www.nytimes.com/2011/01/05/books/05huck.html

Bosman, J. (2013, July 1). Appeals court's ruling helps Google in book-scanning lawsuit. *The New York Times*. Retrieved from http://www.nytimes.com/2013/07/02/business/media/appeals-courts-ruling-helps-google-in-book-scanning-lawsuit.html?ref=googlebooksearch

Boster, F. J., & Mongeau, P. (1984). Fear-arousing persuasive messages. In R. N. Bostrom (Ed.), *Communication yearbook 8* (pp. 330–375). Beverly Hills, CA: Sage Publications.

Bourhis, R. Y. (1985). The sequential nature of language choice in cross-cultural communication. In R. L. Street Jr. & J. N. Cappella (Eds.), *Sequence and pattern in communicative behaviour* (pp. 120–141). London: Arnold.

Boyd, D. (2010). Social network sites as networked publics: Affordances, dynamics, and implications. In Z. Papacharissi (Ed.), *A networked self: Identity, community, and culture on social network sites* (pp. 39–58). New York: Routledge.

Boyle, K. (2012, December 12). The fall and rise of Rockaway: We are still recovering from Hurricane Sandy. *The New York Daily News*. Retrieved from http://www.nydailynews.com/opinion/fall-rise-rockaway-article-1.1217997

Bradac, J. J. (1983). The language of lovers, flovers, and friends: Communicating in social and personal relationships. *Journal of Language and Social Psychology, 2,* 234.

Bradac, J. J., & Giles, H. (2005). Language and social psychology: Conceptual niceties, complexities, curiosities, monstrosities, and how it all works. In K. L. Fitch & R. E. Sanders (Eds.), *The new handbook of language and social psychology* (pp. 201–230). Mahwah, NJ: Erlbaum.

Brandau-Brown, F. E., & Ragsdale, J. D.(2008). Personal, moral, and structural commitment and the repair of marital relationships. *Southern Communication Journal, 73*(1), 68–83.

Brandenburg, C. (2008). The newest way to screen job applicants: A social networker's nightmare. *Federal Communications Law Journal, 60*(3), 597–626.

Brazeel, S. (2009). Networking to top talent or networking your way to top talent. *POWERGRID International, 14*(10), 2.

Brehm, J. W. (1966). *A theory of psychological reactance.* New York: Academic Press.

Brehm, J. W., & Brehm, S. S. (1981). *Psychological reactance: A theory of freedom and control.* San Diego, CA: Academic Press.

Brenneis, D. (1990). Shared and solitary sentiments: The discourse of friendship, play, and anger in Bhatgaon. In C. A. Lutz & L. Abu-Lughod (Eds.), *Language and the politics of emotion* (pp. 113–125). Cambridge: Cambridge University Press.

Brilhart, J. K., & Galanes, G. J. (1992). *Effective group discussion* (7th ed.). Dubuque, IA: Brown.

Britney, F. (2013, July 28). Kate Middleton post-baby body media coverage: Disrespectful to women? *The hollywoodgossip.com.* Retrieved from http://www.thehollywoodgossip .com/2013/07/kate-middleton-post-baby-body-coverage-disrespectful-to-women

Brock, C. (2010, March 17). Padres breaking down language barrier. Retrieved from mlb.com

Brody, L. R. (2000). The socialization of gender differences in emotional expression: Display rules, infant temperament, and differentiation. In A. H. Fischer (Ed.), *Gender and emotion: Social psychological perspectives* (pp. 24–47). Cambridge: Cambridge University Press.

Brooklyn Nine-Nine (2013). Pilot. Retrieved from http://www.baltimoresun.com/entertainment/tv/z-on-tv-blog/bal-andre-braugher-wendell-pierce-fall-tv-20130913,0,2233205 .story#ixzz2qmOapNNm

Bryant, A. (2012, April 7). The phones are out, but the robot is in. *The New York Times.* Retrieved from http://www.nytimes. com/2012/04/08/business/phillibin-of-evernote-on-its-unusual-corporate-culture.html?pagewanted=all&_r=0

Bryant, J., & Pribanic-Smith, E. J. (2010). A historical overview of research in communication science. In C. R. Berger, M. E. Roloff, & D. R. Roskos-Ewoldsen (Eds.), *The handbook of communication science* (2nd ed.). (pp. 21–36.). Thousand Oaks, CA: Sage Publications.

Buck, R. (1988). Emotional education and mass media: A new view of the global village. In R. P. Hawkins, J. M. Wiemann, & S. Pingree (Eds.), *Advancing communication science: Merging mass and interpersonal processes* (pp. 44–76). Beverly Hills, CA: Sage Publications.

Burgoon, J. K. (1978). A communication model of personal space violations: Explication and an initial test. *Human Communication Research, 4,* 129–142.

Burgoon, J. K., & Bacue, A. E. (2003). Nonverbal communication skills. In J. O. Greene & B. R. Burleson (Eds.), *Handbook of communication and social interaction skills* (pp. 179–219). Mahwah, NJ: Erlbaum.

Burgoon, J. K., Blair, J., & Strom, R. E. (2008). Cognitive biases and nonverbal cue availability in detecting deception. *Human Communication Research, 34*(4), 572–599.

Burgoon, J. K., Buller, D. B., & Woodall, W. G. (1989). *Nonverbal communication: The unspoken dialogue.* New York: Harper & Row.

Burgoon, J. K., & Dunbar, N. E. (2006). Nonverbal expressions of dominance and power in human relationships. In V. Manusov & M. L. Patterson (Eds.), *The SAGE handbook of nonverbal communication* (pp. 279–298). Thousand Oaks, CA: Sage Publications.

Burgoon, J. K., Floyd, K., & Guerrero, L. K. (2010). Nonverbal communication theories of interaction adaptation. In C. R. Berger, M. E. Roloff, & D. R. Roskos-Ewoldsen (Eds.), *The handbook of communication science* (pp. 93–108). Thousand Oaks, CA: Sage Publications.

Burgoon, J. K., & Hoobler, G. D. (2002). Nonverbal signals. In M. L. Knapp & J. A. Daly (Eds.), *Handbook of interpersonal communication* (pp. 240–299). Thousand Oaks, CA: Sage Publications.

Burleson, B. R. (2010). The nature of interpersonal communication: A message-centered approach. In C. R. Berger, M. E. Roloff, & D. R. Roskos-Ewoldsen, *The handbook of communication science* (pp. 145–163). Thousand Oaks, CA: SAGE Publications.

Burleson, B. R., Hanasono, L. K., Bodie, G. D., Holmstrom, A. J., Rack, J. J., Gill-Rosier, J., & McCullough, J. D. (2011). Are gender differences in responses to supportive communication a matter of ability, motivation, or both? Reading patterns of situational responses through the lens of a dual-process theory. *Communication Quarterly, 59,* 37–60.

Burleson, B. R., Holmstrom, A. J., & Gilstrap, C. M. (2005). "Guys can't say that to guys": Four experiments assessing the normative motivation account for deficiencies in the emotional support provided by men. *Communication Monographs, 72*(4), 468–501.

Busch, D. (2009). What kind of intercultural competence will contribute to students' future job employability? *Intercultural Education, 20*(5), 429–438.

Bushman, B. J., & Huesmann, L. R. (2001). Effects of televised violence on aggression. In D. G. Singer & J. L. Singer (Eds.), *Handbook of children and the media* (pp. 223–254). Thousand Oaks, CA: Sage Publications.

Business Week (2005). Why most meetings stink. Retrieved from http://www.businessweek.com/stories/2005-10-30/why-most-meetings-stink

Butler, C. W., & Fitzgerald, R. (2011). "My f***ing personality": Swearing as slips and gaffes in live television broadcasts. *Text & Talk, 31*(5), 525–551.

Byrd, D. (2010, January 16). Neil deGrasse Tyson: "Learning how to think is empowerment." Retrieved from http://earthsky.org/human-world/neil-degrasse-tyson

Cacioppo, J. T., Cacioppo, S., Gonzaga, G. C., Ogburn, E. L. & Vander-Weele, T. J. (2013). Marital satisfaction and break-ups differ across on-line and off-line meeting venues. *Psychological and Cognitive Sciences,* www.pnas.org/cgi/doi/10.1073/pnas.1222447110

Cacioppo, J. T., & Petty, R. E. (1984). The need for cognition: Relationships to attitudinal processes. In R. P. McGlynn, J. E. Maddux, C. Stoltenberg, & J. H. Harvey (Eds.), *Social perception in clinical and counseling psychology.* Lubbock, TX: Texas Tech University Press.

Canary, D. J. (2003). Managing interpersonal conflict: A model of events related to strategic choices. In J. O. Greene & B. R. Burleson (Eds.), *Handbook of communication and social interaction skills* (pp. 515–550). Mahwah, NJ: Erlbaum.

Canary, D. J., & Cody, M. J. (1993). *Interpersonal communication: A goals-based approach*. New York: Bedford/St. Martin's Press.

Canary, D. J., Cody, M. J., & Manusov, V. (2008). *Interpersonal communication: A goals-based approach* (4th ed.). New York: Bedford/St. Martin's.

Canary, D. J., Cody, M. J., & Smith, S. (1994). Compliance-gaining goals: An inductive analysis of actors' goal types, strategies, and successes. In J. A. Daly & J. M. Wiemann (Eds.), *Strategic interpersonal communication* (pp. 33–90). Hillsdale, NJ: Erlbaum.

Canary, D. J., Cunningham, E. M., & Cody, M. J. (1988). Goal types, gender, and locus of control in managing interpersonal conflict. *Communication Research, 15,* 426–446.

Canary, D. J., & Dainton, M. (Eds.). (2003). *Maintaining relationships through communication: Relational, contextual, and cultural variations*. Mahwah, NJ: Erlbaum Associates.

Canary, D. J., & Lakey, S. (2012). *Strategic conflict*. London: Routledge.

Canary, D. J., & Spitzberg, B. H. (1993). Loneliness and media gratifications. *Communication Research, 20,* 800–821.

Capella, J. K., & Greene, J. O. (1982). A discrepancy-arousal explanation of mutual influence in expressive behavior for adult and infant–adult interaction. *Communication Monographs, 49,* 89–114.

Caplan, S. (2001). Challenging the mass-interpersonal communication dichotomy: Are we witnessing the emergence of an entirely new communication system? *Electronic Journal of Communication, 11.* Retrieved March 24, 2003, from http://www.cios.org/getfile/CA-PLAN_v11n101

Capozzoli, T. (2002). How to succeed with self-directed work teams. *Super-Vision, 63,* 25–26.

Cappella, J. N., & Schreiber, D. M. (2006). The interaction management function of nonverbal cues: Theory and research about mutual behavioral influence in face-to-face settings. In V. Manusov & M. L. Patterson (Eds.), *The SAGE handbook of nonverbal communication* (pp. 361–380). Thousand Oaks, CA: Sage Publications.

Cargile, A. C., & Giles, H. (1996). Intercultural communication training: Review, critique, and a new theoretical framework. In B. R. Burleson (Ed.), *Communication yearbook 19* (pp. 3835–3423). Newbury Park, CA: Sage Publications.

Carless, S. A., & DePaola, C. (2000). The measurement of cohesion in work teams. *Small Group Research, 31,* 71–88.

Carli, L. L. (1999). Gender, interpersonal power, and social influence. *Journal of Social Issues, 55,* 81–99.

Carter, C. (2011, February 26). Sheen tantrum likely to cost in the millions. *The New York Times,* p. B1.

Casella, J., & Ridgeway, J. (2012, February 1). How many prisoners are in solitary confinement in the United States? *Solitary Watch*. Retrieved from http://solitarywatch.com/2012/02/01/how-many-prisoners-are-in-solitary-confinement-in-the-united-states

Casmir, F. L. (Ed.). (1997). *Ethics in intercultural and international communication*. Mahwah, NJ: Erlbaum.

Cassell, J., Huffaker, D., Tversky, D., & Ferriman, K. (2006). The language of online leadership: Gender and youth engagement on the Internet. *Developmental Psychology, 42*(3), 436–449.

Caughlin, J. (2003). Family communication standards: What counts as excellent family communication, and how are such standards associated with family satisfaction? *Human Communication Research, 29*, 5–40.

CBS News. (2010, November 28). Colin Firth on playing King George VI: Katie Couric talks with *The King's Speech* star about the monarch's battle against a debilitating stutter. Retrieved from http://www.cbsnews.com/stories/2010/11/28/sunday/main7096682.shtml

CBS News. (2011). Texting while driving up 50 percent last year. Retrieved on May 9, 2014, from http://www.cbsnews.com/news/texting-while-driving-up-50-percent-last-year

Cegala, D. (1981). Interaction involvement: A cognitive dimension of communicative competence. *Communication Education, 30*, 109–121.

Census seen lax on diversity. (2010, February 25). *The Washington Times*. Retrieved from http://www.washingtontimes.com/news/2010/feb/25/census-seen-lax-on-diversity

Centers for Disease Control and Prevention (2013). Distracted driving. Retrieved on May 2, 2014, from http://www.cdc.gov/motorvehiclesafety/distracted_driving

Chaiken, S. (1979). Communicator physical attractiveness and persuasion. *Journal of Personality and Social Psychology, 37*, 1387–1397.

Charles, S. T., Piazza, J. R., Luong, G., & Almeida, D. M. (2009). Now you see it, now you don't: Age differences in affective reactivity to social tensions. *Psychology and Aging, 24*(3), 645.

Chen, G., & Starosta, W. J. (1996). Intercultural communication competence: A synthesis. In B. R. Burleson (Ed.), *Communication yearbook* (Vol. 19, pp. 353–383). Thousand Oaks, CA: Sage Publications.

Chen, G-M., & Starosta, W. J. (2008). Intercultural communication competence: A synthesis. In M. K. Asante, Y. Miike, & J. Yin (Eds.), *The global intercultural communication reader* (pp. 215–238). New York: Taylor and Francis Group.

Chen, Y., & Nakazawa, M. (2009). Influences of culture on self-disclosure as relationally situated in intercultural and interracial friendships from a social penetration perspective. *Journal of Intercultural Communication Research, 38*(2), 77–98.

Cherulnik, P. D., Donley, K. A., Wiewel, T. S., & Miller, S. R. (2001). Charisma is contagious: The effect of leaders' charisma on observers' affect. *Journal of Applied Social Psychology, 31,* 2149–2159.

Chidambaram, L., & Bostrom, R. P. (1996). Group development: A review and synthesis of the development models (I). *Group Decision and Negotiation, 16*(2), 159–187.

Child, J. T., & Westermann, D. A. (2013). Let's be facebook friends: Exploring parental facebook friend requests from a communication privacy management (CPM) perspective. *Journal of Family Communication, 13*(1), 46–59.

Childs, C. (2009). Perfect quiet. *Miller-McCune, 2*(4), 58–67.

Chou, G., & Edge, N. (2012, February). They are happier and having better lives than I am: The impact of using Facebook on perceptions of others' lives. *Cyberpsychology, Behavior, and Social Networking,* pp. 117–121.

Chozick, A. (2011, December 12). Athhilezar? Watch your fantasy world language. *The New York Times,* p. A1.

Christenson, P. (1994). Childhood patterns of music uses and preferences. *Communication Reports, 7,* 136–144.

Christians, C., & Traber, C. (Eds.). (1997). *Communication ethics and universal values.* Thousand Oaks, CA: Sage Publications.

Christie, R., & Geis, F. L. (1970). *Studies in Machiavellianism.* New York: Academic Press.

Christophel, D. M. (1990). The relationships among teacher immediacy behaviors, student motivation, and learning. *Communication Education, 39,* 323–340.

Church of Latter Day Saints Gospel Library. (2001). Lessons: Sexual purity. Retrieved from http://www.lds.org/ldsorg/v/index.jsp?vgnextoid=d6371b08f338c010VgnVCM1000004d82620aRCRD&sourceId=1907be335dc20110VgnVCM100000176f620a____ (paragraph 7)

Cialdini, R. (2008). *Influence: Science and practice* (5th ed.). Englewood Cliffs, NJ: Prentice Hall.

Clark, A. J. (1989). Communication confidence and listening competence: An investigation of the relationships of willingness to communicate, communication apprehension, and receiver apprehension to comprehension of content and emotional meaning in spoken messages. *Communication Education, 38,* 237–248.

Clarke, I., Flaherty, T. B., Wright, N. D., & McMillen, R. M. (2009). Student intercultural proficiency from study abroad programs. *Journal of Marketing Education, 31*(2), 173–181.

Clarke, J., LCSW, ACM. (2014, February 23). Personal communication.

Clausell, E., & Roisman, G. I. (2009). Outness, Big Five personality traits, and same-sex relationship quality. *Journal of Social and Personal Relationships, 26*(2–3), 211–226.

CNN.com/living. (2008). Retrieved from www.cnn.com/2007/LIVING/personal/07/30/wlb.quiz.balance/index.html

Cohen, J. (2013, April 27). Reviving an old series the new way: Fan-financing. *The New York Times*. Retrieved from http://www.nytimes.com/2013/04/28/us/veronica-mars-will-return-thanks-to-fan-financing.html

Cohen, M., & Avanzino, S. (2010). We are people first: Framing organizational assimilation experiences of the physically disabled using co-cultural theory. *Communication Studies, 61*(3), 272–303.

The Colbert Report. (2011, March 9). Video clip "Benchpress." Retrieved from http://www.colbertnation.com/the-colbert-report-videos/376920/march-09-2011/bench-press, 3:40

The Colbert Report. (2013, September 12). Better know a district: Washington's 7th-Jim McDermott. Retrieved from http://www.colbertnation.com/better-know-a-district/429042/september-12-2013/better-know-a-district-washingtons-7th-jim-mcdermott, 3:00

Colvin, G. (2012, December 3). The art of the self-managing team. *Fortune, 166*(9), 22.

Comadena, M. E. (1984). Brainstorming groups. *Small Group Research, 15*, 251–264.

Comer, D. R. (1998). A model of social loafing in real work groups. *Human Relations, 48*, 647–667.

Conley, T. D. (2011). Perceived proposer personality characteristics and gender differences in acceptance of casual sex offers. *Journal of Personality & Social Psychology, 100*(2), 309–329.

Conlin, M. (2006, December 11). Online extra: How to kill meetings. *Business Week*. Retrieved from http://www.businessweek.com

Connelly, S. (2009, December 3). Rupert Everett: Coming out of the closet ruined my career in Hollywood. *Daily News*. Retrieved from http://articles.nydailynews.com/2009-12-03/gossip/17940844_1_gay-best-friendcloset-major-stars

Conover, M. D., Ferrara, E., Menczer, F., & Flammini, A. (2013). The digital evolution of Occupy Wall Street. *PLoS ONE 8*(5). Retrieved from e64679. doi:10.1371/journal.pone.0064679

Costa, M. (2010). Interpersonal distances in group walking. *Journal of Nonverbal Behavior, 34*(1), 15–26.

Coulehan, J. L., & Block, M. L. (2006). *The medical interview: Mastering skills for clinical practice*. Philadelphia: Davis.

Cox, P. L., & Brobrowski, P. E. (2000). The team charter assignment: Improving the effectiveness of classroom teams. *Journal of Behavioral and Applied Management, 1*(1), 92.

Cox, S. S., Bennett, R. J., Tripp, T. M., & Aquino, K. (2012). An empirical test of forgiveness motives' effects on employees' health and well-being. *Journal of Occupational Health Psychology, 17*(3), 330.

Cragan, J. F., Wright, D. W., & Kasch, C. R. (2008). *Communication in small groups: Theory, process, and skills* (7th ed.). Boston: Cengage.

Cramton, C. D. (1997). Information problems in dispersed teams. *Academy of Management Best Paper Proceedings*, 298–302.

Crane, D. (2000). *Fashion and its social agendas: Class, gender, and identity in clothing*. Chicago: University of Chicago Press.

Croucher, S. M., Bruno, A., McGrath, P., Adams, C., McGahan, C., Suits, A., & Huckins, A. (2012). Conflict styles and high–low context cultures: A cross-cultural extension. *Communication Research Reports, 29*(1), 64–73.

Culbert, S. A. (2010). *Get rid of the performance review! How companies can stop intimidating, start managing—and focus on what really matters*. New York: Business Plus/Hachette Book Group.

Culbert, S. A. (2011, March 2). Why your boss is wrong about you. *The New York Times*, p. A25.

Culver, S. H., & Seguin, J. (2013). *Media career guide: Preparing for jobs in the 21st century*. New York: Bedford/St. Martin's.

Cupach, W. R., & Spitzberg, B. H. (Eds.) (2011). *The dark side of close relationships II*. New York: Routledge.

Curtis, P. (1997). Mudding: Social phenomena in text-based virtual realities. In S. Kiesler (Ed.), *Culture of the Internet* (pp. 121–142). Mahwah, NJ: Erlbaum.

Cutica, I., & Bucciarelli, M. (2011). "The more you gesture, the less I gesture": Co-speech gestures as a measure of mental model quality. *Journal of Nonverbal Behavior, 35*(3), 173–187.

Cvitanic, O. (2013, February 26). From gangnam style to the Harlem shake, why we just can't resist a dance craze. *Pacific Standard*. Retrieved from http://www.psmag.com/blogs/the-101/from-gangnam-style-to-the-harlem-shake-why-we-just-cant-resist-a-dance-craze-53266

Daft, R. L., & Lengel, R. H. (1984). Informational richness: A new approach to managerial behavior and organizational design. In B. M. Staw & L. L. Cummings (Eds.), *Research in organizational behavior* (Vol. 6, pp. 191–233). Greenwich, CT: JAI.

Daft, R. L., & Lengel, R. H. (1986). Organizational information requirements, media richness, and structural design. *Management Science, 32,* 554–571.

Dailey, R. M., & Palomares, N. A. (2004). Strategic topic avoidance: An investigation of topic avoidance frequency, strategies used, and relational correlates. *Communication Monographs, 71,* 471–496.

Dainton, M., & Gross, J. (2008). The use of negative behaviors to maintain relationships. *Communication Research Reports, 25,* 179–191.

Danet, B., & Herring, S. C. (Eds.). (2007). *The multilingual Internet: Language, culture, and communication online*. New York: Oxford University Press.

Darbonne, A., Uchino, B. N., & Ong, A. D. (2013). What mediates links between age and well-being? A test of social support and interpersonal conflict as potential interpersonal pathways. *Journal of Happiness Studies, 14*(3), 951–963.

Dargis, M. (2012, October 12). Outwitting the Ayatollah with Hollywood's help. *The New York Times*, p. C1.

Daswani, K. (2012, January 9). More men coloring their hair. *The Los Angeles Times*. Retrieved from http://articles.latimes.com/2012/jan/29/image/la-ig-mens-hair-color-20120129

Davies A., Goetz, A. T., & Shackelford, T. K. (2008). Exploiting the beauty in the eye of the beholder: The use of physical attractiveness as a persuasive tactic. *Personality and Individual Differences, 45*, 302–306.

Davies, P. T., Sturge-Apple, M. L., Cicchetti, D., & Cummings, E. M. (2008). Adrenocortical underpinnings of children's psychological reactivity to interparental conflict. *Child Development, 79*, 1693–1706.

Davis, C., & Myers, K. (2012). Communication and member disengagement in planned organizational exit. *Western Journal of Communication, 76*(2), 194–216.

Davis, J., Foley, A., Crigger, N., & Brannigan, M. C. (2008). Healthcare and listening: A relationship for caring. *International Journal of Listening, 22*(2), 168–175.

Davis, M. S. (1973). *Intimate relations.* New York: Free Press.

Davison, W. P. (1983). The third-person effect in communication. *Public Opinion Quarterly, 40*, 1–15.

Day, L. A. (1997). *Ethics in media communications: Cases and controversies.* Belmont, CA: Wadsworth.

DeAndrea, D. C., & Walther, J. B. (2011). Attributions for inconsistencies between online and offline self-presentations. *Communication Research, 38*(6), 805–825.

DeGroot, T., & Gooty, J. (2009). Can nonverbal cues be used to make meaningful personality attributions in employment interviews? *Journal of Business and Psychology, 24*(2), 179–192.

Dehue, F. (2013). Cyberbullying research: New perspectives and alternative methodologies. Introduction to the special issue. *Journal of Community & Applied Social Psychology, 23*(1), 1–6.

DeKay, S. H. (2009). The communication functions of business attire. *Business Communication Quarterly, 72*(3), 349–350.

DeKay, S. H. (2012). Interpersonal communication in the workplace: A largely unexplored region. *Business Communication Quarterly, 75*(4), 449–452.

Dempsey, A. G., Sulkowski, M. L., Dempsey, J., & Storch, E. A. (2011). Has cyber technology produced a new group of peer aggressors? *Cyberpsychology, Behavior and Social Networking, 1*(5), 297–302.

Denniston, L. (2012, June 29). "Wardrobe malfunction" case finally ends. SCOTUSblog. Retrieved from http://www.scotusblog.com/2012/06/wardrobe-malfunction-case-finally-ends

Derks, D., Bos, A. E. R., & von Grumbkow, J. (2008). Emoticons and online message interpretation. *Social Science Computer Review, 26*(3), 379–388.

Derlega, V. J., Winstead, B. A., Mathews, A., & Braitman, A. L. (2008). Why does someone reveal highly personal information? Attributions for and against self-disclosure in close relationships. *Communication Research Reports, 25*(2), 115–130.

Devine, D. J., Clayton, L. D., Phillips, J. L., & Melner, S. B. (1999). Teams in organizations: Prevalence, characteristics, and effectiveness. *Small Group Research, 30,* 678–711.

Dewey, C. (2012, January 17). How many of this year's Oscar nominees passed the Bechdel test? Not many. *The Washington Post.* Retrieved from http://www.washingtonpost.com/blogs/style-blog/wp/2014/01/17/how-many-of-this-years-oscar-nominees-pass-the-bechdel-test-not-many/

Dewey, J. (1933). *How we think.* Lexington, MA: Heath.

DiBiase, R., & Gunnoe, J. (2004). Gender and culture differences in touching behavior. *Journal of Social Psychology, 144*(1), 49–62.

Dillon, R. K., & McKenzie, N. J. (1998). The influence of ethnicity on listening, communication competence, approach, and avoidance. *International Journal of Listening, 12,* 106–121.

Dimmick, J., Chen, Y., & Li, Z. (2004). Competition between the Internet and traditional news media: The gratification-opportunities niche dimension. *Journal of Media Economics, 17,* 19–33.

Ding, H., & Ding, X. (2013). 360-degree rhetorical analysis of job hunting: A four-part, multimodal project. *Business Communication Quarterly, 76*(2), 239–248.

Dipper, L., Black, M., & Bryan, K. (2005). Thinking for speaking and thinking for listening: The interaction of thought and language in typical and non-fluent comprehension and production. *Language and Cognitive Processes, 20,* 417–441.

DiSanza, J. R., & Legge, N. J. (2002). *Business and professional communication: Plans, processes, and performance* (2nd ed.). Boston: Allyn & Bacon.

Dizik, A. (2011, July 11). 8 important tips for Skype interviews. Retrieved from http://www.cnn.com/2011/LIVING/07/11/skype.interview.tips.cb

Doll, B. (1996). Children without friends: Implications for practice and policy. *School Psychology Review, 25,* 165–183.

Dominguez, A. (2013, May 6). Elizabeth Smart speaks out about abstinence education. *Salt Lake City Tribune.* Retrieved from http://www.sltrib.com/sltrib/news/56248622-78/abstinence-smart-elizabeth-trafficking.html.csp

Dominus, S. (2006, September 28). *Extras,* season 2, epsiode 3, Daniel Radcliffe.

Dominus, S. (2012, January 14). *Saturday Night Live,* season 37, episode 12, Daniel Radcliffe and Lana Del Rey.

Dominus, S. (2013, October 6). Daniel Radcliffe's next trick is to make Harry Potter disappear. *The New York Times Magazine,* p 26.

Donnoli, M., & Wertheim, E. H. (2012). Do offender and victim typical conflict styles affect forgiveness? *International Journal of Conflict Management, 23*(1), 57–76.

Don't call me fat! 25 Stars who have lashed out at criticism of their weight. (2013). RadarOnline.com. Retrieved from http://radaronline.com/photos/dont-call-me-fat-celebrities-lash-out-at-criticism-of-weight

Dooling, R. (2011, March 1). Curbing that pesky rude tone. *The New York Times*, p. A27.

Döring, N., & Pöschl, P. (2009). Nonverbal cues in mobile phone text messages: The effects of chronemics and proxemics. In R. Ling & S. W. Campbell (Eds.), *The reconstruction of space and time: Mobile phone practices*. New Brunswick, NJ: Transaction Publishers.

Doris, J. (Ed.). (1991). *The suggestibility of children's recollections*. Washington, DC: American Psychological Association.

Doucé, L., & Janssens, W. (2013). The presence of a pleasant ambient scent in a fashion store: The moderating role of shopping motivation and affect intensity. *Environment & Behavior, 45*(2), 215–238.

Douglas, C. (2002). The effects of managerial influence behavior on the transition to self-directed work teams. *Journal of Managerial Psychology, 17*, 628–635.

Douglas, C., Martin, J. S., & Krapels, R. H. (2006). Communication in the transition to self-directed work teams. *Journal of Business Communication, 43*(4), 295–321.

Dowd, M. (2012, July 1). The wearing of the green. *The New York Times*, p. SR11.

Dragojevic, M., Giles, H., & Watson, B. M. (2013). Language ideologies and language attitudes: A foundational framework. In H. Giles & B. Watson (Eds.), *The social meanings of language, dialect and accent: International perspectives on speech styles* (pp. 1–25). New York: Peter Lang.

Drummond, K. (2010, February 26). New Pentagon sim teaches troops to play nice. *Wired* Danger Room blog. Retrieved from http://www.wired.com/dangerroom/2010/02/newpentagon-sim-teaches-troops-to-play-nice

Ducharme, J., Doyle, A., & Markiewicz, D. (2002). Attachment security with mother and father: Associations with adolescents' reports of interpersonal behavior with parents and peers. *Journal of Social and Personal Relationships, 19*, 203–231.

Duck, S. W. (1984). A perspective on the repair of personal relationships: Repair of what, when? In S. W. Duck (Ed.), *Personal relationships: Vol. 5. Repairing personal relationships*. New York: Macmillan.

Duell, M. (2013). BBC presenter from Middlesbrough claims she gets abuse from viewers because of her northern accent. *Mail Online*, July 16, 2003. Retrieved from http://www.dailymail.co.uk/news/article-2364998/BBC-presenter-Steph-McGovern-claims-gets-abuse-viewers-northern-accent.html#ixzz2cyTVG5I1 [paragraph 8]

Dues, M., & Brown, M. (2004). *Boxing Plato's shadow: An introduction to the study of human communication*. New York: McGraw-Hill.

Duffy, M., Thorson, E., & Vultee, F. (2009). Advocating advocacy: Acknowledging and teaching journalism as persuasion. Paper presented at the annual meeting of the Association for Education in Journalism and Mass Communication, Sheraton Boston, Boston, MA. Retrieved from http://www.allacademic.com/meta/p375952_index.html

DuFrene, D., & Lehman, C. (2004). Concept, content, construction and contingencies: Getting the horse before the PowerPoint cart. *Business Communication Quarterly, 67*(1), 84–88.

Duggan, M. (2013). Cell phone activities 2013. Pew Research Internet Project. Retrieved from http://www.pewinternet.org/2013/09/19/cell-phone-activities-2013

Duke, A. (2013, April 16). Justin Bieber hopes Anne Frank "would have been a belieber." Retrieved from http://www.cnn.com/2013/04/14/showbiz/bieber-anne-frank

Dunbar, N. E., & Abra, G. (2010). Observations of dyadic power in interpersonal interaction. *Communication Monographs, 77*(4), 657–684.

Dunbar, N. E., & Burgoon, J. K. (2005). Perceptions of power and interactional dominance in interpersonal relationships. *Journal of Social and Personal Relationships, 22*(2), 207–233.

Duncan, S., & Fiske, D. (1977). *Face-to-face interaction.* Hillsdale, NJ: Erlbaum.

Dunleavy, V., & Millette, D. (2007). Measuring mentor roles and protégé initiation strategies: Validating instruments in academic mentoring. *Conference Papers—National Communication Association,* 1. Retrieved from http://www.allacademic.com/meta/p194103_index.html

Dwamena, F., Mavis, B., Holmes-Rovner, M., Walsh, K., & Loyson, A. (2009). Teaching medical interviewing to patients: The other side of the encounter. *Patient Education and Counseling, 76*(3), 380–384.

Dwyer, K. K., & Davidson, M. M. (2012). Is public speaking really more feared than death? *Communication Research Reports, 29,* 99–107.

Dwyer, K. M., Fredstrom, B. K., Rubin, K. H., Booth-LaForce, C., Rose-Krasnor, L., & Burgess, K. B. (2010). Attachment, social information processing, and friendship quality of early adolescent girls and boys. *Journal of Social and Personal Relationships, 27*(1), 91–116.

Eagly, A., Karau, S., & Makhijani, M. (1995). Gender and the effectiveness of leaders: A meta-analysis. *Psychological Bulletin, 111,* 3–32.

Eckholm, E. (2010, May 10). What's in a name? A lot, as it turns out. *The New York Times,* p. A12.

Editorial. (2011, April 5). OMG!!! OED!!! LOL!!!. *The New York Times,* p. A22.

Edwards, B. (2013, November 2). Personal communication.

Edwards, C., & Edwards, A. (2009). Communication skills training for elementary school students. *Communication Currents, 4*(4), 1–2.

Edwards, R. (1990). Sensitivity to feedback and the development of self. *Communication Quarterly, 28,* 101–111.

Efran, M. G. (1974). The effect of physical appearance on the judgment of guilt, interpersonal attraction, and severity of recommended punishment in a simulated jury task. *Journal of Research in Personality, 8,* 45–54.

Eibl-Eibesfeldt, I. (1973). The expressive behavior of the deaf-and-blind-born. In M. von Cranach & I. Vine (Eds.), *Social communication and movement: Studies of interaction and expression in man and chimpanzee* (pp. 163–194). New York: Academic Press.

Eisenberg, E., Goodall, H. L., Jr., & Trethewey, A. (2013). *Organizational communication: Balancing creativity and constraint* (7th ed.). Boston: Bedford/St. Martin's.

Ekman, P., & Friesen, W. V. (1969). The repertoire of nonverbal behavior: Categories, origins, usage, and coding. *Semiotica, 1,* 49–98.

Ekman, P., & Friesen, W. V. (1971). Constants across cultures in the face and emotion. *Journal of Personality and Social Psychology, 17,* 124–129.

Ekman, P., Friesen, W. V., & Ellsworth, P. (1972). *Emotion in the human face: Guidelines for research and an integration of findings.* New York: Pergamon Press.

El Ahl, A., & Steinvorth, D. (2006, October 20). Sex and taboos in the Islamic world. *Spiegel Online International.* Retrieved March 12, 2008, from http://www.spiegel.de/international/spiegel/0,1518,443678,00.html

Elliott, S. (2010, June 30). Food brands get sociable on Facebook and Twitter. *The New York Times.* Retrieved from http://mediadecoder.blogs.nytimes.com/2010/06/30/food-brands-get-sociable-on-facebook-and-twitter

Ellison, N. B., Steinfeld, C., & Lampe, C. (2007). The benefits of Facebook "friends": Social capital and college students' use of online social network sites. *Journal of Computer-Mediated Communication, 12,* 1143–1168.

Ellyson, S. L., Dovidio, J. F., & Brown, C. E. (1992). The look of power: Gender differences and similarities in visual dominance behavior. In C. L. Ridgeway (Ed.), *Gender, interaction, and inequality* (pp. 50–80). New York: Springer-Verlag.

eMarketer (2013, March). Digital set to surpass TV in time spent with US media. Retrieved from http://www.emarketer.com/Article/Digital-Set-Surpass-TV-Time-Spent-with-US-Media/1010096

Endo, Y., Heine, S. J., & Lehman, D. R. (2000). Culture and positive illusions in close relationships: How my relationships are better than yours. *Personality and Social Psychology Bulletin, 26,* 1571–1586.

Entertainment Software Association. (2012). Essential facts about the computer and video game industry: 2012 sales, demographic, and usage data. Retrieved from http://www.theesa.com/facts/pdfs/ESA_EF_2012.pdf

Erdur-Baker, O. (2010). Cyberbullying and its correlation to traditional bullying, gender and frequent and risky usage of Internet-mediated communication tools. *New Media and Society, 12*, 109–125.

Ewald, J. (2010). "Do you know where X is?": Direction-giving and male/female direction-givers. *Journal of Pragmatics, 42*(9), 2549–2561.

Ewalt, D. (2005, September 17). Jane Goodall on why words hurt. *Forbes.* Retrieved from http://www.forbes.com

Eyssel, F., & Kuchenbrandt, D. (2012). Social categorization of social robots: Anthropomorphism as a function of robot group membership. *British Journal of Social Psychology, 51*(4), 724–731.

Faiola, A. (2005, September 22). Men in land of samurai find their feminine side. *Washington Post Foreign Service.* Retrieved from http://www.washingtonpost.com/wp-dyn/content/article/2005/09/21/AR2005092102434.html

Farley, S. D. (2008). Attaining status at the expense of likeability: Pilfering power through conversational interruption. *Journal of Nonverbal Behavior, 32*(4), 241–260.

Farnsworth, S. J., & Lichter, S. R. (2010). *The nightly news nightmare: Media coverage of U.S. presidential elections, 1988–2008* (3rd ed.). Lanham, MD: Rowman & Littlefield.

Farroni, T., Csibra, G., Simion, F., & Johnson, M. (2002, July 9). Eye contact detection in humans from birth. *Proceedings of the National Academy of Sciences of the United States of America, 99*, 9602–9605. Retrieved from http://www.pnas.org/cgi/doi/10.1073/pnas.152159999

Faughnder, R. (2014, January 30). TV ratings: "American Idol" dominates; "Super Fun Night" falls. Retrieved from http://www.latimes.com/entertainment/envelope/cotown/la-et-ct-tv-ratings-american-idol-super-fun-night-0140130,0,1521079.story#axzz2s7UZtE00

Fayard, A. (2013, February 13). One approach does not fit all. *The New York Times.* Retrieved from http://www.nytimes.com/roomfordebate/2013/02/27/the-costs-and-benefits-of-telecommuting/in-telecommuting-one-approach-does-not-fit-all

Federal Communications Commission. (2008, January 8). *Understanding workplace harassment.* Retrieved September 3, 2008, from http://www.fcc.gov/owd/understandingharassment.html

Federal Communications Commission v. Pacifica Foundation, 438 U.S. 726 (1978).

Fent, B., & MacGeorge, E. L. (2006). Predicting receptiveness to advice: Characteristics of the problem, the advice-giver, and the recipient. *Southern Communication Journal, 71*, 67–85.

Ferguson, C. J., & Dyck, D. (2012). Paradigm change in aggression research: The time has come to retire the General Aggression Model. *Aggression and Violent Behavior, 17*(3), 220–228. doi:10.1016/j.avb.2012.02.007

Festinger, L. (1954). A theory of social comparison processes. *Human Relations, 7,* 117–140.

Feuer, A. (2012, November 9). Occupy Sandy: A movement moves to relief. *The New York Times.* Retrieved from http://www.nytimes.com/2012/11/11/nyregion/where-fema-fell-short-occupy-sandy-was-there.html?pagewanted=all

Figdor, C. (2010). Objectivity in the news: Finding a way forward. *Journal of Mass Media Ethics, 25,* 19–33.

Finder, A. (2006, June 11). For some, online persona undermines a resume. *The New York Times.*

Fisk, G. M. (2010). "I want it all and I want it now!" An examination of the etiology, expression, and escalation of excessive employee entitlement. *Human Resource Management Review, 20*(2), 102–114.

Fiske, S. T., & Taylor, S. E. (1991). *Social cognition.* New York: McGraw-Hill.

Fitch-Hauser, M., Powers, W. G., O'Brien, K., & Hanson, S. (2007). Extending the conceptualization of listening fidelity. *International Journal of Listening, 21*(2), 81–91.

Flaherty, L. M., Pearce, K., & Rubin, R. B. (1998). Internet and face-to-face communication: Not functional alternatives. *Communication Quarterly, 46,* 250–268.

Flanagin, A. J., & Metzger, M. J. (2007). The role of site features, user attributes, and information verification behaviors on the perceived credibility of Web-based information. *New Media & Society, 9,* 319–342.

Flecha-García, M. (2010). Eyebrow raises in dialogue and their relation to discourse structure, utterance function and pitch accents in English. *Speech Communication, 52*(6), 542–554.

Fletcher, C. (1999). Listening to narratives: The dynamics of capturing police experience. *International Journal of Listening, 13,* 46–61.

Flynn, J., Valikoski, T., & Grau, J. (2008). Listening in the business context: Reviewing the state of research. *International Journal of Listening, 22*(2), 141–151.

Foels, R., Driskell, J. E., Mullen, B., & Salas, E. (2000). The effects of democratic leadership on group member satisfaction. *Small Group Research, 31,* 676–701.

Folger, J. P., Poole, M. S., & Stutman, R. K. (2001). *Working through conflict: Strategies for relationships, groups, and organizations* (4th ed.). New York: Longman.

Forward, G. L., Czech, K., & Lee, C. M. (2011). Assessing Gibb's supportive and defensive communication climate: An examination of measurement and construct validity. *Communication Research Reports, 28*(1), 1–15.

Fox, L. (2013). Poll: Voters ready for a woman president. Retrieved from http://www.usnews.com/news/articles/2013/05/02/poll-voters-ready-for-a-woman-president.

Fox 13 News (Salt Lake City). (2013). Elizabeth Smart speaks at Johns Hopkins University. VIDEO. Retrieved from http://fox13now.com/2013/05/06/video-elizabeth-smart-speaks-at-johns-hopkins-university [11:24]

Fraleigh, D. M., & Tuman, J. S. (2011). *Speak up! An illustrated guide to public speaking* (2nd ed.). New York: Bedford/St. Martin's.

French, J. R. P., & Raven, B. (1959). The bases for power. In D. Cartwright (Ed.), *Studies in social power* (pp. 150–167). Ann Arbor, MI: Institute for Social Research.

Fridlund, A. J., & Russell, J. A. (2006). The functions of facial expressions: What's in a face? In V. Manusov & M. L. Patterson (Eds.), *The SAGE handbook of nonverbal communication* (pp. 299–320). Thousand Oaks, CA: Sage Publications.

Friedman, T. L. (2007). *The world is flat: A brief history of the twenty-first century.* New York: Farrar, Straus & Giroux.

Frisby, B. N., & Sidelinger, R. J. (2013). Violating student expectations: Student disclosures and student reactions in the college classroom. *Communication Studies, 64*(3), 241–258.

Frosch, D. (2013, March 18). Dispute on transgender rights unfolds at a Colorado school. *The New York Times*, p. A10.

Frum, D. (2000). *How we got here: The '70s.* New York: Basic Books.

Frymier, A. B. (1994). A model of immediacy in the classroom. *Communication Quarterly, 42*, 133–144.

Frymier, A. B., & Nadler, M. K. (2013). *Persuasion: Integrating theory, research, and practice* (3rd ed.). Dubuque, IA: Kendall Hunt.

Fuller, B. (2013, July 24). Kate Middleton: Good for you for showing off your post-baby bump. Hollywoodlife.com. Retrieved from http://hollywoodlife.com/2013/07/24/kate-middleton-good-for-you-for-showing-off-your-post-baby-bump

Gabriel, T. (2010, November 4). Learning in dorm, because class is on the Web. *The New York Times*. Retrieved from http://www.nytimes.com/2010/11/05/us/05college.html

Gagnon, M., Gosselin, P., Hudon-ven der Buhs, I., Larocque, K., & Milliard, K. (2010). Children's recognition and discrimination of fear and disgust facial expressions. *Journal of Nonverbal Behavior, 34*(1), 27–42.

Gallois, C., Franklyn-Stokes, A., Giles, H., & Coupland, N. (1988). Communication accommodation in intercultural encounters. In Y. Y. Kim & W. B. Gudykunst (Eds.), *Theories in intercultural communication* (pp. 157–85). Newbury Park, CA: Sage Publications.

Gardner, L. A. (2011). Wat 2 Do Abt Txt'n & Drv'n (aka: What to do about the problem of texting while driving?). *CPCU Journal, 63*, 1–13.

Gardner, W. L., Reithel, B. J., Foley, R. T., Cogliser, C. C., & Walumbwa, F. O. (2009). Attraction to organizational culture profiles: Effects of realistic recruitment and vertical and horizontal individualism–collectivism. *Management Communication Quarterly, 22*(3), 437–472.

Garner, J. T., & Poole, M. S. (2009). Opposites attract: Leadership endorsement as a function of interaction between a leader and a foil. *Western Journal of Communication, 73(3)*, 227–247.

Gates, B. (2009, February). TED Talks: Bill Gates on Mosquitoes, Malaria, and Education. Retrieved from http://www.ted.com/talks/lang/eng/bill_gates_unplugged.html

Gawande, A. (2009). *The checklist manifesto: How to get things right.* New York: Metropolitan Books.

Gay, V. (2014, January). 45 best TV shows to binge-watch. Newsday.com. Retrieved from http://www.newsday.com/entertainment/tv/45-best-tv-shows-to-binge-watch-1.5631924#46

Gayomali, C. (2013, June 14). How typeface influences the way we read and think: And why everyone hates Comic Sans MS. *The Week.* Retrieved from http://theweek.com/article/index/245632/how-typeface-influences-the-way-we-read-and-think

Gearhart, C., & Bodie, G. D. (2011). Active-empathic listening as a general social skill: Evidence from bivariate and canonical correlations. *Communication Reports, 24*, 86–98.

Gehrke, P. J. (2009). Between the Ear and the Eye: A Synaesthetic Introduction to Listening Ethics. *The International Journal of Listening 23*, 1–6.

Gerbner, G., Gross, L., Morgan, M., & Signorielli, N. (1994). Growing up with television: The cultivation perspective. In J. Bryant & D. Zillmann (Eds.), *Media effects: Advances in theory and research* (pp. 17–41). Hillsdale, NJ: Erlbaum.

Gersick, C. J. G. (1988). Time and transition in work teams: Toward a new model of group development. *The Academy of Management Journal, 31(1)*, 9–41.

Gersick, C. J. G., & Hackman, J. R. (1990). Habitual routines in task-performing groups. *Organizational Behavior and Human Decision Processes, 47*, 65–97.

Gettleman, J. (2008, October 18). Rape victims' words help jolt Congo into change. *The New York Times*, p. A1.

Gibb, J. (1961). Defensive communication. *Journal of Communication, 2*, 141–148.

Giles, H., Coupland, J., & Coupland, N. (1991). *Contexts of accommodation: Developments in applied sociolinguistics.* Cambridge, England: Cambridge University Press.

Giles, H., Coupland, N., & Wiemann, J. M. (1992). "Talk is cheap..." but "My word is my bond": Beliefs about talk. In K. Bolton & H. Kwok (Eds.), *Sociolinguistics today: Eastern and Western perspectives* (pp. 218–243). London: Routledge and Kegan Paul.

Giles, H., Fortman, J., Dailey, R. M., Barker, V., Hajek, C., Anderson, M. C., & Rule, N. O. (2006). Communication accommodation: Law enforcement and the public. In R. M. Dailey & B. A. LePoire (Eds.), *Applied interpersonal communication matters: Family, health, and community relations* (pp. 241–269). New York: Peter Lang.

Giles, H., & LePoire, B. A. (2006). Introduction: The ubiquity and social meaningfulness of nonverbal communication. In V. Manusov & M. L. Patterson (Eds.), *The SAGE handbook of nonverbal communication* (pp. xv–xxvii). Thousand Oaks, CA: Sage Publications.

Giles, H., Reid, S., & Harwood, J. (Eds.) (2010). *The dynamics of intergroup communication*. New York: Peter Lang.

Giles, H., & Wiemann, J. M. (1987). Language, social comparison, and power. In C. R. Berger & S. H. Chaffee (Eds.), *Handbook of communication science* (pp. 350–384). Newbury Park, CA: Sage Publications.

Gillath, O., McCall, C., Shaver, P. R., & Blascovich, J. (2008). What can virtual reality teach us about prosocial tendencies in real and virtual environments? *Media Psychology, 11*(2), 259–282.

Gitlow v. New York, 268 U.S. 652 (1925).

Givhan, R. (2013, April 8). The language of Margaret Thatcher's handbags. *The Daily Beast*. Retrieved from http://www.thedailybeast.com/articles/2011/12/19/the-language-of-margaret-thatcher-s-handbags.html

Gladwell, M. (2010, October 4). Small change: Why the revolution will not be tweeted. *The New Yorker*. Retrieved from http://www.newyorker.com/reporting/2010/10/04/101004fa_fact_gladwell?printable=true&currentPage=all#ixzz2Y1RyfEDF

Goffman, E. (1967). *Interaction ritual: Essays on face-to-face behavior*. Garden City, NY: Doubleday.

Gonzaga, G. C., Campos, B., & Bradbury, T. (2007). Similarity, convergence, and relationship satisfaction in dating and married couples. *Journal of Personality & Social Psychology, 93*(1), 34–48.

Gonzales, A. L., & Hancock, J. T. (2011, January/February). Mirror, mirror on my Facebook wall: Effects of exposure to Facebook on self-esteem. *Cyberpsychology, Behavior, and Social Networking, 14*(1–2), 79–83.

Goodman, J. (2013, March 24). Obsessed? You're not alone. *The New York Times*, p. ST9.

Goodrich, A. (2007, March 28). Anxiety about study abroad. *The Georgetown Independent*. Retrieved from http://travel.georgetown.edu/51469.html

Goodwin, D. K. (2002, January 27). How I caused that story. *Time*. Retrieved from http://www.time.com/time/nation/article/0,8599,197614,00.html#ixzz1FMvG5yK9

Gordon, M. E. (2011). The dialectics of the exit interview: A fresh look at conversations about organizational disengagement. *Management Communication Quarterly, 25*(1), 59–86. doi:10.1177/0893318910376914

Gordon, P. (2004, October 15). Numerical cognition without words: Evidence from Amazonia [Supplementary online materials]. *Science Online.* Retrieved March 25, 2008, from http://www.sciencemag.org/cgi/content/full/sci;1094492/DC1

Gore, J. (2009). The interaction of sex, verbal, and nonverbal cues in same-sex first encounters. *Journal of Nonverbal Behavior, 33*(4), 279–299.

Goss, B., & O'Hair, D. (1988). *Communicating in interpersonal relationships.* New York: Macmillan.

Gottman, J. M. (1994). *What predicts divorce? The relationship between marital processes and marital outcomes.* Hillsdale, NJ: Erlbaum.

Gottman, J. M., & Levenson, R. W. (1992). Marital processes predictive of later dissolution: Behavior, physiology, and health. *Journal of Personality and Social Psychology, 63,* 221–233.

Gottman, J. M., & Silver, N. (1999). *The seven principles for making marriages work: A practical guide from the country's foremost relationship expert.* New York: Three Rivers Press.

Goudreau, J. (2013, February 7). The states people are fleeing in 2013. *Forbes.* Retrieved from http://www.forbes.com/sites/jennagoudreau/2013/02/07/the-states-people-are-fleeing-in-2013

Gouran, D. S. (2003). Communication skills for group decision making. In J. O. Greene & B. R. Burleson (Eds.), *Handbook of communication and social interaction skills* (pp. 835–870). Mahwah, NJ: Erlbaum.

Grahe, J. E., & Bernieri, F. J. (1999). The importance of nonverbal cues in judging rapport. *Journal of Nonverbal Behavior, 23,* 253–269.

Gray, F. E. (2010). Specific oral communication skills desired in new accountancy graduates. *Business Communication Quarterly, 73*(1), 40–67.

Greco, B. (1977). Recruiting and retaining high achievers. *Journal of College Placement, 37*(2), 34–40.

Greenberg, B. S., Sherry, J., Lachlan, K., Lucas, K., & Holmstrom, A. (2010). Orientations to video games among gender and age groups. *Simulation & Gaming, 41*(2), 238–259.

Greenhouse, S. (2006, September 3). Now bringing home the leaner bacon: Borrowers we be. *The New York Times.* Retrieved from http://www.nytimes.com

Greenwalk, A. G., Bellezza, F. S., & Banaji, M. R. (1988). Is self-esteem a central ingredient of self-concept? *Personality and Social Psychology Bulletin, 14,* 34–45.

Groeling, T. (2013). Media bias by the numbers: Challenges and opportunities in the empirical study of partisan news. *Political Science, 16*(1), 129.

Grossman, R. B., & Kegl, J. (2007). Moving faces: Categorization of dynamic facial expressions in American Sign Language by deaf and hearing participants. *Journal of Nonverbal Behavior, 31,* 23–28.

Grossman, S. (2013, April 23). Worst first day ever: Rookie TV anchor fired for profanity in first newscast. *Time*. Retrieved from http://newsfeed.time.com/2013/04/23/worst-first-day-ever-rookie-tv-anchor-fired-for-profanity-in-first-newscast

Gudykunst, W. B. (1993). Toward a theory of effective interpersonal and intergroup communication: An anxiety/uncertainty management (AUM) perspective. In R. L. Wiseman & J. Koester (Eds.), *Intercultural communication competence* (pp. 33–71). Newbury Park, CA: Sage Publications.

Gudykunst, W. B. (2004). *Bridging differences: Effective intergroup communication* (4th ed.). Thousand Oaks, CA: Sage Publications.

Gudykunst, W. B., & Ting-Toomey, S. (1988). *Culture and interpersonal communication*. Newbury Park, CA: Sage Publications.

Gudykunst, W. B., Ting-Toomey, S., Sudweeks, S., & Stewart, L. P. (1995). *Building bridges: Interpersonal skills for a changing world*. Boston: Houghton Mifflin Company.

Guéguen, N. (2012). Tattoos, piercings, and sexual activity. *Social Behavior & Personality: An International Journal, 40*(9), 1543–1547.

Guerrero, L. K., & Afifi, W. A. (1995). Some things are better left unsaid: Topic avoidance in family relationships. *Communication Quarterly, 43*, 276–296.

Guerrero, L. K., Andersen, P. A., & Afifi, W. A. (2013). *Close encounters: Communication in relationships*. Los Angeles, CA: Sage Publications.

Guerrero, L. K., Farinelli, L., & McEwan, B. (2009). Attachment and relational satisfaction: The mediating effect of emotional communication. *Communication Monographs, 76*(4), 487–514.

Guerrero, L. K., & Floyd, K. (2006). *Nonverbal communication in close relationships*. Mahwah, NJ: Erlbaum.

Guerrero, L. K., La Valley, A. G., & Farinelli, L. (2008). The experience and expression of anger, guilt, and sadness in marriage: An equity theory explanation. *Journal of Social and Personal Relationships, 25*(5), 699–724.

Haas, J. (2012). Hate speech and stereotypic talk. In H. Giles (Ed.), *The handbook of intergroup communication* (pp. 128–140). New York: Routledge/Taylor and Francis Group.

Hall, E. T. (1959). *The silent language*. New York: Doubleday.

Hall, E. T. (1976). *Beyond culture*. New York: Anchor/Doubleday.

Hall, E. T., & Hall, M. R. (1990). *Understanding cultural differences: Germans, French, and Americans*. Yarmouth, ME: Intercultural Press, Inc.

Hall, J. A. (1998). How big are nonverbal sex differences? The case of smiling and sensitivity to nonverbal cues. In D. J. Canary & K. Dindia (Eds.), *Sex differences and similarities in communication: Critical essays and empirical investigations of sex and gender in interaction* (pp. 155–178). Mahwah, NJ: Erlbaum.

Hall, J. A. (2013). Humor in long-term romantic relationships: The association of general humor styles and relationship-specific functions with relationship satisfaction. *Western Journal of Communication, 77*(3), 272–292.

Hall, J. A., Carter, J. D., & Hogan, T. G. (2000). Gender differences in nonverbal communication of emotion. In A. H. Fischer (Ed.), *Gender and emotion: Social psychological perspectives* (pp. 97–117). Cambridge: Cambridge University Press.

Hallsten, L., Voss, M., Stark, S., & Josephson, M. (2011). Job burnout and job wornout as risk factors for long-term sickness absence. *Work, 38*(2), 181–192.

Halone, K., Cunconan, T. M., Coakley, C. G., and Wolvin, A. D. Toward the establishment of general dimensions underlying the listening process. *International Journal of Listening, 12*, 12–28. (1998).

Hameed, M. (2012, December 20). Team Rubicon: Rebuilding the Rockaways. Thirteen.org, Metro-Focus. Retrieved from http://www.thirteen.org/metrofocus/2012/12/team-rubicon-rebuilding-the-rockaways, 2:30

Hammick, J. K., & Lee, M. J. (in press). Do shy people feel less communication apprehension online? The effects of virtual reality on the relationship between personality characteristics and communication outcomes. *Computers in Human Behavior.*

Hample, D. (1987). Communication and the unconscious. In B. Dervin & M. J. Voight (Eds.), *Progress in communication sciences* (Vol. 8, pp. 83–121). Norwood, NJ: Ablex.

Hample, D., & Dallinger, J. M. (1995). A Lewinian perspective on taking conflict personally: Revision, refinement, and validation of the instrument. *Communication Quarterly, 43*(3), 297–319.

Han, B., & Cai, D. (2010). Face goals in apology: A cross-cultural comparison of Chinese and U.S. Americans. *Journal of Asian Pacific Communication, 20*(1), 101–123.

Hansen, H. V. (2002). The straw thing of fallacy theory: The standard definition of "fallacy." *Argumentation, 16*, 133–155.

Hansmann, R., & Scholz, R. W. (2003). A two-step informational strategy for reducing littering behavior in a cinema. *Environment and Behavior, 35*(6), 752–762.

Hardt, B. (2012, November 8). NY1's Bob Hardt Blogs from Rockaway Beach. Retrieved from http://origin.ny1.com/content/news/171519/ny1-blog-ny1-s-bob-hardt-reports-on-sandy-from-rockaway-beach

Harmon, A. (2011, March 19). On Twitter, "What a party!" brings an envious "Enough, already!" *The New York Times*, p. A1.

Harmon, A. H., & Metaxas, P. T. (2010). *How to create a smart mob: Understanding a social network capital.* Unpublished manuscript, Wellesley College. Retrieved from http://cs.wellesley.edu/~p-metaxas/How-to-create-Smart-Mobs%20eDem2010.pdf

Harrigan, J. A., & Taing, K. T. (1997). Fooled by a smile: Detecting anxiety in others. *Journal of Nonverbal Behavior, 21,* 203–221.

Harris, A. L., & Hahn, U. (2011). Unrealistic optimism about future life events: A cautionary note. *Psychological Review, 118*(1), 135–154.

Harris, G. (2011, July 11). New for aspiring doctors, the people skills test. *The New York Times,* p. A1.

Harris, G. (2013, February 14). In India, kisses are on rise, even in public. *The New York Times,* p. A4.

Harris, T. E. (2002). *Applied organizational communication: Principles and pragmatics for future practice* (2nd ed.). Mahwah, NJ: Erlbaum.

Harrison, K., & Cantor, J. (1997). The relationship between media consumption and eating disorders. *Journal of Communication, 47,* 40–66.

Hartmann, T., & Tanis, M. (2013). Examining the hostile media effect as an intergroup phenomenon: The role of ingroup identification and status. *Journal of Communication, 63*(3), 535–555.

Hartnett, S. J. (2010). Communication, social justice, and joyful commitment. *Western Journal of Communication, 74*(1), 68–93.

Hartup, W. W., & Stevens, N. (1997). Friendships and adaptation in the life course. *Psychological Bulletin, 121,* 355–370.

Harwood, J. (2000). Communication media use in the grandparent-grandchild relationship. *Journal of Communication, 50*(4), 56–78.

Harwood, J., & Giles, H. (Eds.) (2005). *Intergroup communication: Multiple perspectives.* New York: Peter Lang.

Haughney, C. (2012). Time and CNN reinstate journalist after review. Retrieved on May 2, 2014, from http://query.nytimes.com/gst/fullpage.html?res=9C00E7DE103B-F934A2575BC0A9649D-8B63&ref=fareedzakaria

Hawkins, K., & Stewart, R. A. (1991). Effects of communication apprehension on perceptions of leadership and intragroup attraction in small task-oriented groups. *Southern Communication Journal, 57,* 1–10.

Hawkley, L. C., & Cacioppo, J. T. (2010). Loneliness matters: A theoretical and empirical review of consequences and mechanisms. *Annals of Behavioral Medicine, 40*(2), 218–227.

Hayakawa, S. I. (1964). *Language in thought and action.* New York: Harcourt Brace Jovanovich.

Hazel, M., Wongprasert, T. K., & Ayres, J. (2006). Twins: How similar are fraternal and identical twins across four communication variables? *Journal of the Northwest Communication Association, 35,* 46–59.

Hecht, M. L., Jackson, R. L., II, & Ribeau, S. A. (2003). *African American communication: Exploring identity and culture.* Mahwah, NJ: Erlbaum.

Helgesen, S. (1990). *The female advantage: Women's ways of leadership.* Garden City, NY: Doubleday.

Hendrick, S. S., & Hendrick, C. (1992). *Liking, loving, and relating.* Pacific Grove, CA: Brooks/Cole.

Hendriks, A. (2002). Examining the effects of hegemonic depictions of female bodies on television: A call for theory and programmatic research. *Critical Studies in Media Communication, 19,* 106–123.

Henry, A. (2012, May 11). How to choose the best chart for your data. Lifehacker.com. Retrieved from http://lifehacker.com/5909501/how-to-choose-the-best-chart-for-your-data

Herman, M. (2013, January 30). Super Bowl: Are American sports fans the classy ones? *Pacific Standard.* Retrieved from http://www.psmag.com/uncategorized/superbowl-how-to-explain-the-classyness-of-american-sports-fans-52172

Herman, M. (2013, June 13). Crisis-wracked town bets on Smurf-based economy. *Pacific Standard.* Retrieved from http://www.psmag.com/business-economics/crisis-wracked-town-bets-on-smurf-based-economy-60158

Hershatter, A., & Epstein, M. (2010). Millennials and the world of work: An organization and management perspective. *Journal of Business and Psychology, 25*(2), 211–223.

Heslin, R. (1974). *Steps toward a taxonomy of touching.* Paper presented at the Western Psychological Association Convention, Chicago.

Hesse, C., & Rauscher, E. A. (2013). Privacy tendencies and revealing/concealing: The moderating role of emotional competence. *Communication Quarterly, 61*(1), 91–112.

Hicks, A. M., & Diamond, L. M. (2011). Don't go to bed angry: Attachment, conflict, and affective and physiological reactivity. *Personal Relationships, 18*(2), 266–284. doi:http://dx.doi.org/10.1111/j.1475-6811.2011.01355.x

Hinckley, D. (2010, March 14). The price of beauty. *NYDaily News.com.* Retrieved from http://www.nydailynews.com/entertainment/tv/2010/03/14/2010-03-14_vh1s_price_of_beauty_hosted_by_jessica_simpson_is_ditzy_look_at_international_be.html

Hinkle, L. L. (1999). Nonverbal immediacy communication behaviors and liking in marital relationships. *Communication Research Reports, 16,* 81–90.

Hirokawa, R. Y., Gouran, D. S., & Martz, A. E. (1988). Understanding the sources of faulty group decision-making: A lesson from the *Challenger* disaster. *Small Group Behavior, 19,* 411–433.

Hockenbury, D. H., & Hockenbury, S. E. (2009). *Psychology* (5th ed). New York: Worth.

Hoeken, H., Van den Brandt, C., Crijns, R., Dominguez, N., Hendriks, B., Planken, B., & Starren, M. (2003). International advertising in Western Europe: Should differences in uncertainty avoidance be considered when advertising in Belgium, France, the Netherlands and Spain? *Journal of Business Communication, 40*(3), 195–218.

Hofstede, G. (1984). *Culture's consequences: International differences in work-related values.* Beverly Hills, CA: Sage Publications.

Hofstede, G. (2001). *Culture's consequences: Comparing values, behaviors, institutions, and organizations across nations.* Thousand Oaks, CA: Sage Publications.

Hofstede, G., Hofstede, G. J., & Minkov, M. (2010). *Cultures and organizations: Software of the mind* (3rd ed.). New York: McGraw-Hill.

Holland, K. (2006, December 3). Under new management: When work time isn't face time. *The New York Times.* Retrieved from http://www.nytimes.com

Holson, L. M. (2008, March 9). Text generation gap: U r 2 old (jk). *The New York Times.* Retrieved from http://www.nytimes.com/2008/03/09/business/09cell.html

Holson, L. M. (2010, May 8). Tell-all generation learns to keep things offline. *The New York Times,* p. A1.

Homer, P. M. (2006). Relationships among ad-induced affect, beliefs, and attitudes: Another look. *Journal of Advertising, 35,* 35–51.

Honeycutt, J. M., Choi, C. W., & DeBerry, J. R. (2009). Communication apprehension and imagined interactions. *Communication Research Reports, 26*(3), 228–236.

Honeycutt, J. M., & Wiemann, J. M. (1999). Analysis of functions of talk and reports of imagined interactions (IIs) during engagement and marriage. *Human Communication, 25,* 399–419.

Hong, S. M., & Faedda, S. (1996). Refinement of the Hong psychological reactance scale. *Educational and Psychological Measurement, 56,* 173–182.

Hoover, K. (2006, February). Alumni to know: He brought Trader Joe's to Main Street. *Stanford Business Magazine.* Retrieved from http://www.gsb.stanford/edu

Horn, J. (2010, October 31). The production: How *The King's Speech* found its voice. *Los Angeles Times.* Retrieved from http://articles.latimes.com/2010/oct/31/entertainment/laca-sneaks-kings-speech-20101031

Horovitz, B. (2012, May 3). After Gen X, Millennials, what should the next generation be? *USA Today.* Retrieved from http://usatoday30.usatoday.com/money/advertising/story/2012-05-03/naming-the-next-generation/54737518/1

Howard, D. L. (2004, August 2). Silencing Huck Finn. *The Chronicle of Higher Education.* Retrieved from http://chronicle.com/jobs/2004/08/2004080201c.htm

Howe, N. & Strauss, W. (1992). *Generations: The history of America's future, 1584 to 2069.* New York: Quill.

Hseih, T. (2013, March 19). Working from home alone is the real culprit. *Fortune.* Retrieved from http://management.fortune.cnn.com/2013/03/19/working-from-home-telecommuting

Hullman, G. A., Goodnight, A., & Mougeotte, J. (2012). An examination of perceived relational messages that accompany interpersonal communication motivations. *Open Communication Journal, 6,* 1–7.

Husband, C. (2009). Between listening and understanding. *Continuum: Journal of Media & Cultural Studies, 23*(4), 441–443.

Huston, A. C., Bickham, D. S., Lee, J. H., & Wright, J. C. (2007). From attention to comprehension: How children watch and learn from television. In N. Pecora, J. P. Murray, & E. A. Wartella (Eds.), *Children and television: Fifty years of research* (pp. 41–63). Mahwah, NJ: Erlbaum.

Huston, A., & Wright, J. C. (1998). Television and the informational and educational needs of children. *The Annals of the American Academy of Political and Social Science, 557*(1), 9–23.

Huston, D. (2010). Waking up to ourselves: The use of mindfulness meditation and emotional intelligence in the teaching of communications. *New Directions for Community Colleges, 2010*(151), 39–50.

Iedema, R., Jorm, C., Wakefield, J., Ryan, C., & Sorensen, R. (2009). A new structure of attention? Open disclosure of adverse events to patients and their families. *Journal of Language & Social Psychology, 28*(2), 139–157.

Imrov Everywhere. (2014, January 12). No pants subway ride 2014 New York report. Retrieved from http://improveverywhere.com/2014/01/12/no-pants-subway-ride-2014-new-york-reports

Infante, D. A. (1988). *Arguing constructively.* Prospect Heights, IL: Waveland Press.

Infante, D. A., & Rancer, A. S. (1982). A conceptualization and measure of argumentativeness. *Journal of Personality Assessment, 45*, 72–80.

Internet Gaming Disorder. (2013). *DSM5*-org. Retrieved from http://www.dsm5.org/Documents/Internet%20Gaming%20Disorder%20Fact%20Sheet.pdf

"It Gets Better Project" (2013). Retrieved November 1, 2013 from http://www.itgetsbetter.org/pages/about-it-gets-better-project

Ivy, D., & Backlund, P. (2004). *Gender speak: Personal effectiveness in gender communication* (3rd ed.). New York: McGraw-Hill.

Iyengar, S., & Hahn, K. S. (2009). Red media, blue media: Evidence of ideological selectivity in media use. *Journal of Communication, 59*, 19–39.

Jablin, F. M. (1987). Organizational entry, assimilation, and exit. In F. M. Jablin, L. L. Putnam, K. H. Roberts, & L. W. Porter (Eds.), *Handbook of organizational communication* (pp. 679–740). Newbury Park, CA: Sage. Publications.

Jablin, F. M. (2001). Organizational entry, assimilation, and disengagement/exit. In F. M. Jablin & L. L. Putnam (Eds.), *The new handbook of organizational communication: Advances in theory, research, and methods* (pp. 732–818). Thousand Oaks, CA: Sage Publications.

Jablin, F. M., Seibold, D. R., & Sorensen, R. L. (1977). Potential inhibitory effects of group participation on brainstorming preferences. *Central States Speech Journal, 28*, 113–121.

Jablin, F. M., & Sussman, L. (1978). An exploration of communication and productivity in real brainstorming groups. *Human Communication Research, 4*, 329–337.

Jackson, D. (2006, January 29). State of the Union address: A meshing of many ideas. *USA Today.* Retrieved from http://www.usatoday.com/news/washington/2006-01-29-sotu-speech_x.htm?POE=click-refer

Jacobs, C. D., & Heracleous, L. (2006). Constructing shared understanding: The role of embodied metaphors in organization development. *Journal of Applied Behavioral Science, 42,* 207–227.

Jacobs, T. (2012, December 3). "Slut" label refuses to die. *Pacific Standard.* Retrieved from http://www.alternet.org/gender/why-slut-label-refuses-die

Jacobs, T. (2013, January 16, 2013). Chick lit may be hazardous to your self-esteem. *Pacific Standard.* Retrieved from http://www.psmag.com/blogs/news-blog/chick-lit-may-be-hazardous-to-your-self-esteem-51671

Jacobs, T. (2013, February 11). Why you can't stop perusing your Facebook profile. Retrieved from http://www.psmag.com/blogs/news-blog/why-you-cant-stop-checking-your-facebook-profile-52531

Jacobs, T. (2013, March 27). Mindfulness training boosts test scores. *Pacific Standard.* Retrieved from http://www.psmag.com/blogs/news-blog/mindfulness-training-boosts-test-scores-54431

Jacobson, S. (2013). Does audience participation on Facebook influence the news agenda? A case study of *The Rachel Maddow Show. Journal of Broadcasting & Electronic Media, 57*(3), 338–355.

James, C. H., & Minnis, W. C. (2004, July–August). Organizational storytelling: It makes sense. *Business Horizons,* pp. 23–32.

Janis, I. L. (1982). *Groupthink: Psychological studies of policy decisions and fiascoes* (2nd ed.). Boston: Houghton Mifflin.

Janusik, L. (2005). Conversational listening span: A proposed measure of conversational listening. *International Journal of Listening, 19,* 12–28.

Janusik, L. A., & Wolvin, A. D. (2009). 24 hours in a day: A listening update to the time studies. *International Journal of Listening, 23*(2), 104–120.

Jessica Simpson "really, really frustrated" with progress of post-pregnancy weight-loss. (2013, August 13). RadarOnline.com. Retrieved from http://radaronline.com/exclusives/2013/08/jessica-simpson-baby-weight-loss-ok

Jin, B., & Oh, S. (2010). Cultural differences of social network influence on romantic relationships: A comparison of the United States and South Korea. *Communication Studies, 61*(2), 156–171.

Johansson, C., & Stohl, C. (2012). Cultural competence and institutional contradictions: The hydropower referendum. *Journal of Applied Communication Research, 40*(4), 329–349.

Johnson, D. I. (2012). Swearing by peers in the work setting: Expectancy violation valence, perceptions of message, and perceptions of speaker. *Communication Studies, 63*(2), 136–151.

Johnson, D. I., & Lewis, N. (2010). Perceptions of swearing in the work setting: An expectancy violations theory perspective. *Communication Reports, 23,* 106–118.

Johnson, S. (2005, April 24). Watching TV makes you smarter. *The New York Times.* Retrieved from http://www.nytimes.com/2005/04/24/magazine/24TV.html

Johnson, S. D., Suriya, C., Yoon, S. W., Berrett, J. V., & Fleur, J. L. (2002). Team development and group processes of virtual learning teams. *Computers & Education, 39,* 379–393.

Johnson, T. (2010, April 19). Land that job: What interviewers really want you to ask them. *Good Morning America.* Retrieved from http://abcnews.go.com/GMA/Job-Club/questions-job-interview/story?id=10409243

Johnston, M. K., Weaver, J. B., Watson, K. W., & Barker, L. B. (2000). Listening styles: Biological or psychological differences? *International Journal of Listening, 14,* 32–46.

Joiner, R., Gavin, J., Brosnan, M., Cromby, J., Gregory, H., Guiller, J., Maras, P., & Moon, A. (2013). Comparing first and second generation digital natives' Internet use, Internet anxiety, and Internet identification. *Cyberpsychology, Behavior, and Social Networking, 16*(7), 549–552. ISSN 2152-271

Jolie, A. (2009, June 18). Angelina Jolie speaks on World Refugee Day. Video retrieved from http://www.youtube.com/user/AngelinaJolieUN-HCR#p/u/87/qtt1Vs9Lcp0. Quote begins at 0:20 and ends at 1:00.

Jones, C. (2005, May 16). Gay marriage debate still fierce one year later. *USA Today.* Retrieved from http://www.usatoday.com/news/nation/2005-05-16-gay-marriage_x.htm

Jones, D. (2004, November 30). Best friends good for business. *USA Today.* Retrieved May 10, 2008, from http://www.usatoday.com/money/workplace/2004=/=30=best=-friends_x.htm

Jones, E. E. (1990). *Interpersonal perception.* New York: Freeman.

Jordet, G., Hartman, E., & Jelle Vuijk, P. (2012). Team history and choking under pressure in major soccer penalty shootouts. *British Journal of Psychology, 103*(2), 268–283.

Joyce, M. P. (2008). Interviewing techniques used in selected organizations today. *Business Communication Quarterly, 71*(3), 376–380.

Jundi, S., Vrij, A., Hope, L., Mann, S., & Hillman, J. (2013). Establishing evidence through undercover and collective intelligence interviewing. *Psychology, Public Policy, and Law, 19*(3), 297–306. doi:10.1037/a0033571

Kadushin, A., & Kadushin, G. (2013). *The social work interview* (5th ed.). New York: Columbia University Press.

Kaiser Family Foundation. (2010, January 20). Daily media use among children and teens up dramatically from five years ago. In *Generation M2: Media in the lives of 8- to 18-year-olds.* Retrieved from http://www.kff.org/entmedia/8010.cfm

Kalbfleisch, P. J. (2002). Communicating in mentoring relationships: A theory for enactment. *Communication Theory, 12,* 63–69.

Kalman, Y. M., & Rafaeli, S. (2011). Online pauses and silence: Chronemic expectancy violations in written computer-mediated communication. *Communication Research, 38*(1), 54–69.

Kalman, Y. M., Ravid, G., Raban, D. R., & Rafaeli, S. (2006). Pauses and response latencies: A chronemic analysis of asynchronous CMC. *Journal of Computer-Mediated Communication, 12*(1), 1–23.

Kameda, T., Ohtsubo, Y., & Takezawa, M. (1997). Centrality in sociocognitive networks and social influence: An illustration in a group decision-making context. *Journal of Personality and Social Psychology, 73,* 296–309.

Kanter, R. M. (2009). *Supercorp: How vanguard companies create innovation, profits, growth, and social good.* New York: Crown Business.

Karau, S. J., & Williams, K. D. (1993). Social loafing: A meta-analytic review and theoretical integration. *Journal of Personality and Social Psychology, 65*(4), 681–706.

Karau, S. J., & Williams, K. D. (2001). Understanding individual motivation in groups: The collective effort model. In M. E. Turner (Ed.), *Groups at work: Theory and research. Applied social research* (pp. 113–141). Mahwah, NJ: Erlbaum.

Kato, S., Kato, Y., & Scott, D. (2009). Relationships between emotional states and emoticons in mobile phone email communication in Japan. *International Journal on E-Learning, 8*(3), 385–401.

Katzenbach, J. R., & Smith, D. K. (1993). *The wisdom of teams.* Boston: Harvard Business School Press.

Kazemi, D. M., Levine, M. J., Dmochowski, J., Nies, M. A., & Sun, L. (2013). Effects of motivational interviewing intervention on blackouts among college freshmen. *Journal of Nursing Scholarship, 45*(3), 221–229. doi:10.1111/jnu.12022

Keaten, J. A., & Kelly, L. (2008). "Re: We really need to talk": Affect for communication channels, competence, and fear of negative evaluation. *Communication Quarterly, 56*(4), 407–426.

Keating, C. F. (2006). Why and how the silent self speaks volumes: Functional approaches to nonverbal impression management. In V. Manusov & M. L. Patterson (Eds.), *The SAGE handbook of nonverbal communication* (pp. 321–340). Thousand Oaks, CA: Sage Publications.

Keller, E. (2009, September 24). One religion, two faiths. *Slate.* Retrieved from http://www.slate.com/blogs/xx_factor/2009/09/24/a_commitment_to_our_judaism_threatened_our_relationship.html, para 1.

Keller, J. (2013, June 10). "The Internet made me do it." Stop blaming social media for our behavioral problems. *Pacific Standard.* Retrieved from http://www.psmag.com/culture/internet-blaming-social-media-behavioral-problems-59538/#.UbYRNDRH9DQ

Kennedy, R. (2003). *Nigger: The strange career of a troublesome word*. New York: Vintage Books.

Kenrick, D. T., Griskevicius, V., Neuberg, S. L., & Schaller, M. (2010). Renovating the pyramid of needs: Contemporary extensions built upon ancient foundations. *Perspectives on Psychological Science, 5*(3), 292–314.

Keyton, J. (1993). Group termination: Completing the study of group development. *Small Group Research, 24*, 84–100.

Keyton, J., Ferguson, P., & Rhodes, S. C. (2001). Cultural indicators of sexual harassment. *Southern Communication Journal, 67*, 33–50.

Keyton, J., & Frey, L. R. (2002). The state of traits: Predispositions and group communication. In L. R. Frey (Ed.), *New directions in group communication* (pp. 99–120). Thousand Oaks, CA: Sage Publications.

Kiesling, S. F. (1998). Men's identities and sociolinguistic variation: The case of fraternity men. *Journal of Sociolinguistics, 2*(1), 69–99.

Kilmann, P. R. (2012). Personality and interpersonal characteristics within distressed marriages. *The Family Journal, 20*(2), 131–139.

Kirchner, L. (2013, June 10). Brain-scan lie detectors just don't work. *Pacific Standard*. Retrieved from http://www.psmag.com/science/brain-scan-lie-detectors-just-dont-work-59584/#.UbZXyOabDMY

Kissell, R. (2014, January 20). "Sherlock" sees rising ratings in return to PBS on Sunday. Retrieved from http://variety.com/2014/tv/news/sherlock-sees-rising-ratings-in-return-to-pbs-on-sunday-1201065620

Klein, E. (2013, April 28). If this was a pill, you'd do anything to get it. *Washington Post*. http://www.washingtonpost.com/blogs/wonkblog/wp/2013/04/28/if-this-was-a-pill-youd-do-anything-to-get-it/

Kleinmann, M., & Klehe, U. (2011). Selling oneself: Construct and criterion-related validity of impression management in structured interviews. *Human Performance, 24*(1), 29–46. doi:10.1080/08959285.2010.530634

Kline, S., Horton, B., & Zhang, S. (2005). *How we think, feel, and express love: A cross-cultural comparison between American and East Asian cultures*. Paper presented at the annual meeting of the International Communication Association, New York.

Klocke, U. (2007). How to improve decision making in small groups: Effects of dissent and training interventions. *Small Group Research, 38*, 437–468.

Knapp, M. L. (2008). *Lying and deception in human interaction*. Boston: Pearson.

Knapp, M. L., & Hall, J. A. (2010). *Nonverbal communication in human interaction*. Boston, MA: Wadsworth, Cengage Learning.

Knapp, M. L., Hart, R. P., Friedrich, G. W., & Shulman, G. M. (1973). The rhetoric of goodbye: Verbal and nonverbal correlates of human leave-taking. *Communication Monographs, 40*, 182–198.

Knapp, M. L., & Vangelisti, A. (2000). *Interpersonal communication and human relationships* (4th ed.). Newton, MA: Allyn & Bacon.

Knapp, M. L., & Vangelisti, A. L. (2008). *Interpersonal communication and human relationships.* Boston: Allyn and Bacon.

Knobloch, L. K., & Solomon, D. H. (2002). Information seeking beyond initial interaction: Negotiating relational uncertainty within close relationships. *Human Communication Research, 28,* 243–257.

Kobayshi, J., & Viswat, L. (2010). Cultural expectations in expressing disagreement: Differences between Japan and the United States. *Asian EFL Journal, 48.*

Koerner, B. I. (2013, September 26). Forget foreign languages and music. Teach our kids to code. *Wired.* Retrieved from http://www.wired.com/opinion/2013/09/ap_code

Kois, D. (2012, April 1). The payoff. *The New York Times Sunday Magazine,* p. MM18.

Kolb, D. M., & Putnam, L. L. (1992). Introduction: The dialectics of disputing. In D. M. Kolb & J. M. Bartunek (Eds.), *Hidden conflict in organizations: Uncovering behind the scenes disputes.* Newbury Park, CA: Sage Publications.

Kotler, P., & Keller, K. (2011). *Marketing management* (14th ed.). Upper Saddle River, NJ: Prentice Hall.

Kotlyar, I., & Ariely, D. (2013). The effect of nonverbal cues on relationship formation. *Computers in Human Behavior, 29*(3), 544–551.

Kowitz, A. C., & Knutson, T. J. (1980). *Decision making in small groups: The search for alternatives.* Needham Heights, MA: Allyn & Bacon.

Kram, K. E. (1983). Phases of the mentor relationship. *Academy of Management Journal, 12,* 608–625.

Kramer, M. W., & Pier, P. M. (1999). Students' perceptions of effective and ineffective communication by college teachers. *Southern Communication Journal, 65,* 16–33.

Krayer, K. (2010). *Influencing skills for effective leadership.* Dallas: University of Dallas College of Business.

Krcmar, M., & Greene, K. (1999). Predicting exposure to and uses of television violence. *Journal of Communication, 49,* 24–46.

Kreamer, A. (2006, June). Back to my roots: A diary of going gray. *More Magazine.* Retrieved from http://www.more.com/beauty/hair/back-my-roots-diary-going-gray, paragraph 1.

Kreamer, A. (2007, September). Sex and the gray haired woman. *More Magazine.* Retrieved from http://www.more.com/relationships/dating-sex-love/sex-and-gray-haired-woman

Kross, F., Verduyn, P., Demiralp, E., Park, J., Lee, D. S., Lin, N., Shablack, H., Jonides, J., & Ybarra, O. (2013). Facebook use predicts declines in subjective well-being in young adults. *PLoS ONE 8*(8): e69841. doi:10.1371/journal.pone.0069841

Kruger, J., & Dunning, D. (1999). Unskilled and unaware of it: How difficulties in recognizing one's own incompetence lead to inflated self-assessments. *Journal of Personality and Social Psychology, 77*(6), 1121–1134.

Kruglanski, A. W., Chen, X., Pierro, A., Mannetti, L., Erb, H.-P., & Spiegel, S. (2006). Persuasion according to the unimodel: Implications for cancer communication. *Journal of Communication, 56,* 105–122.

Krumhuber, E., Manstead, A., Cosker, D., Marshall, D., & Rosin, P. (2009). Effects of dynamic attributes of smiles in human and synthetic faces: A simulated job interview setting. *Journal of Nonverbal Behavior, 33*(1), 1–15.

Kuhn, T., & Poole, M. S. (2000). Do conflict management styles affect group decision making? Evidence from a longitudinal field study. *Human Communication Research, 26,* 558–590.

LaBarre, S. (2013, September 24). Why we're shutting off our comments. PopularScience.com. Retrieved from http://www.popsci.com/science/article/2013-09/why-were-shutting-our-comments, paragraph 2

Lambert, C. (2012, March–April). Twilight of the lecture: The trend toward "active learning" may overthrow the style of teaching that has ruled universities for 600 years. *Harvard Magazine.* Retrieved from http://harvardmagazine.com/2012/03/twilight-of-the-lecture

Lammers, J., Dubois, D., Rucker, D. D., & Galinsky, A. D. (2013). Power gets the job: Priming power improves interview outcomes. *Journal of Experimental Social Psychology, 49*(4), 776–779. doi:10.1016/j.jesp.2013.02.008.

Lämsä, A.-M., & Sintonen, T. (2006). A narrative approach for organizational learning in a diverse organization. *Journal of Workplace Learning, 18,* 106–120.

Landis, D., Bennett, J. M., and Bennett, M. J. (Eds.). (2004). *Handbook of intercultural training.* Thousand Oaks, CA: Sage Publications.

Landro, L. (April 8, 2013). The talking cure for health care. *The Wall Street Journal.* http://online.wsj.com/news/articles/SB100014241278873236288045783462239607742296

Landsford, J. E., Antonucci, T. C., Akiyama, H., & Takahashi, K. (2005). A quantitative and qualitative approach to social relationships and well-being in the United States and Japan. *Journal of Comparative Family Studies, 36,* 1–22.

Larkey, L., & Hecht, M. (2010). A model of effects of narrative as culture-centric health promotion. *Journal of Health Communication, 15*(2), 114–135.

Latane, B., Williams, K., & Harkins, S. (1979). Many hands make light the work: The causes and consequences of social loafing. *Journal of Personality and Social Psychology, 37*(6), 822–832.

Lawler, K. A., Younger, J. W., Piferi, R. L., Billington, E., Jobe, R., Edmondson, K., & Jones, W. H. (2003). A change of heart: Cardiovascular correlates of forgiveness in response to interpersonal conflict. *Journal of Behavioral Medicine, 26*(5), 373–393.

Le, V. (2011, March 15). Ask an academic: The secret of boys. *The New Yorker* (blog). Retrieved from http://www.newyorker.com/online/blogs/books/2011/03/ask-an-academic-the-deep-secrets-of-boys-friendships.html?printable=true&currentPage=all

Leal, S., & Vrij, A. (2008). Blinking during and after lying. *Journal of Nonverbal Behavior, 32*(4), 187–194.

Leavitt, H. J. (1951). Some effects of certain communication patterns on group performance. *Journal of Abnormal and Social Psychology, 46*, 38–50.

Lebo, B. (2009). Employing millennials: Challenges and opportunities. *New Hampshire Business Review, 31*(26), 21.

Ledbetter, A. M. (2008). Chronemic cues and sex differences in relational e-mail: Perceiving immediacy and supportive message quality. *Social Science Computer Review, 26*(4), 486–482.

Lee, E-J. (2007). Effects of gendered language on gender stereotyping in computer-mediated communication: The moderating role of depersonalization and gender-role orientation. *Human Communication Research, 33*(4), 515–535.

Lee, J. A. (1973). *The colors of love: An exploration of the ways of loving.* Don Mills, Ontario, Canada: New Press.

Leland, J. (2008, October 7). In "sweetie" and "dear," a hurt for the elderly. *The New York Times*, p. A1.

Lemonick, M. (2007, May 3). The *Time* 100: Neil deGrasse Tyson. *Time*. Retrieved from www.time.com/time/specials/2007/time100

le Roux, M. (2006, November 27). Let's talk about sex: Cult South African director shatters taboos. *Namibian*. Retrieved from http://www.namibian.com.na/2006/November/africa/065E8B0EB5.html

Levin, D. (2012, August 4). Beach essentials in China: Flip-flops, a towel and a ski mask. *The New York Times*, p. A1.

Levine, E., & Parks, L. A. (Eds.). (2007). *Undead TV: Essays on Buffy the Vampire Slayer.* Durham, NC: Duke University Press.

Levine, T. R., Serota, K. B., Shulman, H., Clare, D. D., Park, H. S., Shaw, A. S., & Lee J. H. (2011). Sender demeanor: Individual differences in sender believability have a powerful impact on deception detection judgments. *Human Communication Research, 37*, 377–403.

Levit, A. (2010, March 14). Master online searches. The Wall Street Journal Online. Retrieved from http://online.wsj.com/news/articles/SB126852207486461893

Lewis, L. (2005). Foster a loyal workforce. In *Trader Joe's adventure: Turning a unique approach to business into a retail and cultural phenomenon* (pp. 137–152). New York: Dearborn/Kaplan.

Lewis, T., & Manusov, V. (2009). Listening to another's distress in everyday relationships. *Communication Quarterly, 57*(3), 282–301.

Li, L., & Pitts, J. (2009). Does it really matter? Using virtual office hours to enhance student–faculty interaction. *Journal of Information Systems Education, 20*(2).

Ligos, M. (2001, June 20). Getting over the fear-of-speaking hump. *The New York Times*. Retrieved from http://www.nytimes.com

Lim, G. Y., & Roloff, M. E. (1999). Attributing sexual consent. *Journal of Applied Communication Research, 27*, 1–23.

Limon, M. S., & La France, B. H. (2005). Communication traits and leadership emergence: Examining the impact of argumentativeness, communication apprehension, and verbal aggressiveness in work groups. *Southern Communication Journal, 70*(2), 123–133.

Lincoln, A. (1842, February 22). Temperance address. *Repeat After Us.* Retrieved August 14, 2007, from http://www.repeatafterus.com/title.php?i=9700

Lindsley, S. L. (1999). Communication and "the Mexican way": Stability and trust as core symbols in *maquiladoras. Western Journal of Communication, 63,* 1–31.

Lipari, L. (2009). Listening otherwise: The voice of ethics. *International Journal of Listening, 23*(1), 44–59.

Lipinski-Harten, M., & Tafarodi, R. W. (2012). A comparison of conversational quality in online and face-to-face first encounters. *Journal of Language & Social Psychology, 31*(3), 331–341.

Liston, B. (2013, November 20). Charges dropped against girls in Florida cyberbullying case. *Reuters.* Retrieved from http://www.reuters.com/article/2013/11/21/us-usa-florida-cyberbullying-idUSBRE9AK05C20131121

Loden, M., & Rosener, J. B. (1991). *Workforce America! Managing employee diversity as a vital resource.* Chicago: Business One Irwin.

Lohr, S. (2007, October 31). Hello, India? I need help with my math. *The New York Times.* Retrieved from http://www.nytimes.com

Longley, R. (2007, December 31). From time to time: The State of the Union. *About.com: U.S. government info.* Retrieved from http://usgovinfo.about.com/od/thepresidentandcabinet/a/souhistory.htm

Lubell, S. (2004, February 19). On the therapist's couch, a jolt of virtual reality. *The New York Times.* Retrieved from http://www.nytimes.com

Lucas, K., & Sherry, J. L. (2004). Sex differences in video game play: A communication-based explanation. *Communication Research, 31,* 499–523.

Lucero, M. A., Allen, R. E., & Elzweig, B. (2013). Managing employee social networking: Evolving views from the National Labor Relations Board. *Employee Responsibilities and Rights Journal, 25*(3), 143–158.

Luo, M. (2010, March 29). Overqualified? Yes, but happy to have a job. *The New York Times,* p. A1.

Lustig, M. W., & Koester, J. (1993). *Intercultural competence: Interpersonal communication across cultures.* New York: HarperCollins.

Lustig, M. W., & Koester, J. (2006). *Intercultural competence: Interpersonal communication across cultures* (5th ed.). Boston: Allyn & Bacon.

Lutz, C. A. (1996). Engendered emotion: Gender, power, and the rhetoric of emotional control in American discourse. In R. Harre & W. G. Parrott (Eds.), *The emotions: Social, cultural and biological dimensions* (pp. 132–150). Thousand Oaks, CA: Sage Publications.

Macur, J., & Eder, S. (2012, November 4). Runners embrace chance to help residents recover. *The New York Times*. Retrieved from http://www.nytimes.com/2012/11/05/sports/marathon-runners-embrace-chance-to-help-storm-stricken-new-yorkers.html

Madden, M. (2012, February 24). Privacy management on social media sites. Pew Internet & Amerian Life Project. Retrieve from http://www.pewinternet.org/Reports/2012/Privacy-management-on-social-media/Main-findings.aspx?view=all

Madden, M., & Smith, A. (2010, May 26). Reputation management and social media. *Pew Internet & American Life Project*. Retrieved from http://www.pewinternet.org/Reports/2010/Reputation-Management.aspx

Maddux, J.E., & Rogers, R. W. (1983). Protection motivation theory and self-efficacy: A revised theory of fear appeals and attitude change. *Journal of Experimental Social Psychology*, 19, 469-479.

Madlock, P. E., & Kennedy-Lightsey, C. (2010). The effects of supervisors' verbal aggressiveness and mentoring on their subordinates. *Journal of Business Communication*, 47(1), 42–62.

Maguire, K. C., & Kinney, T. A. (2010). When distance is problematic: Communication, coping, and relational satisfaction in female college students' long-distance dating relationships. *Journal of Applied Communication Research*, 38(1), 27–46.

Maiden, B., & Perry, B. (2011). Dealing with free-riders in assessed group work: Results from a study at a UK university. *Assessment & Evaluation in Higher Education*, 36(4), 451–464.

Manroop, L., Boekhorst, J. A., & Harrison, J. A. (2013). The influence of cross-cultural differences on job interview selection decisions. *International Journal of Human Resource Management*, 24(18), 3512–3533. doi:10.1080/09585192.2013.777675.

Mansson, D. H., Myers, S. A., & Turner, L. H. (2010). Relational maintenance behaviors in the grandchild-grandparent relationship. *Communication Research Reports*, 27(1), 68–79.

Marcus, L. (October 4, 2013). How *Project Runway* is getting deafness right. New York Magazine. http://www.vulture.com/2013/10/how-project-runway-is-getting-deafness-right.html

Markoff, J. & Sengupta, S. (November 22, 2011). Separating you and me? 4.74 degrees. *New York Times*, p. B1.

Martinez, E. (2010, March 26). Alexis Pilkington brutally cyber bullied, even after her suicide. *CBS News*. Retrieved from http://www.cbsnews.com/8301-504083_162-20001181-504083.html

Marwick, A., & Boyd, D. (2011, September 12). The drama! Teen conflict, gossip, and bullying in networked publics. A decade in Internet time: Symposium on the dynamics of the Internet and society. Retrieved from SSRN http://ssrn.com/abstract=1926349, p. 18.

Maslach, C. (1982). *Burnout: The cost of caring*. Englewood Cliffs, NJ: Prentice Hall.

Maslow, A. (1954). *Motivation and personality*. New York: Harper & Row.

Mast, M. S. (2002). Dominance as expressed and inferred through speaking time. *Human Communication Research, 28*, 420–450.

Matsumoto, D. (1989). Cultural influences on the perception of emotion. *Journal of Cross-Cultural Psychology, 20*(1), 92–105.

Matsumoto, D., & Hwang, H. (2013). Cultural similarities and differences in emblematic gestures. *Journal of Nonverbal Behavior, 37*(1), 1–27.

Matthes, J. (2013). The affective underpinnings of hostile media perceptions exploring the distinct effects of affective and cognitive involvement. *Communication Research, 40*(3), 360–387.

Mazur, B., Boboryko-Hocazade, J., & Dawidziuk, M. (2012, March). The intercultural competencies of the managers and organization in the global world. *Managerial Challenges of the Contemporary Society, 3*, 117–120.

McCain, J. S. (2008, January 28). John McCain, prisoner of war: A first person account. *U.S. News & World Report*. Retrieved from http://politics.usnews.com/news/articles/2008/01/28/john-mccain-prisoner-of-war-a-first-person-account.html

McClanahan, A. (2006, March 9). What does a feminist "look" like? *Pocono Record*. Retrieved April 8, 2008, from http://www.poconorecord.com

McClintock, E. A. (2010). When does race matter? Race, sex, and dating at an elite university. *Journal of Marriage & Family, 72*(1), 45–72.

McCombs, M. (2005). The agenda-setting function of the press. In G. Overholser & K. H. Jamieson (Eds.), *The press* (pp. 156–168). New York: Oxford University Press.

McConnell, M. (1987). *Challenger: A major malfunction*. Garden City, NY: Doubleday.

McCroskey, J. C. (1970). Measures of communication-bound anxiety. *Speech Monographs, 37*, 269–277.

McCroskey, J. C. (1977). Oral communication apprehension: A summary of recent theory and research. *Human Communication Research, 4*, 78–96.

McCroskey, J. C. (1997). The communication apprehension perspective. In J. A. Daly & J. C. McCroskey (Eds.), *Avoiding communication: Shyness, reticence, and communication apprehension* (pp. 13–38). Cresskill, NJ: Hampton Press.

McCroskey, J. C., & Mehrley, R. S. (1969). The effects of disorganization and nonfluency on attitude change and source credibility. *Speech Monographs, 36*, 13–21.

McCroskey, J. C., & Teven, J. J. (1999). Goodwill: A reexamination of the construct and its measurement. *Communication Monographs, 66*, 90–103.

McDaniel, E., & Andersen, P. A. (1998). International patterns of interpersonal tactile communication: A field study. *Journal of Nonverbal Behavior, 22*, 59–75.

McDonald, M. (2012, September 10). Making Mandarin mandatory—in kindergartens. *The New York Times*. Retrieved from http://rendezvous.blogs.nytimes.com/2012/09/10/making-mandarin-mandatory-in-u-s-kindergartens

McGrane, W. L., Toth, F. J., & Alley, E. B. (1990). The use of interactive media for HIV/AIDS prevention in the military community. *Military Medicine, 155*, 235–240.

McLean, C. (2011, January 24). *Glee*: The making of a musical phenomenon. *The Telegraph*. Retrieved from http://www.telegraph.co.uk/culture/8271318/Glee-the-making-of-a-musical-phenomenon.html

McLeod, D. N., Detenber, B. H., & Eveland, W. P., Jr. (2001). Behind the third-person effect: Differentiating perceptual processes for self and other. *Journal of Communication, 51*, 678–695.

McWhorter, J. (2013, April). Txtng is killing language. JK!!! TED talks. Retrieved from http://www.ted.com/talks/john_mcwhorter_txtng_is_killing_language_jk.html?utm_campaign=&utm_content=ted-androidapp&awesm=on.ted.com_rBl4&utm_source=getpocket.com&utm_medium=on.ted.com-android-share

Mease, J., & Terry, D. (2012). (Organizational [performance) of race]: The co-constitutive performance of race and school board in Durham, NC. *Text & Performance Quarterly, 32*, 121–140.

Mehrabian, A. (1971). *Silent messages*. Belmont, CA: Wadsworth.

Mello, B. (2009). For k-12 educators: Speaking, listening, and media literacy standards. *Spectra, 45*(3), 11.

Merkin, R. S. (2009). Cross-cultural communication patterns—Korean and American communication. *Journal of Intercultural Communication, 20*, 5.

Merolla, A. J. (2010a). Relational maintenance and noncopresence reconsidered: Conceptualizing geographic separation in close relationships. *Communication Theory, 20*(2), 169–193.

Merrill, A. F., & Afifi, T. D. (2012). Examining the bidirectional nature of topic avoidance and relationship dissatisfaction: The moderating role of communication skills. *Communication Monographs, 79*(4), 499–521.

Microsoft, Inc. (2005, March 15). Survey finds workers average only three productive days per week [Press release]. Retrieved April 30, 2008, from http://www.microsoft.com

Miczo, N. (2008). Dependence and independence power, conflict tactics and appraisals in romantic relationships. *Journal of Communication Studies, 1*(1), 56–82.

Mignerey, J. T., Rubin, R. B., & Gorden, W. I. (1995). Organizational entry: An investigation of newcomer communication behavior and uncertainty. *Communication Research, 22*, 54–85.

Miller, C. W., & Roloff, M. E. (2007). The effect of face loss on willingness to confront hurtful messages from romantic partners. *Southern Communication Journal, 72*(3), 247–263.

Miller, D. T., & Morrison, K. R. (2009). Expressing deviant opinions: Believing you are in the majority helps. *Journal of Experimental Social Psychology, 45*(4), 740–747.

Miller, K. (2009). *Organizational communication: Approaches and processes* (5th ed.). Boston: Wadsworth.

Miller, K. I., Birkholt, M., Scott, C., & Stage, C. (1995). Empathy and burnout in human service work: An extension of a communication model. *Communication Research, 22*, 123–147.

Miller, L. C., Cooke, K. K., Tsang, J., & Morgan, F. (1992). Should I brag? Nature and impact of positive boastful disclosures for women and men. *Human Communication Research, 18*, 364–399.

Miller, R. (1991, January 31). Personnel execs reveal the truth about job applicants. *Dallas Morning News*, p. 2D.

Miller, S. K. (2013, November 6). The case for raising your child with two religions. Op Ed, *The New York Times*. Retrieved from http://ideas.time.com/2013/11/06/the-case-for-raising-your-child-with-two-religions

Miller, W. R., & Rollnick, S. (2013). *Motivational interviewing: Helping people change*. New York: Guilford Press.

Minow, N. N. (1961, May 9). Television and the public interest. Speech presented at the meeting of the National Association of Broadcasters, Washington, DC.

Minow, N. N., & Cate, F. H. (2003). Revisiting the vast wasteland. *Federal Communications Law Journal, 55*, 407–434.

Mittel, J. (2006). Narrative complexity in contemporary American television. *The Velvet Light Trap, 58*, 29–40.

Molloy, J. T. (1983). *Molloy's live for success*. New York: Bantam Books.

Money is the top subject for marital spats. (2006, March 20). *Webindia123.com*. Retrieved May 1, 2006, from http://news.webindia123.com/news/ar_showdetails.asp?id=603200038&cat=&n_date=20060320

Monge, P. (1977). The systems perspective as a theoretical basis for the study of human communication. *Communication Quarterly, 25*, 19–29.

Montana Meth Project (2013). Retrieved June 3, 2013, from http://montana.methproject.org

Montepare, J., Koff, E., Zaitchik, D., & Alberet, M. (1999). The use of body movements and gestures as cues to emotions in younger and older adults. *Journal of Nonverbal Behavior, 23*, 133–152.

Montoya, M., Massey, A., Hung, Y., & Crisp, C. (2009). Can you hear me now? Communication in virtual product development teams. *Journal of Product Innovation Management, 26*(2), 139–155.

Moore, G. E. (1903). *Principia ethica*. Cambridge, UK: Cambridge University Press.

Moreland, R. L., & Levine, J. M., (1994). *Understanding small groups*. Boston: Allyn & Bacon.

Morley, D. (2006). Unanswered questions in audience research. *The Communication Review, 9*, 101–121

Morris, D. (1977). *Manwatching*. New York: Abrams.

Morrissey, L. (2010). Trolling is *a* art: Towards a schematic classification of intention in Internet trolling. *Griffith Working Papers in Pragmatics and Intercultural Communications, 3(2)*, 75–82.

Morse, C. R., & Metts, S. (2011). Situational and communicative predictors of forgiveness following a relational transgression. *Western Journal of Communication, 75(3)*, 239–258.

Motley, M. T. (1990). On whether one can(not) communicate: An examination via traditional communication postulates. *Western Journal of Speech Communication, 56*, 1–20.

Motley, M. T., & Reeder, H. M. (1995). Unwanted escalation of sexual intimacy: Male and female perceptions of connotations and relational consequences of resistance messages. *Communication Monographs, 62*, 355–382.

Muir, C. (2008). Job interviewing. *Business Communication Quarterly, 71(3)*, 374–376.

Mulac, A. J., Wiemann, J. M., Widenmann, S. J., & Gibson, T. W. (1988). Male-female language differences and effects in same-sex and mixed-sex dyads: The gender-linked language effect. *Communication Monographs, 55*, 315–335.

Mulgrew, K. E., & Volcevski-Kostas, D. (2012). Short term exposure to attractive and muscular singers in music video clips negatively affects men's body image and mood. *Body Image, 9(4)*, 543–546.

Mumby, D. (2000). Communication, organization, and the public sphere: A feminist perspective. In P. Buzzanell (Ed.), *Rethinking organizational and managerial communication from feminist perspectives* (pp. 3–23). Thousand Oaks, CA: Sage Publications.

Muntigl, P., & Choi, K. T. (2010). Not remembering as a practical epistemic resource in couples therapy. *Discourse Studies, 12(3)*, 331–356.

Murphy, D. R., Daneman, M., & Schneider, B. A. (2006). Do older adults have difficulty following conversations? *Psychology and Aging, 21*, 49–61.

Myhre, K. E., & Adelman, W. (2013). Motivational interviewing: Helping teenaged smokers to quit. *Contemporary Pediatrics, 30(10)*, 18–23.

Nabi, R. L. (2009). Cosmetic surgery makeover programs and intentions to undergo cosmetic enhancements: A consideration of three models of media effects. *Human Communication Research, 35*, 1–27.

National Association of Colleges and Employers (NACE). (2013). Retrieved from http://www2.binghamton.edu/career-development-center/parents/help-your-student/skills-employers-want.html

National Highway Safety Administration. (2014). What is distracted driving? Retrieved on May 9, 2014, from http://www.distraction.gov/content/get-the-facts/facts-and-statistics.html

National Organization for Women. (2006, March 2). *Sexual harassment remains serious problem on campus*. Retrieved May 14, 2008, from http://www.now.org/issues/harass/030206aauwreport.html

Nelson, B. (2002). Making teamwork work. *ABA Bank Marketing, 34,* 10.

Nelson, J. (2011, January 5). Do word changes alter "Huckleberry Finn"? *The New York Times*. Retrieved from http://www.nytimes.com/roomfordebate/2011/01/05/does-one-word-change-huckleberry-finn

Nessen, S. (2012, December 3). In hard-hit areas, Red Cross runs into image issue. WNYC. Retrieved from http://www.wnyc.org/story/254908-red-cross-recovery-efforts

Neuliep, J. W. (2012). The relationship among intercultural communication apprehension, ethnocentrism, uncertainty reduction, and communication satisfaction during initial intercultural interaction: An extension of anxiety and uncertainty management (AUM) theory. *Journal of Intercultural Communication Research, 41*(1), 1–16, DOI: 10.1080/17475759.2011.62323.

Newcomb, A. F., & Bagwell, C. L. (1995). Children's friendship relations: A metaanalytic review. *Psychological Bulletin, 117,* 306–347.

Newman, M. L., Groom, C. J., Handelman, L. D., & Pennebaker, J. W. (2008). Gender differences in language use: An analysis of 14,000 text samples. *Discourse Processes, 45*(3), 211–236.

Ng, S. H., & Ng, T. K. (2012). Power of messages through speech and silence. In H. Giles (Ed.), *The handbook of intergroup communication* (pp. 116–127). New York: Routledge/Taylor and Francis.

Nicholas, S. (2009). "I live Hopi, I just don't speak it"—The critical intersection of language, culture, and identity in the lives of contemporary Hopi youth. *Journal of Language, Identity & Education, 8*(5), 321–334.

Nichols, R. G. (2006). The struggle to be human: Keynote address to first International Listening Association convention, February 17, 1980. *International Journal of Listening, 20,* 4–12.

Nichols, R. G., Brown, J. I., & Keller, R. J. (2006). Measurement of communication skills. *International Journal of Listening, 20,* 13–17.

Nicotera, A. M. (1997). Managing conflict communication groups. In L. R. Frey & J. K. Barge (Eds.), *Managing group life: Communicating in decision-making groups* (pp. 104–130). Boston: Houghton Mifflin.

Nielsen (2013, March—updated October). Free to move across screens: The cross-platform report (Q4). The Nielsen Company. Retrieved from http://www.nielsen.com/content/dam/corporate/us/en/reports-downloads/2013%20Reports/Nielsen-March-2013-Cross-Platform-Report.pdf

Niemann, C. (2014, January). If someone comments on your Facebook post and they're abjectly wrong, are you morally obligated to correct their misinformation? *Wired, 22*(01), 72.

Nierenberg, R. (2009). *Maestro: A surprising story about leadership by listening.* New York: Portfolio.

Nisen, M. (2013, March 14). Zappos' Tony Hseih says creating a great culture is a "five-to-lifetime commitment." *Business Insider.* Retrieved from http://www.businessinsider.com/tony-hsieh-creating-an-amazing-company-culture-2013-3

Nomani, A. Q. (2005, December 14). Tapping Islam's feminist roots. *The Washington Post.* Retrieved March 7, 2008, from http://www.seattletimes.nwsource.com

Northhouse, P. G. (2012). *Leadership: Theory and practice* (6th ed.). Thousand Oaks, CA: Sage Publications.

O'Connor, J., Mumford, M., Clifton, T., Gessner, T., & Connelly, M. (1995). Charismatic leaders and destructiveness: An historiometric study. *Leadership Quarterly, 6,* 529–555.

Office friends: Who needs them? (2005). *Management Today.* Retrieved May 14, 2008, via LexisNexis.

O'Hair, D., & Cody, M. (1994). Deception. In W. R. Cupach & B. H. Spitzberg (Eds.), *The dark side of interpersonal communication* (pp. 181–213). Hillsdale, NJ: Erlbaum.

O'Hair, D., Friedrich, G. W., & Dixon, L. D. (2007). *Strategic communication in business and the professions* (6th ed.). Boston: Houghton Mifflin.

O'Hair, D., Friedrich, G. W., & Dixon, L. D. (2010). *Strategic communication in business and the professions.* (7th ed.) New York: Pearson.

O'Hair, D., & Krayer, K. (1987). *A conversational analysis of reconciliation strategies.* Paper presented at the Western Speech Communication Association, Salt Lake City.

O'Hair, D., O'Rourke, J., & O'Hair, M. J. (2000). *Business communication: A framework for success.* Cincinnati, OH: South-Western.

O'Hair, D., & Stewart, R. (1998). *Public speaking: Challenges and choices.* New York: Bedford/St. Martin's.

O'Hair, D., Stewart, R., & Rubenstein, H. (2007). *A speaker's guidebook* (3rd ed.). New York: Bedford/St. Martin's.

O'Hair, D., Stewart, R., & Rubenstein, H. (2012). *A speaker's guidebook: Text and reference* (5th ed.). New York: Bedford/St. Martin's.

O'Keefe, D. J. (1999). How to handle opposing arguments in persuasive messages: A meta-analytic review of the effects of one-sided and two-sided messages. In M. E. Roloff (Ed.), *Communication yearbook 22* (pp. 209–249). Thousand Oaks, CA: Sage Publications.

O'Keefe, D. J. (2002). *Persuasion: Theory and research* (2nd ed.). Thousand Oaks, CA: Sage Publications.

Okhuysen, G., & Eisenhardt, K. M. (2002). Integrating knowledge in groups: How simple formal interventions enable flexibility. *Organization Science, 13,* 370–386.

Okhuysen, G., & Waller, M. J. (2002). Focusing on midpoint transitions: An analysis of boundary conditions. *Academy of Management Journal, 45,* 1056–1065.

Okoro, E., & Washington, M. C. (2012). Workforce diversity and organizational communication: Analysis of human capital performance and productivity. *Journal of Diversity Management, 7*(1).

Oliver, J. (2010, February). Jamie Oliver's TED Prize wish: Teach every child about food. Video retrieved from http://www.ted.com/talks/jamie_oliver.html

O'Loughlin, J. P. (2010, July 23). Senior HR executive, HR Capital Partners. Personal interview.

O'Neill, B. (2011). A critique of politically correct language. *Independent Review, 16*(2), 279–291.

Ophir, E, Nass, C., & Wagner, A. D. (2009). Cognitive control in media multitaskers. *Proceedings of the National Academy of Sciences, 106* (37), 15583—15587. http://www.pnas.org/content/106/37/15583.short

Oprah.com. (2008). *Oprah's debt diet.* Retrieved from http://www.oprah.com/packages/oprahs-debt-diet.html

O'Sullivan, P. B. (2000). What you don't know won't hurt me: Impression management functions of communication channels in relationships. *Human Communication Research, 26*, 403–431.

Our mission. (2013, December 18). Facebook newsroom. Retrieved from http://newsroom.fb.com/Key-Facts

Pagotto, L., Voci, A., & Maculan, V. (2010). The effectiveness of intergroup contact at work: Mediators and moderators of hospital workers' prejudice towards immigrants. *Journal of Community & Applied Social Psychology, 20*(4), 317–330.

Palacios Martínez, I. M., & Núñez Pertejo, P. (2012). He's absolutely massive. It's a super day. Madonna, she is a wicked singer. Youth language and intensification: A corpus-based study. *Text & Talk, 32*(6), 773–796.

Palomares, N. A. (2009). Women are sort of more tentative than men, aren't they? How men and women use tentative language differently, similarly, and counterstereotypically as a function of gender salience. *Communication Research, 36*(4), 538–560.

Palomares, N. A., & Lee, E-J. (2010). Virtual gender identity: The linguistic assimilation to gendered avatars in computer-mediated communication. *Journal of Language & Social Psychology, 29*(1), 5–23.

Paolini, S., Harwood, J., & Rubin, M. (2010). Negative intergroup contact makes group members salient: Explaining why intergroup conflict endures. *Personality and Social Psychology Bulletin, 36*, 1723–1738.

Parente, D. (2013). *Visual presence.* Retrieved on May 12, 2014, from http://theleadershipstylecenter.com/visual-presence

Park, C. (2003). In other (people's) words: Plagiarism by university students—literature and lessons. *Assessment and Evaluation in Higher Education, 28*, 471–488.

Park, W. (2000). A comprehensive empirical investigation of the relationships among variables of the groupthink model. *Journal of Organizational Behavior, 21*, 874–887.

Parker, A. (2014, February 16). On health act, Democrats run in fix-it mode. *The New York Times*. Retrieved from http://www.nytimes.com/2014/02/17/us/politics/on-health-act-democrats-run-to-mend-what-gop-aims-to-end.html?hp&_r=1

Parker, K., Lenhart, A., & Moore, K. (2012). The digital revolution and higher education. Retrieved on April 29, 2014, from http://www.pewinternet.org/2011/08/28/the-digital-revolution-and-higher-education/4

Parker-Pope, T. (2010a, April 18). Is marriage good for your health? *The New York Times*, p. MM46.

Parker-Pope, T. (2010b, May 11). The science of a happy marriage. *The New York Times*, p. D1.

Partnoy, F. (2012, July 6). Beyond the blink. *The New York Times*, p. SR5.

Patchin, J., & Hinduja, S. (2011). Traditional and nontraditional bullying among youth: A test of general strain theory. *Youth & Society, 43*(2), 727–75.

Patry, M. W. (2008). Attractive but guilty: Deliberation and the physical attractiveness bias. *Psychological Reports, 102*(3), 727–733.

Patterson, B. R., & Gojdycz, T. K. (2000). The relationship between computer-mediated communication and communication-related anxieties. *Communication Research Reports, 17*, 278–287.

Patterson, B. R., & O'Hair, D. (1992). Relational reconciliation: Toward a more comprehensive model of relational development. *Communication Research Reports, 9*, 119–127.

Patterson, T. (2006, November). The Colbert Report: How to beat the host at his own game. *Slate*. Retrieved from http://www.slate.com/articles/arts/television/2006/11/the_colbert_retort.html

Patwardhan, P, & Yang, J. (2003). Internet dependency relations and online consumer behavior: A media system dependency theory perspective on why people shop, chat, and read news online. *Journal of Interactive Advertising, 3*(2), http://jiad.org/article36.html

Paul, P. (2001). Getting inside Gen Y. *American Demographics, 23*(9), 42.

Pauley, P. M., & Emmers-Sommer, T. M. (2007). The impact of Internet technologies on primary and secondary romantic relationship development. *Communication Studies, 58*(4), 411–427.

Pavitt, C. (1999). Theorizing about the group communication-leadership relationship. In L. R. Frey, D. S. Gouran, & M. Poole (Eds.), *Handbook of group communication theory and research* (pp. 313–334). Thousand Oaks, CA: Sage Publications.

Pavley, J. (2013, May 26). Technological literacy: Can everyone learn to code? *Huffington Post*. Retrieved from http://www.huffingtonpost.com/john-pavley/learning-to-code_b_3337098.html

Pavlik, J. V., & McIntosh, S. (2013). *Converging media: A new introduction to mass communication* (3rd ed.). New York: Oxford University Press.

Payne, S. L. (1951). *The art of asking questions*. Princeton, NJ: Princeton University Press.

Pearce, C., & Tuten, T. (2001). Internet recruiting in the banking industry. *Business Communication Quarterly*, 64(1), 9–18.

Pearson, J. C., & Spitzberg, B. H. (1990). *Interpersonal communication: Concepts, components, and contexts* (2nd ed.). Dubuque, IA: Brown.

Pearson, J. C., Turner, L. H., & Todd-Mancillas, W. R. (1991). *Gender and communication* (2nd ed.). Dubuque, IA: Brown.

Peck, J. (2007, December 29). *Top 7 tips for conquering public speaking fear.* Retrieved January 9, 2008, from http://ezinearticles.com/?expert=Jason_Peck

Peluchette, J., Karl, K., & Fertig, J. (2013). A Facebook "friend" request from the boss: Too close for comfort? *Business Horizons, 56,* 291–300.

Pennington, B. (2012, March 29). Arguing over heckling. *The New York Times*, p. B12.

Perry, M. J. (2013, May 13). Stunning college degree gap: Women have earned almost ten million more college degrees than men since 1982. American Enterprise Institute AEIdeas blog. Retrieved from http://www.aei-ideas.org/2013/05/stunning-college-degree-gap-women-have-earned-almost-10-million-more-college-degrees-than-men-since-1982

Petronio, S. (2000). The boundaries of privacy: Praxis of everyday life. In S. Petronio (Ed.), *Balancing the secrets of private disclosures* (pp. 37–50). Mahwah, NJ: Erlbaum.

Petronio, S. (2002). *The boundaries of privacy: Dialectics of disclosure.* Albany: State University of New York Press.

Petronio, S. (2004). Road to developing communication privacy management theory: Narrative in progress, please stand by. *Journal of Family Communication, 4,* 193–207.

Pettigrew, T. F., & Tropp, L. R. (2006). A meta-analytical test of the intergroup contact theory. *Journal of Personality and Social Psychology, 90,* 751–783.

Petty, R. E., & Cacioppo, J. T. (1986). The Elaboration Likelihood Model of persuasion. In L. Berkowitz (Ed.), *Advances in experimental social psychology* (Vol. 19, pp. 123–205). San Diego, CA: Academic Press.

Petty, R. E., & Wegner, D. T. (1998). Matching versus mismatching attitude functions: Implications for scrutiny of persuasive messages. *Personality and Social Psychology Bulletin, 24*(3), 227–240.

Pew Internet (2013). http://www.pew-internet.org/Media-Mentions/2013/Helping-Seniors-Learn-New-Technology.aspx

Pew Research, Religion & Public Life Project. (2008, February 1). U.S. Religious Landscape Project. Retrieved from http://www.pewforum.org/2008/02/01/u-s-religious-landscape-survey-religious-affiliation

Phanor-Faury, A. (2010, June 24). "Nude" doesn't translate in fashion. *Essence.* Retrieved from http://www.essence.com/fashion_beauty/fashion/nude_dresses_racial_bias_fashion_world.php

Piezon, S., & Ferree, W. (2008). Perceptions of social loafing in online learning groups: A study of public university and U.S. Naval War College students. *International Review of Research in Open and Distance Learning, 9*(2), 1–17.

Pines, M. (1997). The civilizing of Genie. In L. F. Kasper (Ed.), *Teaching English through the disciplines: Psychology* (2nd ed.). New York: Whittier.

Planalp, S., & Honeycutt, J. (1985). Events that increase uncertainty in personal relationships. *Human Communication Research, 11,* 593–604.

Pomeroy, R. (2013, April 26). Driving is much deadlier than terrorism—Why isn't it scarier? Retrieved from http://www.realclearscience.com/blog/2013/03/why-we-fear-terrorism-more-than-driving.html

Poole, M. S., & Hollingshead, A. B. (Eds.). (2005). *Theories of small groups: Interdisciplinary perspectives.* Thousand Oaks, CA: Sage Publications.

Potter, W. J. (2008). *Media literacy* (4th ed.). Thousand Oaks, CA: Sage Publications.

Potter, W. J., & Byrne, S. (2009). Media literacy. In R. L. Nabi & M. B. Oliver (Eds.), *The SAGE Handbook of Media Processes and Effects* (pp. 345–360). Thousand Oaks, CA: Sage Publications.

Powers, W. G., & Bodie, G.D. (2003). Listening fidelity: Seeking congruence between cognitions of the receiver and the sender. *International Journal of Listening, 17,* 19–31.

Prager, K. J. (2000). Intimacy in personal relationships. In C. Hendrick & S. S. Hendrick (Eds.), *Close relationships: A sourcebook* (pp. 229–242). Thousand Oaks, CA: Sage Publications.

Pratkanis, A. R., & Aronson, E. (2001). *Age of propaganda: The everyday use and abuse of persuasion.* New York: W. H. Freeman.

Prensky, M. (2012). *From digital natives to digital wisdom: Hopeful essays for 21st century learning.* Thousand Oaks, CA: Corwin.

Preston, D. R. (1998). Language myth #17: They speak really bad English Down South and in New York City. In L. Bauer & P. Trudgill (Eds.), *Language myths* (pp. 139–149). New York: Penguin Putnam.

Priester, J. R., & Petty, R. E. (1995). Source attributions and persuasion: Perceived honesty as a determinant of message scrutiny. *Personality and Social Psychology Bulletin, 21,* 637–654.

Prochaska, J. (1994). Strong and weak principles for progressing from precontemplation to action on the basis of twelve problem behaviors. *Health Psychology, 13,* 47–51.

Prochaska, J. O., & Norcross, J. C. (2001). Stages of change. *Psychotherapy: Theory, Research, Practice, Training, 38,* 443–448.

Punyanunt-Carter, N. M. (2005). Father and daughter motives and satisfaction. *Communication Research Reports, 22,* 293–301.

Quenqua, D. (2012, February 28). They're, like, way ahead of the linguistic currrrve. *The New York Times,* p. D1.

Rabinowitz, J. (1995, July 25). Huckleberry Finn without fear: Teachers gather to learn how to teach an American classic, in context. *The New York Times*. Retrieved from http://www.query.nytimes.com

Ragas, M. W., Tran, H. L., & Martin, J. A. (2014). Media-induced or search-driven? A study of online agenda-setting effects during the BP oil disaster. *Journalism Studies*, *15*(1), 48–63.

Rahim, M. A. (1983). A measure of styles of handling interpersonal conflict. *Academy of Management Journal*, *26*(2), 368–376.

Rainie, L., Smith, A., & Duggan, M. (2013, February 5). Coming and going on Facebook. Pew Internet & Amerian Life Project. Retrieved from http://pewinternet.org/Reports/2013/Coming-and-going-on-facebook/Key-Findings.aspx

Ralph, B. C., Thomson, D. R., Cheyne, J. A., & Smilek, D. (2013). Media multitasking and failures of attention in everyday life. *Psychological Research*, 1–9.

Ralston, S. M., Kirkwood, W. G., & Burant, P. A. (2003). Helping interviewees tell their stories. *Business Communication Quarterly*, *66*, 8–22.

Raman, A. (2007, April 26). Egypt's "Dr. Ruth": Let's talk sex in the Arab world. CNN.com. Retrieved from http://www.cnn.com/2007/WORLD/meast/04/25/muslim.sex-talk/index.html

Ramirez, A., Sunnafrank, M., & Goei, R. (2010). Predicted outcome value theory in ongoing relationships. *Communication Monographs*, *77*(1), 27–50.

Rampell, C. (2013, May 4). College graduates fare well in jobs market, even through recession. *The New York Times*, p. B1.

Rampell, C., & Miller, C. C. (2013, February 25). Yahoo orders home workers back to the office. *The New York Times*. Retrieved from http://www.nytimes.com/2013/02/26/technology/yahoo-orders-home-workers-back-to-the-office.html?ref=business&_r=0

Rappaport, S. D. (2010). Putting listening to work: The essentials of listening. *Journal of Advertising Research*, *50*(1), 30–41.

Rath, A. (2011, February 5). Is the "CSI Effect" influencing courtrooms? NPR News Investigations. Retrieved from http://www.npr.org/2011/02/06/133497696/is-the-csi-effect-influencing-courtrooms

Rawlins, W. K. (1992). *Friendship matters: Communication, dialectics, and the life course*. Piscataway, NJ: Aldine Transaction.

Rawlins, W. K. (1994). Being there and growing apart: Sustaining friendships during adulthood. In D. J. Canary & L. Stafford (Eds.), *Communication and relational maintenance* (pp. 275–294). New York: Academic Press.

Rawlins, W. K. (2008). *The compass of friendship: Narratives, identities, and dialogues*. Thousand Oaks, CA: Sage Publications.

Ray, R., Sanes, M., & Schmitt, J. (2013, May). No-vacation nation revisited. Retrieved from http://www.cepr.net/index.php/publications/reports/no-vacation-nation-2013

Ray, R., & Schmitt, J. (2007, May). No-vacation nation. Washington, DC: Center for Economic and Policy Research. Retrieved from http://www.cepr.net

Rehling, D. L. (2008). Compassionate listening: A framework for listening to the seriously ill. *International Journal of Listening, 22*(1), 83–89.

Reiber, C., & Garcia, J. R. (2010). Hooking up: Gender differences, evolution, and pluralistic ignorance. *Evolutionary Psychology, 8*(3), 390–404.

Reis, H. T. (1998). Gender differences in intimacy and related behaviors: Context and process. In D. J. Canary & K. Dindia (Eds.), *Sex differences and similarities in communication: Critical essays and empirical investigations of sex and gender in interaction* (pp. 203–231). Hillsdale, NJ: Erlbaum.

Rheingold, H. (2002). *Smart mobs: The next social revolution.* New York: Basic Books.

Richmond, V., & McCroskey, J. C. (1998). *Communication apprehension, avoidance, and effectiveness* (5th ed.). Boston: Allyn & Bacon.

Richmond, V. P., McCroskey, J. C., & Johnson, A. D. (2003). Development of the Nonverbal Immediacy Scale (NIS): Measures of self- and other-perceived nonverbal immediacy. *Communication Quarterly, 51,* 502–515.

Richmond, V. P., McCroskey, J. C., & Payne, S. K. (1991). *Nonverbal behavior in interpersonal relations.* Englewood Cliffs, NJ: Prentice Hall.

Richmond, V. P., Smith, R. S., Jr., Heisel,

A. D., & McCroskey, J. C. (2001). Nonverbal immediacy in the physician-patient relationship. *Communication Research Reports, 18,* 211–216.

Richtel, M. (2010, June 6). Attached to technology and paying a price. *The New York Times,* p. A1.

Riffe, D., Lacy, S., & Varouhakis, M. (2008). Media system dependency theory and using the Internet for in-depth, specialized information. *Web Journal of Mass Communication Research, 11.* Retrieved from http://www.scripps.ohiou.edu/wjmcr/vol11/11-b.html

Rill, L., Balocchi, E., Hopper, M., Denker, K., & Olson, L. N. (2009). Exploration of the relationship between self-esteem, commitment, and verbal aggressiveness in romantic dating relationships. *Communication Reports, 22*(2), 102–113.

Riordan, M. A., & Kreuz, R. J. (2010). Cues in computer-mediated communication: A corpus analysis. *Computers in Human Behavior, 26,* 1806–1817.

Ritter, B. A. (2014). Deviant behavior in computer-mediated communication: Development and validation of a measure of cybersexual harassment. *Journal of Computer-Mediated Communication, 19*(2), 197–214.

Roberto, A., Carlyle, K. E., Goodall, C. E., & Castle, J. D. (2009). The relationship between parents' verbal aggressiveness and responsiveness and young adult children's attachment style and relational satisfaction with parents. *Journal of Family Communication, 9*(2), 90–106.

Roberts, S. (2010, November 19). Unlearning to tawk like a New Yorker. *The New York Times*. Retrieved from http://www.nytimes.com/2010/11/21/nyregion/21accent.html

Rochman, B. (2011, December 2). Baby name game: How a name can affect your child's future. *Time*. Retrieved from http://healthland.time.com/2011/12/02/how-baby-names-affect-your-childs-future

Rogers Commission. (1986, June 6). *Report of the presidential commission on the space shuttle* Challenger *accident*. Retrieved from http://science.ksc.nasa.gov/shuttle/missions/51-l/docs/rogers-commission/Chapter-5.txt

Roloff, M. E. (1980). Self-awareness and the persuasion process: Do we really know what we are doing? In M. E. Roloff & G. Miller (Eds.), *Persuasion: New directions in theory and research* (pp. 29–66). Beverly Hills, CA: Sage Publications.

Romans, B. (2011, October 14). The joy of going to the library, from the *Wired* science blog *Clastic Detritis*, Retrieved from http://www.wired.com/wiredscience/2011/10/the-joy-of-going-to-the-library, para. 2.

Rose, G., Evaristo, R., & Staub, D. (2003). Culture and consumer responses to Web download time: A four-continent stoudy of mono and polychronism. *IEEE Transaction on Engineering Management, 50*(1), 31–44.

Rosen, M. (2004, February). Can you truly trust an office friend? When to share and when to shy away—a guide to getting along with your workplace pals (on the job). *Good Housekeeping*, p. 56.

Rosenbloom, S. (2006, August 10). Please don't make me go on vacation. *The New York Times*. Retrieved from http://www.nytimes.com

Rosener, J. (1990). Ways women lead. *Harvard Business Review, 68,* 119–125.

Rosenthal, M. J. (2001). High-performance teams. *Executive Excellence, 18,* 6.

Ross, C. (2007, March 11). Hare interviewed for "Colbert Report." *The Register-Mail*.

Ross, L., & Nisbett, R. E. (1991). *The person and the situation: Perspectives of social psychology*. Philadelphia: Temple University Press.

Roth, A. (2013, February 1). Russia revives the namesake of "Uncle Joe." *The New York Times,* p. A4.

Rothman, A. J., Salovey, P., Turvey, C., & Fishkin, S. A. (1993). Attributions or responsibility and persuasion: Increasing mammography utilization among women over 40 with an internally oriented message. *Health Psychology, 12,* 39–47.

Roup, C. M., & Chiasson, K. E. (2010). Effect of dichotic listening on self-reported state anxiety. *International Journal of Audiology, 49*(2), 88–94.

Rowbotham, S., Holler, J., Lloyd, D., & Wearden, A. (2012). How do we communicate about pain? A systematic analysis of the semantic contribution of co-speech gestures in pain-focused conversations. *Journal of Nonverbal Behavior, 36*(1), 1–21.

Ruben, B. D. (2005). Linking communication scholarship and professional practice in colleges and universities. *Journal of Applied Communication Research, 33,* 294–304.

Rubin, A. M., Perse, E. M., & Powell, R. A. (1985). Loneliness, parasocial interaction, and local television news viewing. *Human Communication Research, 12,* 155–180.

Rubin, D. L., Hafer, T., & Arata, K. (2000). Reading and listening to oral-based versus literate-based discourse. *Communication Education, 49,* 121–133.

Rubin, J. (2013, February 5). The Internet can offer additional intercultural experiences. *The Chronicle of Higher Education.* Retrieved from http://chronicle.com/blogs/letters/the-internet-can-offer-additional-intercultural-experiences

Rudoren, J. (2012, October 1). Proudly bearing elders' scars, their skin says "never forget." *The New York Times,* p. A1.

Rushton, J. P. (1980). *Altruism, socializiation, and society.* Englewood Cliffs, NJ: Prentice Hall.

Russ, T. L. (2012). The relationship between communication apprehension and learning preferences in an organizational setting. *Journal of Business Communication, 49*(4), 312–331.

Russell, J. E., & Adams, D. M. (1997). The changing nature of mentoring in organizations: An introduction to the special issue on mentoring in organizations. *Journal of Vocational Behavior, 51,* 1–14.

Rutherford, S. (2001). Any difference? An analysis of gender and divisional management styles in a large airline. *Gender, Work and Organization, 8*(3), 326–345.

Ryzik, M. (2012, January 4). When an actress prepares (no eye contact, please). *The New York Times,* p. C1.

Safir, M. P., Wallach, H.S., & Bar-Zvi, M. (2012). Virtual reality cognitive-behavior therapy for public speaking anxiety: One-year follow-up. *Behavioral Modification, 36*(2), 235–246. doi: 10.1177/0145445511429999

Sahlstein, E., Maguire, K. C., & Timmerman, L. (2009). Contradictions and praxis contextualized by wartime deployment: Wives' perspectives revealed through relational dialectics. *Communication Monographs, 76*(4), 421–442.

Salazar, A. J. (1996). An analysis of the development and evolution of roles in the small group. *Small Group Research, 27,* 475–503.

Salkever, A. (2003, April 24). Home truths about meetings. *Business Week.* Retrieved from http://www.businessweek.com

Samovar, L. A., Porter, R. E., & Stefani, L. A. (1998). *Communication between cultures.* Belmont, CA: Wadsworth.

Samter, W. (2003). Friendship interaction skills across the life span. In J. O. Greene & B. R. Burleson (Eds.), *Handbook of communication and social interaction skills* (pp. 637–684). Mahwah, NJ: Erlbaum.

Sanchez, J. (2013, December 10). MLB to tackle prospects' language barriers. MLB.com. Retrieved from http://mlb.mlb.com/news/article/mlb/major-league-baseball-works-to-eliminate-language-barriers-for-dominican-prospects?ymd=20131210&content_id=64557052&vkey=news_mlb

Sanderson, J. (2013). From loving the hero to despising the villain: Sports fans, Facebook, and social identity threats. *Mass Communication and Society, 16*(4), 487–509.

Sapir, E., & Whorf, B. L. (1956). The relation of habitual thought and behavior to language. In J. B. Carroll (Ed.), *Language, thought, and reality: Selected writings of Benjamin Lee Whorf* (pp. 134–159). Cambridge, MA: MIT Press.

Sarich, V., & Miele, F. (2004). *Race: The reality of human differences.* Boulder, CO: Westview Press.

Sashkin, M., & Burke, W. W. (1990). Understanding and assessing organizational leadership. In K. E. Clark & M. B. Clark (Eds.), *Measures of leadership* (pp. 297–326). West Orange, NJ: Leadership Library of America.

Sawyer, C., & Behnke, R. (1990). The role of self-monitoring in the communication of public speaking anxiety. *Communication Reports, 3,* 70–74.

Sawyer, C., & Behnke, R. (2002). Behavioral inhibition and communication of public speaking state anxiety. *Western Journal of Communication, 66,* 412–422.

Scheerhorn, D., & Geist, P. (1997). Social dynamics in groups. In L. R. Frey & J. K. Barge (Eds.), *Managing group life: Communicating in decision-making groups* (pp. 81–103). Boston: Houghton Mifflin.

Schelbert, L. (2009). Pathways of human understanding: An inquiry into Western and North American Indian worldview structures. In L. A. Samovar, R. E. Porter, & E. R. McDaniel (Eds.), *Intercultural communication: A reader* (pp. 48–58). Belmont, CA: Wadsworth Cengage Learning.

Schenck v. *United States*, 249 U.S. 47 (1919).

Scheufele, D., & Iyengar, S. (2012). The state of framing research: A call for new directions. *The Oxford Handbook of Political Communication Theories.* New York: Oxford University Press.

Scheufele, D. A., & Tewksbury, D. (2007). Framing, agenda setting, and priming: The evolution of three media effects models. *Journal of Communication, 57*(1), 9–20.

Schiesel, S. (October 25, 2011). Best friends, in fantasy and reality. *New York Times*, p. C1.

Schmidt, R. R., Morr, S., Fitzpatrick, P., & Richardson, M. (2012). Measuring the dynamics of interactional synchrony. *Journal of Nonverbal Behavior, 36*(4), 263–279.

Schofield, T., Parke, R., Castañeda, E., & Coltrane, S. (2008). Patterns of gaze between parents and children in European American and Mexican American families. *Journal of Nonverbal Behavior, 32*(3), 171–186.

Schradie, J. (2013, April 26). 7 myths of the digital divide. The Society Pages: Cyborgology. Retrieved from http://thesocietypages.org/cyborgology/2013/04/26/7-myths-of-the-digital-divide

Schrodt, P. (2009). Family strength and satisfaction as functions of family communication. *Communication Quarterly, 57*(2), 171–186.

Schrodt, P., & Wheeless, L. R. (2001). Aggressive communication and informational reception apprehension: The influence of listening anxiety and intellectual inflexibility on trait argumentativeness and verbal aggressiveness. *Communication Quarterly, 49,* 53–69.

Schrodt, P., Wheeless, L. R., & Ptacek, K. M. (2000). Informational reception apprehension, educational motivation, and achievement. *Communication Quarterly, 48,* 60–73.

Schroeder, L. (2002). The effects of skills training on communication satisfaction and communication anxiety in the basic speech course. *Communication Research Reports, 19,* 380–388.

Schullery, N. M., & Gibson, M. K. (2001). Working in groups: Identification and treatment of students' perceived weaknesses. *Business Communication Quarterly, 64,* 9–30.

Schulman, P. R. (1996). Heroes, organizations, and high reliability. *Journal of Contingencies and Crisis Management, 4,* 72–82.

Schultz, B. (1980). Communicative correlates of perceived leaders. *Small Group Behavior, 11,* 175–191.

Schultz, B. (1982). Argumentativeness: Its effect in group decision-making and its role in leadership perception. *Communication Quarterly, 30,* 368–375.

Schweitzer, T. (2007). *Seven out of 10 employees admit to abusing office computers, phones.* Retrieved May 13, 2008, from http://www.inc.com

Scott, A. O. (November 16, 2011). For one man, Hawaii is a land of problems. *New York Times,* p. C1.

Scott, W. R. (1981). *Organizations: Rational, natural, and open systems.* Englewood Cliffs, NJ: Prentice Hall.

Scully, M. (2005, February 2). Building a better State of the Union address. *The New York Times.* Retrieved from http://www.nytimes.com

Secret of the wild child [Transcript]. (1997, March 4). *Nova.* Public Broadcasting System. Retrieved March 25, 2008, from http://www.pbs.org/wgbh/nova/transcripts/2112gchild.html

Segrin, C., Hanzal, A., & Domschke, T. J. (2009). Accuracy and bias in newlywed couples' perceptions of conflict styles and the association with marital satisfaction. *Communication Monographs, 76,* 207–233.

Segrin, C., & Passalacqua, S. A. (2010). Functions of loneliness, social support, health behaviors, and stress in association with poor health. *Health Communication, 25*(4), 312–322.

Seidler, D. (2011, February 27). Acceptance speech presented at the 83rd Annual Academy of Motion Picture Arts and Sciences Awards, Hollywood, CA.

Shachaf, P., & Hara, N. (2010). Beyond vandalism: Wikipedia trolls. *Journal of Information Science, 36*(3), 357–370.

Shannon, C. E., & Weaver, W. (1949). *The mathematical theory of communication*. Urbana: University of Illinois Press.

Shannon, M., & Stark, C. (2003). The influence of physical appearance on personnel selection. *Social Behavior & Personality: An International Journal, 31*(6), 613.

Shehata, A., & Strömbäck, J. (2013). Not (yet) a new era of minimal effects: A study of setting at the aggregate and individual levels. *The International Journal of Press/Politics, 18*(2), 234–255.

Sheldon, P. (2008). The relationship between unwillingness to communicate and students' Facebook use. *Journal of Media Psychology, 20*, 67–75.

Shepherd, C. A., Giles, H., & LePoire, B. A. (2001). Communication accommodation theory. In W. P. Robinson & H. Giles (Eds.), *The new handbook of language and social psychology* (pp. 33–56). Chichester, UK: Wiley.

Sherif, C. W., Sherif, M. S., & Nebergall, R. E. (1965). *Attitude and attitude change*. Philadelphia: W. B. Saunders.

Sherif, M., & Sherif, C. W. (1967). Attitude as the individual's own categories: The social judgment-involvement approach to attitude and attitude change. In C. W. Sherif & M. Sherif (Eds.), *Attitude, ego-involvement, and change* (pp. 105-139). New York: Wiley.

Shotter, J. (2009). Listening in a way that recognizes/realizes the world of "the other." *International Journal of Listening, 23*(1), 21–43.

Shultz, B. G. (1999). Improving group communication performance: An overview of diagnosis and intervention. In L. Frey, D. Gouran, & M. Poole (Eds.), *Handbook of group communication theory and research* (pp. 371–394). Thousand Oaks, CA: Sage Publications.

Sides, C. H. (2000). Ethics and technical communication: The past quarter century. *Journal of Technical Writing and Communication, 30*, 27–30.

Sillars, A., Canary, D. J., & Tafoya, M. (2004). Communication, conflict, and the quality of family relationships. In A. L. Vangelisti (Ed.), *Handbook of family communication* (pp. 413–446). Mahwah, NJ: Erlbaum.

Simonson, P., Peck, J., Craig, R. T., & Jackson, J. P. (Eds.) (2013). *The handbook of communication history*. New York: Routledge.

Sirolli, E. (September 2012). Want to help someone? Shut up and listen! *TED Talks*: http://www.ted.com/talks/ernesto_sirolli_want_to_help_someone_shut_up_and_listen

Sixel, L. M. (2011, July 7). Manager claims boss asked her to dye gray hair. *The Houston Chronicle*. Retrieved from http://www.chron.com/business/sixel/article/Manager-claims-boss-asked-her-to-dye-gray-hair-2080057.php#ixzz1Rp5iRmra

Smith, P. (2005, February 11). Bullies incorporated. *Sydney Morning Herald*. Retrieved from http://www.smh.com.au

Smith, R., Jr. (2004). Recruit the student: Adapting persuasion to audiences. *Communication Teacher, 18*, 53–56.

Smith, R. E. (1993). Clustering: A way to discover speech topics. *The Speech Teacher, 7*(2), 6–7.

Smith, T. E., & Frymier, A. B. (2006). Get "real": Does practicing speeches before an audience improve performance? *Communication Quarterly, 54,* 111–125.

Smith-Lovin, L., Skvortz, J. K., & Hudson, C. (1986). Status and participation in six-person groups: A test of Skvoret's comparative status model. *Social Forces, 64,* 992–1005.

Snyder, M. (1974). Self-monitoring of expressive behavior. *Journal of Personality and Social Psychology, 30,* 526–537.

Snyder, M. (1979). Self-monitoring processes. In L. Berkowitz (Ed.), *Advances in social psychology* (Vol. 12, pp. 86–128). New York: Academic Press.

Snyder, M., & Klein, O. (2005). Construing and constructing others: On the reality and the generality of the behavioral confirmation scenario. *Interaction Studies, 6,* 53–67.

Sokol, R. I., Webster, K. L., Thompson, N. S., & Stevens, D. A. (2005). Whining as mother-directed speech. *Infant and Child Development, 14,* 478–486.

Soliz, J., & Giles, H. (2010). Language and communication. In C. R. Berger, M. E. Roloff, & D. R. Roskos-Ewoldsen (Eds.), *The handbook of communication science* (pp. 75–91). Thousand Oaks, CA: Sage Publications.

Solomon, D. H., & Vangelisti, A. L. (2010). Establishing and maintaining relationships. In C. R. Berger, M. E. Roloff, & D. R. Roskos-Ewoldsen, *The handbook of communication science* (pp. 327–344). Thousand Oaks, CA: SAGE Publications.

Sonnenfeld, J. (2011, January 23). The genius dilemma. *Newsweek.* Retrieved from http://www.newsweek.com/2011/01/23/the-genius-dilemma.html

Sonnentag, S., Unger, D., & Nägel, I. J. (2013). Workplace conflict and employee well-being: The moderating role of detachment from work during off-job time. *International Journal of Conflict Management, 24*(2), 166–183.

Sorenson, G. A., & McCroskey, J. C. (1977). The prediction of interaction in small groups. *Communication Monographs, 44,* 73–80.

Sosha, T. J. (1997). Group communication across the lifespan. In L. R. Frey & J. K. Barge (Eds.), *Managing group life: Communicating in decision-making groups* (pp. 3–28). Boston: Houghton Mifflin.

Span, P. (2013). Helping seniors learn new technology. Retrieved on May 2, 2014 from http://www.pewinternet.org/Media-Mentions/2013/Helping-Seniors-Learn-New-Technology.aspx

Spillman, B. (2013, September 8). New headquarters for Zappos reflects company's growth, atmosphere. *Las Vegas Review-Journal.* Retrieved from http://www.reviewjournal.com/news/las-vegas/new-headquarters-zappos-reflects-companys-growth-atmosphere.

Spitzberg, B. H., & Cupach, W. R. (2008). Fanning the flames of fandom: Celebrity worship, parasocial interaction, and stalking (pp. 287–324). In J. R. Meloy, L. Sheridan, & J. Hoffman (Eds.), *Stalking, threatening, and attacking of public figures: A psychological and behavioral analysis*. New York: Oxford.

Sprague, J., Stuart, D., and Bodary, D. (2012). *The speaker's handbook*. Boston: Cengage Learning.

Sprain, L., & Boromisza-Habashi, D. (2013). The ethnographer of communication at the table: Building cultural competence, designing strategic action. *Journal of Applied Communication Research, 41*(2), 181–187.

Stafford, L. (2010). Geographic distance and communication during courtship. *Communication Research, 37*(2), 275–297.

Stanley, A. (2012, April 13). There's sex, there's the city, but no Manolos. *The New York Times*, p. C1.

Stapleton, A., & Yan, H. (2013, October 21). Mom of dead Florida teen sends birthday message, promises to fight bullying. CNN.com. Retrieved from http://www.cnn.com/2013/10/20/justice/rebecca-sedwick-bullying-death/index.html

Steil, L. K., Barker, L. L., & Watson, K. W. (1983). *Effective listening: Key to success*. Reading, MA: Addison-Wesley.

Steinberg, B. (2010). Swearing during family hour? Who gives a $#*! *Advertising Age, 81*(22), 2–20.

Stelter, B. (2011, January 2). TV viewing continues to edge up. *The New York Times*. Retrieved from http://www.nytimes.com/2011/01/03/business/media/03ratings.html

Stephens, K. K., & Davis, J. (2009). The social influences on electronic multitasking in organizational meetings. *Management Communication Quarterly, 23*(1), 63–83.

Stewart, C. J., & Cash, W. B., Jr. (2011). *Interviewing: Principles and practices* (12th ed.). New York: McGraw-Hill.

Stewart, C. J., & Cash, W. B., Jr. (2014). *Interviewing: Principles and practices*. New York: McGraw-Hill.

Stewart, L. P., Cooper, P. J., & Steward, A. D. (2003). *Communication and gender*. Boston: Pearson Education.

Stiff, J. B., & Mongeau, P. (2003). *Persuasive communication*. New York: Guilford Press.

Stillion Southard, B. F., & Wolvin, A. D. (2009). Jimmy Carter: A case study in listening leadership. *International Journal of Listening, 23*(2), 141–152.

Stollen, J., & White, C. (2004). The link between labels and experience in romantic relationships among young adults. Paper presented at the International Communication Association, New Orleans Sheraton, New Orleans, LA, LA Online.

Stommel, W., & Koole, T. (2010). The online support group as a community: A micro-analysis of the interaction with a new member. *Discourse Studies, 12*(3), 357–378.

StopBullying.gov. (2013, December 26). State policies and laws. Retrieved from http://www.stopbullying.gov/laws/index.html

Suler, J. (2007). The psychology of cyberspace. Retrieved December 26, 2007, from http://www-usr.rider.edu/~suler/psycyber/psycyber.html (Original work published 1996)

Sullivan, L. (2006, July 26). In U.S. prisons, thousands spend years in isolation [Audio podcast]. In *All Things Considered*. Retrieved from http://www.npr.org/templates/story/story.php?storyId=5582144

Sun, Y., Pan, Z., & Shen, L. (2008). Understanding the third-person perception: Evidence from a meta-analysis. *Journal of Communication, 58*, 280–300.

Sunstein, C. (2007). *Republic.com 2.0.* Princeton, NJ: Princeton University Press.

Sutton, S. R. (1982). Fear arousal and communication: A critical examination of theories and research. In J. Eiser (Ed.), *Social psychology and behavioral medicine* (pp. 303–337). Chichester, UK: Wiley.

Suzuki, B. H. (2002). Revisiting the model minority stereotype: Implications for student affairs practice and higher education. *New Directions for Student Services, 97,* 21.

Tajfel, H., & Turner, J. C. (1986). An integrative theory of intergroup conflict. In S. Worchel & W. Austin (Eds.), *Psychology of intergroup relations* (pp. 2–24). Chicago: Nelson-Hall.

Tamir, D. I., & Mitchell, J. P. (2012). Anchoring and adjustment during social inferences. *Journal of Experimental Psychology, 142*(1), 151–162.

Tannen, D. (1992). *You just don't understand: Women and men in conversation.* London: Virago Press.

Tannen, D. (2009). Framing and face: The relevance of the presentation of self to linguistic discourse analysis. *Social Psychology Quarterly, 72*(4), 300–305.

Tannen, D. (2010). Abduction and identity in family interaction: Ventriloquizing as indirectness. *Journal of Pragmatics, 42*(2), 307–316.

Tannen, D., Kendall, S., & Gorgon, C. (Eds.). (2007). *Family talk: Discourse and identity in four American families.* New York: Oxford University Press.

Taylor, P., & Cohn, D. (2012, November 7). A milestone en route to a majority minority nation. *Pew Research Social & Demographic Trends.* Retrieved from http://www.pewsocialtrends.org/2012/11/07/a-milestone-en-route-to-a-majority-minority-nation

Taylor, P., & Keeter, S. (Eds.) (2010). Millennials: A portrait of generation next. Confident, connected, open to change. Pew Research. Retrieved from http://pewresearch.org/millennials

Team Rubicon. (2014, January 15). Our mission. Retrieved from http://teamrubiconusa.org/about

Ted Prize. (2013). About the TED prize. Retrieved from http://www.ted.com/participate/ted-prize

Tekleab, A. G., Quigley, N. R., & Tesluk, P. E. (2009). A longitudinal study of team conflict, conflict management, cohesion, and team effectiveness. *Group and Organizational Management, 34,* 170–205.

Tell, C. (September 22, 2013). Step away from the phone! *New York Times,* p. ST1.

Teven, J. J. (2007a). Effects of supervisor social influence, nonverbal immediacy, and biological sex on subordinates' perceptions of job satisfaction, liking, and supervisor credibility. *Communication Quarterly, 55*(2), 155–177.

Teven, J. J. (2007b). Teacher temperament: Correlates with teacher caring, burnout, and organizational outcomes. *Communication Education, 56,* 382–400.

Teven, J. J. (2007c). Teacher caring and classroom behavior: Relationships with student affect, teacher evaluation, teacher competence, and trustworthiness. *Communication Quarterly, 55,* 433–450.

Teven, J. J. (2008). An examination of perceived credibility of the 2008 presidential candidates: Relationships with believability, likeability, and deceptiveness. *Human Communication, 11,* 383–400.

Teven, J. J. (2010). The effects of supervisor nonverbal immediacy and power use on employees' ratings of credibility and affect for the supervisor. *Human Communication, 13,* 69–85.

Teven, J. J., & Comadena, M. E. (1996). The effects of office aesthetic quality on students' perceptions of teacher credibility and communicator style. *Communication Research Reports, 13*(1), 101–108.

Teven, J. J., & Hanson, T. L. (2004). The impact of teacher immediacy and perceived caring on teacher competence and trustworthiness. *Communication Quarterly, 52,* 39–53.

Teven, J. J., & McCroskey, J. C. (1997). The relationship of perceived teacher caring with student learning and teacher evaluation. *Communication Education, 46,* 1–9.

Teven, J. J., McCroksey, J. C., & Richmond, V. P. (2006). Communication correlates of perceived Machiavellianism of supervisors: Communication orientations and outcomes. *Communication Quarterly, 54,* 127–142.

Teven, J. J., & Winters, J. L. (2007). Pharmaceutical sales representatives' social influence behaviors and communication orientations: Relationships with adaptive selling, sales performance, and job satisfaction. *Human Communication, 10,* 465–485.

Thacker, S., & Griffiths, M. D. (2012). An exploratory study of trolling in online video gaming. *International Journal of Cyber Behavior, Psychology and Learning (IJCBPL), 2*(4), 17–33.

Theiss, J. A., Knobloch, L. K., Checton, M. G., & Magsamen-Conrad, K. (2009). Relationship characteristics associated with the experience of hurt in romantic relationships: A test of the relational turbulence model. *Human Communication Research, 35*(4), 588–615.

Thibaut, J. W., & Kelley, H. H. (1959). *The social psychology of groups.* New York: Wiley.

Thomas, A. P. (2006, January 31). The CSI effect: Fact or fiction. *The Yale Law Journal Online.* Retrieved from http://www.yalelawjournal.org/the-yale-law-journalpocket-part/criminal-law-and-sentencing/the-csi-effect:-fact-or-fiction

Thomas, D. C., Ravlin, E. C., & Wallace, A. W. (1996). Effect of cultural diversity in work groups. In P. Bamber, M. Erez, & S. Bacharach (Eds.), *Research in the sociology of organizations* (Vol. 14, pp. 1–33). Greenwich, CT: JAI.

Thomas, L. T., & Levine, T. R. (1994). Disentangling listening and verbal recall: Related but separate constructs? *Human Communication Research, 21,* 103–127.

Thompson, A. (2008, April 17). Scientist finds truthiness in "Colbert bump." Livescience.com. Retrieved from http://www.livescience.com/2451-scientist-finds-truthiness-colbert-bump.html

Tidwell, L. C., & Walther, J. B. (2002). Computer-mediated communication effects on disclosure, impressions, and interpersonal evaluations: Getting to know one another a bit at a time. *Human Communication Research, 28*(3), 317–348.

Tierney, J. (2007, July 31). The whys of mating: 237 reasons and counting. *The New York Times,* p. F1.

Tiggemann, M. (2005). Television and adolescent body image: The role of program content and viewing motivation. *Journal of Social & Clinical Psychology, 24,* 361–381.

Ting-Toomey, S., & Oetzel, J. G. (2002). Cross-cultural face concerns and conflict styles. *Handbook of International and Intercultural Communication, 2,* 143–164.

Tjosvold, D. (1992). *The conflict-positive organization: Stimulate diversity and create unity.* Reading, MA: Addison-Wesley.

Tkaczyk, C. (2013, April 19). Marissa Mayer breaks her silence on Yahoo's telecommuting policy. Fortune/CNN.com. Retrieved from http://tech.fortune.cnn.com/2013/04/19/marissa-mayer-telecommuting

Tockett, C. (2012, November 6). How Rockaway Beach Surf Club became a Hurricane Sandy relief center. Treehugger Blog. Retrieved from http://www.treehugger.com/culture/rockaway-beach-surf-club-became-hurricane-sandy-relief-center.html

Tolman, E. G. (2012). Observing cell phone use and enhancing collaborative learning using a wiki. *Communication Teacher, 4,* 1–5.

Toma, C. L. (2013, April). Feeling better but doing worse: Effects of Facebook self-presentation on implicit self-esteem and cognitive task performance. *Media Psychology, 16*(2), 199–220.

Tong, S. T., Van Der Heide, B., Langwell, L., & Walther, J. B. (2008). Too much of a good thing? The relationship between number of friends and interpersonal impressions on Facebook. *Journal of Computer-Mediated Communication, 13*(3), 531–549.

Toobin, J. (2007, May 7). The CSI effect. *The New Yorker.* Retrieved from http://www.newyorker.com/reporting/2007/05/07/070507fa_fact_toobin

Torregrosa, L. L. (2010, August 31). Palin woos women and stirs up foes. *The New York Times.* Retrieved from http://www.nytimes.com/2010/09/01/us/01iht-letter.html

Toussaint, L., & Cheadle, A. C. D. (2009). Unforgiveness and the broken heart: Unforgiving tendencies, problems due to unforgiveness, and 12-month prevalence of cardiovascular health conditions. In M. T. Evans & E. D. Walker (Eds.), *Religion and psychology*. New York: Nova Publishers.

Toussaint, L. L., Owen, A. D., & Cheadle, A. (2012). Forgive to live: Forgiveness, health, and longevity. *Journal of Behavioral Medicine, 35*(4), 375–386.

Tracy, J. L., & Robins, R. W. (2008). The nonverbal expression of pride: Evidence for cross-cultural recognition. *Journal of Personality & Social Psychology, 94*(3), 516–530.

Triandis, H. C. (1986). Collectivism vs. individualism: A reconceptualization of a basic concept in cross-cultural psychology. In C. Bagley & G. Verma (Eds.), *Personality, cognition, and values: Cross-cultural perspectives of childhood and adolescence*. London: Macmillan.

Triandis, H. C. (1988). Collectivism vs. individualism. In G. Verma & C. Bagley (Eds.), *Cross-cultural studies of personality, attitudes, and cognition*. London: Macmillan.

Triandis, H. C. (2000). Culture and conflict. *The International Journal of Psychology, 35*(2), 1435–1452.

Triandis, H. C., Brislin, R., & Hul, C. H. (1988). Cross-cultural training across the individualism-collectivism divide. *International Journal of Intercultural Relations, 12,* 269–289.

Tripathy, J. (2010). How gendered is gender and development? Culture, masculinity, and gender difference. *Development in Practice, 20*(1), 113–121.

Troester, R. L., & Mester, C. S. (2007). *Civility in business and professional communication*. New York: Peter Lang.

Tsa, W. C., Chen, C. C., & Chiu, S. F. (2005). Exploring boundaries of the effects of applicant impression management tactics in job interviews. *Journal of Management, 31*(1), 108–125.

Tse, M., Vong, S., & Tang, S. (2013). Motivational interviewing and exercise programme for community-dwelling older persons with chronic pain: A randomized controlled study. *Journal of Clinical Nursing, 22*(13/14), 1843–1856. doi:10.1111/j.1365-2702.2012.04317.x

Tuckman, B. W., & Jensen, M. A. C. (1977). Stages in small group development revisited. *Groups and Organizational Studies, 2,* 419–427.

Tufte, E. (2003, September). PowerPoint is evil: Power corrupts; PowerPoint corrupts absolutely. *Wired*. Retrieved from http://www.wired.com/wired/archive/11.09/ppt2.html

Ubinger, M. E., Handal, P. J., & Massura, C. E. (2013). Adolescent adjustment: The hazards of conflict avoidance and the benefits of conflict resolution. *Psychology, 4*(1), 50–58.

The ubiquitous PowerPoint. (2013, April). Full text available. *Phi Delta Kappan, 94*(7), 7.

Uhl-Bien, M. (2006). Relational leadership theory: Exploring the social processes of leadership and organizing. *The Leadership Quarterly, 17,* 654–676.

Ulaby, N. (2008, September 2). The "Bechdel Rule," defining pop culture. NPR. Retrieved from http://www.npr.org/templates/story/story.php?storyId=94202522

U.S. Census Bureau. (2012). Census Bureau releases equal employment opportunity tabulation that provides a profile of America's workforce. Retrieved from http://www.census.gov/newsroom/releases/archives/employment_occupations/cb12-225.html

U.S. Department of Justice, Federal Bureau of Investigation. (2010, September). *Crime in the United States, 2009.* Retrieved from http://www2.fbi.gov/ucr/clus2009/index.html

U.S. Equal Employment Opportunity Commission. (2011). Sexual harassment charges. Retrieved from http://www.eeoc.gov/eeoc/statistics/enforcement/sexual_harassment.cfm

Valkenburg, P. M., & Vroone, M. (2004). Developmental changes in infants' and toddlers' attention to television entertainment. *Communication Research, 31,* 288–311.

Van Dick, R., Tissington, P. A., & Hertel, G. (2009). Do many hands make light work? How to overcome social loafing and gain motivation in work teams. *European Business Review, 21*(3), 233–245.

Van Swol, L. M., Braun, M. T., & Kolb, M. R. (2013). Deception detection, demeanor, and truth bias in face-to-face and computer-mediated communication. *Communication Research, 40*(5), 1–27.

Van Swol, L. M., Malhotra, D., & Braun, M. T. (2012). Deception and its detection: Effects of monetary incentives and personal relationship history. *Communication Research, 39*(2), 217–238.

Van Zandt, T. (2004). Information overload and a network of targeted communication. *RAND Journal of Economics, 35,* 542–561.

Vela, L. E., Booth-Butterfield, M., Wanzer, M. B., & Vallade, J. I. (2013). Relationships among humor, coping, relationship stress, and satisfaction in dating relationships: Replication and extension. *Communication Research Reports, 30*(1), 68–75.

Victor, D. A. (1992). *International business communication.* New York: HarperCollins.

Vijayasiri, G. (2008). Reporting sexual harassment: The importance of organizational culture and trust. *Gender Issues, 25*(1), 43–61.

Villaume, W. A., & Bodie, G. D. (2007). Discovering the listener within us: The impact of trait-like personality variables and communicator styles on preferences for listening style. *International Journal of Listening, 21*(2), 102–123.

Villaume, W. A., & Brown, M. H. (1999). The development and validation of the vocalic sensitivity test. *International Journal of Listening, 13,* 24–45.

Vogel, D. R., Dickson, G. W., & Lehman, J. A. (1986). Persuasion and the role of visual presentation support: The UM/3M study (MIS-RC-WP-86-11), Minneapolis, MN: University of Minnesota, Management Information Systems Research Center.

Vogel, H. L. (2011). *Entertainment industry economics: A guide for financial analysis* (8th ed.). New York: Cambridge University Press.

Von Raffler-Engel, W. (1983). *The perception of nonverbal behavior in the career interview*. Philadelphia: Benjamin.

Voorveld, H. A. M., & van der Goot, M. (2013). Age differences in media multitasking: A diary study. *Journal of Broadcasting & Electronic Media, 57*(3), 392–408. doi:http://dx.doi.org/10.1080/08838151.2013.816709

Voss, B. (2010, December 22). Sibling revelry. *TheAdvocate.com*. Retrieved from http://www.advocate.com/Arts_and_Entertainment/Television/Sibling_Revelry

Vrij, A. (2006). Nonverbal communication and deception. In V. Manusov & M. L. Patterson (Eds.), *The Sage handbook of nonverbal communication* (pp. 341–360). Thousand Oaks, CA: Sage Publications.

Wade, N. (2010, January 12). Deciphering the chatter of monkeys and chimps. *The New York Times*, p. D1.

Wailgum, T. (2008, June 8). How Steve Jobs beats presentation panic. *CIO.com*. Retrieved from http://www.cio.com/article/596271/How_Steve_Jobs_Beats_Presentation_Panic

Waldman, K. (2014, January 7). The Bechdel test sets the bar too low. Slate. Retrieved from http://www.slate.com/blogs/xx_factor/2014/01/07/the_bechdel_test_needs_an_update_we_ve_set_the_bar_for_female_representation.html

Waldron, V. R., & Applegate, J. A. (1998). Effects of tactic similarity on social attraction and persuasiveness in dyadic verbal disagreements. *Communication Reports, 11*, 155–166.

Waldron, V. R. , & Kelley, D. L. (2005). Forgiving communication as a response to relational transgressions. *Journal of Social and Personal Relationships, 22*, 723–742.

Wallenfelsz, K. P., & Hample, D. (2010). The role of taking conflict personally in imagined interactions about conflict. *Southern Communication Journal, 75*(5), 471–487.

Wallis, C. (2006, March 27). The multitasking generation. *Time*, pp. 48–55.

Walther, J. B. (1996). Computer-mediated communication: Impersonal, interpersonal, and hyperpersonal interaction. *Communication Research, 23*, 3–43.

Walther, J. B. (2006). Nonverbal dynamics in computer-mediated communication, or: :-(and the net :-('s with you, :-) and you :-) alone. In V. Manusov & M. L. Patterson (Eds.), *Handbook of nonverbal communication* (pp. 461–479). Thousand Oaks, CA: Sage Publications.

Walther, J. B., & Parks, M. R. (2002). Cues filtered out, cues filtered in: Computer-mediated communication and relationships. In M. L. Knapp & J. A. Daly (Eds.), *Handbook of interpersonal communication* (pp. 529–563). Thousand Oaks, CA: Sage Publications.

Walther, J. B., & Ramirez, A., Jr. (2009). New technologies and new directions in online relating. In S. W. Smith & S. R. Wilson (Eds.), *New directions in interpersonal communication research* (pp. 264–284). Newbury Park, CA: Sage Publications.

Walther, J. B., Van Der Heide, B., Kim, S-Y., Westerman, D., & Tong, S. T. (2008). The role of friends' appearance and behavior on evaluations of individuals on Facebook: Are we known by the company we keep? *Human Communication Research*, *34*(1), 28–49.

Walther, J. B., Van Der Heide, B., Tong, S. T., Carr, C. T., & Atkin, C. K. (2010). Effects of interpersonal goals on inadvertent intrapersonal influence in computer-mediated communication. *Human Communication Research*, *36*(3), 323–347.

Waltman, M., & Haas, J. (2011). *The communication of hate*. New York: Peter Lang.

Wang, G., & Liu, Z. (2010). What collective? Collectivism and relationalism from a Chinese perspective. *Chinese Journal of Communication*, *3*(1), 42–63.

Wanzer, M., Booth-Butterfield, M., & Gruber, K. (2004). Perceptions of health care providers' communication: Relationships between patient-centered communication and satisfaction. *Health Communication*, *16*(3), 363–383.

Ward, C. C., & Tracey, T. J. G. (2004). Relation of shyness with aspects of online relationship involvement. *Journal of Social and Personal Relationships, 21*, 611–623.

Wasserman, B., & Weseley, A. (2009). ¿Qué? Quoi? Do languages with grammatical gender promote sexist attitudes? *Sex Roles*, *61*(9/10), 634–643.

Waters, S., & Ackerman, J. (2011). Exploring privacy management on facebook: Motivations and perceived consequences of voluntary disclosure. *Journal of Computer-Mediated Communication*, *17*(1), 101–115.

Watson, K., Barker, L., & Weaver, J. (1995). The listening styles profile (LSP-16): Development and validation of an instrument to assess four listening styles. *International Journal of Listening, 9*, 1–13.

Watts, D. J. (2011). *Everything is obvious once you know the answer: How common sense fails us*. New York: Crown Publishing Group.

Way, N. (2011). *Deep secrets: Boys' friendships and the crisis of connection*. Cambridge, MA: Harvard University Press.

Webster, M. J., & Driskell, J. E., Jr. (1978). Status generalization: A review of some new data. *American Sociological Review, 42*, 220–236.

Webster, M. J., & Driskell, J. E., Jr. (1983). Beauty as status. *American Journal of Sociology, 89*, 140–165.

Wecker, C. (2012). Slide presentations as speech suppressors: When and why learners miss oral information. *Computers and Education, 59*(2), 260–273.

Weger, H., Jr., Castle, G. R., & Emmett, M. C. (2010). Active listening in peer interviews: The influence of message paraphrasing on perceptions of listening skill. *International Journal of Listening, 24*(1), 34–49.

Weisz, C., & Wood, L. F. (2005). Social identity support and friendship outcomes: A longitudinal study predicting who will be friends and best friends 4 years later. *Journal of Social and Personal Relationships, 22,* 416–432.

Welch, B. A., Mossholder, K. W., Stell, R. P., & Bennett, N. (1998). Does work group cohesiveness affect individuals' performance and organizational commitment? *Small Group Research, 29,* 472–494.

Welch, S. A., & Mickelson, W. T. (2013). A listening competence comparison of working professionals. *International Journal of Listening, 27*(2), 85–99.

Werner, J. (2011, February 16). Bucks County teacher suspended for "lazy whiners" comments defends herself in new blog. *The Trentonian.* Retrieved from http://www.trentonian.com

West, A. (2007, August 20). Facebook labeled a $5b waste of time. *Sydney Morning Herald.* Retrieved May 13, 2008, from http://www.smh.com.au

Wheaton, S. (2012, October 13). Missouree? Missouruh? To be politic, say both. *The New York Times,* p. A1.

Wheelan, S. A. (2012). *Creating effective teams: A guide for members and leaders* (4th ed.). Thousand Oaks: Sage Publications.

Wheelan, S. A., & Burchill, C. (1999). Take teamwork to new heights. *Nursing Management, 30*(4), 28–31.

Wherfritz, G., Kinetz, E., & Kent, J. (2008, April 21). Lured into bondage: A growing back channel of global trade tricks millions into forced labor. *Newsweek.* Retrieved from http://www.newsweek.com/id/131707

Widgery, R. A. (1974). Sex of receiver and physical attractiveness of source as determinants of initial credibility perception. *Western Speech Communication Journal, 1,* 13–17.

Wiemann, J. M. (1977). Explication and test of a model of communication competence. *Human Communication Research, 3,* 195–213.

Wiemann, J. M., & Backlund, P. M. (1980). Current theory and research in communication competence. *Review of Educational Research, 50,* 185–189.

Wiemann, J. M., Chen, V., & Giles, H. (1986, November). Beliefs about talk and silence in a cultural context. Paper presented at the annual meeting of the Speech Communication Association, Chicago.

Wiemann, J. M., & Krueger, D. L. (1980). The language of relationships. In H. Giles, W. P. Robinson, & P. M. Smith (Eds.), *Language: Social psychological perspectives* (pp. 55–62). Oxford: Pergamon Press.

Wiemann, J. M., Takai, J., Ota, H., & Wiemann, M. O. (1997). A relational model of communication competence. In B. Kovačić (Ed.), *Emerging theories of human communication* (pp. 25–44). Albany, NY: State University of New York Press.

Wiemann, M. O. (2009). *Love you/hate you: Negotiating intimate relationships*. Barcelona, Spain: Editorial Aresta.

Wierzbicka, A. (2006). *English: Meaning and culture*. New York: Oxford.

Wiesenfeld, D., Bush, K., & Sikdar, R. (2010). The value of listening: Heeding the call of the Snuggie. *Journal of Advertising Research, 50*(1), 16–20.

Willard, G., & Gramzow, R. (2008). Exaggeration in memory: Systematic distortion of self-evaluative information under reduced accessibility. *Journal of Experimental Social Psychology, 44*(2), 246–259.

Williams, D. (2006). On and off the 'net: Scales for social capital in an online era. *Journal of Computer Mediated Communication, 11*, 593–628.

Williams, D., Consalvo, M., Caplan, S., & Yee, N. (2009). Looking for gender: Gender roles and behaviors among online gamers. *Journal of Communication, 59*(4), 700–725.

Williams, D. E., & Hughes, P. C. (2005). Nonverbal communication in Italy: An analysis of interpersonal touch, body position, eye contact, and seating behaviors. *North Dakota Journal of Speech & Theatre, 18*, 17–24.

Williams, J. C. (2014). Women, work, and the art of gender judo. *Washington Post*. Retrieved from http://www.washingtonpost.com/opinions/women-work-and-the-art-of-gender-judo/2014/01/24/29e209b2-82b2-11e3-8099-9181471f7aaf_story.html

Williams, K. D. (2001). *Ostracism: The power of silence*. New York: Guilford Press.

Williams, K. D., Govan, C. L., Croker, V., Tynan, D., Cruickshank, M., & Lam, A. (2002). *Group dynamics: Theory, research, and practice, 6*(1), 65–77.

Williams, K. D., & Sommer, K. L. (1997). Social ostracism by coworkers: Does rejection lead to loafing or compensation? *Personality and Social Psychology Bulletin, 23*(7), 693–706.

Williams, K. N., Herman, R., Gajewski, B., & Wilson, K. (2009). Elderspeak communication: Impact on dementia care. *American Journal of Alzheimer's Disease & Other Dementias, 24*(1), 11–20.

Williams, P. (1993). Surveillance hurts productivity, deprives employees of rights. *Advertising Age, 64*, 14.

Willoughby, B. J., Carroll, J. S., & Busby, D. M. (2012). The different effects of "living together": Determining and comparing types of cohabiting couples. *Journal of Social and Personal Relationships, 29*(3), 397–419.

Wilmot, W. W. (1987). *Dyadic communication* (3rd ed.). New York: Random House.

Wilson, B. J., Smith, S. L., Potter, W. J., Kunkel, D., Linz, D., Colvin, C. M., & Donnerstein, E. (2002). Violence in children's programming: Assessing the risks. *Journal of Communication, 52*, 5–35.

Wilson, G. L., & Hanna, M. S. (1993). *Groups in context: Leadership and participation in small groups* (3rd ed.). New York: McGraw Hill.

Wingfield, N. (2013, October 15). Tech rivals lay down arms for youth coding. *The New York Times*. Retrieved from http://bits.blogs.nytimes.com/2013/10/15/tech-rivals-lay-down-arms-for-youth-coding

Winston, C. (2002, January 28). State of the Union stew. *The Christian Science Monitor*. Retrieved from http://www.csmonitor.com

Winter, J., & Pauwels, A. (2006). Men staying at home looking after their children: Feminist linguistic reform and social change. *International Journal of Applied Linguistics, 16*(1), 16–36.

Witteman, H. (1993). The interface between sexual harassment and organizational romance. In G. Kreps (Ed.), *Sexual harassment: Communication implications* (pp. 27–62). Cresskill, NJ: Hampton Press.

Wittenbaum, G. M., Shulman, H. C., & Braz, M. E. (2010). Social ostracism in task groups: The effects of group composition. *Small Group Research, 41*(3), 330–353.

Wolfram, W., & Schilling-Estes, N. (2006). *American English: Dialects and variation* (2nd ed.)(p. 1). Malden, MA: Blackwell Publishing.

Wolvin, A. (2010). Response: Toward a listening ethos. *International Journal of Listening, 24*(3), 179–180.

Wolvin, A. D., & Coakley, C. G. (1991). A survey of the status of listening training in some *Fortune* 500 corporations. *Communication Education, 40*, 151–164.

Wong, E., & Cheng, M. (2013). Effects of motivational interviewing to promote weight loss in obese children. *Journal of Clinical Nursing, 22*(17/18), 2519–2530. doi:10.1111/jocn.12098

Woo, E. (2011, March 13). Sam Chwat dies at 57; actors lost, and learned, accents under dialect coach's tutelage. *Los Angeles Times*. Retrieved from http://articles.latimes.com/2011/mar/13/local/la-me-sam-chwat-20110313

Wood, B. (1982). *Children and communication: Verbal and nonverbal language development* (2nd ed.). Englewood Cliffs, NJ: Prentice Hall.

Wood, J. T. (2008). Gender, communication, and culture. In L. A. Samovar, R. E. Porter, and E. R. McDaniel (Eds.), *Intercultural communication: A reader* (pp. 170–180). Belmont, CA: Wadsworth Cengage.

Wood, J. T. (2011). *Gendered lives: Communication, gender, and culture* (9th ed.). Boston, MA: Wadsworth Publishing.

Woodzicka, J. (2008). Sex differences in self-awareness of smiling during a mock job interview. *Journal of Nonverbal Behavior, 32*(2), 109–121.

Wrench, J. S., McCroskey, J. C., & Richmond, V. P. (2008). *Human communication in everyday life: Explanations and applications*. Boston: Allyn & Bacon.

Wright, C. N., Holloway, A., & Roloff, M. E. (2007). The dark side of self-monitoring: How high self-monitors view their romantic relationships. *Communication Reports, 20*(2), 101–114.

Wright, K. B., Rosenberg, J., Egbert, N., Ploeger, N. A., Bernard, D. R., & King, S. (2013). Communication competence, social support, and depression among college students: A model of Facebook and face-to-face support network influence. *Journal of Health Communication, 18*(1), 41–57.

Xerxenesky, A. (2013, January 31). When the music stopped. *The New York Times*, p. A23.

Yaguchi, M., Iyeiri, Y., & Baba, Y. (2010). Speech style and gender distinctions in the use of *very* and *real/really*: An analysis of the Corpus of Spoken Professional American English. *Journal of Pragmatics, 42*(3), 585–597.

Yasui, E. (2009, May). Collaborative idea construction: The repetition of gestures and talk during brainstorming. A paper presented at the 59th meeting of the International Communication Association, Chicago, IL.

Yee, N., & Bailenson, J. (2007). The Proteus effect: The effect of transformed self-representation on behavior. *Human Communication Research, 33*(3), 271–290.

Yoffe, E. (2013, February 25). Can we really stop bullying? Slate.com. Retrieved from http://www.slate.com/articles/double_x/doublex/2013/02/sticks_and_stones_emily_yoffe_interviews_emily_bazelon_about_her_new_book.html

Yoo, C. Y. (2007). Implicit memory measures for Web advertising effectiveness. *Journalism & Mass Communication Quarterly, 84*(1), 7–23.

Yook, E. (2004). Any questions? Knowing the audience through question types. *Communication Teacher, 18*, 91–93.

Yoon, K., Kim, C. H., & Kim, M. S. (1998). A cross-cultural comparison of the effects of source credibility on attitudes and behavioral intentions. *Mass Communication and Society, 1*(3–4), 153–173.

Young, J., & Foot, K. (2005). Corporate e-cruiting: The construction of work in *Fortune 500* recruiting Web sites. *Journal of Computer-Mediated Communication, 11*(1), 44–71.

Yukl, G. (1999). An evaluation of conceptual weaknesses in transformational and charismatic leadership theories. *Leadership Quarterly, 10*, 285–305.

Zabava Ford, W. S., & Wolvin, A. D. (1993). The differential impact of a basic communication course on perceived communication competencies in class, work, and social contexts. *Communication Education, 42*(3), 215–223.

Zacchilli, T. L., Hendrick, C., & Hendrick, S. S. (2009). The romantic partner conflict scale: A new scale to measure relationship conflict. *Journal of Social and Personal Relationships, 26*(8), 1073–1096.

Zappos.com. (2014, February 8). Introducing: Core values frog! Retrieved from http://about.zappos.com/jobs/why-work-zappos/core-values

Zarrinabadi, N. (2012). Self-perceived communication competence in Iranian culture. *Communication Research Reports, 29*(4), 292–298.

Zeman, N. (2013, June). The boy who cried dead girlfriend. *Vanity Fair*. Retrieved from http://www.vanity-fair.com/culture/2013/06/manti-teo-girlfriend-nfl-draft

Zhang, J., & Daugherty, T. (2009). Third-person effect and social networking: Implications for on-line marketing and word-of-mouth communication. *American Journal of Business, 24*, 54–63.

Zhang, Q., & Andreychik, M. (2013). Relational closeness in conflict: Effects on interaction goals, emotion, and conflict styles. *Journal of International Communication, 19*(1), 107–116.

Zickuhr, K., Rainie, L., & Purcell, K. (2013, January 22). Libraries in the digital age. Pew Internet and American Life Project. Retrieved from http://libraries.pewinternet.org/2013/01/22/library-services

Zickuhr, K., & Smith, A. (2012). Digital differences. Pew Research Center's Internet & American Life Project. Retrieved from http://www.pewinternet.org/files/old-media/Files/Reports/2012/PIP_Digital_differences_041312.pdf

Zickuhr, K., & Smith, A. (2013). Home broadband 2013. Pew Research Internet Project. Retrieved from http://www.pewinternet.org/2013/08/26/home-broadband-2013

Zimbushka (2008, May 27). *Mike Caro's 10 ultimate poker cues*. Retrieved from http://www.youtube.com/watch?v=QqF8m12JSDE

Zuckerberg, M. (2013, February 26). What schools don't teach. Code.org video. Retrieved from http://www.youtube.com/watch?v=nKIu9y-en5nc; 3:05

■ Acknowledgments

Acknowledgments that follow are taken from Dan O'Hair, Mary Wiemann, Dorothy Imric Mullin, and Jason Teven, *Real Communication*, Third Edition.

Figure 1.5: "The Abstraction Ladder" adapted from *Competent Communication*, Second Edition, Dan O'Hair et al. Copyright © 1997 Bedford/St. Martin's.

Figure 2.10: "Zones of Personal Space" from *Competent Communication*, Second Edition, Dan O'Hair et al., Copyright © 1997 Bedford/St. Martin's.

Figure 28.5: "Complexity of Group Relationships" from *Competent Communication*, Second Edition, Dan O'Hair et al. Copyright © 1997 Bedford/St. Martin's.

Acknowledgments that follow are taken from Andrea A. Lunsford, and John J. Ruszkiewicz, *Everything's an Argument*, Seventh Edition.

Doug Bandow. "A New Military Draft Would Revive a Very Bad Old Idea" from *Forbes*, July 16, 2012, copyright © 2012 by Forbes LLC. All rights reserved. Used by permission and protected by the Copyright Laws of the United States. The printing, copying, redistribution, or retransmission of this Content without express written permission is prohibited.

David Brooks. "It's Not about You" from the *New York Times*, May 31, 2011. Copyright © 2011 by The New York Times. All rights reserved. Used by permission and protected by the Copyright Laws of the United States. The printing, copying, redistribution, or retransmission of this Content without express written permission is prohibited.

Edye Deloch-Hughes. From "So God Made a Black Farmer Too," reprinted by permission of the author. http://eldhughes.com/2013/02/05/so-god-made-a-farmer-dodge-ram/

Walter Russell Mead. From "It All Begins with Football," first published in the *American Interest*, December 4, 2011. Reprinted by permission of the author.

Virginia Postrel. "Let's Charge Politicians for Wasting Our Time" from *Bloomberg View*, June 3, 2014. Reprinted by permission of Bloomberg L.P. Copyright © 2014. All rights reserved.

Deborah Tannen "Why Is 'Compromise' Now a Dirty Word?," first published in *Politico*, June 15, 2011. Copyright © Deborah Tannen. Used by permission of the author.

■ Notes

Notes that follow are taken from Dan O'Hair, Rob Stewart, and Hannah Rubenstein, *A Speakers Guidebook*, Sixth Edition.

Chapter 3

1. Matthew Jacobs, "Celebrities with Stage Fright Include Adele, Hayden Panettiere, Barbra Streisand, Megan Fox, and Many More," *The Huffington Post*, April 5, 2013, www.huffingtonpost.com/2013/04/05/celebrities-with-stage-fright_n_3022146.html. Last accessed July 20, 2013.

2. Michael J. Beatty, "Situational and Predispositional Correlates of Public Speaking Anxiety," *Communication Education* 37 (1988): 28–39.

3. Graham D. Bodie, "A Racing Heart, Rattling Knees, and Ruminative Thoughts: Defining, Explaining, and Treating Public Speaking Anxiety," *Communication Education* 59 (2010): 70–105.

4. Paul L. Witt and Ralph R. Behnke, "Anticipatory Speech Anxiety as a Function of Public Speaking Assignment Type," *Communication Education* 55 (2006): 167–77.

5. Ralph Behnke and Chris R. Sawyer, "Milestones of Anticipatory Public Speaking Anxiety," *Communication Education* 48 (April 1999): 165–72.

6. Christine Kane, "Overcoming Stage Fright—Here's What to Do," *Christinekane* (blog), April 24, 2007, http://christinekane.com/blog/overcoming-stage-fright-heres-what-to-do/.

7. Behnke and Sawyer, "Milestones of Anticipatory Public Speaking Anxiety."

8. David-Paul Pertaub, Mel Slater, and Chris Barker, "An Experiment on Public Speaking Anxiety in Response to Three Different Types of Virtual Audience," *Presence: Teleoperators and Virtual Environments* 11 (2002): 670–78.

9. Lenny Laskowski, "Overcoming Speaking Anxiety in Meetings and Presentations," Speakers Platform website, accessed July 26, 2007, www.speaking.com/articles_html/LennyLaskowski_532.html.

10. John Robert Colombo, "Speech Anxiety: Overcoming the Fear of Public Speaking," SpeechCoachforExecutives.com, accessed July 25, 2007, www.speechcoachforexecutives.com/speech_anxiety.html.

11. Ibid.

12. Joe Ayres, "Coping with Speech Anxiety: The Power of Positive Thinking," *Communication Education* 37 (1988): 289–96; Joe Ayres, "An Examination of the Impact of Anticipated Communication and Communication Apprehension on Negative Thinking, Task-Relevant Thinking, and Recall," *Communication Research Reports* 9 (1992): 3–11.

13. Pamela J. Feldman, Sheldon Cohen, Natalie Hamrick, and Stephen J. Lepore, "Psychological Stress, Appraisal, Emotion, and Cardiovascular Response in a Public Speaking Task," *Psychology and Health* 19 (2004): 353–68.

14. Michael T. Motley, "Public Speaking Anxiety qua Performance Anxiety: A Revised Model and Alternative Therapy," *Journal of Social Behavior and Personality* 5 (1990): 85–104.

15. Joe Ayres, Chia-Fang "Sandy" Hsu, and Tim Hopf, "Does Exposure to Visualization Alter Speech Preparation Processes?" *Communication Research Reports* 17 (2000): 366–74.

16. Elizabeth Quinn, "Visualization in Sport: Imagery Can Improve Performance," About.com: SportsMedicine, accessed August 29, 2007, http://sportsmedicine.about.com/cs/sport_psych/a/aa091700a.htm; Joe Ayres and Tim Hopf, "Visualization: Is It More Than Extra Attention?" *Communication Education* 38 (1989): 1–5; Joe Ayers and Tim Hopf, *Coping with Speech Anxiety* (Norwood, NJ: Ablex, 1993).

17. Ayres and Hopf, "Visualization," 2–3.

18. "Etiology of Anxiety Disorders," Chapter 4, "Adults and Mental Health," Mental Health:A report of the Surgeon General, accessed May 30, 2010, www.surgeongeneral.gov/library/mentalhealth/chapter4/sec2_1.html.

19. Herbert Benson and Miriam Z. Klipper, *The Relaxation Response* (New York: HarperCollins, 2000).

20. Mayo Clinic Staff, "Relaxation Techniques: Learn Ways to Calm Your Stress," MayoClinic.com, accessed May 30, 2010, www.mayoclinic.com/health/relaxation-technique/SR00007.

21. Kane, "Overcoming Stage Fright."

22. Lars-Gunnar Lundh, Britta Berg, Helena Johansson, Linda Kjellén Nilsson, Jenny Sandberg, and Anna Segerstedt, "Social Anxiety Is Associated with a Negatively Distorted Perception of One's Own Voice," *Cognitive Behavior Therapy* 31 (2002): 25–30.

Chapter 4

1. Yogi Berra Quotes on BrainyQuote, accessed January 22, 2014, www.brainyquote.com/quotes/quotes/y/yogiberra124868.html.

Chapter 5

1. For a useful overview of the history of attitudes and attitude change, see Pablo Briñol and Richard. E. Petty, "The History of Attitudes and Persuasion Research," in *Handbook of the History of Social Psychology*, eds. Arie Kruglanski and Wolfgang Stroebe (New York: Psychology Press, 2011).

2. Richard. E. Petty and John T. Cacioppo, *Attitudes and Persuasion: Classic and Contemporary Approaches* (Dubuque, IA: Wm. C. Brown, 1981); M. Fishbein and I. Ajzen, *Belief, Attitude, Intention, and Behavior: An Introduction to Theory and Research* (Reading, MA: Addison-Wesley, 1975); I. Ajzen and M. Fishbein, "The Influence of Attitudes on Behavior," in *The Handbook of Attitudes*, eds. Dolores Albarracín, Blair T. Johnson, and Mark P. Zanna (Mahwah, NJ: Erlbaum, 2005), 173–221.

3. Richard E. Petty, S. Christian Wheeler, and Zakary L. Tormala, "Persuasion and Attitude Change," in *Handbook of Psychology, Personality, and Social Psychology*, Vol. 5, eds. Theodore Millon, Melvin Lerner, and Irving B. Weiner (New York: John Wiley & Sons, 2003).

4. *The Stanford Encyclopedia of Philosophy*, s. v. "Belief," Winter 2011 edition, http://plato.stanford.edu/archives/win2011/entries/belief/.

5. Edward D. Steele and W. Charles Redding, "The American Value System: Premises for Persuasion," *Western Speech* 26 (1962): 83–91; Robin M. Williams Jr., *American Society: A Sociological Interpretation*, 3rd ed. (New York: Alfred A. Knopf, 1970).

6. "Human Values and Nature's Future: Americans' Attitudes on Biological Diversity," BlueStem Communications, accessed January 22, 2014, http://bluestemcommunications.org/changing-behaviors-not-minds-a-communications-workshop/

7. Herbert Simon, *Persuasion in Society*, 2nd ed. Routledge, 2011.

8. Ibid.

9. Kenneth Burke, *A Rhetoric of Motives* (Berkeley, CA: University of California Press, 1969).

10. Hillary Rodham Clinton, "Abortion Is a Tragedy," *Vital Speeches of the Day* 71, no. 9 (2005): 266–70.

11. Kim Parker, "The Big Generation Gap at the Polls Is Echoed in Attitudes on Budget Tradeoffs," Pew Research Social and Demographic Trends, December 20, 2012, www.pewsocialtrends.org/2012/12/20/the-big-generation-gap-at-the-polls-is-echoed-in-attitudes-on-budget-tradeoffs.

12. Jere R. Behrman and Nevzer Stacey, eds., *The Social Benefits of Going to College* (Ann Arbor, MI: University of Michigan Press, 2000).

13. *U.S. Religious Landscape Survey*, Pew Forum on Religion and Public Life, February 2008, accessed July 10, 2013, http://religions.pewforum.org/pdf/report-religious-landscape-study-full.pdf.

14. "Growth of the Nonreligious," Pew Forum on Religion and Public Life, July 2, 2013, www.pewforum.org/2013/07/02/growth-of-the-nonreligious-many-say-trend-is-bad-for-american-society/.

15. Daniel Canary and Kathryn Dindia, eds., *Sex Differences and Similarities in Communication*, 2nd ed. (Mahwah, NJ: Lawrence Erlbaum, 2006).

16. "72% of Online Adults Are Social Networking Site Users," Pew Research Center's Internet and American Life Project, August 5, 2012, http://pewinternet.org/Reports/2013/social-networking-sites.aspx.

17. Matthew W. Brault, Americans With Disabilities: 2010, Current Population Reports, U.S. Census Bureau, accessed Jan 22, 2014, www.census.gov/prod/2012pubs/p70-131.pdf

18. "U.S. Census Quick Facts," U.S. Census, http://quickfacts.census.gov/qfd/states/00000.html; accessed December 12, 2014; New Census Bureau Interactive Map Shows Languages Spoken in America," U.S. Census Bureau, March 13, 2013; U.S. Census, August 6, 2013, www.census.gov/newsroom/releases/archives/education/cb13-143.html

19. "Fact Sheet: Bureau of Intelligence and Research," U.S. Department of State, January 3, 2012, www.state.gov/s/inr/rls/4250.htm

20. Inter-University Consortium for Political and Social Research, *World Values Survey, 1981–1984 and 1990–1993* (Irvine, CA: Social Science Data Archives, University Libraries, University of California, 1997). The 1990 World Values Survey covers four Asian countries (China, India, Japan, and South Korea) and eighteen Western countries.

21. Geert Hofstede, Gert Jan Hofstede, and Michael Minkov, *Culture and Organizations: Software of the Mind*, 3rd ed. (New York: McGraw Hill, 2010).

22. Rushworth M. Kidder, *Shared Values for a Troubled World: Conversations with Men and Women of Conscience* (San Francisco: Jossey-Bass Publishers, 1994).

Chapter 6

1. Ernest Thompson, "An Experimental Investigation of the Relative Effectiveness of Organization Structure in Oral Communication," *Southern Speech Journal* 26 (1960): 59–69; C. Spicer and R. E. Bassett, "The Effects of Organization on Learning from an Informative Message," *Southern Speech Journal* 41 (1976): 290–99.

2. Raymond G. Smith, "Effects of Speech Organization upon Attitudes of College Students," *Speech Monographs* 18 (1951): 292–301.

3. Harry Sharp Jr. and Thomas McClung, "Effects of Organization on the Speaker's Ethos," *Speech Monographs* 33 (1966): 182ff; Eldon E. Baker, "The Immediate Effects of Perceived Speaker Disorganization on Speaker Credibility and Audience Attitude Change in Persuasive Speaking," *Western Speech* 29 (1965): 148–61.

4. Gordon H. Bower, "Organizational Factors in Memory," *Cognitive Psychology* 1 (1970): 18–46.

5. Murray Glanzer and Anita R. Cunitz, "Two Storage Mechanisms in Free Recall," *Journal of Verbal Learning and Verbal Behavior* 5 (1966): 351–60.

Chapter 7

1. William Safire, *Lend Me Your Ears: Great Speeches in History* (New York: Norton, 1992), 676.

2. Bas A. Andeweg, Jaap C. de Jong, and Hans Hoeken, "'May I Have Your Attention?': Exordial Techniques in Informative Oral Presentations," *Technical Communication Quarterly* 7 (2009): 271–84, doi: 10.1080/10572259809364631.

3. "Measuring Intimate Partner (Domestic) Violence," National Institute of Justice, 2012, accessed November 14, 2013, www.nij.gov/topics/crime/intimate-partner-violence/pages/measuring.aspx.

4. Nelson Mandela, "Our March to Freedom Is Irreversible," in *The Penguin Book of Twentieth-Century Speeches,* ed. Brian MacArthur (New York: Penguin, 1992).

5. Oprah Winfrey, (speech, 50th anniversary of March on Washington, DC, August 28, 2013), www.washingtonpost.com/politics/full-transcript-oprah-winfreys-speech-on-50th-anniversary-of-march-on-washington/2013/08/28/3fee1ba4-101d-11e3-8cdd-bcdc09410972_story.html.

6. Charles A. Kiesler and Sara B. Kiesler, "Role of Forewarning in Persuasive Communication," *Journal of Abnormal and Social Psychology* 68 (1964): 547–69. Cited in James C. McCroskey, *An Introduction to Rhetorical Communication*, 8th ed. (Boston, MA: Allyn & Bacon, 2001), 253.

7. Marvin Runyon, "No One Moves the Mail Like the U.S. Postal Service," *Vital Speeches of the Day* 61, no. 2 (1994): 52–55.

8. Bas A. Andeweg, Jaap C. de Jong, and Hans Hoeken, "'May I Have Your Attention?'"

9. Robert L. Darbelnet, "U.S. Roads and Bridges: Highway Funding at a Crossroads," *Vital Speeches of the Day* 63, no. 12 (1997): 379.

Chapter 8

1. Holger Kluge, "Reflections on Diversity," *Vital Speeches of the Day* 63, no. 6 (1997): 171–72.

2. Elpidio Villarreal, "Choosing the Right Path," *Vital Speeches of the Day* 72, no. 26 (2007): 784–86.

3. Hillary Rodham Clinton, "Women's Rights Are Human Rights" (speech, United Nations Fourth World Conference on Women, Beijing, China, September 5, 1995).

4. Sue Suter, "Adapting to Change, While Holding on to Values: *Star Trek*'s Lessons for the Disability Community" (speech, Annual Conference of the Association for the Severely Handicapped, Springfield, IL, September 22, 1999).

5. Oprah Winfrey (speech, Wellesley College commencement, Wellesley, MA, May 30, 1997), academics.wellesley.edu/PublicAffairs/PAhomepage/winfrey.html.

6. James C. May (address, European Aviation Club, Brussels, Belgium, October 30, 2008), www.airlines.org/News/Speeches/Pages/speech_10-30-08May.aspx.

7. Barack Obama's "Remarks by the President on Trayvon Martin," The White House, July 19, 2013, www.whitehouse.gov/the-press-office/2013/07/19/remarks-president-trayvon-martin.

Chapter 9

1. For an enlightening review of the history of outlining from Cicero to electronic software, see Jonathan Price, "STOP: Light on the History of Outlining," *Journal of Computer Documentation* 23, no. 3 (1999): 69–78.

2. Mark B. McClellan (speech, Fifth annual David A. Winston lecture, Washington, DC, October 20, 2003), www.fda.gov/oc/speeches/2003/winston1020.htmlwww.fda.gov/newsevents/speeches/speecharchives/ucm053609.htm.

3. Gratitude goes to Carolyn Clark, Ph.D., of Salt Lake Community College for sharing this assignment with us.

Chapter 10

1. Katherine E. Rowan subdivides informative communication into *informatory discourse,* in which the primary aim is to represent reality by increasing an audience's awareness of some phenomenon; and *explanatory discourse,* with the aim to represent reality by deepening understanding. See Katherine E. Rowan, "Informing and Explaining Skills: Theory and Research on Informative Communication," in *Handbook of Communication and Social Interaction Skills,* eds. John O. Greene and Brant R. Burleson (Mahwah, NJ: Erlbaum, 2003), 403–38.

2. With thanks to Barry Antokoletz, NYC College of Technology, for these comments.

3. Vickie K. Sullivan, "Public Speaking: The Secret Weapon in Career Development," *USA Today,* May 2005, 24.

4. Nick Morgan, "Two Rules for a Successful Presentation," Harvard Business Review Blog ("The Conversation"), May 14, 2010, blogs.hbr.org/2010/05/two-rules-for-a-successful-pre/; Harry E. Chambers, *Effective Communication Skills for Scientific and Technical Professionals* (Cambridge, MA: Perseus Publishing, 2001).

5. Lisa Raehsler, "What People Search For—Most Popular Keywords," Search Engine Watch, March 2, 2013, searchenginewatch.com/article/2066257/What-People-Search-For-Most-Popular-Keywords.

6. Tina Blythe et al., *The Teaching for Understanding Guide* (Hoboken, NJ: Jossey-Bass, 1997); Kenneth D. Frandsen and Donald A. Clement, "The Functions of Human Communication in Informing: Communicating and Processing Information," in *Handbook of Rhetorical and Communication Theory,* eds. Carroll C. Arnold and John Waite Bowers (Needham, MA: Allyn & Bacon, 1984), 334.

7. Ernest Thompson, "An Experimental Investigation of the Relative Effectiveness of Organization Structure in Oral Communication," *Southern Speech Journal* 26 (1966): 59–69.

8. Howard K. Battles and Charles Packard, *Words and Sentences,* bk. 6 (Lexington, MA: Ginn & Company, 1984), 459.

9. Katherine E. Rowan, "A New Pedagogy for Explanatory Public Speaking: Why Arrangement Should Not Substitute for Invention," *Communication Education* 44 (1995): 236–50.

10. Sandra Kujawa and Lynne Huske, *The Strategic Teaching and Reading Project Guidebook,* rev. ed. (Oak Brook, IL: North Central Regional Educational Laboratory, 1995).

11. Shawn M. Glynn et al., "Teaching Science with Analogies: A Resource for Teachers and Textbook Authors," *National Reading Research Center: Instructional Resource,* 7 (Fall 1994).

12. "Altoona List of Medical Analogies: How to Use Analogies," Altoona Family Physicians Residency, accessed August 5, 2010, www.altoona-afp.org/analogies.htm.

13. Shawn M. Glynn et al., "Teaching Science," 19.

14. "Altoona List of Medical Analogies: How to Use Analogies."

15. Wolfgang Porod, "Nanotechnology," *Vital Speeches of the Day* 71, no. 4 (2004): 125–28.

16. Tina A. Grotzer, "How Conceptual Leaps in Understanding the Nature of Causality Can Limit Learning: An Example from Electrical Circuits" (paper presented at the annual conference of the American Educational Research Association, New Orleans, LA, April 2000), pzweb.harvard.edu/Research/UnderCon.htm.

17. Neil D. Fleming and Colleen Mills, "Helping Students Understand How They Learn," *Teaching Professor* 7, no. 4 (1992).

Chapter 11

1. M. L. McLaughlin, Michael J. Cody, and K. French, "Account-Giving and the Attribution of Responsibility: Impressions of Traffic Offenders," in *The Psychology of Tactical Communication*, eds. M. J. Cody and M. L. McLaughlin (Bristol, PA: Multilingual Matters, 1990), 244–67. Cited in Rodney Reynolds and J. Lynn Reynolds, "Evidence," in *The Persuasion Handbook: Developments in Theory and Practice*, eds. James P. Dillard and Michael Pfau (Thousand Oaks, CA: Sage, 2002), 427–44, doi: 10.4135/9781412976046.n22.

2. Ibid.

3. Ralph Underwager and Hollida Wakefield, "The Taint Hearing" (presented at the 13th Annual Symposium in Forensic Psychology, Vancouver, BC, April 17, 1997), www.ipt-forensics.com/journal/volume10/j10_7.htm#en0.

4. Gretchen Livingston, "The Rise of Single Fathers," Pew Research Social and Demographic Trends, July 2, 2013, www.pewsocialtrends.org/2013/07/02/the-rise-of-single-fathers/.

Chapter 12

1. James A. Winans, *Public Speaking* (New York: Century, 1925). Professor Winans was among the first Americans to contribute significantly to the study of rhetoric. His explanation of delivery is considered by many to be the best coverage of the topic in the English language. His perspective infuses this chapter.

2. Judee K. Burgoon, Thomas Birk, and Michael Pfau, "Nonverbal Behaviors, Persuasion, and Credibility," *Human Communication Research* 17, no. 1 (1990): 140+, *Academic OneFile*.

3. Winans, *Public Speaking*, 17.

4. Thomas M. Conley, *Rhetoric in the European Tradition* (New York: Longman, 1990).

5. William Safire, PBS *NewsHour,* aired August 15, 1996 (Public Broadcasting System), www.pbs.org/newshour/gergen/july-dec96/safire_8–15.html.

6. Dan O'Hair, Rob Stewart, Hannah Rubenstein, Robbin Crabtree, and Robert Weissberg, *ESL Students in the Public Speaking Classroom: A Guide for Teachers* (Boston: Bedford/St. Martin's, 2012), 24.

Chapter 13

1. Kyle James Tusing and James Price Dillard, "The Sounds of Dominance: Vocal Precursors of Perceived Dominance during Interpersonal Influence," *Human Communication Research* 26 (2000): 148–71.

2. Caryl Raye Krannich, *101 Secrets of Highly Effective Speakers* (Manassas Park, VA: Impact Publications, 1998), 121–22.

3. Kenneth C. Crannell, *Voice and Articulation,* 4th ed. (Belmont, CA: Wadsworth, 2000), 41.

4. MaryAnn Cunningham Florez, "Improving Adult ESL Learners' Pronunciation Skills," National Clearinghouse for ESL Literacy Education, 1998, accessed July 16, 2005, www.cal.org/caela/digests/Pronun.htm.

5. The digitized audio of King's "I Have a Dream" speech can be accessed at www.americanrhetoric.com/speeches/Ihaveadream.htm.

Chapter 14

1. Robert Rivlin and Karen Gravelle, *Deciphering the Senses: The Expanding World of Human Perception* (New York: Simon & Schuster, 1998), 98; see also Anne Warfield, "Do You Speak Body Language?" *Training & Development* 55, no. 4 (2001): 60.

2. C. F. Bond and the Global Deception Research Team, "A World of Lies," *Journal of Cross-Cultural Psychology* 37 (2006): 60–74; Timothy R. Levine, Kelli Jean K. Asada, and Hee Sun Park, "The Lying Chicken and the Gaze Avoidant Egg: Eye Contact, Deception, and Causal Order," *Southern Communication Journal* 71 (2006): 401–11.

3. Ibid.

4. Eva Krumburger, "Effects of Dynamic Attributes of Smiles in Human and Synthetic Faces: A Simulated Job Interview Setting," *Journal of Nonverbal Behavior* 33 (2009): 1–15.

5. Laurie Schloff and Marcia Yudkin, *Smart Speaking* (New York: Plume, 1991), 108.

6. Alissa Melinger and Willem M. Levelt, "Gesture and the Communicative Intention of the Speaker," *Gesture* 4 (2004): 119–41.

7. Albert Mehrabian, *Silent Messages* (Belmont, CA: Wadsworth, 1981); Mike Allen, Paul L. Witt, and Lawrence R. Wheeless, "The Role of Teacher Immediacy as a Motivational Factor in Student Learning: Using Meta-Analysis to Test a Causal Model," *Communication Education* 55, no. 6 (2006): 21–31.

8. J. P. Davidson, "Shaping an Image That Boosts Your Career," *Marketing Communications* 13 (1988): 55–56.

9. Carmine Gallo, *The Presentation Secrets of Steve Jobs* (New York: McGraw-Hill, 2009), 181.

Chapter 15

1. Jean-Luc Doumont, "The Cognitive Style of PowerPoint: Slides Are Not All Evil," *Technical Communication* 52, no. 1 (2005): 64–70.

2. Richard E. Mayer, *The Multimedia Principle* (New York: Cambridge University Press, 2001).

3. See discussion of the redundancy effect in Richard E. Mayer, ed., *The Cambridge Handbook of Multimedia Learning* (New York: Cambridge University Press, 2005).

4. Dale Cyphert, "Presentation Technology in the Age of Electronic Eloquence: From Visual Aid to Visual Rhetoric," *Communication Education* 56, no. 2 (2007): 168–92.

5. Dale Cyphert, "Presentation Technology."

6. "Line Graph," BusinessDictionary.com, accessed July 10, 2014, www.businessdictionary.com/definition/line-graph.html.

7. Gary Jones, "Message First: Using Films to Power the Point," *Business Communication Quarterly* 67, no. 1 (2004): 88–91.

8. Kulwadee M. Axtell, "The Effect of Presentation Software on Classroom Verbal Interaction and on Student Retention of Higher Education Lecture Content," *Journal of Technology in Teaching and Learning* 4, no. 1 (2008): 21–23.

9. Joel B. Lanir, "The Benefits of More Electronic Screen Space on Students' Retention of Material in Classroom Lectures," *Computers & Education* 55, no. 2 (2010): 892–903.

10. Ronald Larson, "Enhancing the Recall of Presented Material," *Computers & Education* 53, no. 4 (2009): 1278–84.

Chapter 16

1. Nancy Duarte, "Avoiding the Road to Powerpoint Hell," *Wall Street Journal*, January 22, 2011; Rebecca Worley, "Presentations and the PowerPoint Problem," *Business Communication Quarterly* 67, no. 1 (2004): 78–80.

2. Edward Tufte, *The Visual Display of Quantitative Information* (Graphics Press, 2001).

3. A. C. Moller, A. J. Elliot, and M. A. Maier, "Red Is for Failure and Green for Success: Achievement-Related Implicit Associations to Color" (poster presented at the Society for Personality and Social Psychology Conference, Tampa, FL, February 2009).

4. Ronald Larson, "Slide Composition for Electronic Presentations," *Journal of Educational Computing Research*, 31, no. 1 (2004): 61–76.

Chapter 17

1. Jon Thomas, "PowerPoint Is Not the Problem with Presentations Today," Presentation Advisors, March 21, 2010, http://blog.presentationadvisors.com/presentationadvisors/2010/03/powerpoint-is-not-the-problem-with-presentations.html.

2. Dale Cyphert, "Presentation Technology in the Age of Electronic Eloquence: From Visual Aid to Visual Rhetoric," *Communication Education* 56, no. 2 (2007): 168–92; Dale Cyphert, "The Problem of PowerPoint: Visual Aid or Visual Rhetoric?" *Business Communication Quarterly* 67, no. 1 (2004): 80–84.

3. Rebecca B. Worley and Marilyn A. Dyrud, "Presentations and the PowerPoint Problem," *Business Communication Quarterly* 67, no. 1 (2004): 78–80.

4. R. Larson, "Slide Composition for Electronic Presentations," *Journal of Educational Computing Research* 31, no. 1 (2004): 61–76.

Chapter 30

1. Herbert W. Simons, *Persuasion in Society,* 2nd ed. (Routledge, 2011).

2. Alan H. Monroe, *Principles and Types of Speeches* (Chicago: Scott, Foresman, 1935).

3. C. Ilie, "Strategies of Refutation by Definition: A Pragma-Rhetorical Approach to Refutations in a Public Speech," in *Pondering on Problems of Argumentation: Twenty Essays on Theoretical Issues,* eds. F. H. van Eemeren and B. Garssen (Springer Science + Business Media, 2009), doi: 10.1007/978-1-4020-9165-0_4.

Chapter 31

1. Dan O'Hair and Mary Wiemann, *Real Communication,* 2nd ed. (New York: Bedford/St. Martin's, 2012).

2. C. L. Hoyt, "Leadership in Virtual Contexts," in *The Social Net: Understanding Our Online Behavior,* ed. Y. Amichai-hamburger, (Oxford: Oxford University Press, 2003), 180–200.

3. Dan O'Hair, Gustav Friedrich, and Lynda Dixon, *Strategic Communication for Business and the Professions,* 7th ed. (Boston: Allyn Bacon, 2011); Dan O'Hair and Mary Wiemann, *Real Communication.*

4. C. M. Anderson, B. L. Riddle, and M. M. Martin, "Socialization in Groups," in *Handbook of Group Communication Theory and Research*, ed. Lawrence R. Frey, Dennis S. Gouran, and Marshall Scott Poole (Thousand Oaks, CA, Sage, 1999): 139–63; A. J. Salazar, "An Analysis of the Development and Evolution of Roles in the Small Group," *Small Group Research* 27 (1996): 475–503; K. D. Benne and P. Sheats, "Functional Roles of Group Members," *Journal of Social Issues* 4 (1948): 41–49.

5. Ibid.

6. K. Choi and B. Cho, "Competing Hypotheses Analyses of the Associations between Group Task Conflict and Group Relationship Conflict," *Journal of Organizational Behavior* 32 (2011): 1106–26.

7. Dan O'Hair and Mary Wiemann, *Real Communication.*

8. Robert McPhee, Karen Myers, and Angela Thretheway, "On Collective Mind and Conversational Analysis," *Management Communication Quarterly* 19 (2006): 311–26.

9. Geoffrey A. Cross, "Collective Form: An Exploration of Large-Group Writing," *Journal of Business Communication* 37 (2000): 77–100.

10. Claire Ferrais, "Investigating NASA's Intergroup Decision-Making: Groupthink and Intergroup Social Dynamics" (paper presented at the annual meeting of the International Communication Association, 2004); Irving Lester Janis, *Groupthink: Psychological Studies of Policy Decisions and Fiascoes* (Berkeley: University of California Press, 1982).

11. S. Schulz-Hardt, F. C. Bordbeck, A. Mojzisch, R. Kerschreiter, and D. Frey, "Group Decision Making as a Facilitator for Decision Quality," *Journal of Personality and Social Psychology* 91: 1080–93: Dan O'Hair, Gustav Friedrich, and Lynda Dixon, *Strategic Communication for Business and the Professions*.

12. D. Riordan and M. Riordan, "Guarding Against Groupthink in the Professional Work Environment: A Checklist," *Journal of Academic & Business Ethics* (2013): 71–78.

13. S. Ruggieri and C. S. Abbate, "Leadership Style, Self-Sacrifice, and Team Identification," *Social Behavior and Personality* 41 (2013): 1171–78.

14. L. Richard Hoffman and Norman R. F. Maier, "Valence in the Adoption of Solutions by Problem-Solving Groups: Concept, Method, and Results," *Journal of Abnormal and Social Psychology* 69 (1964): 264–71.

15. John Dewey, *How We Think* (Boston: D.C. Heath Co., 1950).

16. Lin Kroeger, *The Complete Idiot's Guide to Successful Business Presentation* (New York: Alpha Books, 1997), 113.

Chapter 32

1. Sheri Jeavons, "Webinars That Wow: How to Deliver a Dynamic Webinar," Citrix GoToMeeting, news.citrixonline.com/download_a_webinar/?attend_a_webinar=Y&paged=2.

2. Kami Griffiths and Chris Peters, "10 Steps for Planning a Successful Webinar," *TechSoup*, January 27, 2009, www.techsoup.org/learningcenter/training/page/1252.cfm.

3. Ken Molay, "Best Practices for Webinars," Adobe Connect, www.adobe.com/products/acrobatconnectpro/webconferencing/pdfs/Best_Practices_for_Webinars_v4_FINAL.pdf.

4. Patricia Fripp, "15 Tips for Webinars: How to Add Impact When You Present Online," *eLearn Magazine*, July 7, 2009, elearnmag.org/featured.cfm?aid=1595445.